INDIANS
of the
PACIFIC NORTHWEST

The Civilization of the American Indian Series

INDIANS
of the
PACIFIC
NORTHWEST

A History

Robert H. Ruby and John A. Brown

With a Foreword by Alvin M. Josephy, Jr.

UNIVERSITY OF OKLAHOMA PRESS
NORMAN

Dedicated to Marion
and to Mary

Library of Congress Cataloging-in-Publication Data

Ruby, Robert H.
  Indians of the Pacific Northwest.

  (The Civilization of the American Indian series; v. 158)
  Bibliography: p. 279.
  Includes index.
  1. Indians of North America—Northwest, Pacific—History. I. Brown,
John Arthur. II. Title. III. Series: Civilization of the American Indian
series; v. 158.
E78.N77R8   979'.00497   80-5946
                               AACR2

ISBN: 0–8061–1731–1
ISBN: 0–8061–2113–0 (pbk.)

Contents

Illustrations

MAPS

Foreword

I am frank to admit that, with a number of pressing commitments of my own, it took me some time, after its authors were kind enough to send me the manuscript of this book, to put all other things aside and get to its reading. Now and again I would dip into it, here and there, and becoming increasingly intrigued with the breadth and depth of the material with which it dealt. Gradually I worked up an interest bordering on suspense—wondering just how monumental a work it was—and at last got to it, beginning with page one and continuing, with mounting awe and respect, to its end.

This is, indeed, a massive synthesis of the history of Indian-white relations throughout the entire Northwest. It is far more than a fitting climax to the authors' previous books on individual Indian tribes in that part of the present-day United States, for it is national history on the grand scale—interweaving and making clear the relationships among numerous Native American groups and between those peoples and succeeding generations of whites who expanded from the East into the various tribal homelands in the Northwest.

Nothing like this book has appeared before. Reflecting an enormous amount of research and a mastery of the huge and scattered literature of primary documents—journals, diaries, government reports, and soon—dealing with a multitude of time periods and geographic areas from the Northwest Pacific Coast to the Missouri River, it brings together in a wondrously organized fashion much that heretofore has been related only in a fractionated and unconnected manner.

I believe that this volume will have an enduring importance for all students and writers on Northwest Indian his-

tory. It should also, I think, be obligatory reading for anyone interested in the history of that portion of our nation. Finally, because it deals so dramatically and sweepingly with a truly stupendous canvas of lively and exciting material, I am sure that the general reading public will find it rewardingly entertaining as well as illuminating.

New York City   ALVIN M. JOSEPHY

Preface

There is no dearth of primary or secondary source material pertaining to the history of Pacific Northwestern Indians. To our knowledge, however, there has been no attempt to assemble this information into a composite regional Indian history. When requested by the University of Oklahoma Press to prepare such a work for The Civilization of the American Indian Series, we set about doing so with some trepidation, fully aware of the magnitude of the task.

The people of whom we write lived in a vast area stretching from the Pacific Ocean to the Rocky Mountains and from British Columbia to the California-Utah-Nevada borderlands—a region of geographical extremes extending from the moist Pacific Coast across the divisive Cascade Mountains to the semiarid Columbia Plateau and the arid Great Basin. The peoples living within this diverse region also differed despite shared elements in their material and nonmaterial cultures and their development. To recognize and record those similarities and differences as they influenced the Indians' history has been a major challenge to us in preparing this manuscript.

Although we are concerned with the natives' history during the period before the first white contacts and with Indian history in recent times, the main time frame of our work is the period from contact until the twentieth century. We leave to others the task of recording the early and recent periods.

In preparing our manuscript, we have utilized the researches of many writers. Not the least important were the anthropologists; we have interlaced our narrative with much material that is anthropological in nature. Because we believe that the life of man involves struggle, conflict becomes a major theme of our story. We have tried to write from the standpoint of our subjects, knowing full well the limitations inherent in such an approach. If we have failed, we can say that, unlike most of the previous non-Indian writers of Pacific Northwestern Indian history, we have tried to portray the Native Americans as the subjects of the history rather than as objects, which is how they appear in most white men's histories. We have sought to appeal to the general reading public. Although our research has been exhaustive and based on numerous sources, we have kept citations to a minimum. We have provided a bibliography including suggested readings which should be helpful to the general reader.

In preparing our manuscript, we have been greatly dependent on and indebted to the many people who made information available to us. Among them are numerous members of the Indian community whose friendships we have cherished in over a quarter century of research among them. We also owe much to the personnel of governmental and private agencies, libraries, and historical societies. Among the individuals representing institutions whom we gratefully acknowledge for their assistance are Nancy Pryor of the Washington State Library; Betty Jean Gibson, Bill Martin, and Terry Sterley of the Wenatchee Valley College Library; Betty Shambrook, Marye Ruth Wood, and Joe Rogers of the Big Bend Community College, Moses Lake; Dan Walters of the North Central Washington Regional Library; Carol McFarland and Dean Marney of the Wenatchee Public Library; Irma McKenzie, Pearl C. Munson, and Mrs. Lawrence Bingham of the Moses Lake Public Library; Bob Pace, Yakima Tribal Media Representative; and Bernice Greene of the U.S. Forest Service. Among the university personnel to whom we owe much for their help are Andrew Jackson, Richard Berner, Patricia Van Mason, and Mrs. Erven Kloostra of the University of Washington and Earle Connette of Washington State University. We also acknowledge the help of the librarians of the Bancroft Library, University of California, and of numerous others in libraries across the country, including the Beinecke Library, Yale University. For reading portions of our manuscript and making helpful suggestions we thank John Fahey, Robert Hitchman, Frank E. Walsh, and Merle Wells.

The satisfaction we have received in preparing our manuscript has more than offset the rigors of our labors. Among our greatest sources of satisfaction are our associations with the people mentioned above and with the countless others who have contributed to our efforts. Nor would we fail to acknowledge our dependence upon our readers, without whom our efforts would be in vain. We trust that we match their expectations.

Moses Lake, Washington ROBERT H. RUBY
Wenatchee, Washington JOHN A. BROWN

INDIANS
of the
PACIFIC NORTHWEST

The American Pacific Northwest

1. CONTACT BY SEA

The Quinault River tumbles into the Pacific Ocean from the jagged Olympic Mountains in northwestern Washington State. For ages natives lived out their days near its mouth in a world of sea grayed by mists and rain and greened occasionally by the sun, a world of forest, mostly evergreen, varying in hue with the disposition of the sky. The Pacific winds were always within their hearing, and the breakers pounded with nonpacific fury against their shores. In the background were the sounds of the creaking and groaning forests. The moods of sea and forest were vital to the people, whose life rhythm followed that of nature herself.

On July 14, 1775, in the white man's measure of time, violence was heard in the natives' world. On that day about two hundred Quinaults (a tribe belonging to the Salishan linguistic group), with bows and arrows and flat spears on long wooden poles, protected by leathern cuirasses called *clamons* and ornamented with many-colored shells hanging from their pierced ears, rushed from their forests to attack and kill a seven-man party from the Spanish schooner *Sonora*. The whites were ashore in a longboat seeking fresh water from the Quinault River. Iron-hungry like all other Northwest Coast peoples, the natives smashed the Spaniards' boat and carried off pieces of the metal from the craft. They carried their attack by canoe to the schooner, where they met fire from the ship's swivel gun and muskets. Seven of their number were killed, matching to a man the number the Spaniards lost (two Spaniards drowned attempting to return to the ship). When the firing ceased, the crew of the undermanned *Sonora*, now in heavy seas, abandoned their wish for revenge, and put out to sea. The natives disappeared into the woods edging their beach, which had been claimed that very day by the Spaniards for their God and country. Bruno de Hezeta of the expedition, memorializing the confrontation, named a small island Isla de Dolores ("the isle of sorrows") off the mouth of the Hoh River in memory of the Spanish dead.

The natives likely did not know that nearly two hundred years earlier Spanish mariners sailing northward had claimed all the lands washed by the Pacific as they sought the mythical Strait of Anian, or Northwest Passage, and the fabulous city Quivira. Natives on the Oregon coast told of ships wrecked off their beaches. One such ship left La Paz, in Baja California, June 16, 1769, with supplies for a Roman Catholic mission at San Diego, in Alta California. Tons of beeswax were deposited ashore from the wreck. Instead of providing candles for solemn ceremonials, the wax littered the shores of "pagan" Oregon, where Indians for years to come would try to sell it to other Indians or to white men who had no more use for it than they did. Although conquistadors in earlier times had treated American natives cruelly, later Spaniards came with orders to deal humanely with them.

For ages the peoples of the Northwest Coast had engaged in intertribal conflict. Often internecine, desultory, and spasmodic in nature, it usually lasted only long enough for the natives to kill their foes, capture human heads as trophies, and enslave prisoners. Traveling in large canoes, which were painted like their own skins, protected by elk-skin cuirasses, and carrying an arsenal of bows and arrows, spears, knives, and clubs, the warriors chanted war songs as they attacked. Meanwhile the enemy villagers tried to defend themselves behind fortifications. After the engagements survivors obtained blood-feud payments for the dead. When wars ceased, memories of them did not. Vengeance-seeking parties would resume the conflict. As a result ownership of the fishing grounds was contested, and tribal boundaries constantly shifted about.

In the area of the 1775 attack on the Spaniards, the Quinaults and the Queets (both Salishan, or Salish, peoples) and the Hohs and the Quileutes, or Quillayutes (both Chimakuan) were, according to their traditions, parties to a confederation extending from Cape Flattery down to Grays Harbor. Occasionally they interrupted their peaceful occupations, such as hunting game in the foothills or on the sea (they hunted fur and hair seals, whales, and sea otters) to war against the Ozettes (Hosetts) and the Makahs, or Kwenetchechat, "people who live on a point of land projecting into the sea" (both Wakashan), who lived near the entrance to the Strait of Juan de Fuca. The Ozettes and Makahs were whale-hunting peoples who, before white contact, had migrated southward from the west coast of Vancouver Island. They served as intermediaries in trade between the Indians of Vancouver Island and those along the coast on the south. Deriving from the Nootkan group of Vancouver Island, they had, with some variations, similar canoes, arms, and implements. The Makahs and Ozettes patched up their differences long enough to join forces against a common foe, the Quileutes. The Quileutes and Quinaults were the only whaling peoples to originate within the present boundaries of the continental United States, excluding Alaska.

The confederation also warred against the Clallams, or Klallams (the latter is the tribal spelling today), a Salishan tribe of the Strait of Juan de Fuca; against the Satsops (Salishan) of the lower Olympic Peninsula; and against the Lower Chinooks (Chinookan) and other coastal and Columbia River peoples. In these wars they often relied on slaves captured from their foes to guide them to the scenes of combat. On the north members of the confederation warred

3

against the fierce peoples of Vancouver and Queen Charlotte islands and against those of the mainland. According to Hoh tradition, shortly before the coming of white men, fighting broke out on the Grays Harbor mud flats, where the Quileutes had pursued their foes intending to raid them for slaves. In the fight many Quileutes were killed when their canoe stuck in the mud after an ebbing tide. Fighting in the open, the Satsops and the Chinookan warriors lost many of their braves, but they returned to their villages with several head trophies.

Although Quileute tradition tells of what were believed to be shipwrecked Spaniards living peacefully for a time among them, native tradition also has it that countrymen of the "Drifting White People" and others shipwrecked on Pacific beaches stormed ashore to prey on them and molest their women. Along aboriginal trade-route grapevines such stories could easily have passed from village to village creating suspicion and belligerence among the natives at the appearance of the white strangers. The molestation of native women helped spoil a meeting that might otherwise have been friendly between Indians and Spaniards north of the Quinault River at Neah Bay (later named for Deeah, a Makah chief), the very northwest tip of the Olympic Peninsula, and the entrance to the Strait of Juan de Fuca. In July, 1790, the Makahs, under their chief, Tutusi (Tatooche?), at the village of Wyacht (Waatch)*, received from the Spanish visitors copper in exchange for salmon, skins, and fruits. The Spaniards were aboard the *Princesa Real*, under the command of Manuel Quimper. Tutusi invited the Spaniards to trade at Neah Bay, saying that six vessels had already bartered there for sea-otter skins. One trader whom they met was the Britisher Charles Duncan, whose sloop, the *Princess Royal*, had lain at anchor in 1788 within the strait at the Classet village near Neah Bay.

Reacting to the molestation of one of their women by a soldier straying from a camp established by Quimper, the natives attacked and painfully wounded the miscreant. In retaliation the Spaniards captured two native canoes and towed them to their ship. On the evening of that event three Makah warriors paddled stealthily to the ship, in an attempt to retrieve the dugouts, only to be scattered when the Spaniards discharged a swivel into the air. Impressed with this show of force, Tutusi kept on peaceful terms with his visitors, telling them that the attackers had been punished. Some of his men continued trading with the visitors.

At Neah Bay, on August 1, 1790, the Spaniards under Quimper performed their traditional religious-political ceremonial of asserting in the name of God, the Trinity, and the King of Spain, that country's "legal sovereignty over these lands and waters," including the bay, Nuñez Gaona, where their ship was anchored. After the ceremonies Quimper sailed off for other shorelines to repeat the ceremonial—in a world of which Spain claimed half as her own. The reaction of the Makahs and other natives to this ceremonial is unknown. They may have been concerned mostly with the physical objects of the ceremonials, such as the crucifixes the Spaniards planted on their shores.

Between August 7 and 11, 1791, Spaniards under Francisco de Eliza visited Neah Bay, where Eliza purchased twenty small native men and women for thirty-three copper sheets. Eliza also established a temporary base farther up the strait in Discovery Bay (near present-day Port Townsend, Washington). On May 28 of the following year Salvador Fidalgo, aboard the frigate *Princesa*, returned to establish the Núñez colony at Neah Bay, not to trade furs but to check British moves on the strait. Watching for ships that were friendly or otherwise, the wary Spaniards did not for long take their eyes off their post and the surrounding natives. Emulating a practice of their hosts, they moored their longboats on the beach for hasty retreats should the natives attack.

With the Spaniards the natives traded furs, fowl, fish, and berries for copper sheeting and learned more of mysterious Christian symbols, such as the cross. Some may have received baptism from Spanish friars. They also learned how food could be grown in gardens and saw domestic animals—cattle, poultry, sheep, goats, and swine—which bore some resemblance to the wild ones that they knew. They could have learned from the Spaniards of even stranger creatures, fearsome beasts roaming steaming jungles on faroff continents.

They could tell their guests of even larger beasts, the whales swimming the broad Pacific. According to Indian mythology the huge mammals were hunted by Thunderbird, or Thlukluts (also called Totooch, Tutush, and other names), who carried the lightning fish, Hahektoak, which seized whales in its powerful claws. So important were the whale hunts that a cut across the nose was the mark of honor among those who killed whales. Beginning with spiritual and physical preparations, the hunts reached their climax when the expeditions of two to five canoes approached the whaling grounds. The canoes were about thirty-five feet long and carried up to eight men. At the whaling ground the key huntsman, the harpooner, or *hoachinicaha*, positioned himself at the bow of the canoe, ready to hurl his weapon, which had been safely blessed by a shaman. The harpoon was up to eighteen feet long and weighed as much as forty pounds. With deadly accuracy the harpooner thrust it sometimes more than fifty feet at the mammoth quarry. Then followed the struggle, man against beast. The whale would lose blood and finally be dispatched and towed ashore, buoyed up by floats. There the body was cut up according to ancient rules and rituals. Choice oil for eating was reserved for chiefs and headmen. The tribe feasted on the flesh and fat. The oil was stored in skinbladders for local use or for trade with neighboring tribes. Some of the tribes south of the strait did not go whaling but processed whales that were tossed on their beaches by storms. The Indians on the coast took a possessive attitude toward such faunal flotsam on their beaches and toward other sea

---

*Other permanent Makah villages were Baadah (Baada), Tekaktus, Deah (Dia and Neah), Klisidatsus (Kehsidatsoos), Tsuess (Tzues), and Ozette (Hosett).

4

and land creatures, such as elk, deer, bear, and smaller game of the forest.*

According to various accounts, in early July, 1792, against the orders of his commander the first pilot of the *Princesa* went ashore to do some shooting in the forests at Neah Bay and did not return. Natives told a search party that a warrior from Tutusi's village had killed a Spaniard with his own gun and carried his body away. Unnerved by the news and aware that his ship was too far offshore to bring her guns into play in case of attack, Fidalgo began to panic. According to the account, two canoes of Indians knifing shoreward toward the fort were hit by shot from Spanish gunners. When the firing ceased, six Indian men and women had been killed. A boy and girl were pulled from the water and questioned by Fidalgo about the missing Spaniard. The lad confirmed the death, and the next day the body was found in a thicket near the outer wall of the fort. Fearing a retaliatory attack, Fidalgo, according to one account, ordered his guns to fire on the village, laying it waste and forcing its occupants to flee across the strait. According to another tradition, the Spaniards, when they claimed land at Neah Bay, had turned liberty to license until a chief whose wife they had stolen rose against them and drove them away. In any case, Fidalgo and his men, on September 26, 1792, abandoned the place to the "warlike, treacherous, and thievish" natives. A few days after the attack natives of a village at Neah Bay yelled and gestured menacingly at the seventy-ton American brig *Hope*, commanded by Joseph Ingraham. The captain, thinking them eager to avenge the men Fidalgo had killed, fired over their heads to quiet their demonstration.

Tradition has it that not all Spanish exploits were of an official nature. Spanish pirates landed at various places along the coast and met various fates at the hands of its natives. One of many Indian traditions tells about a 1,000-man army under a Nisqually (Salishan) chief, Ractamoos, who met 400 freebooting Spaniards storming ashore in northern Puget Sound. According to the tale 150 Spaniards escaped, only to drown in a violent storm in the Strait of Juan de Fuca.*

Natives prevented other whites from establishing na-

tionalist or mercantilist beachheads on the Northwest Coast. In July, 1787, at the mouth of the Hoh River they encountered a party under British trader Charles Barkley. Captain Barkley dispatched two boats from his ship, the *Imperial Eagle*, to trade with the Hohs up their river. The river was too shallow for the larger of the two craft, but the smaller one moved upstream. It never returned. Natives attacked and killed all hands aboard. Barkley named the river Destruction, and gave the same name to the island the Spaniards had called the Isla de Dolores. Because of their attack Barkley described the natives below the strait as of a "Bandity kind."

On the north, off the extremity of the Olympic Peninsula at Tatoosh Island, in late June, 1788, the Makahs met Barkley's countryman, trader John Meares, aboard the British snow *Felice Adventurer*. The Indians were found by Meares, like Barkley, to be of "much more savage aspect" than any that he had seen hitherto in outposts such as the multioutfitting place at Nootka Sound on western Vancouver Island. A contingent of twenty to thirty of them approached the visitors in large oceangoing canoes. Dressed in otter skins, their faces daubed with oil, they were armed with knives, ragged bone-barbed arrows, and mussel-shell-pointed spears. The captain was apprehensive, unable to reconcile in his mind the large population of the island with its barrenness. In fact, the natives had gathered there for summer fishing. Their chief, Tatooche, visited the strangers with white faces. He had entirely blackened his own and covered it with glittering sand. He received the usual small presents from the British, but he made no reciprocal gifts nor could he be persuaded to permit his people to trade with them.

It is Meares's account, rather than the natives', that on a later trip he obtained from the chiefs of the strait promises of free and exclusive trade in the region and the right to build any storehouse or edifice that he deemed necessary. He claimed to have received a similar right from Tatooche. From the latter he also claimed to have purchased a tract of land within the strait, over which one of his officers took possession in the name of the king. Meares named the island for the chief because it was in country held by the Makahs, whose mythical character, Thunderbird, bore the same phonetic name as the chief. The validity of the story of Meare's claims and of the claims themselves is unknown. It can be said only that Meares—with a reputation for deceptiveness—gained his objectives, as one of his biographers writes, by "intrigue or trickery, graft or force."

---

*Whaling, which pitted Pacific Northwestern natives against the vast Pacific Ocean, has intrigued non-Indians from the time of their initial contact with those natives until the present. Among descriptions of whaling written for a geographically wide reading public are James G. Swan, "The Indians of Cape Flattery, at the Entrance to the Strait of Fuca, Washington Territory," *Smithsonian Contributions to Knowledge* 16, no. 8: 8–9, and "Coast Whaling," *The Overland Monthly* 6, no. 2 (February, 1871): 118–25; T. T. Waterman, "The Whaling Equipment of the Makah Indians," *University of Washington Publications in Anthropology* 1 (1920): 1–67. Among descriptions written for regional readers are "Visit to Tatooche Island," *Washington Standard* (Olympia, W.T.), July 20, 1861, p. 1, and "Whaling Off Cape Flattery," *Oregonian* (Portland, Ore.), October 5, 1889, pp. 101–102. A present-day source is Ruth Kirk and Richard Daugherty, *Hunters of the Whale.*

*Because of its probably unofficial nature, Spanish archival sources may never shed light on this confrontation. The native account is related in Lelah Jackson Edson, *Fourth Corner; Highlights from Early Northwest* p. 2.

Wife of Makah Chief Tatooche. Residing where the Strait of Juan de Fuca enters the Pacific Ocean, Tatooche met many white men, including Spaniards, one of whom sketched this picture. Naval Museum, Madrid.

An American trader, Robert Gray—whose relatives would claim that the natives granted him lands also—if he did not employ graft, did on occasion resort to force. In August, 1788, out of Boston in the sloop *Lady Washington*, Gray sailed north along Oregon shores inhabited by the Tillamook (Salishan) Indians, including Tillamooks proper and Nestucca, Nehalem, and Nechesne (or Salmon River) Indians. Gray found them cautious, their weapons at the ready. A few of the weapons were of iron, indicating they had some contact with whites, as did their pock-marked faces. A friendly meeting between the natives and Gray at Tillamook Bay was disrupted when a native made off with a sword that a crewman had carelessly left sticking in the sand. In the ensuing skirmish over it the natives reportedly killed the crewman but lost three of their number in return. Escaping a canoe flotilla, Gray wheeled the *Lady Washington* out of what he called Murderer's Harbor, but not before ordering his crew to fire her guns on plank houses and natives ashore. The natives came to call Americans like Gray "Boston Men," to distinguish them from Britishers, whom they called "King George Men."

Other natives along the Oregon coast appeared hostile to ships' crews seeking trade with them in furs. One midsummer day in 1791, the 78-ton three-masted schooner and former slaver *Jenny*, commanded by Captain James Baker, out of Bristol, England, dropped anchor in an estuary of the Umpqua River to trade. The natives—very possibly Lower Umpquas (Yakonan), also called Kuitshes—were hostile, at least according to Charles Bishop, captain of the *Jenny's* sister ship, the 101-ton *Ruby*, which stopped at that place the following year. According to Bishop, natives there had traded with the *Jenny's* crew but had gestured menacingly at it, flashing bows and arrows and making signs so unfriendly that the crewmen believed that, had they gone ashore, they would have been eaten alive. The captains of the sister ships, not to be intimidated by the Pacific Coast tribes and driven by hopes of great profits, would continue trading for a few more years, amassing furs for the profitable China trade in exchange for precious commodities that ranged from teas to silks. One by-product of the *Jenny's* 1794 trading venture into the mouth of the Columbia River was the birth of a baby to a slave of Chinook chief Shelathwell, a consequence of an affair with the *Jenny's* first mate, a Mr. William. In 1795, Captain Bishop would also enter the river to conduct a brisk trade. Among the items traded to the *Jenny* were cuirasses, which were much in demand among warring northern tribes; Bishop, like other traders, would exchange them for sea-otter pelts for the China trade. In trading, ship captains were constantly aware of what Bishop called the "Wiley guile" of the "Savage race," taking appropriate measures to protect their craft.

Captain Robert Gray did not ingratiate himself with the northern natives by his destruction of a Vancouver Island village of nearly two hundred houses containing priceless images. Word of the captain's action very possibly spread along native trade channels, which stretched from Alaska as far south as California. Sometime after Gray's mercantilist-inspired cataclysm, when a ship out of Boston visited the village of Classet on the strait between Cape Flattery and Neah Bay, the Makah chief Utilla demanded that a hostage board his canoe alongside the ship as he boarded her to trade. In response an assistant to the captain was sent as hostage. After trading had continued for a while, an alarm sounded signifying that a quarrel had erupted between several natives and the ship's crew, which was ashore for water. Several guns were fired toward the watering place. In the confusion the chief sprang to his canoe. Before he could permit the hostage to return to the ship, the chief was fired on by those aboard. Standing calmly erect in his canoe, he ordered his men to paddle ashore amid a shower of bullets, one of which lodged in his thigh. With cannon fire from the ship landing around him, the hostage believed that he would be put to death. Utilla said that he was not the guilty one, releasing him the next day to return to his ship. From then on, the Makah chief would have nothing to do with the Boston ship's captain. Like Utilla, other native traders quickly learned which captains and supercargoes they could trust.

Chief George A. Charley of the Willapa Bay area in south-
western Washington. He is holding a hand-forged knife inherited
from his father, "Lighthouse" Charley Ma-Tote, who said it was a
gift from the early American fur trader Robert Gray. The Colum-
bia River was named after Gray's ship, the Columbia Rediviva.
Pacific County Historical Society, Raymond, Washington.

Some ship captains were known for their unfriendliness to natives. They soon learned to protect their ships and to be cautious of shipboard trading.

On May 7, 1792, large numbers of canoes came off Bulfinch's Harbor (previously Puerto Grek and subsequently Grays Harbor) to meet Captain Gray, now aboard the *Columbia Rediviva*. To him this "savage sett" appeared well armed, with bows and quivers slung over their shoulders much in the style of natives farther up the Northwest Coast. They appeared eager to trade many of their furs for "blankets." Important among the furs of their coasts was sea otter. There were more extensive rookeries, however, farther up the Northwest Coast, where sea-otter pelts had become the main product of the maritime trade. White merchants had discovered their value in China in 1779, after British Capt. James Cook had taken some pelts from the Northwest Coast the previous year. There soon developed a lively unregulated trade in the pelts—in an age when men did not realize the claims of such creatures in the natural environment.

Natives of Grays Harbor, unlike those farther up the coast, appeared to have been ignorant of the use of firearms. Gray and his men could be thankful for this ignorance, for on the night of May 8, 1792, "hooting" sounds carried over the harbor to the *Columbia*, sending her crew to its guns. Several canoes passed the ship in the moonlight and drew fire from the crew's muskets. Fire followed from the ship's mounted guns, which splintered a canoe and sent its occupants to a watery grave. Despite these events the natives still evinced a wish to trade, but Gray backed off, wishing to invite no more trouble.

South of Grays Harbor, on May 11, natives watched as the *Columbia*, for whom the river would be named, inched across the treacherous bar to anchor in Bakers Bay, in the land of the Chinooks. The Chinooks paddled out to the ship in twenty canoes to meet the white men. The appearance of the natives, many of whom had flattened heads, did not shock Gray and his crew as it did later visitors, for the Boston traders had seen similarly misshapen heads in the north.* Trade with Gray and his men continued as the natives exchanged skins for copper, cloths, nails, steel bars, spikes, thimbles, and buttons. The rate of exchange was better for Gray than what he had experienced in the north, perhaps because he was dealing with a people who had few if any contacts with white traders and were ignorant about exchange rates.

As Gray ascended the river to present-day Grays Bay, Washington, word of his presence spread along the mighty stream, bringing other natives down to look and to trade until the ship weighed anchor and slipped across the bar into the Pacific, along whose shores Gray traded below the strait before carrying his furs to China. The Northwest Coast Indians were the vital vortex of a triangular trade from their shores to the Orient, where their furs were exchanged for priceless eastern goods for Boston. With furs supplied him by the Indians, Gray blazed for other New Englanders the route of the long, perilous journey. The traders would return to their New England homelands only

to sail again the first leg of their triangular trade pattern, which took them to the Northwest Coast with goods much cheaper than those that they purchased in the Orient, packed in the holds of their sturdy 100- to 250-ton ships. As skilled mariners, the "Boston Men" and the "King George Men" must have been impressed with the naval architecture of the native canoes which withstood the pounding of the turbulent Pacific tides. Some later believed that the Indian crafts inspired the design of the clipper ships, on which the successors of early-day Boston Men swiftly sailed the oceans of the world.[1]

Although Indians along the coast and outer strait had ample contacts with white mariners, those living along the shores of Puget Sound appear to have had no such frequent meetings with white men before 1792. British Captain George Vancouver is often credited with being the first white man whom they met. He explored their waters en route to a diplomatic mission with the Spanish at Nootka. These natives were not the first Northwest Coast peoples whom Vancouver met. On April 24, 1792, he had encountered a skin-clad people, later called the Rogue Rivers, who were probably Tututnis (Athapascan), near what is now Port Orford on the Oregon coast. In two flat-bottomed canoes, which were unlike the larger Nootkan canoes and which suggested low-tide use, these natives traded skins and bows and arrows with the crews of Vancouver's ships, the 340-ton sloop of war H.M.S. *Discovery* and the 130-ton brig and armed tender H.M.S. *Chatham*. One native had a crude iron knife. Others had copper tubing, from which they had fabricated necklaces embellished with berries and shells. The ears and noses of these "well-limbered" people were perforated and similarly ornamented, and their hair was neatly combed and clubbed.

Vancouver's ships sailed by the deceptive Columbia River bar and entered the strait a few days later. They proceeded eastward up the strait and into Puget Sound for an exploratory tour of less than a month in May and June. The Indians became known not only to the ships' crews but also to the world through the many translations of Vancouver's journals. In the journals he told of a people curious to the minds of his readers, a people whom he and other mariners could compare only with those around Nootka. The natives of the strait and Sound were short of stature. Their long, dark hair was ornamented with wood, bone, shell, and metal. Metal was more common on the outer strait than in the inner Sound, although it was not unknown at the latter place, indicating that the tribes there had received it from those along the Pacific Coast. Their faces were covered with grease and ochre. The aristocracy had flattened heads. Generally they wore skins, and their women had knee-length bark capes; but in warmer, drier weather they wore little clothing. Shorn dogs indicated the use of

---

*Natives of the lower Columbia told the early nineteenth-century fur trader Robert Stuart that Gray was the first white man to enter that river. Kenneth A. Spaulding, ed., *On the Oregon Trail: Robert Stuart's Journey of Discovery, 1812–1813*, p. 42. For an explanation of the head-flattening practice and its consequences see Robert H. Ruby and John A. Brown, *The Chinook Indians*, pp. 47–49, 175, 198, 242, 265–66.

Indians, probably Suquamishes, at a camp near Seattle. Just as horses carried the Indians of the interior, their products, and equipages, canoes performed a similar function for the Indians west of the Cascade Mountains. Pacific Northwest Collections, University of Washington Library.

dog fur for clothing and blankets. Another British traveler in the area in the early nineteenth century provided details about the production of such coverings:

The natives of Tatooch show much ingenuity in manufacturing blankets from the hair of their dogs. On a little island [Tatoosh] a few miles from the coast they have a great number of white dogs which they feed regularly every day. From the wool of these dogs and the fibers of the Cypress they make a very strong blanket. They have also some method of making red & blue stripes in their blankets in imitation of European ones. At a little distance it is difficult to distinguish these Indian blankets from those of Europe.[2]

A traveler among the Clallams up the strait from the Makahs shortly after 1850 noted that they were generally eager to trade whatever they had: short bows (unlike the longer ones of the Columbia Plateau and the Great Plains on the east), flint, bone- or iron-tipped arrows, skins and woolens, and native fishhooks. Some natives along the strait appeared to Vancouver to oppose bartering the favors of their women. Propriety seemed to be the rule among the women, although some Indians offered to sell children (possibly their slaves) to the explorers. In exchange for their goods the natives sought the usual copper, cloth, iron, bells, buttons, and beads. Skulls and head trophies raised on poles in some of the villages made the visitors aware of native conflicts. Presenting a sinister appearance to them were skeletal remains in temporary villages from which woodplank coverings had been stripped. These and other empty villages caused them to speculate whether some catastrophe—conflict or disease—might have stripped them bare. Had Vancouver been among these Indians in winter, he would have found them in permanent villages—small settlements of single dwellings housing four to six families.

The travelers shrewdly observed variations between the

natives of the outer strait and those of the Sound. They observed the former to be oriented toward Nootka in such things as language and transport by their use of the Nootkan canoe. The peoples of the Sound exhibited more wariness than did those of the outer strait, who for several years had had contacts with white mariners. In some cases the natives of the Sound refused to trade with the Vancouver party, and on one occasion they threatened armed conflict. Fighting was an activity to which they were no strangers. They armed themselves with bows and arrows and other weaponry and protected their bodies with tough skin cuirasses. Their enemies were tribes close to home or those from the north, who often swept southward on head and slave hunting expeditions. The Puget Sound peoples seemed to raid less extensively than the natives of the coast, possibly because, with the great natural bounty at their disposal, they were not tempted to take from others, or possibly because their weak political organization precluded such enterprises.

The economic base of the natives in Puget Sound was as strong as their political base was weak. Their seas and forests furnished them abundant wealth and leisure. They were a class-conscious people, and they practiced secret and complex ceremonials revealing the wealth and authority that assured social and economic security. From this existence, which Vancouver witnessed in its florescence, they also developed an advanced technology and a stylized art that is to be seen in their many fine wooden products.

Poles set apart on sand spits with nets strung between — an enigma to Vancouver — were actually clever devices to snare low-flying waterfowl. Several species of salmon, the primary gift of sea and river, provided a basic food, which they ate fresh, smoked, or dried. This source of protein was supplemented by other seafood and by game taken from the nearby forests. They fashioned the light durable cedar from the forests into canoes, house planks, hats, mats, baskets, and a hundred other things. There was scarcely an item from nature that they did not use for food, fiber, or pharmocopoeia. They had a counterpart for nearly every product that the white men brought them. Although some of their tools, utensils, and weapons were inferior to those of white men, others, such as their fishing gear made of the lowly nettle, were superior. Hats and mats made by the deft fingers of Puget Sound Indian women became highly prized in the white community.

These natives did not separate their material objects from things of the spirit. As among other Pacific Northwestern peoples, fruit, root, and salmon ceremonies were conducted properly before food gathering began. Vancouver had proof they were a spiritual people when he observed that their canoe burials contained the bodies of those whose spirits, after failure of doctors to retrieve them, had gone to the other world. Like people everywhere they died naturally, violently, or from diseases. Smallpox had marked the faces of some whom Vancouver saw. Not all were as fortunate as one Salish-speaking family of northern Puget Sound. In an episode reminiscent of the Flood of Noah and the Passover of Moses they were warned by their prophet, Lahailby,

of coming disaster. According to tradition, the prophet had received a warning in a dream that the ministrations of a shaman would be ineffectual and that only group praying could save the family. Obedient to the warning, despite much ridicule from nonbelievers, the prophet was able to save them from the disease. Ironically, it reached many of its victims before they had seen its white purveyors.[3]

The natives' singing and beating on canoes with sticks to ward off evil water spirits were further proof to Vancouver of their spiritual orientation. Had he not been in such haste, he might have learned that they were a people with a well-developed cosmology, who believed in a previous race of "animal people" that included powerful characters, such as Raven, Wolf, and Coyote, whose exploits were well known from myth-legends handed down from the misty past.

Like the natives of Puget Sound, many of the Indians on the Columbia River a few miles beyond its mouth may have seen white people for the first time when they met the Vancouver expedition. Returning homeward from Nootka, Lieutenant William R. Broughton, commanding the *Chatham*, crossed the Columbia River bar on October 20, 1792, to anchor in Bakers Bay near the Chinook village there. Ashore he found the village deserted and fleainfested and noted that its houses appeared to have been more comfortable than those of Nootka and had a greater pitch to their roofs.

These people had come under cultural influences from the coast and also from the traffic on the Columbia River, which descended from the Columbia Plateau in the intermontane West. Their culture rapidly faded along the coast south of the Columbia as it merged with and was replaced by the culture of the California Indians.

A canoe load of natives from Point Ellice (near Knappton, Washington) came out to the *Chatham* evincing a willingness, especially among the women (as would be the case for years to come), to trade skins for copper and other items for ornamentation. The Indians' own inventory of ornaments included dentalia, called *hiqua*, which were milk white, extremely hard, and an inch or so long, tapered at one end and curved slightly to resemble horns of plenty. These shells were collected from sea bottoms in such places as Vancouver Island, the Queen Charlotte Islands, and the mainland coast to Sitka, Alaska. They were more desired when they were of such a size that forty could be strung in a six-foot fathom or the length to which a person could stretch his arms. They were used not only for body decoration but also as a medium of exchange, purchasing one male or two female slaves and paying for services, such as those provided by shamans. They found their way through trade channels far from the place of their origin, to the Columbia River and thence southward and eastward into the interior, that is the area between the Cascade and Rocky mountains.

The flattened heads of the Indian aristocracy were not as shocking perhaps to the early white mariners as they would be to later travelers because the early mariners had seen them on the North Coast. Headflattening was practiced among coastal groups as far south as the Siuslaws

(Yakonan) along the Siuslaw River in Oregon; by groups up the Columbia, such as the Upper Chinooks (Chinookan); and occasionally in the interior among the Shahaptians and allied peoples. Mothers placed infants on cradleboards and applied pressure to the pliable skulls, thus creating their "badge of aristocracy." Some northern peoples, such as the Nitinats (Wakashan) of Barkley Sound on southwestern Vancouver Island, intermarried with flat-headed peoples south of the Strait of Juan de Fuca, but they did not regard the cranial disfigurement as a sign of freedom or high birth. The process, lasting up to a year, was denied to slaves. In the nineteenth century Siuslaw mothers would attempt to introduce the practice among their people. Their ineptness at it brought death to all the children who were treated. Siuslaw men killed three or four mothers when the malpractice continued. When properly carried out, head flattening was neither painful nor harmful. White men interested in cranial studies would be intrigued by its effect on intelligence and personality.

Contact with white men, whether they were Spanish, British, or American, often brought the Indians physical ailments far more damaging than head flattening. Diseases carried by the whites raced up and down the coast. Sometime in the middle of the eighteenth century a wrecked ship that reportedly acquired a contagion in a Chinese port spread it from "far to the north" down the coast to the mouth of the Columbia River, nearly wiping out a village. The survivors put lodges, clothing, and other effects to the torch to prevent its spread. A decade before Gray breached the Columbia, the smallpox had raced along that stream as it had up the Missouri River and across the Rocky Mountains to the upper Columbia.

Natives were also aware of another shipborne threat to their lives and properties, namely, the guns, whose thunder-like blasts were more lethal than their own aboriginal weapons and the few iron battle-axes that they obtained perhaps through coastal trade. The Indians regarded the firearms as evil spirits filling the air with pestilence and death. It was in remembrance of an unpleasant experience with white men's guns that the natives of Neah Bay threatened Captain Ingraham in 1792. But not all their experiences with white men had been bad, for in late July of the following year a friend of Tutusi asked the second pilot of the 46-ton Spanish schooner *Mexicana*, Don Juan Martinez y Zayas, for news of Spanish captains who had been in his country earlier. Farther down the coast, at the mouth of the Quillayute River, six ten-man canoes equipped with two perpendicular prows with holes, paddled out from a cove on August 4. They were on their way to the *Mexicana* to invite her crew to land, and explaining that their chief, Mogos Utpi, had sealskins to exchange for copper and clothing, their "common desire." Declining the invitation because of shifting winds, the Spaniards sailed down the coast to the Grays Harbor area. There, on August 8, a hostile native band under one Canchuk—unlike a friendlier band headed by Putus, tried to seize the Spanish launch by force and then fled when repulsed. Sailing farther south, the Spaniards on August 10 entered the Columbia River, where the natives appeared warlike to them. Although they had trade items aboard, the Spaniards backed off and put out to sea.

The retreat of Martínez y Zayas from the Columbia River was symbolic of Spain's retreat from the Northwest Coast, which was the result of agreements effected by her and Great Britain (known as the Nootka agreements) half a

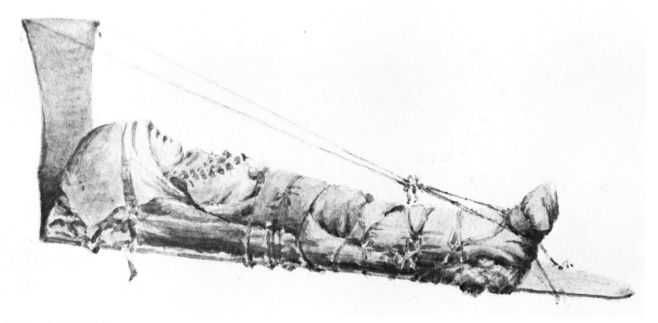

A Chinook child of the lower Columbia River undergoing head flattening. Some tribes near The Dalles just above the Chinookan lands along the Columbia flattened the heads of their infants to a limited extent. Upper-Columbia tribes, such as the Flathead Indians, did not flatten heads at all. Sketch by Paul Kane. Courtesy of the Stark Foundation.

world away from this coast and its people. Trade continued apace between the Indians and the King George and Boston Men because each group possessed things that the other wanted. The natives' shrewdness, developed over years of aboriginal trade, made them aware of the laws of the market-place. They continued to receive, sometimes grudgingly, white traders' metal goods and cloths and, less grudgingly, molasses, which was, as one white trader put it, to "sweeten the tawney stomachs of those savages." Other trade items varied yearly with the Indians' changing tastes in European and American products. Sometimes they used certain goods, such as teapots and buttons, for ornaments, scarcely the use to which white men put them. They continued for a time to trade furs destined for China, as well as cuirasses.

Changing demands in the Orient, as well as declining sea-otter herds, would, by the third decade of the nineteenth century, bring the demise of the trade. Even before then another furry animal was affecting the natives of the Pacific Northwest. Beaver had figured prominently in the legends of the origins of various tribes. Natives had trapped it in modest quantities for fur and meat, but now it came to be much sought by men interested only in its fur. This once lowly but now valuable animal brought overland explorer-trappers and traders searching for it. This quest would cause some of the economic activity to shift from the coasts to inland areas of the Pacific Northwest. Consequently, natives of the inland regions, like the beaver of their lands and lore, would no longer live as they had before.

2. CONTACT BY LAND

One late summer day in 1805 near the Rocky Mountain Lemhi Pass around Horse Prairie Creek, Montana, outrunners of the Northern Shoshonis (here-after referred to as the Shoshonis) were hailed by strange men with white faces. From this meeting some natives fled. An elderly woman and a little girl sat down and held their heads, expecting the strangers to kill them. Captain Meriwether Lewis quieted their fears, for he sought the assistance of their tribe, on whom depended the success of the expedition to the Pacific Ocean led by him and Captain William Clark.[1]

Soon a party of sixty mounted Shoshonis rode up to the strangers at a full gallop. The explorers presented them gifts. In appreciation, the natives caressed Lewis and his men, rubbing the grease on their tawny faces onto the faces of the strangers. Well versed in Indian ways, Lewis offered them the traditional pipe of peace. Before accepting it, the natives removed their moccasins, an act of friendship signifying that the white men could traverse their lands. Among the gifts that they received was a flag for their head chief, Cameahwait (One Who Never Walks, To-oetecone, also Black Gun), as a bond of union. A short distance away women and children of another camp shied from the strangers. Yet the ground of friendship had been broken. The chief gave the party information to help it on its westward journey.

The larger Shoshoni family at that time occupied lands on the northern reaches of the territory that was inhabited by the tribes that are classified as Western, Northern, and Eastern Shoshonis. The Western and Northern Shoshonis' lands stretched roughly from the southern end of the Bitterroot Mountains of western Montana east to the main spur of the Rockies and south to the Colorado River basin, then east of a line beginning at the western end of the Blue Mountains of northeastern Oregon and continuing south on a line about 150 miles east of the Pacific Ocean.

Although the white men's gifts were well received they were not the first such presents to the Shoshonis. They had received others, mostly indirectly, from French and British traders east of the Rocky Mountains, from Spaniards in California and New Mexico, and from white mariners on the Pacific Coast. They did not receive white men's goods as directly as did the Western Shoshonis (hereafter referred to as the Shoshonis), who attended annual markets where the Boise, Payette, and Weiser rivers of Idaho enter the Snake River, a Columbia tributary. At these markets they traded and socialized with other tribes who provided a link with those of the Pacific Coast.

The most treasured of all the foreign imports was the horse. It facilitated the trading process and brought the Shoshonis their goods. Lewis's hosts possessed four hundred of them to break their pedestrian way of life.[2] Just as they had obtained most of their white men's goods indirectly, they had obtained horses from the Spaniards in the eighteenth century through Comanche and possibly Ute intermediaries (both Shoshonean). Horses enabled Cameahwait's people, as they would other western tribes, to travel eastward across the Rocky Mountains to "buffalo" where the shaggy beasts were more numerous. On the heels of Lewis and Clark came American fur hunters driving herds of the big animals farther and farther westward, until in the early 1840s, diminished in numbers, they retreated back across the Rockies.

Across the Rockies, in the Missouri and Yellowstone countries, Shoshonis often hunted buffalo with bows and arrows during the fall and winter, jerking meat and preparing hides before returning west to fish between May and September, earning them the sobriquet "salmon eaters." They were also known on the plains as the "grass-lodge" or "grass-house" people because enemy bands had stolen the hide coverings of their dwellings and forced them to resort to their traditional grass-covered homes.

Cameahwait's people received a promise from Lewis that they would receive more goods if the chief would accompany him to the Beaverhead River, northeast of Lemhi Pass, to meet Clark. Although his people were eager to receive the goods, Cameahwait was wary of strangers. He had reason to be, for his warriors and other mounted Shoshonis fought other Indians across the Rockies, a theater of bloody conflict for red and white men well into the nineteenth century. About sixty years before the Lewis and Clark expedition, the French explorer Pierre Gaultier, Sieur de La Vérendrye, reported that before his own westward trek a Shoshoni band—the Gens des Serpents, or Snakes (a term later applied to all Shoshoni tribes of the Snake River basin)—had destroyed native camps near the Black Hills.* The act was probably committed when the Shoshonis lived east of the Rockies. Those who visited Lewis told him that their people, within their own memories, had lived on the Great Plains, from which they had been driven into the Rockies by the "Pahkees." The latter have been identified as an Algonquian-speaking peoples, such as the Piegans (a Blackfoot [Siksika] subdivision), the Gros Ventres (Atsinas), or the Minnetarees (Atsinas).

Although horses added a mobile dimension to native warfare, they were not its cause. Pacific Northwest and Great Plains tribes fought wars long before the coming of horses. Conflict erupted over contested hunting grounds, the capture of women and children as slaves, the capture of property, the quest for honors and status, and tribal pride. "The People" complex was intensified by a revenge-cycle

---

*The term Snake has also been applied loosely to the Northern Paiutes, Bannocks (a branch of the Northern Paiutes), and the Comanches (all those tribes are of the Shoshonean linguistic family).

mentality in a setting of broken truces. Elderly Piegans told of their wars with Shoshoni bands when both peoples hunted afoot. Around 1730 some Shoshoni war parties traveled north to attack Piegan villages. Unable to secure the aid of other Piegans who had obtained a few guns from Hudson's Bay Company posts, the threatened Piegans were forced to fight with metal and stone weapons. Their Shoshoni attackers had only stone weapons, but they had more effective bows and better-positioned leather shields. After a daylong battle the belligerents disengaged from a rather bloodless confrontation. In an ensuing fight, with about ten guns in the hands of the braves in their front ranks, the Piegans defeated the Shoshonis. Several of the Shoshonis fell victim to "bad spirits" that the Piegans carried onto the field of battle. Terror of battle and of guns caused wars for a period to be carried on by ambush and surprise attacks on small camps.

Horses came earlier to the Shoshonis than to the Blackfoot peoples, who got them, according to their tradition, from the Shoshonis sometime in the 1730s. With their coming, former defensive tactics became obsolete. Bows were shortened, and the use of knives intensified in close-quarter combat. Blackfoot tribes continued to offset their lack of horses with guns obtained from British fur-company traders. Thus they were able to effect surprise ambuscades, such as that at the Three Forks of the Missouri River about five years before the arrival of Lewis and Clark when Cameahwait's people were badly defeated by gun-wielding Gros Ventres. Guns had reduced the Shoshonis whom Lewis and Clark visited to about four hundred souls—which meant that the tribe had even fewer people than horses. Guns, however, did not always tip the balance in favor of the Shoshonis' foes, for the Shoshonis retaliated unwittingly with an even more lethal weapon, the smallpox, which they transmitted to the Blackfeet around 1781. The disease would periodically plague Plains and Pacific Northwest tribes for the next century.[3]

When they met Lewis, Cameahwait and his men had their hair cut short in mourning for tribesmen who had been killed in the desultory trans-Rocky Mountain wars. Cameahwait's wariness increased at the Forks of the Beaverhead River, where, with thirty horses, he had accompanied Lewis to meet Clark. In order to find the Shoshonis and obtain from them horses to get the explorers across the Rocky Mountains to the Columbia River watershed, Lewis had left the main party, who continued along the river route with Clark. When Clark failed to appear, Cameahwait believed Lewis to have been acting on behalf of the Shoshonis' foes. The chief's apprehension was somewhat relieved when Lewis in a dramatic show of sincerity yielded him his party's guns. The following day, August 17, 1805, was a memorable one. There were two reunions: Lewis with Clark and the much heralded meeting of Sacajawea with her people. Captured at the Three Forks confrontation, she had been traded by her captors until she reached the Mandan Siouan Indians of North Dakota, where she was employed to guide Lewis and Clark. Sucking her fingers, which was the sign for "my people," and swinging her hands in a wide circle, mean-

ing "my nation," she held a tearful but joyful reunion with them. Despite later controversy about her effectiveness as expedition guide, she did serve it well because she provided an entrée to peoples of her own race. Most of the expedition party were fair-skinned, except for the member with the "buffalo hair on his head," Clark's black servant, York, who helped keep natives along the way more curious than contentious.

Nowhere on the trek was Sacajawea's presence more helpful to the explorers than it was at this reunion. Any chill between the two parties was broken by her presence, along with more gifts of clothing and tobacco. Tobacco was always sought by American natives, and especially by Cameahwait's people, who were dependent on others for it. Silver medals of friendship from the Great Father, President Thomas Jefferson, capped off the happy occasion. The Shoshonis invited the explorers to remain with them. Because they were under orders, they could not oblige, but they did promise to open trade channels so that the Shoshonis could receive goods "necessary either for their comfort or defense." At that time it appeared that Cameahwait's people were more interested in defense than in comfort, especially since the white men had brought them no arms. The Spaniards to the southwest, although willing to trade the Shoshonis horse trappings, had not traded them guns, possibly fearing that with the weapons they would become involved in bloody conflicts and kill themselves off. On his return to St. Louis, expedition member John Colter met fur trader Manuel Lisa, who lost little time in following the Lewis and Clark trail. In 1807 he built a trading post on the Yellowstone River at the mouth of the Bighorn River in Montana, east of the Rockies, to supply natives with "necessary articles on reasonable terms." Not the least important of the articles were guns, which Lisa feared would disturb the balance of tribal powers and jeopardize the trade that he sought with his native clientele.

For the moment, without guns, the Shoshonis' best hope was their horses, which they had husbanded closely from the time the Minnetarees had stolen many of them in the spring of 1804. Horses were of equal concern to Lewis and Clark for traveling westward. The fiddle which Lewis ordered to be played to amuse the natives did not ease the problem.

The next people whom the explorers met helped somewhat to meet their need for horse transport. Flathead (Salishan) Indians would tell for years to come of the confrontation of their ancestors with the Americans. One of their chiefs, Three Eagles (Cheleskaiyimi), left their camp at Ross' Hole, or Ross' Fork, at the head of the Bitterroot Valley to scout the country because he feared that Indian foes were prowling about seeking to steal horses, an action that plains, mountain, and plateau tribes equated with war. In the distance Three Eagles saw several men who were leading two pack horses. Two men, Lewis and Clark, were riding ahead. Because the two did not wear blankets, the chief believed that they had been robbed of them, but he soon learned the identity and the mission of the *sama*, or *seme*—a native term meaning "not human" when applied to whites—and gave

Flathead Indians playing the ring game. Pacific Northwestern Indians, especially during slack periods in hunting, fishing, and gathering activities, played many games, often attended by gam- *bling. From a sketch by Gustavus Sohon, probably made in 1854 or 1855. Smithsonian Institution National Anthropological Archives, Neg. No. 37,644.*

them tobacco to smoke. Not liking the native tobacco, the explorers told the natives to fill their pipes with some that they had brought, mixing it with the native kinnikinnick. After three days of friendly meetings the explorers and their party pushed on.

The Flatheads who treated their guests so hospitably were known by various names, including Selish, or Salish, a designation that is applied to a wider linguistic group. They were called Têtes-Plates by the French-Canadian fur traders. They denied that their ancestors flattened heads, but accepted the theory that they were called Flatheads because the sign language identified them as pressing both sides of the head with the hands so that white men thought that they did. A mountain man later claimed that the word Salish meant "we the people," which was signified by striking the head with the flat of the hand, and that the people received their name from that gesture. The identification and explanation of the origins of native names is fraught with many pitfalls, as is shown in the classic statement of W. A. Ferris, an American Fur Company employee:

Several tribes of [Rocky] mountain Indians, it will be observed, have names that would be supposed descriptive of some national peculiarity. Among these are the Black-feet, Flat-heads, Bored-noses, Ear-bobs, Big-belly's, etc., and yet it is a fact, that of these, the first have the whitest feet; there is not among the next a de-

formed head; and if the practice of compressing the skull so as to make it grow in a peculiar shape ever did exist among them, it must have been many years since, for there is not one living proof to be found of any such custom. There is not among the Nez-perces an individual having any part of the nose perforated; nor do any of the Pen-d'orulles wear ornaments in their ears; and finally, the Gros-vents are as slim as any other Indians, and corpulency among them is rare.[4] Equally fraught with pitfalls is the explanation of individual Indian names. The observation of a mid-nineteenth-century government explorer has some merit despite its oversimplification:

Their adoption of names is arbitrary, and a fortuitous circumstance is frequently seized upon to gratify the passion for a change. The first name they bear is generally taken from some circumstance at the child's birth, and in after life, others are added to the first, and there are few individuals but are well supplied with them.[5]

The Flatheads, who for hundreds of years had been Salish-speaking peoples, may have drifted east of the Rocky Mountains before returning west across that range to their historic homeland. Causes for their westward movement were smallpox and the acquisition of guns by restless Blackfoot peoples, which shifted the power balance on the plains. Their lands in the Bitterroot valley were about eighty miles long and three to ten miles wide. Although the valley was a thoroughfare for people and goods passing to and from the plains, the Flatheads had ample space to run their horses, many of which were acquired from the Shoshonis, largely through peaceful exchange. When Lewis and Clark met the Flatheads, they had at least five hundred horses, slightly more than the 450 lodges that Lewis believed they possessed. They spoke a tongue more guttural than that of their Shoshoni horse suppliers, but there was little difference in the dress of the two peoples. Their complexion was lighter than that of most of the Indians that the expedition had met hitherto.

The explorers met peoples of yet another linguistic stock as they dropped down from the Bitterroot on the Lolo Trail to the more gentle prairie country on the lower Columbia Plateau. The peoples there were no strangers to the Flatheads and were identified by them by their linguistic family name, Shahaptian, which meant Travelers to the Buffalo Country. At Wieppe Prairie, in present-day Idaho, upland Shahaptian groups extended friendly greetings to the explorers, setting before them foods that included the two staples of their lands, dried salmon and the root of the camas. On the first day of autumn more villagers, from thirty double lodges, met the strangers and identified themselves as "Chopunnish of Perced-nose," or Nez Percés. They were also called by some the "green wood" or "blue earth" people; they called themselves Nimipu, or Noon-neemepoo, and the like, meaning "The People." It has been suggested that the name Nez Percé was a distortion of the words *nez près*, meaning "flat nose," a name given to them by French-Canadian trappers in early days. According to their mythology, they were created at Kamiah on a branch of the Clearwater River. On his return, Lewis recorded that they wore in their noses "a single shell of Wampom," a practice not observed by all the Shahaptian peoples, who occupied many villages in lands stretching southward and westward from the Rockies to the Blue and Cascade mountains.

The amiable Twisted Hair was chief of the village. Farther down the Clearwater at a fishing camp, he had a long smoke with Clark. Clark gave him a medal, a well-deserved gift because he drew for Clark a map of the Clearwater-Snake-Columbia river system, which was the explorers' outlet to the sea. The expedition's horses were to be left in the care of the chief. The explorers learned how to burn out the hulls of logs for their canoe transport on the waterways. More natives, some from the Snake River, came to see them downriver, for word of their coming had spread. From the Nez Percés the explorers received the epithet "dog-eaters" because they preferred the meat of that animal to fish, a preference not shared by their hosts. Other Nez Percés met the explorers at the confluence of the Snake and Clearwater rivers. They were darker than the Flatheads but, like them, they were fond of adornment. Shells and metal pieces indicated some indirect contact with the Pacific. Opposed to this apparent opulence was their simple economy: they fished and gathered from spring to fall, hunted on snowshoes in winter, and crossed the Rockies in spring to hunt buffalo.

They had to fend off not only the attacks of plainsmen but also, closer to home, the marauding Northern Paiutes, a Shoshonean people of southwestern Idaho and southern and eastern Oregon. The Paiutes (as they will be called here) were the scourge of the lower Columbia River peoples. What appeared to the explorers to be Nez Percé avarice was in reality a niggardliness born of a meager existence.

Nez Percé living patterns had changed considerably during the three-quarter century before their meeting with Lewis and Clark. The most important change was the acquisition of the horse, which reached them indirectly from the Spaniards around 1740 through intermediary peoples, such as the Shoshonis and the Cayuses (Waiilatpuan). The latter tribe is believed to have acquired the horse from the former. The Nez Percés later captured horses from the Blackfeet, who could ill afford to lose them because cold winters and cunning foes prevented them from raising many colts to maturity. The Blackfeet were forced to replenish their herds by raiding other peoples, including those west of the Rockies.

In their protected valleys and on their lush hillsides the Nez Percés became first-rate, if stern, horsemen, practicing such techniques as gelding (the "quieting operation," in the words of a Lewis and Clark Expedition member). It was no handicap to the Nez Percés that they had no guns with which to kill buffalo: like the other native buffalo hunters they could fire several arrows into the animals in the time it took a ball from an awkward muzzle-loading rifle to rip into the beasts, whose only defense was their lunging hulks. Armed plainsmen were far more dangerous to the Nez Percés. From the returning explorers the tribe obtained powder and balls, as well as a firearm or two to supplement the half-dozen guns that one of their bands had obtained from the Minnetarees. About six years later they obtained guns from white traders in such areas as Spokane country and thus were able to cope more successfully with their foes on the plains.

Not all the Nez Percés were buffalo hunters. Some clung to a fishing-and-gathering economy. It has been estimated that fish constituted about 80 percent of the Nez Percé diet even after the coming of the horse. The fishing Nez Percés were separated geographically from their buffalo-hunting fellows by Lapwai Creek, a tributary of the Clearwater near its confluence with the Snake. Nonbuffalo-hunting Nez Percés below this line exchanged dried camas, salmon pemmican, horn bows, and bags with hunter Nez Percés for buffalo robes, feathered trappings, and other accoutrements of plains culture. Non-material items, such as songs, dances, and ceremonials were exchanged as well. The buffalo-hunting tribes became a link not only between plains tribes and the fisher Nez Percés, but also between the plainsmen and dwellers of the Pacific Coast.

Near Lapwai Creek, which was the Nez Percé dividing line, and in the Clearwater country the explorers on their return journey learned much about the Nez Percés, especially about their conflicts with their foes. Visible evidence was on the person of an important chief of that place, Neeshnepahkeook, or Cut-Nose, so called because of a lance stroke he had received in a fight with the Shoshonis. Thus it was not strange that natives of his village believed the explorers to be on some mission of murder. Their apprehensiveness was quickly dispelled when they received kindnesses, which helped ensure friendly relations between the Nez Percés and Americans not only then but for years to come. The villagers told the Americans how the Shoshonis had killed some Nez Percé emissaries and how they had swiftly avenged the act by killing, by their count, forty-two of their foe. With the score now more than even, they said that they planned another attempt at reconciliation. They also said that they wanted peace with the Blackfeet. Fearing treachery from those plainsmen, they sought to maintain alliances with other western tribesmen, especially Salish tribes who also had scores to settle with common foes. Three Coeur d'Alêne (Salishan) allies from the north visited Cut-Nose's village at the time of Lewis and Clark's return home. According to one account, the Coeur d'Alênes were named for a niggardly French Canadian with the "heart of an awl": a French interpreter rendered the Coeur d'Alêne word meaning "pin" or some other trifling object as *alêne*, or awl, and the phrase *coeur d'alêne*, or "heart of an awl," so amused his companians that they applied it to the tribe.

Down on the Snake River natives displayed to the traveling visitors objects to whet their curiosity such as President Jefferson would have wished to see. Among them was a sweathouse, one of several devices that purified and purged natives to withstand the rigors of their lives. It was a hollow square, six to eight feet deep, formed in the riverbank. Three sides were dammed with mud. The hole on the fourth side was covered completely except for an opening about two feet wide at the top, through which bathers descended into the interior with heating stones and water jugs. Such houses were used for body conditioning and warding off disease, but they proved to be death chambers for those exposed to diseases such as smallpox and measles. The curious travelers were further impressed that they were among a cleanly people by other structures set aside for women in the menses. Such buildings and others set aside for child bearing were widespread among Pacific Northwestern Indians. Other structures caught the visitors' eyes: racks for drying the life-sustaining salmon and the graves into which the natives placed their dead. The corpses were wrapped in skins, covered with earth, and marked or secured by wooden pickets, which some white men, less judicious than Lewis and Clark, would pull up and use for firewood.

On October 13, 1805, the explorers passed an Indian fishing village near the mouth of a stream that entered the Snake River from the north. The stream later bore the name of the Palouse (Shahaptian) Indians who fished there. The name derives, some believe, from the French word *pelouse*, meaning "greensward": the river and its people were in a country of grassy hills. But possibly the name has some connection with the rocks at the mouth of the river. The explorers reached the Columbia-Snake confluence, where large numbers of natives, down from summer camps, had gathered for late-fall salmon runs. One group of nearly two hundred, assembled in a seimcircle, drummed and chanted

a welcome to their guests, for which their chief received some clothing and medals. The next day their head chief returned with several men to smoke. They called themselves Sokulks, and they represented, on Clark's map, about 2,400 souls in 120 lodges which were situated on the Columbia River considerably north of the point where the Snake entered the big river. They were, in fact, the Wanapums (Shahaptian), who lived along the Columbia from Priest Rapids to the mouth of the Yakima. The early designations of these and other Pacific Northwestern natives by white men have puzzled later students. Many of the numerous tribes that the explorers cataloged along the Columbia between the mouth of the Snake and the Pacific later bore designations other than those that they gave them. Several, through extinction or intermarriage with other peoples, lost their tribal identity altogether before the end of the nineteenth century.

Accompanying the Sokulks were another people who spoke virtually the same language. Called by the explorers Chimnapums, they are believed to have been a branch of the Yakimas (Shahaptian), who were also called Yahahkimas, Eyakemas, and the like by Salish Indians. The explorers were apparently interested in comparing the people on the lower Columbia with those at the river's headwaters, and they singled them out for close examination. The

Indian sweathouse from the upper Columbia River area. North Central Washington Museum Association.

Mat houses belonging to the Wanapum Indians near Priest Rapids on the Columbia River. With some deference to white men's materials, such houses were used by the Wanapums until the 1950s. The second photograph shows the matting applied to the house frame. United States Bureau of Reclamation.

women were pictured as more inclined to corpulence than those on the east, having broad faces and flattened heads with eyes of "a dirty sable" and coarse hair braided without ornaments. In contrast to the Nez Percé women, who wore long bead-and-shell-decorated leather shirts, the Sokulk women allowed no covering except a truss, or piece of leather, tied around the hips and drawn tightly between the legs. They did not completely foreswear ornamentation, for both sexes wore large blue or white beads hanging from their ears, their necks, their wrists, and their arms, and they sported brass and copper bracelets, as well as shell and bone trinkets and feathers. By trading dogs to their visitors, they received thimbles and knitting needles, which were never to be used as their donors intended but were mixed and matched with native ornaments. They lived in large mat or rush houses, which varied in length from fifteen to sixty feet. Six-foot-high forked poles supported the matted roofs, which were adapted to the climate, the most arid of all the lands traversed by Lewis and Clark.

Everywhere there was ample evidence that the natives were a salmon-eating people. The explorers observed their fish-catching and processing paraphernalia and the mixing of roots and berries with the salmon to form a highly nutritious food. Salmon ingested with dirt and sand wore the Indians' teeth to the gums. Like other river and plateau peoples, they also suffered eye diseases, for which the explorers administered "eye water," the most frequently administered medication of their journey. The explorers attributed the malady to exposure to sun reflected on the water and snow, but it was also due to inadequate protective headware, campfire smoke, and alkali dust.

Although the Americans' most immediate needs, like the natives', were sustenance and transportation, they were under orders to explore and classify the human and natural resources of the regions through which they passed. At the confluence of the Columbia and the Snake, the natives used charcoal to sketch for them on a robe a map of the upper Columbia and its affluents. Communication between the natives and fact finders was anything but perfect, and inaccuracies in the explorers' maps and journals increased in direct proportion to the distance of the things described from their trail. Thus the natives were unable to trace adequately for them the course of the upper Columbia, which the explorers confused with the Okanogan, a tributary that enters the Columbia from the north, which they believed to be the main course of the big river.

To welcome them near the confluence were other native dignitaries, such as Chief Yelleppit, a "handsome well-proportioned man" with a "bold and dignified countenance," whom the Americans ascribed to the Walla Walla (Shahaptian) nation but who may have been Chief Ollicott of the Cayuses. The Cayuses were called *Cailloux*, or "People of the Stones or Pebbles," by French-Canadian fur men. They were closely associated with the Wallawallas, whom they regarded as inferiors, and also with the Nez Percés, with whom they intermarried and whose flexible language they eventually adopted in preference to their own. In 1806 peoples calling themselves Yellept, or Yelleppit, who are believed to

have been a Cayuse band, met the homebound explorers in Nez Percé country; as did Ollicott, whose friendliness won him Clark's sword, a hundred balls, some powder, and sundry other goods.

The natives downstream from the confluence, who were often raided by Shoshonis and Paiutes, cowered in their lodges expecting similar treatment from the Americans. Again timely gifts quieted their fears. Watching Clark bring down a fowl with his musket confirmed their belief that he had in some way descended from the clouds; the belief was reinforced when his magnifying glass brought down fire from the sky.

The sound of the party's fiddle music was exciting to the natives, but it was but a respite for the explorers before they witnessed a somber sight the next day. On an island in the Columbia they found several grave houses containing leather-wrapped bodies. The bodies were arranged on mat-covered boards, from which were suspended tools, utensils, and trinkets to accompany the dead to the other world. Skeletons of horses outside the native mausoleums indicated that the animals had been killed to carry their deceased masters—a practice observed by many tribes of the Columbia Plateau.

The traveling Americans were soon met by natives along a narrow, turbulent stretch of river from Celilo Falls down through The Dalles. Nature was scarcely more turbulent than man along this stretch, for it had been the scene of fighting between the peoples who lived above and below it. Two of the party's Nez Percé chieftain guides, whose people had been involved in the conflicts, wanted to terminate their services at the beginning of the precipitous waterway, stating that they did not understand the language of the tribes below. Those below Celilo Falls spoke the Chinookan tongue, which was alien to the Shahaptian Nez Percés. A Sahaptin-speaking village of Eneeshurs (the Skin, or Skeen, tribe) was located at the falls. The "Echeloot" village of Upper Chinookan Wishrams was a scant six miles below.

At The Dalles the arid environment of the interior suddenly gave way to the marine-influenced environment of the lower Columbia. The division was as sharp as the roar of the nearby river, which was like a crashing tower of Babel, dividing the tongues. The Nez Percé guides did not wish to become involved in the conflicts that often erupted between their own tribe and others who lived upriver and the tribes who lived below the falls, whom they treated with contempt. Later a fur trader recalled that, in passing the place, his leader condescendingly threw a bag of leaf tobacco to some proudly mounted Nez Percés. When they rode off offended, refusing the proffered gift, the fish-eating Indians rushed in to appropriate the tobacco.[6]

Thanks to the good offices of Lewis and Clark, a truce was effected between the feuding Shahaptians and Chinookans before their guides turned back. It was ceremoniously sealed with gifts of clothing and medals and topped off with fiddle music and dancing, to the delight of the natives. Again, the fiddle music did not quiet the explorers' apprehension at this stretch of river, where they feared pillage and plunder. Fortunately for them, Pacific Northwest natives were often more friendly to strangers than they were to each other. Lower Chinookans near the mouth of the Columbia were among those who often raided the Dalles peoples, whom they regarded as inferiors. Such conflict and the conduct of the lower Columbia peoples caused one expedition member to opine that all the natives from the Rockies to the falls were "honest, ingenious and well disposed," unlike those downriver and along the coast, whom he considered "a rascally, thieving set." Shortly after the middle of the eighteenth century, the Lower Chinooks had fought a battle with the Upper Chinooks, who came annually to the lower Columbia for clams. After the Upper Chinooks had failed to heed the warnings of the lower-river people not to invade the latter's clam beds, the lower Chinooks lured them into waist-high sword grass and then pounced upon them. For years the victims' bones littered an eroding Columbia shoreline. Nor did the Chinooks confine their aggressions to the Upper Chinooks. About fifteen years before the coming of Lewis and Clark, a large canoe flotilla of the lower-river peoples traveled twenty days up the Columbia, past "some great waterfall," to a lake, where they destroyed

the men of a large tribe that inhabited its shores and enslaved the women and children.

The Dalles peoples feared no foe more than the marauding Northern Paiutes. Over the years the latter tribe had helped precipitate a human flux in the intermontane Pacific Northwest. They are believed by some anthropologists possibly to have forced the Shahaptians north of the Columbia by the beginning of the eighteenth century. The Molalas (Waiilatpuan), who formerly occupied lands south of the Columbia, were split from their Cayuse neighbors. From along the Deschutes, a Columbia River tributary, one Molala band moved southwest to the headwaters of the Umpqua River. The other band moved west beyond the Cascade Mountains to the valleys of the Molalla and Santiam rivers, which are tributaries of the Willamette (itself a Columbia tributary). Salishan informants of the upper-middle Columbia later claim that their ancestors, around perhaps the middle of the eighteenth century, had occupied lands in the area of The Dalles and farther north, as well as lands on the east in the valley of the Umatilla, a tributary of the Columbia. Various peoples, such as the Cayuses and the

Indians curing salmon at The Dalles on the Columbia River. Sketch from Northwest Magazine, *April, 1894.*

Shahaptian Umatillas and Nez Percés, had pushed the Salishans northward. Some anthropologists believe more likely that horse-riding Shahaptians rebounded in the nineteenth century and extended their territory east and south at the expense of adjacent Paiute bands, who were horseless until around the middle of the century. Thus there were feuds among the Paiutes and the Shahaptian and non-Shahaptian northern peoples until well into the nineteenth century. Some scholars believe it was the Teninos, a Shahaptian people of the lower-middle Columbia, who drove the Molalas from their homelands.

Swept up in this flux, natives of the Columbia buffered themselves with the river itself, and with a strip south of it, from foes such as the Paiutes who settled on the upper Deschutes. Occasionally river peoples ventured into the buffer zone, which was southwest of The Dalles, to hunt in the timbered mountains, but not to establish permanent villages. On their journeys they passed the sites of ancient fights with their foe. Warriors of aggressive tribes, such as the Nez Percés and the Cayuses, also journeyed into the Willamette Valley to hunt and trade.

An Upper Chinookan who was returning from fighting with natives of the Deschutes (possibly Paiutes) met the explorers. Another displayed for them his medicine bag, which contained fourteen forefingers, digital trophies that he had stripped from foes slain in the southeast, where the Paiutes roamed. All the warring tribes returned from battle with these visible proofs of victory. Even tribes who were friendly to white men, such as the Flatheads and the Nez Percés, proudly displayed fingers and scalps of slain foes.

The river dwellers intimated to their visitors that the conflicts with the Paiutes restricted their fishing villages to the north bank of the Columbia; and, in fact, in later times fisheries would be found on both sides of the river. At one Eneeshur village of seventeen huts natives on scaffolds with long-handled scoop nets up to four feet wide caught salmon swimming through shore eddies. The fishermen gutted their catches and placed the flannel-red flesh on scaffolds to dry in the sun. Then they pulverized the meat between stones and placed it in large rush-and-grass baskets lined with salmon skin. Continuing the processing, they compressed the meat, covering the tops of the containers with fish skins that were secured with cords through holes in the baskets, which they corded in dry places. Next they wrapped the cords in mats, piling them in stacks that weighed ninety to one hundred pounds. They traded some of their well-preserved product to surrounding tribes. For example, the representatives of fourteen different tribes who met Lewis and Clark at the Long Narrows between The Dalles and Celilo Falls probably purchased salmon there. Traveling natives who purchased the Columbia River delicacy might trade it in turn to the salmon-hungry tribes of the plains, but much of the processed salmon was consumed on the spot. At the Wishram village on the north side of the river at Celillo Falls there were gabled wooden houses pitted to a depth of six feet (among other Pacific Northwestern Indians the depth of the pitting varied, as did architectural styles). The explorers estimated that the stock of processed fish in the village was in excess of two tons.

It was customary for the Wishram villagers to celebrate the arrival of salmon by ceremoniously cutting the fish into small pieces that were given to children. The natives of The Dalles believed that they should not take the first salmon running because those fish had been endowed by the Great Spirit with powers that made them bolder and better able to swim to the spawning grounds, from which their fingerlings would return to the sea. Elsewhere on the Columbia and its tributaries "salmon chiefs" saw to it that rituals were rigidly observed with dances and first-run taboos to ensure good subsequent runs. The Chinooks believed that they should place a berry in the mouth of the first salmon caught to nourish it on what they believed to be its foodless journey to the spawning grounds. To ensure further success in their fishing, they cut the salmon crosswise. Important Tillamook men ate the first salmon from head to tail, throwing the bones and the roasting racks into the fire. Up the Columbia, at Kettle Falls, (known as Schwanatekoo, or Deep Sounding Water, below the Canadian border), an elderly shaman supervised the catching and the distribution of the fish to the various families. It was forbidden to throw into the river the bones of the salmon first caught. Offenders had to purify themselves with a bark concoction.

Several species of salmon flashed upriver to their home streams. Besides the humpbacked, or pink, salmon (*Oncorhynchus gorbuscha*), whose Columbia runs were never large, others that ran the stream were the royal Chinook, or king, salmon (*O. tshawytscha*), from February, March, and April to November; the blueback, or sockeye (*O. nerka*), in May and June and often July; the silver, silversides, or coho (*O. kisutch*), in August; and the dog, or chum (*O. keta*), in early September, which often came in with the last Chinook runs and the first runs of silvers. The steelhead (*Salmo gairdnerii*), a trout, ran in December and January and often heavily in July, after which its run fell off till its return in December.

When runs were poor, fish stocks became depleted, forcing natives to move away from the rivers in search of other food. Despite the severe stricture at the Celilo-Dalles stretch that made it a good fishery, many fish escaped up the Columbia. With an assortment of traps, weirs, gaffs, gigs, and nets the natives caught them at The Cascades, The Dalles, Priest Rapids, Rock Island, and Kettle Falls, as well as at other rapids on the big stream and on a score of its tributaries. Large falls in the Columbia watershed, such as those of the Spokane, Pend Oreille (at Clark Fork), Willamette, and Snake rivers, made it difficult if not impossible for salmon to escape beyond them. On the Snake, salmon ascended about 650 miles from the Pacific Ocean.

Since large numbers of Indians gathered to fish at those points, they were good places for concourse. The last of the major fishing and gathering places that the westbound explorers reached (the first obstacle for salmon returning from the sea) was a two-and-a-half-mile stretch of rapids called The Cascades, about forty miles below The Dalles. As others did who traversed the stretch later, they noted tree stumps standing in the river. Indian tradition had it that, within the memories of their fathers, the mountain had

SALMON FISHING AT CHENOOK.

Indians fishing for salmon at Chinook on the north bank of the Columbia River near its mouth. The sketch was made by James

Swan, who was an early settler, agent, and friend of Indians.

crashed down to the river, creating the phenomenon. Tradition also had it that beneath the obstruction a stream flowed, forming the "Bridge of the Gods." In a mythological and geological mix, the phenomena were attributed to everything from the collective wrongdoing of the people, who had angered the Earth Mother, to a rock-throwing lovers' quarrel between Mount Hood, which flanked the south shore, and Mount Saint Helens on the north shore, with Mount Adams on the east joining in to form a lovers' triangle.

Not all the material goods of the Pacific Northwestern Indians were employed for the support of the living, as the explorers discovered. Nowhere was this more evident to them than at The Cascades, a wild, gloomy place where wooden images and native and white men's goods were strangely mixed to accoutre tombs. The burial places were not the only evidence of desolation on the river: along its course to the sea, pocked faces showed where the smallpox epidemic of 1782–83 had swept through. Cases of scrofula, gastric disorders, blindness, tooth decay, and swelling of limbs and inevitable accidents gave ample proof that—even without imported diseases, such as smallpox, measles, venereal disease, and possibly influenza and malaria—the Indians were as susceptible to sickness as human beings are everywhere. They also suffered mental diseases, about which little is known. At the time of first contact, whites reported cases of extreme mental aberration, but they often regarded cultural practices that differed from their own as

mental disorders. In dances the Indians emulated animals (such as the zany bluejay) from which, they believed, they received special powers. This was viewed by whites as deviation from sanity, as was the potlatch ceremony, in which the giver disposed of his possessions, a custom that was practiced with varying degrees of benevolence and viciousness from the upper Northwest coast down to the Columbia River. White men also regarded the death wish of an elderly person as a suicidal mental aberration.

It appears that the longer the explorers were among the natives the more familiar the natives became. If familiarity did not breed contempt, it did breed a possessive attitude toward the explorers' things that exasperated the latter greatly, especially as they prepared to return home. Such familiarity was characteristic of the Chinooks (especially the Chinook women) who often visited the expedition party, who wintered across the Columbia from them during the soggy winter of 1805–1806. The Clatsops, also a Lower Chinookan people, were not as shrewd in the arts of trade with white men because they lived on the less accessible south shore of the Columbia, where ships did not pass as they did Bakers Bay on the north. They outwitted their Chinook neighbors by inviting the Lewis and Clark party, the "cloth men soldiers," to winter among them, and because of advantages to the Americans of sojourning in their lands, the offer was accepted. Trying to keep in the good graces of their guests, the Clatsops cried, "No Chinook!" when approaching the fort named for them, Fort

Potlach house on the Skokomish Reservation, 1875. Its dimensions were 40 by 200 feet. Penrose Library, Whitman College.

Clatsop, in order to distinguish themselves from their more aggressive Chinook neighbors, who had more intimate exposure to white men than they did and who thought nothing of canoeing approximately four miles across the river from the south shore.

Both the Clatsops and the Chinooks, along with their neighbors, such as the Kathlamets (Chinookan), traded with the "cloth men soldiers." They offered food products of their lands, such as fish and elk, and expected something in return. Fortunately the American visitors had a few leftover medals to give, perhaps not so much as media of exchange as tokens of good will. They regretted the skimpiness of their

A Kalapooia Indian sketched by A. T. Agate of the United States exploring expedition of the early 1840s under Lieutenant Charles Wilkes, U.S.N. At the time of the expedition the Kalapooia tribes had recently been greatly reduced in numbers. They were victims of epidemics, including what was believed by some authorities to be Asian Influenza. Reproduced from Harold Mackey, The Kalapuyans *(Salem, Ore.: 1974).*

supply of blue beads. They were apparently unaware of the natives' preference for them. One trade item that Lewis and Clark did not wish for their men was provided by a Chinook madam, whom they dubbed "Old Boud." A by-product of the services of her girls was "the venereal," which left the men in a debilitated condition. A British trader who lived in the near area of the party's winter quarters in 1814 blamed Americans who entered the river in 1810 for bringing the disease there from New York and the Sandwich Islands.[7] It actually had been transmitted to coastal natives by sailors long before the Lewis and Clark visit, by which time it had reached epidemic proportions along the Northwest Coast. Because of the pandering of Chinook women to white men sailing into the lower Columbia, the Chinooks developed a reputation as disseminators of the disease. White men came to apply the word Chinook to many things for which the Indians were not really responsible, such as chinook winds (a misnomer) and the Chinook jargon, while Indians at great distances from the mouth of the Columbia equated the word in the privacy of their camps with the venereal.

On the expedition's return journey in 1806, Clark ascended the lower Willamette River (which he called the Multnomah and which was also called by some McKay's River) to a point near present-day Portland, Oregon. The tribes that inhabited the river valley were numerous despite the smallpox. Natives told Clark of other Willamette Valley peoples, such as the Kalapooias, or Kalapuyas, of whom there were about two thousand by the explorers' estimates living in forty villages. The Kalapooian speakers were in several bands, of which the more important were, from north to south, the Atfalati Tualatins, the Yamhills (Yamels), the Pudding Rivers (Ahantchuyuks), the Luckiamutes (Lackmiuts), the Santiams, the Marys Rivers (Chepenefas), the Long Tom Creeks (Chelamelas), the Kalapooias proper, and the Yoncallas (Yonkallas).

For years the natives whom Lewis and Clark visited would tell of the strangers, venerating the things they had brought. In 1853, for instance, a Palouse chief, Wattaiwattaihowlis, proudly exhibited to the leader of a railroad survey party a medal that the explorers had presented to his father, Kepowhkan. A flesh-and-blood reminder of their visit, according to the Nez Percés, was Halpatokit, Clark's red-haired, thin-lipped son, born in 1807 to one of their women. Of greater consequence to the explorers' countrymen — to the "Bostons" — was the news of their trek, which stimulated the Americans to extend their mercantile horizons to the West. Their rivals, the men of King George, were also seeking such horizons and were already making mercantile tracks overland to the Pacific. Soon the strangers from the "Land of the Sun's Rising" would meet and trade with the natives in the lands where it set.

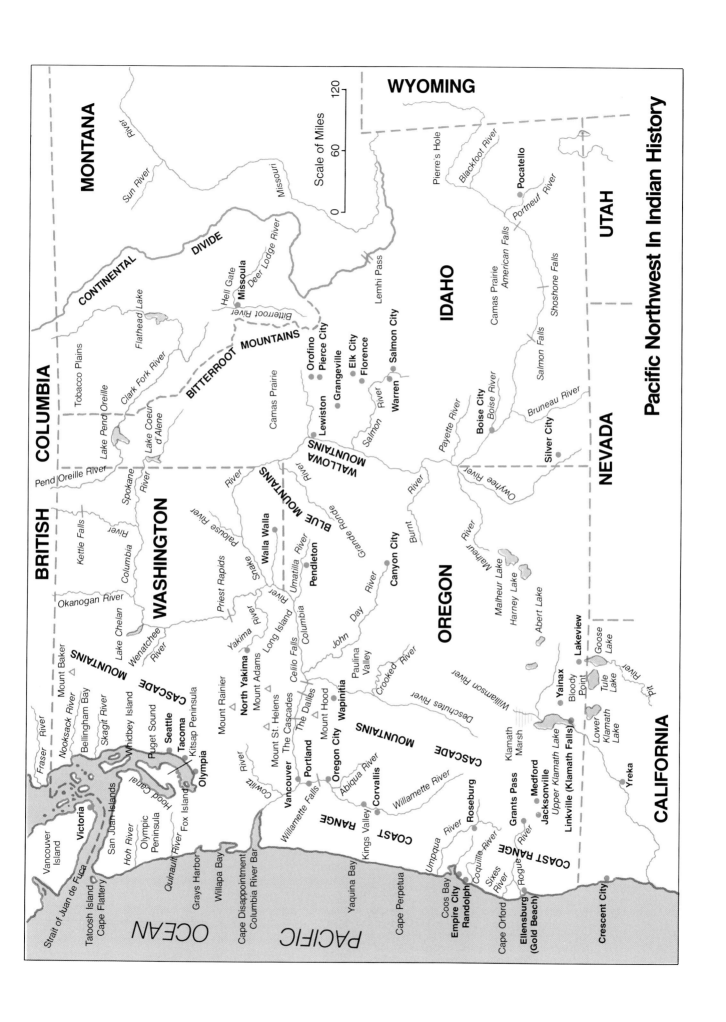

Pacific Northwest In Indian History

3. FURS AND FURIES

To the north in New Caledonia (later British Columbia), natives met a King George man traveling across the continent more than a decade before those to the south met Lewis and Clark. In 1793 the bold Alexander MacKenzie of the British North West Company completed his arduous trek to the Pacific Ocean. He found the natives near the coast unfriendly, perhaps because of some unpleasant confrontation with white seamen earlier. Unfriendly Piegans in the area between the routes of the rival British and American explorers prevented another Nor'Wester, David Thompson, from opening a westward route between the two east-west tracks. This did not prevent the aggressive Thompson from learning of lands to the west, for around 1800 he sent two men, Le Blanc and La Gasse, apparently to assess the possibilities of the fur trade in that region. They traveled with a party of Kutenais (Kootenays, or Kootenais) (Kitunahan)—a tribe, also known as the Flatbows, who lived along the Kootenay River across the Rocky Mountains on the west.* Spokane (Salishan) Indians have a tradition that two *sama* (Frenchmen, or other whites), possibly Le Blanc and La Gasse, spent time with them. The Spokanes dubbed one of them Noweaquanoore, which means Face Upside Down, because he was bald and bearded. They called the other Chekualkua because their first impression of him was that he "couldn't figure things out for himself." He may have been the one whom the Kutenais called Bad Fire because he liked a small campfire, in contrast to the other who preferred a big one.[1]

The Americans inadvertently had eased the way for their rival, Thompson, to cross the Rockies. After Captain Meriwether Lewis fought Blackfeet on July 27, 1806, the Piegans, who buffered the Blackfeet and other Indian allies from Salish attacks, rushed down to help them, allowing Thompson to slip past the Piegans through the Rockies to the very source of the Columbia River. There, in the land of his Kutenai friends, he built his Kootenai House near Lake Windermere during the summer of 1807.

The Kutenais were happy with the goods and protection that Thompson brought, and they were also happy to have among them this restless man with a short nose and black hair "worn long all around, and cut square, as if by one stroke of the shears just above the eyebrows." They called his Nor'Westers the "Long Hairs" for the way he cut his hair. They also called him Kookoosint, a corruption of their word for star, possibly meaning the "star man." They were intrigued by his seemingly magical instruments to measure the earth and sky, and, more practically, they were eager to buy from him guns and ammunition to defend themselves more adequately against the Piegans on their annual buffalo hunts. Although their benefactor supplied them with firepower, he saw to it that they received no firewater. He

knew it would make their difficult ventures on the plains even more difficult. It worked to the Kutenais' advantage that their Piegan foes had been inflamed by liquor since their contacts with white traders, even to the point of bartering the favors of their women to obtain it. A Shoshoni chief most eloquently described the baneful effects of liquor on red men in peace and war when he said: "Send it not to us, we would rather die by the arrows of the Blackfeet. It unmans us for the hunt and for defending ourselves against our enemies; it causes unnatural dissensions among ourselves; it makes the Chief less than his Indians; and by its use [come] imbecility and ruin..."[2]

Eager to prevent the Kutenais from receiving firearms, the Piegans crossed the Rockies to kill Thompson. Thompson's sojourn among the Kutenais and his gifts to them prevented the killing. The Kutenais and Flatheads traded with Thompson in the following year, 1808, as he explored farther south into Salish country seeking potential trade. That winter and the next, natives near Kootenai Falls on the Kootenai River (near present-day Libby, Montana) met one of Thompson's faithful aides, Finan McDonald. Unlike Thompson, McDonald was massive, with a bushy beard, flowing red hair, and a fiery temperament to match. Natives soon learned that a long house that he built protected a store of precious goods that had been carried over a long, arduous route from the east.

Word of Thompson's coming had reached natives farther south. In early September, 1809, on the Clark Fork, or Salish River, which flowed into Lake Pend Oreille, about eighty men and their families, representing the Flatheads, Kutenais, and Coeur d'Alênes, provided Thompson with food. On a point jutting into the lake near present-day Hope, Idaho, Thompson established Kullyspell (or Kalispel) House. The horse-riding, Salish-speaking Kalispels, or Pend d'Oreilles, lived around Lake Pend Oreille.* They and the

---

*The Kutenais have been divided into two general groups on the basis of their different subsistence patterns. The two groups are divided along a line running roughly north and south through present-day Libby, Montana. Those on the east on the upper Kootenay River were the Upper Kutenais, who subsisted mainly by hunting the buffalo. Those on the west were lower down the Columbia River system from those in Montana and were known as the Lower Kutenais. They subsisted largely on fish. The Kutenais are thought to have resided originally east of the Rocky Mountains until they were pushed westward by the Blackfeet, although some authorities believe their migration westward occurred at an earlier time. Today the Kutenais in the United States reside on the Flathead Reservation and in the vicinity of Bonners Ferry, Idaho. For the most part there is no distinction in this text between the Upper and Lower Kutenais.

*According to John R. Swanton, *The Indian Tribes of North America*, pp. 399–400, the names Kalispel and Pend d'Oreille are synonymous; the latter is not a subdivision of the former. Thus in this volume we use the one term, Kalispel.

Upper Spokanes went to hunt buffalo more than the Lower Spokanes and other neighboring tribes, who obtained their subsistence mostly from local salmon, roots, berries, and game. Their women, who married into Salish families farther east, of course, went with them after the buffalo.

The buffalo-hunting Salishans welcomed the new arms that replaced their lances and flint-headed arrows, which were relatively harmless against the leather shields of their foes. Taking to firearms readily, they became better marksmen than their Piegan rivals. They had to be better hunters because the game in their lands were smaller targets than the buffaloes, which the Piegans shot at close quarters. The canny Thompson warned his customers that the arms and other goods were not gifts, that they would have to pay for them by killing fur-bearing animals to trade.

The most important of the fur-bearing animals was the beaver. Until the money nexus entered the fur trade in the late nineteenth century, beaver pelts were the standard medium of exchange for not ony furs and goods but also services. The beaver weighs about thirty-five pounds when fully grown. It has chisel-like teeth and a broad tail. Its fur has supporting stiff hair over a shorter underlayer, which is soft, thick, and beautifully glossy. The fur was sought by traders for the European market, where it was processed into hats. Soon natives obtained metal traps, in which they could catch the beaver more quickly and surely than in the baskets that they had used for ages.

Kullyspell House remained in operation no more than two winters, perhaps because there were other posts that were more suitably located for the trade. One of those was Saleesh House near present-day Thompson Falls, Montana, which Thompson established shortly after the closing of Kullyspell House. It was on a bench overlooking the north bank of the Clark Fork River. In olden times the Flatheads and their allies had sought refuge at this place when pursued by their foes. Below lay Bad Rock, beyond which their foes dared not pass. Bones scattered on meadow lands below were ghastly evidence that battles had been fought there. For nearly forty years fur trade in Flathead country would center at Saleesh House. After 1812 it was called Flathead Post or, occasionally, Fort Flathead and was moved near to present-day Eddy, Montana, about fifteen miles east of Thompson Falls. It was never fortified and was relocated three times. It was secondary to posts at Spokane and Colville in the movements of the trade. Despite its name, it was the Kalispels and Kutenais who were regarded by white traders as indolent, who collected more than half the post's beaver pelts; the Flatheads trapped mainly in the spring, when Blackfoot raids abated. To encourage Indians to trap, Finan McDonald, who succeeded James McMillan at Flathead Post, extended them credit in winter to be repaid in pelts in summer.

The natives received instruction from McDonald in the use of their newly acquired weapons. Better yet, their instructor, spoiling for a good fight, like his Scottish Highlander ancestors, fought alongside his Salish pupils in the summer of 1810 against the Piegans, whose numbers had recouped from the late eighteenth-century smallpox

Family of Bannock Indians in front of a grass lodge, 1872. Photograph by William H. Jackson. Oregon Historical Society.

epidemics. When their ammunition was spent, the Piegans were forced to defend themselves with stones. In the fighting, seven Piegans were killed (more, by some accounts), and thirteen were wounded. The Salish lost five killed and nine wounded. Both parties had been more intent on killing and maiming than on taking scalps.

This was not the first time that the Flatheads acted in concert with white men against their Plains Indian foes. Two years earlier they had joined Manuel Lisa's trader, John Colter, in skirmishes against the Blackfeet, and they were propositioned by other Lisa men to help fight Indians who were hindering white traders in the collection of furs.

Colter is believed to have been the first white man to enter the homelands of the Bannocks (Shoshonean), who were called Panahki by some Shoshonean peoples. In precontact times the Bannocks had taken more readily to horse culture than the other Paiutes had. They hunted big game on horseback and separated themselves from other Paiutes to settle in present-day southeastern Idaho and associate with upper-class mounted Shoshonis, in a plains setting that was broken by lush bottomlands along the Snake, Portneuf, and Blackfoot rivers. The use of horses enabled them to live in large permanent groups instead of smaller ones confined to the vicinity of food caches. Tall and warlike, the Bannocks contrasted sharply with the fishing

Shoshonis along the Snake River below Salmon Falls. The latter were regarded contemptuously both by other natives and by whites as a lower class, the Digger Indians; they had few technical cultural elements and inhabited a stingy environment that permitted them few horses. In contrast, the skilled mountain Bannocks raided the Blackfeet and, among other enterprises, served as middlemen between other tribes, such as the Nez Percés and the Cayuses.

The Bannocks have sometimes been confused with the Sheepeater (Tukuadüka) Indians, who were also Shoshonean. Archaeological evidence indicates that the Sheepeaters maintained a cultural continuity for hundreds of years, inhabiting a mountainous area twenty thousand miles square that conforms roughly to the Salmon River drainage area of central Idaho. There is some evidence that they may have been driven by Blackfeet to their rugged country, but this theory is contradicted by the long occupation of their conservative culture and by their long-established mountain-sheep economy. Shoshoni-Blackfoot shifts on the plains came in the eighteenth century; it is likely that any Blackfoot pressure on the Sheepeaters was against small groups who ventured onto the plains to hunt buffalo after the tribe acquired horses. Those mounted Sheepeater groups would in time join the Shoshonis from the Lemhi River area of Idaho. The less-mobile body became associated with the Shoshonis from the Weiser River area in Idaho.

Andrew Henry of the Missouri Fur Company was a Lisa partner. He established Fort Henry on the upper Snake, where he spent the winter of 1810–11. Abandoning his post in the spring of 1811, he proposed rallying the Shoshonis and Flatheads to fight the Blackfeet, not unaware of the dangers the Blackfeet posed to his trapping operations. The 1810 Salish-Piegan fight had proved that the Piegans were unable to meet the armed challenge of their Salish foes. They blamed the white men for their defeat because these whites supplied their enemies with arms and ammunition, but they found it more politic to swear vengeance on their Salish foes rather than the whites, on whom they depended for arms, tobacco, and liquor. To curb the hunting aggressions of the Salish and the better to steal their horses, the Piegans made a temporary peace with the Kutenais. The Kutenais' lands did not support horses well, and the Kutenais were therefore less threatening. Also, there were fewer of them; a white trader estimated in 1811 that there were no more than fifty families. By making peace with the Kutenais, the Piegans hoped to continue raiding the Flatheads, from whom they stole many horses.

Spokane Indians traveling from their homelands to Nor'Wester posts were happy in the summer of 1810 when clerk Finan McDonald and Jacques ("Joco" or "Jocko") Raphael Finlay, came among them to build a post called Spokane House, a half mile up the Spokane River from its juncture with the Little Spokane. Finlay, a "blood," had been trading among the Kutenais and the Flatheads. Proud of their newly acquired guns and their iron-headed weapons, the Spokanes were eager to try them out. With a band of Kalispels who were camping nearby, they proposed attacking some of the Okanagon (Salishan) Indians who

lived along the river of the same name. According to tradition, the Spokanes had raided these peoples in early times, as they had the peaceful San Poils (Salishan), killing them but also suffering losses themselves.

Spokane House became a mart and mecca for not only native peoples in its immediate environs but also Salish peoples on the Columbia River to the west and Shahaptians, who brought horses to trade there along with beaver, otter, and other skins. Very likely their appearance at the post stimulated Thompson to extend his operations farther to the southwest.

Thompson's activities had confined him to the western American hinterland, but his rivals, the American "Short Hairs," continued their Pacific Coast trading monopoly while the British "Long Hairs" were involved in the Napoleonic wars. Selling furs and cuirasses (the latter were traded to natives to the north), coastal natives continued to receive in exchange an ever-expanding variety of goods, such as metals, cloths, beads, breads, and molasses. Included in the trade of some Boston Men with the natives were slaves captured along the Pacific Coast from Alaska south. The coastal red men were no strangers to traffic in this human commodity. They purchased slaves from the intermediary Makahs, who in turn raided for them across the Strait of Juan de Fuca on Vancouver Island. From their distant northern homeland in the Queen Charlotte Islands, the Haida (Skittagetan) natives raided for slaves as far south as Cape Mendecino, California. Perhaps the most notorious American slaver on the Northwest Coast was George W. Eayers (or Eayrs), who was under contract with the Russians to hunt sea otter from the Columbia to California. From the lower Columbia (where male slaves brought native sellers ten to a dozen blankets in 1810) north along the coast of present-day Washington, Eayers spirited away a dozen males, seven of whom escaped by stealing a boat and making for shore.*

Needing food more than fortune, Eayers's Russian contractors hoped to escape their barren Sitkan quarters and sustain themselves farther south at such places as the Strait of Juan de Fuca, Grays Harbor, and the mouth of the Columbia River. They must have believed their claim to the latter place difficult to prove. At the very time when Lewis and Clark planned to leave it, the Russian (formerly, American) ship *Juno* had staggered off the Columbia bar; the same gale that denied the Americans their planned start for home also denied the Russians entry to the river. Russian American Company official Alexander A. Baranov sent three ships southward on September 20, 1808. One of them, the *Saint Nicholas*, was wrecked on November 1 near the mouth of the Quillayute River, where natives harassed the crew. She was carrying twenty-one Russians and Aleut (Eskimauan) Indians, three of whom were women. Six days later, the Hohs,

---

*There is some speculation about how widespread Eayers's slave taking was along the West Coast. The Makahs have several traditional accounts of such activities by people like Eayers. Eric Blinman, Elizabeth Colson, and Robert Heizer, "A Makah Epic Journey," *Pacific Northwest Quarterly* 68, no. 4 (October, 1977): 153-63.

Quilleutes, and Quinaults attacked the Russian party as it crossed the Hoh River. In the attack the Indians captured an Aleut woman and a boy, and in the ensuing fight two Indians and a Russian were killed. The Russians retreated up the Hoh River, where they built a blockhouse. They remained there until they descended the river again and the Indians captured them. After the natives had passed the Russians to other bands, they were finally ransomed in May, 1811, by an American trader.

When their plans failed on the lower coast, the Russians contracted with Yankee traders Jonathan and Nathan Winship to transport a hundred Aleuts from Alaska to California, where the natives were to take sea otter off the coast in their small craft called *baidarkas*. The Winships, their brother Abiel, and an associate, Benjamin P. Horner, had heard, no doubt, of the possibilities in the inland fur trade. They planned a permanent "fur colony" up the Columbia a short distance from the sea. Perhaps this was to be not too far from where their countryman Allen Weir and a party of trappers had spent the winter of 1809–10 in the vicinity of the Columbia-Willamette river confluence.

A site was chosen on the left bank of the Columbia at Oak Point about thirty miles from the sea, but before the projected post could be built, the seasonal June cresting of the river forced the traders from a cabin that they had built. Before they could build another downstream, the Indians chased them to the shelter of the trees. The natives were said to have been Chinooks and Chilwitzes (also called Chilwitses, Hellwitses, and the like; perhaps Chinookan). They were armed with bows and arrows and muskets and scatter-fired their missiles. They also dogged the crew that had been sent to clear brush for the new post, driving them to their ship, the *Albatross*. The natives' response stemmed from their opposition to rivals on the lower river, which they regarded as an exclusive domain of theirs that could be neither violated nor traversed without payment of tolls.

In the following year, 1811, the Chinooks downriver extended a friendlier welcome to seaborne Astorians in the employ of American fur tycoon John Jacob Astor, proprietor of the Pacific Fur Company.[3] In early April they rescued from a watery grave and took to their village Duncan McDougall and David Stuart, who were partners of Astor. Seeking wider geographic and economic opportunities, McDougall and Stuart sought to establish a post for the company at the mouth of the Columbia River—the western anchor of a chain of posts across the continent. Astor wished to monopolize the fur trade on the Columbia and ship the furs to China along with those secured from the Russians in Alaska. Fur-company partners, factors, traders, and clerks were known among traders as bourgeois in contrast to the *engagés*, the employees in the lower echelons of the trade.

The Astorians were grateful to the natives for saving them from death—a far better fate than some of the crew of their ship, the *Tonquin*. The *Tonquin's* captain, Jonathan Thorn, was known as "the nautical despot." A fortnight before McDougall and Stuart's rescue, he had ordered his crew to sound the treacherous Columbia River bar in a

March gale, and it proved to be their graveyard. Unlike the natives, mariners for years to come were unable to make their peace with the bar. Their frustrations while crossing it or awaiting suitable winds and tides to escape through its treacherous breakers were expressed by Oregon poet C. H. Joaquin Miller: "Mercy! the savage old Columbia pitches us out of her mouth into the sea, as if glad to get rid of us—as if we were a sort of Jonah."

In mid-April curious natives visited the Astorians at Youngs Bay on the south bank of the Columbia in Clatsop country. They were trying to forget the tragic events of recent days as they attacked the brush and giant trees to win a clearing in the stingy wilderness for a post, which was to be Fort Astoria. Among those who visited the strangers was the one-eyed Comcomly (Madsu, or "Thunder"), the intellectually and physically powerful Chinook chief. He possessed many wives and slaves, some of whom paddled him in a sturdy canoe across the broad Columbia to see the Astorians. He got along tolerably well with them, but since he himself took goods to peoples upriver to exchange for their furs, he was fearful lest his suppliers eliminate him as a middleman by bringing their goods directly to the Astorians. One stratagem he employed to keep his native clientele from visiting the Astorians was to tell them that bad men would carry them off as slaves. The knowledge that maritime traders, such as Eayers, had taken Indian slaves in exchange for sea otter pelts gave credence to his stories.

Communication with the natives near the fort was mostly in the Chinook jargon, a language developed for conducting the trade. This lingua franca was composed primarily of Nootkan and other Indian words, as well as words from the languages of the various foreign nationals who visited or settled along the Northwest Coast. The language was simply structured and augmented by signs; it evolved to admit new words to match new goods and practices in the trade. Some words entered it in a bizarre fashion. The word *pehlten*, meaning something unusual or absurd, possibly stemmed from the irrational behavior of one Archibald ("Judge") Pelton, an American living along the lower Columbia. Perhaps stemming from *pehlten* was the Chinook word *partelum*, meaning drunk or full of rum (or "lum," as the Chinooks called it because they could not pronounce their Rs). It appears that as drunkenness was new to the Chinooks, so was their new word to match it. White trade with the Indians limped along in the jargon, and in future years the natives were hard pressed to understand less tangible matters that the whites attempted to explain, such as landholding and religion. Despite the shortcomings of Chinook, it would be spoken until the late nineteenth century from Canada to California and from the Pacific to the Rockies.

Other natives soon met Astorian parties probing the region for furs. Somewhere above Grays Harbor, natives met Astorian partner Robert Stuart, who was guided there by the Clatsop chief Coalpo. Stuart found the natives "insolent," although few in numbers. Those at The Dalles received in May a visit from him and his fellow partner Alexander McKay and two clerks and welcomed the gifts that they brought to win their friendship. Coalpo refused to travel further upstream; understandably, since on one occasion he had burned a village in that area. His refusal to proceed disappointed the Astorians, who hoped to locate near a Nor'Wester settlement, Spokane House. On this journey the Astorians met Soto, the son of a shipwrecked sailor and a native woman. Detouring homeward on the Cowlitz River, which enters the Columbia from the north below its confluence with the Willamette, the party met some native warriors, who dishevelled their shirts and trousers to see if their bodies were as white as their hands and faces. At some undesignated spot north of Fort Astoria, natives killed an Astorian and later cut to pieces an eight-man trading party. Small wonder that the Astorians were apprehensive of natives crowding around their post; they were far outnumbered in the area by an estimated 214 Chinooks, 180 Clatsops, 234 Chehalises (Salishan), and 200 Tillamooks. One trader estimated the number of warriors within a hundred miles of the fort at 2,000. The situation might have been more frightening to the Astorians if many of the surrounding peoples had not been commercially oriented.

The Astorians were put further on edge and on guard by the June 5 departure of the *Tonquin* for the north. They strengthened their fortifications. Large numbers of natives from the Strait of Juan de Fuca and Grays Harbor were camping across the river at Bakers Bay. They frightened the traders with news of some disaster striking the ship in the north. The fur men feared that the bearers of the news might seek some kind of retaliation on them. About that time Comcomly's son, Casacas ("Prince of Wales"), seriously injured a Chehalis chief while playing ball. The Astorians feared the incident might push the Chinooks into war with the Chehalises, whose friendly gestures toward the Astorians were resented by the Chinooks. Fearing Chehalis encroachment on their trading monopoly, the Chinooks showed the Astorians more than the usual amount of goodwill despite Comcomly's displeasure at the defensive preparations that were underway at the fort.

Rumors of some disaster befalling the *Tonquin* continued to filter down the coast. In August, 1812, a native named George Ramsay (Lamazu) told—by means of voice, gesture, and sign language—how he had been on the scene at Clayoquot Sound on the west shore of Vancouver Island when Captain Thorn had struck a head chief and expelled him from the ship. Smarting from the insult to their chief, the natives had plotted to kill the crew and take over the ship. Later, with large numbers of natives aboard and around her, she had exploded with a frightful roar, and parts of bodies flew in all directions.

Helping to engender ill feelings between the Astorians and the natives was head man McDougall, a peevish character. On one occasion the irritable Scot incarcerated a native who helped himself to some tobacco. Astorian clerk Alexander Ross wrote that when Comcomly came across the river the next day, McDougall brandished a blunderbuss in order to impress him. The gun accidentally discharged, blowing off a corner of the chief's robe. In response to his yells, his people rushed war-whooping to his aid. Believing

Comcomly had killed McDougall, the Astorians fired on the beleaguered chief. Two clerks finally placed themselves between the opposing forces, preventing what might have been a catastrophe.

McDougall's policies were based on medicine and matrimony. On receipt of confirmation of the *Tonquin* disaster, he flashed before the frightened natives a vial containing, he said, the virulent and dreaded smallpox. He married Comcomly's daughter, Ilchee, purchasing her in the native way in hopes of cementing better relations between the company and her chieftain father and his people—a practice other white traders would imitate. Some of the white husbands would leave their wives, as McDougall did. Others remained to have Christian clergymen solemnize the unions. The latter unions were generally harmonious, but not always so, especially when aristocratic women, wishing to flatten the heads of their offspring, were opposed by their husbands.

Surrounded by raw nature and natives, McDougall warmly greeted Thompson on July 14, 1811, as Thompson completed his "Journey of a Summer Moon," the last leg of his journey across the continent to open trade channels for his company.[7] The expedition to the mouth of the Columbia had been launched less than two weeks earlier. With a bateau crew of five French Canadians, two Iroquois (Iroquoian), and two Nespelem Sanpoil interpreters, he had set out from Kettle Falls, homeland of another Salish people, the Colvilles. The Colvilles were known as "Les Chaudières" among the French Canadians and Squeeryerpe (or Schuelpi, Chualpay, and the like) among themselves. They were also called Kettles for the depressions in the rocks that gave the Kettle Falls their name. Thompson's record of his journey among the natives along the Columbia, whom he guessed totaled roughly 13,615 souls, provides an intimate glimpse of these peoples in the early nineteenth century, especially those between Kettle Falls and the Columbia-Snake confluence, an area that is believed to have been untraveled by white men before his arrival.

Natives of the Columbia below Kettle Falls (Salishan Sanpoils, Nespelems, and Wenatchees) regarded Thompson with awe, offering prayers to the Great Spirit for his safe journey downstream and his return with the white men's goods that he promised to bring them. The first tribe that he met, the Sanpoils, had repulsed, with Colville aid, an attack of the Nez Percés and their Shahaptian allies, the Yakimas, in the late eighteenth century. They welcomed Thompson in a much friendlier fashion. They told him that they had "only their hands" to procure food and clothing, but wanted some iron-tipped arrows, which, unlike guns, did not frighten off game nor pose the danger of cross-fire when hunters encircled their quarry. Like all peoples along the river, they were hungry for tobacco, calling it "their friend."

Below the Columbia-Wenatchee confluence natives met the downriver travelers in a village that contained a 240-foot rush-mat lodge (this was not as long as some of the plank houses on Puget Sound, where one at Port Madison Bay measured over 500 feet in length). Apparently at least one villager had never seen white men, for he felt Thompson's

Colville Indians trapping salmon at Kettle Falls on the Colum-
bia River. From a painting by Paul Kane, who visited the
Pacific Northwest in the late 1840s. Royal Ontario Museum.

limbs to make sure that he was like the natives.

Thompson reached the Columbia-Snake confluence, which was in Shahaptian country south of the Wenatchees. There his Salish San Poils ceased their guiding and interpreting. The visit of Lewis and Clark had apparently only whetted the appetite of the natives for white men's goods. The ornament-minded women were especially delighted with the things that Thompson carried, such as "the Kettle, the Axe, the Awl, and the Needle." Their men appeared to be more concerned with securing firearms to defend themselves from the Paiutes, who were denying them access to buffalo grounds in the lower Snake River country.

With greater exposure to white traders, natives below the Columbia-Snake confluence had increased their wariness of whites from the time of Lewis and Clark. They were especially wary of the Astorians. Those below The Cascades believed that Astor's men had brought them the smallpox, a belief that was confirmed in their thinking by the prophecies of a Kutenai Indian, named Kocomene Peca, who traveled on the lower Columbia at the time of Thompson's journey. Saying that she had changed her sex, the

prophetess led her people against the Piegans in a mannish fashion like Joan of Arc, about whom she may have learned from French Canadians. A short distance upstream from Fort Astoria were the Clatskanies (Klatskanis, or Tlatskanais; Athapascan), who earlier had migrated from north of the Columbia River. They were hostile not only to Astorians who sought to pass their shores without paying tolls but also to their successors in the trade, the Nor'Westers and men of the Hudson's Bay Company, who passed their shores only in large armed convoys.

A most troublesome spot on the Columbia for passersby was The Dalles, which was known as a "general theatre of gambling and roguery." At that place the natives demanded an increased tariff on goods, as well as tolls for portaging canoes and their contents. When David Stuart, leading an Astorian party upriver with Thompson from Fort Astoria, hesitated to comply with their demands, they flashed sharp, two-bladed daggers, threw stones, and fired arrows, forcing him to part with some cheap leaf tobacco and a few trifling presents for their headmen. Wiser heads among the natives prevented their aggressive fellows from

Mat-covered lodges of Colville Indians near Kettle Falls on the Columbia River. Salmon is shown hanging to dry. From a paint- *ing by Paul Kane. Royal Ontario Museum.*

committing a violent act. Above The Cascades natives met the travelers flourishing daggers and bows, from which they might have fired arrows dipped in rattlesnake venom. In early 1814 a trader, Alexander Stuart, would be badly wounded by one of the poisoned arrows.

Rattlesnake venom was collected by elderly women. Besides using it to poison arrows, the natives prepared a concoction from it to induce abortions. This was perhaps a more medicinal and humane approach than another method that was sometimes used, that of placing the belly over a stick or tree trunk and pressing heavily.

At the Columbia-Snake confluence Chiefs Tumatapum of the Wallawallas, Quill-Quills-Tuck-a-Pesten of the Nez Percés, and Ollicott of the Cayuses met the Astorians. The traders found the Indian men "generally tall, raw-boned and well-dressed" in buffalo robes and deerskin leggings. Their moccasins were garnished with porcupine quills, trimmed, and painted red. The women were clothed in heel-length deerskin garments, leggings, and moccasins like those of the men. The men garnished themselves with dentalia and

other beads and trinkets and decorated their faces with red paint. The chiefs cleverly worked the Astorians against their rival Thompson by telling them that the Nor'Wester had given them presents and that, if Stuart did likewise, he could travel wherever he wished. Their insatiable thirst for white men's goods had obviously sharpened their ability in the competitive trading game. Ross believed that goods would never satisfy their desire for more of the same nor bring them happiness.

On August 31, 1811, at the Columbia-Okanogan confluence, natives met the Astorians with pledges of friendship and gifts of beaver. Their friendly disposition encouraged the Astorians to establish Fort Okanogan there that year and to extend their fur quests among the Shushwaps (Salishan) of the Thompson River country in present-day British Columbia. The Palouses met Thompson as he proceeded up the Snake, and he purchased horses from them for his journey over the plateau to Spokane House. To those who brought him a horse for his northward passage he gave a piece of paper worth ten beaver skins at any North West Company post. Unable to fathom how a piece of paper

Reeds, such as those being sorted by this Indian woman on the banks of the Columbia River near White Bluffs, Washington, were put to various uses. They were especially important as matting for floors and house coverings. U.S. Bureau of Reclamation.

could purchase goods, the natives were filled with awe, as were other Pacific Northwestern Indians who received papers from white men for one reason or another.

In the Spokane country several Kalispels and Coeur d'Alênes came to see the returning Star Man, only to discover he had brought them none of the goods, such as guns and axes, that they wanted. One Coeur d'Alêne chief complained of a lack of ammunition that prevented his people from protecting themselves as they hunted buffalo cows. Thompson gave them some ammunition and sent a note to Finan McDonald at Kullyspell House to supply their needs. In October, Thompson found Saleesh House in bad repair and learned that the Piegans had broken their truce with the Kutenais, sent a war party to intercept him, and killed every person in a Kutenai lodge.

Aware of the success of their Salish foes in procuring arms, the Piegans sought to make peace with them. At a council that included one Spokane warrior, a Salish tribesman harangued his listeners, naming those who had fallen in previous battles with their Plains foes. A Flathead chief stated that he wanted peace because the Salish had achieved an equality in arms with the Piegans. The Great Spirit, he said, the one who made the ground green, did not want it stained red with blood. It had, indeed, been stained: besides Indian losses, the desultory wars alone had killed 350

free trappers, by Thompson's estimates; they paid their chronic debts to the company with their very lives. After a lengthy council the Flatheads and their allies decided to cross the Rockies in summer, when the bull bisons were fat, to lands that the Salish claimed as their own and also to extend their hunts into Piegan lands, in what amounted to a declaration of war. They sent runners to ready their allies for the venture, expecting little aid from the Shahaptians. The latter had their hands full fighting the Shoshonis. When August came and the bull bisons were fat, the chief and a party of about 350 went to hunt the buffalo, approaching equal numbers of the Piegan foes. Both the Salish and the Piegan warriors were singing and dancing till they came within one hundred yards of each other. Then the songs and dances gave way to war cries as they rushed toward each other in mortal combat. When the fight was over, many on both sides lay dead or wounded. The Piegans withdrew, defeated. The last of the free buffalo hunters was slain (the free hunters were those who owned their own equipment). Thompson — the quiet, peaceful man who supplied guns and ammunition to his red allies — had helped to turn the tide of battle.[8]

In late August, 1812, some natives whose previous dealings had been with Nor'Westers encountered an Astorian party led by a former Nor'Wester, John Clarke. It was descending on Spokane House to build a post, Fort Spokane, right under the noses of the rival Nor'Westers. The Astorians brought with them a variety of goods to trade not only to natives in the immediate vicinity of the post but also to those more distant, such as the Kutenais and the Flatheads, into whose country Clarke sent men who boldly opposed the Nor'Westers. Natives of the area were eager to trade with anyone who provided them with guns — a good gun at that time went for no less than twenty beaver skins. Astorians made a good profit in such transactions, as they did in exchanging clothes for beaver.

According to one of the traders, the two companies each dispatched scouts to spy on and foil the other. From their example the natives became well trained in such tactics, playing one party off against the other to their own advantage. Besides tobacco, one commodity often used in such competitive situations was liquor. It was watered down but still potent enough for the newly initiated native imbibers. On one occasion the influential Spokane chief Illim-Spokanee, who diplomatically beat a path between the rival posts, was induced to drink some liquor. In a few days he returned for more. Subsequently, since it would never have done for white traders to have such an important chief set an example of drunkenness, both parties adhered to an 1812 agreement banning liquor traffic with the Indians, sparing them the drinking bouts that elsewhere resulted in maimings and loss of life.

In another quarter of Astorian operations, natives of the Willamette Valley in late 1811 and early 1812 saw parties probing the region in response to native reports that beaver there were "very abundant." Possibly the same natives who saw the Astorians had, a half dozen years earlier, met Captain Clark and informed him of the numerous peoples of

Kalapooian stock living up the Willamette. The natives would have met Astorian partner Donald McKenzie. In the spring of 1812, he probed briefly but deeply south into the valley. Its bountiful aboreal and faunal resources may have caused him to overestimate its beaver potential. Natives also must have met another party led by Astorian clerks William Wallace and John C. Halsey. In late 1812 or early 1813 Wallace and Halsey established a post near present-day Salem, Oregon. There they took furs mostly from free hunters rather than from the natives of the area, who were possibly unfamiliar with fur-gathering activities. The Astorians regarded the latter as too "lazy" to trap; in reality they did not wish to alter their ancient hunting practices to garner furs.

Two Astorian clerks, John Reed and Alfred Seton, with "a portion of the hands," entered the Willamette Valley to winter with Wallace and Halsey. On March 20, 1813, they were back at Astoria, bringing a quantity of dried venison. A June, 1813, company inventory on the Willamette showed about a thousand beaver skins taken. An inventory for September 17 of that same year for the Willamette regions show the receipt of seven beaver skins, two thousand pounds of dried meat, and a hundred pounds of tallow.

Because of their absence hunting buffalos, Nez Percé bands, such as those who met Lewis and Clark near the Snake-Clearwater confluence, did not meet McKenzie and his men, who went there in September, 1812, to build a crude post. To Astorian thinking, the "quiet and peaceable folk" contrasted sharply with those of The Dalles, where early the previous year natives had attacked a seventeen-man Astorian party under Robert Stuart, who injudiciously had tried to slip his brigade past portages at night. In an ensuing fight two Indians had been killed, and John Reed was nearly war-clubbed to death. The natives demanded that Reed be delivered "to cover the dead" as they expressed it. The Astorians refused, paying in native fashion for the human losses with blankets and tobacco, after which the natives disengaged from the confrontation.

In the fall of 1812, on learning of the outbreak of the War of 1812 between Britain and the United States, Astorians cached their goods and hurried to their post at the mouth of the Columbia. The war in many respects climaxed troubles that had beset the Astorian enterprise. It helped to destroy the venture—which had been marked by failure—to supply and deliver ample goods of suitable quality to native customers. More tragic were the deaths of sixty-one men in the enterprise. Natives at The Dalles gave the returning Astorians under McKenzie a cool reception in the spring of 1813, expressing displeasure at his failure to keep his promise to exchange blankets, knives, and axes for pelts, glaring at the *pashiskiukx*, or white men, who had been many moons in their country by then but were purveyors of no goods, only death to their people (they meant those killed two years previously). The natives withdrew when the Astorians raised and cocked their rifles. At the cry of "à l'eau, à l'eau, Camarades," the Astorians moved upstream.

Returning to their caches, McKenzie and his men discovered that a band of young Tushepaws (or Tashepas and

Charley Celila, a Wishram Indian. His people lived about five miles upriver from The Dalles on the north side of the Columbia River. University of Oregon Library.

the like), possibly a Nez Percé band from below the Snake River, had been rummaging about the post.* The party retrieved some of its stolen goods and searched several Nez Percé villages, finding but little in the camps of those who unanimously claimed that the robbers were the Tushepaws. Shortly after, McKenzie and his men boldly rushed a Tushepaw village, declaring they had not come to fight, but to supply goods. They recovered some of their own goods, firing a salute to impress the villagers with their firepower. A few days later, a friendly band of Scietogas arrived. Although

*The Tushepaws have not been positively identified. Lewis and Clark placed their spring and summer residence on the North Fork of the Clark River and their winter residence on the Missouri, believing perhaps that they were Flatheads. The ethnologist Albert S. Gatschet states that Tushepaw is a Shoshonean term applied to northern tribes, including the Nez Percés and the Kutenais (Frederick Webb Hodge, ed., *Handbook of American Indians North of Mexico* 2: 853). For additional information on the Tushepaws, see A. W. Thompson, "New Light on Donald Mackenzie's Post on the Clearwater, 1812–1813," *Idaho Yesterdays* 18, no. 3 (Fall, 1974): 28–32, in which Thompson concludes that the Tushepaws were most likely Nez Percés.

they bore a Paiute-Shoshoni name which translated as "camass eater," they were most likely a Cayuse band living in mat lodges on the Umatilla River. In January, 1812, when Astorian business manager Wilson Price Hunt straggled westward to Astoria, these people befriended him, unlike the Bannocks and the Shoshonis, who fled at his approach. Their welcome placed them high in his opinion as a noble people who never ate dogs, had hundreds of horses, wore buckskin clothing and robes, and possessed white men's goods, such as pots, kettles, and axes, which indicated that they had obtained them through trading furs. When a Tushepaw chief tried to induce the Scietoga chief to annihilate McKenzie's expedition, the Scietoga chief refused, reminding the Tushepaws that with guns obtained from white men they could fight their foes on the buffalo plains.

As the Astorian enterprise had begun on a tragic note at the mouth of the Columbia River, it ended on an equally tragic note far to the east near the Snake River and its affluent, the Boise. In January, 1814, John Reed and eight others were killed by natives there, where they had gone seeking Astorian stragglers and horses to help them leave the country. Only the wife of trapper Pierre Dorion and her two children survived to reach the Columbia. She told how at the first post that Reed built natives had greatly importuned them and how members of the Dog-rib tribe (Shosho-nean) had committed the treacherous act. In fact, the killings have been ascribed to various other tribes. The treachery of the act, regardless of who perpetrated it, was overshadowed by the heroism of this woman and her children. Their story became one of the most often told stories to come out of the American West—a story not only in the white community but also in the red, for she was an Indian.

A salmon in the stylized form of Pacific Northwest Indian art. The salmon was the staple food of coastal natives and also important in the diet of Columbia Plateau Indians. From a graphic by Henry Ruby.

4. NATIVES AND NOR'WESTERS

Natives at Astorian posts in late 1813 must have been confused when American flags were lowered and Union Jacks were hoisted in their stead; they were unaware perhaps of the policies by which the North West Company appropriated the Astorian posts. On learning that Astoria was to be transferred to the British company, Comcomly believed that a ship approaching the mouth of the Columbia River on November 29, 1813, had come to carry off the Astorians as slaves. To prevent this, he promised to hide about eight hundred warriors in the woods, where, in concert with Astorian guns, they might hold off the British "invaders." A key figure in the transfer, which was precipitated by Astorian fears of a British takeover in the course of the War of 1812, was Duncan McDougall, who persuaded his father-in-law to abandon his earlier plans.

With McDougall's assurance that no harm would befall him, the chief boarded the British sloop of war *Raccoon*, which was at anchor in Bakers Bay to welcome the King George Men. Comcomly felt an affinity with them because he too was of royal blood. For his welcome he received from the *Raccoon*'s captain, W. Black, a bumper of wine, as well as an old flag, a laced coat, a cocked hat, and a sword which he proudly but awkwardly displayed. He was absent when on December 13 the British took over the post amidst cheers and gunfire. From clerk Gabriele Franchère, the only Astorian who understood their language, the curious natives learned what was transpiring. When Black left the river in late December without slaves, Comcomly realized he had misjudged the captain's mission. He also had misjudged the loyalty of British Astorians to Astor; with the transfer of the post, like its flagpole, they showed their true British colors.

From their Astorian rivals the Nor'Westers inherited more than physical posts and properties. Most important to them was the native clientele with whom they had to deal to secure their venture. The change of flags and management, however, meant less to the natives than it did to the new owners. The economics and policies of the trade had not changed, nor had the attitudes of native traders. Losing none of his shrewdness, Comcomly earned from the new proprietors of the fur post, which was renamed Fort George, such epithets as "troublesome beggar" and "niggardly fellow." The ending of the truce prohibiting the sale of liquor to Indians did not help the situation. Liquor had flowed freely on the *Raccoon*, and tipsy tars venturing from ship to shore had set a poor example to the natives. One Fort George trader induced one of Comcomly's sons to become drunk, and in that state he became the object of laughter among the slaves. This was possibly the occasion when the chief, finding him staggering, foaming, and blabbering at the mouth, ordered him shot. Fortunately, the youth sobered in time to avoid such a fate.

The Nor'Westers believed that their predecessors had pampered the chaffering Chief Comcomly and other natives, yet tried to keep in their good graces by supplying them various goods and services. They did balk at the chief's request that their blacksmith make him some iron arrow points, the likes of which, they feared, might someday be directed at them. The fear was justified on January 9, 1814, when Alexander Stuart staggered into the fort half dead from wounds from such an arrow. The trouble had begun earlier that month when a Nor'Wester party sailed upstream to carry arms and supplies into the interior and search out the Reed party in the Snake River country. At the mouth of the Willamette a party with David Stuart warned them of trouble ahead. Natives at The Cascades had been stopped by fire from the party's three-pounder. Ignoring this warning to travel no farther upstream, the Nor'Westers pushed on. Natives at The Cascades, already angered at Nor'Westers for furnishing arms to their enemies upstream and taking advantage of the party's preoccupation with portaging its properties, helped themselves to its guns, powder, kettles, and other goods. Although two of the natives died, they still disrupted the trading party's upriver passage. They did so with aboriginal arms, on which they had to depend not only because of their isolation from the source of guns but also because their toll-gathering left them little time to seek furs to exchange for firearms.

The natives probably expected the Nor'Westers to seek their lost goods and wreak punishment on them. They did not have long to wait. By mid-January, 1814, those near The Cascades met a polyglot party of nearly a hundred men led by Chief Coalpo's wife, who acted also as an interpreter and mediator, and Fort George headman John George McTavish, along with Chief Casino (or Casenove, Keisno, and the like), a powerful chief of the Columbia-Willamette confluence. Weakening the expedition's resolve to punish the killers were rivalries among its Indian members, two of whom got on poorly with Casino, as did Coalpo's wife and other Indians of the lower river. The two natives retrieved some of the stolen guns, but were told that most of the missing goods were at the village of a Chief Canook at the Upper Cascades. There the punitive party took a chief as hostage to ensure return of the missing articles. Unwilling to challenge Canook at the strategic Cascades, the party returned home, ending what a former Astorian would call an "inglorious expedition."[1]

Nor'Westers inherited a legacy of troubles not only from their own brashness but also from the brashness of the Astorians around the Pacific Northwest. The department of former Nor'Wester and Astor partner John Clarke was typical. His party came near the confluence of the Snake and the Palouse rivers in late May, 1813, with thirty-two horses loaded with furs from the Spokane district. Some native, or

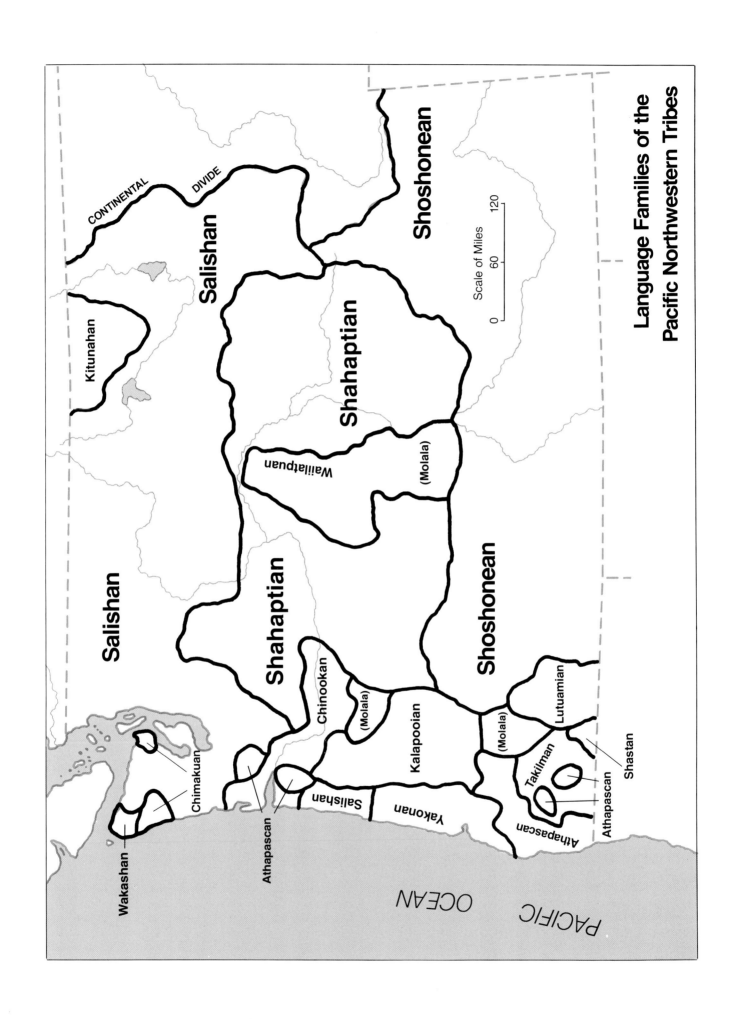

Language Families of the
Pacific Northwestern Tribes

PACIFIC OCEAN

Salishan

Shahaptian

Shoshonean

Waiilatpuan

(Molala)

Kitunahan

Continental Divide

Scale of Miles

0   60   120

Wakashan

Chimakuan

Athapascan

Chinookan

(Molala)

Kalapooian

Salishan

Yakonan

(Molala)

Takilman

Lutuamian

Athapascan

Shastan

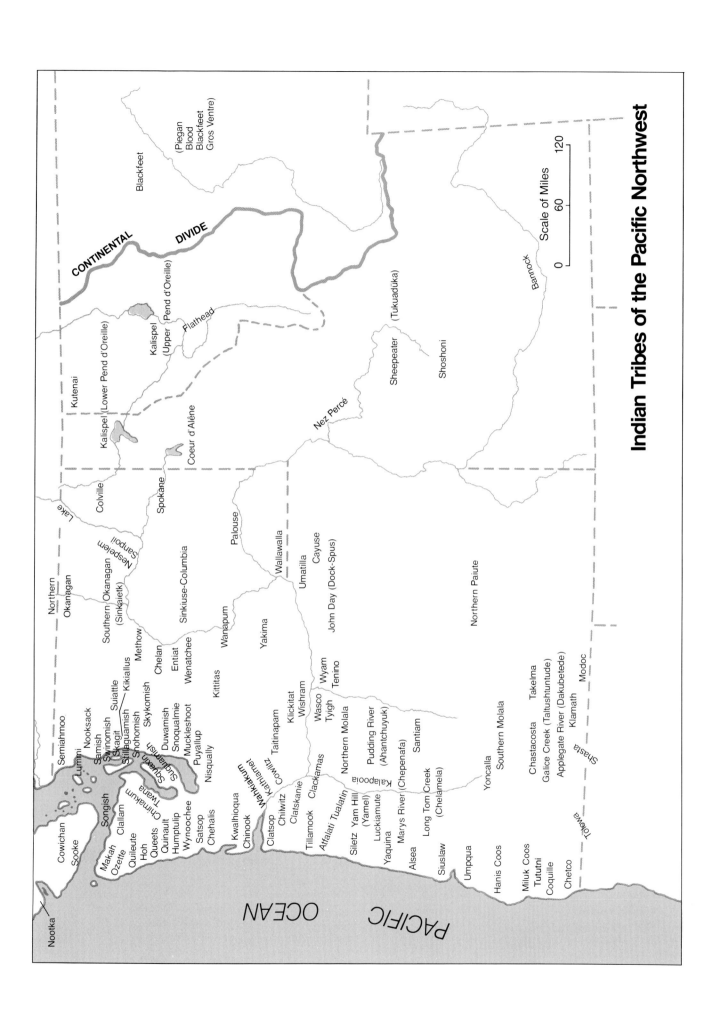

Indian Tribes of the Pacific Northwest

natives, stole the party's goods. Among them was Clarke's prized silver goblet from which at Fort Spokane he customarily drank with much ceremony. Clarke had earned a reputation among whites and Indians as an indulgent popularity seeker. Normally he was unmoved by thefts of company property, but he became enraged at the loss of his goblet. Assembling the natives, he vowed that, if the utensil was not returned, he would hang those found guilty. A native, believed to be a Nez Percé, was caught shortly after, and the goblet was returned. Nevertheless, in keeping with Clarke's decree, Clarke's men pinioned the victim and hung him on a makeshift gallows. To an Indian this was the most frightful and despicable way to die, and having taken Clarke's threat lightly, the natives were stunned by his action. After a harangue from their chief, they rode their fastest horses spreading word of the deed in all directions and assembling the tribes for vengeance.[2]

A few days later an Indian camp at the Columbia-Snake confluence bristled with anger over the hanging. On May 30, Tumatapum, the Wallawalla chief, rode up to Clarke crying: "What have you done, my friends? You have spilt blood on our lands." Had not Meriwether Lewis and William Clark said that there would be perpetual peace between reds and whites? John Clarke's party, fearing for their lives, pushed off for Astoria. Tumatapum told the 1813 summer brigade, on its return upriver to the interior posts, that he had tried so hard to appease the "bad hearted" Indians smarting from the affair that he had talked himself hoarse. He urged the traders to turn back. The brigade was forced ashore from its midriver course, where it sought to escape attack, by natives singing and dancing in what the brigade believed to be a prelude to their deaths. The natives let them move on after a smoke, but they did not forget the hanging. In 1814, near the same place, they fired warning shots at a bateau crew passing downstream and jumped into the river to heel the craft landward high and dry on the beach, from which they would not let it proceed until its crew had "smoked themselves drunk." Near the end of June, 1815, when another Nor'Wester brigade failed to beach its craft, natives engaged them in a fight, in which two natives were killed and a third badly injured. The next day the crew "covered the dead" with goods and moved quickly on.

In the spring of 1814 at a populous sprawling rootgrounds camp in the "Eyakema" (upper Yakima, or Kittitas) valley northeast of present-day Ellensburg, Washington, the Cayuses, Nez Percés, and other tribesmen found Alexander Ross, now a Nor'Wester, in their midst seeking to buy horses for his brigades. Earlier the friendly Wenatchee chief Sopa, to whom Ross had exchanged cloth and gartering for horses three years before, had his men warn Ross and his party not to enter such a hostile camp, crying, "Samah! Samah! Pedcousm, pedcousm" ("White men, white men, turn back, turn back, you are all dead men!"). Wishing to prove his loyalty to the Nor'Westers as he had to the Astorians, Ross brushed the warning aside and pushed on to the Indian camp.

In the center of the huge temporary village, where it was customary for head chiefs to pitch their lodges, the native leaders told him that traders like him were the "men who kill our relations, the people who have caused us to mourn." Aware of the Indians' desire for trade goods, and that the goods could "cover the dead," Ross obliged the natives by yielding a knife, beads, buttons, and rings; he was happy to escape with his life. Sometime later a trader would attribute the death of trapper John Reed to the hanging ordered by Clarke. The Indians were not only angry at the hanging but also at the general failure of the Nor'Westers to abide by the protocol requiring pay for passage through Indian country.

In the upper interior, to which the brigades passed, Salish peoples, such as the Spokanes and Flatheads, extended the Nor'Westers a better reception than that given them elsewhere. Yet, there were troubles there also. The natives were displeased with the tariff, which was subject to vagaries in a distant marketplace. Native males resented company personnel taking their women for wives. At the same time, the natives' wish for the white men's "medicine" helped to check their aggressions against the suppliers of the seemingly magical substances, and on one occasion young Spokane braves even offered to wage "war" against the Nez Percés for threatening some of Clarke's men for the hanging. The Astorians declined the offer, for, like the Nor'Westers, they wanted peace among the tribes so that their energies could be diverted from war to the work of hunting furs.

A Nor'Wester party reached Fort Spokane, a more commodious place than Spokane House, in late August, 1814. The Spokanes assembled to meet them. With typical chieftain's oratory, Illim-Spokanee declaimed, "The white men made us love tobacco almost as much as we love our children." He also revealed that in anticipation of other more powerful "medicine," especially guns, on the return of the brigades, his people had "broken their arrows" almost to the point of forgetting how to use them. The white men, he declared, had deceived the people by failing to bring the guns and "fire powder" in their big canoes. Yet, not daring to slouch from his diplomatic posture, he remained on good terms with the whites, as would his famous son, Chief Spokane Garry, at a later time. The Spokanes best expressed their feelings about the white men as they danced before them and chanted:

The good white men, the good white men,
Our hearts are glad for the good white men.
The good white men, the good white men,
Dance and sing for the good white men.[3]

Down on the lower Columbia, Nor'Wester operations encountered both opportunities and obstacles. On January 21, 1814, a native party, including Wallawallas, Cayuses, and others from The Cascades, visited Fort George, asking its traders to come to their lands; which, they said, abounded with beaver. On the other hand, swift-riding horsemen, very possibly Nez Percés and Cayuses, gave company personnel to understand that they wanted no white men and guns in the Willamette Valley, where the two tribes came to hunt. They were painted—as were their mounts— and they were armed with bows and arrows and iron-shod

Indian burial place on the Cowlitz River. From a painting by Paul Kane.
Pacific Northwest Collections, University of Washington Library.

lances about six feet long. They feared that the guns with which the traders killed deer and other game to supply Fort George would frighten away the game and make it impossible for them to hunt there with their own weapons.

Although they were not a threat to the safety of Fort George, Chinook women continued to threaten the health of its men. Despite an April 19, 1814 quarantine against their entry to the establishment, they moved in during the fall, occupying small huts that ringed the fort and bartering their favors to the men of the brigades coming down from the interior. The shortage of trade goods had made the natives in the area restless. The problem was relieved somewhat in April, 1814, with the arrival of a long-awaited supply ship, *Isaac Todd*. The biggest surprise aboard was a white woman named Jane Barnes; "the greatest curiosity," wrote one trader, "that ever gratified the wondering eyes of the blubber-loving aboriginals of the north-west coast of

America." She became the object of the affections of both white and red men around the fort, including one of Comcomly's sons, who sought to kidnap her and make her his special wife. Considering the debilitated condition of the men at the fort, a Dr. Swan, who also arrived on the *Isaac Todd*, was a more valuable, albeit less attractive, addition than Jane.

Word reached the fort in March, 1814, that the Nez Percés and the Cayuses had destroyed a native village at The Dalles. Later natives nearer the fort—allegedly Tillamooks or, possibly, Clatskanies—killed some Astorians. They were tracked down in May and ordered executed by headman Donald McTavish, an action that did little to improve Company-Indian relations. Petty wars along the lower Columbia and in its environs continued to hamper the trade. In early April a war party of three hundred Cowlitzes (Salishan) and their allies in forty canoes fought Casino's braves at the mouth of the Willamette River. That chief and his men had guns. The Cowlitzes had none. The affair, in which the parties sought satisfaction for some wrong, was bloodless. More arrows and lead were spent than blood. Fortunately for Fort George traders, a much publicized showdown between the Chinooks and the Chehalises that was scheduled for early spring, 1814, never took place. About that time a native from somewhere around The Dalles shot at Comcomly while he was bathing in a river. The chief dispatched his slave to destroy the attacker. The obedient slave laid the assailant low with a bludgeon and finished him off with a knife.

There were other irritants to company operations. In Comcomly's own household was his son, the treacherous Casacas, who often advised his father to attack the fort. Another source of trouble to the company was the Iroquois, who killed company livestock with reckless abandon. They also destroyed the natives' game and sometimes killed natives who stood in their way.

In 1816 natives of Kalapooian linguistic stock warned a ten-man Nor'Wester trapping party not to continue up the Willamette until they paid tribute for their passage. During an ensuing fight they caught the free-loading passersby in a hail of arrows fired from the shore. Returning the fire with their guns, the trappers killed a native. Shortly, the Kalapooians met a larger party of twenty-five men under a clerk, who "covered the dead" by giving merchandise to the dead man's survivors. Company trappers became embroiled in another fight in the vicinity, killing three natives and frustrating for a time Nor'Wester operations in the Willamette Valley. Sometime around 1817 the natives met an even stronger Nor'Wester party of forty-five armed men and two clerks. This time the natives smoked the pipe and received trade goods to "cover the dead" as the parties patched together a crude treaty. By its terms the Nor'Westers were promised ingress and egress past the falls of the Willamette (which were twenty miles from the confluence of the Willamette with the Columbia) to and from its watershed. Like the Astorians before them, they were eager to trap the fur-bearing animals there and in the beaver-rich Umpqua country of southwestern Oregon. By one provision of the treaty Willamette chiefs were to address their grievances to company "chiefs" at Fort George. The Willamette natives apparently abided by the terms of the "peace."

One of the greatest threats to trading operations out of Fort George was the Cowlitz War of 1818, which was precipitated by Iroquois molestation of native women on the Cowlitz River. Before the confrontation was over, the Iroquois had killed a dozen Cowlitzes. Shortly after the killings, Fort George trader James Keith brought the Cowlitz chief, How How, to the establishment. There Keith and others sought to appease him for the losses sustained by his people by arranging a marriage between his daughter and one of the men. Some of the Chinooks, who were never on good terms with the upriver people, fired on How How and his braves. Thinking the Cowlitz chief and his men were attacking in retaliation for the Cowlitz killings, fort personnel turned the bastion guns on them, wounding one of their number.

In 1819 the Iroquois apparently duplicated their Cowlitz treachery on the natives of the Umpqua Valley. A sixty-man Nor'Wester party had been led there by two clerks. On the verge of harvesting a beaver-pelt bonanza, the unruly Iroquois killed a dozen natives, sending panicky fellow trappers scurrying back to Fort George, not only those in the Umpqua party but also others who were on the Willamette. In 1820 the fort managers sent hardy Thomas McKay beyond the Willamette headwaters, where he appeared to have more success both with the natives and with the hunt.

North West Company traders hoped to experience fewer troubles in the beaver-rich Snake River country as they sought to extend their operations into that region. Aware of Astorian difficulties in the area, they prepared for their venture with some trepidation, unsure how they would be received by some of the Snake River peoples, for instance, the Shoshonis in the far-distant Snake-Colorado river borderlands. Had the peoples lived along the company communication lines, which ran east to the headquarters at Fort William on Lake Superior, their disposition would have been better known.

The person chosen to conduct the Snake venture was Donald McKenzie, a man of physical strength, mental acuity, and a "dauntless intrepedity" balanced by "cautious prudence"; a man full of "plans and projects." In 1817 he visited company posts in the interior, looking for one near the Columbia-Snake confluence to serve as a collection depot in anticipation of a fur harvest up the Snake. Returning from that journey, Perpetual Motion, as his colleagues called him, was off again barely a week later. With a forty-five-man party he traversed rugged snow-covered lands in search of an understanding with aggressive tribes, whose good will and permission were essential for passage to a vast storehouse of furs. A line of communication stretched from a proposed anchor post near the Columbia-Snake confluence to the upper Snake. Indians anywhere along it could jeopardize company operations. Success depended on the willingness of the natives at the proposed post to permit the traders to assemble their furs there as much as it did on permission from Snake River natives to enter their lands to gather them.

Laid out in 1818, Fort Nez Percés stood on the left bank of the Columbia a half mile upstream from the Columbia-Walla Walla confluence, which was below the confluence of the Columbia and the Snake. The fort was surrounded by barren, silent hills and overshadowed by frowning, rugged basalt bluffs. Nez Percés, Wallawallas, Yakimas, Wanapums, and other Columbia River peoples gathered to watch as an assortment of nearly a hundred company men assembled to build a post in their lands—French Canadians, patient Owyhees from the Sandwich Islands, and Iroquois and other Indians from the East. As the natives had sought compensation from white traders who traversed their lands, they also sought the favors of the builders and payment for the driftwood logs that were rafted to build the post in its treeless setting. Until their demands were met, they decreed no hunting, fishing, or trading for the preemptors of their lands. Aware that the success of the trade from east to west depended on this western anchor, the builders yielded to their demands and proceeded to build their fort on the small beachhead that was grudgingly given them.

The natives' permission to build the fort in no way guaranteed its security nor its operations. They disapproved of the company's policy of seeking peace with their ancient, troublesome Shoshoni foes. One day they broke off talks with chief trader Ross to welcome home Chief Tumatapum from fighting the Shoshonis. The noisy mounted war parties were frightening to the company men as the braves gyrated in and out of their saddles among the lodges, yelling at the top of their voices. Tumatapum's homecoming was no exception. The warriors' heads were covered with wolf head-dresses (worth two horses), which were ornaments with bear claws or feathers trailing to the ground. Their owners carried prized black leather girdles, wore painted shirts, and held medicine bags, pipes, and other articles. In their proper places in the regalia were lances, scalping knives, bows, quivers of arrows, and most valuable of all, guns. Equally highly prized were their favorite horses. White or mottled black and white, they were caparisoned from head to tail, painted and decorated like their riders to create a physical unity between man and beast that matched the mystical union between the red man and his horse.

The natives rushed to meet the returning warriors in a happy reception. No tearing of hair, no wailing this time: there were Shoshoni captives on which to vent their emotions. On such occasions it was customary for women to pull captives from horses; trample them; tear out their hair and flesh; jab them with knives, sticks, and stones or any other weapons they could find; before driving them to camp, where the people turned out en masse for the scalp dance. In this ceremony the men stood about fifteen feet apart facing each other, forming two rows at least a hundred yards long. Inside the rows were two rows of women facing each other, with a five-foot space in the middle. In the five-foot space male and female captives, naked to the waist, held long poles, atop which were scalps of their relatives. On such occasions, when the dancing and chanting began, captive and captor alike moved alternately to the right and to the left to the rhythm of a loud drum, while the jeering women threatened their human quarry with still more torture should they not "laugh and huzza." Before the dancing ceased at dusk, captives were usually cared for in friendly fashion to gird them for more cruel treatment the next day. After that they were no longer regarded as common property but as slaves under the care of masters, from whom they received better treatment.

Flushed with victory, Tumatapum said in council with Ross: "If we make peace, how shall I employ my young men? They delight in nothing but war, and besides, our enemies, the Snakes, never observe a peace." Pausing and pointing to his newly captured slaves, scalps, and weapons, he said: "Look, am I to throw all these trophies away? Shall Tum-a-tap-um forget the glory of his forefathers, and become a woman?" A Cayuse chief, whom Ross identified as Quahat (perhaps Ollicott), spoke from an authority greater than

Although described as a Chinook Indian, the man in this photograph has the facial characteristics of foreigners who came to the Chinook shores in early days. The different ethnic groups included Hawaiian Islanders, blacks, and natives of other Pacific Islands, as well as Britishers and Americans. Smithsonian Institution National Anthropological Archives, Bureau of American Ethnology, Neg. no. 3083-A.

that of other chiefs of the region, even the Nez Percés, when he asked, "Will the whites in opening a trade with our enemies promise not to give them guns or balls?" Other chiefs speaking in the same vein were answered by the traders' argument that peace and comfort would follow the trade.

Other councils followed. Finally an entourage of natives from the area assembled at the fort, smoked the pipe, and promised to make peace with the Shoshonis. This gave the Nor'Westers their much needed passage to Shoshoni lands. To seal the council, the natives threw off their garments, a gesture with mercantile overtones, for they wanted new ones; seldom did they allow ceremony to interfere with economic considerations. The smoke to seal the accord also signaled their need for more tobacco.

The ceremony was scarcely a love feast between Nor'Westers and natives, for the latter continued to react coolly to the fort, which Ross called the Gibraltar of the Columbia. The first objects to greet their eyes as they approached it were its loopholed palisades. To gain access, the natives had to pass through an outer gate, then through double doors, which led to a twelve-foot-high interior wall with portholes and slip doors, which stood in turn beneath two strong wood bastions and a long cannon. Trade was carried on through a wall opening eighteen inches square that was secured by an iron door, behind which was a trading shop. The Indians regarded as a mild affront a house that was erected at the fort gate strictly for Indian use. They were also offended at fort restrictions, especially restrictions of the sale of guns, ammunition, flints, and other goods. They taunted the strangers in their lands with such remarks as "Why are the whites so stingy with their goods? They hate us or they would be more liberal." They teased the traders by rapping on the big door. When their call was answered, they laughed in the face of the attendants and jeered: "Are the whites afraid of us? If so, we will leave our arms outside. Are the whites afraid we will steal anything?" Ross tried to calm them with assurances of goodwill, even getting them to admit that brash young braves might cause trouble anytime.

The natives sauntered around the fort, demanding its goods with threats that they would force its occupants to leave their lands. They engaged in activities that the fort traders considered both barbarous and time-wasting: scalp dancing; horse racing; gambling; and, "on every hillock," painting their faces, more easily now with the cheap paper-rimmed mirrors obtained at the posts (the post managers contributed to the very vanity that they decried).

The Indians obviously wanted the best of two worlds: the benefits of the trade and the trade goods while they retained their traditional life-style of hunting, fishing, gathering, and war. In remote recesses of the Pacific Northwest, such as the middle and upper Snake watersheds, natives were even less willing to surrender their life-styles. McKenzie was aware of their disposition as he left Fort Nez Percés to open trade in the area in late September, 1818, traveling with a caravan of 55 men, 195 horses, 300 beaver traps, and much trade merchandise. His fear that the natives would be poor fur gatherers prompted him to take along several Iroquois, whom he brought from the east not only to gather furs but also perhaps to set an example of such activity to the red men in the faraway Pacific Northwest. At Boise River, McKenzie fitted them out to trap while he pushed on up the Snake. The charms of Shoshoni women proved greater for the free trappers than the lure of soft beaver hides. Later McKenzie would round up some who had forgotten their company debts, abandoned their mounts and traps, and scattered with Shoshoni women to live off the land. Before the termination of their service in the Snake River country, one of the freemen would be killed in a scuffle with natives, two would desert, and seven would defect to the Shoshonis.

The natives in the Snake River country did not fancy gathering furs, considering it an occupation fit for women and slaves. Thus trading posts proved impractical. On his return from the Bear River in southeastern Idaho and northeastern Utah, McKenzie began building a post in the summer of 1819 near the one that Reed had built a half-dozen years earlier. Two of his men were killed, and the post remained unfinished because of the natives' hostility. They harassed not only the Nor'Wester venture in Snake country

at this time but also the Nor'Wester supply lines down to Fort Nez Percés. Taking advantage of the over confidence of a trader named William Kittson, they stole his horses, which were *en route* to supply McKenzie. To them this was an act of bravery, but to the Nor'Westers it was a disruption of trade. Realizing the importance of the trade lifeline, McKenzie assigned most of his men to retrieve the stolen horses. Natives would later kill two of Kittson's men returning to Fort Nez Percés.

During the absence of Kittson's party, a band of "mountain Snakes," who were actually Bannocks, approached McKenzie's camp. He tried to ensure its safety by presenting gifts to them, but to no avail. Attacking, the Bannocks tried to breach a makeshift breastwork. They were foiled when McKenzie and his men sprang over the obstruction, lighted a match, and placed a keg of powder between themselves and the foe. The frustrated attackers fled. Shortly, a two-hundred-man Nez Percé party under one Red Feather appeared, which might explain the sudden departure at that point of the Bannocks. Unhappy with Nor'Wester penetration into the lands of their traditional foes, a Nez Percé war party rode off because they were unable to cross a swift river separating them from the company men.

Farther up the Snake River, natives frequently encountered McKenzie and his men as the traders made their way to the Bear River country. One day the traders learned from a friendly Shoshoni band that a large Blackfoot party was nearby. As natives were communicating this information to McKenzie, a runner brought word that five Nez Percé parties nearby had killed several Shoshonis a few days before. The Shoshonis sought protection with McKenzie and his men, but the traders avoided this in their wish to stay clear of the native conflicts swirling about them. The Nor'Wester dilemma in that arena of intertribal conflict elicited from Ross the statement that, with "The Nez Percés behind, the Blackfeet before, the hostile Snakes everywhere around; our people were completely surrounded."*

At the end of a Shoshoni-Blackfoot fight the grim tally showed more Blackfeet dead than their foes. Many Shoshonis celebrated their victory in full view of McKenzie's uneasy men, scalp dancing, singing, and shouting far into the night in the eery glow of their campfires. At the battlefield a native chieftain gruesomely pointed out the anthropological fact that the "heads of the Blackfeet are much smaller than those of the Snakes, and not so round." The same applied to their scalps.

As yet, the principal chiefs of the large Shoshoni nations had not confronted McKenzie's party as it approached their camps. The party stopped to camp at wooded and watered places, from which they set out afoot and on horses each morning, traversing distances of about twenty miles in all directions to set their traps and return with their catches. In early spring, 1820, two Shoshoni chieftains, Pee-eye-em

---

*Present-day anthropologists take issue with Ross's delineation of the three Shoshoni groups. See Julian H. Steward, *Basin-Plateau Aboriginal Sociopolitical Groups*, Smithsonian Institution, Bureau of American Ethnology Bulletin no. 120, p. 267.

(Peim) and Amaquiem, met McKenzie, three of his men, and their Indian guides. The chieftains were described by Ross as the most powerful leaders of the three divisions of "the great Snake nation": the Sherrydikas (Northern Shoshonis), whose warriors were mounted upper-class men called "dog-eaters"; the Wararereekas (Western Shoshonis), known as "fish eaters"; and the Bannocks, whom Ross called Banatees (Northern Paiutes), who were known as "robbers." The Sherrydikas were tall and slender. They were a warring and buffalo-hunting people, rich in horses. By contrast, the Wararereekas were less imposing in appearance. They were numerous, but disunited and poorly armed. They seldom took the offensive in war and were prey to the Blackfeet. The Bannocks, who generally frequented the northern frontier of the Shoshoni country in small bands, were regarded as outlaws by the proud Sherrydikas.[5]

On learning of the fur seekers in their midst, large numbers of the three groups gathered to form a massive tipi village. The Sherrydikas occupied the center of the aboriginal sprawl. The Wararereekas and the Bannocks were in peripheral locations. Like most natives, the Shoshonis refused to reveal their numbers. Pee-eye-em rose in council to clarify for McKenzie some basic facts of Shoshoni inner culture, namely, that his own people fought the Nez Percés and plundered white men. He explained that he had no time to inflict punishment for the depredations and torments inflicted by the "mosquitoe"-like Bannocks, who were not even admitted to the council.

Far away from the council, natives, such as those whom Pee-eye-em described as troublesome, were extending their hostilities to the very doors of Fort Nez Percés. On a raid a band that was possibly Shoshoni killed stragglers from a nearby Wallawalla camp—a man, four women, and five children—and then quickly fled. In response, about four hundred Nez Percés, Wallawallas, and Cayuses approached the fort, shrieking, cutting themselves, and laying on the ground the bloated bodies of their people who had fallen in the raid. Chanting the death song, the brother of one of the women kidnapped by the attackers pitched a lodge within fifty yards of the fort. Tumatapum blamed the attack on whites for trading guns and balls to the foes of his people and their allies. Ross emerged from the fort with red cloth, laying six inches of it on each body as an expression of sympathy, but it took two weeks of smokes and palaver to calm the Indians down.

Back at the Shoshoni council, McKenzie had to settle for Sherrydika and Wararereeka good intentions. A Wararereeka chief, Amaketsa, gave assurances of peace, denouncing the Bannocks as a "predatory race" and the main cause of all Shoshoni-Nez Percé troubles. Pee-eye-em's brother, Amaquiem, spoke to four Bannocks, who had been invited to the council later, to denounce them as "robbers, and murderers," scolding and warning them to mend their ways on pain of death. The accused trembled, silent before their accuser. When Amaquiem sat down, they asserted their friendship to whites. When the council was over, McKenzie presented to Pee-eye-em and Amaquiem moccasins that were beaded with an emblem of peace. At their request they received from McKenzie a blanket, belt, and skillet, and after some hesitation the whites accepted Amaquiem's word that it was the Bannocks who had plundered and murdered the Reed party in the fall of 1813.

There followed a brisk trade between the natives and their fur-gathering visitors. The Wararereekas and Bannocks brought to trade the four- or five-foot-long beaver-skin garments with which they covered themselves in winter. In a sense they took the very clothes off their backs to exchange for a knife or awl, and they sold the horses from under themselves for an axe apiece. In these exchanges they revealed not only a value system different from that of whites but also an anxiety to trade, which some Pacific Northwestern natives were beginning to lose as they became more sated with white men's goods.

Visiting the Shoshonis a little later, Ross provided an eye-witness description of their trade with white men:

But it was truly Indian-like to see these people dispose of articles of real value so cheap while the articles of comparatively no value at all, at least in the estimation of the whites were esteemed highly by them. When any of our people through mere curiosity wished to purchase an Indian headdress composed of feathers, or a necklace of bear's claws or a little red earth or ochre out of any of their mystical medicine bags, the price was enormous. But a beaver skin worth twenty-five shillings in the English market might have been purchased for a brass finger ring scarcely worth a farthing. A dozen of the same rings was refused for a necklace of bird claws not worth half a farthing.[6]

The two powerful Shoshoni chieftain brothers accompanied the homeward-bound McKenzie brigade, trailing off from it short of the Blue Mountains. There the caravan met a large Cayuse escort for its triumphant return to Fort Nez Percés. The furs were loaded on 150 horses strung out in a line over two miles long. Only time would tell if the peaceful arrangements between the tribes around Fort Nez Percés and the Shoshonia bands—so ceremoniously sealed with peace pipes—would go up in smoke.

Time alone would also decide the fate not only of the Snake expeditions but the rest of the North West Company operations as well. Conflict with Pacific Northwestern natives had made the quest for furs hazardous and had resulted in the loss of human lives—losses that were not as meticulously recorded as were the economic losses. The latter in one year, in the opinion of Ross, amounted to four thousand beaver, worth six thousand pounds sterling. A host of management problems, of which the natives may have been unaware, foreshadowed troubles ahead for the company. Perhaps the greatest threat to its continued operations was its competition with the Hudson's Bay Company, with which it fought for control of the vast northern inland American fur trade. Along the path of the struggle in Canada east of the Rocky Mountains, natives had become pawns in a deadly game played with liquor and guns that sent them to their deaths. Unless some peace were effected between the two firms, natives of the Pacific Northwest stood a good chance of becoming casualties as well as customers.

5. TRIBES, TRAPS, AND TROUBLES

In 1821 the North West Company merged with the Hudson's Bay Company, whose London directors retained that name. As a result, Pacific Northwestern natives found themselves dealing with a monopoly; unlike in Canada, where competition between the two firms had nearly torn them and the natives apart. It remained to be seen how the monopolistic position of the company would affect its far-western native clientele. In fact, relations between the natives and the people of the "Bay" soon proved friendlier than previous contacts between Indians and fur seekers, although there remained many possibilities for trouble. Company personnel knew that their operations depended on the goodwill of the natives as much as it did on the bounties of nature and their monopolistic position. The greatest threat to the company's position was the Americans, who were also moving westward across the continent in search of furs.

Optimistic reports of Pacific Northwestern fur potentials came from the company's new Columbia district. Trader John L. Lewes wrote on April 2, 1822, that the fur trade could be secured by advances into unexplored tracts around Puget Sound and the Snake River country. George Simpson, governor in charge of the western operations, believed the company's fur trade in the Snake country and other deep reaches of the Columbia watershed could check Americans who had access to the Snake via the South Pass through the Rockies in southern Wyoming. He also encouraged company pursuit of furs in what he believed to be richer fur grounds to the north in New Caledonia, although prospects in the coastal areas there had been hampered by conflict between natives and white coastal traders.[1]

Three years had passed since McKenzie worked out his 1820 truce with the powerful Sherrydika chiefs, Pee-eye-em and Amaquiem, who held the key to the vast treasure house of furs within the Shoshoni hinterland. The perennial Alexander Ross was selected to ensure their goodwill in what were hoped to be final negotiations. Under company strategy, he was to approach Shoshoni lands from the north, exploring and trapping along the way. In late 1823 he began the first leg of his journey. At his departure point, Fort Spokane, there was evidence that new fur horizons had to be sought. The furs that natives of that vicinity were bringing to the post were, in the company's thinking, too little and too late, especially when the natives demanded so many of the company's precious stores of clothing, tobacco, ammunition, and medicine. They did, however, supply Ross with horses, which were basic to the success of interior fur brigades. Horses were more important to him than the salmon that natives at nearby Kettle Falls sometimes supplied in exchange for trifling articles of British manufacture and tobacco, which was now almost a necessity to them.

At the Flathead Post natives met Ross as he completed the organization of his Snake brigade. His expedition, which set out on February 10, 1824, was an amalgam of different human groups, much like others in the Pacific Northwest. The brigades usually were an assortment of French Canadians, Iroquois, half bloods from both sides of the Rockies, native men and women from the West, Indian slaves who were the property of trappers' wives (among whom there were considerable jealousies), and also children. For the horse-riding brigade members home was wherever they camped on their various journeys, just as it was for the native horsemen of the mountains, plains, and plateaus. Their equipment consisted of traps slung on their saddles, other horse gear, items to trade, and not least important, guns; for such ventures were of a both "military and mercantile" nature.

The caravan did not impress its leader, not because it was motley but because it lacked the discipline that Ross believed necessary for successful trapping and for coping with hostile Indians and competing Americans. The Iroquois, who were noted for not only deceptions but also defections, plagued him on the journey, where all hands were needed to face hostile men and nature. Especially to be feared along the route that Ross projected were the raiding Blackfeet. That tribe struck the Salish lands to its west, easily crossing the lofty Rocky Mountains by northern passes, and the lands of the Shoshonis to its south at such places as the Lost, Wood, and Boise rivers of southern Idaho. Blackfoot depredations threatened the brigade at every turn of the trail, although Finan McDonald, now in the Hudson's Bay Company's employ, had defeated those plainsmen in 1823 on the upper Lemhi, a tributary of the Salmon River (itself a tributary of the Snake). Not satisfied with a simple skirmish, McDonald and a brigade pursued the Blackfeet with superior firepower and killed several of their number, including one who had the audacity to wave a scalp on a pole before the infuriated Scot. This head-on encounter proved costly, however, for the brigade lost about a half-dozen of its own people. The Ross Snake brigade crisscrossed the Rockies, hunting and trapping in relative freedom. Advancing as a unit, it reached the Portneuf River of southern Idaho. There the Iroquois went their separate ways to trap.

During that summer of 1824, Pee-eye-em met Ross in council near present-day Boise, Idaho. A Cayuse delegation was present, with whom Ross was acquainted from his trading days at Fort Nez Percés. They had come from that fort. In a ceremony as dramatic as that which McKenzie celebrated with the Shoshonis four years earlier, Pee-eye-em and the Cayuses effected a truce in a pipe-smoking ritual, allowing the company access to the Shoshoni country. Yet there was no guarantee that the other Shoshonean peoples, the Wararereekas and the Bannocks, over whom Pee-eye-em had no more control than he had four years earlier, might not frustrate company fur quests as they had those of the North West Company.

On October 24, 1824, an Iroquois party that had left the brigade rejoined it on Salmon River in company with Jedediah Smith's American party of Rocky Mountain Fur Company trappers. At this time it came to light that a Sheepeater band, angered that Ross had recovered traps that they had stolen, avenged his action in a fight with the Iroquois. The attackers lost a chief, and the Iroquois lost their traps, guns, and a large quantity of furs. Wandering aimlessly after the fight, the Iroquois attached themselves to Smith's party; whom, they reported, relieved them of nearly all of their furs in exchange for leading them to the Pierre's Hole country (west of South Pass in the Teton Basin in Idaho), where they were to have met Ross. Ross and his brigade returned to the Flathead Post in November with five thousand beaver and other pelts.[2]

The company's operations in the Snake River Basin in the winter of 1824-25, which replaced the rather-useless summer hunts, were under Peter Skene Ogden. Ogden was charged not only with gathering furs but also with saving company operations from the encroaching Americans. Simpson in a July 12, 1823, communication had written that Ross should be cautioned not to open the way to Americans. In company with Smith (who had returned with Ross), Ogden and his brigade left the Flathead Post on December 20, 1824, for the Snake country. As though the terrain were not difficult enough for the travelers, an advance party, led by François Payette and thirteen trappers, ran into trouble as it sought to outrun Smith to get its share of beaver along the Blackfoot River. In April, 1825, the Blackfeet attacked Ogden's brigade although they had maintained that they were at war with the Shoshonis, not whites; possibly they remembered Finan McDonald's attack on their people. To make matters worse, American trading parties tried to spirit the Iroquois away. Some freemen did slip off, hoping to shed their company debts. On May 29 two freemen ran off, leaving not only their horses, traps, and furs but also their women and children.

The spread of buffalo intensified conflict of tribes on subsistence hunts west of the Rockies at this time. The animals moved into the Green and Bear river valleys and into the area of the Salmon and Lemhi rivers, which were roughly the western limits of their range. The buffalo disappeared from the upper Snake around 1840 after such tribes as the Nez Percés hunted out the western fringes of that range. Nez Percé chief Old Joseph (also known as Tuekakas and Walamuitkin, or Hair Knotted in Front) was credited with killing a buffalo on Burnt River, a Snake tributary, in 1847. The Bannocks and other tribes west of the Rockies would begin returning east around 1840 to follow buffalo migrations in that direction.*

The Blackfoot hands-off policy toward Ogden and his brigade allowed the brigade to spend three months reconnoitering dangerous country on the upper Missouri River.

Although claimed by Americans, this country was unbreached by St. Louis trappers because the Blackfeet there vented more opposition on the Americans than the British, who were their primary suppliers of white men's goods. Returning to the upper Snake in late September, Ogden trapped his way across present-day Idaho for a month, en route to Fort Nez Percés—which would soon be called Fort Walla Walla because of the merger.

The greatest threat to Ogden's journeys was the desertion of nearly forty of his fifty-eight trappers. Because of such desertions, Ogden relied for help on the Flatheads. American traders had sought vainly to win over that tribe in their fur-hunting efforts, but they remained loyal to their British allies. For their loyalty they were rewarded at Flathead Post on December 18, 1825, with powder, balls, and tobacco—commodities that the company supplied more freely to loyal tribes than to others. On the previous day about sixty or seventy Flatheads had approached the fort in their customary manner: singing, flying flags, and firing guns. These gestures were countered by a musket-fire salute from the post.

Just as ranks existed in the Hudson's Bay Company organization, so did they also among native peoples. This was evident during trading sessions at various posts and Indian villages. At Flathead Post some headmen smoked in the "gentleman" house; while lesser braves smoked in the "Indian" house, trading beaver, horse gear, buffalo tongues, saddle blankets of buffalo calfskin (called apichements, apichemons, apichamores, and the like),* and pemmican. Company traders at the post were pleased that bad trails and weak horses during the winter of 1825-26 had kept the Flatheads away from the buffalo country, where they had gone on summer hunts, and forced them to remain at home to hunt beaver. This did not free them and their Salish allies from troubles, for the Blackfeet stalked their lands freely to steal horses. That winter the Piegans stole seven Kalispel horses. Not only did men of the Bay discourage their native traders from crossing the Rockies; they also discouraged their own men from venturing across the mountains onto the plains because they feared American traders might spirit them away.

Staying home did not necessarily mean larger fur harvests by the Indians. That December those at Flathead Post spent considerable time gambling, a diversion to which they were so addicted that they carried it on in the snow,

---

*The buffalo, Bison bison, which began migrating to western slopes of the Rocky Mountains in the second decade of the nineteenth century, were pushed there by American fur hunters east of the Continental Divide. Receding eastward in the third decade of the nineteenth century, buffalo became extinct on the western slopes after the 1840s. In prehistoric times, however, different species of the animal, bison occidentalis and Bison antiquus, roamed as far to the west as the present state of Washington.

*Reuban Gold Thwaites states that apichements were mats made of rushes used for constructing lodges and for beds and coverings. Early Western Travels 1748-1846 21:145 n. 17. Clifford M. Drury states that apishmore and apishamore were words used by Plains Indians for saddle blankets made from buffalo-calf skins. Nine Years with the Spokane Indians The Diary, 1838-1848, of Elkanah Walker, p. 239, n. 49.

much to the disgust of the fort traders. The freemen continued to irritate the company traders; in Simpson's words, they were "the very scum of the country." Between expeditions they quarreled with local natives and engaged in other nonproductive activities that only increased their debts and their indisposition to the company. John W. Dease wintered among the Flatheads from 1825 to 1829; he was retained there because of his influence over Iroquois freemen.

Simpson came west in 1824 to initiate an economic overhaul of the Columbia Department, which had been on shaky grounds since fur operations began there. On reaching Fort Spokane on October 28, he noted that, although Indians came there to trade, they also came to gamble and race horses with other Indians of the area and with the Nez Percés, who often came to trade horses and have a good time with their Salish friends. Simpson was critical not only of the natives but also of fort personnel. The latter seemed to him more interested in fun than furs in a setting more enervated than energized. Within two years the Spokane post fell victim to Simpson's economy axe; it was removed near to Kettle Falls, where it was called Fort Colvile (Colville). Bastioned and picketed, it became the company's largest and strongest area post next to Fort Vancouver.

The greatest outward show of opposition to the proposed move came from an influential Nez Percé known as "scoundrel Charley." Complaining that his people would have to travel seventy miles farther from their homelands to the new post, he threatened an embargo on its supply of horses from Snake River. Company officials lulled the Spokanes into thinking the change was best for them. It was at least better for other tribes, for instance, the Lower Kutenais; for they now would have a post nearer their homelands.

Simpson shrewdly detected various threats to fur trade on the Columbia, where the furs were less numerous and less well prepared than those gathered east of the Rocky Mountains. The Flatheads living near the crossings of the mountains might become spoiled as company traders sought to retain their goodwill in the face of American competitors who wished Flathead lands for the United States. Another serious threat to the Columbia trade was the continuing intertribal conflict. Warriors of the interior on swift mounts raided peoples of the Columbia area and the sedentary villagers of The Dalles, taking scalps, slaves, and horses. Company officials had no illusions that they could immediately break up traditional war and hunting expeditions; instead they sought to minimize them in the best interests of the trade.

Simpson's economy axe cut down the Columbia River to Fort George. In his words, it was "not at all suitable to an Indian Trading Post," and by decree he scheduled it for removal to some place farther upriver. Natives around that fort perhaps did not understand the economics of the move, which placed the fort at Vancouver on the north bank of the Columbia across from its confluence with the Willamette. Nor did they understand the politics of the move. The fort would be more safely in British lands if Joint Occupation agreements were terminated. Those agreements, which

were first negotiated in 1818, safeguarded both British and American territorial rights from the Pacific Northwest to Alaska.

On March 16, 1825, Comcomly wept when Simpson officially broke the new of the move to the natives. The chief's tears may have been genuinely shed at the prospect of the departure of the King George Men from his homelands, or they may have been shed at the inconvenience and loss of position such a move would cause for him and his people. By the same token removal would enhance the position of rival chieftains farther up the Columbia in the direction of Vancouver. Among the latter were Schannaway, a Cowlitz—whose village lay astride the route leading down to the Columbia from Puget Sound—and Casino, in whose lands the new Fort Vancouver would be established. Happy with the move, Casino announced his King George citizenship.

Simpson believed that the Chinooks and other lower Columbia and coastal natives were so eager to barter furs that they would bring them upriver to The Cascades and even beyond to Fort Walla Walla. He did not know that countless Columbia floods rushing to the sea had not covered the bad blood between the Chinooks and other lower-country peoples and those of The Cascades-Dalles area, whom they would have to pass to reach Fort Walla Walla. Fortunately for the company, the Cascades-Dalles toll gatherers had been tamed by what Simpson called the "judicious firm and conciliatory measures" pursued by British traders. For instance, firmness, tempered by diplomacy, had helped curb their aggressiveness to the point where they were now happy merely to trade salmon for tobacco. The Columbia River itself proved more turbulent than its people. Its treacherous reaches continued to exact a high toll of the lives of company men shooting downstream on their annual brigades to company headquarters at Fort Vancouver.

Natives were perhaps unaware that Simpson was encouraged by his London superiors—who were themselves influenced by evangelical-humanitarian movements in Great Britain—to extend Christian probity and sobriety to the red man. Simpson somewhat naively believed that his arrival on the Columbia had dried up the flow of liquor on that stream. In his opinion the liquor had deprived the natives of the will and wherewithal to sell their furs and garnish themselves with goods of British manufacture. In fact, the *regales* were as boisterous as ever. In early August, 1824, trader John Work tells of stopping with an upriver-bound brigade a short distance from Fort George possibly just to remove from the sight of its natives an event in which the men spent the better part of a day drinking and fighting. It would take more than Simpson's optimism to dry up the liquor flowing from ships at the mouth of the Columbia; from which, as though through the neck of a whiskey bottle, it flowed upstream, debauching natives in its way. Early in the century a trader had written that "all Indians on the Columbia entertain a strong aversion to ardent spirits, which they regard as poison."[3] No more: where Spaniards had offered Northwest Coast natives only tea, coffee, and chocolate to drink, the red men now easily obtained alcoholic beverages from British and American mariner-traders. Stemming from Nor'Wester days, the practice of "giving the dram" had become fairly general to set natives in a good, albeit unsteady, mood for trading sessions. In some quarters along the Columbia they received a bottle of rum for every ten skins brought in. Very likely, in Simpson's thinking, keeping a dry operation would contribute as much to company efficiency as it would to the natives' sobriety.

Natives north of the Columbia, up to and along the shores of Puget Sound and the lower Fraser River, were exposed to fewer white men than were those of the lower Columbia watercourse. Yet the isolation of those peoples continued to be breached. In late November, 1824, natives of that region, such as the Chehalises, met a company expedition that was probing for fur prospects. The Chehalises were no strangers to the men of the Bay, but they were meeting them this rainy season in their villages. The houses were of planks set vertically and fashioned neatly at their tops. There was, according to one description, "a complete bank of filth and nastiness . . . mixed with the offal of fish and dirt of every kind. . . ." At one Chehalis village the nearly naked natives, hiding behind trees, threatened to attack the party with bows and arrows, an attitude that surprised the travelers because they had traded peaceably with the Chehalises before. Their unfriendly disposition stemmed from a report spread by Comcomly's son, Casacas, that the party had come to attack them. Gifts of tobacco helped to dispel their suspicions. The importance of this weed in the trade was expressed by a company official who implied that the firm's short supply threatened to jeopardize the entire trade on the Columbia.

Meeting the party on the lower reaches of the sound were other natives. A trader, Pierre Charles, had been among them for some time. Salishans met the northbound travelers farther up the sound, including Nisquallis, Suquamishes, Snohomishes, and Skagits. Some of them fled to the woods at the traders' approach, fearing, as others had along the route, that the party had come to attack them in the manner of northern tribesmen, such as the Cowichans (Salishan) of the lower Fraser River and the Haidas of the Queen Charlotte Islands.

It was evident from their weaponry that the Puget Sound peoples had changed but little since their initial contact with white men. They had bows, arrows, spears, and bludgeons, but few guns. The Skagits continued to flatten the heads of their infants, but not as severely as the natives of the lower Columbia did theirs. As winter approached, they covered their nakedness with blankets hung around their shoulders. Some wore cloaks of hair and feathers in lieu of such coverings.

Like other peoples in the area that extended west of the Cascade Mountains, south to the Columbia River, and north to Alaska, the Puget Sound Indians held potlatches.[4] The wealth-destroying institution reached its highest form in the northern quarters. The motivations behind it ranged from the economic to various aspects of the social. It served to hold groups together and was a means of achieving identification and integration. More practically, it served as a

weapon against rival families or contenders for power in the group. In the potlatch, a guest chieftain and his people lost face and "power" if they did not return in a future potlatch one hundred percent of the value of the gifts received from a rival host and did not destroy even more wealth in even larger fires.

The isolation of natives of the lower Fraser River was evident in their blankets, which they manufactured of hair or coarse wool, and in their short cedar-bark cloaks. Their weaponry was primitive. What goods of white manufacture they had were apparently obtained indirectly through native trade channels. Probably it was in the same way that they contracted the smallpox.

Relations between the natives of the lower Fraser and Vancouver Island and the tribes of Puget Sound were not very friendly at this time. Around 1825 one of the sound's most powerful shaman chiefs, a Suquamish named Kitsap, organized a 200-canoe war party to seek revenge on the northern foes. According to one version, the attackers stroked their canoes across the strait to the site of present-day Victoria, British Columbia. There they killed natives and plundered every camp that they could find. When they returned south across the strait to Dungeness, a fog lifted and revealed to them some homeward-bound Cowichan warriors with prisoners and plunder from the Sound. The two war parties killed their prisoners in front of each other and then began a general six-hour fight. When it was over, Kitsap's party and the Cowichans had each lost all but about forty canoes.

If the fight occurred in 1825, it was just two years before the company established Fort Langley on the lower Fraser. Such an attack at that time would have hampered company operations in the general area. Operations were then centered at Fort Vancouver on the south. The move from Fort George was delayed because of a threatening Indian war near the abandoned post. The trouble began when Comcomly placed two of his sick sons under the care of a neighboring shaman. Despite the shaman's ministrations, the two reportedly died. Whereupon the unpleasant Casacas ordered a slave to kill the unsuccessful practitioner—the usual practice among Pacific Northwestern Indians (and a root cause of the Whitman massacre nearly a quarter-century later). Tensions increased at Fort George at the time of removal when natives killed two company employees. On April 14, 1825, war-painted Indians, decked out in elkskin cuirasses and armed with guns, bows and arrows, and knives, held a war dance near the fort punctuated by chanting and the rattling of shells. Although no war erupted from the demonstration, it did provide an unpleasant send-off to Vancouver for the company.

Troubles continued for the British firm after removal to its new post. A company physician, Dr. John Scouler, observed, "The Indians continue to behave very peac[e]ably toward us, although it is apparent that the utmost distrust prevails among themselves." In mid-July, 1825, the botanist David Douglas (Olla-piska, or Fire; The Grass Man) stepped into the midst of a continuing Chinook-Clatsop feud as he probed the floral riches of the lower Columbia. His host,

Coqua, whom he described as a chief of the Chinooks and Chehalises, was extremely solicitous for his safety as the botanist watched war preparations. A reported 300 warriors prepared on the beach to meet an expected Clatsop invasion. Members of Comcomly's own family apparently were victims of the feudings.

The marriage of Ilchee—Comcomly's daughter and Mc-Dougall's ex-wife—to Casino did little to cement relations between her father and her new husband. Flaunting his newly found importance, Casino raised a fuss when the company assured Comcomly of passage upstream beyond Casino's village, which was about six miles below Fort Vancouver on the Columbia north bank, to trade at Fort Vancouver. The chief factor of the company was Dr. John McLoughlin, a tall, impressive man with a florid complexion, gray hair, and blue eyes. He acted with an authority based on a knowledge of the native mind gained from experience in the trade over nearly half his forty-one years. He warned Casino that the company would not stand by and let his guns obstruct Chinook flotillas en route to the fort. The crafty Casino countered McLoughlin's proposal with one of his own, namely, that the Columbia become a free river in the vicinity of the fort, a proposal that gave him a much stronger position on the river than that of his Chinook rivals, who would be far from their home villages. Believing the Comcomly-Casino feud to have blocked nine-tenths of the natives' trade that summer, McLoughlin diligently sought to effect a truce between the contending parties. In this he was apparently successful. The chief factor was aware of Casino's machinations, which involved the hiring of a functionary to assassinate those obnoxious to him. He even tried to have Ilchee killed, thinking she had caused the death of their son, and he might have succeeded had McLoughlin not taken her into protective custody.

Other Indians were unhappy with changes set in motion by Simpson. After a subpost was moved to Fort Walla Walla from The Dalles area, the Wascos (Chinookan) from The Dalles assembled a large canoe flotilla reportedly in retaliation and sailed downstream to seize Fort Vancouver. A chief at The Cascades friendly to McLoughlin tipped him off to the planned invasion. Immediately the chief factor sent for Casino to assemble his warriors and canoes on an inlet a short distance below the fort and repel the attack. As the Wasco fleet approached the fort, its warriors drummed the sides of their craft, beat drums, blew on shells, and chanted war songs. The Indians of the lower Willamette were on good terms with the invaders, and they warned them of the big medicine of the King George Men. After attending the meeting of the two peoples, Casino hurried to the fort to inform McLoughlin of the developments. Shortly after McLoughlin put the fort on alert, three Wasco chiefs approached its big postern. A stern, kilted Highlander was standing guard nearby, sporting a broad sword. When the chiefs entered the great reception hall, they found another Highlander bagpiping what they believed to be some strange, ominous medicine. Thoroughly frightened by this time, they accepted some gifts from McLoughlin and departed too shaken to carry out their designs.[5]

Although concerted action failed, isolated moves against the company continued. In March, 1827, four Indians of The Dalles area attacked a company express. They were seeking to pillage the tempting goods en route to an interior post, but were cut off by the expressmen. Indians at Fort Walla Walla appeared threatening to the trade. That post stood at the doorway to the Snake country, to which the company now looked more than ever to salvage its Pacific Northwestern fur operations. At Fort Walla Walla, on his downriver journey, Simpson had disregarded the natives' pipe-smoking professions of peace, writing, "[as soon as] we turn our backs they are ready to pillage each others Women and Horses and cut each others throats." He believed the Indians no more on his homeward journey in late March, 1825, when he found himself in a 300-lodge camp with plenty of trouble brewing. Trader John Dease had reprimanded an interpreter for "over intimacy with the natives and indiscreet amours both in the Camp and at *Home*." At this rebuke the interpreter sought to incite the tribes against the fur company. A rumor quickly spread that the interpreter was in league with Cayuse chief Umtippe (Cut, or Split Lip) to massacre the fort personnel, including Dease and eleven other men. Simpson met on March 27 with 300 warriors under nine chiefs (five Cayuses, three Nez Percés, and a Wallawalla) and succeeded in calming them down with a long speech and long fathoms of tobacco, as well as fifty loads of powder and ball. The Indian demonstration was possibly an ominous prelude or merely a ploy to obtain some badly needed goods. It convinced Simpson that "9 Murders out of 10 Committed on Whites by Indians have arisen through Women."

Despite such incidents Indians of the Columbia were actually more tractable, conformable, and dependent on white traders than ever before, bearing out John Lewes's words of April 2, 1822, that they had "become so much accustomed to the produce of the Civilized world, that they find it necessary to exert themselves to procure their wants and this they know can only be by their hunting the beaver." They had, however, no such dependence on their native foes, especially the Shoshonis. Despite Pee-eye-em's gestures of peace, conflict between Columbia River and Shoshoni bands continued. In May, 1825, the Cayuses skirmished with the Shoshonis over horses, losing one of their braves, but severely wounding a Shoshoni chief. That summer, under pressure from Dease, a Cayuse-Nez Percé delegation effected a truce with the Shoshonis in an effort to cool their mutual enmity. The effort may have been successful, for about six weeks later nearly eight hundred beaver skins were brought to Fort Walla Walla. The number might have been larger had not some "mortality" broken out among the Cayuses. The illness may have prevented the catch from approximating the estimated 2,000-beaver harvest of 1824, the largest ever brought to the post. On the other hand, the malady may have prevented more Cayuse-Shoshoni conflict.

Indians around Fort Walla Walla confided in Dease. Simpson regarded such rapport as indulgence on the trader's part. It was, in fact, good public relations. Some insight into

Dease's concern for his clientele is visible in an anecdote involving an elderly chief. Having suffered a chain of misfortunes, including the loss of his sons—his "bow string broken," as the old chief put it—he ordered his people to bury him alive. They and Dease quite naturally shied from carrying out such a request. Not wishing to interfere with native mores that did not hamper trade, Dease acquiesced to the chief's request and even saw to it that a flag was placed over his grave. For his gesture he received ten of the chief's finest horses, the hallmark of his earthly wealth and status.

The chief's bequest was symbolic of the role of the horse in the natives' culture. Their lives revolved around this animal rather than the beaver. Recognizing this, the company brigades accepted their fine horseflesh for company brigades to travel to the fur country and return with pelts. More practically, fort personnel ate horsemeat provided them by the Indians. Around 1825 horses brought more to their Cayuse, Wallawalla, Palouse, and Nez Percé owners near Fort Walla Walla than they did to the tribesmen farther up the Snake River, where they were not only more numerous but also in better condition.

On the east, where the horses carried the fur seekers and transported their prizes homeward, Shoshoni bands continued to plague traders and trappers, especially Americans. Ogden stated that, in the last months of 1825 and into 1826, Shoshonis killed about thirteen Americans—who were known to plateau and mountain Indians as the "Long Knives" of the Rocky Mountain Fur Company. Ogden also stated that the Shoshonis had stolen nearly 200 of the company's traps and that for three years after 1823 no less than thirty-two Americans were killed and their traps, horses, and beaver pelts lost. Such depredations were committed largely by Shoshoni bands, "who appear determined to destroy and annoy . . . wherever an opportunity affords." To make matters worse, the Blackfeet were as dangerous as ever. On Sunday, September 26, 1830, John Work buried one of his brigadesmen, Pierre L'Etang, who had been cut down by Blackfeet. Work lamented, "Thus are the people wandering through this country in quest of beaver continually in danger of falling into the hands of these ruthless savages and certain of losing their lives in the most barbarous manner, independent of the privations and hardships of every other kind they subject themselves to . . . ."

Trappers, traps, and the trapped were truly being taken with a vengeance; men gave little attention to conserving life, human or animal. One old-time Rocky Mountain trapper wrote:

When the beaver are cut [caught] they will twist their foot off. They won't bite it off. They are the most harmless thing in the world. They are just like a little baby. Catch a beaver and touch it and it will just turn up its head; a little one will just turn up and cry like a little baby. I hated to kill them, but says I, "it is $5."

In a similar vein another mountain man said, "Traders do not go to the mountains to preach sermons, sing psalms to Indians, but to make money . . ."

The vagaries of human life in those regions were evident when Shoshoni bands, who were not always on good terms with Americans, joined them in fighting the Blackfeet. In one battle, before which Shoshoni shamans had prophesied the coming of their foe, the combined Shoshoni-American force met the Blackfeet near the Snake-Portneuf river confluence. When the fighting ended, the Shoshonis reportedly had lost sixteen men as they routed their enemy. The Blackfeet suffered heavy losses, but perhaps not as many as is indicated by the 173 scalps that a white man reported they had taken. Shoshoni exhilaration at these victories did not check the decline of their numbers. An American fur trader in 1831 observed, with obvious exaggeration, that the Shoshonis, like the Flatheads, had been almost annihilated by the vengeful Blackfeet, who were by then well armed with guns.

Another ingredient in the human cauldron was the Bannocks, who were still not inclined to adhere to Pee-eye-em's injunction that they make peace with white men. In 1826, Captain William Sublette, who was in command of the Rocky Mountain Fur Company trappers, was near the juncture of the Snake and the Salt rivers. He told some Shoshonis who were friendly to whites to warn a nearby camp of "thievish" Bannocks that, if they stole horses from whites, he would devastate their lands. In the winter of 1825–26, after marauding Bannocks stole some Rocky Mountain Fur Company horses near the mouth of the Weber River (an Ogden River tributary in northeastern Idaho), a band of the company's trappers under Thomas Fitzpatrick charged their camp. Another band under James Bridger stampeded their horses, recovering some that belonged to the company and some of the Indians. In another conflict, the Bannocks killed a Shoshoni and two white men. A Rocky Mountain Fur Company party tracked down and mauled the Bannocks. Losses in that engagement are unknown. There still may have been many Bannocks left, however. Ogden met Indians whom he identified as Bannocks on Camas Prairie in south-central Idaho; he estimated their numbers at 1,500 souls living in thirty lodges and owning 3,000 horses. Very likely those Bannocks were mixed with the more numerous Shoshonis because the two peoples by then were becoming closely interrelated, often camping, hunting, and fighting together.

On November 25, 1827, the Bannock head chief, The Horse, visited Ogden carrying an American flag. The flag was American and not British, but that would not have concerned Ogden, who was seeking Bannock goodwill by giving them presents. Bannock aggressions against white trappers continued with less punishment than Hudson's Bay Company traders believed they deserved. Company policy was partly responsible for the situation, for it was believed that punishment should be meted out only after the greatest provocations on the part of red men. The latter often misinterpreted this policy as one of appeasement. Under the blanket of tolerance the Bannocks, with about four hundred guns captured in Blackfoot wars and in forays against white trappers, were emboldened to continue their depredations.[6]

In the spring of 1825, Ogden realized a good fur harvest from the southern Snake tributaries. Meanwhile, a Snake expedition under Finan McDonald was forced to turn back when natives warned him of the presence of hostile Indians. Intertribal conflict continued to threaten the trade and showed no signs of lessening. On April 1, 1826, some Cayuses from Fort Walla Walla, en route to steal Shoshoni horses, were disappointed to learn that Blackfeet had beaten them to the prizes. The company was not disappointed that the Shoshonis were helping it create a beaver-barren zone in the Bruneau and Owyhee river countries of southwestern Idaho and eastern Oregon. Such exploitation conformed to the company policy of stripping the area of furs to deprive the Americans of them and frustrate American operations north of the Snake and in the Boise country.

West of the scene of those developments, the natives of the Oregon interior became alarmed at the fur seekers pushing their operations into their lands. In October, 1826, on Ogden's third Snake expedition, natives of the upper Crooked River, a Deschutes tributary in central Oregon, set fire to the grass a scant ten yards from his camp. A few days later the Paiutes attacked his brigade, stole some of its horses and guns, and scuffled with one of the men over the theft. In the Malheur country in southeastern Oregon natives huddled six or eight to a sagebrush-and-grass lodge, trying to protect themselves from such winters as that of 1825, which reduced them to cannibalism and to plaguing Odgen's brigade by threatening to steal its horses. After painful arrowhead wounds sustained in a scuffle with a small band over guns and horses, two of the brigadesmen were too ill to contest the aggressions of natives along the way. What food the natives of that bareboned country were able to find consisted mainly of fish from their lake, which they caught in scoop nets of peeled sagebrush bark. Because there were few beaver in their lands, they had little means of procuring arms through trade with white men. Had they such weapons, they might have been tempted to go to hunt the buffalo. In that case the warring Plains tribes would have destroyed them more effectively than the harsh environment of their homelands.

Farther to the southwest were the Klamath Indians (Lutuamian). They called themselves Eukshikni maklaks and were called La Lakes by Canadian trappers. They lived around Upper Klamath Lake, Klamath Marsh, and the Williamson and Sprague rivers. Like other poorer tribes they sought to isolate themselves from both red and white men. The absence of horses kept them from contact with the horse-riding Cayuses and Nez Percés, who tried to reach them in the summer of 1826, possibly to raid them for slaves. Shoshonis had traveled to Klamath country from as far away as the plains, but on returning east had nearly starved. They had been convinced that they should continue their annual treks, on which they traded for leather goods from the Spaniards and purchased other goods and horses from Americans. Fur traders were beginning to probe Klamath lands. After that the lands were traversed by roads, over which men traveled and broke the Klamath isolation. By 1825 the tribesmen had met one fur prober, Finan McDonald. Later Ogden moved through their country on his Snake expedition.

Unlike many Shoshonis and Paiutes, the Klamaths pur-

sued a sedentary existence, which was fostered by the natural richness of their lands. Like other peoples so endowed, they put the land's resources to work to amply provide themselves food, clothing, and shelter. The villagers of Klamath Lake lived in earthen houses, which were entered from flat tops. On Williamson River at the lower end of Klamath Marsh about Upper Klamath Lake, they lived in log houses, which were built on the water atop stone and gravel foundations. The foundations were secured by pilings that were sunk about six feet into the ground. In summer they subsisted on antelope from nearby plains. Unlike natives whose contact with white traders had put guns in their hands, they armed themselves with bows and arrows for hunting and defense. In late summer they collected *wocus*, the seed of a water lily, from Klamath Marsh. They processed this into a nutritious food which was used in soups or mixed into a flour to make cakes. Like other native food-gathering grounds, the *wocus* marshes were the scenes of many councils and were marketplaces where goods and slaves were exchanged. (The establishment of a reservation for the Klamaths and United States government's assistance to them have not prevented them from gathering at *wocus* grounds as their ancesters did for ages.)

The Klamaths, as Ogden observed, were a "happy race" with but few wants. Even as he broke their isolation, Ogden feared that their disposition would with "two years intimacy with Whites . . . make them like all other Indian villains." He believed that the bones of their dead lying above ground warned them of their own mortality. They were not a morbid people, but did observe rigid taboos against mentioning the names and deeds of their dead.

Also seeking isolation from white men were the natives of the upper Rogue River, of which the lower reaches had already been opened by fur men. On the upper Applegate River, a Rogue tributary, natives late in the winter of 1826–27 fled at the approach of Ogden's party. He warned his men to take nothing from their village. These natives seemed to have had no direct contact with those of the Umpqua River to the north. Instead, through neighbors trading with the Umpquas—possibly the Upper Umpquas (Athapascan)—they obtained such goods as knives and axes, which they in turn bartered for beaver and dentalia. An Umpqua chief, guiding six trappers from the Willamette, reached the upper Rogue near present-day Grants Pass, Oregon, and exhausted the beaver supply of the area. As a result Ogden dispatched Joseph Gervais and four men to trap their way to the Umpqua and thence to the Willamette "so as to open communication" between the Umpqua and Fort Vancouver.

Back in the Snake River country, furs had begun to diminish, but conflict had not. McKenzie's tradition of peace still protected the British from the depredations of many of the Shoshonis. Americans had less protection. The Shoshonis took credit for the demise of four of a forty-man American trapping party who wandered off from the Boise. Unlike the Shoshonis, the Blackfeet were under no obligation to spare either British or American trappers. On May 20, 1828, one of their war parties attacked Ogden's brigade on the Owyhee, killing a woman and stealing all the horses. On June 24, another war party killed one of Ogden's French Canadians. A decade after the 1819 brigade traveled into the Snake country, only two of its members had died naturally. In September, 1830, Blackfeet brushed with Shoshonis in the Camas Prairie country, and that same month they attacked a company party under John Work, who had replaced Ogden as the leader of the Snake brigades. It was in that engagement that the Blackfeet struck down Pierre L'Etang and an Indian slave, whose valiant stand allowed two others of the party to escape. In the winter of 1831–32 the Blackfeet mauled Work's brigade as it sought furs to the north on Flathead-Blackfoot borderlands, killing seven and wounding others of the party, who were already weakened by "intermittent fever."

One of the most violent clashes in the turbulent Snake country occurred at Pierre's Hole in eastern Idaho near the Wyoming border at the summer rendezvous of 1832. The annual rendezvous gatherings were variously located from year to year throughout the Rockies and attracted natives and trappers from far and near to exchange furs for staple goods and trinkets, which the American traders freighted up from St. Louis. The gatherings were enlivened by socializing and revels amidst din and dissipation. Liquor flowed freely, as it had at the gatherings since shortly before the earliest recorded rendezvous in 1825 on Henry's Fork, a Green River tributary in southwestern Wyoming. Near there an American exchanged whiskey from a keg for the year's fur catch of some drunken trappers.

The volatile atmosphere at Pierre's Hole needed only a spark to ignite a general melee. This was furnished by an Iroquois, Antoine Goddin, whom Ogden had released from his service and whose father the Blackfeet had killed. With an equally vengeful Flathead, Goddin confronted a Blackfoot party who was approaching the Hole, mostly afoot, in search of Shoshonis. The Flathead leveled his gun at a chief who was peacefully approaching and fired, killing him instantly. Thus the fight began on July 18. Nez Percés and Flatheads from a reported hundred lodges joined American trappers in the struggle. When it ended, the Blackfeet carried off their dead, reportedly leaving ten on the field. On the other side the reported body count was six trappers and up to seven Nez Perceés. One Nez Percé wounded was an important chief, Hallalhotsoot, known later as Lawyer, whose mother was a Flathead and whose father was the Nez Percé chief Twisted Hair. The battlefield lay silent afterwards except for the noise of vultures and the howling of masterless dogs. Over all lay the stench of death.*

That fall Shoshonis and Bannocks, although branding each other as killers of the Long Knives, combined at the head of the Goddin or Big Lost River in central Idaho to defeat the Blackfeet. In the fight the Shoshoni-Bannock

coalition reportedly killed forty Blackfeet. They lost nine of their own number, including The Horse, whom they had believed to be bulletproof and invincible. Ironically, The Horse had restrained his Bannocks from reprisals after losing one of his family in a similar attack. His death made the Bannocks all the more eager for revenge.

Among the Bannocks at this time was Captain B. L. E. Bonneville, an American explorer and fur seeker on leave from the United States Army.[7] He found his native hosts "fuffling and brandishing their arms..." as they recited how the Blackfeet had "drenched their villages in tears and blood!" The Bannocks seemed to gain courage and energy to kill in proportion to the quantity of buffalo meat they gorged. Thus they fortified themselves to kill more buffalo or more Blackfeet; it made little difference to them which they killed.

In hunting buffalo, the Bannocks followed well-established rules of the chase. Posting front and rear guards, they hid in hollows and ravines downwind of their quarry. At a lookout's signal they rode yelling into the shaggy, moving mass. The herd's hooves beat the sod as it moved like a mighty river, swirling, crowding, and stampeding to escape the pursuers. To match movements of the buffalo, huntsmen wheeled and coursed their mounts, selecting their targets from the mass. Bulls charged, enraged by arrows sticking in their thick hides. Sometimes in flight they stumbled and fell. Then the rider-huntsmen avoided entanglements by keeping one or two of the beasts between themselves and their quarry and thus keep it from falling in front of their horses. If the ground was dry, the buffalo, horses, and men were covered with dust; when it was wet, they were peppered with mud clods from flying hooves. Finally, from well-placed missiles fired directly behind their foreshoulders in their most vulnerable spot, the buffalo writhed and died. As hunters pursued the herd remnant, women moved in to process the meat and hides and transport them to their camps.

The various buffalo-hunting tribes pursued their quarry with equal vigor, but Bonneville noted a disparity among them in their dealings with white men. When Bonneville was on the Snake River, one of his parties reported to him in early February, 1833, the death of one of its members and the capture of two others. He believed the Bannocks to be guilty and not the Nez Percés and their Salish hunter allies. On the Salmon River during the previous fall Nez Percé hunters had welcomed Bonneville to their camp with shouting, singing and gunfire. Having scoured the region for buffalo and other game, they were short of food, yet offered him some of their meager supply of dried salmon. From them he learned that roots and plants sustained them when there was no game. To obtain game and beaver, they bartered their horses, which were the main source of their wealth, to various tribes, even the Bannocks, at a native mart below the headwaters of the Boise and Payette rivers. Their customers did not tend horses as well as they did. They were horsemen par excellence and were described as a people "more like a nation of saints than a horde of savages."

Visiting Bonneville's winter quarters on the Salmon River were the Kalispels, a 300-lodge people who, like the

---

*Estimates of the deaths of trappers and their native allies are more accurate in white men's records than in those of the defeated native foes, who often removed their dead from the field of battle. For an account of this fight, see Willard C. Hayden, "The Battle of Pierre's Hole," *Idaho Yesterdays* 16, no. 2 (Summer, 1972): 2–11.

Nez Percés, were religious. Also like the Nez Percés and the Flatheads, they were armed and mounted. They sought to remain so by staking their horses nightly before their lodges, both to defend themselves and to use on the summer and fall buffalo hunts. They hunted around the headwaters of the Missouri River, around Henry's Fork on the Snake, and around the northern branches of the Salmon River. They wintered around Flathead Post, where they susbisted on roots and dried buffalo meat.

With "noise and mummery" the Nez Percés and their Salish allies rejected Bonneville's suggestion that by sweating and bleeding they cure themselves of a disease that he believed to be pneumonia. They were even less willing to accept his good offices to help end their Blackfoot wars, reminding him that with a foe of lying hearts and traplike tongues there could be no peace. "Let there be war!" they cried. They were especially fearful lest Nez Percés who had been captured previously by the Blackfeet lead their captors in search-and-destroy missions on their own people, a practice that was employed by Indians of the Northwest Coast, as has been noted.

Shortly the Nez Percés' belief in Blackfoot treachery was confirmed. The plains marauders drove off eighty-six mounts, sending their unhorsed Nez Percé masters down the Columbia River to replenish their stock. The new horses would in time become more prizes for the Blackfeet because the Nez Percé found it easier to replenish their stock than to risk their necks retrieving them. When they felt compelled to fight to save their necks, if not their horses, they showed a bravery that earned for them, like their Salish allies, the reputation that one of their number was a match for three Blackfeet.

In March, 1833, the Nez Percés withstood a withering Blackfoot attack, in which a Nez Percé woman figured prominently in their defense, shooting arrows into the foe with great accuracy. After the fight the Nez Percé held a rendez-vouslike celebration, a "regular blow out." Later some of them took up the suggestion of one Kosato, a Blackfoot defector wounded in the fight, that they resume their Blackfoot wars. In an ensuing fight with their foe only one of a party under Chief Blue John lived to carry the news of the deaths to the victims' relatives.

Few, if any, Indian assessments of those turbulent times remain. We do have an incisive analysis of them as they affected native populations from the pen of an on-the-spot observer, an American scientist named John K. Townsend. Although not absolving the Indians from a share of the violence, he admitted, as did few others of his race at that time, that the troubles were "fomented and kept alive from year to year by incessant provocatives on the part of white hunters, trappers, and traders, who are at best but intruders on the rightful domains of the red men of the wilderness..." Smashing each other's traps and beaver lodges and killing each other outright had become a way of life.[8]

Townsend had come west with New Englander Nathaniel J. Wyeth. In 1834 Wyeth established Fort Hall on the Snake near the mouth of the Portneuf River above American Falls, seeking to salvage what was left of the fur trade there. His fort builders had to be wary of both the Blackfeet and their foes, although shortly after the fort was built a Shoshoni contingent arrived and was apparently pleased with the fort, as was a 250-lodge Bannock party that also arrived to trade. The following year Wyeth was reminded that the Bannocks had lost none of their aggressiveness. At that time one of his trappers and a companion were en route to the Columbia with a large load of beaver pelts. They were entertained in the lodge of a Bannock chief, who with several young braves ambushed and killed the pair. White men seldom probed the motivations for such actions. Perhaps in this case like so many others, as Townsend observed, the whites had committed some wrong.

The establishment of his post gave Wyeth no monopoly on the fur trade in the area. In 1835 even the Kutenais joined the Flatheads and the Nez Percés in collecting and selling beaver to the British right under the noses of the Americans. To counter the American post, McLoughlin in 1836 sent the trusted Thomas McKay to build Fort Boise on the north bank of the Snake a mile below its confluence with the Boise. In 1837 the Hudson's Bay Company bought out Fort Hall. In 1834, Wyeth built Fort William on Sauvies Island in the Columbia, within the shadow of Fort Vancouver. Both Bonneville and Wyeth, like other Americans, found it difficult if not impossible to deal with the natives without government support as they attempted to extend their trading operations into the Columbia River Valley. Would-be American entrepreneurs found to their sorrow, as would

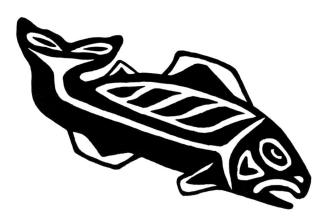

other challengers of the Bay, that they were dealing with a firm with more knowledge of the country and its human and animal resources than they had, knowledge that enabled it to conduct aggressive policies geared to satisfy the needs of the trade. They also discovered that the company not only attempted to save its own and native peoples from destruction but also the furry objects of its quests. It trapped in areas under its control only as many animals as the traffic would bear without decimating the breeding stock.

The Hudson's Bay Company's policies did not, however, leave the natives' life-styles untouched. Company trading and posts disrupted native trading patterns. For example, trade at Fort Hall and Fort Boise changed the trade in the Grande Ronde, a lush valley fifteen miles long and twelve miles wide in northeastern Oregon. The Cayuses, Wallawallas, and Nez Percés met there to trade horses and salmon to the Shoshonis in return for roots, skin lodges, and elk and buffalo meat. The company's greatest imposition on the natives was the fur-trading nexus that brought the red men fabricated goods: they wanted the goods but were less inclined to gather the furs to pay for them.

Despite the shortcomings of the trade the natives would have to reckon with the Bay until the American population increased and international negotiations curtailed the company's efforts. Until then, whether they liked it or not, the native inhabitants had to deal with this trading concern in their lands.

6. BARTER WITH THE "BAY"

The natives of the Snake country felt the presence of the Hudson's Bay Company less with each passing year, but those in other areas of the Pacific Northwest felt it more, especially the power of the company's chief factor, Dr. John McLoughlin. His authoritarian hand became especially heavy when he believed his firm's operations to be in jeopardy. In January, 1828, Clallams murdered Alexander McKenzie and four other company men and enslaved a native woman as the party returned from the lower Fraser River. McLoughlin dispatched an expedition in June to avenge the act. The operation was marine in nature and involved the company ship *Cadboro*. The ship was armed with light artillery, which acted in concert with a land party composed of four clerks and a motley crew of over fifty men, including Owyhees, Iroquois, and Chinook slaves. The latter two groups were well fitted for such an undertaking. When their punitive task was finished, the vengeance seekers had killed about twenty-five Clallams. They destroyed two villages as well as several canoes in what one expedition leader later characterized as a shameful overreaction.[1]

On July 14, 1828, Lower Umpqua Indians, the Kuitshes, who bore a bad reputation among white traders even before Astorian days, attacked a seventeen-man party under Jedediah Smith who were seeking a road from California to Oregon. They killed all but four members of the party. Before the attack a chief had stolen an axe from the party and Smith had ordered him tied as though he were to be hanged. The axe was recovered, but the chief was humiliated and resentful. Smith and the other survivors had been absent at the time of the massacre. They finally reached Fort Vancouver, where sanctuary was provided by McLoughlin. Had Smith recapitulated his journey to the tragic scene, he would have told how he and his men reached the coast and on June 27 came to the Rogue River. There they committed a provocative act, building a raft from a native house. The natives fled at the party's approach, as others had along its northward coastal route. Women abandoned their basket chores and other tasks until the strangers passed by. Farther north at Port Orford the party came upon the "Quatomas" (Kwataimes?), a subdivision of the Tututnis (Athapascan) usually referred to as the Lower Rogue River Indians. They lived along the lower Rogue River and the coast and along the Pistol, Elk, and Sixes rivers. They had traded with the crews of vessels off Port Orford at least since George Vancouver had named that headland in 1792. At that place in July, 1817, a quarter-century later, well-formed men dressed in deerskins and carrying green boughs and bunches of white feathers canoed toward a trader ship. Apparently frightened, they did not board her, but traded to her crew land furs, berries, fish, and handsome baskets for beads and knives.[2]

Had Smith recounted further, he would have told how at the mouth of the Coquille River on July 3, Lower Coquilles, or Miluks (Kusan), were frightened by him and his men and scurried before them to a canoe that they paddled upstream. When Smith's party caught up with them, the natives damaged the canoe that the party had used to cross the river. After that the party moved on to Coos Bay. The natives there were Hanises (Kusan). Like the Tututnis they were no strangers to white men, having traded with them from the time of Vancouver. Subsequent trading with men of the Hudson's Bay Company had resulted in little acculturation. They were primitive and wary of strangers. When Smith traversed their lands, he found only one fusee among them; all the rest of the tribe were armed with native weapons, such as knives and tomahawks. They subsisted largely on fish and mussels.

With Smith's arrival at Fort Vancouver, McLoughlin—with more vigor than investigation—immediately dispatched an expedition to the mouth of the Umpqua to punish the attackers and recover as much stolen property as possible. In a generous move he paid Smith about $20,000 for his furs. How many goods the Umpquas retained from the attack is not known. In late May, 1829, natives of the Modoc tribe (Lutuamian), who lived along the central Oregon-California border, confronted Ogden's party with guns and ammunition which that trader believed to have been plundered from Smith.

The Clatsops were also on the receiving end of company punishment. In keeping with their ancient custom, they claimed whatever washed up on their shores. Thus they appropriated goods from the company ship *William and Ann*, which was wrecked on March 10, 1829, on Clatsop Spit. In her assorted cargo was rum, which provided the Clatsops a regale. Besides the loss of twenty-six crewmen the company was deprived of the ship's goods. The trading stock was badly needed to lower prices to meet the American competition along the coast and on the Columbia River. When the company demanded the return of the goods, the Clatsops sent "an old Brush and a Swap" to the leader of a fifty-five man punitive and recovery party. In response to what an historian would call "aggressive impudence rather than murder" on the part of the Clatsops, the party killed four natives and burned Clatsop Village. Word went out that not just four but several more natives had lost their lives to company vengeance. According to stories that made the rounds, a chief's head was sent to Honolulu. Ironically, the Tillamooks down the coast, to whose lands Smith escaped and who escorted him overland and down the Willamette to Fort Vancouver, were among the natives who felt the company's punitive hand.

A woman of the Nehalems, a Tillamook band, 1915. Tillamook County Pioneer Museum.

In ordering his punishments, McLoughlin followed the legal codes of Britain, which his company represented in that part of the world. The codes differed sharply from those of the natives. For instance, the Clatsop affair revealed different codes of possessory rights. In matters of crime and punishment the Clatsops and other Indians followed a familial system, whereby goods or money were paid to relatives of the slain to "cover the deaths."

A company policy worked out in various articles dated July, 1825, required that natives be not only treated in a Christian manner but also encouraged to pursue the faith. Company policy also forbade discharged personnel to settle among the Indians to become vagabonds. The performance of errant Iroquois had perhaps helped shape company policy in that regard. Like its North West Company predecessor the company encouraged its men to marry native women. Some of the native women whom they married were slaves, who, following native custom, owned slaves themselves. Slave women especially sought the mixed marriages because they were less bound in them than they had been in their native marriages. Indian men continued to oppose marriages of their women to non-Indians. Thus a double standard prevailed in the fur-trading community. Chiefs and headmen continued to encourage marriages of their daughters to important fur men, such as factors, traders, and clerks, when they believed the unions would work to their own regal advantage. McLoughlin himself was married to a half-blood woman. More numerous than those aristocratic unions were the marriages between native women and company *engagés*.

According to a Protestant missionary who visited Fort Vancouver in 1835 and 1836, white men called their Indian mates women rather than wives. White husbands claimed it was difficult for them to return to white communities with their Indian spouses and offspring. Moreover, they claimed that the Indian women came from cultures where marital arrangements were less formal than among whites and that the Indians did not understand "the obligations of the marriage covenant." Thus there developed in the Willamette Valley at French Prairie—as there would near other company posts, such as those at Walla Walla and Colville—settlements containing a racial mix. Sometimes when parents separated, half-blood children suffered dislocation. Generally they were not stigmatized and could, if qualified, become company officials. For many years most of the interpreters were recruited from their ranks. The interracial mixes, rather than obstructing company operations, tended to strengthen them.

Despite occasional disciplinary action by the company, it and the Indians generally got along with but little violence. They naturally grumbled as prices slid downward from the highs of the early 1830s in the European fur market, where beaver hats were being replaced by silk ones. Locked in as they were to a company-imposed monopolistic fur nexus, the Indians had little choice but to sell their furs and skins to the company. As much as possible, the company tried to standardize prices in fairness to its far-flung red clientele, which was clustered around its various western posts from New Caledonia to Spanish territory and from the Rockies to the Pacific. Over the years, price standardization became more difficult as goods traveled from the company entrepôt at Fort Vancouver to its outposts, where at times they advanced in value by as much as one-third.[3]

With time the Indians became more discriminating in their tastes for the goods that the company supplied to them. They soon discovered the difference between its goods and those supplied by the Americans. An American settler wrote: "Whoever had traded with an Indian must have often heard the remark [in the Chinook jargon] 'Wake close okoke Boston mámoke, wake car'qua King George, quánisum close kon'away icktas King George mámoke'— 'This is not good, this American manufacture; it is not like the English; that is always good.'" British goods were also giving native ones a run for their money. In 1846 a Britisher noted that Indian demand for British blankets was so strong that their own blankets of dog hair were discounted; eight or ten Indian blankets were going for a single sea-otter skin.

Guns were always a lively item in trade with Indians, if they could meet the tariff. One gun went for as many skins as a fully loaded pack of other goods. They were almost a necessity now, since with their introduction they frightened animals, making it difficult for Indians to position themselves closely enough to kill with native weapons. Once the natives acquired guns, there was always the possibility that they would turn them on their suppliers, a possibility that was checked somewhat by company control of their sale. In coming years arms and ammunition supplied to Indians in the Pacific Northwest by the company and also by Americans would cause anxiety among the increasing American population, who believed guns in Indian hands were pointed at them.

The Pacific Northwestern Indians, like those elsewhere across the American continent, were unwitting victims of Anglo-American rivalries, which began in the East and were intensified by the American Revolution and the War of 1812. The latter war, as has been noted, caused a shift from American to British fur operations in the Pacific Northwest. Ironically, the natives had no voice in the policies of the two powers seeking mercantile and political advantage in their country. Not until nearly the last quarter of the nineteenth century would the rivalries be resolved by the 1872 San Juan Islands boundary settlement, which implemented the settlement of 1846 by setting the boundary at the Canal de Haro between Vancouver Island and the San Juan group.

At times Indians were caught in the middle of the international rivalries. In the late 1820s when two American

ships, the *Owhyee* and the *Convoy*, traded goods for Indian furs in the very heart of the company domain on the lower Columbia River, their decks became floating marketplaces for the natives, who were contacted by parties from the ships seeking to snatch their trade from the British. To prevent this encroachment, McLoughlin dispatched his own parties to keep the Indians from the Americans and lowered the tariff to meet that of his competitors until their ships left the river.

Any benefit Indians of the lower Columbia received from this competition was, in their thinking, temporarily offset in a most bizarre fashion. Word went up and down the river in 1829 that a Captain John Dominis of the *Owhyee* had brought what natives called the Cold Sick to avenge some dispute he had with them over the tariff. According to one Indian version, a native swam ashore with a stick that the captain had placed in the river to mark its deceptive channels. The native had barely reached the shore when he was seized with violent chills and fever and fell dead. His fellows examined the marker, "found it guilty," beat it with clubs, and dragged it over rocks and through water. They finally placed it over a fire, reducing it to ashes, which they carefully gathered and threw upon the water to destroy the evil spirit, in the belief that the Tlchachie (the spirits of the dead) did not like dust or ashes and would not pass through them (a Roman Catholic missionary told of a similar ritual among the Coeur d'Alênes). In another version of the story of the Cold Sick, natives were said to have contracted the disease on the left bank of the Columbia near present-day St. Helens, Oregon, where they received contaminated clothing off the *Convoy*, the *Owyhee's* consort in the trade. For some time natives were wary of boarding ships entering the river, fearing a similar catastrophe. Remembering McDougall's virulent vial, they naturally attributed the malady to Captain Dominis and demons, although other epidemics (for instance, one in 1823–24) had spread along the lower Columbia and Willamette valleys in recent times.

The Cold Sick disease, called The Intermittent Fever, was formerly believed by non-Indians to have been malaria. Some present-day students of the disease believe it to have been some strain of influenza. It ravaged natives most violently from 1829 until 1833 and struck intermittently throughout the 1830s and into the following decade. In the Pacific Northwest it struck natives most violently from The Dalles downriver, especially around the lower Cowlitz and Fort Vancouver and in the Willamette Valley. With little immunity and trusting to native doctors and native remedies, such as sweat bathing, the natives had little chance for survival. One notable exception was Casino, who received medications at Fort Vancouver. The remedies administered there were quinine and a quinine substitute from the bark of dogwood trees. Not so fortunate was Casino's rival, Comcomly, who was apparently a victim of the epidemic. His skull became one of the most famous exports from the Columbia River. It was taken in 1835 by a company doctor, Meredith Gairdner, for craniological and phrenological study. After Gairdner's death in the Hawaiian Islands, it went to Britain. Finally, after nearly 120 years, and after barely surviving the World War II blitz, it was sent for study in 1956 to the Smithsonian Institution, which returned it for burial in the Ilwaco, Washington Community Cemetery.

Missionaries among the Kalapooia bands found that nearly 70 percent of them died from fevers between 1830 and 1833. Estimates of Indian losses in the Willamette and lower Columbia river valleys and in the other areas of the illness's greatest ravages ranged from 50 to 90 percent. According to John Work, who led an expedition in August, 1832, from Fort Vancouver to the Bonaventura, or Sacramento, River, the greatest threat was not hostile man but disease, which literally plagued the expedition coming and going. Indians between the Columbia and the Sacramento threatened to kill anyone bringing the fever among them. At the southern terminus of the expedition the disease took a heavy toll of natives, as it did in the San Joaquin Valley and around Tulare Lake. It has been suggested that it was spread to the latter areas from northern quarters, at least partly by southbound brigades like that led by Work.

With decreased numbers of Indians, the company faced a reduced market in the Pacific Northwest. Life and death continued, however (as, for instance, when the Black Death ravaged Europe in the late fourteenth century). Sadder than the economic losses were the human ones. Ghastly reminders were the remains of villages burned to the ground to check the spread of the disease. Survivors rebuilt houses, but on a smaller scale than before because they believed the disease would strike them again in their dwellings. Denied the usual meticulous funerary care, disease victims lay along dreary shorelines to bleach like so many pieces of driftwood.

Had disease not reduced their numbers in the Willamette Valley, the Indians there might have resisted company operations more strongly. After Simpson and McLoughlin had checked the agricultural and waterpower potentials along that stream, they sent workers there in the fall of 1830. Two years later they opened a millrace at Willamette Falls. The water powered wheels for saws which were to cut lumber from trees in the very woods that once had been a mecca for both red and white hunters. Not until 1843, however, was the mill erected. Indians of the valley were temporarily spared further encroachments when the London directors vetoed McLoughlin's plan to establish an agricultural enterprise there. The enterprise was the incubus of the Puget Sound Agricultural Company formed in 1838, a subsidiary of the Hudson's Bay Company. The agricultural company operated on prairie lands around Fort Vancouver and below Puget Sound. Its operations furnished the parent company with wheat, which, with fish and lumber, was consumed not only locally but also exported to California, Alaska, and the Hawaiian Islands.

South of the Willamette the company continued searching for pelts, believing them more plentiful there than in the lower Columbia and Willamette valleys. Natives in remote areas, such as the Siuslaws on the Oregon coast, were aware of the explorations of company man Alexander McLeod in the summer of 1826. His men trapped among the Lower Umpquas that fall. Similarly, the Coquille Indians were aware of him along their river, which he explored while his men trapped there. In January, 1827, he canoed down the Coquille to its mouth, searching for the Rogue River, and, turning inland, walked and canoed to the Sixes River, north of the Rogue. Following the directions of Indian guides and natives along the way, he came on January 11 to the Rogue, calling it the Toototenez. The botanist David Douglas noted of McLeod's travels that, although natives viewed him "narrowly and with much curiosity," they were hospitable and performed his camp chores, happy to receive in exchange the "smallest trifle of European manufacture."

Some indications of the continuing primitiveness of natives in that remote section of Oregon were their preferences for their own knives to those sold by the company and for dentalia. Dentalia was so popular among them that McLeod wrote McLoughlin on November 5, 1826, requesting some for trade. They were sought both as money and for ornamentation and were prized by not only the natives in those remote regions but also those in more frequent contact with company operations. At one time the company attempted to satisfy the natives' demands by importing synthetic dentalia, but, quickly detecting them as counterfeit, the natives refused to accept them.

In the winter of 1830–31 Lower Umpquas met company trader Michel La Framboise with three other men seeking furs. In early 1832 they met him again in their country. They also met there the trapper Gagnier, who was apparently accompanied by free trapper Jean Baptiste Desportes McKay. In keeping with the company's policy encouraging unions with native women, Gagnier married the daughter of a prominent Umpqua chief. La Framboise went him several wives better by boasting one in every tribe. Small wonder that he was said to be the only white man able to move alone in security in the lands of his wife's people, the Umpquas.* In 1832 natives in those lands began to trade at a newly established company post, Fort Umpqua, on Calapooya Creek at its confluence with the Umpqua.

The company policy encouraging its men to marry native women drew the Indians closer to the British than the Americans who were now beginning to enter their country. The red men did not favor the American presence on their lands south of the Columbia River, and the territory there threatened to fall to the Americans more than the lands on the north. Among those opposing the American presence were the peoples of the Rogue River and its tributaries: Takelmas and Latgawas (Takilman); Chastacostas; Taltushtuntudes, or Galice Creeks; and Dakubetedes, or Applegate Rivers. Those tribes are usually lumped together with other Athapascans on the coast as Rogue River Indians, or Rogues, a term that is mostly used hereafter despite

*In 1836 a new Fort Umpqua was established on the south bank of the Umpqua River near the mouth of Elk Creek at a point about forty miles from the Pacific Ocean. It was across the river from a trappers' camp located there in 1832 and used by trader John Work. It was abandoned in the late 1840s when its personnel were lured away by gold discoveries in California. The old post is often called McKay's Fort, presumably because Nor'Wester Thomas McKay was sent in 1820 with a party to explore the country south of the Willamette River and he selected the site of the fort.

the involvement of two language groups.

Many of the white men who traveled through the Rogue River Indians' lands believed that the name Rogue befitted those peoples. They were so named by French Canadians in the company employ because of their "roguish" behavior. One who so believed was the Kentuckian John Turner. In June, 1835, the Rogues attacked Turner's party of eight trappers with clubs, bows, and knives on the south side of the Rogue River below Rock Point on the California Trail, killing two and wounding several others. Other natives attacked the survivors in their northward flight to the Willamette, which they reached minus all but two of their guns and half their party. In September, 1837, the Rogues attacked the American entrepreneur Ewing Young and a party who were driving about seven hundred cattle on a 600-mile journey from California to the Willamette. During the fight two arrows ripped into Young's horses, and one ripped into the back of one of his men, who survived. From the place of the fight to the Umpqua River, natives continued to harass the party as it struggled northward to the Willamette, which it reached with three men reported killed and about seventy cattle missing.

In the 1830s natives south of the Willamette Valley afforded safer passage to company trapping and trading expeditions bound for California. But this route did not free them from such troubles as McLeod faced in his attempt to open a southward route in 1829. Returning over the Siskiyou Mountains in northwestern California and southwestern Oregon, he lost his horses and was forced to contend with rebellious freemen in his party.

Mounted caravans of about sixty souls, including French Canadians as well as other "bloods" and Indians of both sexes and all ages, carried British merchandise to barter for furs with natives along the way and for furs and horses with white settlers in California valleys. These groups were very colorful as they trekked the American West. They were especially so when, on approaching the Sacramento Valley, they removed the stains of their long journey and dressed in their finest, seeking to outdo each other like ladies of a European court. While they wintered in the valley hundreds of miles from their base at Fort Vancouver, they hunted and trapped, and their skillful women fashioned deerskin moccasins, shirts, and pantaloons, which were much in demand among the Californians. With spring they loaded their horses with furs (mostly beaver and otter) in bales weighing up to 180 pounds per pack animal. To the sound of the tinkling bells of their horses, which were herded by young drovers, they began their homeward journeys. Often they drove horses purchased from California Indians, who had stolen some of them from other red men. As they approached Fort Vancouver, they prepared for reentry in the grand manner of their Sacramento arrival. Duties placed on fur exports by Mexican authorities and other international complications ended these colorful ventures.

Most American attempts to encroach on company operations in the Pacific Northwest failed, but this did not lessen Yankee attacks on company policies, especially those pertaining to Indians. An American at the mouth of the

Columbia in 1834, Hall H. Kelley, saw, "little there but darkness and blackness and desolation; heard but little more than the sighs and cries of the misery in the perishing remnants of the Clotsop and Chenook tribes, and the roar and rage of mighty waters." Indians below Vancouver, he wrote, lived "in the most brutal, sottish, and degraded manner." Kelley had sought to establish an American colony at the mouth of the Columbia, envisioning exclusive possession by Americans of that stream. In his plan American possession would follow trade with Indians, whose wants would be stimulated by concourse with Americans and by the introduction of agriculture. This sounds very fine, but it was not by chance that in his plan for a proposed town at the mouth of the river Indians were to live on the back streets. Although demeaning, such an attitude was still better than driving them off, as other whites sometimes did under similar circumstances.

As might be expected, the company sought to defend itself from its American critics. One who took the offensive against the company's detractors was John Dunn, who served as clerk during the 1830s at Fort George. The fort was used then as a subpost at the strategic Columbia River entrance. Critical of what he termed "buccanneering commerce" by the Americans on the Northwest Coast, demoralizing to its natives, he boasted that his firm had done much to civilize those in its commercial care. He was proud of his own self-professed role in stopping certain barbarous practices in the secret societies (*tamanawas*), such as the "impostures of [native] priests." To show divine approbation, the shamans stuck daggers into flabby parts of their patients' chest and stomach flesh without drawing blood. Dunn claimed to have curbed that practice and also the killing of slaves to serve their dead masters in the other world.

The arguments of company apologists did not satisfy the Americans, who countered with more criticism. Especially critical of company influence, where native practices were concerned, was special United States agent Lieutenant William A. Slacum, who was in the Pacific Northwest in 1836 and 1837 on a naval reconnaissance. He condemned the British firm for permitting such native practices as those that Dunn claimed to have stopped. In reality the company was no more responsible for native intemperance than the American traders, who carried on a lively ship-to-shore traffic in liquor. McLoughlin told a missionary at Fort Vancouver in the mid-1830s that rum was the stock in trade for salmon of an American company (perhaps Wyeth's)—so much of it was exchanged to Indians for fish that they spent more time drinking than fishing. Under McLoughlin's urging, Ewing Young abandoned a whiskey still, which he had pieced together with equipment salvaged from Wyeth's abandoned Fort William. Aware that alcohol was the "Easiest-Cheapest and Quickest means . . . to acquire influence over Indians," McLoughlin took measures to curb its consumption among his clientele and personnel by locking up the stores at Fort Vancouver, opening them only on special occasions. It was perhaps before his prohibitions that two Indians of The Cascades, Pahklah and Walamitwachochino, exchanged a slave girl for a small barrel of whiskey. They brought it upriver, where "all the chiefs got drunk."

Slacum also criticized the company for permitting slavery among its Indians. He was apparently unmindful that such a practice, long woven into the fabric of native mores, could not be easily eliminated. On the Columbia when the lieutenant was there a slave could be purchased for eight to fifty blankets, depending upon the quality of the animate and inanimate merchandise involved. The situation was no worse than in the rest of America, where white men held slaves for nearly 220 years. If anything, the company discouraged slavery by presenting gifts to chiefs who liberated slaves. The slaves' commitments to their masters included killing enemies and other nasty business. Company personnel were not unmindful that they themselves were potential targets for slaves who were carrying out the evil designs of the native masters.

The thousands of miles separating the company's operations in the Pacific Northwest from its British headquarters afforded it some protection from homeland critics breathing the air of evangelical-humanitarian winds blowing across Britain at that time. The winds were strong enough, however, to blow the Anglican Reverend Herbert Beaver aboard the company ship *Nereide*. Beaver traveled with his wife to the outpost of British civilization at Fort Vancouver in May, 1836, to see how the company's representatives were upholding their mandate to protect the "aboriginals" in their care. Where he had expected, as he wrote, to find "red savages," or "dirty brutes" as his wife called them, he soon found himself among white "savages." McLoughlin had espoused the Catholic faith, and perhaps as bad in Beaver's thinking, he had married a half-blood woman. Beaver laid aside his criticisms of the place as "the very stronghold of Popery," but he was critical of the "many acts of cruelty and murder committed upon natives by persons in the Company's service."

Beaver's observations of natives at the post were in keeping with his incensed attitude toward conditions there. Among the tribes frequenting the establishment were the Klickitats, a Shahaptian tribe called Robber People by the Chinookans. They were a vigorous hunting people who had been less exposed to the company, as Beaver recorded it, than the far-less vigorous Chinooks had. He may not have known that the Klickitats in precontact times were believed to have moved up from the south or from the western slopes of the Rockies to the eastern slopes of the Cascades. Their removal was hastened by pressure from the Cayuses, who had been themselves pressured by the Paiutes. Their new location was dominated by Mount Adams, the "Mountain of the Klickitats," which was also called, by the Klickitats and the Yakimas, Pot-to, or "standing up," and Quch Whyamnay, meaning White Eagle. The Klickitats, who deified a "White Bird in the Sun," made a mark for themselves on earth. They became culturally similar to the Yakimas and, like them, ranged their horses on grassy, rich hills. Their women became expert at basketry, and their men expert in the manufacture and use of bows and arrows and other weapons of the chase. With increased contact

with whites, such as those at Fort Vancouver where they gravitated for trade, they supplemented their native weapons with firearms.

Some Klickitats had separated from the main body of the tribe. One such group was the Taitinapums (or Titon-nap-pams, and the like), who lived on or about the headwaters of the Cowlitz and Lewis rivers. They were called "wild" or "wood" Indians by the main Klickitat bands. They may have been the natives whom a Nor'Wester in 1814 noted living near Mount Saint Helens, west of Mount Adams and northeast of the Columbia-Willamette confluence, who had broken their isolation to hunt in the Willamette Valley. Pockets of such semiisolated hill and mountain peoples were not unusual in the Pacific Northwest. West of the Taitinapums in the Willapa Hills lived a small band of Kwalhioquas, an Athapascan people who occasionally broke their isolation to travel to the lands of lower-river and coastal natives, such as the Chinooks. Over the years such peoples as the Taitinapums had gathered about them a certain mystique; the lower-river natives circulated tales that they stole and ate children and traveled invisibly. The main body of the Klickitats, on the other hand, became very visible on the lower Columbia and in the Willamette valley. Some of them intermarried with lower-river peoples, such as the Cowlitzes. As natives of the lower valleys succumbed to epidemic diseases in the 1820s and 1830s, the aggressive Klickitats stepped into the vacuum to hunt and trade.

Compared with the Klickitat women, Chinookan females became, in Reverend Beaver's words, "as accomplished courtesans as any upon the face of the whole earth: inferior to none in profligacy, disease, and extravagance." This was a result of more associations with sailors (by no means all British) and with the lower classes of company personnel. They resorted to infanticides and abortions when their white husbands deserted them or the fathers were unwilling to support unwanted offspring. Beaver was unaware of the facts of native life or intellectually dishonest in not reporting that native women practiced abortions long before white men appeared in the Pacific Northwest. With little historical perspective he also blamed company men for venereal diseases, which his modesty would not permit him to identify by name. He condemned the company's slowness in abolishing slavery and was critical of its policy of binding *engagés* for periods of servitude, which was, in his thinking, a form of slavery. As if those were not criticisms enough, he accused the company of trading to natives for pelts and other native goods various items of which were "useless, one quarter pernicious, and the remainder of doubtful utility." Two and a half years after his arrival Beaver's fervor dissipated into frustration. Unwilling to face or fathom the facts of life on a fur-trading frontier, he sailed for England, retaining but few fond memories of the fort—except one perhaps, his sideboard well stocked with liquors from its cellar.

Fort Vancouver was a center of civilization if there was one on the wild Northwest coast. If not highly civilized in Beaver's sense of the word, it tried to be—as American

1845 sketch of the Hudson's Bay Company Fort Vancouver. From the 1820s until the 1840s the fort was the primary emporium of *the Pacific Northwestern fur trade. University of Oregon Library.*

travelers would attest. It was at least cosmopolitan. The lowly Indians who lived unthreateningly in the fort village were joined by many newcomers to the region: the managerial Britishers; the carefree, colorfully garbed French Canadians; the half-bloods homebred from unions with Indian women; the Owyhees (who were so faithful that a river in Idaho was named for them after natives in the winter of 1819-20 killed three of them there); and the visiting Indian tribes. The fort hummed with industry and trade. Indians passed freely to the courtyard during business hours and into the Indian shop to exchange furs, salmon, venison, baskets, and canoes for blankets, guns, tobacco, and assorted baubles.

Evidence of the company's concern for those under its care was its school for the children of its men and native women and orphaned Indian and half-blood children. One child who attended was Ranald McDonald, son of Comcomly's daughter, Princess Sunday, and clerk Archibald McDonald (MacDonald). Among the unusual pupils at one time were three survivors of a Japanese junk, which, straying illegally from its homeland, had in 1833 beached near Cape Flattery, where Makah Indians enslaved the survivors. McLoughlin learned of their plight when an Indian brought him a small piece of rice paper on which was sketched a junk wreck on the beach with three figures standing nearby.

After inquiry McLoughlin dispatched an expedition to ransom and rescue them. Their presence in the school helped inspire Ranald to journey in 1848 to the mysterious land of Japan, an adventure that provided him an education more exciting than that of the Fort Vancouver school or the continuing formal education that his father sought for his "young Chinook." McDonald's stay in Japan would help Commodore Matthew Perry gain entrance to that land and open it to the world.

With such cultural amenities and with continuing company control at the fort, the resident and visiting natives feared it less than they formerly had. It lost its military character despite its silent-but-frowning guns, and during the 1830s it became increasingly, in the words of a company clerk, "the grand mart, and rendezvous for the company's trade." Regional furs and other native goods were brought to it for shipment to Pacific destinations and Britain. British processed and manufactured goods arrived there for trade to the local personnel and the Indians and for transshipment to a similar market at various interior posts. Among the goods from Britain were those made of cotton grown and harvested by American slaves. Many American Indians covered their bodies with this cloth, although most Pacific Northwestern Indians did not adopt white men's clothing until later.

At some interior posts, such as Fort Colvile, security and weaponry had become as superfluous as at Fort Vancouver. This was not the case at Fort Nisqually, which was established in 1833 at the head of Puget Sound and was the terminus of an overland route northward from Fort Vancouver.[4] Northern tribes were always threatening the post. Along the route to it from Fort Vancouver attacks against the company personnel and properties were less likely than intertribal conflict. On the right bank of the Columbia south of Vancouver stood the lodge of an Indian who had killed a fellow tribesman. After the deed was committed, about three or four hundred of his people assembled in an attempt to convince him that he should cover the dead. This he did by expending considerable property, remarking at the conclusion of his payment: "The sun was high when I killed him. It was not in the dark. I have paid the price of his blood and what more can I do?" To an Indian there was little more that he should do. Farther north on the Fort Nisqually route a chief (who was decked out in blanket, capot, blue vest, trousers "a foot too long," an English hat, and blucher shoes) traveled on May 23 to a council to deliberate on the propriety of accepting two slaves as a peace offering from northern tribes for the murder of his kinsfolk. Sometime in the 1830s or 1840s the Upper Chehalises, after six months of preparations, raided the Snohomishes to the north.

Realizing the harmful effects on trade of the continuing intertribal feudings, company officials redoubled their efforts to stop it. Natives had usually congregated in large numbers at the site of Fort Nisqually in August. During that month in the year of the fort's founding they were assembled there by a trader, George Herron, to hear his pleas to them to stop their feuds. With a Nisqually named Lachalet (or Lahlet and the like) as an interpreter, Herron tried to make them confess their murders and thefts. Some did confess, accepting his admonition never to commit such wrongs except in self-defense. To seal the promise, they marked their names with an X on a sheet of paper. As the Indians and the trader both knew, the signing was a gesture that was not binding on other members of the signatories' tribes.

In September, 1834, several tribes of the Fort Nisqually trading area fought the Twanas (Salishan) of the Hood Canal west of Puget Sound. One of the Twana bands was the Skokomishes of the upper Hood Canal (after whom an Indian reservation was later named). At the fort rumor had it that the son of a Clallam chief killed in the company's 1828 retaliation against his tribe was seeking retribution from the fort for the death. Personnel there quickly began installing pickets to protect the post from attack and, should that not occur, to protect it at least from the natives' pilferings. Bastions were installed, and other precautions were taken, including the construction of a small court where Indians had to wait their turn to trade.

The arrival of Indians with word of an American presence in Puget Sound alarmed fort personnel. The fort's chief trader, Dr. William Fraser Tolmie, believed the Indians' news to be a ploy to effect a reduction in the tariff, such as had occurred when the *Owhyhee* and the *Convoy* were on the Columbia. The presence of the American ships had reduced the tariff and, in the native's thinking, their own populations as well. On September 28, 1833, they told Tolmie of the arrival of two American ships, saying that the captains threatened to bring disease among them if they did not trade their beaver.

"Robust, fierce-looking, burly," well-armed Clallams were among those especially angered at the tariff, which was "robbing the Indians of one beaver," as they put it. One native offered to help Tolmie should the Clallams or others get out of hand. He was Challicoom (or Shallicu), a person "of some note & well disposed toward the whites." He had befriended the trader when the latter was traveling to Fort Nisqually; unlike most natives of that area, he had not demanded payment or some bargain before giving food to the traveling white men. In early October a Makah chief appeared at the fort seeking a better price in order to buy more goods, but departed with only a "common" gun, for which he had traded a small sea otter and five beaver.

On October 21, disgruntled at the tariff, the Clallams set out for their homes with sixty to eighty beaver that they might have traded had the post been adequately stocked with goods. Its short supply was occasioned by the failure of a company ship to arrive with the goods. With such a scarcity the company may have been tempted to raise its tariff, but refrained from such action. The natives in the area might have reacted more strongly to company pricing policies had they not continued to subsist on the fruits of their richly endowed ocean, strait, and sound homelands. Keen tradesmen that they were, they continued to play the waiting and haggling game. In order to entice their trade, Tolmie dispatched parties to the Clallams in February, 1834, and returned shortly with about fifty beaver pelts. This was not a large number; the Clallams possibly withheld their pelts, waiting for Americans to come along and give them a better price.

The natives were aware of the June 9, 1834, arrival of the company ship *Llama* off Fort Nisqually because her sails signaled her approach. The goods she carried eased somewhat the supply problem, but there remained other worries for company merchants. In August the Clallams returned. Men at the fort, previously engaged to agrarian and other tasks, prepared for trouble. Still angered at the tariff, the Clallams demanded a blanket per beaver with such vehemence that the trader had to turn them out of the shop. Fortunately they left without resisting. Surprisingly, the son of the Clallam chief slain in 1828 thought the death well "covered" and became a trusted company messenger. On October 9 thirty Makahs visiting the fort reported trading some canoes and a few skins to Captain Dominis. To keep them trading at the post, Tolmie purchased from them not only some of their beaver but also dentalia.

Hunting, fishing, and other wintertime activities kept natives from the post, but, as noted, large numbers came there during the late summer. One Sunday, August 24, 1834, about 300 natives assembled, representing eight different tribes. They were not identified, but they may have included Makahs from the far tip of the Olympic Peninsula, although at about this time the Makahs sold the products of

A woman of the Skagit tribe working on a mat. Skagit County Historical Museum.

their country, including oil, directly to the company ships that carried them to markets. The other Indians may have been Clallams from the Strait of Juan de Fuca, Twanas from Hood Canal, Skagits and Snohomishes from northern Puget Sound, Duwamishes (Salishan) and Suquamishes from farther south on that body of water, Chinooks from the Columbia, Chehalises and Cowlitzes from along their rivers south of the fort, Snoqualmies (Salishan) from the western slopes of the Cascade Mountains, and Wenatchees and Yakimas from the interior. With horses and beaver to barter, the latter two tribes came to this fort in the land of the Nisquallis, with whom they had marital and other close ties. As Klickitats had driven horses westward through the Cowlitz Pass of the Cascade Mountains to Fort Vancouver, these tribesmen, especially the Yakimas, drove horses over the Naches Pass of the same mountains to Fort Nisqually, where they ranged on prairies around that post. As was the custom in the interior, horses were killed to accompany the dead to hunting grounds in the other world. Thus several horses were killed over the grave of Sophy, a Nisqually of royal blood. On March 25, 1835 a Yakima chief, Takill, arrived with but one beaver to sell—an event no more unusual than his earlier imprisonment by the Kalispels.

Considering the large number of Indians gathered at

Fort Nisqually during the summertimes, things remained relatively peaceful, although occasionally an obstreperous Indian would be ejected from the fort. Besides trading, Indians gathered around the post to gamble, often with bone and stick markers. Such gaming set poorly with company traders, who believed that it contributed to the Indians' beggary, intransigence, and other troubles. Anticipating trouble on New Year's Day, 1835, Tolmie wrote that it would never do to dispense rum "amongst such brutes," libations were thus reserved for company employees. This company-imposed abstinence for Indians must not have been observed always, for on April 7, after exchanging furs for rum, some Chehalises began to fight amongst themselves on the beach. They may have obtained the liquor from sources other than company.

Seeking to minimize such troubles, Tolmie and Herron instructed the Indians in the doctrines of the Christian faith. Herron claimed that at Fort Colville he had done much to "civilize" its Indians. Some tribesmen there had even offered to trade their furs for his prayers. Perhaps he and Tolmie believed such instruction would eliminate or at least curb such practices as the *tamanawas* ceremonies, which the British trader Dunn claimed to have eliminated on the lower Columbia. The Indian congregation of the Nisqually white traders found it difficult to comprehend Christian concepts as they were explained in the Chinook jargon. The latter was characterized by Tolmie as a "vile compound of English, French, American & the Chinook dialect"; he should have added Russian and Spanish. A classic account, possibly contrived, of an innocent white man's confrontation with the jargon originated at a later time on the Yakima Indian Reservation. The Yakimas, not liking the man, referred to him as a hyas cultus Boston man, which the visitor took to mean "highly cultured man from Boston." In fact, when translated from the jargon, the phrase meant "very bad American." Tolmie found a more satisfactory vehicle of communication in the "Flathead" language (Salish), which was interpreted to traders at the fort by The Frenchman, a European-clothed, bushy-bearded Snohomish chief, named Witskalatche. Clallam head chief Lughkinum had already furnished Tolmie a vocabulary of his people's language.

Before the 1846 Anglo-American boundary settlement northern Puget Sound Indians, besides trading at Fort Nisqually, also traded at such company posts as Fort Langley on the lower Fraser River and Fort Victoria on lower Vancouver Island. Built in 1843, Fort Victoria received the trade of the Lower Skagits and others. A Semiahmoo (Salishan) chief, Kwetiseleq, near the Canadian border became rich selling furs at Fort Langley, buying slaves with his earnings. Indians continued to patronize Fort Nisqually, which was moved inland a short distance from the beach after the

boundary settlement; operations continued there as at other company posts. After 1843, Fort Victoria supplanted Fort Langley as a trade center for peoples of the strait.

Such changes were affecting the formerly bustling entrepôt Fort Vancouver. Even before the boundary settlement it was losing its importance as a locus of the fur trade. Forced to diversify operations there, the company increasingly exported flour, lumber, and Columbia River salmon. Indians took their salmon catches to company stations on the lower Columbia, such as the Cascade-Dalles area and Willamette Falls. After the fish were tallied, the native women received tickets to exchange at the close of the fishing season for cottons, calicoes, blankets, beads, ammunition, tobacco, and other goods. In the meantime they prepared the salmon by a rather complicated pickling process for company shipment to the Hawaiian Islands.

The increased attention of the company to fish and farms instead of furs indicated that its original purpose was beginning to change. Yet until the end of its operations around 1872 in what was American territory the company would continue fur trading. Long before its fur posts decayed and its traders departed the natives had to reckon with other white men, who were more interested in the soil of the Indians' lands and their souls than their furs. How they responded to the new seekers was most important to their history, for after they met them, their lives were changed more than ever before.

7. A STRANGE NEW THING

It is not known where or when Pacific Northwestern natives were introduced to the Christian faith. Spanish friars were recorded among them in 1792 at the colony of Núñez Gaona at Neah Bay. Indian lore tells of shipwrecked white men, from whom the natives may have learned something of the faith. Crucifixes excavated along the coast indicate that ships carried the symbols of the faith if not the message. There is some evidence that priests from Alta California missions visited the valleys of southern Oregon before the eighteenth century. With the coming of the horse interior tribes traded along the Spanish borderlands, experiencing perhaps some awareness of the faith as it was extended by the priests—a spiritual antidote to the Spanish conquistadors' extension of it by the sword. Two Spanish Franciscan friars, Silvestre Vélez de Escalante and Francisco Atanasio Domínguez, failed to penetrate north of present-day Utah on a missionary journey in 1776. Thus it appears that in the main direct proselytizing of natives north of that point awaited the coming of missionaries from other quarters. Along a ribbon of the interior the ministrations of Lewis and Clark, although primarily humanitarian rather than Christian, created among the Nez Percés a stir which, a quarter-century later, encouraged them to search for the white man's religion. In 1831 a delegation, largely Nez Percé, journeyed to St. Louis to seek out William Clark, then a general and superintendent of Indian affairs—which suggests that on his western journey he may have told them of the Christian god.

In the late eighteenth and early nineteenth centuries Pacific Northwestern natives appear to have received little more than an inkling of the faith from maritime traders, whose efforts were mercantilist, not missionary. Landbased fur traders, such as David Thompson, Alexander Ross (whose Bible consoled him one lonely winter at Fort Okanogan), and Peter Skene Ogden, saw the lands of their fur quests as a field, though a difficult one, for Christian missionary endeavor. Fur clerk Ross Cox, who had enough exuberance for them all, looked forward to the day when missionaries would, "meet on the Rocky Mountains, and from their ice-covered summits, proclaim to the benighted savages 'Glory to God in the highest, and on earth peace and good-will towards men.'"

It is more than a little paradoxical that the haughty, often treacherous Iroquois would, as Ross put it, "sing hymns oftener than paddle-songs" and that they gave many of the natives of the interior, especially those of the Pacific Northwest, their first introduction, albeit rudimentary, to the Roman Catholic branch of the Christian faith. Although these primitive outriders of the faith knew their limitations in it, even refusing to teach Christian prayers to natives "for fear they would get them wrong," they gave Christian doctrine a nativist cast, believing, for example, that souls were the linings of bodies. From the Iroquois the Pacific Northwestern natives pieced together a religious mix; the nativist yielded slowly to the Christian until in the twentieth century some effort was made to recombine them in a new mix.

The appearance of a fabulous messianic figure called Shining Shirt, who was possibly an Iroquois, gave the Iroquois enhanced status among the Pacific Northwestern natives. He had prophesied among the Flatheads the coming of men with white skins and long, black robes who would teach them religion, give them new names, change their lives, and cause wars to cease. After that an irresistible tide of white men was to come. Especially appealing to the natives was his prediction that the black robes would aid them in a material way; such aid was equated with spiritual benefits, such as divine protection for themselves and destruction of their foes. Before critical battles warriors kissed or bit the prophet's talisman, a metal-inscribed cross.

Spokane tradition tells of their prophets predicting the coming of white peoples. Perhaps sharpening the prophecies were natural phenomena such as the Mount Saint Helens Ash Storm around 1800. Nespelem tradition tells of this shower of dry dust covering the earth to a depth of three or four inches. It drove the people to pray and dance to the "dry snow," calling it Chief and Mystery. Such activity left them no time for their customary food gathering, and some of the elderly fell victims to the "snow." Even their traditional starvation food—a black, pasty moss mixture—could not save them. In 1853 elderly Kalispels recalled, as had elderly Spokanes in 1841, the eruption, which rained cinders and fire. They believed the sun had burned up; happy to see it shining the next day, they held a great feast and dance.

Yakima lore has similar stories of the coming of white men, the Kooyawowculth, who were to wrest the land from its original inhabitants. After one of their prophets, Temteiquin, had "died" for three days, he returned to earth and predicted the coming not only of a black robe but also of other white peoples. The black robe of the prophecy and the three-day death possibly indicate a knowledge of Christian forms and traditions, perhaps acquired through direct or indirect association with Spaniards in the southwest. An exponent of the nativist Dreamer, or Pom-Pom, religion, Temteiquin believed that the coming of whites boded ill for his people, as did another Yakima prophet, Wat-tilki.

There had been, as has been noted, sizable importations of Iroquois during the era of the North West Company, which they served in menial capacities as boatmen and fur-gathering freemen. Nearly forty of them, for instance, had been present at the building of Fort Nez Percés. Because of their lowly rank in the company, they exerted more religious influence on the natives than did the managerial personnel who espoused the Roman Catholic, Anglican, and Presbyterian faiths. Their wish to escape their contractual obligations to the fur companies, to which they were chronically in debt, drove them back and forth between the company's employ and the native villages, to which they attached themselves when the fur trade waned. There, along with the imported eastern Indians and French Canadians, they exerted considerable secular as well as religious influence on native peoples.

On his "Journey of a Summer Moon" in 1811, Thompson learned that Indians of the Columbia River acknowledged a Great Spirit dwelling in the clouds, who was Master of everything and the Maker of lightning, thunder, and rain. It was to him that their souls went on their deaths. In contrast to Christian believers they recognized as solar deities the sun, moon, and stars, of which the greatest was the sun. At about the time when George Simpson visited the Spokanes they held religious services in their chief's lodge, kneeling before a religious picture obtained from some white traders and praying to Quilentsatmen (the Maker or, literally, He Made Us) to protect and rescue them at last from the Black One below.

In the early 1830s a Shoshoni chief, Hiding Bear (Pahdasherwahundah), said that, since the Nez Percés rated so highly with white men, he would learn their moral code and religion and hold Christian devotionals so that his people might gain superiority over their "ignorant rivals," the Utes.[1] The chief began dutifully practicing what the Nez Percés preached, observing their holy days as Sundays and marking them on crude calendars. Sundays (erroneously termed sabbaths by white men) were observed quite commonly by natives, but not with the solemnity of devout Christians, for on those days they gambled and raced horses. For them Sundays were never days of rest. Some Indians said that their observances of special days of worship antedated the coming of white men. The Yakimas were said to have observed the Sapálwit, or "Indian Sunday," which they "did not get...from any books—from no white man." Besides their first-salmon and root ceremonies, which were reminiscent of Jewish rituals, they had a dualistic belief in good and evil forces in this world and the next, where people were divided according to their deeds.

Although natives had been aware of the competition among the fur seekers in their lands, they were less aware of the competition that was developing among religious denominations for the salvation of their souls. As has been noted, George Simpson and the company he represented had some concern for the spiritual welfare of natives in the company's economic care. He ceremonialized his responsibility as the guardian of Indian souls in April, 1825, on his return east by baptizing the sons of a Kutenai chief and of the Spokane chief Illim-Spokanee before taking them on the difficult trans-Rocky Mountain journey to the Anglican Mission Society School. The school was held in conjunction with company operations at Fort Garry on the Red River near present-day Winnepeg, Canada. There in the early 1820s the Reverend John West hoped that Anglican mis-

sions could be extended to tribes as far west as the Pacific Coast. Until such a time western chieftains' sons came from their mountains to the mission shepherded by Simpson. The latter, before a change of policy (but not of heart), had said, "I have always remarked that an enlightened Indian is good for nothing." Simpson hybridized the tribal names of his two young Kutenai and Spokane charges with those of company managers: Spokane Garry was a lad of about fourteen; Kootenay Pelly was perhaps slightly younger. Among other chiefs who requested Simpson to take their sons east were the treacherous Casacas and Casino. The fur man refused their request, fearing that, if some accident befell them on the arduous journey, it might not sit well with Casino or Comcomly, "the principal Men below the Walla Walla."

The journey of Garry and Pelly to the Red River and their furlough four years later encouraged other chieftain fathers to send their sons east to learn the white man's ways. In the spring of 1830 they sent to the mission Kootenay Collins, Spokane Berens, Cayuse Halket, and the Nez Percé lads Ellis (or Ellice) and Pitt. Simpson judged rightly the responsibility involved in taking the lads so far from their homes: in 1831, Kootenay Pelly died at the school; Spokane Berens died there in 1834; and Kootenay Collins died soon after his return home in 1833. Although no Kutenai bitterness is recorded at the deaths of their two boys, Pelly's death from a horse fall saddened his Lower Kutenai chieftain father, the Grand Queue. Visiting the chief in 1841, Simpson recorded that, although the chief dared not mention the name of the deceased, he had suffered a blow from which he never recovered. In 1837, Cayuse Halket, who had been furloughed to his Cayuse people in 1833, died accidentally at the mission, causing considerable consternation and anger among his people.

Spokane Garry, the most noted of the Red River scholars from the Pacific Northwest, furloughed with his people in 1829 and returned home two years later armed with an Anglican Book of Common Prayer and a King James Bible. For a time Garry kept his knowledge sharp by Christian prayers, ceremonials, and missionary efforts among his own and allied peoples. Among those who heard his words were Coeur d'Alênes, Flatheads, and middle and upper Columbia River peoples, as well as the Nez Percés. Language differences between the Salish and Shahaptian peoples had not prevented their intermarriage and other forms of mingling at numerous fishing, hunting, and root-gathering grounds, where they had ample time to learn and talk about Garry's words. Such gathering places, like tribal villages and trading posts, were marketplaces where religious wares were exchanged. At the time of Garry's ministrations trader George Herron exerted his Christianizing and "civilizing" influence at Fort Colvile, which was near one of those cosmopolitan gathering places, Kettle Falls. So many people gathered there that they observed Sundays and traveled considerable distances without so much as a knife for protection. They might have used such weapons had they not called on Herron to arbitrate their disputes.

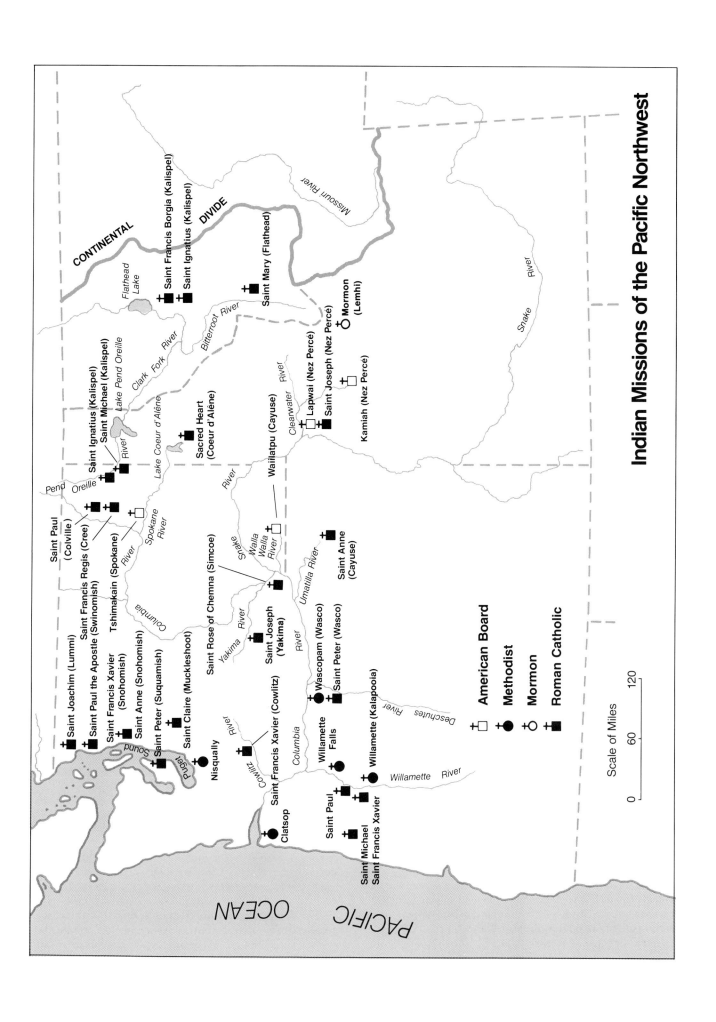

Indian Missions of the Pacific Northwest

CONTINENTAL DIVIDE

Saint Francis Borgia (Kalispel)
Saint Ignatius (Kalispel)

Flathead Lake

Saint Mary (Flathead)

Missouri River

Mormon (Lemhi)

Clark Fork River

Bitterroot River

Lake Pend Oreille

Saint Ignatius (Kalispel)
Saint Michael (Kalispel)

Lake Coeur d'Alêne

Sacred Heart (Coeur d'Alêne)

Clearwater River

Lapwai (Nez Percé)
Saint Joseph (Nez Percé)

Kamiah (Nez Percé)

Snake River

Pend Oreille

Saint Paul (Colville)

Saint Francis Regis (Cree)

Tshimakain (Spokane)

Spokane River

River

Waiilatpu (Cayuse)

Walla Walla River

Umatilla River

Saint Anne (Cayuse)

Columbia

Saint Rose of Chemna (Simcoe)

Yakima River

Saint Joseph (Yakima)

Snake River

Saint Joachim (Lummi)
Saint Paul the Apostle (Swinomish)
Saint Francis Xavier (Snohomish)
Saint Anne (Snohomish)
Saint Peter (Suquamish)
Saint Claire (Muckleshoot)

Puget Sound

Nisqually

Nisqually River

Saint Francis Xavier (Cowlitz)

Cowlitz River

Wascopam (Wasco)
Saint Peter (Wasco)

Deschutes River

Willamette (Kalapooia)

Willamette Falls

Columbia

Saint Paul
Saint Michael
Saint Francis Xavier

Clatsop

Willamette River

PACIFIC OCEAN

American Board
Methodist
Mormon
Roman Catholic

Scale of Miles
0   60   120

It would take more than Garry's words to win over to Anglicanism the Iroquois-influenced Flatheads. Once when visiting them the youthful Garry deferred to his father to convey his words, among which was the statement that Catholic priests ate the dead. Since the promised priests did not come, some Flatheads may have believed Garry. At any rate he disturbed many Flatheads, who temporarily abandoned the faith of their absent fathers.

This Flathead religious disturbance may have been instrumental in the resurgence among them and among other tribes of the Prophet Dance, variations of which had appeared at other times and places among American natives. From the northern peoples it spread around 1830 to other Pacific Northwestern tribes, increasing in vigor and variety. The prophets' increased exposure to Christianity, which had a part in the revival of their dance, and the increasing white encroachment on their lands gave impetus to their teaching, which included the belief that the earth had to be wrested from the interlopers and returned to its aboriginal purity to its native inhabitants, living and dead.[2]

Pacific Northwestern natives were seekers of medicine — wealth and power in things material as well as spiritual. Examples of this are legion, but one will suffice: in 1835 a young Suquamish dreamed that he was given a written paper and eighteen blankets from heaven and, later, a coat covered with dollars. He then presented clothes to his people in a potlatch ceremony, carrying out with a vengeance the Christian concept that it is better to give than to receive. He hoped that his bread cast on the water would return with the volume of a bakery.[3]

To gain power the young were sent out on lonely vigils. During such spirit quests the novitiates received in dreams or trances special powers from birds and other nonhuman things, mostly animate. The powers were revealed later in winter dances and were guarded even to the point of killing those suspected of stealing them.

If not the most poignant, perhaps the longest and most publicized (both in America and Europe) of the power quests was the voyage of the Nez Percé-Flathead delegation to St. Louis in 1831. They were seeking what the *Christian Advocate and Journal* in 1833 emotionally termed the "white man's Book of Heaven." Since the delegation spoke languages that were strange to white men, their mission was not very clear, but they did make the Roman Catholic sign of the cross and other signs relating to baptism. Episcopalian William Clark sent them to a Catholic cathedral, where they received baptism and kissed the cross. Making their journey especially poignant was the death and Christian burial of two of the delegation at St. Louis, far from their homelands, and the disappearance of some of the others somewhere between that city and the Pacific Northwest.

The Nez Percé-Flathead journey not only stimulated the Christian community to convert Indians but also stimulated other Indians to trek to St. Louis for missionary help. In 1835, 1837, 1838, and 1839, influenced by Iroquois, such as Ignace La Mousse (who came west around 1816), Flathead delegations journeyed to St. Louis for missionary help for not only themselves but also the Nez Percés, Kalispels,

Kutenais, Spokanes, Colvilles, and Cayuses, all of whom, they said, wanted priests. John Gray, who was a deserter from Ogden's employ, and several families in an Iroquois group that emigrated to the west in 1816 left the Rocky Mountains purportedly to save their souls,[4] although it is well known that many Iroquois defected to save their necks. All of the Flathead delegation of the 1837 quest except Old Ignace were killed by Sioux (Lakota) Indians. Young Ignace (Ignace Chapped Lips), who went to St. Louis in 1838, remained there to accompany black robes to the Flatheads in 1840 to teach them the doctrines and songs of the faith on their home grounds.

A half-dozen years before the Catholic missionaries responded, Protestant missionaries heeded the Macedonian calls of the Nez Percés and Flatheads by sending missionaries to the Pacific Northwest. Before their arrival the natives continued Christian worship without benefit of clergy. Observing them at worship were frontier-roughened white men. Laying no claims to sainthood, they were surprised at the natives' zeal in worship, which was characterized by one white as "a strange medly; civilized and barbarous." Sometimes traders and trappers sold them playing cards, telling them they were Bibles. Indians who knew better chided their fellows for this, as they did for gambling. They also chided white men for such diversions and misdeeds, saying that untutored "savages" had a higher morality than they.

As the fur-trade and missionary eras overlapped, it was quite common for natives to cluster around the far-flung company posts to conduct their devotionals. They were often found speaking and singing prayers beneath the frowning bastions of Fort Walla Walla, at Flathead Post, and at Fort Colvile. At Fort Vancouver, on Sunday, May 5, 1833, they danced from side to side in circles two-deep, simulating with their arms and bodies the movements of their feet. The dance rose to a crescendo until they dropped to their knees. Then after a short prayer they resumed their gyrations. Possibly the Cold Sick gave impetus and urgency to their devotionals at that time. Natives performed a similar ceremony at Fort Nisqually that same year, dancing, as did those at Vancouver, on Christian grounds but unconcerned with abstract redemptive and trinitarian concepts of the Christian faith. From trader William Fraser Tolmie they heard more appealing words about the creation of man, the expulsion of their first parents from a garden paradise, and the Great Flood. Variations of the Biblical account of the Deluge and myths of man's creation may have had a place in their lore before the coming of white men. White settlers chuckled when an Indian told ethnologist George Gibbs of the land being covered by water "many moons ago" in the time of Noah; they believed the Indian informant had gotten the story from some trader or missionary rather than his own native lore. In fact, Yakima lore held that Mount Ararat was a Satus-Toppenish mountain, and to the Flatheads, Flathead Lake was the central point of the Flood from which the Nez Percés climbed a high mountain east of Kamiah to save themselves.

At Fort Hall, Nez Percé and Cayuse Indians attended services with a Hudson's Bay Company brigade on Sunday,

July 27, 1834. The services were conducted by the Methodist Jason Lee, who was traveling with the trader Wyeth. Lee was the first missionary to respond in person to the Indians trek to St. Louis for help. With his nephew, Daniel Lee, Jason was commissioned to serve "the Flatheads," meaning all tribes in a large, ill-defined area west of the Rocky Mountains. Lee's native congregation did not understand a word that he said, but they maintained "the most strict and decorous silence," rising and kneeling when he did. The meeting followed one of their own in which a chief had reminded them of their obligation to the Great Spirit, who was the maker of light and darkness in contrast to the evil workings of the Black Chief below. A month later, observing a similar service among the Cayuses, Captain Bonneville concluded that, like the Nez Percés and the Flatheads, the Cayuses had strong devotional feelings that had been cultivated by some "resident personages" of the Hudson's Bay Company since they observed Sundays and the cardinal holidays of the Roman Catholic Church.

The Indians' welcome of the Lees, their desire that Jason Lee remain in their lands, and their willingness to help him seek a mission site came from their wish, as they often expressed it, to hear "a strange new thing." Possibly they remembered prophecies and promises that white men would come with powers even greater than those that they had sought on vigils in their youths. At any rate they were pleased with Lee's promise to establish a school where they and their children might learn the ways of white men and their god.[5]

Listening to Lee preach at Fort Vancouver on Sunday, September 28, was a motley congregation of races and classes, including the survivors of the wrecked Japanese junk. Lee had been invited by McLoughlin to hold the service. The chief factor advised him to abandon the idea of establishing a mission among the real Flathead Indians because their nomadism and wars would make a mission difficult to maintain. Seeking "the identicle place that the Lord designs" was difficult for Lee. The spot that finally seemed best to fit the divine prerequisites was the Willamette Valley; he established his mission there in a rich-bottomed, tree-bordered prairie near present-day Salem, Oregon.

The means of subsistence near the mission site appeared promising to the optimistic Lee. He believed that he could extend his ministry to natives on the mountain and coastal perimeters of the Willamette Valley and to American immigrants, who surely would be lured to the valley by its fertile soils. Before the mission house was properly roofed—a necessity in that rainy land—the Indian pupils arrived. They and later arrivals received Lee's instruction not only in reading and writing but also in vocational pursuits, of which the most important was farming, the prevailing American occupation at that time. Very soon the "strange new thing" proved stranger than the Indians expected; they became disillusioned with the radical changes that the school sought to make in their lives. Disease and defection seriously disrupted the school's operations. Lee reported that of the fifty-two pupils admitted in the first four years eight died, some ran off, and others were withdrawn by their parents.

After an Indian lad named Kenoteesh died at the mission in August, 1835, his brother sought to kill Daniel Lee and lay worker Cyrus Shepard to avenge the death. He was dissuaded from the act by another Indian who had accompanied him to the school, but he satisfied his need for vengeance by killing some unarmed Indians nearby. So great were the hopes of one Waileptuleek for the mission that he not only accompanied the Lee party from Fort Hall to Fort Walla Walla but also sent his children to the mission school; only to have two of them die from fever in February, 1837, and another die as he attempted to flee the contagion of the place.

As Indians died at the mission, so in a sense did their culture as the missionaries tried to replace it with their own. Natives were forbidden to speak their own languages in the school. This practice was also adopted by the United States government when it established Indian schools nearly three decades later. Like the missionaries, the government equated native tongues with barbarism. A teacher at the school, Medorem Crawford, commented that not even the English language lifted the students from barbarism, for as fast as they learned it they learned to swear in it. Indians also clung to the hope that they could exchange spiritual gifts for material ones. In 1880 a Columbia River chief remembered his response to a sermon preached by a Methodist missionary at Willamette Falls: "Yes, my friend," he recalled saying, "if you give us plenty of blankets, pantaloons, flour and meat, and tobacco, and lots of other good things, we will pray to God all the time, and always."

While the number of Indians around the mission and the signs of their culture decreased, reinforcements of mission workers increased. One party arrived in May, 1837, by ship at the mouth of the Columbia and ascended from the juncture of that river and the Willamette to the station. It discovered much work to do the day after its arrival, for a Chief Samnik of one of the Kalapooia bands was brought there badly wounded by the gunfire of another Indian. In order to prevent such tragedies, the mission workers had to reach not only the Kalapooias but also such tribes as the Umpquas, Tillamooks, Klickitats, Nisquallis, and Upper and Lower Chinooks.

In August, 1837, natives received instruction from the Lees and from Shepard as the missionaries made a circuitous journey from the Willamette to its Molalla River tributary and back, a trek that restored the missionaries' health as much as it may have advanced the spiritual health of the natives. In that same month the Tillamooks met and heard the words of Jason Lee, whose party was guided to their coastal country by Joseph Gervais. In late summer, 1838, at Fort Umpqua about forty miles up the Umpqua River Lee was met by some Kalapooias from the Willamette in the place of a hoped-for delegation of local natives. In response to Lee's words, the Kalapooia chief who was interpreting them said that he had curbed adultery among his people and would put away one of his wives on his return home.

Protestant and Roman Catholic clerics had little sympathy or understanding of native marital practices. They frowned, for instance, on the bridegroom's indemnification

The Methodist Mission near The Dalles, where missionaries of that faith in the 1830s and 1840s ministered to the Wascos and other Indians. Reproduced from the journal of Major Osborne Cross, who traveled with a military corps from Fort Kearney to Oregon in 1849. University of Oregon Library.

of a bride's parents for services she would no longer provide them. They severely condemned polygamy and never felt comfortable with the natives' familial system, in which sisters of deceased wives came to live in the households of widowed brothers-in-law or widowers joined the households of deceased wives, depending on local custom. The reverse also took place as widows went to live with brothers-in-law as their wives.

On the trek to the coastal country natives admitted to Lee and his traveling companion, the Reverend Gustavus Hines, that they had killed many people, both whites and Indians, and that murder, along with disease, had carried off many red men. They had other words for the Methodist preachers: "We have been called a bad people, and we are glad that you have come to see us for yourselves. We have seen some white people before, but they came to get our beaver. None ever came before to instruct us. We are glad to see you; we want to learn; we wish to throw away our bad things, and become good." After hearing Lee's words, they said, "It was all very good," and presented him with a woman's cedar-bark dress and a beaver skin. Skeptical of their words, Hines feared that trade in skins was their motivation for permitting a mission among them. Neither the natives nor the missionaries had a chance to prove Hines right or wrong, for he and Lee turned their backs on that remote spot for the safety of the Willamette Valley. At Fort Umpqua they heard a rumor spread by a chief that in McDougallian fashion they had brought medicines in a bag to kill off the Indians. As if this news was not ominous enough, they also learned that an Umpqua chief, on hearing a rumor that his wife had been unfaithful, had shot her through the heart. Not long after the missionaries left, natives unsuccessfully attacked the fort.

The Dalles was astride a better-beaten track for white men than any other place among the more remote peoples, such as the Umpquas, and it was surrounded by about fifteen hundred Wascos. It seemed a more promising field to the Methodists than the Fort Umpqua area. At about the time of the founding of the Wasco, or Wascopam, Mission there in 1838, one of the missionaries exuberantly reported that over a thousand of the natives had embraced the Christian faith. At this place, where the Shahaptian and Chinookan tongues merged, Daniel Lee had some success in communicating in Sahaptin. He contented himself with communicating with the Chinookan speakers in the jargon bearing their name.

It did not take long for the missionaries to discover that their field, like the Indian languages, was as hard as the nearby basaltic rocks. The Indians had abandoned the flesh cutting of earlier times, but they shocked the missionaries by rattling doors and windows for entry into the mission house. Especially shocking was the fate of the native healers: when they failed to cure the victims of disease, they became victims themselves of vengeance-seeking relatives. In 1839, Lee prevented what might have been a nasty confrontation between Thomas Farnham, who was traveling through the area, and an Indian by stepping in to return to Farnham a great deal of horse gear that the Indian had appropriated.

Some aboriginality was knocked off the natives by revival meetings in 1838 and 1839. It would take more to mold them in the Methodist image. The missionaries hung on, preaching and teaching to about two thousand Wascos and other Upper Chinooks, Wallawallas, Klickitats, and others. With abundant fish runs in the Columbia, the natives could not be induced to become farmers, but they were content to consume produce from the missionaries' gardens. When the fishing runs were over, they moved into the mountains to gather berries. During their absence, marauding Indians entered their deserted villages and stole salmon that they had carefully cached, leaving them virtually starving by spring. Horses that the missionaries hoped to use in farming proved to be a source of trouble as Indians stole them and then demanded shirts for their return. On swift cayuses the Indians of the same name and the Nez Percés swooped down on the fisher Indians' villages, shrieking wildly and frightening them half to death despite the riders' assurances that they were not bent on war, just practicing for it.

Jason Lee, on his return from an eastern journey to reinforce the Oregon mission, preached at a camp meeting at the Wascopam Mission in the fall of 1841. He reported that 130 natives were baptized and 500 took the sacrament. Coming to the mission about that time were the Klamaths, far from their homes. In 1873 one of their subchiefs stated that a Klamath named Link River Jo had visited The Dalles "thirty years ago" and learned from missionaries about the Holy Spirit, from which he sought gifts for all the tribes. He said that in the Spirit's absence the tribes proved unworthy of the gifts because of their continuing murders and killings.*

In hopes that the Oregon mission's labors would be successful and furthered by support from the East, Lee took five Indians with him on his journey back there in 1838, including William Brooks (Stum-manu), a Chinookan speaker, and Thomas Adams, a Kalapooian. Brooks had been trained at the Willamette mission, as had a younger brother and sister of his. His presence on the eastern tour and his words at various church meetings gave the tour not only promotional impetus but also poignancy because on the trip he succumbed to some disease, possibly tuberculosis. His denouncements of whites plying his people with rum and of clergymen more interested in the economic than the spiritual resources of his homeland helped to raise both cash and conscience among his listeners. In Peoria, Illinois, the graphic description given by Adams of the quantity and quality of lower Columbia River salmon and Lee's favorable description of Willamette soils prompted the organization of Farnham's Oregon-bound "Peoria Party," the group that had horse troubles at The Dalles. Only a handful of those who set out in 1839 with the party ever arrived at their destination. Although they never reached the place where salmon entered the Columbia from the Pacific, where they had hoped to build a large city, the remnants of the party settled in the Willamette Valley to become virtually the first American settlers in the Pacific Northwest.

The days of the Methodist mission were numbered. After several complaints from church officials about Lee's spiritual and secular conduct, he returned east in 1843, never to return, and the mission closed the next year. It is not known how much the closure may be attributed to the Reverend Joseph Williams of Indiana, who spent 1841 and

1842 preaching "to the people...and...to the Indians," as well as seeing the country. Even if they had little impact, his words at least were incisive: "I fear our missionaries are too scornful with the poor naked Indians...I fear the world and speculation has too much influence over these missionaries...I believe that it is brother Lee's intention to do good for the heathen; but it seems he had a great deal of business on hand, which seems a hindreance to the work of religion."[6] Lee and his supporters, of course, would not have agreed with this assessment.

As easterners pondered the words of William Brooks about the plight of the Indians, they also pondered those of the opening volumes of a magazine, *Oregonian and Indian's Advocate*, published in 1838. This was the first publication ever established, in the editor's words, "to defend Indian rights," although at the same time it encouraged American emigration to their lands. Greatly influenced by letters from Methodist missionaries in the Pacific Northwest, the editor believed there was still time to save the natives there from the evils that had befallen their eastern brothers. "Neither rum nor oppression has yet affected the tribes of Oregon," wrote the editor hopefully. William Brooks, at least, had known better.

Toward the end of the eighteenth century Europeans had advocated a Christian mission on the Northwest Coast. By 1810 and 1811 plans had been formed in New England in the circles of the American Board of Commissioners for Foreign Missions (of the Congregationalist, Presbyterian, and Reformed churches) for a mission to the coast, and by 1817 plans were made for one specifically "near the falls of the Columbia." Further evidence of New England concern for the welfare of the Northwest Coast Indians was expressed by Nathan Whiting in his *Religious Intelligencer* (published in New Haven, Connecticut). He wrote on November 6, 1824: "The natives have already been exposed too long to the contaminating influence of such men [adventurers]. It is time to exert a counteracting influence, and the sooner this is done, the easier and the better."

Circumstance—or providence, as Calvinist members of the American Board would call it—prevented one of the board's representatives, Jonathan S. Green, from establishing a mission on the Northwest Coast. In late summer, 1829, the Chinooks met Green aboard the *Owhyhee*. It was a pleasant encounter, but it caused the minister to think that American Indians from Norfolk Sound to the Columbia River had learned all the vices of white men and none of their virtues. In the thinking of Green and his American Board colleagues the Pacific Northwestern natives needed what those of the Hawaiian Islands had received a decade before the much-publicized trek to St. Louis, namely, a new spiritual breath to soften that of mercantilism. The captain of the *Owhyhee*, fearing the challenge of the Columbia River entrance, denied Green the privilege of carrying his faith to the natives beyond it. Not for another seven years did the natives of the Pacific Northwest have an American Board mission in their lands, and then it was in the interior reaches rather than along the coast.[7]

On September 28, 1835, the Nez Percés on the Clear-

---

*In 1847 the mission was sold to Dr. Marcus Whitman. Whitman had planned to move his own mission there, but his untimely death prevented the move. During the Yakima war the Wascopam Mission's buildings were purposely burned to keep Indians from occupying them after Fort Dalles was built nearby in 1850.

water River fired a welcome salute and then feasted a westbound American Board missionary, Reverend Samuel Parker,[8] who was reconnoitering the region for mission sites. On Sunday, October 4, a three-lodge band of natives heard him preach. Near Fort Walla Walla, with protocol equaling that of a royal court, Cayuse villagers, like those Indians at the mouth of the Deschutes River who met Parker, arranged themselves in a reception line for him in descending order from headmen to women and children. Greeting him the next day were the Wallawallas, who were no longer stigmatized by other tribes. Parker believed that they were descended from former Nez Percé slaves. In a small village on the Columbia north bank above the Cascades he was met by "the only real Flatheads and Nez Percés": their heads were flattened slightly, and their noses pierced with dentalia. On October 16 he reached the stockaded Fort Vancouver, which was inhabited by a hundred white personnel, with three times that number of Indians "in a small compass contiguous."

Chief Moses of the Sinkiuse tribe, astride a cayuse. The chief, who weighed well over 200 pounds, appears too large for his mount. Such horses stand from twelve to fifteen hands high. Courtesy of Grace Christianson Wenzel.

That fall and winter natives from the mouth of the Columbia to The Dalles and up the Willamette above The Falls to the Methodist mission heard Parker preach about the Great Spirit. Their practices and their belief in this deity and the "Black Chief" below suggested to Parker that they were possible descendants of the lost tribes of Israel, a subject of considerable speculation in the United States at the time.

As there had been a division among Biblical tribes, Parker noted a division among those of the Pacific Northwest. He believed, as did so many other white travelers in the region, that the Indians of the coast were less stalwart and noble than those of the interior, although no less worthy of salvation. At The Dalles, which was between the two regions, the chief, Tilki, was possibly rendered penitent by Methodist preachings and therefore seeking to avoid the fires of hell, such as those spewing from volcanic Mount Saint Helens. Parker was brought close to tears as he beheld the tearful chief pleading for someone to "teach them the right way to worship God and to be saved." When they met Parker in April, 1836, as he journeyed into the interior, many of Tilki's fellows claimed to have abandoned their former practice of dancing on Sundays. Their first request of him, even when "suffering with hunger and nakedness," was for tobacco.

Natives met Parker at Fort Walla Walla in late April and early May, 1836. They were happy that he had kept his promise to return and ready to hear his words, some of which must have resembled those of the Catholic fort trader Pierre Pambrun. Pambrun had introduced them not only to basic church teachings but also to a tough code of laws that included, on sentencing by chiefs, hanging for theft. The laws pertaining to polygamy must not have been strictly obeyed. One chief told Parker that he was too old to give up either his ways or his wives, and if that meant going to hell, he would just have to go. Several Nez Percés in the gathering escorted the missionary to their country. Along the way he saw evidence that his society had much work to do. Under Catholic influence Indians sometimes placed crosses over graves, as they did other objects with "medicine," or charms. In a burst of iconoclastic fury at an Indian camp near the mouth of the Snake River, Parker smashed the cross protecting the grave of a little girl who had just died.

Not in Parker's itinerary was Waiilatpu, The Place of the Rye Grass, which was twenty-five miles east of Fort Walla Walla in the fertile Walla Walla Valley, on the lands of three Cayuse chiefs—Umtippe, Waptashtakmahl (Red Cloak or Feathercap), and Tiloukaikt. Later that year the American Board established a mission there, which eleven years later became its best-known mission because of a massacre. An interpreter at Fort Walla Walla, the Catholic John Toupin, would later claim that in 1835 he and Pambrun accompanied Parker to the site and that the missionary told the natives that a doctor or medicine man would come to preach and teach there, after which ships annually would bring free goods, including hoes, which they would be taught how to use.

Later in 1836 another American Board mission was established at Lapwai Creek near the confluence of the

caused an even greater stir among the Cayuses than the coming of her mother; a stir that was equaled among the Nez Percés when Mrs. Spalding gave birth to a girl, Eliza, in November of the same year. Children were a boon to Protestant missionaries, as they were to other whites, when there was tension between the races. The day after the birth of the Whitmans' daughter Chief Tiloukaikt came to see the baby. He called her a Cayuse *temi*, or girl, because she was born on Cayuse land, but asked why she was clothed in a dress and why she was lying in a bed with her mother and not on a cradleboard in a maternity lodge.

The initial harmony at the mission began to break down. Interpreter Toupin later claimed that he was present when Umtippe, placing his ailing wife in Whitman's care, said: "Doctor, you have come here to give us bad medicines; you come to kill us, and you steal our lands. You had promised to pay me every year, and you have been here already two years, and have, as yet, given me nothing. You had better go away; if my wife dies, you shall die also." Umtippe then summoned a well-known Wallawalla *tewat*. The *tewat* ministered over the woman, pronounced her cured, and received a horse and blanket for his fee. Ironically, when Umtippe fell ill, he came to Whitman for aid and survived — a fate better than dying at the hands of a Wallawalla *tewat*. When a relative of Umtippe died after treatment by a *tewat*, Umtippe's brother Isaichalakis shot the *tewat* dead.

Cayuse chiefs noted that Whitman, like Spalding, had but one wife; a poor arrangement, they believed, because, as they put it, where there were many wives they all "had more to eat." Cayuse women — "slaves" Mrs. Whitman called them — performed menial tasks, as did all native women. Their men did not want them to work for the Whitmans. Consequently, those working at the mission were mainly Wallawallas. "The Kayuse ladies," in Mrs. Whitman's words, were "too proud to be seen usefully employed."

Like Spalding, Whitman hoped that the natives' tillage of the fertile Walla Walla Valley soils would make it unnecessary for them to migrate. More than Spalding's Nez Percés, the Cayuses disdained agriculture as a hindrance to their traditional means of subsistence. Tillage of the soil was not proving to be the "strange new thing" they expected from their tutors. They wanted goods and power — "medicine." Thinking the missionaries' words could help them acquire "medicine," they asked for their instructions. The Whitmans responded by teaching lessons and songs in church and school in the flexible Nez Percé language. By adopting that language, the Cayuses followed a pattern not unusual among the Pacific Northwestern Indians. The Chinooks, for instance, adopted the language of their Chehalis neighbors; the Clatsops, that of the neighboring Tillamooks; and the Chimakums, that of the nearby Clallams.

In preaching, Whitman entrusted to a well-coached "rehearser" the task of repeating his sermons line for line. Despite this safeguard, the missionary believed that his words were misunderstood by both chiefs and Indians — not because of the hardness of the language but because of the hardness of their hearts. When in 1840 he told them so, they were pricked to the core. Some even threatened to whip

him. During the summer of 1841 an Indian named Tilkanaik struck him in the chest in the continuing wrangle over ownership of the mission lands. Angry that Whitman was diverting the waters of Mill Creek to irrigate his gardens, the Indians diverted water from his ditches until he convinced them there was enough for all. Later Chief Tiloukaikt struck him, pulled his ears, and threw his hat into the mud, condemning him for trying to change Cayuse ways. "Doctor," he said in substance, "I am mad at you. Before you came, we fought with each other, killed each other and enjoyed it. You have taught us that it is wrong, and we have in great measure ceased. So I am mad at you for preventing our doing what we enjoyed."

In October, 1841, there was another round of unpleasantries. Archibald McKinlay, who had become chief trader at Fort Walla Walla after Pambrun's death in a horse accident, compared the Cayuses' behavior to that of a pack of dogs. Stung by the insult, several Cayuses powwowed, rode to the mission, and stormed the mission house. One was armed with a hammer; another with an axe and later a club and gun. They boycotted services, broke windows, and troubled the animals. The arrival of Cayuse chief Camaspelo from his Umatilla River village helped to calm them, as did Tiloukaikt, who had calmed himself down. Whitman's controversial ride to the East in 1842-43 to save his mission saved it during his absence from further such confrontations. "But why," asked the Indians, "did Whitman go East? Was it to get soldiers to fight them?" Suspicions of Whitman's motives had also spread to some of the Nez Percés. H. K. W. Perkins, a Methodist missionary at The Dalles, revealed the disturbing news conveyed to him by the Wascos and Wallawallas. They said that the Nez Percés had dispatched one of their chiefs in the winter of 1842-43 to the Indians east of Fort Hall in order to excite them to cut off the party that Whitman was expected to bring with him. Whitman's return to his mission in 1843 at the head of an immigrant party caused the Nez Percés and Cayuses to question the missionary's motives all the more. Were American Board missionaries and white men reserving all the "medicine" for themselves? Brothers of the now-deceased Umtippe asked if the missionaries were not rich and getting richer. Whitman's new house and the clothes that the family wore and hung out to dry displayed opulence for all red men to see. Their suspicions were deepened by the agitations of Joe Gray, a half-blood Iroquois, and Tom Hill, a Delaware.

The Reverend Elkanah Walker and the Reverend Cushing Eells with their wives established their Tshimakain, The Place of the Springs, on lands of the Middle Spokane Indians on Chamokane Creek, a Spokane River tributary,[10] about twenty-five miles west of present-day Spokane, Washington. The Middle Spokanes were considerably less refractory to them than the Cayuses were to their missionaries. They had eagerly sought their presence, encouraged to do so by Fort Colvile trader Alexander McDonald. He had warned Indians around his post not to pray to the sun and had set aside a room at the post for them to conduct morning and evening prayers. He had also promised help in building a house for the missionaries.

The mission was well located. It was within reach of about two thousand Indians—Spokanes and other Salish peoples—within a radius of about sixty miles. Nonetheless, developments followed the pattern observed at the other American Board stations: initially both the Indians and their clerical mentors were optimistic over the mission's prospects; then followed the inevitable cultural clashes. The first conflict was with the Spokanes and involved litters of mongrel dogs. The Indians never killed the puppies but permitted them to pilfer. The dogs ate game scraps and fish offal, destroyed mission chickens and gardens, and yelped at night. On one occasion Walker put the Indians under an interdict until they promised to kill the dogs. When that did not work, he hired an Indian to do the job. Somehow the dogs kept coming back.

The natives at Tshimakain, like those at the other missions, were irregular attenders of church and school. In food-gathering periods during the first year of the mission's operation congregations varied from thirty to a hundred souls, with no more than half the congregation remaining at the mission during the week. The natives usually came from up to thirty miles away on Saturdays and departed on Mondays. Some came from greater distances for sojourns of one to two weeks. Occasionally the missionaries carried their ministrations to the root and fishing grounds. Suffering poor health, Walker found it difficult to do so.

The Spokane language was characterized by the missionaries as one of "crooked" and "hissing" sounds, and they found it difficult to communicate with their flock. Small wonder that Mrs. Walker regarded November 25, 1839 as "an eventful day to the Flat Heads," for the Indians then received their first reading lessons. The printed words were not as exciting to them as the pictures in the missionary lady's book; one was of an animal that they had never seen before, an elephant. Although they loved to sing, they often tired of sitting and lost interest. Some of their elders, who also attended school, not only fell asleep but also fell behind the children in attainments. In December, 1842, the scholars saw a sixteen-page book that was "the first ever printed in the Flathead [at Lapwai]," as Mrs. Walker described it. It introduced its readers to letters and figures and included a key to pronunciation, lessons in spelling and numbers, and stories featuring biblical characters.

Spokane chief Big Head (Old Chief, Cornelius) was a visitor to the lower missions and helped to translate the mission book. Some of his other activities were not so welcome to the missionaries—especially his polygamy. Like other chiefs he believed that if one wife was good two were better. Polygamy was an institution too deeply engrained among the older Indian headmen for the missionaries to eradicate it. They had to content themselves with encouraging young Indian men to take but one wife. Big Head also insisted on taking his daughter to a medicine man when she was sick. It must have been most shocking to the missionaries when the Indians suggested that one of their Indian doctors might cure the Reverend Eells's sickly wife, Myra.

A growing scarcity of game over the years helped to send

Big Head across the Rockies to hunt buffalo in the winter of 1840-41 where increasing numbers of Middle and Upper Spokanes were going in search of food and hides. In 1846 the chief was reported as having a herd of fifty cattle to help ease the meat shortage somewhat, but most Indians showed little enthusiasm for raising cattle. In some areas of the Columbia Plateau, cattle of the "Spanish breed" ran wild in the hills. These cattle had been obtained from the Hudson's Bay Company. They were inferior to the small herds that American Board missionaries had driven west in 1836. To natives their meat was less tasty than their own game. Similarly they preferred the native fowl to the poultry imported by the company, which shattered the early-morning stillness with their crowing, and they preferred their own roots to the company-introduced potatoes. Most obnoxious of all imports, vegetable or animal, were the hogs, which tore up the Indians' lands snorting about for roots.

The roots that the Indians sought to keep from the hogs made up an important part of the diet of the Spokanes and other tribes. As soon as the snow melted, they gathered the pohpoh, a small onionlike root with a dry, spicy taste; and the *spetlan*, or *spatlum*, the delicious and easily dissolved bitterroot. In June they sought the tasty camas. Because of the importance of root-digging, it was not uncommon for Spokane men to join the bands of their root-digging women instead of vice versa. Fortunately for the Spokanes, Walker gave up trying to raise potatoes and abandoned hog raising. Lack of plows and harness, which had to be imported from great distances for the horses, made it difficult for the Spokanes to farm at Tshimakain. As in other northern Salishan lands crop-damaging frosts could strike any month of the year.

The Spokanes' gambling annoyed the missionaries, as did such ceremonials as the *huwash*, which was a singing, dancing, feasting affair. The Indians went from lodge to lodge until they finally entered one that was darkened save for a small topside opening. Through the opening the spirit descended in the form of a small bone. A shaman laid this bone over the heart of his subject, from whom the spirit had departed. The spirit then returned to ensure the subject against death. There was also the *tohua*, which involved dancing and walking barefoot. It was performed in the spring to ensure an abundance of deer, fish, roots, and berries.

Whether it was treated with missionary or native medicine, disease was a common threat to mission success. Walker was prompted to report that, although he and his colleagues had administered all the medicines they had, the real antidote for the Indians' "greatest disease"—that of "superstition"—would be "settling and civilization." The Indians attributed their attrition to one particular superstition, as Walker reported to Secretary Greene on April 16, 1840. The Indians, he wrote, believed in a race of giants, "men stealers," who inhabited the top of a perpetually snow-covered mountain on the west, from whose lofty heights they descended nightly to steal salmon and eat the fish raw. Approaching nearby villages and smelling strongly, the monsters gave three whistles, hurled stones on houses, and snatched people away, leaving a "track . . . about a foot & a half long."

Natives also believed in a race of "little people," the Elequas Tern (Stick Indians), who inhabited high places, such as the Cascade Mountains. The Yakimas believed in a race of such people on the western edges of their lands in the Cascades. They called them the Techum. Tribes bordering Mount Rainier, Mount Saint Helens, Mount Adams, and Mount Baker in the Cascade Range also believed in a race of mountain people. Fears of such beings, real or imagined, did not keep natives over the years from crossing the mountains on missions of war or peace. The Salish peoples of Lake Chelan, which pierces arrowlike into the heart of the Cascade Mountains, fought and traded in early times with coastal peoples. The Okanagons crossed the mountains to the coast, carrying hemp from their country to sell to marine natives, who used it to make fish nets. Then the Okanagons returned to their homelands laden with marine goods.

Spokane Garry exerted considerable influence among the Upper and Middle Spokanes after he became chief on the death of his father. He paid his first visit to the mission on January 5, 1841, but did not help the missionaries to teach the natives. They had hoped he would because he had taught school using pictures that Spalding had left him in the spring of 1837. Possibly he shied from helping the missionaries because he preferred Anglican doctrine and ritual to the American Board's Calvinism and lack of ritual, or possibly he was confused by the differences between the two faiths. He appeared at the mission from time to time to talk, interpret, and help to translate portions of the Bible into Salish. His appearances became more infrequent because he believed the Indians opposed them. They "jawed him so much about it" was the explanation given to George Simpson when the latter revisited the country in 1841. At that time Garry did not convey his feelings directly to his former spiritual benefactor, for Simpson surprised him in a gambling game, which so shamed the chief that he did not even come out of his lodge. Garry had taken to wrapping himself in a buffalo robe and had reverted to native ways, including the practice of spirit medicine. He remained friendly to the missionaries, but they no longer sought his help. Big Head rendered them much more assistance, but as long as he did not become a Christian, neither did his people. Thus the Walkers and Eellses had to content themselves with a "decade of dedication" to the "sowing of the seed."

To the American Board missionaries like the Methodists, the "paganism" of their flocks was scarcely a greater menace than what they called the "popery" and "religious idolatry" of the Roman Catholic Church. Their fears of its previous influence among the natives were small compared with what they suffered at the appearance of Roman Catholic priests in the Pacific Northwest. Many natives, on the other hand, welcomed the priests and their lay workers. They believed that they could receive from them powers that forerunning natives of the Catholic faith for so many years had told them they would receive.

8. BLACK-ROBE MEDICINE

In 1838 two Roman Catholic secular priests, François Norbert Blanchet and Modeste Demers, arrived in the Pacific Northwest. They were French Canadians and represented that part of the diocese of Quebec between the Rocky Mountains and the Pacific Ocean. Apparently the clerics did not come on any spiritual quest, such as the journey of the Nez Percés and Flatheads to St. Louis in 1831.[1] Instead requests for the black robes had come from the French-Canadian farmers of French Prairie in the Willamette Valley. The Methodist mission in the valley was never popular with those Catholic ex-Hudson's Bay Company employees. Chief Factor Dr. John McLoughlin of that company favored the coming of the priests, believing that they might not only prevent American missionaries from acquiring influence over the French Canadians but also exert a benevolent influence on the Indians. Still, McLoughlin had a higher regard for organized Protestant missionary efforts than he had for itinerant Protestant emissaries, such as the Reverend Joseph Williams. In McLoughlin's words, Williams had come to the Pacific Northwest "to bewilder our poor Indians already perplexed beyond measure by the number and variety of their instructors."

The Indians of the region would not know that the London directors of the Hudson's Bay Company doubted the wisdom of permitting Catholic priests in the Willamette settlement. The directors believed the field of missionary endeavor to be limited and that competing Protestant and Catholic efforts in the same area might lead to Indian troubles. Nevertheless, natives at Fort Colvile greeted Blanchet and Demers when they arrived there on November 6, 1838, after a six-month journey of about five thousand miles. Word of their coming had reached the Pacific Northwest some weeks before. Interior tribes, such as the Colvilles, Sanpoils, Spokanes, Wenatchees, and Okanagons, had ample time to gather at the fort to meet the "French chiefs." At last with their own eyes they were seeing the "chiefs" about whom the Iroquois and Canadians had spoken: the black robes—men of real cloth, not of leather, which American Board missionaries often wore—carrying crucifixes and other symbols of worship that the Protestant missionaries sought to disparage if not destroy. For the two priests the magnitude of their task was mitigated by their zeal. They immediately set to work to fulfill the two objects of their coming: to rescue the "savages" from "barbarism and its disorders" (from the French word *sauvage* the denigrating expression siwash evolved) and to extend help to poor Christians, such as the French Canadians, Iroquois, and other immigrants, who had allowed this western land and its natives to tarnish their faith and make them licentious and forgetful of their duties to the church.

During their four-day stay at Fort Colvile the two priests baptized native children. Baptism was the initial sacrament of the Catholic church, washing away the taint of original sin; but, except for the very elderly and those on the verge of death, adult Indians shied from receiving the sacrament. The two priests celebrated mass many times in the presence of the chiefs, who attended "with as great a respect as if they had been fervent Christians." Encouraged by this response, the black robes believed that a fruitful mission could be established among the rather homogenous Salish peoples. The mission, they believed, could be more fruitful than that of Elkanah Walker and Cushing Eells, who, among other failings, in the priests' view were too permissive with older chiefs in not demanding that they shed all wives but one. They were also critical of Protestant missionaries for distributing Bibles "in profusion . . . a ridiculous means of conversion for the inhabitants of the forest," bearing no fruit for their colporteurs. In July of the following year, 1839, Demers traveled itinerantly up the Columbia River Valley and returned to Fort Colvile to gather the gleanings from his brief harvest at that place. He baptized more children, heard confessions, and condemned French Canadians for "country marrying" Indian women.

Moving swiftly on their journey from Fort Colville to Fort Vancouver to rescue Columbia River Indians from Protestants and perdition, the two priests appeared on November 18 at Fort Walla Walla. During a 24-hour stay there as guests of Pierre Pambrun, they received Cayuse and Wallawalla chiefs and their peoples. One baby baptized at that time was the child of Cayuse chief Young Chief (Tauitau). This baptism shocked the Reverend Spalding: the American Board clergyman, although he did baptize children, did not believe as the Catholics did that the rite was necessary for salvation. Dr. Marcus Whitman had less influence over Young Chief's people in their Umatilla River camps than he did over those at Waiilatpu and could do little to prevent the Catholic ministrations to the Cayuses at the fort. On his journey to Fort Colvile the following year Demers found much work to do. There were Canadians to marry, infants to baptize, and children to teach and to tell that the Protestant missionaries (whom the priests called teachers, not preachers) had talked too long and baptized too late.

Since the French Canadians had taken Indian wives, the priests' efforts had to be directed to Indians and "bloods." They wasted no time in ministering to the natives around Fort Vancouver. They founded the mission of Saint Francis Xavier in the Cowlitz Valley near a company subpost that Blanchet had visited in December, 1838, shortly after his arrival in Vancouver. Demers was in residence at Saint Francis Xavier when not on his journeys. The French Canadians extended Blanchet a hearty welcome at French Prairie, a response that was not shared by all the Indians. The Kala-pooias, perhaps because of Methodist influence, avoided the black robes on their lands. In January, 1839, Saint Paul's Church of the Willamette was dedicated within a dozen miles of the Methodist mission. During that month, at the first mass in the valley, native women and their children heard the black robes explain the symbols and doctrines of the church, which were translated from the French and interpreted to them in their own dialects. After three weeks' instruction from Blanchet twenty-five Indian women received baptism "in excellent frame of mind" and were married. Also receiving baptism were an elderly man and women and a girl, all of whom died shortly.

At Fort Vancouver, Indians learned the catechism from Demers and heard his teachings in the Chinook jargon. Realizing the Chinook's imperfections, the priests set out to learn the more difficult native languages. In March, 1839, Blanchet was met at the Cowlitz station—where he had been in December of the previous year—by important chiefs from as far away as Puget Sound. In April natives of twenty-two different tribes of the Fort Nisqually trading area met Demers at the fort, where they deposited their furs and listened to his teachings. He had gone there to forestall the plans of the Methodist Reverend David Leslie to establish a mission. His hearers, as has been noted, had been given Christian teachings earlier by fort managers. Following their usual procedure the priests baptized some Indian children, and some French Canadians confessed their sins. Most Indians contented themselves with merely hearing their words.

Natives of the upper Chehalis River received Demers's ministrations in August, as did others shortly at Fort Nisqually. Although few were at the fort to meet him, word soon spread of his presence, and large numbers hurried there to give the black-robed visitor a ceremonious welcome. They arranged themselves in order of rank, painted and bedecked with feather trappings; their ears and noses adorned with dentalia. Deferring to their stratification of themselves, Demers dispensed crucifixes of different values according to the ranks of the recipients. In teaching he used what he termed the "historical ladder." The Indians called this device the sahale stick from the French *bois d'en haut*—meaning "wood from above" or "wood from heaven or God." On it the great events of the church were marked. Since Indians noted historical events on knotted thongs and notched sticks and as certain sticks were believed to have special powers, the sahale stick had relevance for them.

From the sahale stick the missionaries evolved the "Catholic ladder," a large chart of strong wrapping paper pasted on white cloth. It showed the great events of church history and doctrine—for instance, the Flood, the Tower of Babel, the Ten Commandments, the Twelve Apostles, and the Seven Sacraments—as well as various precepts of the faith. Since many Indians did not stay with the missionaries long enough in one place to understand its contents, tribal leaders took it to their villages and attempted to explain it to their people, some of whom had never seen the priests. At one time the Nez Percés saw a ladder made by Spalding, who

recognized its effectiveness as a teaching aid. As might be expected, his ladder contained the precepts of the American Board; it did not portray Protestants withering away on its lower rungs, as the Catholic ladder did. On one occasion Whitman smeared the blood of a steer on a Catholic ladder, warning with greater insight than he realized that Cayuse country would be bathed in blood.

Despite an optimism that was characteristic of most Catholic missionaries, Blanchet and Demers were also realistic; they were aware that the large numbers of Indians coming to see and hear them were no indication of immediate success. Their would-be parishioners still continued their "unholy" practices. Most pernicious to the priests was the *tamanawas*. Its practicioners could, the natives believed, cast spells on their enemies *"even if one is fifty leagues away."* Even though natives did not fight general wars as white men did, they fought many petty ones. In the priests' view the "demon of discord" sent to perdition those who otherwise might have been rescued by their ministries. In fact, on the very day in May, 1840, that Blanchet reached Whidbey Island, he learned of a recent fight there between the Clallams and the Skykomishes or Skeywhamishes, a Salishan tribe. Tslalakom (Tzallicum?), a Suquamish chief living on the island, was involved in the fight (the Suquamishes also lived on the west side of Puget Sound). Tslalakom was a former visitor to the Cowlitz, where he had received a sahale stick, and he attributed the Clallams' defeat to their ignorance of God and their failure to sing canticles and make the sign of the cross—all of which proved to him that "Christian medicine" had empowered his own people to defeat them. A few days later the missionary acted as peacemaker and effected a truce between the warring factions. The victors were to give two guns to "cover the deaths" of two Clallams killed in the fight. Under the aegis of the Clallam defeat, Tslalakom and his camp welcomed the priest. They crowded around a crude chapel that Blanchet had built and embellished with religious objects, including a "ladder" six feet high. Also gathering to worship with the black robe was Skagit chief Netlam (also called Snietlam, Swusskanam, George Snatlem, and the like) and his people, who lived on Whidbey Island. Snohomish chief Witskalatche was also in attendance with his people. The assembled throng heard the priest tell of heaven and of earth. He said that he would help them to plant grains and would send horses, other animals, and plows to replace their only tool, which was a crude stick for planting potatoes (which they obtained, no doubt, from the company) and for rooting oysters from the bay.

On Sunday, May 31, 1840, four hundred natives from all over the island presented themselves to Blanchet, each in his proper rank as was their practice. Singing canticles, they bore a heavy twenty-foot cross prepared the previous evening to give dramatic symbolism to the meeting. Jesus bore some resemblance to the deity of native lore Dokibatl, the Transformer, or Changer (whose name was spelled differently among the tribes). Some natives believed that Dokibatl had returned to earth in the ships of the early white men who entered the Strait of Juan de Fuca. With some variations most peoples of the Olympic Peninsula and Puget Sound believed in him. His cult appeared to be associated with the Prophet Dance of the Columbia Plateau. Both flourished in the 1830s. The missionary's words about life after death were familiar to his listeners, for they believed in such a life. In healing ceremonies they sought to rescue souls gone to the other world. According to tradition an elderly man, influenced either by early white men or by natives, canoed north from Puget Sound with a cargo of coppers to tell natives of those northern regions that they would die but afterwards rise to live again.

Caught up in the pageantry of the ceremony and in the conviction that Blanchet expressed in his words, the natives promised to follow the black robes and to serve the "Great Master." As Indians were meeting Blanchet on Whidbey Island, those of the lower Columbia, who were fewer than those in the north, were gathering around Demers. "The scourge of God [the Cold Sick, or influenza] having stricken these unfortunate savages because of their abominable lives," Demers recorded that, "with a little bell in one hand and a 'Catholic Ladder' in the other," he conducted a three-weeks' mission, "instructing the adults [in the Chinook jargon], baptizing the children and doing much good." By his teachings Demers sought to check the natives' religious practices and make a dent in their mercantilism; he claimed that they bartered any Christian faith they might have "for a shelter or a shirt." The following spring natives of the Fort Langley area listened to Demers preach, permitting him to baptize many children. At the same time those around Fort Vancouver, the Willamette, the Cowlitz, and The Cascades of the Columbia provided Blanchet more gleanings in his harvest of souls.

On September, 28, 1841, Blanchet reported that in the spring Demers won over an entire village at Willamette Falls from the Methodists. One of the Methodist ministers had lamented the previous year that it would take many years to elevate the village's 150 natives from the "depth of their pollution into a civilized and Christian people." Natives in the Willamette Valley and other places where Catholic and Protestant missionaries stepped on each others' toes must have benefited at times materially if not spiritually from the rivalry. The opening rounds of the contest began in 1841, and ensuing rounds were fought with little "dignity or Christian charity." Blanchet tried to win over the Clackamas Indians (Chinookan) on the Clackamas River in the northern Willamette Valley with rosaries, religious medals, and other gifts. Meanwhile the Methodist Reverend Alvin F. Waller tried to win them over with trousers, shirts, and dresses—and warnings that diseases, whose recent ravages had made them deathly afraid, would be their lot for gambling, cohabiting unlawfully, failing to keep the sabbath, or succumbing to Roman Catholicism.

In the summer of 1840, Blanchet received a letter stating that the "Shoshones and Snakes" wanted a mission, that the Flatheads and Kalispels had nothing more important at heart, and that the Nez Percés were tired of their "self-styled" ministers with wives, greatly preferring Catholic priests. The writer of the letter was Peter De Smet, S.J., who exerted more influence in the area than many of his profession.[2] His superiors had been touched by the appeals of the Flatheads visiting St. Louis in their quests for a mission, especially the visit in 1839 of two young French-speaking Iroquois, Pierre Caseveta (or Gauche) and Young Ignace. Thus the romantic, yet stocky and physically enduring, enthusiast De Smet left St. Louis the following year to lay the groundwork for a desired Paraguayan-type reduction for a Rocky Mountain mission.[3]

According to both whites and Indians, a Kalispel medicine man named Chalax (White Robe) could predict the times and magnitude of Blackfoot attacks by means of his prayers. Under his influence his people and some Flatheads met De Smet at a rendezvous on the Green River in southwestern Wyoming early in the summer of 1840. Also on hand to meet the black robe were some Shoshonis preparing for an expedition against the Blackfeet. The Kalispels and Flatheads remained at the rendezvous less than a week. In the open air De Smet performed a mass, whose Latin words were stranger to the Indians than their tongues were to him. The natives sang in response to the black robe, whose spiritual power appeared like that of their own spirit power, the *sumesh*. The songs may have been more religious in nature than some of the aboriginal lays or the bacchanalian songs that were sung at the rendezvous by carousing mountain men in cacophonous accompaniment to the wild celebrations at such meetings. As the rendezvous were an exciting sensory mix, the fathers wished to use the meetings for the religious good of the Indians—well aware that noise and singing were essential to their enjoyment of life along with eye-appealing colors. The best instruction was of little value without those accompaniments. At Pierre's Hole, a place filled with raucous noises and glittering colors, about 1,600 natives greeted the missionary. Among them was a Flathead chief who was largely of Kalispel extraction named Bear Looking Up or Standing Grizzly Bear. De Smet called him Big Face and christened him Paul. "From time to time," said the chief to the black robe, "good white men have given us advice and we have followed it.... Blackrobe, we will follow the words of your mouth." Big Face had received baptism, which was not an unusual thing because he was aging and near death and therefore wanted all options kept open to ensure his safe entry to a happy hereafter.

Responding to a request from Big Face, De Smet visited the chief's people to survey their needs on their home grounds. He had already come to admire them for their courage in fighting the Blackfeet. At a later time a Kalispel chief, Michel, recalled that, when the priests first came, they asked the people if they prayed to the sun, to which they replied in the negative. They were known, however, to have offered large pieces of flesh to the sun god Natosa, especially when going to war. The priests told them not to pray to such chiefs. Michel explained that the people believed that after death the good people went to the east and the bad to the west. He added that they had learned of The Good Chief in the East about five hundred years earlier, when a man had seen the world and the people therein as he climbed a tree to heaven. Michel explained that the man returned to tell the people about it. Thus, when white men came to their country, they said that the Good Man of the East was God above and that they knew about Him long before the white men came.[4]

During De Smet's first visit to the mountains, as he recorded it, Chalax, leading only sixty men, routed a 200-lodge Blackfoot party in a tough five-day battle, killing eighty with but one of his own people wounded. De Smet also recorded that shortly before his arrival among the Flatheads seven of their number, finding themselves confronted by "a thousand" Blackfoot warriors, held off the attackers for five days fortified by prayers to the Great Spirit. When the fighting was over, many Blackfeet lay dead or wounded, and only one Flathead had died of his wounds—and that was after receiving baptism.

On one occasion, also recorded by the black robe, the Flathead war chief Insula (Red Feather), or Michael (surnamed "The Little Chief") sustained the assault of an entire village attacking his own. On another occasion, after some Bannocks had been guilty "of the blackest treason," Insula marched against them with but a tenth of their number. Invoking "the protection of heaven," Insula rushed the foe and killed nine of them. In one engagement, possibly the same one, he killed the brother of a Bannock chief and might have killed more of the enemy had he not announced to his men that fighting must cease because it was the sabbath, the hour of prayer. Returning to camp without dressing their wounds, Insula's men fell on their knees to "render to the Lord of Hosts the honor of the victory." Although a ball through his right hand rendered it useless, Insula aided two comrades more seriously wounded than he. On other occasions he acted with such courage that certain Nez Percés, who were also involved in the Bannock wars, extended to him the honor of being their principal chief. Saying it was by God's will that he was chief of the Flatheads, he refused the invitation.

The arrival in September, 1841, of the Flathead-De Smet party at a cottonwood- and pine-shaded grassy meadow on the right bank of the Bitterroot River, the planting of a wooden cross there, and the naming of the spot Saint Mary's were singular events to the black robe and his clerical corps. They were no less so to the Flatheads.

De Smet was one of many white men who admired these peoples. The Astorian Ross Cox noted that except for their cruel treatment of prisoners they had fewer failings than any tribe he had met. That sentiment was echoed by Nor'Wester Alexander Henry, who characterized them as "a brave and virtuous people." Female chastity among them, wrote another, was a "national medicine." De Smet's description of the Flatheads as a people among whom "dissentions, quarrels, injuries, and enmities" were unknown was obviously an oversimplification. Everyone knew that such a description did not apply to their dealings with their foes, let alone to occasional intratribal squabbles. The black robe, exulting in the power of his own "medicine," also exulted in Flathead victories over their enemies. With medieval zeal he was apparently undisturbed that their spiritual preparations for war, let alone the wars themselves, were un-Christian. In re-

counting their exploits, he stated that their prayers had given them victories over superior forces, perhaps because he did not wish to jeopardize his rapport with the Salish peoples. When the battle statistics were obviously exaggerated in their favor, he did not condemn them or question their reports of heavy enemy losses compared with their own.

The Flatheads and their Salish allies proudly carried wounds and scars from enemy knives, spears, clubs, arrows, and balls. Not to have done so would have been a sign of cowardice. Especially honored, if they were fortunate enough to survive to show their wounds, were the dog soldiers, who, in advance of main war parties, sniffed out and entered enemy camps with only their medicine and rattles. If they were killed, the parties turned back. The Flatheads also sent into enemy country spies dressed like their foes.

Many battle scars would have been covered had De Smet achieved his antinudity goal among the Flatheads and among other tribes who sought to avoid the discomfort of clothing in warm weather. To protect his flock at Saint Mary's from Blackfoot "wolves," De Smet trusted not only in prayers but also in palisades. He ordered the latter to buffer the establishment physically from the incursions of the raiders of the plains. Out on those plains his flock had no palisades to protect them—only their prayers and prowess, vigils and vigilance. Other Salish tribes had to establish their own systems of protection from the Blackfeet, whose foremost objectives were the fine Salish herds of horses. To help protect the animals from Blackfeet, the Kutenais concealed a large stallion in the mountains.

When Big Face sought to defer to De Smet as chief because the latter had superior "medicine," the cleric declined the offer, shrewdly choosing to work through the native chiefs in building his mission and leading its people in his regimen of devotionals, which was as rigid as that of a cloister. Helping the priests in the performance of their tasks was their use of rewards—not just words of praise, but more visible rewards, such as crucifixes, medals, ribbons, pictures, and the like, distributed publicly for all to see. When Big Face died, his people, in keeping with his request, wrapped him in a prayer flag, such as was raised on Sundays to announce the day, and buried him at the foot of the cross that had been erected at the founding of the mission. His successor, Victor, was prefect of the Flathead men's group, the Society of the Sacred Heart. A Flathead bearing the name Standing Grizzly, who was christened Loyola after the founder of De Smet's Jesuit Order, helped the black robe cause among the Kalispels. Among the Kutenais the missionaries relied on Ignace, a New York Iroquois, to assist them in their Christianizing endeavors.

With the zeal of a medieval scribe the Reverend Gregory Mengarini, S.J., who had come west with De Smet, began translating the catechism into the Salish. He found that tongue:

. . . truly very difficult and complicated. Furthermore, it is in no was related to European languages. One might say that brevity of expression is carried to excess. For them, one word is really a com-

Peter Adams, a Flathead Indian. Early Catholic missionaries   *garb. Museum of Native American Cultures.*
among the Flatheads opposed their appearing seminude in native

plete phrase. Often the Salish closely combine two, three, or four words with the singular result that the word composed is shorter than the . . .words which made it. This . . .constitutes a richness in vocabulary unequalled by other languages.[5]

The richness of the language received a severe test when put to the music that the missionaries taught the Indians. A visiting bishop later recorded that their singing "sounded as if a dozen, at least, of harmonious wolves were scattered among the congregation." It probably resembled the war chants that were sung over the graves of the fallen, set to music with Christian words.

More Indians would have gathered around the Flathead mission had they not been occupied that fall at their customary food-gathering places. A chapel was being built with pediment, colonnade, gallery, balustrade, and choir seats, replete with lighting and an organ. Aware of the realities of Indian subsistence patterns, De Smet took his ministry to his catechumens, visiting, baptizing, educating, and indoctrinating as he went. Some had come under the influence of "American ministers," most likely those of the American Board. He knew as well as those American missionaries did that the vagaries of nomadism threatened the natives with possible extinction. Some whom De Smet met that year, such as the Kutenais, depended for survival on black moss. To De Smet's thinking, the natives' reliance on the uncertainties of nature would have to yield, albeit painfully slowly, to a sedentary agrarian economy, one of the legs on which a successful reduction could stand.

In late 1841, De Smet made a 42-day journey down the Clark Fork River to Camas Prairie and Lake Pend Oreille and over to Fort Colville, the very back door of Walker and Eells's mission. He baptized 190 persons, among whom were 26 sick and elderly Indians, and over 2,000 people heard him preach. Among evidences of faith that he saw among them were wooden crosses placed over the graves of the dead—a Christian gesture negated somewhat by nearby offerings to the dead and provisions for their journeys into the next world. Other native practices were not easily abandoned, for instance, their gambling, which at least one Catholic cleric believed to be a greater evil than liquor. At a Kalispel camp that year a white traveler found a party of braves playing cards that they had obtained from American trappers in the Snake River country.

Back on the more sacred grounds of Saint Mary's which was like the center of a halo encircling many bands, the Flatheads received baptism in December, 1841; 150 of them on Christmas Day alone. To show her favor to the Flathead tribe, the Blessed Virgin appeared in a vision to a little orphan, Paul, in the hut of an aged and pious woman. In De Smet's words, "the Flatheads merited the glorious title of true children of God." When the Flatheads, other Salish tribes, and the Nez Percés journeyed to the plains that winter, the Reverend Nicholas Point, S.J., accompanied them. Point saw in the trek, which was dedicated to Mary, an opportunity to instruct and baptize those who had not previously received that rite, providing, of course, that they showed the proper "disposition." The hunters wanted the

black robe along for his "medicine," to ensure a good hunt and to protect them from the Blackfeet. On the hunt they were so busy guarding their horses—and so concerned about returning home with their buffalo hides and their own skins intact—that they paid little attention to his words. Moreover, his "medicine" did not prevent some of them from being killed or injured, nor from stealing women from passing hands, which further isolated them from his ministrations.

During that winter's hunt the Nez Percés killed a dozen Blackfeet. Suddenly faced with annihilation at the hands of those raiders, the Kalispels rallied behind a woman, Kuilix (or Red, for the color of her robe), in the fashion of the followers of Joan of Arc, whose exploits the Indians may have learned from the French Canadians. Inspired by Kuilix's leadership, the Kalispels killed twenty-eight of the foe. The Blackfoot survivors called off their attacks against the Salish buffalo hunters for the rest of the winter, believing them protected by black robe "magic." Believing such powers were meant to protect them alone and not other children of the Great Spirit, the Salish hunters became angered at Point's insistence that they spare the Blackfeet whom they surrounded in battle. They obeyed the order most reluctantly, incensed with Point "for meddling." So incensed were they with Mengarini's concern for Blackfoot souls that on one occasion they threatened to abandon him on the plains. They might not have concurred with Point's assessment of the 1842 summer hunt as "more like a pious pilgrimage than a hunt of the ordinary kind."

The pilgrimage to buffalo may not have been pious, but it was at least picturesque. Point wrote of the natives:

Generally the Indian loves everything that flutters in the wind. Thus he wears his hair long; his horse's tail and mane are long. He loves to have hides fringed and uses colored ribbons. Every kind of fringe and feather, but especially eagle feathers, please him so much that very often he would not relinquish things of this kind for a whole world full of useful goods. And it must be admitted that in the eyes of a vain man the costume of an Indian riding through camp at full gallop is not without its charm.[6]

From the time when some Coeur d'Alênes visited the mission site in 1841 a few days after De Smet's party arrived there, it was clear that it would be a mecca for surrounding peoples. Stirred by De Smet's travels, native peoples gathered there that winter, some from considerable distances. A San Poil came from the west wishing to learn prayers that the black robe had taught the Flatheads. Before spring a Spokane band visited De Smet, expressing happiness that the "right kind of Black-gown" intended to establish a mission in their country. He had already baptized one of their dying children—in contrast to Eells and Walker, who performed the rite only on their own children. Other Salish peoples visited the mission besides the Flatheads and the Kalispels but with somewhat less zeal. Even Shoshonis and Bannocks came. The missionaries had journeyed through their lands to the Bitterroot Valley, and they had received the black robes more charitably on that journey than the Flatheads had.

The many journeys of the Indians were short compared with those of De Smet, who traveled about 180,000 miles, not only throughout the Great Plains and stretches of the intermontane West but also across the Atlantic on several occasions, seeking support for his mission. In mid-April, 1842, he baptized all the children and nine adults of a thirty-lodge Kutenai band. In his absence they had been instructed by an Iroquois, the wife of an Iroquois, and a Canadian. Accompanying him farther on his journey were a dozen Kutenai warriors and some "blood" Crees (Algonquian), whom he had baptized in 1840. At a Kalispel camp a chief of Nez Percé parentage confessed that he had killed one of his relatives, which in De Smet's view was an act prompted by the devil.

The Coeur d'Alênes were among the tribes who met De Smet. He called them "a small but interesting tribe, animated with much fervour." Most of those who met him at Lake Coeur d'Alêne were seeing a Catholic missionary for the first time. On the morning after De Smet's arrival a chief tersely addressed the visitor: "Black-gown, we come here very early to observe you — we wish to imitate what you do. Your prayer is good; we wish to adopt it." The chief's people listened to the black robe, especially the children. De Smet baptized all of the latter, along with twenty-four sick and aged adults. One of those baptized was an eighty-year-old chief, Jesse. To be sure that their people did not forget De Smet's teachings, the chiefs from time to time harangued them with reminders to keep the black robe's words.

On May 1, 1842, De Smet was again at Fort Colvile baptizing a chief and his wife, whom he named Martin and Mary. As he moved westward to minister to the living, he saw a well-accoutred burial ground and observed that many of its occupants perhaps had died outside the Christian faith. Natives on the upper Sanpoil River received his instructions and had their children baptized. Farther west many sick Okanagons came to him for baptism.

One result of De Smet's visit to Vancouver in June, 1842, was a look at Blanchet's Catholic ladder, one of which he carried back to Saint Mary's. Later he would commission a Paris publisher to print quantities of them. From the harangues of chiefs and parents, Indian families learned in their own camps more of the meaning of the missionaries' words and the pictures illustrating them. They also received visits from the fathers, who came to see that the Christian message had not been lost or watered down in transmission.

Father Point was especially eager in the follow-up work. Perhaps his greatest challenge came in November, 1842, when he began the Mission of the Sacred Heart among the Coeur d'Alênes on St. Joseph's River (St. Joe River), a tributary to Lake Coeur d'Alêne near Saint Maries, Idaho. Those Coeur d'Alênes had a tradition that one of their chiefs, Whirling Black Crow, had dreamed that a black robe would come to them. Whirling Black Crow did not live to see his dream fulfilled, but according to the tradition his son did when he met De Smet at a Flathead camp.

The Coeur d'Alênes did not enjoy the best of reputations among fur traders, whom they kept out of their lands, or among other tribes. Point himself described them as a lazy, squalid, idolatrous, gluttonous, dishonest people noted for "dissimulation, egotism, and cruelty." De Smet described them as having "great power in juggling and other idolatrous practices," a more constrained characterization than that of his neurotic coworker. Later the Coeur d'Alênes would confess to De Smet that they had venerated a calico shirt that was spotted like smallpox and a white coat. They had secured these items from the first white man in their lands in exchange for several of their best horses. Continuing their confession, they said that they had imagined the spotted shirt to be the Great Spirit Himself, the master of the smallpox scourge, and the white coat to be the Great Spirit of the Snow. They had believed that the spotted shirt would protect them from more smallpox and the coat, white like snow, would guarantee them successful winter hunts. They admitted further that they had incorporated these garments into their various rites, offering to them the great medicine pipe representing the sun, fire, earth, and water, after which they held a great dance in which they gyrated, gestured, and chanted.

With a mission in their lands, the Coeur d'Alênes were more securely drawn into the Catholic orbit than they had been earlier that year when, on February 9, 1842, one of their chiefs had visited Tshimakain with Spokane Garry and had invited Eells to teach his people. That chief represented half of his followers as favoring the priests and the other half, Walker and Eells. In Point's thinking the Coeur d'Alêne mission, like Saint Mary's, would be the focal point of a reduction where natives would cluster to receive spiritual and physical help from the fathers. Like other natives the Coeur d'Alênes found it difficult to persevere at the agrarian tasks that a reduction demanded. The nearest thing they had to an agricultural tool was a digging stick used by their women. The confinement accompanying a soil-tilling existence in time would only cause moroseness and melancholia to increase among them, as it did among other natives also. The cost and difficulty of obtaining agricultural tools were great, but that never bothered Indians as much as it did the fathers.

Point believed that the cultivation of the physical and spiritual soil was blocked by "redoubled efforts of Hell" and by strongly ingrained "tribal instinct," but that it could in time be loosened by work, faith, and reason. Before that happy day not only the natives' resistance to change but also a host of other problems (ranging from floods and enemy raids to devilish mosquitoes) caused the Mission of the Sacred Heart to be moved three times. The missions of Saint Ignatius among the Kalispels and Saint Paul among the Colviles were moved also. With Indian help the fathers labored to erect and maintain church structures. Resembling those of Europe, the church buildings stood exotically in the Pacific Northwestern wilderness, painted and protected from its sun and storms. If churches lasted longer by being painted, why, asked the Kalispel Michel, should not an Indian paint his face. The implication was that such practices would likewise ensure him longevity.

Opposition to mission progress among the Coeur d'Alênes was personalized in the behavior of such chiefs as

Stellam (Thunder). He had been skeptical of Garry's teachings as well as Point's, believing missionaries need do no more than distribute powder and tobacco among the people. It was of no small moment in enhancing his importance among his people that his lodge was the tribal distribution point for fish and game. Among the Kalispels, De Smet recorded, the chiefs distributed game from their lodges with "rigid impartiality" in addition to their other duties, which included services as marriage counselors.

Despite Stellam's recalcitrance, the Coeur d'Alênes hailed the cross, surrendering to it their fetishes more readily than their chiefs did their multiple wives, whom they acquired or lost through informally arranged transactions. On two occasions in 1843, when he thought that they were not living up to their promises, Point threatened to close the mission, as would other priests there at later times. The continued resistance of such traditionalists as Stellam helped little to ease the priestly hard line. On one occasion Stellam started a rumor that several Flatheads who received baptism had died. To save the mission, he and other chiefs were administered the sacrament, although at the time they continued their old practices of polygamy and gambling. As far as the Indians were concerned, the priests had not won a victory, only a truce. Over the years, however, that truce slowly turned to victory for the priests. Utilizing the Coeur d'Alêne tendency to isolation, the fathers guided them more deeply into farming and into the faith. One cleric maintained that Christianity was the means by which less-traditional tribesmen were induced to abandon their roving life, including the dangerous treks to hunt the buffalo. Worse than possible death at the hands of the Blackfeet, their priests told them, were the immoralities committed along the way, and worst of all the danger of dying without the sacraments of the church. After 1876, on a vow of younger tribesmen to abandon the eastward journeys, one black robe proudly hailed the Coeur d'Alênes as "the tribe which has now made the greatest advances in civilization."[7]

The clerics generally enjoyed the good will of their flocks. They did, however, face a constant danger that chiefs such as Stellam and his counterparts in every other tribe would retard if not undo the propagation of the faith. Besides this there was the omnipresent threat from nature, as moody and difficult as her children. Like a typical medieval man De Smet saw little in her to enchant him. The physical hardships that he and his colleagues endured were legion. On one occasion Blanchet nearly drowned ascending the Willamette River to visit Demers. Pacific Northwestern Indians might not have been the objects of a concerted plan for their conversion if De Smet had not escaped drowning in a Columbia River boat wreck in the spring of 1842 on the way to a meeting at Vancouver with Blanchet and Demers, or if he and other members of a Catholic reinforcement had not safely crossed the Columbia bar inbound on July 31, 1844. The *Infatigable*, the ship on which they rode, on the latter occasion entered the Columbia through a dangerous unused channel. Natives watching her entrance were so certain that she would sink that they rent their clothes in mourning for those aboard. Living up to her name and aided by "Divine Pilotage," she successfully escaped the treacherous bar. Aboriginally adorned Clatsops and Chinooks boarded her, bringing gifts of fresh salmon and potatoes, evoking from the weary passengers an evening Te Deum.

The passengers responded to the natives' welcome with considerably less cultural shock than had members of the Methodist "Great Reinforcement" at a similar reception by the natives. When their ship, the *Lausanne*, had inched across the bar on May 21, 1840, the approximately fifty passengers led by Jason Lee had been as shocked by the natives' welcome as they had been by the perils of their passage. Chinooks clambered aboard asking for "lum" (rum), with Clatsops "savage in their appearance." All were painted and singing and dancing their own kind of welcome to the passengers. The entry of the "Great Reinforcement" was made all the more ominous for its passengers by the realization that they had to compete with the Catholics for Indian souls. At that very moment at that very same place Demers was conducting his mission among the natives.

The Catholic "Reinforcement" of 1844 was not the first for its mission. De Smet had journeyed east for additional workers. In response Jesuits Peter De Vos and Adrian Hoecken had arrived in the Pacific Northwest in the fall of 1843 and with De Smet had founded Saint Michael's Mission among the Kalispels in September, 1844, on the Pend Oreille River (formerly the Clark Fork) at Kalispel Bay (in northeastern Washington near the Idaho border). In the spring of 1845 the two moved the mission a short way downriver (to a site above Cusick, Washington). There they established Saint Ignatius, which would be reestablished on September 24, 1854, at St. Ignatius, Montana. The Coeur d'Alênes got along scarcely better with Hoecken than they did with Point. The latter had been removed from the mission by his superior.

Secular priests Antoine Langlois and Jean Bolduc arrived in September, 1842, to reinforce the missions on the Willamette and Cowlitz. In March, 1843, twelve hundred Clallams, Cowichans, and Songishes (all Salishan tribes) gathered around Bolduc in the Songish village on the lower tip of Vancouver Island. The village of long, board houses and carved posts was surrounded by palisades to protect its inhabitants from nocturnal attacks by Cowichans seeking to kill the men and enslave the women and children. During the priest's visit some truce must have been in effect between the Cowichans and their Songish foes.

The Skagits controlled the mouth of their river and the central parts of Whidbey Island around Penn Cove. Several Skagits and Clallams met Bolduc on the island in late March under what must have been strained circumstances. The two peoples had long been at odds as the Clallams tried to encroach on Skagit lands. The son of the Skagit chief deferred to the priest to preach and say mass. The son's preaching and mass-saying would have amounted to a recital of religious history, while he showed his people how to make numerous signs of the cross, and the singing of a few canticles with the Kyrie eleison.

Pitching his camp near the cross that Blanchet had planted when he first landed on the island in 1840, Bolduc soon found himself engulfed in a tide of worshippers totalling seven hundred souls, largely Skagits. On March 26, 1843, at the request of several parents he baptized their children in a little meadow. The rite lasted from noon until sunset. The following day the Skagit chief, saying the priest should not be lodged in a "cotton house" (a tent), promised that, "tomorrow you must tell me in what place we shall construct thee an abode, and thou wilt see how powerful is the effect of my words when I speak to my people." The chief may have been Netlem. After his death a few years later, as well as the deaths of several of his tribesmen, the Skagits lost much of the power that the chief had flaunted. Soon two hundred workmen, dividing their labors among tree-cutting, hauling, and building, provided Bolduc a 25-by-28-foot house covered with cedar bark and floored with rush mats. During the week they heard his instructions and learned several canticles. "Without singing," observed the priest, "the best things are of little value; noise is essential to their enjoyment." At the close of his mission several natives from the mainland fell to their knees and exclaimed: "Priest, priest, during four days we have travelled to behold thee, we have walked night and day, and have scarcely tasted any food; now that we see thee our hearts are joyful, take pity on us; we have learned that there is a Master on high, but we know not how to speak to him. Come with us, thou wilt baptize our children as thou didst those of the Skadjats." Although moved by this display, Bolduc was committed to return to the Fort Nisqually area and could not respond to their plea.

Like others of the cloth, Bolduc knew that as natives sought the standard of the cross they also pursued a double one—namely, baptism for their children but hesitancy in receiving it for themselves—in the belief that prayers and canticles alone would remove from them the taint of original sin. "As soon as we touch this chord," wrote Bolduc, "their ardor is changed into indifference." "In vain," he continued, "the chieftains harangue their inferiors; how can they expect to make any impression where they are themselves the more guilty!" The best opportunities for missionary endeavor, he believed, were among the coastal peoples, such as those with whom the Reverend Joseph Menetrey, S.J., worked in Oregon in 1846, and among the tribes who were settled at the mouths of various rivers. The Reverend John H. Frost of the Methodist Great Reinforcement had experienced much disappointment at his Clatsop Mission near the mouth of the Columbia River. Under the cape bearing the name Disappointment he had put out to sea on August 21, 1843, trying to convince himself that natives of the lower Columbia were better off than when he came among them. Suffering less discouragement, Catholic missionaries in the 1850s penetrated the Umpqua Valley and other areas of the central and southern Oregon interior, as well as such areas as the Yakima country north and west of the Columbia River.

Indians of the Lower Columbia region gave ample proof to both Protestant and Catholic missionaries that they could not be easily dislodged from their traditional beliefs and practices. Their reduced numbers forced them to abandon their former large-scale wars for petty ones. They engaged in much in-fighting under the life-taking stimulus of whiskey and rum, which made them preying rather than praying men whom Lee had pictured to his superiors. He had claimed that, if the Methodist mission had done nothing else, it had stopped all petty wars from The Dalles to the sea. By contrast Dr. John Richmond of the Great Reinforcement opined that, "Extinction seems to be their inevitable doom, and their habits are such that I am fearful that they will never be reached by the gospel." De Smet, on the other hand, expressed "transports of delight" at the prospects for a harvest of Indian souls, while at the same time he was paradoxically fearful for the success of the reductions. Not even the fever raging upriver to The Cascades as late as 1844 could prevent the soul harvest: aided by the exertions of reinforcement priests, such as the Reverend John Nobili, S.J., "they all had the consolation of receiving baptism before expiring."

In 1844 the Kalispels met De Smet at a camp on Clark Fork River where the Coeur d'Alène deputation awaited his return to their Mission of the Sacred Heart, to which he went in November. The Flatheads were denied his presence during the winter of 1844–45 when ice and floods kept him from Saint Mary's. The tribes were apart on Christmas Day as were their priests. Yet they fitly observed the occasion. The entire Flathead tribe approached the "Holy Table," and twelve young Indians tutored by Mengarini performed several musical pieces during a midnight mass. At their mission the Coeur d'Alênes were permitted their first communion. After a second high mass all the Kalispels received baptism under the sponsorship of the elderly, for whom De Smet had performed the rite two years earlier. In Paraguayan fashion, which fitted Salish sex-segregation practices, men and women lined up on opposite sides to receive baptism.

In February, 1845, the Flatheads came from Saint Mary's to the Saint Ignatius Mission to meet De Smet arriving there by bark canoe. About three hundred Kalispels were present, mostly adults belonging to the station of Saint Francis Borgia near Flathead Lake (slightly north of present-day St. Ignatius, Montana). They presented themselves at the baptismal font. By July, Indians at Saint Ignatius Mission had helped to build fourteen log houses and a barn, besides preparing timber for a church. They also fenced three hundred acres of grain and raised a few hogs and domestic fowl, as well as thirty head of horned cattle. The women had learned to milk the cows and had also learned to churn butter. It was a great solace to their spiritual fathers that the number of converts there had doubled since Christmas. Among the Kalispels who visited De Smet were five headmen, including Selpisto, Stiettiedloodsho, and the prophet Chalax, who was surnamed The Juggler. The latter told De Smet that, his surname notwithstanding, he had never given himself up to "juggling" nor to deceptive practices, offering instead "his heart and soul to the Master . . . ." It was none too soon either, for three months after his baptism with the name Peter he died. Partly through The Juggler's influence De Smet had baptized three hundred of his people.

In 1845 tribes of the interior gathered around various missions, particularly those among the Flatheads, Coeur d'Alênes, Kalispels, and Kutenais. That same year the Sanpoils, Spokanes, and Okanagons were served by a resident priest from Saint Ignatius. Near Kettle Falls the Crees were served from the station of Saint Francis Regis established by De Smet in 1845. In August of that year natives of Kettle Falls joined many others to meet De Smet, who placed them in the care of Saint Paul, for whom a mission there was named. As De Smet "fished" for men, including eleven elderly ones who were borne to him on skins, the natives garnered their own harvest of salmon. Like the priests who endangered their lives in their soul harvests, the natives jeopardized theirs as they crawled over foaming water on poles to large baskets where they clubbed the salmon and threw them onto the beach. In that same year, 1845, at the request of the Indians of Kettle Falls, the Reverend Anthony Ravalli, S.J., built the first chapel in their lands. Other black robes followed him there. Some disease that raged in 1846 gave more urgency to De Smet's efforts, which he extended to Fort Okanogan and into Canada.

At the same time the natives continued to receive the ministrations of Catholic missionaries in the Willamette and Cowlitz valleys, at Fort Vancouver and Whidbey Island, and in New Caledonia. Before 1848 the Yakimas and Cayuses also received the ministrations of the priests. About six thousand Indians, French Canadians, and half bloods were served from all these missions. The continual establishment and relocation of the various missions made their presence anything but static. The Indians adjusted to the changes, for they were accustomed to shifting their domiciles with the seasons. Intermarriage among the tribes also kept their populations in flux. Keeping up with their charges challenged the fathers and also worried them because the shiftings threatened the establishment of successful reductions.

De Smet called Saint Mary's Mission "the nursery of our first missionary operations in the Far West." Of all the interior missions, it remained the most cosmopolitan. It was like a little Rome, continuing to attract not only Salish and Shahaptian peoples but also the Shoshonis, Bannocks, and even the Blackfeet. One of the Blackfoot bands was badly mauled by the Flatheads and Kalispels in the summer of 1845. Because of so many losses at the hands of Shoshonis in the Bear River country, the Blackfeet had ceased to go there. All were drawn to Saint Mary's by the power of the god of battle and black robe "medicine," which they believed had rewarded the resident Flatheads in their wars.

Some of the Blackfoot bands were recent losers in encounters with Salishan speakers. Away from the holy ground of the Marian sanctuary, Crow Indians (Siouan) handed the Blackfeet several losses, although they themselves had been battered by incessant wars. The Crows were well known for sending taunting insults at their foes with the same rapidity that they fired their missiles. Despite an alliance with the Shoshonis, they were contemptuous of western peoples, especially the fish eaters of the Columbia River. The Crow haughtiness contrasted sharply with their humility in an earlier era, when according to a centenarian Nez Percé woman they had come from the plains seeking a home among her people. When told that the country was too mountainous for them, they turned back to occupy lands between the Yellowstone and North Platte rivers until the Sioux drove them from the southern part of that area. In 1846 the Crows were very much jarred by defeat at the hands of a Flathead-Nez Percé war party. Their loss was rendered even more humiliating when a Flathead mother put a Crow to flight with a knife. The fight may have been the same reported in late July, 1846, when the Flatheads and Nez Percés were joined by a Piegan band of Small Robes. The Small Robes had closed ranks with their erstwhile foes, thanks to their wish for black robe "medicine," the ravages of an 1837 smallpox epidemic, and, not unimportantly, a common hatred of the Crows. In the fight the Small Robes as well as the Flatheads attributed the death of a Nez Percé brave to his failure to make the sign of the cross and to the failure of his people to pray before engaging in combat. Arriving at the Flathead camp one day after the fight, De Smet sent a message to the Crows to effect a reconciliation. He received no reply: the haughty plainsmen had withdrawn after burying their dead.

Continuing Nez Percé involvement in Blackfoot wars made De Smet fearful lest the Nez Percés become a spiritual drag on the Flatheads. At the same time the Nez Percés were less than enthusiastic at the Blackfeet's conversion to the faith of the priests. Black robes were especially eager to extend the faith. They realized that the diminishing buffalo herds threatened to cause ever greater conflict with potentially disastrous results to the Shahaptians, Salish, and Blackfeet alike. The Flatheads were especially threatened; they were now greatly outnumbered by approximately fourteen thousand Blackfoot souls, by De Smet's count. Shortly, the good relations that the black robes had hoped to establish between the Flatheads and the Small Robes collapsed, possibly because non-Christian elements gained control of the Piegan band. By 1848 the Small Robes had again gone to war with the Flatheads, frustrating all the more the missionaries' hopes of bringing all warring factions together under the Christian standard. During the 1860s the Flatheads killed the youthful Small Robe warrior woman Pitamakan (Running Eagle), who was that band's most noted member.[8]

Nevertheless, gestures of peace by some Blackfoot bands and the softening of some of the Flathead's revenge-seeking practices gave encouragement to the black robes. Blackfoot treachery continued. Sometime around 1849 the mid-Columbia chief Sukltalthscosum was felled by the Blackfeet after seeking to unite various interior tribes against them. They reportedly cut out his heart, cut off his limbs, and worst of all, took his once-proud head across the border to an agency in Canada.[9]

De Smet knew that the Flathead lamb would not readily lie down with the Blackfoot lion as long as the lion left his lair to raid Salish villages and as long as the huntsmen of those Salish villages continued to beard the lion on the plains. As he left Saint Mary's in 1846, De Smet prayed for a miracle to soften Blackfoot and Salish hearts and permit the establishment of mission reductions among them before they were reduced to extinction. The miracle seemed less likely on the Flathead side when those tribesmen reluctantly received the ministratons of De Smet's successor, Father Mengarini. They did not appreciate his bluntness, nor his wish to spread the gospel to the predatory Blackfeet.

Great as the Blackfoot threat was to the Indians of the Pacific Northwestern interior, it was not as great as the impending invasion of Americans. Motivated by a sense of national destiny, the Americans cast their eyes on Indian lands. Occupation of them was, in their thinking, more important than saving the souls of their original owners. Ironically, their drive to occupy Indian lands—first, west of the Cascade Mountains, then in the interior—was abetted by the Protestant missionaries who tried to prepare the Indians for their coming. It remained to be seen how the Indians, with the Protestant promotion and the Catholic protection, would respond to the American tide that was about to sweep in upon them.

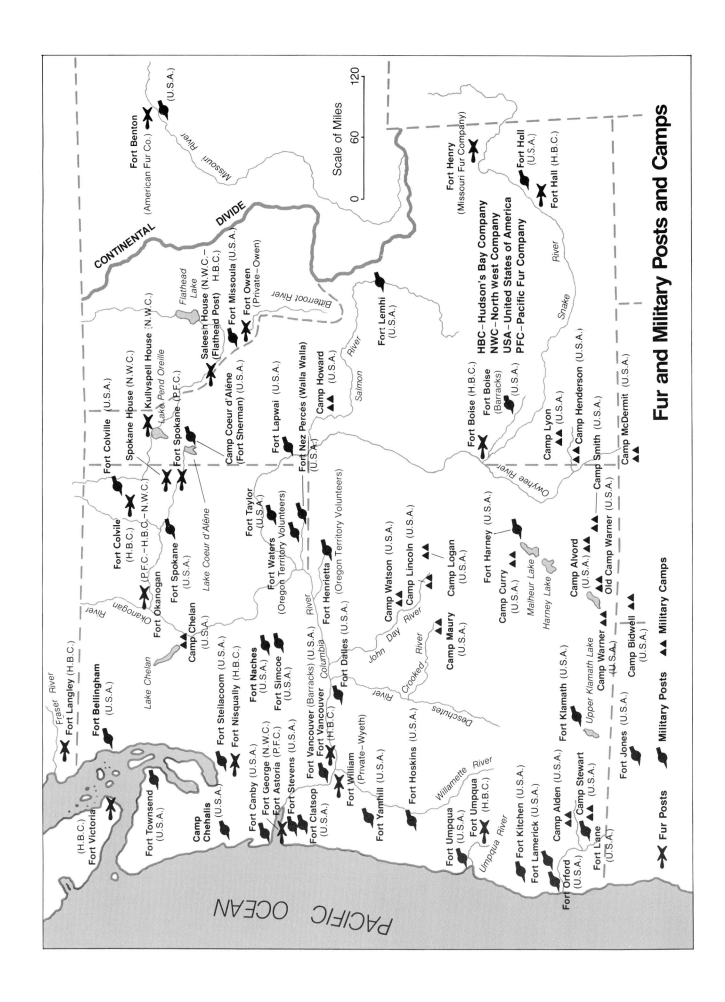

Fur and Military Posts and Camps

Scale of Miles

0   60   120

PACIFIC OCEAN

CONTINENTAL DIVIDE

HBC – Hudson's Bay Company
NWC – North West Company
USA – United States of America
PFC – Pacific Fur Company

Fort Victoria (H.B.C.)

Fort Townsend (U.S.A.)

Fort Bellingham (U.S.A.)

Camp Chehalis (U.S.A.)

Fort Langley (H.B.C.)

Fraser River

Fort Steilacoom (U.S.A.)
Fort Nisqually (H.B.C.)

Fort Naches (U.S.A.)
Fort Simcoe (U.S.A.)

Fort Canby (U.S.A.)
Fort George (N.W.C.)
Fort Astoria (P.F.C.)
Fort Stevens (U.S.A.)
Fort Clatsop (U.S.A.)

Fort Vancouver (Barracks) (U.S.A.)
Fort Vancouver (H.B.C.)

Fort William (Private–Wyeth)

Fort Yamhill (U.S.A.)

Fort Hoskins (U.S.A.)

Willamette River

Fort Umpqua (U.S.A.)
Fort Umpqua (H.B.C.)
Umpqua River

Fort Orford (U.S.A.)

Fort Kitchen (U.S.A.)
Fort Lamerick (U.S.A.)

Camp Alden (U.S.A.)
Camp Stewart (U.S.A.)
Fort Lane (U.S.A.)

Fort Klamath (U.S.A.)

Upper Klamath Lake

Fort Jones (U.S.A.)

Camp Bidwell (U.S.A.)

Lake Chelan

Camp Chelan (U.S.A.)

Fort Okanogan (P.F.C.–H.B.C.–N.W.C.)
Okanogan River

Fort Colvile (H.B.C.)
Fort Colville (U.S.A.)

Fort Spokane (U.S.A.)

Spokane House (N.W.C.)
Fort Spokane (P.F.C.)
Kullyspell House (N.W.C.)
Lake Pend Oreille

Lake Coeur d'Aléne

Camp Coeur d'Alène (Fort Sherman) (U.S.A.)

Fort Taylor (U.S.A.)

Fort Waters (Oregon Territory Volunteers)

Fort Lapwai (U.S.A.)

Fort Nez Percés (Walla Walla) (U.S.A.)

Camp Howard (U.S.A.)

Saleesh House (N.W.C.– Flathead Post) H.B.C.

Fort Missoula (U.S.A.)
Fort Owen (Private–Owen)

Flathead Lake

Bitterroot River

Salmon River

Fort Lemhi (U.S.A.)

Fort Benton (American Fur Co.) (U.S.A.)

Missouri River

Fort Henry (Missouri Fur Company)

Fort Hall (U.S.A.)
Fort Hall (H.B.C.)

Snake River

Fort Boise (H.B.C.)
Fort Boise (Barracks) (U.S.A.)

Owyhee River

Camp Lyon (U.S.A.)

Camp Henderson (U.S.A.)

Camp Smith (U.S.A.)

Camp McDermit (U.S.A.)

Fort Henrietta (Oregon Territory Volunteers)

Fort Dalles (U.S.A.)

Columbia River

Deschutes River

John Day River

Crooked River

Camp Watson (U.S.A.)
Camp Lincoln (U.S.A.)
Camp Logan (U.S.A.)
Camp Maury (U.S.A.)

Fort Harney (U.S.A.)

Camp Curry (U.S.A.)

Malheur Lake
Harney Lake

Camp Alvord (U.S.A.)
Camp Warner (U.S.A.)
Old Camp Warner (U.S.A.)

Military Posts   Military Camps

Fur Posts

9. AMERICAN SETTLERS AND UNSETTLED INDIANS

It is not known when Pacific Northwestern natives first saw white settlers on their lands. The stories of the first settlements are shrouded in mystery like so many other traditional tales on the hazy borderline between fact and fancy. Natives had a tradition that four men escaped from a Spanish galleon which wrecked near the mouth of the Columbia River sometime around the middle of the eighteenth century. It was believed that they traveled up the Columbia to The Cascades or The Dalles, where they married native women and settled down. Tradition also tells of other sailors who were shipwrecked or abandoned their craft to live among the natives of the Northwest Coast. A white man living east of the northern Puget Sound city of Bellingham, Washington, in July, 1908, told of cutting a tree on which was carved the name Gilhinly Killan beneath 145 rings of annual growth. Killan appeared to have settled there around 1750, about one hundred years before white men were known to have been in the area.[1] Tradition also has it that about 1812 a free trapper named Montour drifted into the Willamette Valley and established himself on what later became French Prairie. After farming there and making convenient alliances with native women, he abandoned the place around 1826 when, with the arrival of another settler, he found it too crowded for him.

The Hudson's Bay Company tried to keep its French-Canadian exemployees out of the Willamette Valley, but had little legal power to do so. Around 1831 and 1832 there were at least three former employees of the fur company living there with Indian women. A half dozen years later there were about fourteen such families. The Indian women helped to attract and hold the French Canadians in the valley because they did much of the white's work, having been purchased as slaves from valley natives, who shunned white men's work. A white visitor in 1841 reported a Mr. Johnson living above Willamette Falls with two such "slaves."

Those early settlers found themselves among a native population as primitive as the Indians along the coast. Having abandoned some of the more elaborate pit houses of an earlier era, Willamette Valley natives at the time of white contact lived in simple, often temporary structures of bark and boards, sometimes covered with skins and blankets. Their clothing, like that of the coastal natives, was sparse until the missionaries in the 1830s tried to put more covering on them. Their food was easily obtained. Larger animals, such as deer, were corralled in large circular hunts, or surrounds, and driven to central points where bowmen dispatched them. The natives also ate fish, a variety of small game, and even insects, such as tent caterpillars and whole wasps' nests. The only crop that they planted was a native tobacco. They also prepared black, sweet-tasting foxtail tubers to trade to coastal peoples, such as the Umpqua bands, for sugar-pine nuts. It was their practice to burn prairies and woodlands to clear them for hunts and to stimulate the growth of roots and berries. That practice produced conflict with white settlers in the valley and later with forestry officials in the mountains, where the Indians burned off timbered areas to hunt and graze animals without permits. In contrast to the natives below Willamette Falls and on the lower Columbia and its navigable tributaries, the upper-Willamette tribes were reported as having no canoes in the early nineteenth century. Unlike interior peoples coming into the valley to hunt, they had no horses and crossed the river on large reed bundles.

The Willamette natives' life-styles seemed crude to whites; yet before the advent of the whites their food supplies were more ample and secure than those of natives in other areas, including much of the interior and even the Columbia River Valley, where the salmon runs sometimes failed. As the nineteenth century progressed, the food supply on the Willamette became increasingly threatened. Fur hunters stripped the area of game, and after 1828 the Hudson's Bay Company accepted contracts with the Russian American Company for grains. Thus the natives' land base began to alter. At the same time the French Canadians were enlarging their farms, reducing still further the lands on which the natives had traditionally depended for survival.[2]

The diminution of food supplies was not the only factor causing the decline of Willamette Valley natives. As noted, epidemics, such as the Intermittent Fever in 1829 and 1830, devastated the native populations. In 1838 there were but 1,200 Kalapooian speakers, in 1841 but 600, and in 1844 but 300. Among the many problems facing the Methodist mission was the difficulty of operating in the midst of this decline. When white settlements in the valley reached sizable proportions in the 1840s, the few natives left there could hardly contest it. They suffered a fate not unlike that of their predecessors, the Multnomahs (Chinookan), who according to tradition, grew peaceful by residence in the valley and had to give way in the eighteenth century to the more aggressive Kalapooian peoples sweeping up from the south. Like other restless peoples settling in river valleys, the Kalapooias also became sedentary, which made them targets for warlike western and southern coastal tribes, who swept over the valley to rob and plunder as much as to kill. On at least one occasion around 1810 the Kalapooias were said to have laid aside their peaceful stance to battle the Klamaths and repulse them from the valley. Starvation and disease rendered them powerless to resist white encroachment and caused them to suffer a loss of spirit as well as a breakdown of tribal organization and customs. Even though whites had not disturbed the land base of such tribes

Be-ell, an Indian of the Kalapooian-speaking Yoncalla tribe of the Willamette Valley in Oregon.

as the Klamaths, Rogues, and Modocs, their diseases killed off many of them, helping to prepare the way for white occupation of their lands.

As native populations declined, Americans prepared to move into the vacuum created by the native's deterioration. They were stimulated by glowing reports, especially of the Willamette Valley and its soils, coming from the lips and pens of Protestant missionaries and other Americans. American expansionist thought had been conditioned even before the missionary era by Hall Kelley's impassioned writings and by petitions to Congress for American occupation of the region. Official government surveys followed. As noted, the survey of Lieutenant William A. Slacum revealed much about the country and its natives. Like most other American reports his was nationalistic in tone—good reading for his countrymen, whose growing sense of national destiny made some of them eager to claim the continent for the United States. Like Jason Lee, Slacum minimized the dangers of Indian conflict as an obstacle to American expansion, noting that the numbers of the Willamette natives had greatly dwindled.

Like natives in other parts of America the Indians of the Pacific Northwest had little knowledge of Anglo-American policies pertaining to their own lands. They often did not know to which country the ships arriving on the coast belonged. When the American brig *Loriot* carrying Lieutenant Slacum was chopping at anchor in Bakers Bay one December day in 1836, Chinook Indians coming aboard asked, "Is this 'King George' or 'Boston' ship?" When H. M. S. *Sulphur* crossed the bar on July 29, 1839, the natives were so long conditioned to trading with white men from ships that they did not understand that the mission of the men on board was to survey the lower Columbia for Britain. Wishing to remain on good terms with local natives, especially in the light of increasing Anglo-American rivalry over the region, the *Sulphur's* crew entertained aboard ship royal Chinook and Chehalis personages, for whom special rooms and cabins were provided.

From the *Sulphur's* assistant surgeon, Dr. Richard Brinsley Hinds, we have a most intimate account of lower-river peoples at the time of the first American immigrations. Hinds visited the house of Comcomly's successor, Chenamus. The powers of the new chief were modest despite the assertion of two visiting white men that he held sway over tribes west of the Cascade Mountains from southern Oregon to Puget Sound. If he did not have power, he did have pomp. He sat at the rear of his long house on a platform, backdropped by a board painted in rings of high relief. Behind that was a gigantic red and black figure, against which he customarily sat to ward off evil spells. The figure indicated that the natives at least maintained an outward show of traditional religious beliefs. Hinds learned, however, from the Fort George company manager, James Birnie, that, "the prosperity of Europeans had struck deeply at the root of their customs." This was Hinds's way of saying that time and Pacific tides had brought increased numbers of foreigners and their culture to the natives' shores, causing a waning of the old ways and crafts, such as the carving of wooden images like that adorning Chenamus's house.

When natives of Cape Flattery boarded the ship carrying the American naval lieutenant Charles Wilkes in the summer of 1841, they were surprised that so large a vessel had not come for furs. Moreover, they could not understand the purpose of a man-of-war—which they would come to know only too well in those northern waters in years to come. Wilkes tabulated about twenty thousand native souls in the region, including those of Vancouver Island, the adjacent mainland, and the Blackfeet, who in his opinion were no hindrance to American settlement. Of particularly little hindrance were the Indians of lower Puget Sound, the lower Columbia River, and the Willamette—the regions where Americans were most likely to settle. Natives in more remote areas were not always so friendly. In the Rogue River country one of them fired on a member of the Wilkes expedition for cutting up a deer. In return a naval officer summarily shot and killed the native.

Wilkes pictured the natives as relatively harmless because of their weakness for gambling, laziness, squalor, the institution of slavery, and continuing petty feuds. He

Interior of a Chinook lodge. From a sketch by A. T. Agate with the United States exploring expedition in the early 1840s under Lieutenant Charles Wilkes, U.S.N. Reproduced from Charles Wilkes, U.S.N., Narrative of the United States Exploring Expedition During the Years 1838, 1839, 1840, 1841, 1842.

believed that they had also been rendered harmless by the exertions of the Hudson's Bay Company, whom he complimented for having checked the liquor trade.[3] In this effort the company had been assisted by Methodist missionaries and by the Oregon Provisional Government. That body had been organized by American settlers in the Willamette Valley and patterned on American governments in the East. Established in 1843, it provided law and order and authorized land claims until the United States extended its jurisdiction over the region. With little or no consultation with native inhabitants, law-abiding citizens were assured possession of 640-acre sections if they recorded metes and bounds, improved the property within six months, and resided on it within a year. In 1845, with grudging Hudson's Bay Company participation, the government's territory extended from Mexican lands in the south to Russian lands in the north. In 1844 it passed a law forbidding the importation or introduction of ardent spirits and the erections of distilleries. All violations were subject to fines. With continued American occupation, arrests of those selling liquor to Indians were numerous; convictions, few.*

*When Jason Lee organized a temperance society to save natives from extinction from drink, Ewing Young (who had proven the stock-raising potential of the Willamette Valley) abandoned his liquor still under McLoughlin's urging. He had salvaged the equipment for it from Wyeth's deserted Fort William. Nevertheless, liquor continued to be sold to natives in a no man's land under the Anglo-American joint occupation of Oregon.

Wilkes believed the efforts of Methodist missionaries among the Indian remnant in the Willamette Valley to have failed. He offered the suggestion that they shift their operations further north to Puget Sound and the Strait of Juan de Fuca, where they could do the Indians more good. Even the once-feared Casino was pictured by Wilkes as having come so much under the influence of Fort Vancouver and having lost so much influence over Indians that, instead of using his canoe flotillas for war as he once had, he was reduced to having his Indians carry passengers and messages up and down rivers and thus posed no threat to American immigrants. Just below the Columbia-Cowlitz confluence were the once fastidiously kept sepulchres at Coffin Rock. Canoes holding dead bodies lay on the summit, where offerings of cloth ornaments, baskets, and other utensils hung atop poles. They were, in Wilkes's words, "fast going to decay as [were] the living." In earlier times desecration of that much-noticed place would have stung natives to bodily retaliation against its violators. When one of Wilkes's party accidentally set fire to the rock, the action did little more than anger the survivors of the dead. Desecrations of sacred burials in the Cascades–Dalles area became more evident with increased travel by whites. De Smet reported in 1846 that Christian travelers had stolen the very boards covering the dead, leaving them prey to crows and vultures.

Before the publication of Wilkes's narrative in 1845, Americans had been seeking routes over which to emigrate to this faraway land about which they were hearing so much. The Western portions of routes to the region had been proved possible by such early traders as the Astorian Wilson Price Hunt. In 1811 and 1812, Hunt had blazed a path to Oregon utilizing the strategic South Pass to breach the Rockies. There remained the problem of conducting wagons along the far-western portions of that route to the Pacific. In 1840 three Indian women and several children were in a party that included mountain men Robert Newell, William Craig, and Joe (or Joesph) Meek. The group took wagons from Fort Hall and Fort Boise over the Blue Mountains to Fort Walla Walla.

In 1839, Farnham's Peoria Party, who were supposedly the first Americans to emigrate to Oregon, straggled through the lands of the Bannocks, whom Farnham viewed as a treacherous and dangerous race, especially to foot-weary travelers such as the splintered remnant of his original party, who were plodding on without benefit of wagons. Contempt of Digger Paiutes below Fort Boise did not prevent one group of Peorians from purchasing from them a bale of well-processed salmon for three knives.

The immigration of over a hundred whites in 1842 may be considered the first of the 1840s, a decade in which about twelve thousand Americans traversed Indian country in their "walking lodges" to settle farther west in the Willamette Valley. As might be expected, their arrival caused great consternation among the natives along their route and in the Willamette terminus. At the very time when the 1842 immigration was moving toward the end of its long journey, rumors were rife that aggressive tribesmen of the interior—Cayuses, Wallawallas, and Nez Percés—were about to take to the warpath against the embryonic Willamette white settlement, from which the expanding white population threatened the existence of the Willamette natives and the natives of the interior. From their experience with Whitman and Spalding, the interior tribes already had a preview of the troubles that could develop over ownership of their lands. Rumors continued to circulate among the Cayuses that Whitman would bring fifty soldiers to the Pacific Northwest to fight them. If this were true, they vowed to attack mission stations and settlements in the Willamette Valley. At Fort Walla Walla, which was the scene of increased tension between Indians and traders, security was tightened. In late October, 1842, during her husband's visit to the United States, an Indian tried to assault Mrs. Whitman, causing her to flee to the Methodist mission at The Dalles.

In the following month, November, 1842, snow-capped Mount Saint Helens, known to the Yakimas as Low-wenat Klah (Throwing Up Smoke), scattered smoke and blew ashes. Was the mountain god expressing anger at his children? Or, like a Sinai in the Oregon wilderness, was it saluting the American Moses, Dr. Elijah White?[4] White was commissioned as Indian agent for the territory west of Iowa. He was en route from the Willamette to the interior to hand down the law to the natives there; in essence, to control them and to provide means for punishing offenses hampering American settlement. The Cayuses were scattered in the

Walla Walla Valley at the time of his arrival and were understandably less than enthusiastic over his statutes. More tractable, yet frightfully caparisoned, the Nez Percés ratified the laws in December and bade farewell to White as he began his journey to the Willamette, his task only partially completed.

To complete the lawgiving and to calm the Wallawallas, Cayuses, and Nez Percés, whom he called "the only three tribes from which much is to be hoped, or anything to be feared, in this part of Oregon"—White revisited those tribes the following spring. He found the Cayuses "brave, active, tempestuous, and war-like...independent in manner" and often "boisterous, saucy, and troublesome in language and behavior." He found the more numerous but less affluent Wallawallas not much different. The Nez Percés were noble in every American's book, but, in White's thinking, could become "contaminated" and cause trouble because of intermarriage and other contacts with the Cayuses and Wallawallas.

The Cayuses accepted the laws reluctantly. One of their chiefs stated that Indians wanted something more tangible. When he was informed that the laws were recognized by God, Wallawalla Chief Peopeomoxmox (Yellow Serpent) was happy that he would not have to go to hell for whipping his people as some of them had said he would. On May 24, 1843, the chiefs approved the laws, after witnessing an object lesson in the need for law and order when an Indian dented the head of a Hawaiian named John with the wadding from his rifle.

It would be wrong to think that before accepting White's legislation the three tribes were without laws, although some travelers at that time (including the visitors in the Pacific Northwest) believed that all Indians were lawless except for brief periods. Dr. Hinds, for instance, wrote that the Chinooks "appeared to live under no government or proper controls." More permanent observers among them noted their long-standing moral codes and rules, over which lay restrictions and taboos more numerous and strict than those of societies supposedly more civilized. Overlaying those structures, among some natives, were those handed down by fur traders and later by missionaries. An examination of White's laws reveals a silence on matters pertaining to adultery, about which the three peoples had traditionally strict codes. Instead, White's code dealt with such things as murder, theft, and destruction of property. The punishment for anyone who willfully took a life or burned a dwelling was death by hanging—a provision strange indeed to Indian families, who punished murderers by retaliation in kind or by exacting payment from their people for lives taken. Illegally entering a dwelling (for the white man, his castle) was forbidden under White's code. Such an entry never annoyed natives, who intermingled closely in extended family villages. Peering through windows or failing to knock on the doors of white men's houses before entering seemed no breach of etiquette to these people living in tipis, who had borrowed this type of dwelling with some variation from Plains tribes.

In order to enforce the laws, Dr. White urged the Indians to choose head chiefs to assume responsibility for them, as government officials would subsequently urge for the sake of expediency. Chiefs had assumed specialized responsibilities before, for instance, in times of emergency. But now they were being compelled to impose group control, punish nonconformists, and act as official spokesmen for the groups in various matters. Before the coming of settlers, fur companies had also preferred to work with tribes through individual spokesmen. Running counter to traditional native policies, White and his successors were laying the foundation for intratribal jealousy and strife in Indian dealing with white men. White was apparently oblivious to this; it was simply his wish to deal with individual spokesmen rather than numerous chiefs, whom it would prove difficult to bring around to the Americans' point of view.

Under White's direction the Nez Percés elected as head chief Ellis, the former Red River Mission scholar. Like Spokane Garry his association with white men was an important consideration in his election. As the first head chief of all the Nez Percés in their history, he diligently sought to impose the new legal order, until measles took his life on a buffalo hunt. Although his election appeared on the surface to be a unifying force, it further widened the division between the Nez Percé Christians and the non-Christian bloc under the influence of Looking Glass. In 1848, Lawyer assumed the position after the chieftaincy of one named Richard. Also elected under White's direction was Young Chief of the Cayuses. That tribe's governance had previously rested among three chiefs. Young Chief immediately deferred to Five Crows (Achekaia, or the similar-sounding Hezekiah), the possessor of many wives, slaves, and cattle and a recent Spalding convert.

White must have believed that his laws were timely, for in that same year, 1843, nearly a thousand immigrants traveled the Immigrant Road from Independence, Missouri, to The Dalles. By 1848 about ten times that number had traversed the route—the Oregon Trail. Their passage through Indian lands worked hardships both on them and on the natives. In their haste to traverse the country, especially between Fort Hall and Fort Boise, where alkali dust and sand swirled across an ever more deeply rutted road, immigrants gave little heed to the effect of their passage on the Indians. Their guns killed or frightened game, and their livestock consumed the grasses.

At best natives of the region were hard pressed to find subsistence. Contributing to their hunger was the disappearance of the last vestiges of the buffalo from west of the Rockies. Hunters were forced to confront Plains tribes east of the mountains, creating not only competition for the animals but also shifting alliances among the tribes. Disastrous defeats had kept Blackfeet out of the Snake River country. Thus the Shoshonis, who were not parties to White's laws, were free to prey on the immigrants, forcing them to move in larger trains for safety. Such depredations caused Lieutenant John C. Frémont and his party of United States Topographical Engineers in 1843 to move along the road with an eye to locating fortifications to secure it from Indian attacks.

Despite occasional troubles from Indians travel was safer for the immigrants of the early forties than it would be later when the red men had suffered more greatly from American migrations and responded more violently to them. Many times during the early migrations the fish- and root-eating natives along the Snake at such spots as Salmon Falls (halfway between Fort Hall and Fort Boise) provided the immigrants salmon from the runs that gave that place its name. The salmon runs saved not only many trail-weary travelers from starvation in the late-summer or early-fall seasons but also the Indians themselves. Had immigrants not negotiated that stretch of trail, they would have perished or, at best, become like its natives, whom one immigrant called "the filthiest, most depraved, and degraded creatures, any where to be found among the dregs of human nature."

Along the stretch of road running west from the Snake River where it begins its northwesterly arc to join the Columbia, natives of the Burnt and Powder river countries sought to acquire the immigrants' goods, especially ammunition, for which they had little to trade, since beaver, which formerly were used in such exchanges, had been virtually wiped out of their country. Farther along the road—west of the rugged Blue Mountains, over which the road passed from the Grande Ronde Valley—Cayuse Indians on the Umatilla River traded horses from their numerous herds for worn-out cattle. They also traded fish and vegetables so that the immigrants could gird themselves to continue straggling towards the Columbia River. Cayuse chiefs were known to offer their daughters as wives to immigrant men whether the latter were married or not. The statement of the guidebook writer Lansford W. Hastings that the Cayuses were a "villanous and treacherous race of thieves," is, of course, overdrawn.[5] It was the practice of the Indians to cut stock from wagon trains with an eye to reselling it. They regarded this as legitimate pay for the consumption of pasturage on Indian lands.

Nursed from childhood on stories of Indian wars and strained by their journey through Indian country, the immigrants, who were mostly frontiersmen, expected the worst from natives along the way. They knew scarcely more about the natives of the Pacific Northwest than the latter knew about them. The plethora of emigrant guidebooks dumped on the market to intensify the Oregon Fever was generally silent on how to deal with Indians. If the writers and other promoters of Oregon emigration had stressed the Indian dangers, it would have frightened people from hazarding the journey. In the advice for readers, oxen were recommended not only as the best means of locomotion but also as the animal least likely to be driven off by Indians. Emigrants were told to travel in companies small enough not to arouse Indian suspicions but large enough for the common defense. It was recommended that they avoid the appearance of fear and show no familiarity with the red men. Presents were to be given not for placation but for peace. In order not to frighten readers, guidebook writers often described Indians along the way as "friendly," although Lansford Hastings warned that the term friendly when used by mountaineers to describe Indians implied only that they were not arrayed in armed and hostile opposition to whites.[6]

Arriving at The Dalles in exhausted and starving condition, travelers were hardly in a position to judge the natives there and on the lower-Columbia route to the Willamette. The character of some immigrants was not improved by their long journey, and they exerted a bad moral influence on their native hosts. Traveling under less strain in 1846, De Smet with a judgmental twitch described those Indians as dwelling in "a few poor huts, constructed of rush, bark, bushes, or of pine branches, sometimes covered with skins or rags—around these miserable habitations...[surrounded by] bones of animals and the offal of fishes of every tribe, amidst accumulated filth of every description." He said they were a people whose hands fulfilled "in rapid succession, the varied functions of the comb, the pocket-handkerchief, the knife, fork, and spoon—while eating... loudly indicated by the crackling and discordant sounds that issue from the nose, mouth, throat, etc., a sight, the bare recollection of which is enough to sicken any person."[7]

The Dalles had long been a native mart and a resting place for travelers and their goods. It became in the 1840s a new kind of thoroughfare where immigrants and Indians met, in De Smet's words, "for the purpose of affording mutual aid." Indians had goods and services to offer the immigrants arriving there, who were in need of food, horses, canoes, and guides. As Indians hired out to carry immigrants and their effects across the often-dangerous rivers between the Snake and the Deschutes, those of The Dalles hired out to perform similar service on the Columbia, which was the most dangerous leg of the immigrants' journey of nearly two thousand miles. The precipitous cliffs on the Columbia forced them to take to the river, sometimes on driftwood rafts.

The revenues earned at The Dalles had considerable effect on the outward appearance of its natives. They went from their summer-and-fall near nakedness of preimmigrant days to an opposite extreme, adorning themselves most ludicrously in highly priced shirts, tights, dresses, and even ladies' old-fashioned frilly night caps, atop which they sometimes set sailors' glazed caps. Boots and brogans now occasionally covered their bare feet, which normally carried them surefootedly over the treacherous rocky stretches of that country. Atop copious accretions of fish oil, the women loaded themselves with calico gowns, vests, flannels, and heavy overcoats. Pairs of pantaloons and vests obtained from immigrants helped the Indians to purchase slaves, who were brought up from the south and sold at The Dalles; or, if an Indian were not fortunate enough to have such items to purchase a slave, he could secure one for a horse, six beaver skins or two blankets. At one time Paiute boy and girl slaves were sold at The Dalles to the Yakimas and other natives for six or seven horses or a good canoe.

The Dalles most aptly fitted De Smet's description of it as a "kind of masquerading thoroughfare where emigrants and Indians meet." In the summer of 1845, Yakima chiefs Kamiakin and Showaway (Ice), stopped off there en route to the Willamette to sell their horses, as did Ellis, homebound

from trading horses for cattle in that valley. Around the middle of the century a horse was exchanged in the interior above The Dalles for six blankets worth ten dollars apiece.

When they reached Fort Vancouver, immigrants benefited from McLoughlin's well-known hospitality and benevolence. In fact, his efforts on their behalf preceded their arrival. It was his practice to send orders to the company traders along "the communication" from Fort Walla Walla to Fort Boise and Fort Hall not to let immigrants suffer and urging the company officials to teach the Indians to treat travelers kindly. Indians had little trouble distinguishing immigrants from company men and sometimes stole from traveling Americans at The Dalles and The Cascades as their predecessors had from fur men before the advent of the Hudson's Bay Company. In 1843 when some American stragglers reached Fort Vancouver in canoes, the white-haired factor patriarch chided an Indian who wished to kill the "Bostons," and he chided others at The Dalles, calling them dogs for expressing a similar wish.

The enervation of Kalapooian speakers in the Willamette Valley, induced by their decline, was interpreted by the white community as lethargy to such an extent that, when other Oregon tribes were called lazy, they responded that they were not of Kalapooian stock. White immigration did not in any way check the decline of other Willamette peoples. The Clackamas, who were estimated by Lewis and Clark in 1806 at 1,800 souls, had dwindled to less than 100 by the middle of the century. The immigrants had little previous exposure to these native populations; unlike fur traders and missionaries, they had not seen their demise, only its consequences. Moreover, most appeared to be little concerned with it. Although not subscribing to the punishment-of-God concept, many believed the decline of the Indians to be ordained by a higher power and would have agreed with the commissioners of the Oregon Provisional Government, who stated in 1844: "This country has been populated by powerful Indian tribes, but it has pleased the Great Dispenser of human events to reduce them to mere shadows of their former greatness. Thus removing the chief obstruction to the entrance of civilization, and opening a way for the introduction of Christianity where ignorance and idolatry have reigned uncontrolled for many ages."

Those who lived intimately with the natives for years, such as Joseph Gervais, would not have agreed with that assessment. During plagues he watched the occupants of several lodges die of fevers and starvation, infants sucking the breasts of dead mothers and adults on occasion choking their children to death for hindering their mothers from digging the roots that were the chief source of food. Before the plague of the 1830s infanticides and abortions did not seriously disturb the maintenance of stable native populations. Carried over into the plague and postplague periods, such practices were a threat to the very survival of many tribes.

By the time of the coming of American immigrants conflict between the red and white races in the Pacific Northwest had been minimized not only by the decreased numbers of the Indians but also by the Hudson's Bay Company, whose policies were enlightened (with some lapses) and firm. The American community arrived with little such understanding, tolerance, or need to conduct mutually agreeable relations with the Indians. Thus tense situations were created, such as the Cockstock affair of 1844.* A Wasco Indian, Cockstock, according to one account, was angered that one of his relatives had been sentenced by the Wascos to be punished according to the laws of Dr. White for mistreating the Reverend H. K. W. Perkins at The Dalles. With a band of young Molala braves Cockstock rode around the village at Willamette Falls frightening women and children and taunting the Methodist missionaries who reprimanded him for his misbehavior. On March 4 his anger was deepened by some dispute involving a land claim and by the reported implications of his involvement in an Indian killing that had resulted from his provoking a quarrel between Klamaths and Molalas over acceptance of White's laws. He and four Molalas rode into the village at Willamette Falls armed with guns, bows, and arrows. They had no thought of making their vendetta public by attacking the settlement, which had mills belonging to Americans and Dr. McLoughlin, as well as several stores, shops, a schoolhouse, a public library, doctors, lawyers, and all other requisites for a successful frontier community.

Resisting arrest, Cockstock was butted to death by a gun muzzle, or killed by gunfire according to some accounts. In the fracas two settlers were also killed; one by gunshot, the other by poisoned arrow. The response to the affair was immediate in both the white and Indian communities. The whites anticipating Indian retaliation, organized with the authorization of the government a mounted rifle company, the Oregon Rangers. Using the ancient method of covering the dead, Dr. White placated Cockstock's widow with two blankets, a dress, and a handkerchief in lieu of making restitution to her people. Then with others of the American community he waited, fearing similar troubles from nonresident Indians, who continued to gather around the settlements to satisfy a labor shortage. During slack periods the whites regarded these Indians as a nuisance.

As long as Indians remained in the valley, they disputed the white man's encroachment on their lands, but it should be remembered that the encroachment of native tribes on each other's lands antedated the white man's coming. The natives' anguish at the loss of their lands was voiced by one elderly woman; pointing an accusing finger at some settlers who had appropriated the lands of her people, she cried:

*As might be expected, there is considerable discrepancy among the accounts of the Cockstock incident. Among the references that record it from its many sources is Charles H. Carey, *General History of Oregon Through Early Statehood*, pp. 521–24.

"Before the white men came, we owned all the country; we hunted, fished and dug camas where we liked, but the white man has taken our hunting grounds and will not even let us dig camas. Now the poor Indians will starve." Sometimes chiefs, unsanctioned by their people, signed agreements with white men to take claims on Indians lands. One such arrangement was made between an Indian chief, Wanaxka, and a Major Robert Moore for a mile-square tract up and down the Willamette River opposite Oregon City, where Dr. McLoughlin claimed a similar-sized tract. On the death of his wife, who never came west, the major had to relinquish half his claim.

The concept of cultivated farms was alien to the natives. Also alien to them was the concept of individual land ownership sanctioned by the laws of the Oregon Provisional Government permitting whites to occupy sections if metes and bounds were established and if properties were improved within six months and occupied for a year. In implementing these acts there were many Indian-white confrontations, most of which went unrecorded. In 1845 and 1846 settlers ran off Indians in the Santiam Valley, a Willamette tributary and appropriated their lands, to which they never returned. Helping to condition Indians to a grudging acceptance of the white man's land practices were the French Canadians who established farms for themselves and their families. Sometimes Indians negotiated formal arrangements with whites, receiving pay for their lands in produce and other commodities. Nevertheless, there were numerous conflicts between Indians and settlers over the land. Exercising considerable conscience, Oregon Provisional Governor George Abernethy asked the Legislative Assembly: "Cannot some method be devised by which their villages can be surveyed, and stakes set, inside of which whites may not be permitted to enter and build. The Indians inhabited their villages previous to our arrival, and should be protected by us." About all that Abernethy could do was await the arrival of agents of the United States and hope that they could solve the problem.

By the middle forties not only the natives of the Willamette and its tributaries had discovered settlers on their lands but also those in more remote areas such as the Umpqua River Valley. The Hudson's Bay Company men at their station on that river were alarmed that settlers were causing its natives to shift locations and neglect their hunting, thus creating a poor business climate at the post.

In the Umpqua Valley, as well as in other remote areas on both sides of the Cascade Mountains, natives stood aloof, restive and warlike, vowing to resist the encroaching white men. Had not the white men, their diseases, and their liquor destroyed the Indians of the lower Columbia and Willamette? To keep their vow, some of them would shortly kill and be killed.

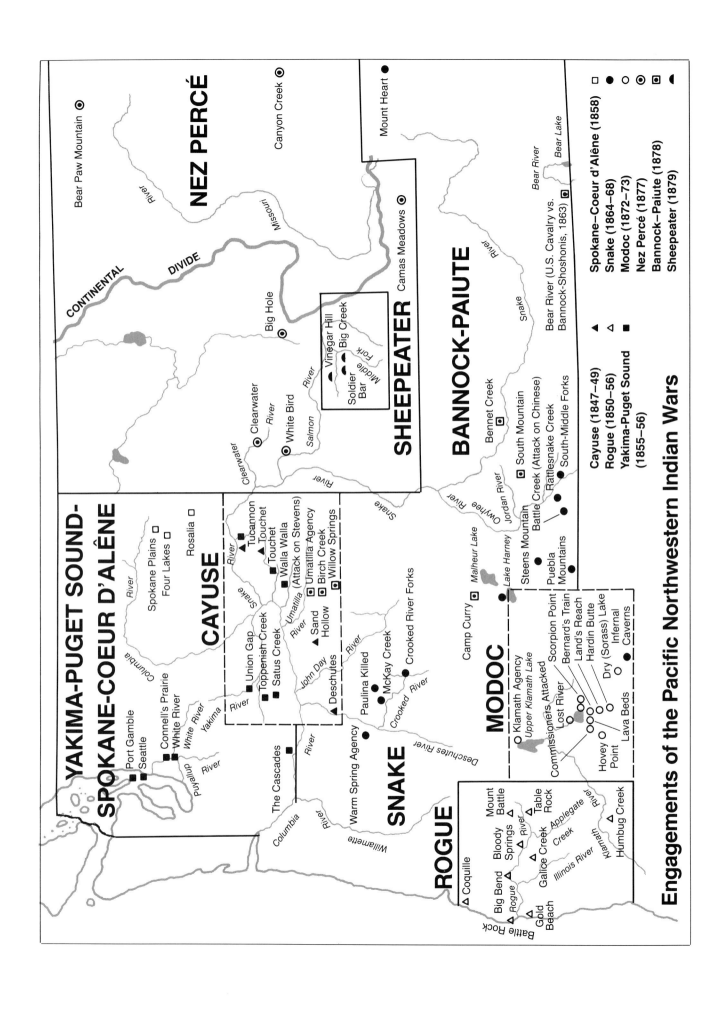

Engagements of the Pacific Northwestern Indian Wars

10. BLOOD IN THE RYE GRASS

The quiet summer of 1844 belied the increasing discontent among the Indians of the interior. The restraining hand of some Cayuse and Wallawalla chiefs was absent; they had gone to California to trade furs and horses for cattle. In the absence of his chieftain father a young Cayuse and other young braves rode to The Dalles to raid the people there. Back at Waiilatpu mission the son called on Dr. Marcus Whitman. The missionary told him he did not "shake hands with robbers." Two years later a Cayuse–Nez Percé band raided, plundered, and killed defenseless villagers south of The Dalles. Whitman's warning to the Cayuses to cease their aboriginal ways was falling on deaf ears. One young Cayuse, the killer of a Wasco chief, later died. It was believed that he choked to death on a piece of dried buffalo meat. Since mission personnel had put emetics in melons to discourage thievery and had put out wolf bait to kill the Indians' dogs, the Indians feared that Whitman, like a vengeful medicine man, was trying to kill them.

Particularly galling to the Indians were the increasing numbers of immigrants moving west, some of whom stopped off at Waiilatpu to recoup their strength before continuing down the Columbia. Some of those stopping off in 1844 took all the available space in the mission house, occupying rooms that Indians were forbidden to enter. Putting the Indians further on edge was the death of Elijah Hedding, son of Wallawalla Chief Peopeomoxmox. In the winter of 1844–45, Hedding was shot in a dispute over a horse by an American at Sutter's Fort in the Sacramento Valley. When word of the death reached his people and their Cayuse allies, they talked about seeking revenge in kind by taking the life of the preacher Whitman, since Elijah Hedding had been a Methodist mission student and preacher of sorts. In September, 1846, a rumor spread through California that a thousand Wallawallas armed by the Hudson's Bay Company had returned under Peopeomoxmox to avenge the death of his son (Wallawalla was a designation that Californians applied to several northern interior tribes). When they arrived, the old chief said they had no such designs. They were, in fact, too few in numbers and had been too weakened by disease in their camps to wreak much vengeance. Ten of their number joined Frémont's California Battalion in fighting that annexed California to the United States.[1]

As the natives grieved over Elijah's death in 1847, more immigrants rolled westward, the largest Oregon-bound migration yet. As if the numbers of the immigrants were not enough to alarm the natives, the settlers also carried measles with them. The natives tried to cure the disease with Whitman's medicine and their own treatments, including the now-lethal sweatbath and cold-river plunge. In the summer of 1843, Cayuses in the Rockies contracted a disease that had spread to the Wallawallas and to natives at The Dalles. During the measles plague a grim four-act drama unfolded in Cayuse lodges: fever, breaking out, dysentery, and death. In those lodges eastern Indians Joe Lewis and Tom Hill and a former Hudson's Bay Company employee, Nicholas Finlay, who was married to a Cayuse woman, rehearsed all the old stories of whites uncorking bottles to release germs in order to kill Indians and of Whitman's "plotting" to poison them.*

Seeking some medicine or charm better than their own or Whitman's, some Cayuses turned to the black robes, who tried to unite the religiously divided Cayuse house under the Catholic standard. Whitman's anger at this defection of his red parishioners alienated them still further from him. On the very day, November 27, 1847, that Whitman returned to his mission station from the Umatilla, where he had ministered to sick Indians, the Catholic Mission of Saint Anne was established on that stream to worry him further. That same fall the Mission of Saint Rose was established near the confluence of the Columbia and the Yakima. Seven years earlier a Yakima chief, Harkeley, had returned from Saint Paul's Mission in the Willamette Valley to instruct his people on Sundays. Another Indian, Pierre, also returned from Saint Paul's to baptize Cayuse children and adults who were in danger of dying.

A threat greater than the competition of the two arms of the Christian faith was about to come to Waiilatpu on Whitman's return there. The Grim Reaper, the unhorser of the free-riding Cayuse Indians, had prepared by measles for murder. Now he sharpened his scythe and rode a pale horse through the "Place of the Rye Grass." In the annals of Pacific-Northwestern Indian-white relations few events were more singularly tragic than that of November 29, 1847. At the Place of the Rye Grass the trees lining the creeks had surrendered their burnished gold to autumn gray. The sun's rays failed to burst over the Blue Mountains into the valley, as the day began with a cold mist—a fit setting for the tragedy to follow. Before the day was over, Whitman lay dead from a tomahawk blow, and Mrs. Whitman, always fearful for her husband's life but not for her own, fell victim to gunshots and blows. Before the massacre had run its bloody course, the mission was sacked, and fourteen whites, including mission personnel and immigrants, were killed. Two died of exposure.

*The Whitman massacre is narrated in Ruby and Brown, *The Cayuse Indians,* in a chapter entitled "Ride a Pale Horse," pp. 109–112. Subsequent events are narrated in pp. 113–71. The Cayuses and their allies became involved in a war with volunteers of the Oregon Provisional Government, who captured and hung those whom the provisional government deemed guilty of the act.

Flaunting the laws both of Moses and Dr. White, a small group of malcontents with tomahawks and guns had wreaked vengeance on the missionaries, from whom they had expected bold magic but received bad "medicine." By one Indian estimate nearly two hundred of their people had died in the plague. Exhilarated over their vengeance for these deaths, the killers may have failed to foresee that the white men would seek a retribution of their own. On December 1 the Catholic Reverend Jean Baptiste Abraham Brouillet buried the Protestant bodies in a common grave and warned Spalding (who was en route to his mission from Umatilla) of the tragedy. The Cayuses had marked him for death also. The Indians treated the survivors as slaves forcing several women to become their wives. For years Protestants would erroneously assert Catholic culpability in the massacre. The bishop of Walla Walla, Augustin Magloire Blanchet, summoned Cayuse chiefs Five Crows and Young Chief and others, telling them how grieved he was at the atrocious act and expressing hopes that the women and children would be spared and sent on to the Willamette.

The response of the Oregon Provisional Government legislature to the massacre was immediate. It authorized the raising of a 500-man mounted volunteer force and within ten days of the killings nearly fifty men were en route to The Dalles. Cayuse chief Camaspelo was so frightened by the event and by the white reaction to it that he visited Bishop Blanchet on December 18 to tell him that his people were doomed to die—that he favored killing the horses and leaving the country. Other Cayuses were also filled with consternation, as were their Nez Percé allies, on learning of the white reaction to the deed perpetrated by a handful of malcontents. The bishop warned Camaspelo that the longer his people delayed in ferreting out those responsible the more difficult it would be to make their peace with white men. After agonizing conferences with the peacemaking bishop, Camaspelo warned the Cayuse chiefs to give up "the American girls." All of them did except Five Crows, who resisted pleas from his fellows to relinquish his "wife."

On December 23 the chiefs met in council with Peter Skene Ogden of the Hudson's Bay Company, who had come up from Fort Vancouver to seek the release of forty-seven Cayuse-held hostages, thirty-seven of whom were children. Ogden warned the captors that he was acting for the company and not for the American community and that refusal to release them might well push the Americans into an all-out war against the tribe. The mercenary Tilou-kaikt and Young Chief, who were longtime hagglers with the company in trade, offered to release the captives for a price. Their offer was accepted. In exchange for their prisoners Ogden promised them fifty blankets, fifty shirts, ten guns, ten fathoms of tobacco, ten handkerchiefs, and a hundred rounds of powder and ball. Had there not been lives at stake, the Cayuse chiefs would never have won a trading bout so handily. Fulfilling their end of the bargain, they delivered the hostages to Fort Walla Walla to join five Americans who had already fled there.

On New Year's day, 1848, Spalding arrived at the fort with a delegation of fifty Nez Percés and ten whites whom they were holding, perhaps in protective custody. On the next day the ransomed whites set out by boat with Ogden for the Willamette Valley, where he was hailed by the American community as a hero for his intercession on behalf of their fellow countrymen. Shortly after the party left, fifty armed Cayuses rode to the fort threatening to kill Spalding. Fearing such actions or, worse yet, a general uprising of natives all over the Pacific Northwest, the frightened American community sent frantic appeals for help to their countrymen in other quarters. Joe Meek, whose daughter had sickened and died after the massacre, was sent to Washington D.C., for aid from the government. He faced hostile Bannock demonstrators en route there until, seeing his company disguise (a red belt and Canadian cap), they allowed him to proceed.

In their traditional browbeating fashion, fractious Cayuse war parties warned the Tyighs (a Shahaptian tribe on the lower and middle Deschutes River), the Teninos (a tribe at the mouth of the Deschutes and across from it on the Columbia north bank), and the Wascos that they should join them against the Americans or suffer the consequences. Under the pressure some of them did. On January 29, 1848, retreating Teninos and Cayuses near a small creek about thirty-five miles up the Deschutes from The Dalles met and repulsed a volunteer party led by Major Henry A. G. Lee. The volunteers killed a brave and captured two women and a number of horses before retreating. The following day, short of where Meek Cutoff crossed the Deschutes, Indians with rifles and bows and arrows skirmished their way out of defeat at the hands of a 130-man volunteer party commanded by Colonel Cornelius Gilliam. (The cutoff was a road between Fort Boise and The Dalles that bypassed the Blue Mountains and ran across southeastern and central Oregon east of the Deschutes, which it crossed south of the Columbia). The soldiers burned the Indians' camp. Indians claimed that it was in retaliation for this deed that they put the torch to buildings at the Whitman mission.

Because few were actively joining them in their fight, the Cayuses scurried frantically for allies, even contacting their ancient foe, the Molalas. Contacted, in turn, by the Molalas, the Klamaths refused to join the fighting. The Cayuses sent runners to natives of the interior, asking them to make common cause against the Americans. Suffering some disease at the time, the Colvilles below the Canadian border had a good excuse for not going to war. The Spokanes made no commitment to fight. Among their neighbors were some Coeur d'Alênes, Flatheads, and Kalispels who went to the scene of the conflict, having been told that whites had killed all Catholics and company men, including Thomas McKay. In the middle of February two Yakimas brought word to The Dalles that despite Cayuse pleas for help they would not enter the fight because they had no quarrel with whites, especially with those who were keeping out of their country. Like other interior peoples, who from precontact times built earth and stone fortifications, the Yakimas built two such structures to protect themselves from the Cayuses pressuring them to enter the conflict. These fortifications were located near where the United States Army later established its own Fort Simcoe on August 8, 1856, at Mool Mool ("Many Springs" or "Bubbling Water") on Simcoe Creek, a Toppenish Creek tributary in the middle of the Yakima country about sixty-five miles north of The Dalles.

Joining the Cayuses were elements of the Nez Percés, Wallawallas, and Umatillas and most of the Palouses. Thus strengthened, the combatants set out to confront the soldiers under Colonel Gilliam, leaving The Dalles on February 15. Two groups with different objectives were traveling awkwardly toward the Cayuse country under orders from the Provisional Government: the volunteers under legislative authorization to capture the Whitman killers and three peace commissioners charged with preventing a coalition of Cayuses and other Indians.

The Indians kept the white forces under surveillance as they moved eastward into the barren interior south of the Columbia River. On February 20, Indians burned the Saint Anne Mission, and about four hundred of them moved west of the Umatilla to make their stand against the advancing whites. On February 24 near Sand Hollow, eight miles east of Wells Springs on the Immigrant Road, they warned off the three commissioners, who were riding out ahead of the volunteers with a white flag. Some distance away were elderly Indians who had come to see the showdown slaughter of the whites. The Coeur d'Alênes, Flatheads, and Kalispels were also in the vicinity. When they found Thomas McKay alive and well with the volunteers, they knew that the information was false that the Cayuses had brought them of his death and discounted the inducements of Catholics and company men to fight. They apparently kept out of the struggle.

The red belligerents began the three-hour Sand Hollow fight confident of victory. They rushed their foe, backed off, and came on again at full speed. They shouted that they would beat the Americans to death with clubs and then proceed to the Willamette and take their women and property. Five Crows and another Cayuse chief, Grey Eagle, shouted to their men that, like their mother the earth, they would let no harm befall them. Their foe, they cried, would never reach the Umatilla River. Believing himself invulnerable to bullets, Grey Eagle ventured too close to the volunteers and was felled by rifle fire. A company interpreter, Baptiste Dorion, ran out, stomping on Grey Eagle's face. Grey Eagle's death and the wounding of other chiefs threw their braves into confusion. Urged on by the wounded Five Crows, they continued to fight, and their fusees threw balls farther than those of the soldiers. The Indians received no hits from the volunteers' long-barreled nine-pound cannon, but may have been frightened by the "big-medicine" gun. After moves and countermoves on both sides, the Indians retreated to recoup in nearby hills, minus eight men killed.

At this juncture the failure of others of their race to join their cause was most disappointing to the red fighters. Word of the Sand Hollow defeat had a sobering effect on the Spokanes. In early April, Reverend Eells in a dramatic gesture had Big Head and the Columbia River chief Sulktalthscosum place their hands on a New Testament and promise to abide by their commitment to remain at peace. The Cayuses

had offered Sulktalthscosum sixty horses and forty cows from Whitman's mission to enter the war on their side. In early June the volunteers escorted the missionaries out of the Spokane country, terminating their mission there. The war also terminated Spalding's mission to the Nez Percés, although most of them refrained from fighting.

On the Umatilla River a Nez Percé deputation bearing a white flag was permitted inside the volunteers' line, although Gilliam thought it was a ruse to allow the retreating Indians time to put more distance between themselves and the soldiers. The commissioners finally convinced the colonel of the Nez Percés' good faith. By late February some retreating Indians had trailed off toward the Blue Mountains, while others fell back toward the Walla Walla. At Fort Walla Walla, Peopeomoxmox reiterated his peaceful intent to the troops, expressing anger, however, that the legislature of the Oregon Provisional Government, thinking every gun in Indian hands was pointed at them, had passed an act preventing the introduction of firearms among the Indians. Most Indians by this time had found guns a necessity in hunting game.

Near the mission, where troops in early March looked over the evidence of the recent carnage, a Cayuse named Stickus, who was a friend of Whitman and other white men, parlayed with the commissioners and the volunteers. Unnerved by this peaceful gesture, the Cayuses sent runners to the Nez Percés, seeking to prevent them from joining the troops; they had apparently learned that the Nez Percés were to meet the commissioners at Waiilatpu to prevent a Cayuse-Nez Percé coalition. On March 6, two hundred and fifty Nez Percés with Camaspelo and a few other Cayuses met Colonel Gilliam and the commissioners in council near the newly erected Fort Waters, where soldiers had converted the fire-blackened mission into a hospital and living quarters. Camaspelo and the Nez Percés gave assurances of peace. After the council a Nez Percé delegation tried to persuade the Cayuses to surrender the Whitman killers, who at that very moment were in the Cayuse camps. The Cayuses would not surrender them. At the same time Gilliam, believing the Cayuses would never surrender the guilty, would have nothing to do with Stickus. The pursuers of the Cayuses called the killers the "five murderers." Believing the Cayuses would never surrender them, Gilliam offered to take the troublesome Joe Lewis, a suggestion that undermined the position of the commissioners, who had maintained all along that the Cayuses should turn over all of the guilty in order to protect their innocent fellows from white recriminations.

Frustrated by Gilliam's inflexible bargaining, the commissioners returned to the Willamette, as Stickus and his party went east to tell the Cayuses of the troops' deployment. Young Chief separated his followers from their warring brothers, who were now trailing to the mouth of the Tucannon, a Snake tributary and their old tribal boundary line, in order to join their Palouse allies. When the volunteers, still pursuing the Cayuses, reached the crossing of the Touchet River (near Waitsburg, Washington, about twenty miles north of Waiilatpu), Stickus met them with livestock, other properties, and cash which the Cayuses had appropriated. He also implicated Joe Lewis in the Whitman massacre. Combatant Indians who had camped there the previous night were already hurrying off in different directions. The Cayuse Tamsucky went east. Tiloukaikt led the main body of Cayuse combatants with some Palouses, Wallawallas, Umatillas, and Nez Percés to the mouth of the Tucannon, about thirty miles to the north.

At that place four hundred Indians, mostly Palouses, looked up to see Gilliam's command riding boldly into their camp. The armed Palouses, professing friendship, succeeded in convincing the troops that the murderers were on the north, across the Snake River, when actually they were close by. On March 14, deciding to abandon the chase, Gilliam ordered his men to round up enemy horses and cattle, after which he and his troops turned and rode off for the Touchet River. Before the command withdrew, the Cayuses had begun swimming cattle across the Snake, outwitting the Americans. After the troops had gone but a mile, the Cayuses rode in to join the Palouses and turn on the troops in an all-day running fight. As in previous encounters the Indians exchanged verbal insults with their foe. Using the services of one Mungo Antoine Ansure as an interpreter, the volunteers hurled insults at the fighting Indians that day and the next while the Indians chased them to the Touchet. The pursuers came off poorly in a fierce hour-long fight because they persisted in their traditional way of fighting: the braves selected individual targets as buffalo hunters did instead of massing their attack. They also relied more on noise and threats than on careful marksmanship. The Indians lost four killed and fourteen wounded. The latter were carried off groaning to the accompaniment of the death chants of the survivors.

The failure of other tribes to come to their aid doomed the Cayuses. They were so reduced in numbers, even before the beginning of the conflict—which was known as the Cayuse War—that they could not have waged a successful contest without substantial help. Realizing their precarious situation, Tiloukaikt and others fled to the Palouses, and his sons left for Fort Boise with Tamsucky and Joe Lewis. Others fled to the upper Burnt River. Five Crows went to the Wallowa Valley in northeastern Oregon to nurse his wounds in company with Old Joseph, the Nez Percé chief. The Cayuses friendly to whites remained in the Walla Walla Valley. The most noteworthy of the soldiers' losses—which were less than those of the Indians—was Colonel Gilliam, who was accidentally shot to death. The peace commissioners also suffered a loss in their failure to induce the Cayuses to deliver the murderers. If their fighting counterparts had sought to kill some Indians during the campaign, it may be said they succeeded.

On May 9, Colonel James Waters, commanding the First Company Oregon Rifles, met Cayuse and Nez Percé chiefs and Peopeomoxmox at Fort Waters, which was named for him. The colonel warned them that the soldiers would hold the country until the murderers were punished, stolen property was returned, and the destroyed property was paid for. Since March, Tiloukaikt and his band of com-

batants had sat tight with their Palouse allies on the right bank of the Snake. As Waters and his troops approached the mouth of the Tucannon, which they reached on May 19, they discovered that Tiloukaikt had fled to the Clearwater country; he had eluded a trap that Lee and Waters had set by dividing their forces to catch him. On May 21, Nez Percés near the mouth of the Clearwater told Lee and his men that Tiloukaikt had fled from there on May 19 for the Lapwai area. Lee was no stranger to the Nez Percés, having taught at the Spalding mission in the winter of 1843–44; he told his listeners that, since the troops had failed to punish the Cayuses, they had seized their properties. The Nez Percés in turn told Lee of the eastward flight of the Whitman killers and then helped him round up several of the killers' horses and cattle.

Before leaving Lapwai, Lee's command offered the Nez Percés several hundred dollars' worth of enticing merchandise for the apprehension of the killers or any two of their leaders. Half the sum was to be paid for any of them, and a quarter of it for the capture and delivery of certain Indians less responsible for the crime. Most wanted were Tiloukaikt, Tamsucky, Tomahas, Joe Lewis, and Tiloukaikt's son, Edward. Unaware of the reward, Peopeomoxmox in the middle of June learned that two of the wanted ones were near the Columbia-Yakima river confluence and ordered his men to run them down and hang them. One was captured and hanged; the other escaped. With the help of the Wallawalla chief and his men, Lee's command pursued the escapee, Tomahas.

As Tiloukaikt kept to the mountains to avoid capture, Waters departed the interior for the Willamette on June 8, leaving Captain William Martin in charge of a 55-man force. Since the Provisional Government had been unable to check the Indians with rifles and bullets, it continued its attempt to do so with bans and rulings. There had been the ban on sales of guns and powder; there now followed a prohibition on further missionary activity in the interior. Disregarding Lee's order to advance no farther than The Dalles, the zealous Bishop Blanchet, taking orders from a Higher Power, returned in an attempt to regain Catholic prestige and Cayuse souls. In that year, 1848, Saint Peter's Mission was established at The Dalles. The tribesmen, however, believed that Blanchet's power had failed them in their time of trouble. American Board missionaries made no attempt to return to the scene of their labors. In their absence some Spokanes, Nez Percés, and Cayuses tried to follow their precepts.

The soldiers remaining that summer to guard the Walla Walla Valley were authorized by the Provisional Government, through Waters and Lee, to claim Cayuse lands, which the government maintained the Indians had forfeited by their hostile acts. The authorization was another of the free-wheeling actions of the Provisional Government, which took matters into its own hands while the United States Government was preoccupied in the Mexican War. The editor of the *Oregon Spectator* (Oregon City) lamented on July 13, 1848, that the fertile Walla Walla Valley had not been settled much earlier because Whitman on behalf of the

Cayuse Indians had prevented it. After the last of the Fort Waters garrison left for home, a few straggling Cayuses returned to the valley.

After the Anglo-American boundary settlement in 1846, Indians of the interior met in April, 1849, with Joseph Lane, the new governor of Oregon Territory, which was established August 14, 1848, and encompassed present-day Oregon, Washington, Idaho and western Montana.[2] Lane sought to stabilize the Indians so that they would not attack immigrants or ally with the hunted Cayuses. In his first message to the territorial legislature on May 7, 1850, he declared the entire Cayuse tribe responsible for the Whitman massacre until those guilty of it should be surrendered for punishment.

Having peacefully traversed Cayuse country, the Mounted Rifle Regiment arrived at Fort Vancouver in October, 1849. Two companies of the First Artillery arrived also from the United States by sea. Thus Lane had leverage on Cayuses to deliver up the murderers. He also expected support from the Hudson's Bay Company, which sought to keep peace among the tribes in order to stabilize what was left of its business below the forty-ninth parallel. An increasing number of Cayuses, Wallawallas, Nez Percés, and even Palouses were beginning to jump on the "catch-the-killers" bandwagon. In late October, 1849, the Nez Percé Timothy and others of his tribe persuaded Young Chief to come out openly on their side after acquainting him with Lane's intentions. Like a desperate animal trapped in a hunters' circle, Tomahas would have killed Chief Timothy if Fort Walla Walla trader William McBean had not intervened. One twenty-man Nez Percé party under Timothy decided to attack the murderers in the belief that they had killed the Cayuse chief Tintinemetsa, but abstained from doing so on finding that chief very much alive at Waiilatpu. Aware of Nez Percé designs on them and growing increasingly desperate, the hunted Cayuses and their families moved deeper into the mountains. Leading the chase were Timothy and his men, sixty Cayuses under Young Chief, and others, including the Wallawallas.

Late in 1849, the Indian posse overtook the fugitives at the headwaters of the John Day River, where they captured their livestock and confronted the hunted ones hiding behind makeshift fortifications. A Nez Percé, Hoot Hoosha, shot and killed Tamsucky. A "blood" named Pierre and an Indian named Chappylie shot the Cayuse Shumkain. Four others were captured: Tamsucky's son, Klokamas (Tlocoomots), Eyoweahnish, and Kimasumpkin. At the posse's suggestion the women, children, and elderly were separated from the other fugitives. Surrounded, the murderers had exchanged gunfire with their pursuers, wounding a Wallawalla. Tomahas, the slayer of Dr. Whitman, escaped, as did Tiloukaikt, who was present when Tomahas killed the doctor; also Estonish, Isaichalakis, and a Shoshoni, Tsooyoohah, who had killed an American near Fort Boise. Only partly successful in trying to capture its quarry, the posse returned to Young Chief's camp on the Umatilla to discuss further action and to divide the spoils taken from the fugitives. A deep undercurrent of dissension developed between the Cayuses and Nez Percés; the latter believed that the Cayuses had cheated them in the distribution of the spoils.

On learning that Lane could offer no peace terms to the Cayuses until all the Cayuse murderers were apprehended, Young Chief, wishing to pursue them, asked the Nez Percés to choose the time for the chase. The latter were slow to respond. A discussion between the Cayuses and Nez Percés followed, in which the latter deemed guilty anyone in hiding. The Cayuses disagreed. In January, 1850, smarting because his people had received no spoils from the pursuit of the killers, Nez Percé Chief Red Wolf informed Lane that his people considered the Cayuses accountable for the murderers because they held some of them as well as their properties. Stripped of their goods and starving, some of the murderers rode toward Young Chief's camp to surrender. Young Chief decoyed the others in, catching the wiliest of them, Tiloukaikt and Tomahas. In his continuing ill humor against the Nez Percés, Young Chief said that the captured Tomahas was a Nez Percé relative of Looking Glass.

Softening his position somewhat, Lane in a January 25, 1850, letter to Young Chief said he wanted the murderers, but that he also wanted to be a friend and protector of the Cayuses and he could not be so until the guilty were surrendered. Aware of Nez Percé–Cayuse tensions, Lane in a January 28 letter warned the Nez Percés not to make war against the friendly Cayuses. In a February 7 letter to the governor, McBean suggested that he send someone to gather the prisoners held by Young Chief. On receipt of the letter about two weeks later, Lane instructed Major J. Samuel Hatheway, who had arrived on the transport *Massachusetts* with two companies of artillery, that he should proceed to Young Chief's village to collect the prisoners; thus removing, in Lane's words, "The only barrier to a permanent peace with the Cayuses." What he was really saying was that peace had been secured on the terms of the white community he represented. The weary Cayuses had no other choice than to accept those terms.

In early April, 1850, Lane went to The Dalles to bring in the five accused murderers, who had been brought there. With a military escort he returned to the village at Willamette Falls, Oregon City, with three of them; the other two followed in custody. The Cayuses implied that there could have been no more than five since all others responsible for the Whitman killings were dead and the others whom the Cayuses had rounded up as suspects had been released. Some of the suspects perhaps had no part in the murders. The important thing was that Lane had his five murderers; that is what mattered. There were varying opinions about the guilt of the five and the reasons for going to Oregon City. For instance, some believed that they surrendered themselves in lieu of the real murderers so that the Cayuses could have peace. Nevertheless, the five were in fact delivered up by the Cayuses, and the pursuit of them is well documented.

In Oregon City the captives were bound over to Joe Meek, the first United States marshal of Oregon Territory. They were taken from the mainland across a guarded bridge to Abernethy Island in the middle of the Willamette Falls.

They could have understood but little of the pretrial maneuverings, but were aware of their need for legal defense, offering fifty horses for that service. A true bill was returned on May 13 and filed on May 21 indicting each of the five for the murder of Dr. Whitman. Several indictments were issued for the other deaths at Waiilatpu. On May 22 the defense counsel filed a "plea in bar of jurisdiction" claiming that at the time of the alleged felony the Cayuse nation was outside the Indian territory over which the United States claimed jurisdiction. The prosecution answered that with the Anglo-American boundary settlement all territory south of the forty-ninth parallel belonged to the United States, which consequently had jurisdiction over it.

Judge O. C. Pratt rejected that plea, as he also did a request for a change of venue from the highly charged Oregon City to Clark County across the Columbia. Considerable testimony followed from massacre eyewitnesses. After the prosecution witnesses had testified, an article appeared in the *Oregon Spectator* on May 30, 1850, stating that Tiloukaikt admitted striking Whitman with his hatchet as attested by one of the witnesses, that Tomahas admitted shooting Whitman, and that Klokamas (the smallest of the five) admitted helping to kill young John Sager. The article further reported that Kimasumpkin was reported as being present at the massacre but not a participant in it. The so-called confessions were carried all over America to a citizenry stunned by the news of the Whitman killings. Publications in England and France also carried stories of the outrage that had snuffed out a Protestant community in far-off Oregon.

Continuing its case, the defense claimed not only that the accused did not murder the Whitmans but also that the killings were justified on the grounds that the missionary was "killing" the Indians. Called as a witness, McLoughlin testified that he had warned Whitman of danger; he maintained, as did other witnesses, that the Cayuses killed their medicine men for failure to cure patients.

Other witnesses were called. Fast-moving frontier justice did not validate their claims that after Whitman had given medicines to the Indians they had died. Neither did it take into account tribal custom, which might have been considered more carefully in an age more enlightened by anthropological studies. The prosecution's task was much simpler and shorter. On Friday, May 24, Judge Pratt denied the defense's motion for an arrest in judgment of the court and its request for a new trial. The court convened at 4:00 P.M. to receive the jury's verdict: prisoners guilty as charged. Pratt sentenced them to hang, Monday, June 3, 1850 at 2:00 P.M. — a convenient time for the crowd of two to three hundred persons who had packed into the 500-soul river boom town to see them die. A group of whites tried to obtain acquittal of the accused. Governor Lane, who might have pardoned them, had left for California immediately after the trial. Secretary Knitzing Prichett, acting in the governor's absence, refused to grant a reprieve, giving as a reason his uncertainty whether or not the governor was yet out of the territory. In his pocket the secretary carried the death warrant signed by Lane.

Since the petitioners could not save the lives of the condemned, Archbishop Francis N. Blanchet sought to save their souls. They refused to see Spalding. Blanchet brought a Catholic ladder to aid in their instruction so that they could be spiritually fortified to climb the ladder to their deaths. Twice daily for eight days the Reverend Mr. August Veyret visited the doomed Indians. According to Meek, Kimasumpkin declared his innocence to the very end. According to Blanchet's declarations Tiloukaikt maintained that all the Indians who had committed the crimes were dead. On the day of the execution the archbishop baptized the five condemned men. At 2:00 P.M. they were brought to the scaffold by a squad of soldiers. Meek arranged them in order for the drop. As he gave a last blessing and exhortation, Veyret was reported to have said: "Now then, Children of God! Onward, onward to heaven! O Lord Jesus, into they hands I commend my spirit, have mercy on my soul." He then fell to his knees, praying for the condemned. Three died instantly; two struggled—Tomahas, the longer. Said Meek, "It was he [Tomahas] who was cruel to my little girl at the time of the massacre; so I just put my foot on the knot to tighten it, and he got quiet." According to a well-known story Meek once shot an Indian dead on sight and explained it to a puzzled Nathaniel Wyeth as an action to keep the natives from stealing traps. When Wyeth asked him if the dead man had indeed stolen any, the old mountaineer replied, "No, but he looked as if he war going to."

Thirty-five minutes later the bodies were taken down and buried. Two months later the aloof *New York Tribune* commented: "Much doubt was felt as to the policy of hanging them, but the *popularity* of doing so was undeniable.... They were hanged, greatly to the satisfaction of the ladies who had traveled so far to witness the spectacle." And in 1879 a contributor to a publication in the East—where Indian-white hatreds had had many years to cool—wrote an epitaph for Oregon City:

The little nasty town...was the scene of a self-immolation as great as any of which we read in history, and there were not three persons there who appreciated it. The accursed town is, we hear, still nastier than ever, and the intelligent jury—no man of whom dared to have a word of pity or admiration for those poor Indians—with the spectators of that horrid scene, are either dead or damned, or they are sunk in the oblivion that is the fate of those who are born without souls.

As the killers dangled on the scaffold, a thoughtful person in the vengeful gallery who assembled in Oregon City that day might have pondered the words of the well-known divine Dr. Lyman Beecher, who in Cincinnati in 1836 had told some Oregon-bound missionaries, "Go on and do the present generation of Indians all the good you can, and get as many to heaven as possible, for you will be the means of sending the next generation all to hell."

11. RAVAGE ON THE ROGUE

Like the Indians of the northern interior those in southern Oregon faced whites traversing their lands between the Willamette settlements and California. The numbers of the whites were to increase with the opening of a new route from the East bringing them into the Willamette Valley. In 1846 Jesse and Lindsay Applegate, Levi and John Scott, and eleven other men searched out a route into the valley as an alternative to the trail from Fort Hall to The Dalles and down the Columbia River.[1] In June, following an old Indian trail, the party crossed the Calapooya Mountains into the Umpqua watershed. Farther south Rogue River natives, keeping them under surveillance, fired at them ineffectually on June 26 with dew-moistened muzzle-loading rifles. After the party crossed the Rogue River at the California Trail crossing (near Grants Pass, Oregon), large numbers of Rogues came from hiding to taunt them as they made their way up Rogue River. When they had harassed them out of the vicinity, the natives turned their attention to taunting another party of white travelers. Along the Oregon-California border near the foot of the Siskiyou Mountains, which the California Trail crossed, the Applegate party broke east through unexplored country via Green Springs.

In the Lower Klamath Lake region in northern California, Modoc smoke signals warned natives of the passage of the white party. The Modocs still smarted from losses that they sustained two years earlier in the Lost River–Tule Lake country in a fight with the better-armed Bill Williams party, who had brushed with various Indians throughout the American West. Now the Modocs were greatly agitated, thinking the Applegate men had come to punish them for an attack that they had made on Colonel John C. Frémont's camp on Upper Klamath Lake only a few nights before, when a Lieutenant A. H. Gillespie had brought Frémont a dispatch stating that his services were needed in the Mexican War. In the attack on Frémont's party three of his Indian guides were killed, but the famous frontiersman Kit Carson escaped. Gillespie reported that nine Klamaths were killed when the Frémont party attacked a Klamath band and destroyed their village. That those killed were perhaps innocent of the attack on the party was of little moment to it.

The Applegate party moved east to the Humboldt (Nevada) section of the Fort Hall–California branch of the Immigrant Road, following this route to Fort Hall, where it was hoped Oregon-bound immigrants would be induced to travel down the California Road before breaking westward on the South Road blazed for them by the Applegate party. Critics of the route condemned it because it traversed a desert "as dry and blasted, as if it had just been heaved upon from some infernal volcano."

Reaching the Humboldt River on its return, the Applegate party led a train of 150 immigrants to the Willamette. As they rolled in their wagons via Robert and Blue Rock springs, they discovered the natives to be as volcanic as their land. At Clear Lake in California, then called Lost, or Modoc, Lake, the Modocs swooped down early one morning on the immigrant camp, shouting and waving blankets, stampeding cattle and horses over wagons, and tearing down tents. The Modocs pierced the body of one white with over two dozen arrows. The immigrants hurried on. Near Tule Lake (California), where the meadows were narrowed by bluffs, gashed by gullies, and thickened with tules, about three hundred natives hid in a trench that they had dug, waiting for the travelers to pass through the place. As the party approached, the natives waved blankets and stampeded stock firing volleys of poisoned arrows at the trespassers through their lands. As the arrows were no match for the immigrants' muzzle-loading rifles, the natives were forced to seek refuge in nearby hills. They returned to the scene of the fight on hearing the anguished cries of one of their captured warriors. Whites had fed him red pepper. Fighting resumed and continued all day. Pools of the blood of the slain—many of whom were Indians—dotted the grisly scene, which was known thereafter as Bloody Point. Carnage lay strewn there for years. Travelers on the South Road were warned of the danger along the route by the words "Look out for the Indians" scrawled on bleached cattle skulls.

Although about five thousand souls immigrated in 1847, only eighty wagons traversed the South Road. The Klamaths, Modocs, and Rogues continued harassing immigrants, sending them hurrying to the Willamette instead of settling on the lands of those tribes.

The few Americans who settled on the south side of the Calapooya Mountains at the northern rim of this forbidden country might have suffered attacks by its natives if the Klickitat war chief Socklate Tyee and his braves, who were armed with Hudson's Bay Company guns, had not forayed south to fight the Rogues. The Klickitats also sold guns to southern Oregon Indians, stole their women, and buffered white settlers from the attacks of other Indians. Around 1839, crossing the Columbia River, the Klickitats overran the Willamette Valley, killing game in defiance of the weakened Kalapooias, whom they boasted they had taught to ride and hunt. Shortly before 1841 in Kings Valley (north of Corvallis, Oregon) they had defeated the Kalapooias in a skirmish, although outnumbered. They rented lands from

John Ponsee, a Rogue River Indian. His people futilely fought to preserve their southwestern Oregon lands from white encroachment during the 1850s. Lincoln County Historical Society, Newport, Oregon.

the Kalapooias, trading horses and other things to them for hunting grounds and privileges. They were known to have established depots for collecting furs and to have levied tribute from conquered native bands. Their restlessness propelled them into hunting grounds as far west as Oregon's Coast Range.

The Klickitats are credited with trading "civilized" clothing to the five-band, 200-soul Upper Umpquas in the area of the south fork of the Umpqua River, teaching them words of the Chinook jargon. They helped whites less from love than from love of gain. Some Klickitat men hired out as farm hands, and sometimes they sold the services of their women to white settlers, in hopes that the settlers would let them continue hunting in the Willamette Valley and let them keep a small tract that they claimed on the west side of

the river at the head of the valley. When a white man came among them around 1845, they asked him his intentions. When told that he intended to settle, the Klickitat chief said, "You can if you don't meddle with us." In Oregon in 1851 they numbered nearly six hundred.

In early 1848 the Indians of western Oregon were more threatening to whites than usual. Many young white men of that region had joined militia outfits fighting the Cayuse Indians far from that place. Word spread through the valley that a Molala chief, Crooked Finger, was angered at whites (especially at Frémont for his attack on the Molalas' allies, the Klamaths) and that Crooked Finger had gathered a force of 150 Klamaths, Umpquas, Rogues, Atsugewis, Achomawis, and Modocs to strike a blow in the valley that year. (The Atsugawis and Achomawis were Shastan tribes living along the Fall and Pit rivers in northern California; hereafter they are referred to as the Pit River Indians.) In response some settlers and friendly Indians ambushed a force of combatant Molalas and other Indians who were advancing along Butte Creek (in present-day Marion and Clackamas counties in Oregon). The Molalas had been joined by some Klamaths, possibly upper Klamaths (who had been residents for several years of the Willamette Valley). The Klamaths had traversed the Klamath Trail to the Silverton country (east of present-day Salem, Oregon) to camp with the Molalas. After they arrived, the Indians were ordered by whites to leave the area. When they refused, the whites on March 5, 1848, attacked their camp on Abiqua Creek, killed two of them, and the next day killed seven fleeing warriors, one of whom was a woman armed with bow and arrow. Two other women were wounded. One account placed the Indian losses at thirteen dead and one wounded. One white man was wounded. Much controversy raged over the Battle of Abiqua. Some whites called it a justifiable action to remove "dangerous" Klamaths from the Willamette.

After placer mining on California streams, Oregonians returned home with a little dust to seek their fortunes on the lands that they had abandoned for the glitter of gold. Along their homeward route the Rogues sometimes appropriated their properties. After they had relieved one such group of their gold pouches, the whites requested Oregon Territorial Governor Joseph Lane to recover their stolen treasure. In response, Lane and a fifteen-man party of whites with Klickitat chief Quatley (also known as Quarterly and the like) and ten braves traveled in June, 1850, to the Rogue Valley to retrieve the gold. On the south bank of the Rogue the governor and his party were met by armed bands of Rogues, specifically the Takelmas. The latter were a people divided into two major groups: the Dagelmas, or "those living alongside the Rogue River," and the Latgawas, or "those living in the uplands").* One band was under Chief Apserkahar. Ordered to return the gold, the natives delivered only empty pouches, believing them to have been the only things of value. They had thrown the gold dust away.

At a critical point in the confrontation Apserkahar signaled his warriors to arms. Quatley and his followers perhaps felt that they had little to lose in this action against the Rogues because the Klickitats were encroaching more heavily on Rogue and Klamath lands as whites began to disrupt Klickitat hunting grounds on the Willamette. At this time Apserkahar was so impressed with Lane's bold action and with his extraction of a peace from the Rogues that he asked him if he might not take his name. He was granted permission to take only Lane's first name, Jo (Joe). In exchange the natives presented Lane with a Modoc slave boy.

After this event involving the Lane party, Quatley in 1851 expressed to Oregon Superintendent of Indian Affairs

Anson Dart a wish to extend the Klickitat hunting grounds southward rather than have them forced to return to their original homelands in the interior north of the Columbia River. The natives' wish was not granted, for, with the increasing hostility of natives below the Columbia, the Klickitats in 1855 were forced to remove to their old homelands, although they pleaded their rights and exerted their claims in the white men's courts.

The confrontation involving Lane, the Klickitats and the Rogues did nothing to improve relations between the many Rogue bands and the whites. It did not take long for the natives to learn that the white men's lust for gold sent them running like quicksilver globules from panned-out Sacramento streams to all corners of the American West. The natives of northern California and southern Oregon were among the first to feel the impact of that invasion. Early in 1851 gold was discovered on the Shasta River, and thousands were attracted into northern California. Provoked by the incursions, the Rogues laid aside their treaty with Lane to increase their attacks on whites traversing their lands. They killed a number of packers and miners. One of their victims was Captain James Stuart, who was with a detachment of regulars that Major Philip Kearney led from Fort Vancouver to Benicia on San Francisco Bay. The ten-day fight began on June 17, a few miles up the Rogue River from Table Rock (about ten miles north of present-day Medford, Oregon). Stuart was felled by an arrow. Lane came down to join in the fighting, in which fifty natives were reported killed or wounded. Kearney took thirty women and children prisoners, and Lane delivered them to Oregon Territorial Governor John. P. Gaines. A few years earlier the natives had had but few firearms; now they had accumulated several. The increase augured more trouble for the future.

The Rogues were finding their homelands invaded not only by land but also by sea. In September, 1849, the ship *William G. Hagstaff*, bound from Astoria to San Francisco, foundered as she tried to enter the Rogue River for water. The Indians burned her, but salvaged her chain plates to make knives. The next year the *Samuel Roberts* landed on the lower Rogue. About thirty-five passengers were aboard under a Dr. Fiske, "an odd genius full of enthusiasm and brandy." They tumbled ashore, eager to acquire land. One passenger described the Lower Rogues who met them as "about five feet tall, with low foreheads and an expression of inveterate duplicity, and . . . an incarnation of every savage vice." The natives had pierced noses, from which they suspended ornaments of "everything that tickled their fancy." The Lower Rogues swarmed around the vessel, offering bows, arrows, pelts, baskets, mussels, fish, berries, and any other articles that they possessed in exchange for beads, trinkets, and fire-damaged cutlery. They confronted expeditions from off the *Samuel Roberts* with much gesticulation, whooping, and pointing of arrows. Their actions, accentuated by their frightening appearance, made the visitors feel unwelcome.[2]

Along the southern Oregon coast the confrontations continued. At dawn on June 10, 1851, natives gathered for a

---

*The ensuing Rogue War, precipitated by these events, is well narrated by Stephen Dow Beckham, using primary and secondary sources, in his *Requiem For a People: The Rogue Indians and the Frontiersmen.*

war dance to ready themselves to challenge a party of whites who had landed with cannon the previous day at a rock (Rock Island; later Battle, or Battle Rock, Island) at Port Orford. The whites were from the ship *Sea Gull*, under Captain William Tichenor. They had come to lay out a townsite and search out a trail eastward through the Coast Range. After the ship sailed off, the natives attacked those who had disembarked, firing arrows at them on the rocks. Most of the missiles passed over the heads of the settlers. The natives then rushed the rocky beachhead on which the tiny party held its ground. After a brief skirmish, in which twenty natives were reported killed, the Indians retreated to plan a counterattack. Some days later they returned, reinforced in numbers and in bows and arrows. After a harangue from their chief, they broke into a prolonged yell and then

Molly Carmichael and her mother, who were both Tututnis, or Lower Rogue River Indians. Like other Pacific Northwest native women, these western-Oregon Indians were adept at handicrafts, especially basketry. Lincoln County Historical Society, Newport, Oregon.

swarmed down the bank, across the beach, and up a narrow path to the driftwood breastworks. The whites fired their cannon into the breastworks, forcing the natives to retreat. From behind rocks and trees the natives arched their arrows into Battle Rock. During the night the whites stole away, eventually reaching the Willamette. Later seventy armed men returned to Battle Rock with Captain Tichenor. Among them was William G. T'Vault, who set out with a party from the coast to explore a road eastward over the Coast Range to meet the Oregon-California Road. On the Coquille, T'Vault and half his party survived an attack by the Coquille Indians, who were enraged at trappers and miners corrupting their women and at settlers plugging their game trails, felling trees, and digging up their lands. They may well have recalled their traditional tale of a wrecked Russian whaler crew in 1830, whom they believed had carried a disease that raced through their villages at that time, but the illness may have been only an outbreak of the Intermittent Fever.

On September 14, Superintendent Dart arrived at Port Orford to persuade about five hundred Coquilles and Tututnis to cede their lands to the government. Within a few weeks he concluded two treaties with them. The troops dispatched to Port Orford were reinforced for two planned expeditions: one against nontreaty Coquilles on the north side of their river and the other to survey a route across the Coast Range to the Oregon-California Road. On November 5 the Coquilles exchanged shots with the military party under Colonel Silas Casey, and on November 22 they lost fifteen killed and many wounded in a twenty-minute fight with the troops.

The settlers represented the greatest threat to the natives' security. The whites occupied their lands as they had Indian lands on previous American frontiers, aided by generous government land policies. Nowhere were the government's policies more generous than in Oregon Territory after Congress's enactment of the Donation Land Law in 1850. Under its provisions half-sections of land were granted to male settlers (including American half-bloods) if they were over eighteen years of age, were citizens or had declared their intention of becoming so before December 1, 1851, and had occupied and cultivated their lands for four consecutive years before December 1, 1850. If married by December 1, 1851, their wives were granted a half-section also. White males twenty-one years of age and over and their wives were each granted 160 acres if they settled between December 1, 1850, and December 1, 1853. In western Oregon the Donation Law appropriated two and a half million acres from the Indians' land base. Designed to encourage and reward settlement of the Pacific Northwest, the laws were extraordinarily disastrous to the region's natives and violated the American principle of government that individuals' lands should not be taken from them without their consent. Not even fur traders had made such demands on the Indians' lands.

Quickening the white men's exploitation of Indian lands was their failure to find a unity between themselves and nature. In their haste to exploit, white men believed that only soil-tilling hard work fitted one for rewards in this and the other world. Although concerned with things of the spirit, Indians were also deeply concerned with their own physical survival in a delicately balanced environment, which the encroaching settlers and their tools could easily disturb. Nevertheless, the Indians found themselves unwittingly and unwillingly drawn into the white men's agrarian pattern of survival; they scarred the earth themselves on a limited scale by planting and harvesting crops at various places in the Pacific Northwest. In so doing they were careful not to disturb the bones of their ancestors. Natives on the south Umpqua in 1852 became angry when a white man, more interested in bushels than in bones, plowed up a field containing their dead.

When they saw what the white men's economy was doing to the natives of the Willamette, natives in other places vowed to resist the process. In 1851 the Paiutes rushed a sleeping immigrant camp at Bloody Point, where the South Road ran between overhanging cliffs near Tule Lake. At dawn they killed thirty-five men, women, and children, wounding others and appropriating eighteen thousand dollars' worth of property. If the Paiutes had not then been warring against the Nez Percés, and the Rogues against the Klamaths, they would have been more free to attack white travelers.

Governor Lane and the Oregon territorial delegate to Congress, Samuel R. Thurston, were without authorization to conclude treaties with the Indians for title to their lands—only to give them presents and to obtain their friendship. They proposed removing the Indians from west of the Cascade Mountains to lands east of that range. Whites called the policy "colonization." Some of them honestly believed it essential to safeguard and protect the Indians to be removed. For many whites, however, it was a segregation policy to rid their communities of unwanted red men. To the Indians it was a form of genocide.

The natives in the region to which the Indians were to be removed—the Yakimas, Cayuses, and others—feared that an influx of Indians from west of the Cascade Mountains into their semiarid country would upset the land-man ratio, which was more delicately balanced there than in the Willamette Valley. They also feared that an influx would bring venereal and other diseases.

Targeted for removal by the territorial government, the Willamette Indians had no choice but to meet the three-man commission headed by former Governor Gaines authorized to deal with them for the sale of their lands. The commission in May, 1851, treated with Santiam, Tualatin, Yamhill, and Luckiamiute bands of Kalapooias and with two Molala bands—all of whom surrendered their valley homelands. The occasional whites and half-bloods who urged the Indians to make no deals with white men were thorns in the flesh of the white treaty makers in the valley, as elsewhere. In early August, Superintendent Dart, assisted by the Reverend Henry Spalding and the Reverend Josiah Parrish, concluded ten treaties at Tansey Point in Clatsop country with Indians living near the mouth of the Columbia River. As noted above, they had concluded two other treaties at

OREGON INDIAN.

"Oregon Indian." The garb attests to the rigors of the climate of Oregon, much of which is mountains and plateaus. Reproduced from James F. Rusling, The Great West and Pacific Coast *(New York: 1877).*

Port Orford and one with the Clackamas of the Willamette Valley. By their treaties the Willamette Indians surrendered lands from Oregon City south to Mary's River in Benton County, Oregon.[3]

The treaties involved a total of $91,300, which was to be paid to the Indians in ten annual installments of clothing, flour and other groceries, other goods, and small amounts of money. In exchange the whites received an estimated six million acres of land. Because of the destruction of their economy, the food to be received was vital to the Indians' survival. Although Lane had urged in 1849 that they be allowed guns and ammunition to hunt what game was left to them, government bans made it almost impossible for them to hunt for food on their lands. Until the full amount could be obtained of the goods provided by the treaties, government officials dispensed some of the items at gatherings which they called potlatches. This practice of aiding the subsistence of Indians with whom treaties had been made or were to be made was continued among other Pacific North-

Princess, or Lady, Oscharwasha, also known as Jennie; a Rogue River Indian. Her dress resembles that of the Plains Indians rather than that of her ancestors, who stubbornly resisted the encroachments of whites on their southern-Oregon lands in the 1850s. Southern Oregon Historical Society.

western tribes. The policy was expressed in the words of one government official: "They must be fed or fought," or they would, in the words of another, resort to "the tomahawk and scalping knife." Often the foods and goods were too little and too late. In 1847, Lieutenant Neil Howison of an American naval reconnaissance expedition to Oregon suggested annual distributions to natives of a few thousand flannel frocks and good blankets, stating that "an Indian would rather go naked than wear a bad one." Concerned lest natives believe the gifts were from the Hudson's Bay Company, government officials quickly instructed their agents to dispel that misunderstanding by purchasing the goods from American merchants wherever possible. This did not raise the blankets' quality in the natives' thinking, for they continued to favor those of the company—to cover not only the living but also the dead.

Of as much concern to Dart as the legal goods were the illegal ones, especially liquor. When negotiating his treaties, he asked Major Hatheway, the commander of the First Artillery forces at Fort Vancouver, to stop the introduction of liquor at Astoria. Judges of the Oregon Territorial Supreme Court had held that the Intercourse Act of 1834 (4 Stat 729) did not apply to the country west of the Rocky Mountains as it pertained to liquor sales. The congressional act of June 5, 1850, however, authorizing the negotiation of treaties in Oregon, did contain sections extending the laws "regulating trade and intercourse" to Indian tribes west of the Rockies.

Treaty-making agents were customarily accompanied by American troops to give them extra leverage on the Indians. When Dart was preparing to effect treaties with the tribes of the lower Columbia, the secretary of the interior requested that troops accompany him there, only to be informed by the war department that the only troops in the general area were two companies of artillery—one stationed on Puget Sound (at Fort Steilacoom, established in August, 1849) and the other dividing its duties between Astoria and Fort Vancouver.

In his treaties Dart included the provision that Indian villages or bands receive certain portions of their ceded lands as permanent homes, a policy that was at odds with that of the government. Some have cynically noted that Article 4 of the Clatsop (Tansey Point) Treaty permitted Indians to "pick up whales that may be cast away on the beach." In fact, it was one of the best things the government could have done for the Clatsops. Their ancestors believed that supernatural beings on the far side of the ocean sent the huge mammals to their shores. Some peoples of the central Oregon coast believed that the myth figure Suku had come ashore in the belly of a whale. Thus the people observed strict taboos in cutting and processing these gifts. After learning that "novel provisions" of the treaties displeased the settlers, the United States Senate failed to ratify them.

With gold discoveries in the Rogue Valley in 1851 the place was no longer merely traversed by outsiders but occupied by them. Because of the Rogues' reaction to incursions in their valley, Governor Gaines met with them in July of that year, shortly after their defeat by Major Kearney, to get them to renew the 1850 peace promises that they had

made to Lane. Superintendent Dart shortly ordered Alonzo A. Skinner, the newly appointed agent for southern Oregon, to settle in the valley with his headquarters near Table Rock on the Rogue right bank opposite its confluence with Bear Creek. With increased occupation and spoilation of their lands, the Rogues regarded very lightly the treaty effected with Gaines.

In January, 1852, fifty people were taking donation claims in Jackson County in Rogue country. Among them were Agent Skinner and his interpreter, Chesley Gray, and Samuel H. Culver, whom Dart had left as agent at Port Orford in the fall of 1851. On the heels of the land seekers and miners, the town of Jacksonville was established, from which whites could move more easily onto Indian lands or supply miners and settlers with goods and services.

The Rogues prepared for trouble, among other ways by seeking aid and allies among neighboring tribes. Among those they visited were the Cow Creek Umpquas under Chief Miwaleta, who declined to help them. The following year, his body scarred from fighting the Shastas (a Shastan tribe), he died fever-ridden from an 1852–53 plague, along with half his band. His son and sucessor, Quentousa, continued the fight against the white foe.

In July, 1852, after the Rogues resumed hostilities, whites in Jacksonville organized a volunteer force under John K. Lamerick, for whom Fort Lamerick on Rogue River would be named. At this time Agent Skinner called for a council of volunteers and Rogues at Big Bar below Table Rock to prevent hostilities between the two groups. At the council were volunteers under Elijah Steele from the mushrooming mining town of Yreka, California. They had organized to curb the Shastas as the Jacksonville volunteers had organized to curb the Rogues. Most Shastas lived in northern California along the middle Klamath River and its tributaries, the Scott and Shasta rivers. A small portion of the tribe lived in Oregon on the northern slopes of the Siskiyou Mountains and in the Rogue drainage area from present-day Ashland, Oregon, to Table Rock. Despite a November 4, 1851, treaty with the Shastas, calling for a reservation for them along the lower Scott River, the Shastas, like the Rogues, were angered at white incursions in their country.

On July 21, 1852, the Oregon Shastas in a tenuous peace with their Rogue allies, the Takelma and Latgawa bands, said that they would not communicate with other Shastas who had been at enmity with the Oregon bands, although the latter had also fought with the miners searching for gold. On the night of June 2, some miners who were seeking the killers of a white man captured the son of Shasta chief Sullix. The next month the son was shot in the head at close range when accused by a Yreka volunteer of attempting to escape. On July 17 another native was shot by one John Calvin as he resisted accompanying volunteers to the council. That event precipitated immediate firing between Indians and volunteers. The Rogues escaped under Chief Sam (Toquahear). The following day Lamerick's volunteers attacked a Rogue village at the mouth of Evans Creek, a Rogue tributary. The day following that, they discovered Sam and his band in some thickets along the Rogue near Table Rock. Sam dispatched two women toward the advancing volunteers with word that he wished two whites to come without firearms to parley with him. After that, on July 20, some Indians broke loose to cross the river. Their escape was frustrated by gunfire from the troops. At this turn of events the Indians strongly appealed for a treaty to prevent further aggressions on the part of the volunteers. Consequently, peace was established with the Rogues, who agreed that whites could settle anywhere in Rogue country. The Rogues were not to molest white men's cattle; they were to return stolen properties; and they were to have no further communications with the Shastas nor seek protection among them after committing depredations against whites. Because of poor cooperation from volunteers out to destroy the Indians, Skinner resigned.

To protect themselves from extinction, the Rogues continued to seek allies among neighboring tribes. Their sources of subsistence were rapidly disappearing, forcing them to eat the white men's cattle and wear his cast-off clothing. In the month before they established peace with Skinner, Rogue bands, such as that led by the aggressive Chief Sam, had made a pact with the Modocs to exterminate the ever-increasing numbers of whites entering their lands over the South Road. California natives had also made similar pacts to exterminate whites.

After their agreement with Skinner, the Rogues lessened their aggressions against whites. The same did not hold for the Modocs, who increased their attacks. At their ambuscade position, Bloody Point at Tule Lake, they attacked several immigrant parties in the fall of 1852. In one attack they killed all the persons in a wagon train except one man and mutilated the bodies of women and children. When word of those attacks reached Yreka, Benjamin Wright, a former revivalist and whiskey seller, led a party of volunteers to the scene of the troubles to protect the trains. In the group were five Shasta foes of the Modocs; Mary, a turncoat Modoc; and two other Indians. In an August confrontation with the Modocs at Bloody Point the volunteers killed over thirty of the tribe, forcing their survivors to flee to the tules for safety.

The Modocs were put in further jeopardy when Wright's volunteers were joined by others from Jacksonville. Wright also secured boats from Yreka with which to reach the Modocs in their tule hideout, but the latter escaped to lava beds on the south. The Shastas, with Wright and Mary, destroyed all the Modoc winter stores. In November the Indians received word from Wright that, if they brought in two captured immigrant women and the stock that they had captured, he would leave their country. In response Modoc chiefs Schonchin and Curley Headed Doctor came to Wright's camp on the north side of Lost River. Schonchin's forty-five warriors outnumbered Wright's eighteen men, since most of the volunteers had returned to Yreka. Fearing the Modocs were about to kill him and his men, Wright outmaneuvered them during the night by sending six men across the river to prevent the Indians from escaping an attack that he planned on them. At dawn the Indians found themselves trapped by the attack. Schonchin and Curley Headed Doctor escaped. Forty of their men were reported killed by Wright's men, who suffered only four wounded. The scalps of the Modoc dead were paraded through Yreka. Years later Indians claimed that Wright had attacked the Modocs when they came to hold a truce with him. Whites disagreed whether or not it had been Wright's intention to invite the Indians to a feast in order to poison them and force them into flight while he and his men shot them down.

Miners were just as guilty of treachery. When they captured Indians, they hanged them, or they tied their hands, then told them to run for their lives and shot them down. In one attack near present-day Ashland, Oregon, miners killed six Indians. Chiefs Jo, Sam, Jim (Anachaharah), and several other headmen then pledged themselves to exterminate the whites. Precipitating the Rogue War of 1853, the Rogues in early August broke into the cabin of a settler named Edward Edwards. When he returned home, they shot him and mutilated his body. Then they went on to kill another white man, wound another, plunder cabins, steal cattle, and ambush whites on the very outskirts of Jacksonville. In retaliation miners attacked a band of Shastas on Bear Creek. Fearing that miners would extend and continue their attacks on the Rogues, Chief Jo sent runners as far north as the coastal Siuslaws to seek help for his Rogues, as well as to the Klamaths, Shastas, and Modocs. When they failed to heed the warning of Shasta Chief Tipsu (Tipsey), who lived at the foot of the Siskiyou Mountains, to leave the country, whites found themselves in a hundred-mile swath of burned buildings and other pillage, from Cow Creek south across the Siskiyous and along the South Road, where Indians killed nearly forty white travelers.

Rogue attacks were now widespread. On August 11 at Willow Creek, a tributary of lower Bear Creek, they attacked five men, including Wiliam G. T'Vault, who escaped as he had the Coquille attack two years before. They swept through the valley firing cabins and foraying against volunteers on the Applegate, a Rogue tributary. Volunteers had routed an Indian camp near the mouth of Sterling Creek, a tributary of the Little Applegate River. On August 12 on Williams Creek, another Applegate tributary, the Rogues ambushed volunteers and attacked miners holed up in a cabin. A few days later they ambushed other miners fleeing to Jacksonville, killing one. On the night of August 17, Sam's band killed two volunteers in a three-hour skirmish. The Indians might have made a rout of it had not a volunteer company from Yreka chased them off. Before the volunteers arrived, the red men had captured eighteen horses and mules loaded with blankets, guns, and ammunition. That same day the Rogues killed five more whites in the valley and attacked white men's cabins and immigrants on the South Road, killing one.

On August 22, General Lane, commanding Oregon volunteers, left Camp Stewart (on Bear Creek near Phoenix, Oregon) accompanied by Lieutenant Bradford R. Alden with ten regulars from Fort Jones. They ascended the Rogue near Table Rock, picking up the trail of the now-retreating Indians. Colonel John E. Ross, commanding two companies of volunteers, led one batallion down Rogue River and up Evans Creek into the mountains over a route made difficult by rocks, underbrush, and trees which the Indians felled to impede the progress of their pursuers. They also set fires, choking the lungs of their pursuers and reducing their visibility.

Veering from Evans Creek, the Indians ascended a high ridge near its headwaters to camp at a spring on the side of Battle Mountain. Taken by surprise, they took to the cover of trees and underbrush as the troops opened fire on them from a distance of thirty yards. After four hours of sharp fighting the Indians sued for peace. In the fight Lane was wounded in the right shoulder by a Minie ball. The Indian losses were eight killed. Seven of the twenty Indians wounded would die, confirming the challenge that Jo had hurled at the soldiers that they would fight and die defending their lands. In response to a summons from Jo, Sam arrived on the scene, but was too late to be of any help.

The Indians asked to see General Lane, whom they respected. In the ensuing parleys, Jo, Sam, and Jim agreed to a cease-fire and to meet in seven days at Table Rock to negotiate. That night Indians and soldiers camped uneasily four hundred yards apart, fearing treachery from each other. At that very time there was treachery down the Rogue, where a volunteer company lured several of Jo's Grave Creeks to a cabin with an offer of food and friendship. When they appeared, the volunteers killed several of them. In revenge those who escaped burned cabins along Jump Off Joe Creek (in northeastern Josephine County, Oregon) and on August 28 ambushed volunteers at Long's Ferry (west of Grants Pass).

On September 1, Indians and soldiers assembled near Table Rock at Camp Alden. The next day Captain Andrew Jackson Smith arrived with his dragoons from Fort Orford. On September 3, Jo, Sam, and Jim's wife, Mary, entered Lane's headquarters to engage in talks. An Oregon volunteer company under Lieutenant L. F. Grover arrived accompanied by General Joel Palmer, Oregon superintendent of Indian affairs. Palmer had been appointed to his post in March after Dart resigned futilely trying to explain to the Indians why the government had failed to fulfill its treaty obligations. Giving more force to whites' assemblage were Agent Culver and a United States District Court judge, Matthew P. Deady.

As some Indians were absent, the red negotiators were given three more days to assemble in council. They were warned that, if they were not on the grounds by then, hostilities would commence. By agreement only ten unarmed men, no troops, were to be at the council grounds. Chiefs were to be present, but were to keep their men and arms at a distance. On September 9, Lieutenant August V. Kautz and his regulars from Fort Vancouver arrived dragging a howitzer to further augment American clout at the council.

On September 10, under the frowning perpendicular cliffs at Table Rock, with "seven hundred hostile savages" in war paint and feathers some distance away, the chiefs listened to speeches by General Lane and Superintendent Palmer, which were rendered in English, translated by James W. Nesmith into the Chinook jargon, and finally translated from that language into that of the Rogues. In the middle of the afternoon a young brave ran onto the council grounds, sweat streaming from his naked body, to harangue his fellows with the news that volunteers under one Elias A. Owens had captured the Indian Jim Taylor, tied him to a tree, and shot him to death. On hearing this, the Indians threatened to tie each white man in council to trees with lasso ropes, readying the ropes as they did their guns, which they pulled from skin cases. Seeking to extricate the whites from this threatened attack, Lane assured the Indians that Owens was not one of his soldiers, but a bad man violating the truce, for which he would be caught and punished. Perhaps out of desperation, his arm still in a sling from his gunshot wound, Lane admitted that the Indians could easily kill him and his fellows, but warned that, should they do so, whites would hunt them down from tribe to tribe wiping them from the face of the earth. The natives appeared calmed by Lane's words, as they were by promises of shirts and blankets to be paid to Taylor's relatives to cover his death. With the air thus cleared, the council proceeded.

The treaty of Table Rock was signed by Superintendent Palmer, Agent Culver, and eight headmen representing 287 Indians. The treaty specified a temporary reservation (until a permanent one should be established) extending up Evans Creek to a small prairie, across mountains to Upper Table Rock, south to Rogue River, and down that stream to the mouth of Evans Creek. Lane set payment for all lands in the valley at $60,000. In a preliminary peace treaty signed on October 8 with Jo, Jim, and Sam, a quarter of that sum was to be withdrawn to indemnify whites suffering property losses at the hands of Indians. Under the provisions of the Table Rock Treaty the government promised to build houses on a reservation for all head chiefs. The Senate would ratify the document on April 12, 1854. In late September the military established Fort Lane a mile below Table Rock on the south bank of the Rogue with Captain Smith in command.

As in other negotiations with Indians, whites learned in the Pacific Northwest that natives living in independent bands or villages had not combined into large units. Thus the treaty-making process was complicated for white officials. While Palmer treated with the Cow Creek band of Umpquas on September 19, providing them a temporary reservation in their homelands until a permanent one should be established, Chief Tipsu and his band, who claimed ownership of the upper Rogue Valley, hid in the Siskiyous and did not sign the September 10 treaty. After the council Lane struck off to find Tipsu, with whom he signed an agreement in which the chief promised to respect the rights of settlers.

Indians and whites continued to clash on the Applegate. On the Illinois, a lower Rogue tributary, a band under Chief John, who were not a party to the recent treaty, skirmished with miners. The chief maintained that he was fighting because he "lost more of his people in one year of peace than in two years of war."

The presence of miners and settlers on the Oregon coast extended Indian-white conflict into that area. Gold discoveries there in the summer of 1853 resulted in the establishment of the towns of Elizabethtown, Logstown, Prattsville, Whalesburg (later called Ellensburg and Gold Beach), and Empire City and spelled doom to neighboring Indians. Tolowa bands (Athapascan) at the present-day Oregon-California border were driven from their homes up the Smith River in northern California under the continuing white attacks. In those forays seventy natives were killed, and their village burned. In January, 1854, more Indians were killed there.

A troublesome town for the Nasomah (Nasum) band of Lower Coquilles was Randolph, six miles north of the mouth of the Coquille, where gold was discovered in the winter of 1852. Indians living in huts at the mouth of that stream had abandoned their animal skins for cotton clothing, but had yielded little else of their native way of life, including resentment of whites. In the winter of 1853–54 they killed isolated settlers, burned cabins, and drove off and killed cattle. In retaliation the whites sent an ultimatum to Coquille chief Tyee-John to make his Indians cease their attacks. The chief returned the ultimatum with one of his own—that he would kill every white man coming against him. Shortly, as they were sleeping in an unguarded camp, the Coquilles were attacked by a volunteer outfit, the Randolph Minute Men. Under a musket-fire barrage some of the Indians, who had an arsenal of only three guns plus bows and arrows, jumped into the cold river trying to escape their attackers, as others fled into the woods. In their flight sixteen of their number, one a woman, were killed and four wounded, and their village burned. The hostilities were over by the time Lieutenant Kautz and his troops arrived that evening from Port Orford accompanied by Indian agent S. M. Smith. Three Coquilles were hanged, victims of swift frontier justice. Their survivors would be moved in 1856 to the Siletz Reservation, established by executive order, November 9, 1855.

Angered by attacks on them in early 1854, the Coquilles retaliated by killing trappers and ambushing other whites, who in turn continued the revenge cycle by hanging two Coquilles. Shortly whites massacred some Nasomahs. The Chetcos (Athapascans of the group referred to as Coast Rogue) were still angry at the loss of their ferrying business, which whites appropriated, and at attacks on their villages, such as that made by one A. F. Miller and some of his cronies in 1853. After appropriating the natives' guns, the attackers had assaulted the main Chetco village. Allowing its women and children to escape, they killed two of the men while two more burned to death in houses which had been fired. When Superintendent Palmer visited the Chetcos and Coquilles in May, 1864, they were understandably cool and noncommittal toward him.

The flurry of coastal mining was nearly over. Not so the flurries between reds and whites. Back in the Rogue and Klamath river valleys Indian-miner clashes caused troops to be dispatched from Fort Jones, California in January, 1854, to quash the Indians. With the troops was one soldier who

later gained a reputation as America's greatest Indian fighter: George Crook, then cutting his military eyeteeth as a young army lieutenant. Before terminating his service in the West, Crook learned to his discomfort that the Indians' aboriginal weapons were still effective. In the spring of 1857—shortly after killing, as he called them "my first Indians"—he was wounded in the Pit River country by an arrow whose head he carried to the grave. At the time of his wounding he was concerned that natives of that area fired arrows impregnated with the livers of deer and antelope bitten by rattlesnakes. Wishing to shatter the Shastas, troops with Crook fired balls from a Fort Lane cannon into a cave. Shortly, the Indians sued for peace. Ironically, their rifles were superior to those of many whites.[4]

One victim of the struggle was Chief Tipsu. A call went out from the military to thirty-eight Tyighs of north-central Oregon to join a Fort Jones detachment in running down the chief and his followers. The soldiers and their red mercenaries were denied the glory of bringing on his demise, for he died at the hands of his own Shastas, so weary were they of fleeing their white foes. On May 24, volunteers tried to force the Shastas to Fort Jones. The prospect of going there was none too pleasing to them, especially since the Rogues confined there were starving. Sixty pitiful Shastas were rounded up. As they paused at Klamath Ferry to bathe in the river, whites shot five of them, including a head chief, Bill. Before expiring he was beaten, scalped, and tossed into the rapids.

In the spring of 1854, Superintendent Palmer, touring the scene of the troubles, attributed them to the Donation Land Act. He returned that fall to extinguish title to the remaining Indian lands. On November 18 he persuaded the Rogues at Table Rock to permit other bands to come on their reservation. That same day at the mouth of the Applegate he treated with the Shastas and with the as-yet-untreated Upper Umpqua bands for cession of their lands and their removal to Table Rock Reservation. Eleven days later at Calapooya Creek (in Douglas County, Oregon) he treated with certain Kalapooia bands of the Umpqua Valley and with other Upper Umpquas who were without treaties, to persuade them to cede their lands. After ceding they were expected to remove to a permanent home at a time and place chosen by the government. Through treaties the government had acquired title to all Indian lands between the Calapooya Mountains and the southern Oregon border. On January 22, 1855, at Dayton in Oregon Territory the few remaining Kalapooia bands of the Willamette Valley treated with Palmer. When the treaty making was over, the Willamette Indians had turned over to the United States 7.5 million acres in exchange for $200,000 and had agreed to remove to a reservation. Signing the treaties meant the loss of their land base; yet, since they had been unable to prevent its loss, they hoped that removal to reservations would let them survive a little longer.

The treaties did not mean the end of conflict. Klamath country was the scene of more troubles in 1855 and 1856 when holdout Rogues made two incursions against their Klamath foes. The latter continued fighting the Shastas and

Rogues, stealing women and selling them as slaves to tribes as far north as the Cayuses and Nez Percés. As was so often the case in the Pacific Northwest, such intertribal animosities hastened the demise of the contesting Indians at the hands of the military. The 147 Rogue warriors represented 523 of their people remaining in the valley, where two years earlier there had been 406 warriors out of a total nine-band population of 1,154. Instead of dissipating what strength they had left in fighting red foes, they should have reserved it to fight white volunteers and to harass the whites in general.

In the spring of 1855, after a miner was killed on Indian Creek near Klamath River—for which whites blamed the Rogues of the Illinois Valley—revenge-seeking volunteers crossed the Siskiyous, moving down Althouse Creek Canyon near the California border to the mining town of Kerbyville on the upper Illinois River. They succeeded in killing four Indian men and women. For their own safety several Indian families were hustled out of the area by their new Table Rock agent, Dr. George Ambrose.

In July of that year conflict again erupted on the Klamath when Indians killed a dozen miners near the Scott and Shasta rivers and Humbug Creek in northern California, which are Klamath tributaries. In retaliation a posse indiscriminately killed twenty-five Indians in what whites called the Humbug War. Again volunteer companies formed to drive the Indians into the mountains. In August, the Klamaths on the northeast tried to run down members of the U.S. Army Corps of Topographical Engineers, who were exploring a railroad route to the Pacific. The natives met them yelling, shaking their bows and arrows and their few guns. Finally, assured that the explorers meant no harm, they visited their camps, where they communicated with them in the Chinook jargon.

In June, Palmer attended a Walla Walla Treaty council at which he joined Washington Territorial Governor and Superintendent of Indian Affairs General Isaac I. Stevens in dealing with interior tribes of the Washington and northern Oregon territories. After that, he treated with confederated bands of middle Oregon: the Shahaptian-speaking Teninos (or Teninos proper), Wyams (Wiams or Lower Deschutes), Tyighs (Tighs and Upper Deschutes), and Dock-spus (Tukspushes and or John Day River Indians) and with upper Chinookan-speaking Dalles Wascos (Wascos Proper), Hood River Wascos (Smock-shops) and with some Cascade Wascos (Kigaltwallas). He then went to the coast, where he treated with the Alseas (Yakonan) on Alsea River and Alsea Bay, the Tututnis, the Chastacostas (on both sides of the Rogue in the area of the Illinois), Siuslaws, Lower Coquilles, and Chetcos for half the frontage of the Oregon coast—five million acres—which those tribes agreed to cede for $90,000 in a treaty that the Senate never ratified. The Tillamooks, Lower Coquilles, Tututnis, and Chetcos were forced onto the Siletz Reservation (formerly the "coast reservation"). The Grand Ronde Reservation (not to be confused with the Grande Ronde Valley of northeastern Oregon) was established in June, 1856, for Indians removed from the Table Rock Reservation. Military posts were established to keep an eye on the removed Indians. One of the posts, Fort Hos-

Annie Rock, an oyster gatherer on the Oregon coast, with the tools of her trade. Her people, the Chetcos, were among those dislodged by wars with whites in southwestern Oregon in the 1850s. They were sent north to the coastal Siletz Reservation. Lincoln County Historical Society, Newport, Oregon.

kins, was established under the supervision of Lieutenant Philip Sheridan in July, 1856, in upper Kings Valley on the Luckiamute River, "to keep the Indians [of the Siletz Reservation] a way from the Settlements and the whites from the reservation, and to afford protection to Settlers in case the Indians ever break out..."[5]

Among the Shastas were six Rogues from the Table Rock Reservation whom whites suspected of helping the Shastas. When the six fled to their reservation, a posse of

Yreka volunteers pursued them to the confine. Refused admittance to it, the volunteers had to abandon their demand that the six be surrendered in three days. Smarting from such rebuffs, volunteers held meetings in October, 1855, in Jacksonville, divided their forces, and then moved on a Rogue band under one Jake who were encamped in a village on Big, or Butte, Creek, an upper Rogue tributary. In the early morning hours of October 8 the band was pounced upon by a posse, who killed the elderly and children—twenty-three in all. A band under one Sambo was attacked by the other force, and one Indian was killed. In revenge roving bands, acting in concert on various fronts, attacked settlers, sparing neither men, women, nor children. One attacking band was that of Chief John. They decamped from near the mouth of Ward Creek (a Rogue tributary) for the mountains between Rogue River and the Illinois Valley, attacking whites and burning houses. The bands of Limpy and George joined in the concerted attack, stationing themselves farther down the Rogue near the settlements. The bands seemed bent on fulfilling plans formulated in the Klamath Council of June, 1854, where it was decided that Indians of southern Oregon and northern California were to exterminate whites and reclaim lost Indian lands. Only Sam's band on the Table Rock Reservation was noncombatant. Completing the cordon of outposts around Rogue River Valley, the Modocs and Rogues of Butte Creek occupied country along its eastern borders. The result of the maneuvers was the October 9 "massacre" of Evans Ferry, in which Indians slew twenty whites. The Rogues pushed downriver toward the Coast Range, killing a rancher's wife, his daughter, and the owner of another ranch, wounding his daughter. The killings that day sent miners fleeing into Jacksonville.

On October 15, Oregon Territorial Governor George Curry issued a proclamation calling for five companies of mounted volunteers to constitute a northern battalion and four companies for a southern battalion to control the Rogues. Before the troops could get into action, the Rogue bands of George, Limpy, and John and Tenas Tyee fought a sharp eight-hour skirmish on October 17 against miners and packers on Galice Creek, a Rogue tributary. Failing to dislodge their foe, they withdrew, dragging off their dead. A week later the Rogues attacked supply wagons on Cow Creek, killing a white man and burning more cabins. Citizens from Althouse and Sucker creeks in the Siskiyous scoured the hillsides for Indians who were ambushing the trains moving toward the coast along a route Lieutenant Kautz had opened that month. On October 31 a Rogue party near Leland, Oregon, ambushed Captain Smith and his regulars in an all-day fight known variously as the Battle of Bloody Springs, Grave Creek Hills, or Hungry Hill. With inferior smooth-bore, short-range musketoons that errantly fired heavy, round bullets, the troops barely escaped the better-armed Indians, who broke off action on November 1 after a four-hour fight in which fifteen Indians and thirty-one whites were killed.

The skirmishes had been costly for both sides, especially for the Rogues, whose fighting had prevented them from laying winter food supplies. They faced the prospect of starving. From their forest and canyon strongholds they forayed briefly into the river valley in early November firing at express riders and burning cabins. On November 22 volunteers burned twenty-five abandoned huts six miles down the Rogue from the mouth of Grave Creek. Because of their friendliness to whites, Sam's people incurred the wrath of other Rogues, who went on the Table Rock Reservation burning every article they could find that was of any value to Sam's people, as well as killing agency cattle. On November 25, 150 warriors and their families fortified themselves at Black Bar, five miles upstream from Little Meadows, where they came under the surveillance of volunteers. The volunteers had devised with the regulars a plan to drive the Rogues from the mountains to the Rogue river. The Rogues south of the river were apparently unaware that 386 volunteers and 50 regulars were within three miles of their camp and preparing to raft across to the south bank. Discovering the approaching troops, the Rogues repulsed them, ending for the soldiers the first Meadows Campaign on November 26.

On December 2 in another theater of operations a band of noncombatant Cow Creek Umpquas were defeated at Deer Creek, a south Umpqua tributary. On Christmas Day troops were especially active, as though expecting victory to celebrate the occasion. On that day Jake's band from Butte Creek were fired on without warning while they were encamped along Little Butte Creek, an upper Rogue tributary. A number were killed, and the rest captured or dispersed. Another camp four miles north of Rogue River was also fired upon. When the shooting ended, a number of Indians were killed, and twenty were captured. Five days before the new year arrived, soldiers attacked part of old Chief John's band east of Williams Creek, killing three braves and putting others to flight. Another band sought shelter in miners' cabins at the forks of the Applegate and eluded a party of potential attackers.

The 314 Indians camped at Fort Lane and the 300 under an agent on the Umpqua were scarcely better off than those continuing the fight. Lacking food, clothing, and shelter, they suffered from malnutrition, tuberculosis, and measles. Palmer hoped to get them removed to the Siletz and Grand Ronde. Before he could move his Indians, combatant Umpquas attacked settlers' cabins in Douglas County in early December, stealing and killing livestock.

In the following week well-armed volunteers marched unsuccessfully to the Applegate, where they could not return the Indians' fire in an attack because the mules carrying their ammunition and a howitzer had fallen off a cliff. The mules had drowned. Indians of John's band escaped from a miners' cabin near the forks of the Applegate, where troops had pinned them down. On the night of January 4, 1856, before ammunition and a howitzer replacement reached the besiegers, the natives escaped, after exchanging some shots. On January 21, when fired at by reinforced volunteers on Murphy Creek (an Applegate tributary), they returned the fire and moved into the mountains.

That January the Oregon Territorial legislature petitioned for Agent Palmer's removal because he did not ad-

Umpqua Chief Solomon Riggs, who was taken with his people to Grand Ronde Reservation in 1855-56.

vocate an Indian extermination policy. It also asked for the recall of General John E. Wool, who commanded the Department of the Pacific with headquarters in Benicia, California. Wool's policies also clashed with those of officials and other citizens of Oregon Territory and Washington Territory (which was established March 2, 1853) who believed the general favored a soft line against Indians. When Palmer was to be removed in August, 1856, and replaced by Absalom F. Hedges, who served until May 1, 1857, Chief Sam, puzzled by the rapid shifting of white chiefs, remarked, "With us [unlike with you] we are born chiefs; once a chief we are a chief for life."

In late January, 1856, Palmer began removing Indians from the Umpqua. By the second week of February nearly five hundred Indians—Umpquas, Molalas, and Kalapooias—had reached the Grand Ronde Reservation. Four hundred others trekked the long distance from Table Rock to the Grand Ronde through a snowy countryside.

Over on the coast, as word spread northward of the Indian-troop and miner-troop clashes on the Rogue, the gold seekers fled their sluices on Whiskey Run (between Coquille and Coos rivers) to Empire City on Coos Bay, abandoning forts there when the Tututnis, Chetcos, and Lower Coquilles seemed restrained. Although the Chetcos

retreated to the mountains, the Lower Coquilles held out against the whites. They were still smarting from the loss of the fifteen warriors killed and the women and children captured by volunteers the previous spring. On October 21, 1855, after the Lower Coquilles burned a settler cabin, whites organized the Coquille Guard. Under such pressures the Lower Coquilles agreed to follow the directions of David Hall, who was subagent under Ben Wright, and reluctantly moved onto a temporary reservation at Port Orford. They remembered, no doubt, the Casey expedition of November, 1851, and the massacre of the Nasomah band in 1854.

In November and December, 1855, the Coquille Guard marched up- and downriver from its headquarters at Fort Kitchen (on the south fork of the Coquille near Myrtle Point, Oregon), skirmishing with Indians. They killed four natives and hung another. After Agent Wright had ridden into the camp of the Coquille Guard on Christmas Eve, ordering them to disperse, they reluctantly disbanded in late January, 1856. Near dawn on the night of February 22, when most miners along the beaches from Cape Sebastian to Euchre Creek had gathered in Gold Beach (just south of the Rogue mouth) to celebrate George Washington's birthday, Tututnis struck the camp of another volunteer outfit, the Gold Beach Guard, killing nine of its fourteen men. They also burned every building that they could find and then fanned out to continue their pillage. Six miles up the coast from Gold Beach at Elizabethtown, they killed a German immigrant and his three sons and captured his wife and two daughters, who were later ransomed. At a cabin on the treaty grounds where the Guard had located, Enos, a half-blood Indian from back East and a former Frémont guide, was reportedly tipped off by Benjamin Wright's common-law wife, Chetco Jennie, and he laid Wright low with an axe. In their tradition, the Tututnis ate his heart and mutilated his body as though in retribution for his Modoc killings. They also killed an officer of the Guard and twenty-three other people. The party goers took refuge in a half-built structure, Fort Miner, on the north bank of the Rogue near its mouth, where the women helped their men to melt lead and poured Minie balls.

In hills east of Fort Miner, Enos harangued warriors to continue their attacks. Unable to take the offensive, the Tututnis still managed to keep the whites at bay. Indians as far south as the Tolowas joined in the uprising, making lines of communication with California difficult for their white foes. As troops moved north from California and south from Fort Vancouver to converge on their quarry, Tututnis in sand dunes on the south bank of the Pistol River ambushed volunteers from Crescent City, California, who were pushing ahead of the regulars on their way north. Back at Fort Miner white women and children were removed by schooner as most of their men remained with the regulars to fight the Indians.

With spring, 1856, the Indians of the Rogue River Valley, joined by others from the coast, formed a stronghold near the junction of the Rogue and Illinois rivers. There on March 19, after surviving the winter on such food as oxen taken from settlers, the Chastacostas lost five warriors in a

Indians of the Siletz Reservation representing the Chetco, Rogue, Coquille, and Coos tribes of western Oregon. Note the dentalium in nose of the man, front row left; the traditional square drum, right; and the Typso feather wands held by the women. Lincoln County Historical Society, Newport, Oregon.

skirmish with Captain Christopher C. Augur and regulars from Fort Orford. On the 22nd the Rogues exchanged fire with troops of Captain Smith from Fort Lane, who were coming to rendezvous at the Illinois with those of Augur and Colonel Robert Buchanan moving up from the south. In fighting Smith's troops, the Indians suffered two casualties. As the Tututnis up the Rogue discovered troops moving to meet them, they returned fire and fled. In close combat five of their number were killed, and three others were drowned attempting to flee in a canoe. When the three military units failed to link up for a showdown against their red foe, their troops disengaged and marched down to the coast.

As soldiers scoured the Rogue Valley, many Lower Coquilles left their temporary reservation at Port Orford. For the next month the Rogues moved about their valley, and some harassed whites beyond its confines. On April 27, under a heavy fog, Indians between Big and Little Meadow at the Big Bend of the Rogue were surprised when attacked by volunteers concealed in brush across the river. From behind rocks and trees the warriors returned the fire as women and children ran for cover. Reinforced, the volunteers continued attacking until evening. When the firing ceased, over twenty Indians lay dead. Several times during the fight they had vainly sued for peace. On the next day, April 28, they fought for three hours, losing two of their number. The soldiers disengaged.

The Indians' request for peace was eventually accepted, and a treaty council arranged. On May 15, Chetco and Tututni chiefs parleyed with Colonel Buchanan, who found them at Oak Flat on the Illinois. They agreed to negotiate there at council grounds surrounded by snow-covered mountains. When preliminary discussions were concluded, Rogue chiefs George and Limpy met Buchanan on May 19 at the council grounds. On May 21 and 22 the chiefs were asked in council to surrender their arms and to assemble their people within the week at the meadows at Big Bend. John had expressed a willingness to cease fighting, but not to leave his homeland for the Siletz. Defiantly he addressed Buchanan:

You are a great chief; So am I. This is my country. I was in it when these large trees were very small not higher than my head. My heart is sick with fighting, but I want to live in my country. If the white people are willing I will go back to Deer Creek and live among them as I used to do; they can visit my camp, and I will visit theirs; but I will not lay down my arms and go with you on the reserve. I will fight. Good-by.

A detachment of infantry from Fort Lane under Captain Smith marched upriver to receive the surrendering Indians at the Big Bend. Even getting to the council grounds was hazardous for the Indians. One group who made their way there by canoe was raked by gunfire from reinforcing

WINTER LODGE OF THE UMPQUA INDIANS.

A winter lodge of Umpqua Indians. Like other lodges of the Pacific Northwest coast, it was made of planking. Frank Leslie's Illustrated Newspaper, *April 24, 1858.*

SUMMER LODGES OF THE UMPQUA INDIANS.

A summer lodge of the Umpqua Indians sketched for Frank Leslie's Illustrated Newspaper, *April 24, 1858.*

troops. Others were also fired upon as they hurried along trails.

In George's camp, where Applegate, Galice, and Cow Creek survivors prepared for the May 26 meeting, the Indians plotted to attack the soldiers. John reportedly instigated the move. The next day they charged the soldiers' front and rear. Some climbed steep slopes to attack, and others tauntingly dangled ropes in front of their foe, emulating the way whites hanged Indians. About an hour before noon they charged the ridge, only to be repulsed. From positions atop hills they kept up a withering day-long crossfire on Smith's company, killing four troops and wounding sixteen others. The Indians continued firing until after dark. After a four-hour lull, they resumed the attack at daylight, continuing it until late afternoon. After several futile thrusts, the Rogues were repulsed to the riverbank and forced to surrender. The arrival of Augur's troops had spelled their defeat. George and Limpy surrendered May 29 at Big Bend. For several days Superintendent Palmer conferred with headmen as Indians straggled in and soldiers flushed others from the hills. Later one company burned a Chastacosta village, killing four men fishing. Others were killed or captured as troops sought to tighten their net. John escaped that snare. His actions confirmed his defiant words to Buchanan.

In hot June weather on the tenth about 242 Rogue captives set out with soldiers for Port Orford. Moving out, they wept and wailed at being forced to leave their homelands without their tools and other properties, to live, die, and be buried in a strange land. Although Palmer believed that the remoteness of their destination, the Siletz Reservation, would help protect them from whites, there was no assurance of protection from the natives of that place. At Port Orford, Enos unsuccessfully tried to stir them to resist. On June 20 about 600 Indians embarked on the northern journey aboard the steamer *Columbia*.* Because John had refused to surrender his arms in May, he was the last Rogue chief to come in, joining his fellow tribesmen in surrender near Port Orford on June 29. As an added indignity he and over 200 others were forced to walk 125 miles up the coast to the reservation. A steamer carrying nearly another 600 Indians had sailed without him. This experience and confinement did not break John's spirit. In May, 1858, because authorities believed he had received emissaries from Sam to plot a general uprising, he and his son were sent to Fort Vancouver. From there they were sent for incarceration to the Presidio at San Francisco, where the army detained and in-

doctrinated many recalcitrant Indians.†

The Indians of southwestern Oregon had not been completely exterminated as some whites had hoped. Yet warring and peaceful Indians alike had failed to hold their homelands inviolate. Abandoning large areas of ancestral lands, natives of the upper Umpqua were on the Grand Ronde Reservation along with those of the Willamette. Those of the southern coast and Rogue River Valley were on both the Grand Ronde and the Siletz. There was little chance that the internees could successfully challenge the white men and regain their lost lands. From the Columbia River northward other natives sought to avoid the same fate. Like the quarry they surrounded in their hunts, they felt a circle narrowing about them. Sometimes their prey escaped the surrounds. Could the Indians also escape those that the white men were preparing for them?

---

*Oregon Superintendent of Indian Affairs Absalom F. Hedges assigned R. B. Metcalfe as the first agent to the Siletz, where he assumed his duties on August 20, 1856. On that reservation of about one thousand square miles were the Rogues from the bands of Chiefs John, George, and Jo; Chastacostas; and some coast tribes. Problems arose when Indians of tribes with unratified treaties did not receive rations as did such tribes as the Cow Creek Umpquas and the Rogues, treated, September 19, 1853, whose ratified treaties provided them with rations. Many Oregon coast tribes were not yet on the Siletz. Oregon Superintendent of Indian Affairs James Nesmith, who succeeded Hedges, appointed two subagents to the Umpqua and Port Orford districts to oversee Indians who were not yet removed. Until his murder by Indians, Ben Wright, who was assigned to the Port Orford district as subagent, had under his care all the natives from the California border north to the Port Orford area and as far as the Coquille River. North of the Coquille was the Umpqua district, which extended north to the Siletz Reservation, where subagent E. P. Drew had 690 Indians under his care.

†Rogue River John and his son Adam are thought to have been the first Indians detained for punishment by the military at its installations in the San Francisco Bay area. The two were most likely confined in the guardhouse at the Presidio. Years later it was common practice for the army to take "difficult" Indians from their homelands for incarceration at Alcatraz. In 1858 the Presidio had the only guardhouse in the Bay area and a garrison to supply the daily guard. At Alcatraz only an army engineer and a civilian labor force constructed the first set of fortifications. The island was not garrisoned until December, 1859, when barracks and officers' quarters were erected. John and his son were released and returned to Oregon in May, 1862. Orders for John's release were sent to the commanding officer of the Presidio, not to the commander of the island. When returned, John and Adam went to the Grand Ronde (although when they were sent from Oregon five years before they had been on the Siletz). On the Grand Ronde they served as model Indians, exerting influence over other Indians to remain on the reservation.

12. NARROWING CIRCLES

In the spring of 1848, Chief Patkanin of the Snoqualmies summoned the peoples of Puget Sound to a deer drive on Whidbey Island. He had a brush-and-seaweed fence built across a narrow portion of the island from Penn Cove on the east of Ebeys Landing on the west, into which dogs drove the deer. Sixty deer were snared from the drive to provide the natives a great feast. On the third day of the feasting Patkanin warned that an American, Thomas W. Glasgow, had claimed lands bordering on the eastern end of the fence. The chief warned that whites soon would be so numerous that they would carry natives off in "fire-ships" (steamers) to perish in a distant country called Pelaky Illehee, the land of darkness. He exhorted the people to rise up against the whites and take the settlers' properties before they became too numerous to exterminate. One target that he proposed attacking was the Hudson's Bay Company post Fort Nisqually. Foreseeing that the Americans would appropriate Indian lands north of the Columbia as they had done in the Willamette Valley on the south, he suggested attacking a small American settlement at Tumwater (which was first called New Market) near Olympia, Washington, on southern Puget Sound near Fort Nisqually.

Not all the natives concurred in the plan. One who opposed it was a Nisqually chief named Gray Head. One reason perhaps for his opposition was that, in exchange for Indians' abandoning such practices as killing slaves and horses, company traders had agreed to protect them from northern Puget Sound natives raiding the southern Puget Sound country for booty and slaves. Gray Head also feared that attacks of the northern Puget Sound Indians would stimulate Patkanin's Snoqualmies and other tribes to encroach more on the weaker peoples of the southern Sound. A Duwamish chief also opposed attacking the Tumwater settlement. For the moment the council agreed to kill Glasgow and another white man, A. B. Rabbeson. The plan failed when Glasgow's Indian wife apprized him of it, causing him to flee the island as Rabbeson did with the help of a friendly Indian.

To avenge beatings inflicted on the Snoqualmie wife of the Nisqually Lachalet, Patkanin descended on Fort Nisqually with about a hundred warriors, mostly Snoqualmies, Snohomishes, and Skykomishes. On May 1, 1849, as Patkanin was admitted to the fort grounds, his brother, Kussass, readied an assault on the post. Washington territorial pioneer Ezra Meeker later claimed that Patkanin had landed that month at Budd Inlet (Olympia, Washington) with a war-canoe flotilla. According to Meeker, Patkanin had made it known that he was going to destroy the whites, and, when a squad of white men told him that one of their race had a "terrible great gun" (actually an oversized rifle), that could sink his canoes, Patkanin and his party withdrew.[1] At the fort the natives spurned the usual gift of tobacco to put them in a good mood. A gunshot, fired by a fort guard in jest as much as in warning, signaled Kussass and four natives to rush the gate. Inside they shoved fort personnel around and fired shots and insults. By the time fort personnel had armed themselves, the attackers had fled. An American, Leander Wallace, who had come there to trade, was left dead from a gunshot wound. Their fire also perforated a small postern gate that fort personnel called The Watergate. In the scuffle a Skykomish shaman was killed, and two Snoqualmies were wounded, one in the shoulder and the other in the neck.

After the fracas Patkanin, who reportedly had slipped away during the excitement, discovered that he would have to deal not only with company personnel but also with officials of the United States, which now claimed the country below the forty-ninth parallel. On learning of the attack Americans built blockhouse forts in areas as diverse as the Tumwater River near the fort and the Cowlitz. On receipt of a message from the Puget Sound trader Tolmie, Governor Lane promptly dispatched a Lieutenant Hawkins northward to the Sound. In July an artillery company under Captain Bennett H. Hill, recently arrived from the East, was dispatched to the Sound. Other troops following were garrisoned at Fort Steilacoom.

Patkanin offered what was by native standards a large gift of eighty three-point blankets to settle the affair, but the Americans, following their own system of justice, took their own retribution on the attackers. Six were brought before a judge at Fort Steilacoom. Two of them, namely Kussass and Qullahwout (the latter was a Skykomish chief and a brother of Patkanin), were found guilty of murder by a jury. In October they were hanged, the first such "legal" hanging on Puget Sound. Four were exonerated—Tatum, Quailthlumkyne, Whyeck, and Sterhawai (Stuhanie). The last was an innocent slave whom the Indians had hoped to substitute for the guilty in keeping with an ancient practice.

Patkanin could find no slave to take his place when the military shipped him off to San Francisco for a short incarceration. If they sent him less to punish him than to impress him with the large number of whites who were gathered there in response to the gold rush, it might be said that the punishment was successful. On returning home he caused Americans no more trouble; in fact, he became their ally. The Snoqualmies and their allies kept coming to the Fort Nisqually to ascertain the plans of white men and to trade, although not as much in weapons as formerly because of the Oregon territorial government's restriction on their sale to Indians. The ban was intended for the protection of the American settlers, whose numbers were augmented by continuing immigration from the East and by miners returning from California. On November 13, 1851, twenty-four whites, half of them children, landed at Alki Point, in present-day Seattle. Patkanin befriended them, especially their leader, Arthur A. Denny, the founder of Seattle, which was to become the largest city in the Pacific Northwest before the end of the century. Each additional newcomer, however, filled the Indians with alarm, for the whites brazenly encroached on potato patches, root grounds, and clam beaches. Some new arrivals brought liquor and diseases and forced natives into submission by physically beating them when they got in the way. Control over Indian lives was exerted not only by the immigrants but also by the government, which placed agents over the red inhabitants.

Like the natives of the Sound the Makahs and Clallams of the Strait of Juan de Fuca were especially opposed to white men entering their country. In 1853, after a Clallam named Natcherni killed a white man (a Mr. Pettingale), who was one of three whites whom the Indians of the strait had recently killed, the Clallams came under the surveillance of the government steamer *Active* cruising into New Dungeness to seek out the killer. Several native chiefs were hauled aboard ship at the nearby settlement of Port Townsend and held hostage until the killer was delivered. The one who was finally turned over proved to be an innocent lad. Besting the whites in this manner did not blind Indians to the fact that in days ahead they would have to reckon with the government, whose gunboats proved its determination to make its authority felt.

As if those events did not augur trouble enough for Indians, the natives witnessed a decline in the fur-trading system, to which they had finally learned to adjust despite some conflict. The Hudson's Bay Company already had changed its traditional operations, among other ways, from strict fur gathering to agriculture. The fall in the price of beaver, which in 1853 was but a dollar for the skin of a large animal, paralleled the decline in its pursuit, although by the fifties the animals' numbers had increased because of a decline in trapping. In 1834 the Columbia River district harvest was 21,000 pelts; by 1845 it was reduced to 17,290, and by 1848 to 12,756.[2] Another indication of the rapidly diminishing fur trade below the Canadian border is seen in an official report stating that company posts below the border were operating at a loss, with the exception of Fort Colville, the greater portion of whose furs came from Canada. The high prices that the Indians of the Walla Walla and Snake countries demanded for their horseflesh further hampered company operations in the interior. By the middle of the century Indians were passing from a barter system to one of cash received in exchange for their goods and services.

Seeking some permanency in this time of change, Indians continued to receive the ministrations of the Roman Catholic fathers. In 1857 the Reverend Eugene Casimere Chirouse, O.M.I., established a mission in the Snohomish country. He and the Reverend Louis J. D'Herbomez of the same order established other missions among the Nooksacks, Lummis, and Samishes (all Salishan) from Puget Sound north to the Canadian border. The presence of the priests—as well as other factors, such as the ravages of the diseases reducing native numbers—served to limit the intertribal warfare that formerly erupted among the tribes. Very closely related to the Lummis, the Samishes lived peacefully with their mainland neighbors, the once powerful and warlike Nuwhahas (erroneously called Upper Samishes), and were lumped together with the Skagits for the convenience of white treaty makers. Between the sixties and the early eighties churches were built among such Salish speakers as the Lummis, Swinomishes, Suquamishes, and Muckleshoots. In 1857, however, the Squaxins (Salishan) of southern Puget Sound would have nothing to do with a priest.[3]

The reservations on which the fathers ministered already were being planned for the Indians as much to allow whites to procure their lands as to protect the natives from white encroachment. Puget Sound Indians commiserated over their prospects with the Yakimas and the Klickitats, who traveled routinely, when snow conditions permitted, westward across the Cascade Mountains to Fort Nisqually to trade horses for marine products and other goods. By 1853 deer in the Yakima country had become so scarce—not so much because of white hunters as, ironically, because of Indian ones—that a horse was exchanged for as few as ten deerskins. The Yakimas were greatly agitated lest whites seize their garden spots, as they had those west of the Cascade Mountains, and lest they appropriate grasslands on which to graze their stock.

In a June 5, 1851, council with Indians at The Dalles and in another on the twenty-seventh with the Nez Percés, Superintendent Dart assured them that whites would not drive them from their lands, for which he promised they would be paid. The natives were disturbed to hear from him of the plan to remove Indians from west of the Cascade Mountains into the interior. Former Governor Lane had been aware of the importance of stabilizing the potentially explosive situation in the interior, which threatened destruction to both whites and Indians. In his first message to the Oregon Territory legislature on July 17, 1849, he had happily reported that on a recent journey to the interior he had effected a peace between the Yakimas and the Wallawallas to end one of the many petty wars fought by tribes of that region. The establishment shortly of an agency among the Cayuses was calculated not only to help them survive but also to ensure their good behavior toward whites who traversed their lands astride the Immigrant Road.

As on other inland frontiers white settlers in certain areas of the Pacific Northwest interior were preceded shortly after mid-century by cattlemen driving herds onto their lush grasslands. Lieutenant Ulysses S. Grant, serving as an officer at Vancouver Barracks, was a silent partner of one cattle outfit in the Walla Walla Valley. Unhappy with the land takers, the Cayuses and Wallawallas held councils in the winter and spring of 1852–53 to discuss plans to rid themselves of the intruders. Major Benjamin Alvord, commanding an army garrison at The Dalles, warned General Ethan Allen Hitchcock, commanding the Pacific Division in San Francisco, that the Yakimas, who previously had fortified themselves against the Cayuses, were now par-

Lummi Indian dancers of Northwest Washington, circa 1921. Whatcom Musem of History and Art, Bellingham, Washington.

ticipating in Cayuse-Walla Walla councils, as they were in councils with Puget Sound tribes to defy the settlers, the Kooyawowculth whom Yakima prophets had predicted would wrest their lands from them.

Kamiakin, who was the son of a Nez Percé–Palouse father and a Yakima mother, emerged as the leader in preparing for the eventual native defiance of the whites. In many respects he was a landless chief who happened to be at the right place at the right time to asume Yakima leadership.[4] He was friendly to the Reverend Charles Pandosy, O.M.I., and D'Herbomez, unlike Lower Yakima chiefs Skloom and his brother Showaway. Still he failed to heed the priests' admonition to give up all but one of his wives. Theodore Winthrop, author of the classic *The Canoe and the Saddle*, traversed Yakima country on a journey from Puget Sound to The Dalles in the summer of 1853 and described Kamiakin at his camp on the Ahtanum, a Yakima tributary: "a tall, large man, very dark, with a massive square face, and

grave, reflective look"—a contrast to natives of the Sound, who appeared ignoble to this aristocratically reared scion of an old Puritan family, who traveled awkwardly among the western "savages." Because of Kamiakin's animosity toward them, whites would call him Sullen Chief.

In contrast to his own, Theodore Winthrop disdained the natives' aristocracy, which in his words bore as its stamp the "coxcombries and deformities" of the "skull-crushing system." Whites often wrote on paper for Indians words that were highly prized by them, such as their new names, verifying them as the names of white dignitaries. One important Clallam bearing such a name was Chief Chitsamakhan (Chetzamokha), who was dubbed Duke of York. Winthrop wrote that civilization came to Chitsamakhan with "stepmother kindness" baptizing him with rum and clothing him in discarded "slops." One of Duke's wives bore the name Queen Victoria. The chanting of his other wife, dubbed Jenny Lind, must have made her in Winthrop's thinking little like her operatic namesake. Both she and her husband, like so many other natives of the strait and Puget Sound, had succumbed to "liquor of the fieriest," devil-sent on lumber brigs and by other means to prostrate the natives as the smallpox had. Winthrop considered alcohol to be "the fatalist foe of the Indian." Had he been as interested in the Indians' genealogical roots and traditions as he probably was in his own, he might have learned that the nearby Chimakum Indians (Chimakuan) were, according to their traditions, a remnant of a Quileute band, who fled the Pacific Coast because of a high tide that took four days to ebb. The Chimakum village Tsetsibus (near Port Hadlock, Washington) had been a gathering place for Puget Sound natives, although the Chimakums were never numerous, especially after they sustained heavy losses in conflicts with neighboring tribes around 1790. In a fight with the Suquamishes around 1850 the Chimakum braves were either slaughtered or captured.

Yakima fears were given added substance in 1853 by whites moving across their lands toward Puget Sound. Citizens of that region began that summer to hack out a road eastward over the Cascade Mountains. These efforts were enough in themselves to increase the gravity on Kamiakin's face. Government officials tried to make him believe that such a road through his country would greatly benefit him and his people. Neither he nor they believed it would.

Tribes of the interior invited others—from the Chinooks of the lower Columbia to the Blackfeet on the east—to join in a coalition against the whites. Father Chirouse understood the volatility of the interior Indians and tried to protect the Cayuses from white inroads, as he later would the natives of Puget Sound. Father Pandosy made similar efforts on behalf of the Yakimas. After Wiemashet, a son of Upper Yakima Chief Owhi told his father in the spring of 1850 that he would kill the black robe if he did not take the priest away, Owhi took the cleric for safekeeping to the Selah Valley and Naneum Creek in Upper Yakima country.

On April 17, 1853, Pandosy wrote Catholic priest Toussaint Mesplié at The Dalles: "The clouds are gathering upon all hands.... The Tempest is pent up ready to burst." "*The cause of this war*," emphasized Pandosy, "*is that the Americans are going to seize their lands.*" Demonstrating that complaints voiced in councils were not merely campfire talk, the Indians began gathering and husbanding guns and ammunition in much the same way that the Rogues had on the south. Rumors persisted among the whites in the now predominantly Protestant Willamette community that the priests were arming the Indians to destroy their Protestant rivals.

The tribes' apprehensions were increased in the summer

An Indian family near Chimakum Creek at the foot of the Hood Canal below present-day Port Townsend, Washington. Pacific *Northwest Collections, University of Washington Library.*

126

of 1853 by the appearance of Captain George McClellan leading a northern Pacific railroad survey party along the western portions of a line that was to run from St. Paul to Puget Sound. McClellan broke the news to the Yakimas that their country would soon become a thoroughfare for white travel, warning their chiefs not to retaliate against whites for such travel but to forward complaints to Isaac I. Stevens when he arrived to assume the governorship of the newly established Washington Territory. That same summer word spread among Indians of the interior that the command of Lieutenant Rufus Saxton, protecting the surveyors, had come to seize the Indians' lands, horses, and other properties along the soldiers' route from The Dalles to Fort Benton on the upper Missouri River. The Cayuses, Wallawallas, Palouses, Nez Percés, and other tribesmen met with him to ascertain why he was crossing their lands. He appeared to have calmed their fears with his low-keyed responses to their questions. Near the mouth of the Palouse, Saxton would not punish a Spokane Indian suspected of stealing horses from his command, fearing that punishment would alienate the Spokanes from any association with the troops.

Moving northward cross-country from the Yakima to the Columbia River, McClellan continued his surveys en route to join Stevens, who was moving westward toward the Spokane country. At the mouth of the Wenatchee River, McClellan accepted the word of the natives that it was impossible to open a road along that stream and over a mountain pass to Puget Sound. Trains of the Great Northern Railroad would be running over that route within a scant forty years. The captain had its natives select a chief to represent them in a forthcoming council with Stevens. They chose Tecolekun, who ousted Sulktalthscosum's son, Quiltenenoc, in an election. At McClellan's suggestion natives of the lower Okanogan selected a leader named Kekehtumnouse (or Pierre) as their chief for purposes of dealing with government officials.

Having no voice in selecting their chiefs were the many smallpox victims whose bodies were literally scattered that summer along the mid-Columbia, as they were at other points in the Pacific Northwest. The disease, like a grim reaper cutting a swath, struck down Indians and helped clear the way for whites to traverse and occupy the Indian lands. Their dead bodies were morbid proof that white men had disease as their ally, besides guns and liquor, to help them eliminate red men standing in their way. Along the Snake River at such places as Salmon Falls many had died the previous year after sweat-bathing and plunging into the river. The smallpox nearly wiped out the Makahs in 1853. It had been carried to them by two Makahs who were told to burn a pile of old clothing in San Francisco and instead carried it home aboard a ship. Hoping to escape their infected village, some natives fled across the Strait of Juan de Fuca to Vancouver Island, infecting tribes there. As the contagion ran its course, the Makahs offered, in return for a cure, to become the slaves of John Hancock, a white trader at Neah Bay. The gesture reveals their plight, for they had frowned on his presence there. Hancock hauled the dead away, bury-

George and Jennie, Methow Indians. The Methows were interior Salish. They lived along the Methow River, a Columbia Tributary. North Central Washington Museum Association.

ing them in two trenches he had dug for that purpose. Two chiefs who succumbed were Flattery Jack and Klehsitt, a Russian half blood. At the Makah village of Baadah the dead lay unburied. Indian agent E. A. Starling reported in December, 1853, to Governor Stevens that the epidemic had spread to every tribe on Puget Sound and had been most devastating among the Makahs, whose numbers it had halved. For years Makahs believed whites had put the disease in bottles and buried it in the sand.[5]

Ravages of the disease on the Columbia River below the Canadian border, severe as they were, would have been worse had Catholic priests not vaccinated the Indians. In the words of the Flathead missionary, the Reverend Adrian Hoecken, S.J., the immunization prevented the Spokanes and "other converted Indians" from being "swept away by the hundreds" like their nonimmunized fellows. More Indians might have received inoculations had they not believed that evil spirits entered bodies through poisoned darts like those that were used in vaccinations. Indians with such beliefs sought immunity by fleeing to the hills or in severe hydropathic practices. When McClellan was on the upper Columbia, Indians of the Methow River, a Columbia tributary, had abandoned their country seeking to avoid the plague.

Indians sometimes received inoculations from white

neighbors. George Luther Boone, living west of the Coast Range in Oregon Territory, vaccinated several Indians, including Klickitats. At one village natives crowded around Winthrop and Dr. Tolmie praying to be vaccinated and offering a salmon for the service. Another white man of whom Indians sought aid at the time was Major Alvord. In 1853 several Wasco, Wishram, and Tenino chiefs asked him to help them suppress the custom of killing doctors if they did not cure their patients, a practice that had just cost them the lives of three of their practitioners. Three months later the smallpox destroyed a large segment of the Wishrams. When a doctor boasted of shamanist powers, the indignant tribe, believing him guilty of the plague, hanged him from off a horse.[6]

Although frowning on doctor killings, Hudson's Bay Company officials did not interfere greatly with the practice, especially in the interior. Company officials appeared to frown more on the practice when killings occurred closer to the company headquarters, Fort Vancouver. Sometimes Indians turned to territorial officials and to army personnel to help solve the problem of Indian deaths. A chief in The Dalles area, Kaskillah, wrote Governor John P. Gaines in June, 1852, seeking his support in sparing natives from diseases carried overland and upriver from the coast. A concoction of Oregon grape helped natives of the area check the ravages of gonorrhea, which was cutting an infectious swath up the Columbia. Eye ailments continued to plague Columbia River peoples. Columbia Plateau peoples suffered atrophy of leg muscles because of their overdependence on horses for transport.

As the railroad surveyors assayed diseases, Indians in general, and Indian lands in particular, Stevens met in that summer of 1853 with Blackfeet at Fort Benton, hoping to knock the edge off their belligerence. The small segment of that people with whom he talked offered to use their influence to induce their nation to cease sending war parties against other tribes—a task too great for even the optimistic Stevens to believe possible. Yet he held out hopes of assembling tribes from both sides of the Rockies to effect a lasting peace. On September 8, 1853, he requested Lieutenant John Mullan to carry a message to the Flatheads assuring them that the president, the Great Father, would protect them from the Blackfeet, who had helped reduce their numbers to only 325 souls. At the same time the Plains raiders had reduced their horse herds by theft. In a letter of October 2, 1853, Mullan replied to Stevens that he had found the Flatheads in buffalo country, where it was their practice to go in April in company with the Kalispels and Nez Percés to hunt bulls. They would return west and then go again to the plains later in the summer to kill cows. They returned west of the Rockies through the latter part of the year with meat and buffalo robes.

As the buffalo-hunting era moved toward its close, western tribesmen, especially the Salishans, increased, if anything, their hunts on the plains as they sought subsistence in traditional ways. A look at the buffalo-hunting phenomenon is therefore in order. The Nez Percés and Salishans, who lived farther from the northern plains than

such tribes as the Flatheads, often wintered east of the Rockies. Westerners reached the hunting grounds in Montana over diverse routes. Some of the more important ones were between Hell Gate near Missoula, Montana, and the plains. One route was up the Blackfoot River on the western slope of the Rockies to Cadottes Pass on the upper Sun River. A second route was up the Little Blackfoot through Mullan Pass and down Smith River to the Musselshell and Judith countries. A third route was up the Deer Lodge River. The Deer Lodge Valley, like the Big Hole, Beaverhead, and Jefferson river valleys, had been neutral ground for Shoshoni, Salishan, and Shahaptian peoples. From the Deer Lodge valley a route crossed Pipestone Pass and continued down the Jefferson by Sixteen-Mile Creek and on to Twenty-Five-Mile Creek (Shields River) to the country surrounding that stream. An important route for the Nez Percés was over Lolo Pass.[7]

Some tribes sojourned on Horse and Camas prairies on the Clark Fork during annual migrations to and from the buffalo country. The Upper Kalispels under Ambrose were one such tribe. They numbered 280, including intermarried Spokanes, Kalispels proper, and Flatheads. The Lower Kalispels, numbering 420 souls under Chief Victor, continued their treks to hunt buffalo. Although they had come under the influence of mission agriculture, they were willing to risk their own hides to obtain the hides of the big beasts of the plains.

The physical and spiritual preparations for the hunts continued as they had in times past. The physical preparations involved the gathering of weapons. Increasingly used now were flintlock guns obtained from white traders. A white traveler at Fort Kootenay near Jennings, Montana, in 1854 demonstrated to the Kutenais a six-shooter, a weapon they had apparently never seen before. The buffalo hunters also had to gather their horses and gear. Their sojourns on the plains sometimes kept them up to three years from their western villages and took them far beyond traditional hunting grounds, such as the Musselshell, Yellowstone, and Judith Basin countries, to points as far east as Lake Superior. Spiritual preparations among Salish hunters included the *kaseesum* (also *skasitsum* and the like), a ceremonial act in which hunters beat sticks on "power" blankets, indicating their commitment to the always-dangerous journey to the buffalo country. The aged, the infirm, and the cowardly remained behind. The Nez Percés observed a three- to seven-day ceremony of preparation, purging food from their stomachs, sweat-bathing, and plunging into cold water to overcome *wawash*, the spirit of fatigue.

Reaching the plains required no small amount of skill. Crossing rivers that were frozen solid was not difficult, but crossing at other times was. Some natives crossed such wide rivers as the Missouri on horses. Often they floated properties across rivers on round, basket-shaped frameworks of willow, over which buffalo hides were tightly stretched to form boatlike floats. Women and children often perched precariously atop balloon-shaped bundles of their belongings encased in lodge skins as their ponies towed them across. They usually spent a day or so drying out and repacking belongings before moving out onto the always-dangerous buffalo ranges.

Sometimes when trading with the Blackfeet the products from the west, such as pounded salmon, in exchange for buffalo hides, arguments erupted that led to fights. These were usually brief, seldom lasting more than two or three days, after which truces were declared. Memories of such encounters remained, however, to bring contending parties together again in conflict. At other times braves summoned their powers to enable them to creep into the skin-covered Blackfoot "barns" and silently purloin horses after carefully removing bells tied to their hooves. Whenever the Blackfeet stole Salishan horses, their owners were hard pressed to return home with their own skins and those of the buffalo intact. Honors were won by performing valorous acts on the hunts. Young braves eagerly sought entrance into warrior societies, which were structured in emulation of those of their Plains foes, from whom they borrowed many forms and trappings. On returning home after successful hunts, they celebrated the scalp dance and other victory dances. Returning from the buffalo hunt, a member of the Nez Percé band of Chief Ellis brought Blackfoot scalps and muskets that had been taken in revenge for the death of the member's only brother at their hands. In the center of a circle he displayed his trophies for all to see, reciting the manner in which each was taken. A mock battle followed in emulation of that in which he had garnered the trophies.[8]

The Coeur d'Alênes impressed all survey-party members with their agricultural endeavors, which had helped to spare them the dangerous buffalo trips but not intertribal conflict closer to home. Visiting them in early October, 1853, Stevens noted their uneasy relationship with the Upper Spokanes over a joint boundary line west of Lake Coeur d'Alêne. Relations between the two peoples were not as strained as they had been in earlier times, when they occasionally warred against each other. Chief Garry may have told Stevens how the Roman Catholic Coeur d'Alênes had taunted his people as heretic believers of a worthless faith. Garry impressed Stevens, who described him as a man "of education, of strict probity, and great influence over his tribe." His position was enhanced by a Dantelike appearance and the ability to speak English, which his people recognized as an asset in communicating with white men. It was he who told Stevens of the movements of other survey-party members in the area and who supplied Stevens with horses when he left it. With the Stevens surveyors was the artist John Mix Stanley. Seven years previously he had painted portraits of interior tribesmen, as did another equally famous artist, George Catlin, on his "last rambles" in the region two years after the Stevens surveys. Before Catlin the artist Paul Kane in 1847 painted Pacific Northwest Indian life.

Moving to Olympia, the seat of the Washington territorial government, Stevens left Indian affairs on both sides of the Rockies in a state of suspended animation. Lieutenant Saxton late in summer of 1853 found the country east of Kalispel Lake deserted by Indians fearing Blackfoot raids. In the country of those raiders James Doty of the survey party

noted that about five hundred natives, mostly Piegans, had passed Fort Benton between the first of October and the last of December en route to war. Although about one hundred of them were induced to turn back, an estimated eight hundred to a thousand above and below Fort Benton moved toward the Flathead, Shoshoni, and Crow countries.

Survey-party members well knew the troubles that the Blackfeet had brought on the Flatheads, whom the surveyors regarded as a friendly people who had been too long and too much oppressed by the Plains raiders. The latter they characterized as "Arabs of the North" and, more sharply, as "formidable freebooters," "develish fiends," and "hellhounds of the mountains." To keep the aggressive plainsmen under control, Mullan recommended to Stevens the building of a military post at or near Fort Benton. To survey officials, the Flatheads expressed a willingness to abandon ·their roving and accept agents, tools, and other government aid—a willingness stemming from the knowledge that further plains hunts threatened them with extinction. The many people they had lost to the Blackfeet, as well as the many horses (and the cattle that the Blackfeet sometimes killed for spite), were threatening to confine them west of the Rockies. They were at the point where they had little chance for survival without subsistence from other sources.

Both Stevens and Mullan encouraged the Flatheads to remain at home in the Bitterroot and rebuild their Saint Mary's Mission, closed in November, 1850. Stevens's plans to open the Bitterroot to white settlement save for a small reservation would have made it all the more difficult for the Flatheads to survive. His thinking revealed that his responsibility as superintendent of Indian affairs to protect Indians conflicted sharply with his railroad surveys and his governorship, both of which were dedicated to preserving the interests of whites over those of red men. In short, he failed to see any conflict of interest. The Indians were not so blind. Using the French words of a priest, they called him "un homme a doubles bouches"—a man with a forked tongue.

Mullan would have had agents of his own Catholic faith appointed to administer Indian affairs. Taking issue with him was George Gibbs. Like the governor, Gibbs saw Mullan's priestly orientation as inconsistent with settlement of the country and with established Indian policies. From two large agencies, one on each side of the Cascade Mountains, Gibbs would have established reservations near to where the Indians lived, where under responsible chiefs they might "raise their vegetables and bury their dead"—in reality, little islands washed by a sea of whites and watered by the Donation Land laws. Stevens, on the contrary, believed the fewer reservations the better. It appeared to most survey officials that outside of fertile river valleys the vast semiarid Columbia Plateau would be safe for Indian habitation for a long time to come, although cattlemen were already casting covetous eyes on its bunch-grass richness. What they failed to see was its potential for dry-land farming, which was to be under way there within a quarter century.

In matters of Indian governance Gibbs followed the thinking of the missionary Dr. White, Stevens, and McClellan, who implemented Stevens's thinking; he wanted the bands to choose their own chiefs to treat with the government. He wrote:

One principle of policy, in particular, should be observed—the union of small bands under a single head. The maxim of divide and conquer does not apply among these people. They are never so disposed to mischief as when scattered and beyond control; whereas it is always in the power of the government to secure the influence of chiefs, and through them to manage their people. Those who at present bear the name have not influence enough, and no proper opportunity should be spared of encouraging and supporting them in its extension. This policy, long pursued by the Hudson's Bay Company, was one secret of their former great influence.⁹

When Cayuse Indians in 1853 appealed to their agent, Robert R. Thompson of the Oregon superintendency, to choose a chief for them, he declined, saying it was their responsibility to do so. With such a response, they reverted to their traditional practice of seeking company assistance in the selection, turning to Fort Walla Walla trader Andrew D. Pambrun. He suggested they choose Five Crows as their leader. Remembering that chief's belligerent posture during the Cayuse War, Thompson wrote Pambrun on October 21, 1853, that the Cayuses and Nez Percés would henceforth look to his agency for guidance in selecting a chief. Peter Skene Ogden, now chief factor for the Hudson's Bay Company at Fort Vancouver, assured Superintendent Palmer that Pambrun would be informed that he had, as Ogden put it, "nothing whatever to do with the political affairs of the natives."

Portions of the multivolume report of the Pacific railroad surveys pertained to natives west of the Rockies. Because those surveys might affect the building of a transcontinental railroad, the Indians were favorably pictured to offset a host of criticisms of the railroad that included the possibility of Indians plundering passing trains. Ironically neither Indians nor lack of technology delayed the building of the first transcontinental railroad—the Union Pacific-Central Pacific, completed in 1869—but sectional conflict within the United States itself did. Stevens had felt the impact of such conflict in 1853 when his superior, the secretary of war, southerner Jefferson Davis, limited funds for surveys along the northern route. The consequences of the conflict proved far more tragic to Stevens, for he was killed in the early stages of the Civil War.

Without written words the Indians had no multivolume report to record their own reaction to the surveys. After a period of initial surprise they had by 1854 settled into an uglier mood. This became evident at the beginning of that year, when, after whites killed five Indians near The Dalles, the Indians retaliated by attacking and robbing immigrant parties along the well-beaten Immigrant Road. Compounding the conflict were the increasing numbers of whiskey peddlers, who operated in poorly policed and protected local jurisdictions whose courts, refusing to accept Indian testimony, failed to prosecute them. Major Gabriel Rains succeeded Major Alvord as commander of Fort Dalles in 1854. He was so concerned by the deteriorating situation that he called for prompt action by the militia to prevent what he believed would be a general Indian uprising from the Cascade to the Rocky Mountains.

In the meantime Kamiakin continued to rally the tribes, including his own divided Yakimas. His efforts were hampered by continuing intertribal raids, which caused ill will to fester among the natives despite the attempts of Hudson's Bay company officials and Indian agents to prevent them. Kamiakin hoped that the threat of a white invasion faced by all tribes in common would produce enough cohesion to hold them together at least long enough to oppose it.

In the summer of 1854, Stevens expressed to the chiefs his wish to meet them in council to discuss government purchase of their lands. According to Indian accounts Kamiakin then called a council of interior tribes in the Grande Ronde Valley to map out a strategy to oppose such a move. At that council the interior was reportedly divided into bounded areas corresponding to the reservations that the government would establish, so that, when the tribes met with the governor, they could hold out for reserves corresponding to those they had marked out in their council. Foreseeing trouble ahead, Pandosy warned Kamiakin that Indians could fight and delay whites, but could never stop them.

The Indians did not have long to wait to employ their stratagems on Stevens. Before the year of 1854 was out, the aggressive surveyor–governor–Indian superintendent began his treaty making with the Indians of Washington Territory. He hoped to complete his task quickly, for the sooner smoke wisped from treaty pipes the sooner it would roll from white men's chimneys. The red men understandably did not share the governor's sense of expedience as they prepared to meet him in council. Around village campfire councils they talked of the possible consequences of the forthcoming meeting. One that they could not fail to contemplate was that white men by pacts or power might wrest from them their lands—even the very ground on which they held their solemn councils.

13. TREATIES OR TREATMENT?

Many of the basic provisions of the treaties signed by Columbia River and Oregon tribes had been formulated by Superintendent Joel Palmer under guidelines established in drafts of treaties effected with Missouri and Omaha Indians (10 Stat. 1043). When commissioned to treat with the Indians of his territory, Governor Isaac Stevens followed Palmer's basic formula. Following guidelines laid down by a commission and by local agents, he planned to begin his treaty making on Puget Sound, proceed to the coast, and thence across the Cascade Mountains to the interior. In 1850 and 1852, Indians on the north side of the Strait of Juan de Fuca had met with British Columbia Governor James Douglas to negotiate a series of treaties, by which they ceded all their lands except their accustomed village camps and fishing sites, most of which would later become reserves.

In exchange for the lands ceded, the Indians with whom Stevens proposed to treat were to receive goods (rather than money) and services, such as instruction in the white men's agricultural and mechanical arts. Chiefs were to receive annuities. Fisheries were to be preserved. Tribal warfare and drunkenness were to be abolished, and also slavery, which some chiefs north of the strait had promised government officials they would end as early as 1849. In return Indians were to be placed on as few reservations as possible for the sake of expediency and economy of administration. The reservations were as yet unsurveyed. That peoples of diverse cultures and contentions were to be grouped together was of little concern to the white treaty makers. The chiefs who emerged as spokesmen for the diverse groups were those who cooperated with whites. Promises of annuities and the gifts distributed to them and to their peoples, as well as the presence of the military, were all calculated to bring the chiefs and their Indians into line with the policies of the government. The type of tribal leader that evolved after years of dealing with government officials was an autocrat whose position the government destroyed once the Indians were settled on reservations, at which time and place it came to regard them as obstacles to its administration of Indian affairs. Thus before the end of the century the United States government virtually destroyed the office of chief, although certain Indians continue to bear that title in the twentieth century.

Because of the many language differences among the tribes and because of the white men's difficulties in mastering their tongues, Stevens, like traders and missionaries before him, employed the Chinook jargon at his councils. By now in the areas where white men had settled, most Pacific Northwest Indians had learned to communicate with them in the jargon. Swinomish informants stated that the Indian who interpreted at the Point Elliott Treaty Council at present-day Mukilteo, Washington, was the first one in their area to learn the jargon. Steven's words were translated into that lingua franca, which was poorly suited to treaty negotiations, and were reinterpreted in the various tribal tongues. The process was then reversed as the Indians' words were retranslated into English, making the negotiations burdensome. Despite the use of the time-consuming jargon, Stevens continued in his resolve to consummate the treaties as quickly as possible.

In response to Stevens's summons, Nisquallis, Squaxins, Puyallups (Salishan), and Indians of six other tribes assembled on the day before Christmas, 1854, at Medicine (now McAllister) Creek in present-day Mason County, Washington.[1] The Indians were prepared to deliberate at length the treaty proposals enunciated there, but on the day after Christmas a young Puyallup named Linawah (also called Richard and Tyee Dick) made an impassioned speech in favor of it. Consequently, sixty-two chiefs and headmen affixed their signature marks to it. By its terms three reservations were established of about 1,280 acres each: the Puyallup at the mouth of the Puyallup River (near Tacoma, Washington), the Nisqually above the mouth of the Nisqually River (near Olympia, Washington), and the 1,494.15-acre Squaxin on Squaxin Island in southern Puget Sound (near Shelton, Washington). Within two years recommendations were made to enlarge the Puyallup to 18,062 acres (done by executive orders dated January 20, 1857, and September 6, 1873), to relocate the Nisqually and enlarge it to 4,718 acres (done by executive order on January 20, 1857), and to create the Muckleshoot Reservation of 3,440 acres near the confluence of the White and Green rivers (near Auburn, Washington).* A century later, during controversy over Indian fishing rights, the state of Washington unsuccessfully contended that the Muckleshoots were not a party to the treaty. The name Muckleshoot was an Anglicized form of the native name, Buklshuhl, and was not applied to the people until after the treaty.

The third signature on the treaty was that of Nisqually Chief Leschi (Lesh-high, Laschyach, and the like), who was to lead Puget Sound Indians against the Americans in war. Leschi declared to his death that he had never signed the document. During negotiations, when each chief was expected to make a map of his country in preparations for a composite map, Leschi reportedly refused to complete his and tore up a paper commissioning him as chief. By contrast most Indians eagerly sought such papers. Quiltenenock, son

---

*The Muckleshoot Reservation was set aside by executive order on January 20, 1857 (and modified by order on April 9, 1874). The Nisqually Reservation was relocated and enlarged, and the Puyallup Reservation was enlarged by executive order, January 20, 1857, under provision of the sixth article of the Medicine Creek Treaty, December 26, 1854.

A Nooksack Indian leader, Indian Jim, of northwestern Washington, with young Nooksacks. Whatcom Museum of History and Art, Bellingham, Washington.

of the late Columbia River chief Sulktalthscosum, had journeyed to Puget Sound and the Willamette Valley around 1850 seeking such a paper commissioning him as chief of scattered mid-Columbia bands. When the chief of the Queets Indians (Salishan) of the Olympic Peninsula lost the written commission that he had received in 1854, he requested another one fifteen years later. As we have noted, Indians treasured papers delineating their relationship to white dignitaries.

On January 22, 1855, 2,300 Indians assembled at Point Elliott (Mukilteo, near Everett, Washington) to treat for the cession of their lands. They came from the area between the Puyallup River and the Canadian border and included, from south to north, Duwamishes, Suquamishes, Snoqualmies, Snohomishes, Stillaguamishes, Swinomishes, Skagits, and Lummis. The council began and ended in a single day. After some remarks by Stevens and his party the Indians sang Catholic canticles and recited prayers. Chief Seattle (Sealth) responded to some remarks by the governor. Seattle was a Suquamish-Duwamish son of the warrior chief Schweabe. He lived mainly among the Duwamishes, having become their chief after proving his leadership qualities in a war that pitted them and other saltwater tribes against those of the Green and White rivers. Seattle said to Stevens:

I look upon you as my father. All of the Indians have the same good feeling toward you and will send it on the paper to the Great Father in Washington. All of them, men, women, and children, are glad that he has sent you to take care of them. My mind is like yours; I don't want to say more. My heart is always good toward Doctor Maynard. I want to get medicine from him.

Seattle was referring to Dr. David S. Maynard of Seattle, the town named for the chief. Stevens assured Seattle that under the treaty the Indians would have a doctor to care for them.

The treaty had actually been written before the council convened. It was read to the Indians, who were asked to sign if satisfied. They signed and the next day received presents. Seattle presented Stevens a white flag, which some might regard as a symbol of surrender, saying:

"Now, by this we make friends and put away all bad feelings, if we ever had any. We are the friends of the Americans. All the In-

Dr. Joe, a Swinomish medicine man. As an infant he went through the head-flattening process. Skagit County Historical Society.

dians are of the same mind. We look upon you as our father. We will never change our minds; as you have seen us we will always be the same. Now! now! do you send this paper of our hearts to the Great Chief. That is all I have to say."

Eighty-two headmen signed the treaty. Among them were Patkanin and Goliah of the Skagits.* An important signatory was the Lummi chief Chowitshoot (also Chowitsut and the like). Because of the smallpox, his people had abandoned settlements in the San Juan Islands to join others of their tribe on the mainland. The ancestors of the mainland Lummis had moved from the San Juans in pre-contact times to occupy lands near present-day Bellingham, Washington. There, according to tradition, they all but exterminated the native inhabitants of the area, the Hulhwa-

luq and the Skalakhan, in a war to secure fishing rights in the Nooksack River.[2] Chowitshoot was credited with exerting control over peoples from the Swinomish lands north to the Canadian border. His fame as a potlatch giver caused jealousy among other chiefs. Around 1859 or 1860 he was murdered by a half brother while pursuing his young Swinomish wife, who had run off with a thousand dollars.

The lands ceded under the treaty encompassed roughly the area of the several present-day Washington counties: King, Snohomish, Skagit, Whatcom Island, San Juan, and part of Kitsap. Several reservations were established under the treaty for tribes listed in 1980 by the Bureau of Indian Affairs. The Lummi reservation was enlarged by executive order, November 22, 1873, at the mouth of the Nooksack River for the Lummis. The Swinomish Reservation was on the peninsula at the southeastern end of Perry's Island (now Fidalgo Island). Its northern boundaries were clarified by executive order, September 9, 1873. The reservation was for the main Skagit village, for the Swinomishes, and for what white treaty makers regarded as Skagit subdivisions, the Suiattles and the Kikialluses. The Tulalip, or Snohomish, Reservation was enlarged by executive order, December 23, 1873. It was near the mouth of the Snohomish River and was for the Snohomishes, Snoqualmies, Skagits, Suiattles, Samishes, and allied bands. The Port Madison Reservation (also called the Suquamish, Fort Kitsap, and Seattle Reser-

---

*Stevens thought the Lower Skagits (who inhabited lands down the North Fork of the Skagit River and the central portions of Whidbey Island) were Swinomishes. He therefore did not extend a separate invitation to them to sign the treaty to cede their lands. When informed of his error after the document was signed, Stevens promptly sought an Indian among the Lower Skagits to sign. That Indian's unawareness of the intent of the treaty paper caused misunderstanding for years between the Lower Skagits and the government. With no reservation of their own the Skagits moved to the Swinomish and Tulalip reservations. For years the government considered the Swinomishes a subgroup of the Lower Skagits. The Swinomishes denied the relationship.

Fishing camp of Lummi Indians of northwestern Washington shortly after the turn of the century. Whatcom Museum of History and Art, Bellingham, Washington.

vation) was enlarged by executive order on October 21, 1864. Located on the Kitsap Peninsula, it was for the "Swamishes," "Etakmurs," Lummis, Snohomishes, and Suquamishes.*

On January 25, 1855, at Point No Point on a northern tip of the Kitsap Peninsula twelve hundred Indians assembled in council. They represented Clallam, Chimakum, and Twana bands living on the west side of Puget Sound from a point across from Steilacoom to a point at or near

---

*More land was set aside later for reservations that had not been provided by the treaty. The Port Gamble Reservation (located near the entrance to Hood Canal on its eastern shore) was purchased March 12, 1936, for the Suquamish and Clallam Indians. The Nooksack Community was also established later. It was not a true reservation, but an aggregate of individual allotments comprising 2,906 acres. It was set aside for the Nooksacks in Whatcom County, Washington, northeast of Bellingham.

Dungeness. After their treaty had been read and interpreted, Stevens asked if they had anything to say. Most of the opposition was voiced by the Twanas, who were unwilling to sell their lands. Like other Indians they regarded them as a religious heritage and, unlike whites, believed them something not to be traded or sold. Yet, through contact with whites, they were beginning to recognize the commercial value of the lands. One chief expressed the changing view when he said: "I do not want to sell my land, because it is valuable. The whites pay a great deal for a small piece, and they get money by selling the sticks [timber]." "Formerly," he continued, "the Indians slept, but the whites came among them and woke them up, and we now know that the lands are worth much." One chief opposed having to leave accustomed food-gathering places for the uncertainties of a reservation. Another opposed having to go to a place where he said his people would have to live with the more numerous Clallams. Their complaints notwithstanding, but after seeking a delay, the Twanas changed their position. Accompanying the Duke of York on January 26, they came bearing white flags as gifts for Stevens, saying their hearts had become white. They then proceeded to sign the treaty. By so doing they agreed to the usual stipulations, including the stipulation that they would not trade outside the United States. In lieu of going on the Skokomish Reservation, which was established under the treaty and by executive order on February 25, 1874, most Clallams integrated themselves into surrounding white communities. Three main bands—the Jamestown, Port Gamble, and Lower Elwha—remained on accustomed tribal sites in the nineteenth century.

On the evening of January 30 the Makahs at Stevens's invitation boarded his schooner in Neah Bay to hear him explain the main features of the proposed treaty. Chief Kalchote and several others expressed fears at the possible loss of their fishing grounds. On the morning of December 31 provisions of the treaty were read and interpreted. After presenting the governor a white flag symbolizing their acceptance of the document, the Indians signed the treaty and received the usual presents. The Makah Reservation created by the treaty was enlarged by executive orders on October 26, 1872, and January 2 and October 21, 1873.

Most other Indians of the Olympic Peninsula and south to the Columbia River were summoned to a council set for February 25, 1855, on the Chehalis River just east of Grays Harbor. One white man of the fourteen of his race attending the gathering recorded that the Indians noisily approached the grounds, faces painted, hair groomed, and best clothes donned. Within a large cleared square stood the white men's tents, surrounded by 350 Indians arranged tribally: Chinooks, Lower Chehalises, Quinaults, Queets, Satsops, Upper Chehalises, and Cowlitzes, representing about 843 souls in all. The council opening found the Indians assembled in front of Stevens's tent. That night they enjoyed, although they did not understand them, stories the white men told. After the customary warming-up period the next day, they learned through the semantic maze of interpretation the terms of the treaty. They then dismissed themselves to discuss them. Still angered that treaties Dart had made with lower Columbia River tribes at Tansey Point in 1851 had never been ratified by the Senate, the Chehalises refused to sign. The next day Narkarty (Nahcotta), a Chinook chief who also was disillusioned by the government's failure to live up to its Tansey Point treaty obligations, movingly told of the natives' wish to remain in their homelands:

Our fathers, and mothers, and ancestors are buried there, and by them we wish to bury our dead and be buried ourselves. We wish, therefore, each to have a place on our own land where we can live, and you may have the rest; but we can't go to the north among the other tribes [to a reservation that Stevens proposed stretching from Grays Harbor to Cape Flattery]. We are not friends, and if we went together we should fight, and soon we would all be killed.[3]

Narkarty's apparent liberality regarding the whites' posses-

sion of Indian lands except for those containing the graves of the dead is interesting in the light of a statement of an early-day white settler. With perhaps some exaggeration he wrote, "If I or any of the settlers had been allowed to have purchased the Indian titles to the land when we first went there, the whole tract from the Columbia to Fuca Straits could have been bought for a few trifling presents."

Native Americans plucked beautiful feathers from the eagle to adorn various pieces of their clothing and ceremonial objects. From a painting by Alden Metcalf.

One white man at the council, James Swan, opined that Stevens might have obtained signatures from Chinook and Chehalis headmen had it not been for the antics of one Tleyuk, the son of an old Chehalis chief, Carcowan. Since the proposed reservation did not include Tleyuk's homelands, and because he sought the head chieftaincy of the tribes, and also because he voiced strong opposition to ceding his lands, Tleyuk stirred dissension among the assembled tribesmen. The turmoil was carried further by his father, who smuggled whiskey onto the grounds in defiance of a prohibition by Stevens, before whom he appeared quite drunk. The next morning, after an evening approaching bedlam, Stevens severely reprimanded Tleyuk, tearing up before the assemblage a paper recognizing him as chief. On March 3 the Chehalis Council ended in failure.* On July 1 special Indian agent Michael Simmons effected the Quinault River Treaty with the Quinaults, Queets, Hohs, and Quileutes, by which those tribes surrendered their lands for the Quinault Reservation. The treaty did not receive Stevens's signature until January 25, 1856, when he returned to Olympia from treaty making east of the Cascade Mountains. The Quinault Reservation for the Quinault Treaty

---

*A reservation for the Chehalises, Chinooks, and a few other small tribes was established on the Chehalis and Black rivers by executive order, July 8, 1864. On October 1, 1886, by executive order 3,753.63 acres of the Chehalis Reservation were restored to the public domain for Indian homestead entry.

tribes was established in 1861 at the mouth of the Quinault River and enlarged by executive order, November 4, 1873. A reservation for the Quileutes was established at the mouth of the Quillayute River by executive order, February 19, 1889. A reservation for the Hohs, who were closely related to the Quileutes, was established at the mouth of the Hoh River by executive order, September 11, 1893.

On September 22, 1866, the small, 335-acre Shoalwater Bay Reservation was set aside by executive order on the north shore of Willapa Bay for about thirty or forty families in that area. Since the tract was unproductive, the Indians scheduled to go there stayed away. Some worked for whites in the oyster industry of Willapa Bay. Some who were entitled to allotments on the reservation took them instead on the Quinault. Superintendent Dart had treated with the Willopahs (Athapascan) on August 9, 1851, for their lands, which stretched east from Willapa Bay into the Willapa River watershed. By 1855 the tribe had become nearly extinct. Their demise was hastened by intermarriage with other tribes and by the smallpox plague of 1853. Chinook and Chehalis Indians appropriated their old village sites.

On April 1, 1855, James Doty, Stevens's secretary, and A. J. Bolon, his subagent, persuaded Kamiakin to participate in a council at which the government wished to treat with interior tribes for their lands. It was the Yakima chief who chose the meeting place—the old Indian grounds on Mill Creek, six miles above Waiilatpu in the Walla Walla Valley. Eventually representatives of the tribes agreed to meet there with both Stevens and Superintendent Palmer because the peoples involved lay within the Washington and Oregon superintendencies. The tribesmen opposed the forthcoming council. Stevens was warned of their disposition by the Reverend Paschal Ricard, O.M.I., among others. Ricard was then superior of the Catholic mission in the Yakima and Cayuse countries. At The Dalles, Major Rains was unconvinced of the need to provide troops for the council, another indication of the differing federal and territorial views in the conduct of Indian affairs. Yet he did accede to Stevens's request by sending along a detachment of thirty-seven troops, who were increased by another ten who had been chasing Indians in the Umatilla country. In late May word spread that the Cayuses, Wallawallas, and Yakimas were determined to retain their lands.

Known for their friendship for whites from the time of Lewis and Clark, the Nez Percés rode onto the council grounds[4] on May 24, carrying a flag given them in 1848 by

Nez Percés arriving for the Walla Walla Council in May, 1855. More Nez Percés were on the council grounds than all the other tribesmen there. From a drawing by Gustavus Sohon. Smith-sonian Institution National Anthropological Archives, Bureau of American Ethnology Collection, Neg. No. 45,734.

May. 1855. *Walla Walla Council.* Governor Stevens with Indians.

Indians meet in the Walla Walla Valley to council with Washington Territorial Governor and Superintendent of Indian Affairs Isaac I. Stevens and Oregon Territorial Superintendent of Indian Affairs Joel Palmer. As a result of their deliberations three major reservations were established: one for the Nez Percés; one for the Cayuses, Umatillas, and Wallawallas; and one for those under the Yakima standard. Yakima Nation Media Center.

their friend the former mountain man Robert Newell in appreciation for their help to whites in the Cayuse War. When the tribes were assembled, there were more Nez Percés on the grounds than all the other tribes combined. Chief Lawyer, still suffering from the wound inflicted by the Blackfeet, was banqueted by Stevens and Palmer. Other chiefs shown favored treatment were the lesser Cayuse chief Stickus, who was a friend of the departed Whitman, and Garry, who was on the grounds as an observer only. On May 26 the Cayuses and Wallawallas, gaily dressed and whooping and shouting, circled the 2,500-person camp three times in their fashion, making no attempt to disguise their hostility at the prospect of losing their lands. The chiefs—Weatenatanamy, Five Crows, Umhowlish, Howlish Wampo, Stickus, and Camaspelo— dismounted at the tent of Stevens and Palmer, to which they were invited. They shook hands, in the words of a white observer, in a "decidedly offish" manner. They declined an invitation to smoke, saying that they had not come that day to talk. On May 28 large numbers of Yakimas, Wallawallas, and Palouses arrived to encamp some distance from the council grounds. When the friendly chief Lawyer revealed to Stevens and Palmer the Cayuse and Wallawalla plans to resist, the commissioners were forced to plan countermoves. They needed the prayers that Spalding's convert, Chief Timothy, had uttered in church the previous day, for the Wallawallas, Cayuses, and Yakimas sent word they would accept no provisions and gifts, not even the seldom-refused strands of tobacco. By the twenty-ninth the council was obviously one of the largest such gatherings in Indian-American history with nearly five thousand Indians encamped in the valley. That the commissioners felt outnumbered is an understatement.

Peopeomoxmox asked for more than one interpreter to ensure Indian understanding of the council proceedings. Interpreters were ready to assist. Their role has too often been overlooked. Not only did their task call for a conversance with the native tongues but also with the English language and the Chinook jargon. Often interpreters, such as William Craig at the Walla Walla council, were married to Indian women, causing the white community contemptuously to call them squaw men. Half bloods like Andrew Pambrun, who was also at the council, also served as interpreters. Half bloods were usually the sons of white traders and Indian women. They often lacked formal education, relying instead on an acuity nurtured by their wits-sharpening life in two cultures. The interpreters at times did misinterpret, but a host of them—Joseph Gervais, Gabriel Prudhomme, George Montour, and others too numerous to mention—served to lessen conflict between the two races of which they were a part.

Through the interpreters the words of Peopeomoxmox were translated for the commissioners:

In one day the Americans became as numerous as the grass. This I learned in California. I know it is not right; you have spoken in a roundabout way. Speak straight. I have ears to hear you and here is my heart. Suppose you show me goods; shall I run up and take them? Goods and the earth are not equal. Goods are for using on the earth. I do not know where they have given lands for goods. We require time to think quietly, slowly. You have spoken in a manner partly tending to evil... Show me charity. I should be very much ashamed if the Americans did anything wrong... Think over what I have said.[5]

The Cayuses agreed with the words of the Wallawalla chief, but sought redress with arms, not words. After several months of spearheading a plan to rid the country of whites, they now hatched a plot with Wallawalla and Yakima help to kill the tiny knot of whites at the council and then ride down to capture the military garrison at The Dalles. On June 1 a fierce thunder and lightening storm, followed by strong winds, presaged something ominous about to happen. At midnight Lawyer, who had been absent from the war councils but apprized of them, brought word of the plot to Stevens. He had pitched his own lodge near the tent of his white friend as an expression of loyalty. Instead of working through the head chief, Lawyer, whom they thought of as a turncoat, the plotters sought to spread disaffection by stirring up some lesser chiefs in an anti-American Nez Percé faction. One of those, Spotted Eagle, told the commissioners of the maneuverings.

Particularly galling to the Cayuses was Stevens's plan to place them as well as the Nez Percés, Wallawallas, Umatillas, and Spokanes on a proposed reservation extending from the Blue Mountains to the spur of the Bitterroots and from the Palouse River part way up the Grande Ronde and Salmon rivers. Stevens tried to assure the tribes that such a reservation would be to their advantage, but the plan was so odious that even the friendly Stickus was offended by it. The tribes also found it difficult to accept Palmer's argument that they should go on a reservation to protect themselves from whites. Cayuse–Nez Percé interculture was no guarantee that those tribes wished to live on the same land. As his people were slated for the proposed reserve, Peopeomoxmox asked for delays while Stevens daily countered with the words, "Give me your hearts"—which meant in essence, "Give me your lands." To surrender them, as the Indians explained to Stevens, meant scarring the earth mother. In

response to the Indians' stiffening stance the governor was forced to jettison his two proposed reservations and propose three instead: one for Nez Percés, one for Yakimas, and now one for the Cayuses, Wallawallas, and Umatillas.

Submersed in tension, the Indians debated with anguish the reservation proposals as the commissioners continued to pressure them for their acceptance. Having ridden about three hundred miles in seven days from Blackfoot country, Looking Glass, the aged leader of the militant Nez Percé faction, rode onto the council grounds dangling a Blackfoot scalp to scold the Nez Percés for considering Stevens's plan for a Nez Percé reservation. After a conference nonreservation advocates under the elderly chief tried to depose Lawyer. Segments of the tribe friendlier to whites prevailed, retaining Lawyer as the Nez Percé spokesman. To obtain the signature of Looking Glass on the treaty, Stevens promised to make him war chief next to Lawyer in authority.

The failure of Looking Glass to persuade the Nez Percés to accept his viewpoint allowed the commissioners to proceed with the help of Lawyer. Helping to influence the Nez Percés was the commissioners' proposal of the separate reservation (the Umatilla) for the Cayuses, Wallawallas, and Umatilas—a prospect that was more satisfactory to the Cayuses than to the other two tribes because the confine was to be in Cayuse lands. Creating a more favorable disposition among the Nez Percés to sign a treaty was the belief that was beginning to gain ground among them that it would be cowardly not to do so.

On June 9, after Stevens had talked privately with Kamiakin and Peopeomoxmox, the two agreed to sign a treaty. According to Doty, when Kamiakin saw that the commissioners had brought presents for the Indians, he said he would accept them only after the president approved the documents and after the Indians had removed to the reservation. Apparently the Yakima chief feared that acceptance of gifts, even token ones, for signing would make the treaty more binding.

Witnessing the council, William Cameron McKay, the son of trader-interpreter Thomas McKay, wrote of Kamiakin's signing:

When the Indians hesitated, the Governor said to tell the chief, "if they don't sign this treaty, they will walk in blood knee deep." To illustrate, Mam-ia-kin [Kamiakin] was about the last to sign by making his cross. When he returned to his seat, his lips were covered with blood, having bitten them with suppressed rage. Father Chaurause [Chirouse] the Catholic Priest was standing by me at the time, and he drew my attention to the blood, remarking "I am afraid we will all be murdered before we leave these grounds."

By June 11 all had signed. A white man in attendance wrote with some irony, "Uncle Sam has got 22,000,000 acres more of land, and a few thousand more of Indians to take care of, and a lot of money to pay...." On the following night and the morning of the next day a violent gale blew across the council grounds, marking the council's end as it had its beginning, as though nature had frowned on the proceedings there. With pens in hands and tongues in cheeks the chiefs had marked their Xs on the treaty, with the exception of Lawyer, who wrote his name. As *x* symbolizes an unknown quantity, the Indians' marks reflected their unknown future. To some their marks were calculated to forestall events long enough to spill the blood of the white men and avenge the blood on Kamiakin's lips. It was of little moment to them as they returned to their peoples that Stevens was then en route to treat with the natives in the northeastern portions of his territory and the Blackfeet beyond.

The chiefs, representing fourteen tribes under the Yakima standard, had signed away the greater portion of their lands: an empire of nearly ten million acres in present-day Washington from the Cascade Mountain ridge on the west to the Chelan-Methow-Cascade mountain ridge on the north, to the Palouse and Snake rivers on the southeast, and back to the Columbia. Within the vast treaty cession two places were reserved for the peoples called the Yakimas: the ancient, vital, six-mile-square Wenatchee fisheries, which were about twenty-five miles up the Wenatchee River from its mouth, and the Yakima Reservation of nearly a million and a quarter acres between the Yakima River and the Cascade Mountains. The Cayuses, Wallawallas, and Umatillas received an 800-square-mile reservation in present-day northeastern Oregon. Within it flowed the Umatilla River. Along it they could raise their gardens, but mostly grazed their horses on the hill and plateau grasslands. The Nez Percés received a reservation of approximately 7,694,270 acres in present-day Oregon and Idaho, which was later reduced to about 756,968 acres.

It was at Wasco, or Wascopam Springs, near The Dalles that Superintendent Palmer treated with the Middle Oregon tribes in the summer of 1855. A half-dozen years later their supervision was to be briefly under the Washington Superintendency, whose jurisdiction extended all the way from Olympia on the west to present-day Montana. On June 25 those bands yielded about 11,000 square miles in exchange for the Warm Springs Reservation in present-day north-central Oregon. It then consisted of 464,000 acres, half mountainous and timbered, with but small portions of farming land; ten years after removal its Indians raised annual crops of less than four hundred bushels. Finally under threats and intimidation they agreed to accept the confine. About twenty years later certain Teninos still had received no compensation for improvements made near The Dalles prior to their removal.

Under the treaty Indians destined for the Warm Springs Reservation were guaranteed the right to journey to their usual and customary fishing places between Celilo Falls to The Dalles. Sidetracking them onto reservations did not keep them or other Indians in similar situations out of the way of whites. Their roving proved an annoyance to settlers, who pressured the government to confine them to their reservation. Consequently in 1865, Oregon Superintendent of Indian Affairs J. W. Perit Huntington told them that, if they signed an agreement to leave the Warm Springs only with passes, he would issue them a hundred blankets and

John Harmelt, the Wenatchee chief who led the fight for redress after the sale of the Wenatchee fisheries. Funds from the sale were used to build the Erwin Irrigation Ditch on the Yakima Indian Reservation. North Central Washington Museum Association.

thirty head of oxen. Thinking the offer an inducement merely to obtain passes to leave the reservation to fish, the Indians agreed to it on November 15 with their signatures to a treaty, not foreseeing difficulties in obtaining the passes from future agents. Fortunately for them, the treaty was never ratified. If it had been, they in effect might have lost their freedom to fish off the reservation. The signatures of chiefs to treaties, ratified or not, did not alter living patterns that their peoples had developed over generations. On February 9, 1929 (45 Stat 1148), the government set aside a village site near Celilo Falls for a small band of Indians assigned to the Warm Springs Reservation.

In the meantime the chieftains who were signatories to the Walla Walla Treaty were incurring the wrath of bands who claimed that the Walla Walla negotiations had been conducted without their approval. Nez Percé, Cayuses, Wallawalla, and Umatilla elements were especially bitter at

Lawyer's cooperation with the white treaty makers. The bitterness remains to the present. Having refused to attend the council, the Klickitats were enraged at the sale of their lands in the southern portion of the Yakima cession, as they were also at their expulsion from Oregon Territory in the summer of 1855. Pressure from whites forcing them from Oregon had also created the Yakima Reservation, on which they were to be confined. At the same time their expulsion and confinement created a large reservoir of malcontents, auguring future trouble.

Discontent among the Indians was never greater. Now, they cried, was the time to strike their white foe. About a month after the Walla Walla Council, Kamiakin, emerging as chief spokesman of the dissidents, failing to make peace with whites, declaimed: "The white man is coming among us, we will soon be driven away. The best way is to keep him out of our country." Heeding his admonition, runners, and Kamiakin himself, went among the various tribes to recruit braves for war with promises of horses, cattle, and blankets. At Fort Colville, garbed in Hudson's Bay Company broadcloth with red trimmings and brass buttons, Kamiakin received from the fort trader, Angus McDonald (as he also had from Father Pandosy), the warning that it was hopeless to fight the whites—that eventually hundreds more of them would swarm over Indian country. Undaunted, Kamiakin and his braves went among the Wallawallas, Cayuses, and Palouses offering up to five hundred horses and two hundred cattle to entice them into war. Lower Yakima Chief Skloom visited Indians of The Dalles area seeking their aid. As a token of support, Looking Glass gave Kamiakin his war horse. The Yakima chief bestowed it on Chief Owhi's son, the tall, light-complexioned Qualchan, telling him, in the words of its Nez Percé donor, that white men had pushed the Indians into the sea and were going to take their remaining lands. Leschi was credited with stories of whites shipping Indians far away from their homes. The son of a Yakima-Klickitat mother, Leschi often crossed Naches Pass to the interior to visit his mother's people and attend their war councils with the Cayuses. To help him and his brother Quiemuth to incite the Nisquallis against the whites on Puget Sound, the Yakimas initially offered Leschi 150 head of horses and 100 head of cattle. He hurried home to Puget Sound to attempt to entice its natives into war by threats and warnings of their possible expulsion to the "Land of Darkness," stating that, should they refuse to enter the war coalition, whites would exterminate or at least enslave them. Leschi further sought to entice Puget Sound peoples to enter the war by promising them spoils in the form of the white men's buildings and their other improvements. At the same time certain squaw men and influential Puget Sound chiefs told natives that King George Men would help them drive the Bostons from the land and that after that the Britishers would return. Then Americans would no longer take and fence the lands of Indians and run cattle and hogs over their potato patches, nor desecrate their peoples' graves, nor appropriate their fisheries as the Americans had. Moreover, they assured their listeners, the British would pay them more for their goods and services than the Americans, besides supplying them arms and ammunition.

Qualchan played a similar role in the interior as Leschi's on Puget Sound. He recalled the words of his own father at the Walla Walla council that, were Indians to surrender their mountains, they would have nothing to eat, their women and children would be crying for food, because it was from those mountains that they received roots, berries, deer, and other game for their food, clothing, and shelter.

The impending crises revealed not only the Indian-white rift but also the deepening rift among the Yakimas. Jealous of Kamiakin's leadership among the Yakimas was the Upper Yakima Kittitas (Teias), the elder brother of Owhi. The latter also was jealous of Kamiakin's leadership role. Owhi opposed killing whites traversing Yakima lands; he would kill only those settling on them. In the summer of 1855 a packmaster leading a company train from Fort Nisqually to Fort Colville reportedly gave ammunition to the Klickitats, urging them to take up arms against the Americans. Their Yakima neighbors had large quantities of ammunition but were short of guns. Some of the arms came from sources as far distant as the Mormons. Yet the Yakimas had arms enough to kill miners traversing their lands to gold fields in the Colville country. Gold rumors floated down from the Colville to the Willamette, where hard times gave the yellow metal more glitter. An envoy of the French government in the Oregon country in 1851 and 1852 wrote that the "rascally Spokanes" had refused to divulge its location. McClellan's men had looked for "colors" at stream crossings, and at the Walla Walla council there had been much talk among whites of gold in the Colville country.

Gold talk sent men scurrying through Indian country, risking their necks for the metal—a scurrying that increased in 1858 with rushes through the interior to the Fraser River. Especially galling to interior tribes was the passage of miners through their lands before their treaties were approved by the United States. Until such a time the land was still theirs. Stevens had not told them that the treaties would be ineffective until ratified by the United States Senate. Some miners mixed lust for gold and lust for native women, further incensing hotblood braves. In that summer of 1855, at a ford in the Yakima River, Qualchan and his followers killed six white men. By late summer and early fall their toll of gold seekers had reached twenty, including two killed by Wenatchee Indians on the Umtanum Ridge between the Columbia and Yakima rivers. Taking advantage of the absence of the cautious Owhi in buffalo country, Qualchan and his braves were unrestrained from killing miners and appropriating their goods. Qualchan took the goods to settlements, such as The Dalles, to buy ammunition and calicoes for his people. Sulktalthscosum's sons, Moses and Quiltenenock, also committed depredations on passing miners. Like Qualchan they had been enticed into attempting to eliminate whites with Kamiakin's promises of guns, horses, and blankets. The two Sinkiuse warriors went among northern tribes, such as the Wenatchees, Chelans, Methows, and Okanagons, entreating them to enter the planned war against the whites, agreeing with Yakima warriors to form a defense line between Rock Island on the mid-Columbia and the Wenas Creek in the Yakima country. Moses later confessed of his activities during this period that his hands had been "dipped in blood."

Threatening the effectiveness of this war mobilization effort was the increasing concern of some tribes felt with the warlike actions of the Yakimas and their allies. After witnessing the killing of a white prospector, a Spokane chief offered his warriors to a party of miners to help them run down the killers. Qualchan met opposition when, decked out in his best war finery, he dashed through the Cowiche country on the upper Yakima River. There his paternal half brother, Wienshet, rebuked him for being Kamiakin's lackey. The two drew knives. A warrior named Eneas jumped between them, begging them not to spill each other's blood.

Many of these developments were unknown to Stevens that summer as he moved from the Walla Walla eastward toward the Rockies. In late June the Coeur d'Alène head chief, Stellam, met him and his entourage at a camas prairie where about two hundred and fifty Coeur d'Alènes from twenty-nine lodges were drying roots. Stellam received Stevens's invitation to meet him and the other chiefs at the Coeur d'Alène mission to learn of the treaty that the Great Father wished to make with his people. At the mission the tribesmen, their priests, and lay workers heard the governor explain his wish to purchase Coeur d'Alène and Spokane lands on his return from the Blackfoot country. In response to his invitation a Coeur d'Alène delegation accompanied him on his journey toward the plains.

On July 7 that delegation along with the Flatheads under their chief, Victor, the Kalispels under Alexander (No Horses), and the Kutenais under Michelle—a 300-man delegation in all—escorted Stevens and his party to Council Grove near Hell Gate.[6] In keeping with the government policy of consolidating tribes under certain leaders to facilitate dealing with them, Stevens passed over other chiefs in favor of Victor as a spokesman for the three tribes, although, in fact, he treated him rather shabbily in council. His choice was not based on a numerical superiority of Victor's Flatheads. He estimated the band at 450 souls in contrast to 600 Kalispels. By his estimates the Kutenais numbered 350. His decision to combine them with the Fleatheads and Kalispels was based on the geographical accident that one Kutenai band happened to reside on Dayton Creek on the west shores of Flathead Lake, although their historical homeland was Tobacco Plains on the west. Making no claims to Salish links, their relatives lived in scattered villages in northeastern Washington Territory and Canada. Previously the Kutenais and Flatheads had often fought one another. Thus their inclusion together in the treaty helped to make it disgusting to both tribes.

On July 9, as the Hell Gate Council opened with about 1,200 Indians, Victor was undoubtedly surprised that Stevens said he had come not so much to ask for his lands as to aid his people against the Blackfeet. Victor told him how Blackfoot raiders had recently killed twelve Flathead hunters and stolen Flathead horses. He might have added

that during the year the Blackfeet had also taken the scalps of twenty-five Nez Percés right there at Hell Gate, orphaning their children as they had those of his own people.

As at the Walla Walla Council Stevens sought one common reservation for the tribes. That, in fact, meant putting them in either the Flathead or the Kalispel country—alien grounds for one or the other. He foresaw trouble in getting the Kalispels to move south from around their Saint Ignatius Mission and its Jesuit influence and in getting the Flatheads to move north from the Bitterroot to around that mission, where the priests sought to make them cease their roamings.

On the second day of the council a second-ranking Kalispel, Big Canoe, pointedly asked why a treaty was needed since his people had never spilled the blood of white men. Stevens's talk about the gifts that the Indians would receive must have seemed hollow to Big Canoe's people, especially to those living around Saint Ignatius, where black robes had already provided them goods like those that Stevens promised them. His bait of five hundred dollars for each chief who signed was, however, something that the priests could not provide. By the third day it was evident that Victor did not want to live on Kalispel land and that

Kutenai Chief David and his wife, Rebecca, at Bonners Ferry, Idaho. Museum of Native American Cultures.

Victor, head chief of the Flatheads, drawn by Gustavus Sohon in the spring of 1854.
Smithsonian Institution National Anthropological Archives, Neg. No. 37,417.

Alexander and Michelle wanted to remain near the Saint Ignatius Mission, although Stevens, by reversing himself, was now trying to persuade Alexander to join the Flathead chief in the Bitterroot Valley. In council Flathead chief Red Wolf (or Isaac), the son of a Kutenai father, complained of Stevens's attempts to gather the tribes in one place where before they had been in three.

To help break the deadlock, Stevens sent for Father Hoecken of Saint Ignatius Mission. The priest understandably opposed any move to the Bitterroot, which would have ended his Saint Ignatius reduction. Red Wolf suggested that, if Victor were to join the Kalispels, his people would not go with him. On July 12 in private council Victor and Alexander seemed willing to make concessions, but in open councils with Stevens they resumed their inflexibility. On Friday 13, when Victor continued to resist removal from the Bitterroot, Stevens tried to humiliate him. After the governor called him "an old bitch," he left the council. Victor refused to meet on Saturday. To keep from being removed from his own lands, Alexander tried to persuade Victor to move to the Saint Ignatius Mission by promising him the head chieftaincy of all Indians there. Victor returned to the council, Monday, July 16.

The stormy Hell Gate Council became in essence a contest between Victor and Alexander to decide which chief would remove to the other's homeland. The Kutenais presumably had little input in that deliberation. Stevens prepared to leave the council grounds on July 16 when the deadlock between the two chiefs seemed unbreakable; each chief was trying to place the other in uncompromising positions. At that point Victor weakened his stance by making remarks that Stevens interpreted to mean that he would accept a reservation in the Bitterroot Valley if the president ruled that place the better site for the Flatheads. Stevens

142

added this stipulation as a provision of the treaty.

On that same Monday eighteen chiefs and headmen affixed their marks to a twelve-article treaty. Under the document (which was ratified March 8, 1859) the confederated nation of Flatheads, Kalispels, and Kutenais was combined under Chief Victor. Their reservation was about 1,242,969 acres and was called the Jocko (for the North West Company trader "Jocko" Finlay) or the Flathead reservation. In return for it the tribes exchanged a large tract west of the Rockies within the Columbia River drainage area. The treaty also stipulated that other tribes might settle on untaken reservation lands with the occupants' consent. As the council closed, Stevens wrote the commissioner of Indian affairs that the Jocko Reservation posed no difficulties because Victor was promise-bound to remove there.

Several of the tribesmen accompanied Stevens on his five-day journey across the Rockies and down to Fort Benton to treat with the Blackfeet, including Victor, Alexander, and Nez Percé Chiefs Looking Glass, Spotted Eagle, and Eagle from the Light (also called Eagle Against the Light and, by his own people, Tippealahanokaupoo). Until the council convened, the Indians may have felt safe in company with Stevens, wary as they were of the Blackfeet, whose hearts they believed to be a lie and their tongues a trap—a treacherous people, they believed, whose pipes puffed the smoke of deceit. At Fort Benton, Stevens had to await the arrival of goods, including presents for the Indians, which had been shipped by steamer up the Missouri River. Many of the Indians who accompanied him scattered to hunt buffalo, using bows and arrows more effectively than smoothbore rifles. The council grounds were moved a hundred miles down the Missouri to a point below the mouth of the Judith River to meet the Indians hunting in that direction and the boats unloading their cargoes. The council opened on October 16 with small segments of the Blackfoot nation present—Bloods (Kainah), Piegans, Blackfeet proper, allied Gros Ventres—and the tribesmen accompanying Stevens.

The Indians approached the council with misgivings—even the bold Blackfeet, who feared they would be wrested from their lands and sent north to the Saskatchewan country. Measles had scattered the Crows, who had also been invited to the council. At its opening a sharp difference became evident—not primarily among the Indians but between Stevens and Colonel Alfred Cumming, who was the superintendent of Indian affairs for much of the trans-Mis-

Kalispel (Pend d'Oreille) Chief Alexander (Tumclehotcutse) sketched by Gustavus Sohon in April, 1854. In July 1855, Alexander became one of the principals of Governor Isaac I. Stevens's Flathead Treaty Council. Smithsonian Institution National Anthropological Archives, Neg. No. 37,417-B.

sissippi West and the senior commissioner at the council. Where Cumming saw the Blackfeet as savages in a country too poor to support white settlers, the ever-optimistic Stevens had great hopes for their lands. He warned the Indians that the buffalo, around which much of their economy centered, were very limited, implying that the Indians would have to become agrarians like whites.

The treaty effected with the Flathead Confederation (Flatheads, Kalispels, and Kutenais) and the Nez Percés and the Blackfeet was basically a peace document. In it, unlike Stevens's other treaties, the Indians did not cede their lands. The Blackfeet were to keep the peace by not warring with Assiniboins (Siouan), Shoshonis, Crees, Dakotas (Siouan), or other tribes. Since the tribes still believed the buffalo to be necessary for their survival, the treaty stipulated that all the country south of a line from the Hell Gate or Medicine Rock passes to the Musselshell River was to be kept open as common hunting grounds where no tribes were to settle. Territory from this line north to the Canadian border was to be exclusively for the Blackfeet.

In protest Alexander said it was his ancestral right to hunt north of that line—that the common hunting grounds were too small. He also opposed the proposed closure of the northern passes, the Cut Bank and the Marias, which were customarily used by his people in going to hunt buffalo. Little Dog, a noted Piegan warrior and a friend of Father Hoecken, realized that Indian hunting days were nearing an end and said that, since Alexander made such a point of it, they would let him come out via those northern passes. Another Piegan chief, Lame Bull, pointed to the objecting western Indians and noted that, unlike those tribesmen, the Blackfeet were willing to abide by the treaty provisions.

The treaty recognized the confederation and the other tribes as sovereign entities and at the same time their dependence on the government of the United States, with which they were to live in peace. Signed October 17, 1855, it would be ratified six months later.* The absence of many tribesmen from the council (although 3,500 attended), and the tribal rivalries that the treaty could not resolve posed serious problems for the future. After the council the. Flatheads killed two Crows and lost a man to the Bannocks and another to the Gros Ventres. The Coeur d'Alênes brought down six Bannocks, losing five of their Spokane allies in the process. Five days after the treaty the Bloods went to war with the Crees.

Stevens may have been unaware of the breaches of the treaty as he happily turned homeward to Olympia, having tucked away in his pocket within a year a dozen treaties with Indians of the Pacific Northwest. His joy was short lived. On the Teton River a messenger told him that tribes on the west were already at war with a large force who were waiting to kill him near Walla Walla. Brushing off suggestions that he return by way of the east, he decided to push on to Olympia to face the music—that of dancing Indians at war.

---

*The United States was to pay the confederated tribes $120,000 over a twenty-year period. Although the second Flathead chief, Moses (Moise), owned a farm near the Saint Ignatius Mission, as did Insula and others, Moses refused to sign the treaty.

14. THE TEMPEST UNLEASHED

On November 24, 1855, the Coeur d'Alênes were surprised to find Territorial Governor Isaac I. Stevens at their mission with two of his men and four Nez Percé chiefs. Yakima emissaries had been there a few days before trying to induce the Coeur d'Alênes to enter their war against the Americans. At best not all the Coeur d'Alênes were friendly to the whites. Chief Stellam had appropriated some of Stevens's supply wagons, which were later regained with the help of the more friendly Spokanes. The Spokanes had also recently been approached by Yakima emissaries to enter the war, and they were as surprised when the governor visited them as the Coeur d'Alênes had been. On December 4 several Indians met Stevens in the cabin of one Antoine Plante above Spokane Falls. Among those present were some Colvilles with their priest, the Reverend Joseph Joset, S.J.; the Coeur d'Alênes with the Reverend Anthony Ravalli, S.J.; some Spokanes and San Poils; and a white miner-volunteer outfit, the Spokane Invincibles.

Still warmed by the speeches of Kamiakin's envoys, the assembled tribesmen treated Stevens as cooly as the autumn weather did. Several chided him for his fast-moving land-taking policies. With neutral coolness even Garry told him: "Those Indians have gone to war, and I don't know myself how to fix it up. That is your business." Thinking it a poor time for treating, the chief concluded, "These matters should be tied up like a bundle of sticks." It was Garry who broke to Stevens the news of the killing of Andrew J. Bolon, his agent for tribes between the Cascade and Rocky mountains. Bolon was to have prepared the way for Stevens to

Two sons of Yakima war chief Kamiakin: Tomeo Tesh, left, and Cleveland, right. Missing is Kamiakin's third son, Snake River. Grace Christianson Wenzel Collection, Adam East Museum, Moses Lake, Washington.

treat with northern tribes. Garry, in fact, had talked with Bolon at The Dalles shortly before the agent had struck off alone to the north to investigate the deaths of miners at the hands of Qualchan and his braves. Shunning the offers of the chiefs to escort him to Lapwai, Stevens with his own Stevens Guard set out for that place, from which he returned to Olympia, January 19, 1856. There he received a thirty-eight-gun salute, one for each state of the union. In the meantime less-ceremonial guns had been fired in the interior as the "pent up Tempest," in Father Mesplié's words, had finally become unleashed.[1]

In early October at Walla Walla, Peopeomoxmox, surrounded by dancing braves waving miners' scalps, refused to meet Indian agent Nathan Olney. When Stevens's emissary, Bolon, reached the lodge of his friend Showaway a few miles from Toppenish Creek (a lower Yakima tributary), Bolon was warned to return to The Dalles. Heeding the warning, he quickly set out for that place. On the morning of September 23, 1856, he overtook an Indian party coming over the Ahsoom Trail (which ran between the Yakima country and Celilo Falls) near the summit of the Wahshum Mountains (north of Goldendale, Washington). They were en route to fishing grounds at Celilo. Mosheil, a Methodist mission-school dropout, harangued the others in the party, saying that Bolon had hanged some Indians, for which he should die. Aware of something about to happen, the women of the party rode on ahead. Suddenly Mosheil, Wahpiwahpilah, and Soquiekt attacked the agent. Disregarding his pleas in the Chinook jargon that they spare his life, Soquiekt tossed a knife to one Stahkin (also called Stockun and the like). Stahkin slit Bolon's throat. The agent struggled briefly and fell dead. They buried him in a shallow grave a quarter mile from the spot, shot his horse, and divided his goods. A Klickitat woman, Wantah, later pointed out the killers to soldiers at Fort Simcoe. The soldiers captured and hung Wahpiwahpilah and Stahkin. With her own gun Wantah shot Mosheil as he approached her and some soldiers.*

The killing of Mosheil by Wantah, a Klickitat woman, is evidence that Kamiakin was unable to gather to his war standard all of the geographically divided Klickitat people. To keep them from warring Indians, the military rounded up some of them at Vancouver, including Taitinapams from their mountain fastnesses on the Cowlitz and Lewis River headwaters. Kamiakin sent two men to entice other Klickitat bands to enter the war. One group under Yakatowit (Yah-ho-towit) refused their request. Yakatowit had advised whites to man the forts at The Dalles, Vancouver, and Steilacoom with many soldiers. The Klickitats under Umtuch agreed to join the Yakima chief in his war. They left for the scene of action only to be overtaken by volunteers and

returned to Fort Vancouver. As Umtuch tried to reach his scouts ahead, one of them killed him. The scout had failed to recognize his chief. Umtuch's incarcerated people were moved to the White Salmon area on the Columbia right bank below The Dalles.

The Bolon killing disrupted Kamiakin's war timetable. He had planned to begin hostilities when the Columbia was frozen and the mountain passes snow-covered in order to prevent the military from coming upriver from Fort Vancouver or across the mountains from Fort Steilacoom. The Indians were forced to call quickly into play their intelligence system to apprize them of the soldiers' moves. During troubled times Owhi, a master of such an intelligence system at home or on the plains, customarily stationed his spies about a mile apart along well-worn trails. He stationed them more distantly at less stressful times. Only recently his spies had jumped a Blackfoot party attempting to attack his sleeping band. With poles and knives his men had defeated the attackers, enslaving two of their women.

On the evening of October 3 a rider burst into Kamiakin's camp with word that soldiers had crossed the Columbia at The Dalles that morning and were marching toward Yakima country. Fires atop the highest peak signaled the Indians to gather and post scouts at strategic points between the Yakima and The Dalles. Kamiakin moved his camp to below the gap on the Ahsoom Trail, a short distance southeast of Fort Simcoe between Toppenish Creek and The Dalles. Two days later three hundred painted braves were assembled and ready to hide in brush, ravines, and rocks near where the creek crossed the trail (which was later The Dalles–Fort Simcoe military road). On October 5, as was typical of so many unexpected events attending such confrontations, the Indians killed a soldier of an advance party. In returning the fire, the troops killed a chief, Wahtahkin, as he crept across the brushy creek.

Near midafternoon the Indians met the main body of the troops of Major Granville O. Haller's Fourth Infantry. With slightly more than a hundred officers and men, less than a quarter of all the regulars stationed in the Pacific Northwest, Haller hoped to make some show of force against the warring natives. As in other Indian fights large numbers of natives gathered to watch the action at the Battle of Toppenish, leading whites to assume they were fighting a force of up to a thousand. Among the warriors were the Yakimas, Columbia Sinkiuses, Wallawallas, Cayuses, Palouses, Chelans, and Spokanes. Just in from buffalo country, Owhi was among those present. Few, if any, Okanagons were there. They had been restrained by the influential Okanagan chief, Walking Grizzly-bear, who advised the Okanagan headmen to withhold ammunition from their young braves.[2]

Many of the braves wore *tamanawas* head caps, whose powers they believed would shield them from bullets. More practically, they tried to disrupt the troops' formations by stampeding their horses, then splitting off individually to deny their attackers a concentrated target. On October 6 fighting resumed sharply. Lack of guns denied the Indians the quick victory that they sought. Above the noise of battle

---

*For a long time it was believed among whites that the Yakima Qualchan was the killer of Bolon. Lucullus Virgil McWhorter identifies his killers in *Tragedy of the Wahk-Shum: The Death of Andrew J. Bolon, Indian Agent to The Yakima Nation*, in mid-September, 1855. From McWhorter's voluminous notes (in Holland Library, Washington State University, Pullman, Washington), we have accounts by the Indians themselves of the incidents of the Yakima War.

Cayuse Dr. Whirlwind and Wallawalla Chief No Shirt. Also known as Shaplish, Dr. Whirlwind toured with a medicine show in the late 1890s. Smithsonian Institution National Anthropological Archives, Bureau of American Ethnology Collection, Neg. No. 2902-B-33.

Kamiakin could be heard exhorting his men to hold on. About noon, as they began to lag, he sent an express north to Qualchan telling him to hurry with reinforcements from the Selah Valley. Until that help arrived, Quiltenenock and Skloom were among those helping Kamiakin maintain the momentum of battle. A signal finally was received from a rock on the east that the 200-man reinforcement had passed Union Gap (just above the village Pakiut below present-day Yakima, Washington). The warriors' spirits were renewed. With the arrival of reinforcements the braves were able to cut the soldiers off from their pack mules and their provisions, including food and blankets. The Indians refused to eat the food, thinking it poisoned. That night they again disengaged—to eat, and to sleep as best they could amidst the raucous braying of captured mules. They left the battleground a vacuum, into which Haller moved his men. His Indian scout, Cut Mouth John, slipped out of camp early in the morning for The Dalles to seek reinforcements. He was named for a wound received in trying to capture the Whitman killers.

Scouting on horseback for the Indians, two of their number, Twiwash and Kookonee, stumbled on some soldiers. In a skirmish Kookonee was wounded, and his horse was shot down, trapping him by the leg. Early the next morning he straggled into camp. By then the soldiers had abandoned that battle area. Qualchan restrained some braves wanting to chase them. On the third morning of the seesaw fight the warriors pushed Haller's troops to an eminence, where they surrounded and pinned them down all day without food or water. The Indians were confident that they would destroy the remaining troops by the next morning. They had already killed eight soldiers and wounded about thirteen others. Haller had lost his horses, cattle, and a howitzer, which the Indians found partly buried. He also had lost his pride.

The humiliating defeat bore little resemblance to an expedition that Haller had led from The Dalles in July, 1855, against the natives, who on August 20, 1854, had killed members of the Ward immigrant party twenty miles from Fort Boise. That bumbling raid had netted Haller one Indian shot dead and three hanged. It also forced Fort Boise trader William Charles to abandon his post, as the Indians believed he had sent for the Haller party. Thus the area, later known as southern Idaho, was literally given back to the Indians.

After his defeat by Kamiakin, Haller had no choice but to retreat from the Toppenish to The Dalles, one jump ahead of an Indian detail pursuing, harassing, and reminding him and his troops, with more insult than injury, that they had been whipped. Some years later the warrior Moses gave a terse resumé of the action: "Then we started a war here and we whipped most of the soldiers; we kept fighting the soldiers right here at Toppenish on the little river that runs into the big river. We kept fighting the soldiers and drove them to The Dalles and then we quit and came back." How many casualties the Indians suffered is not known. Some later sources placed them at around forty.

To prevent more casualties, Agent Olney hurried to head off the main body of Cayuses and Wallawallas from joining the Yakimas, but with little success. At the very time he was with Peopeomoxmox and his Wallawallas, they and the Cayuses were completing their war plans. The Palouses were poised for war at the mouth of their river. At Olney's insistence personnel were forced to abandon Fort Walla Walla to the Wallawallas and other tribes in the area. The Indians moved in to sack the post and appropriate its livestock and other properties, leaving it a shambles. Fort Hall and Fort Boise were completely disorganized. The Teninos burned agency buildings on the Umatilla, and the Cayuses burned several buildings, including sawmills and gristmills at Fort Waters. The settlers who had not already fled the Walla Walla Valley now did so, abandoning livestock to the Indians. As in the Colville Valley, French-Canadian former employees of the fur companies remained along the Walla Walla in relative safety with their Indian wives. Most of them had married before the passage of a Washington Territorial law of January 29, 1855 (*Washington Territory Laws*, 1854, page 33), which declared void any marriage between a white person and an Indian who was more than a half blood. Unlike many Pacific Northwestern Indians, the Bannock chief Le Grand Coquin (Shoowoohoo) and the Eastern Shoshoni chief Washakie were among Indian leaders staunchly opposing miscegenation.

On learning on October 7 that Lieutenant W. A. Slaughter had left Fort Steilacoom with troops for Naches Pass to join Haller, Kamiakin dispatched Qualchan and Teias with 250 braves to meet the challenge from Puget Sound. Near the top of the pass Qualchan's men captured an Indian scout whom Slaughter had sent on ahead. The scout begged for his freedom since he was related to Teias, and he was released to Slaughter to tell him of Haller's retreat. Slaughter then retraced his steps back to Puget Sound. Angered at the release of the relative of Teias, Qualchan summarily banned that elderly chief from the warrior ranks, forcing him to join the women for the rest of the war.

On November 8, Kamiakin and about fifty warriors were reconnoitering near where Satus Creek enters the Yakima. On returning north they came upon an advance detachment of Oregon Mounted Volunteers. Two of the volunteers drowned pursuing the Indians, who crossed the Yakima River. The troops withdrew to the right bank of the river. Hearing gunfire at Union Gap, about a hundred braves rode out to skirmish with the advance volunteer party until dark. Kamiakin's scouts told him and his braves that a much larger force was moving northward from The Dalles under a Major Gabriel Rains, with cannon and 334 regular soldiers plus 500 mounted Oregon and Washington territorials. The Indians chose to make their stand on the Yakima at Union Gap, a more defendable site than the Toppenish or the Satus.

The news that regulars and volunteers were again approaching the interior via Naches Pass posed a serious problem to the defenders. Several of their warriors were in the Walla Walla Valley reinforcing Peopeomoxmox, leaving but three hundred to face the troops at Union Gap. Although many families were tending livestock in the Selah, Wenas, and Moxee valleys, a large gallery of Indians assembled to witness the impending fight. Among the leaders poised to lead their warriors in combat were Kamiakin, Skloom, Showaway, Moses, Quiltenenock, Nanamkin of the Entiats (a Wenatchee subdivision), and Big Star of the Spokanes (Big Star's Indian name was Kwittilkokusam; he was also known as the "elder Lot").

The Indians had fewer men and far fewer guns than their foes, but as defenders they at least had horses that were more rested than the jaded mounts of the troops. About noon on November 9 the troops reached the gap. On their approach the Indians crouched behind rocks and brush. Suddenly the unfamiliar tones of a bugle pierced the air. The troops divided their forces. One column moved up the hillside canyon. The other proceeded along the river at the break in the hill, a maneuver that the defenders had not foreseen. To meet it, Owhi defended the river edge. Showaway stood ready to defend the east bank. With but one of the few Indian guns and four or five braves, Qualchan guarded the canyon entrance at the top of the ridge. In the face of the charging troops and breastwork-splintering fire from a howitzer, the warriors, thinking the big gun some kind of evil spirit, scattered to the brush a short distance above the gap. A soldier was about to overtake the mounted Kamiakin atop the west side of the hill when Qualchan shot the trooper off his horse, killing him. Unable to fend off troops moving up the canyon, Qualchan and his braves fled up the Ahtanum a short distance above the gap. Unable to hold his ground, Owhi managed to escape the troops pursuing him. Other warriors atop the hill fled down its north side with the troops pursuing. On the next morning a few warriors returned to the gap as decoys to cover the retreat of the braves and their families from the area. Abandoning their cattle, some of the refugees went with Kamiakin to White Bluffs on the east bank of the Columbia above the mouth of the Yakima. Owhi and Teias moved their people across the Columbia to the mouth of Crab Creek near Beverly, Washington. In their ensuing flight they lost many horses in the swift-flowing river.

The rearguard braves who were acting as decoys fell back from the soldiers charging through the defile. Retreating northward toward the Naches River, the Indians kept up a running fight through present-day Yakima, Washington. Abandoning the chase, the troops rode back to the mouth of the Ahtanum and up that stream to Saint Joseph's Mission, which had been established there three years previously. At Saint Joseph's, Cut Mouth John, who had the dubious honor of having killed a lone, elderly Indian left at the gap, paraded sacrilegiously in vestments that Father Pandosy had abandoned when he fled to the Colville country. Later the Yakimas remembered the priest with a cultlike reverence. On October 14 the volunteers uncovered a half keg of powder in a potato patch. They thought the departed priest had planted it for Indians to use against whites and vented their wrath by firing the mission. In a few minutes the settlement was in ashes. Even dissident Indians had not resorted to arson when they had previously plundered the mission. Father Chirouse quite naturally condemned the

act, as he did the lust of the volunteers driving them to it. The mission was not restored until the middle of the 1860s, when Bishop Blanchet sent the Reverend L. N. St. Onge from Vancouver to reopen it. In the later, happier times the Indians were fascinated by the mysterious "singing machine," an organ that Father Jean Baptiste Abraham Brouillet brought to the mission. St. Onge made considerable progress in translating the Yakima language.[3]

The troops moved up the Naches. They thought the main body of Indians had fled over Naches Pass because their rearguard on November 10 had decoyed the troops from the gap in that direction. In three days they returned from the Naches having missed a large Indian encampment on the Wenas Creek. They then withdrew to The Dalles, and troops that had been dispatched from Puget Sound for the interior were turned back because of troubles on Green River. Qualchan salvaged some glory and popularity among his people by driving off a large number of the soldier's horses to Priest Rapids.

Ten days after the Battle of Union Gap, Major Mark A. Chinn and 150 Oregon Mounted Volunteers reached the Umatilla River. Their purpose was to establish Fort Henrietta (later Echo, Oregon) at the site of the former Utilla Indian Agency.[4] A large force of mounted Wallawallas, Cayuses, and Umatillas were keeping the fort under constant surveillance. When soldier scouts left it, the Indians decoyed them into Umatilla and Wallawalla camps—from which they escaped. The Indians kept apprized of troop movements by flaring signal fires. On the night of November 28, 1855, such fires may have warned Indians that enemy reinforcements were heading toward the Wallawalla country. On December 2, Colonel James K. Kelly, who had assumed Chinn's command, was joined by Captain Charles Bennett and his command from The Dalles. The soldiers rode through a cold night rain to Fort Walla Walla. Finding it deserted, they pressed up the Walla Walla Valley, where the main body of Cayuses and their allies were gathered under Peopeomoxmox. Not until December 3 did Captains Thomas Cornelius and Absalom J. Hembree and their Oregon Mounted Volunteers reach the Walla Walla Valley. Nearing the camp of Peopeomoxmox, they may not have known of that Chief's efforts to rally dissident Indians to his standard—efforts in which he was only partially successful. Although Five Crows and Camaspelo joined him, not all the Cayuses did so. Among the prominent Nez Percés who refused to join the combatants were Lawyer, Old Joseph, and Red Wolf. On December 4 warriors skirmished troops in the Walla Walla Valley. That evening a small band of scouts raided the exposed Fort Henrietta, killing and scalping a guard and running off a pack string en route to the Walla Walla Valley. From his camp on the Touchet River the outmanned Peopeomoxmox, seeking to give his people time to move farther from the troops, entered Kelly's camp with about fifty men and a flag. Questioning his peaceful motives, Kelly had him taken into custody. Before dawn the Indians abandoned their camp and the staples that they had purloined at the sack of Fort Walla Walla. Peopeomoxmox offered to pay for the stolen goods.

On December 7 about three hundred warriors attacked the volunteers in an all-day fight at the mouth of the Touchet. Under troop pressure they retreated, the soldiers pursuing. Before nightfall Peopeomoxmox was tied and bound. When a fellow captive, unable to bear this indignity to his chief, drew his knife, the Wallawalla chief and those around him were mowed down by rifle fire. The volunteers scalped the chief, dividing their hairy trophy into twenty pieces. They divided his skull for buttons, preserved his ears in a bottle of spirits, and stripped the skin from his back for razor strops. "Such is Indian warfare," wrote company trader James Sinclair, a witness to the volunteers' grisly vengeance. Their retaliation may have been partly in vengeance for the Whitman massacre, for which the chief had no responsibility. That made no difference to the volunteers. They had gotten themselves a very influential "good"— that is, dead—Indian. Stevens later affirmed that Peopeomoxmox had been "slain fairly."

The next morning, December 8, the Indians were reinforced by a hundred Palouses. A total of five hundred braves fought until darkness ended the conflict—and the lives of nearly fifty Indians. Two days later, when the troops were reinforced by others from Fort Henrietta, the Indians withdrew, and the troops "forted up" two miles above Waiilatpu. The combatant Indians crossed Snake River to camp with their Palouse allies, from whose camps they spied on troops in the Walla Walla Valley. At the time noncombatant Cayuses were at a winter camp three miles above the Wallawalla treaty grounds on Mill Creek, about nine miles above Kelly's camp. "Hostiles" daily visited the neutrals, attempting to entice them into the war, reminding them that whites were killing their people and stealing their lands.

The Indians who harassed troops during the winter of 1855–56 suffered losses in their attempts to protect their lands and people. The Cayuses abandoned many horses when forced to flee the Walla Walla Valley. Many horses starved for want of forage or, in weakened condition, drowned at river crossings. Robbed of their usual food caches, some Indians began to weary of the war. In January, 1856, those who were resolved to continue it stole nine horses from Colonel Kelly as he moved from the Umatilla to the Walla Walla. In February they captured thirteen wagonloads of supplies along that same route, including ammunition, and they continued raiding the rest of the winter. With spring approaching, the volunteers resumed their pursuit of the "hostiles," killing nine of them in a mid-March fight at the mouth of the Tucannon. When the soldiers crossed the Snake River, the Indians, abandoning many cattle to their pursuers, fled to the Nez Percé country, stealing horses along the way. Some fled northward as far as the Spokane. They returned only after the volunteers had moved west out of the Walla Walla Valley.

Indian spies reported inactivity in Rains's winter camp, which was on the Klickitat River about twenty-five miles from The Dalles. Troops had built a blockhouse there on one of Skloom's favorite hunting grounds. During the hiatus Owhi and his people returned to their homes and food caches. Some of Kamiakin's followers had returned to

the Yakima, leaving their chief to winter at White Bluffs.

In January, Leschi sent a messenger to Qualchan, requesting reinforcements for a proposed attack on the town of Seattle. Responding, Qualchan and about a hundred warriors crossed the Cascade Mountains to Leschi's war camp near Lake Washington, just east of Seattle. The Indians, like the whites, attempted to coordinate military movements between Puget Sound and the interior. Yet the two regions were in essence separate theaters of war. Developments on the Sound involved a flurry of conflict.[5] Leschi and his followers were prepared to attack whites on the upper White River until regulars under Captain Maurice Maloney and Washington territorials under Captain Gilmore Hayes moved eastward on October 24, 1855, over Naches Pass to assist Rains in his campaign against the Indians of the interior. That same month Captain Charles Eaton of the newly organized mounted Puget Sound Rangers began patrolling from Snoqualmie Pass to Lewis River Pass. With eighteen men Eaton travelled through the Cascade Mountains south of Mount Saint Helens with orders to kill "suspicious" Indians or send them in irons to Fort Steilacoom. Also targeted by Acting Governor Charles H. Mason for the iron-chain treatment were two of Patkanin's brothers living with other Snoqualmies in Seattle. They were to have been returned to Fort Steilacoom on the thirty-gun navy sloop of war *Decatur*, but escaped capture by the intervention of Arthur Denny, who knew not only Patkanin's new loyalty to Americans but also the need to keep friendly Indians in Seattle to work for whites. To prove his friendliness, Patkanin gave venison, mountain sheep, and hides to the captain of the *Decatur*. After the chief and his braves were mustered into the white man's service as scouts, Patkanin was to receive a twenty-dollar bounty for each enemy head and four times that amount for the heads of chiefs, a practice familiar to him and other Puget Sound Indians.

Governor Mason geared for hostilities by calling for more volunteers to ride horses that the government requisitioned from their Indian owners, promising to pay for their use. Meanwhile, the *Decatur* cruised around Puget Sound firing into woods, splintering trees to impress the Indians. Leschi and Quiemuth escaped patrolling horsemen by fleeing to Green River, where they encamped on Thursday, October 25. They abandoned fields, from which soldiers took their horses. At the same time a large body of warriors camped on White River (near Auburn, Washington). That Thursday, Eaton's company crossed the Puyallup River and camped a mile east of that stream, and the next day his command divided and marched along each side of the river.

The warriors now moved on Eaton's troops—a mere eleven men holed up in an abandoned cabin. From this impromptu fortification they withstood Indian gunfire on the night of October 27, futilely returning it. Their red foes were hidden in the dark, brushy landscape. Early on Sunday morning, October 28, the Muckleshoot Indian Nelson led an attack on settlers between present-day Kent and Auburn, Washington. Acting on the assurances of Mason, the settlers had believed themselves safe in their homes on

Patkanin, a Snoqualmie chief. Initially opposed to Americans, he later became their friend. From a painting by an unknown artist. Seattle Historical Society.

He had worked for the combination diligently, using threats and persuasion to combine the tribes and rid Puget Sound of its white invaders. He assured its natives that they could appropriate the properties and improvements of the Americans. If they wavered from their attacks, he warned, powerful tribes from east of the mountains would come and enslave them.

On October 31 near the Massacre site at Connell's Prairie the Indians surrounded an advance party of six troops from Hays's volunteers and Maloney's regulars. The troops had been dispatched earlier to help Major Rains, but called back. Kitsap and Quiemuth detained them with professions of friendship while other Indians prepared an ambush. In ensuing hand-to-hand fighting they killed two soldiers, Benton Moses and Joseph Miles. On November 3 they met fifty regulars under Lieutenant Slaughter and an equal number of volunteers under Captain Hays, who were searching out their camping places. From a camp atop a bluff on the right bank of White River the Indians prepared to meet the searchers. In an ensuing general six-hour, cross-river fight, from behind log-and-driftwood cover the Indians killed one regular, wounded another, and wounded a volunteer. They nearly missed killing one soldier, whose hat they shot off, and another, whose hat they rimmed with rifle fire. As was the common practice, officials reported Indian losses as heavy: "no doubt...from 25 to 30 Indians" and "no telling how many were wounded." At the war's end Indians claimed they had lost no men—that the numbers reported killed were obtained by counting holes shot in hats held up by their owners while the owners were safely hidden

White River. In the attack, which Americans would call the White River Massacre, the Indians broke down cabin doors and, with old muskets, killed a reported eight persons, capturing a two-year-old child. Among the attackers was a band led by the Klickitat chief Kitsap (not to be confused with the earlier Suquamish chief of the same name), and another band led by Klickitat Chief Kenasket (Tenascot, and the like). On the twenty-ninth, Lieutenant James McAllister of Eaton's command and a Michael Connell set out to dissuade Leschi from attacking whites. The Indians expressed contempt for their peacemaking attempts by killing the two.

The White River Massacre, ordered by Leschi and carried out by Kitsap and Nelson, was premature. The blow was made before Leschi could induce all the Puget Sound tribes to join in the uprising. Indian forces at the time were approximately as follows: Leschi's sixty-five Nisquallis and Lower Puyallups; thirty-five Muckleshoots, Duwamishes, and Suquamishes combined with thirty-five Snoqualmies under the leadership of Kitsap and Nelson; thirty-five braves under Kenasket; and twenty Upper Puyallups under Quilquilton (also known as Coquilton and the like). In February, 1856, forty Yakimas under Qualchan reinforced the coalition. After the Massacre, Puget Sound tribes began withdrawing support from Leschi's hoped-for combination.

Illga Adams, subchief under the Tillamook chieftain Kilchis. Tillamook County Pioneer Museum.

behind logs. Encamped on Green River, the braves were approached by regulars and volunteers on November 4. Unenthusiastic for a fight, they prepared to hit and run, as the troops, disinclined to pursue them, pulled out for the Puyallup River. On November 6 a small warrior party ambushed a detachment of Slaughter's regulars moving toward the Puyallup, killing one and wounding four others.

Strengthening of regular and volunteer forces at this time filled the valleys with troops, making the Indians aware that the Americans had not been deterred from their pursuit despite recent losses. Swollen rivers and worn-out pack animals delayed further pursuit for a time. The numbers of the combatants reportedly swelled to three hundred under Kitsap, Kenasket, Quiemuth, his fellow Nisqually Klowowit, and Nelson. On the night of November 25 they surrounded the Slaughter-Hays camp of regulars and volunteers near Stuck River, a Puyallup tributary, near where McAllister had been killed. The troops were en route to White River. In dense fog, yelling and shrieking, the Indians exchanged shots with the troops, killing one and driving off forty horses. After his capture February 29, 1856, a soldier shot out Kenasket's brains.

Warring Indians kept troops under constant surveillance. From the confluence of the Stuck and the Puyallup (at Sumner, Washington) Slaughter reconnoitered north to join forces with a volunteer company at present-day Auburn, where Indians watched soldiers warming themselves and drying their clothes around a large fire. On the morning of November 26, 1855, creeping past sentries, they fired on their prey, killing Slaughter and twelve others and wounding several. The suddenness of the attack, which prevented the soldiers from returning fire, allowed the attackers to slip away without casualties.

Runners had contacted scattered tribes south of Puget Sound and in Oregon, seeking to entice them into the war. Most of the tribes kept out of it. When hostile Klickitats warned the Tillamooks to rise up and fight the whites, their chief, Kilchis, had his people bring in their guns to allay white fears that they were about to enter the conflict. To prevent noncombatant Indians from south of Puget Sound from joining their warring fellows, government authorities approved a policy (credited to Indian agent John Cain) of separating them from those at war. Under the Cain plan Klickitats and Chinooks were collected at Vancouver, Klickitats at the White Salmon, Yakimas opposite The Dalles, Cowlitzes at Cowlitz Farms, and Chehalises at a point on their river. To keep tabs on their internees—because of their ties with hostile Klickitat, Yakima, and Puget Sound Indians—agents not only confined them but also confiscated their guns.*

In the Puget Sound country authorities set about removing nonwarring Indians from east of the Sound to five temporary reservations on that body of water to separate them from the warring factions. Although hunted by whites, Leschi and thirty-eight men in six large canoes paddled to one of those reservations—Fox Island (near Tacoma, Washington)—where they tied up the agent, John Swan, and tried to entice 806 Puyallups and Nisquallis confined

there to leave the island and join them in war.

Jittery authorities and settlers wanted the Indians removed, especially from the Seattle area. Many Indians opposed removal. Leschi planned to storm the town and then lead his braves down to Fort Steilacoom to give it the same treatment. Fearing troubles for the remaining friendlies, Arthur Denny and Doctor David S. Maynard hustled them across Elliott Bay. It was Denny who earlier had objected to the plan of having a *Decatur* crew seize and hold hostage relatives of Patkanin, for whose good behavior Denny had said he would assume responsibility.* Chief Seattle remained friendly to whites and remembered also the death of his nephew, Almos, who was killed by Owhi in the early forties. Seattle and his warriors retaliated for the death by killing ten men and capturing their women and children.

On January 21, 1856, Indians friendly to whites brought word that Owhi and an Indian party had crossed the Cascade Mountains. On the twenty-fifth the party, a reported eight hundred Indians under Owhi and Quilquilton, crossed Lake Washington and moved toward the town of Seattle. That evening several spies slipped into Seattle to gather what intelligence they could, preparatory to an early morning attack. The infiltrators talked with two Indians—Curley (Suquardle), a former Duwamish chief who had succumbed to Chief Seattle's rule, and Jim. Both were workers at the Henry Yesler sawmill. Curley and Jim, in turn, talked the spies out of attacking at 2:00 A.M. in favor of a later morning attack. The two suggested the delay to give the townsfolk time to be up and to give the two time to alert the crew of the *Decatur* as well as Yesler and C. C. Hewitt, captain of the local volunteers. Early on the morning of the twenty-sixth Jim carried word of the plot to Yesler in time to alert the townsfolk.

With dawn the Indians readied themselves to attack. The resounding noise of a howitzer fired into their ranks signaled the beginning of the Battle of Seattle. The Indians set up a howl. Townsfolk scurried to a blockhouse. Indians loaded their cumbersome muskets. From over two miles of deep woods on the far side of a 200-yard swamp they fired their muskets into the town. Their women prodded hesitant ones to the attack. Added to the crackling of the Indians' muskets was the small-arms fire from townspeople and the continual booming of the *Decatur*'s guns pouring shot,

---

*Some Klickitats at Vancouver, who were regarded by whites as friendly, received a tip from an Indian party returning from California (where it had been making buckskin clothing for Spaniards) that Rogues and Shastas had stolen their horses. The "friendlies" included Spencer, Lumly, and Klickitat Peter. They decided to punish the robbers during the war, which they did by killing several Rogues in an ensuing foray.

*Another prominent citizen of Seattle, the Reverend David E. Blaine, believed that lack of cohesion among the Indians would prevent more conflict. Blaine also observed that Indians who spoke the Chinook jargon were the most "immoral" of their race because of their association with white men and that the country would have been a good place in which to live if the Indians and alcohol were removed—a case of throwing out the Indians with the firewater. David E. Blaine and Kate P. Blaine, *Letters From the Pacific Northwest Written by David E. Blaine and Kate P. Blaine 1854–1858.* Mimeographed copy in University of Washington Library, Seattle, Wash.

SEATTLE. BATTLE of '56

Sketch in the Seattle Post Intelligencer, July 5, 1892, of the Battle of Seattle, January 26, 1856. The settlers were previously warned and aided by a gunboat in the harbor, and they escaped what the Indians hoped would be a massacre of the whites.

grape, and canister ashore. During the fight the attackers shifted their position northward toward a blockhouse, where settlers huddled. Subsequently some of the settlers were moved to the *Decatur*, and others to the bark *Bronte*. After a short pause the Indians charged the town, firing bullets into houses. The *Decatur's* guns kept firing, most of their missiles crashing harmlessly into trees. The Indians fell back. Men from the *Decatur* pursued to trap them, as Indian leaders, such as Leschi, had hoped they would. As the Indians prepared to effect their ambuscade, the seamen escaped to return to their ship. The red attackers continued desultory firing throughout the afternoon. By evening they had melted into the woods, burning houses and barns as they went. How many losses did they sustain? Yesler later claimed that not one of them was hurt—perhaps an underestimation. Two whites (some say three) were killed. Later, Indians claimed that it had not been the *Decatur's* guns that frightened them but their "poohing" or "twice shot" (the noise of the detonation and the impact of the missile), which had mystified and terrified them.*

On February 7, Leschi reappeared there in keeping with his warnings after the Seattle defeat, but with fewer numbers than in the January attack. This time fire from ships kept the Indians at bay. They ineffectively fired their muskets in an all-day semicircular maneuver from Third Avenue of present-day downtown Seattle past Marion Street. Witness-

*Pacific Northwestern Indians had been familiar with "fire ships" (steamers) as early as 1836 when the Hudson's Bay Company steamer *Beaver* appeared on the Columbia River. The *Beaver* sailed the Northwest Coast after that with Indians among her crew. Indians also served on the steamers that later plied the Columbia River, Pacific Ocean, Strait of Juan de Fuca, and Puget Sound. By shortly after midcentury the steamers had virtually destroyed the Indian canoe transport business by carrying passengers and cargo on those larger bodies of water. Besides the *Decatur*, whose guns disrupted their Seattle fight, natives felt pressure from other such craft on Puget Sound: the *Hancock*, the *Massachusetts*, and the revenue cutter *Jefferson Davis*. The *Active*, of which the natives had bad memories, was dispatched from Olympia after the Seattle fight to cruise around Elliott Bay. The *Republic* was dispatched from California for Fort Steilacoom with 250 troops. Among the numerous works in which the Battle of Seattle is narrated is Bernard C. Nalty and Truman R. Strobridge, "The Defense of Seattle, 1856, 'And Down Came the Indians,'" *Pacific Northwest Quarterly* 55, no. 3 (July, 1964): 105–110, and "Seattle's First Taste of Battle, 1856," *Pacific Northwest Quarterly* 47, no. 1 (January, 1956): 1–8.

ing the action, Chief Seattle again took no part in it, and, again, frightened Seattleites took to the blockhouse.

Out in the countryside some whites remained on their claims. Some even assisted the warring Indians in one way or another in exchange for their protection. In March, Stevens arrested certain settlers for refusing to turn themselves in for aiding the enemy. Early in the war Leschi had sent word that no whites were to be harmed west of the Deschutes River, which flows into Budd Inlet near Olympia. Non-American citizens (mostly British) suffered no harm from the Indians unless the latter believed them to have aided the Americans. Reinforced by the Klickitats and other Indians of the interior, the Puget Sound warriors continued to drive off American livestock and burn buildings. Along the Duwamish River they left only two or three buildings standing.

With seventy-six Snoqualmies and Snohomishes, Patkanin, who was commissioned by Stevens to round up the warring Indians, sought out the combatants still following their leader, Leschi. At that chief's camp at the fork of a small stream on White River, the barking of dogs signaled Patkanin's approach with his men. Taunting the approaching Patkanin, Leschi called out, "I have understood that you were coming to attack me, and I am prepared for you, I think I will have your head before tomorrow noon." To which Patkanin replied, "I don't know, but I think that before that time I will have your head." The day following that verbal exchange, Patkanin's men, trying to make good his boast, stormed a house where Leschi's men had fortified themselves. After a sharp fight the surrounded ones were driven from their structure. Before the day ended Patkanin's men ran out of ammunition and withdrew, thinking they had killed six of Leschi's men, including a chief. Better proof to white authorities were the heads of two of their victims in that fight. They displayed them along with four others collected after a skirmish near Snoqualmie Falls.

Patkanin and his braves were encouraged by their recent successes and by the receipt of money, blankets, and other goods for turning over to American officials the grisly tokens from the bodies of their slain foes. They swept the forests from the Snoqualmie River to Connell's Prairie and up the Cascade Mountains to Naches Pass and into other mountain fastnesses seeking to snare the hiding combatants. In early March about fifty warriors killed several whites south of Fort Steilacoom, a place that held bad memories for Indians. Whenever possible, Americans retaliated for those attacks. On March 4 their volunteers fired on a canoe on the Duwamish, killing two Indians and wounding others. Such skirmishes in February and March, 1856, severely harassed and hampered the Indians.

On March 10, 150 Indians, reinforced by Qualchan and Eneas from east of the Cascade Mountains, discovered at White River Crossing on Connell's Prairie a detachment of volunteers, who had come there to build a blockhouse and install a ferry. From behind brush and logs the Indians, outflanking their foe, fired a musket volley into their midst. On learning that reinforcements were coming to their aid, the troops withdrew to a hilltop, a maneuver that the In-

dians took for weakness. They then charged the troops, fighting them into midafternoon. Although the 150 braves outnumbered the 100 troops, the Indians were now outflanked when frontally attacked and were defeated. Retreating, they abandoned withes and ropes for dragging off their dead, who perhaps were not so numerous as the military exaggerated them to be. The Indians had wounded only four soldiers. In the litter of their defeat was a drum whose beats would never again gird warriors to battle. With the sounds of the injured and dying in his ears, Qualchan left for home. Wearying of war, Leschi and his braves eventually fled up the White River and through Naches Pass into the Yakima country, where Kamiakan fed the hungry refugees. From there Leschi made peace overtures to U.S. Army Colonel George Wright. In May, Stevens reported that Leschi and his people had been on Naches Pass, from which the chief kept in communication with his spies west of the mountains.

Defeat virtually broke Indian resistance on Puget Sound. Those who continued the fight fragmented into small units, from which they continued to kill isolated settlers whom they deemed unfriendly, burning their houses, barns, and other properties and running off their stock. In April, Captain H. J. G. Maxon (promoted to Major, April 20, 1856) and his company of volunteers killed eight Indians and took fourteen prisoners between Yelm Prairie and the area known as Nisqually Pass (possibly the area approaching Mount Rainier carved out by the Nisqually River). While scouting up Michael's Fork (perhaps Mashel Creek, a Nisqually tributary near Mount Rainier), Maxon killed eight more, took three prisoners, and sent the women and children to the settlements.

With the combatants fragmented, many Indians in April and May, 1856, joined in the search for them. They wore red-trimmed blue caps, which Olympia ladies had made to help distinguish the friendlies from the warriors as much as to appeal to their vanity. Among the searchers were Chehalises under Captain Sydney Ford and members of other tribes under Agent Wesley Gosnell from the Squaxin Reservation. They scouted Nisqually and Puyallup swamps for their quarry. Close ties between the pursuers and the pursued made the warfare civil in nature. The noncombatant Indians, like whites contracting with the military, discovered that war could be profitable when they were paid for renting horses to transport the Indian chasers. Most Indians who rented out their animals did not, however, receive the pay promised them for providing this service. The hoped-for combination of the tribes of the interior with those of Puget Sound had failed. Thus Indian resistance west of the Cascade Mountains was brought virtually to an end. If further resistence was to be successful, it would have to come from tribes east of those mountains. More populous and aggressive, those tribes prepared to resume the fight, determined to resist the advances of the soldier representatives of American civilization. In so doing, they were aware that their destiny and the destiny of other Indians of the Pacific Northwest depended on their success.

15. THE SHIRT STILL BLOODIED

It was in January, 1856, that the Oregon Territorial Legislature sent its memorial to the president calling for the removal of General John E. Wool, whose official reports told of outrages committed against Indians. The memorial was only the tip of the iceberg of coolness between Oregon and Washington territorials and the United States Army in the conduct of the war. John Beeson, an Oregon immigrant of 1853, was among the very few whites in the Pacific Northwest who came to the defense of its Indians at this time of fear and hysteria. His letters to newspapers and his speeches defending the Indians in their struggle, and his condemnation of those seeking to prolong the war for monetary gain, brought down on his head the wrath of the white community. In his *Plea For the Indian; With Facts and Features of the Late War in Oregon* (published in 1857), he warned that, if Indian "exterminators" did not desist from their course of action, they would bring down not only Indian society but also American society on top of it.

In February, 1856, the Yakimas went south to visit Indians at the mouth of White Salmon River, carrying news that warriors of Kamiakin's confederacy were about to launch an attack downstream at The Cascades. The Yakima chief seemed to realize the strategic importance of that location more than Colonel George Wright did. Wright commanded the Columbia River District, and was now Kamiakin's principal adversary. All military goods destined for the interior had to pass through this strategic corridor.

By March, 1856, all but nine of the soldiers had been withdrawn from a blockhouse built the previous year at the Middle Cascades, leaving the Upper and Lower Cascades with their mills, warehouses, boat landings, and transportation projects exposed to attack. At the same time some inkling of what could happen in that area came after a Klickitat attack on the small white settlement at the mouth of the White Salmon River. On March 5, Indians had also fired on the steamer *Wasco* near the mouth of Hood River and had committed other depredations. Those at The Cascades, hitherto believed friendly, painted themselves and slipped into the woods to confer with Yakima warriors led by Bolon's killer, Stahkin, who was the coordinator of the planned attack on The Cascades.

Suddenly on the sunny morning of March 26, Indians simultaneously attacked both the Middle and Upper Cascades. At the Middle Cascades they killed a soldier. They captured another, whom they tortured, finally bashing in his face. They also burned houses and pillaged goods. They cached the goods, but were never to retrieve them. In an all-day fight at the Upper Cascades they attacked Bradford's store, where about forty whites had taken refuge, and burned houses, a sawmill, and a lumber yard. The attackers were short of ammunition and thus forced to cut endgate

wagon rods for their muzzle-loader bullets. Besides firing their guns, they rolled huge rocks and threw dry-moss firebrands down on the store, whose occupants were kept busy extinguishing the fires, by dousing brine on them from pork barrels or shoving them off with long sticks. The attackers kept barely out of the range of the guns that the defenders had found in the store.

At the outset of the attack the crew of the little steamer *Mary* fired up their ship for a hasty retreat. Realizing that the *Mary* would summon help from The Dalles, the Indians attacked her as she moved out into the Columbia with her whistle screaming to summon help. Before she got under way, Indian guns wounded a fireman. A cook drowned when he fell overboard wounded. The steamer crew had some fence rails aboard for fuel—which was a fortunate thing for it, as Indians had taken over the woodyards between the Upper Cascades and The Dalles. More of the defenders of Bradford's store would have been killed had it not been for a sixteen-year-old interpreter, John McBean, who risked his life carrying water from the river to the thirsty ones in the store during the three-day siege. When relief troops arrived on the *Mary* and *Wasco*, they plunged into the woods, firing howitzers in all directions. James Sinclair, traveling with young McBean, was shot and killed in the attack.

Indians also fired on buildings at the Lower Cascades. Warned in time, whites had pushed off in boats for Vancouver. After the fight at the Lower Cascades, the steamer *Belle* landed on March 28 with ammunition for the blockhouse. At the same time the steamer *Fashion* landed to disembark a company of troops from Fort Vancouver under Lieutenant Philip Sheridan. Indians blocked Sheridan's narrow passage, and one of their bullets grazed his nose, nearly depriving the Civil War of one of its generals and the daughter of a Rogue chief a husband. Another bullet killed a soldier at his side. As Sheridan was about to surprise a number of Indians at the Middle Cascades blockhouse, an inadvertant bugle call sent them scurrying into the woods. At nearby Bradford's Island thirteen Indians, who had fled there for protection from Indians as much as from whites, were corralled by Sheridan. Largely on Indian evidence, despite their pleas of innocence, the warriors were indicted for treason since they were alleged to have been parties to the June 25, 1855, treaty with Middle Oregon tribes. Shouting "Wake nika kwass kopa memaloose! [I am not afraid to die!]," one chief, Old Chenoweth, was hung despite his offer to purchase his freedom with, among other things, ten horses and two wives. On the following day Tecomeoc and Cap Joe were hung, and in the days following that Tsy, Sim Lasselas, Four-fingered Johnny, Jim, Tumalth, and Old Skein were hung. Including Chenoweth, nine in all were executed. Kanewake was reprieved on the scaffold, and Banaha was taken to Vancouver and "decorated with ball and chain." Ironically those who suffered those fates were Cascade Indians. They were believed to have been lured into hostilities by a combination of Klickitats and Yakimas, the main perpetrators of the attack on The Cascades. The total of Indian casualties in or as a result of the fighting is unknown. Their enemy counted fifteen dead or missing, including three soldiers, a blood and a black.

After the fighting, troops guarded 800 "friendly" Indians on the so-called White Salmon Reservation established by Governor Stevens near present-day Bingen, Washington. In 1858 its agency, under Dr. Richard H. Lansdale, was moved north to Fort Simcoe. Sheridan's triumph was offset the following year on a sortie to an Indian village. With frictions arising from the displacement of so many tribes in the wake of Indian wars in western Oregon, such killings appear to have been more numerous than ever. At a critical moment Sheridan discovered that his pistol had been stolen, compelling him to a display of diplomacy rather than force. To add to his embarrassment, the Indians, in his own words, responded to his predicament with "contemptuous laughter," and he returned to Fort Yamhill "rather crestfallen."[2]

The Yakimas were exuberant, but not complacent over their part in the attack at The Cascades. Their scouts closely watched a troop detachment under Thomas Cornelius, now a colonel, who had assumed command of the Oregon Mounted Volunteers from Colonel Nesmith. On April 9, 1856, the detachment, 241-men-strong, reached the mouth of Satus Creek, moving up that stream several miles to encamp in a narrow canyon. That evening Cornelius and Captain Absolem J. Hembree rode into an Indian trap. Hembree was shot in the abdomen above the hip. As he rode off, he wheeled, shot his attacker dead, and fell dead himself. The Indians scalped him, stripped off his clothes, and then rushed toward the volunteers' camp, but the soldiers gained an eminence from which to counterattack. Fighting lasted until noon, when the Indians, withdrawing from the rocky terrain, rode up the creek to another eminence, on which three hundred warriors had by now fortified themselves among the rocks. The troops dismounted, ran uphill, dropped to reload, then charged, firing their superior rifles. The Indians broke, leaving one killed and three wounded. A warrior, Yellow-wash, slipped into the camp of the returning volunteers, driving most of their horses out of reach of their riders.

In May, Wright moved north from Fort Dalles toward Yakima country to search out those whom the military believed deserving of peace or punishment, a difficult task since the army found it hard to make the distinction. Often the soldiers shot peaceful Indians pointed out to them by government scouts who had personal grudges against the victims. To hide their own misdeeds, Indians sometimes blamed innocent ones who had already been hung. Two of Qualchan's men were shot because it was presumed that they had killed miners passing through Yakima country.

Kamiakin advised his Indians not to meet Wright's soldiers until those troops reached Simcoe. In case things went badly the Indians gathered their horses and prepared their families for evacuation east of the Columbia. When word came that troops had reached Simcoe, Qualchan in full feathered regalia led four hundred mounted warriors as far as the Naches River. Wright's troops encamped on the south of the Cowiche. At this time the rift between Kamiakin and Owhi deepened, as the latter, returning from Puget Sound, realized the futility of continuing the war. Some warriors began aligning themselves with the peace-seeking group. Others with Kamiakin vowed to continue the struggle. In response to Owhi's call for a peace council, Kamiakin said the war had just begun—that only the women would stop fighting. "I am a warrior, and not a woman," he declaimed. "I say let us fight today. If you conclude today to ask for peace from the invaders of your country and forever after become slaves to the white race and a disgrace to your proud ancestry, I cannot help it. I will leave my country and among the Palouses and Spokanes hope to find true warriors. With them I will fight."

After Wright had received Owhi's word that he would bring in his people, the colonel ordered him to bring in horses, mules, and other properties taken from whites. The chief demurred. To surrender the booty would have run counter to Indian practice pertaining to the disposition of spoils of war. In the spring of 1858, Owhi lost a large number of horses stolen by David (Kiyuyu), an Indian scouting for Major Robert Garnett, the commander of Fort Simcoe. On June 11 eight companies of troops crossed the Naches on a bridge that they built over that stream. From there Wright and Major Edward J. Steptoe journeyed northward to the Kittitas and over to the Wenatchee—a journey prompted by Owhi and Quiltenenock, who, fearing retaliation, had failed to gather their people to surrender.

In July, Wright removed throngs of Indians from the Wenatchee fisheries to quarantine them from their "bad chiefs," who might yet try to entice them into war. As they moved bag and baggage to the Kittitas, the Indians and their mounts formed a five-mile-long procession moving circuitously to that place. It was a remarkably large cavalcade, considering that others had traveled directly south to the Kittitas over intervening hills (Swauk-Blewitt, Washington). In the meantime, Qualchan, Moses, and Quiltenenock kept in touch with Kamiakin, all the time keeping options open for war—or peace should that become a necessity. In his continuing conflict with the army, Stevens received two Indian emissaries that month in Olympia, Patkanin and the Yakima Eneas. The latter rejected the governor's offer of money for the capture of Leschi and Quiemuth, who were then among the Yakimas.

Some indication of the desperation of the combatant Cayuses at this time was their condescension to seek allies among their ancient Shoshoni foes. They were rewarded for their efforts by attacks from those peoples. The Cayuses were more successful in keeping the war cauldron boiling among their own tribesmen, some of whom had hitherto been peacefuly disposed, and among their allies. That July about 2,500 Indians gathered in Nez Percé country to powwow over the state of affairs. They met in a setting charged by "excitable tales" from the Cayuses. A number of Nez Percé chiefs angrily refused American packtrains further entry to their lands.

The Cayuses learned that the Shoshonis had no monopoly on surprise attacks. Some Cayuse families, camped at root grounds in the Grande Ronde Valley (near Elgin, Oregon), were attacked on the morning of July 17 by the right wing of the Washington Territorial Volunteers under the command of Colonel Benjamin F. Shaw. Fresh from victories on Puget Sound and itching for more action, the volunteers had little apparent cause to attack, other than to let off steam and scald some Indians in the process. As the few young braves rode out to meet the troops to defend their camp, some families fled to brush along the river, and others fled downstream. In an engagement as brief as it was deadly, the troops killed nearly forty Indians, many of whom were old men, women, and children. They also destroyed provisions and plundered horses and cattle. As late as February 9, 1908, a writer in the *Portland Oregonian* called Shaw's attack "a master stroke to rescue the country from barbarism."

On August 2, Wool issued his order restricting white settlement in Indian country east of the Cascade Mountains. Wishing to keep that area open, Stevens sought a second Walla Walla council to, as he put it, "restrain the doubtful and wavering [Nez Percés] from active hostility." The Coeur d'Alenes and Spokanes refused to attend the council, which got under way on September 11. In the vicinity, but possibly not at the council, were Kamiakin; Owhi; Qualchan and his younger brother the warrior Lokout; and Moses. When Quiltenenock showed Stevens an endorsement that Wright had given him on the Naches River, the governor brushed him aside, as he had the Chehalis Tleyuk. He also spurned the request of a Nez Percé, Speaking Owl, for the return of his people's lands, deferring instead to Lawyer who urged the Nez Percés to stand by the 1855 treaty. Old Joseph and Red Wolf said they did not understand the treaty and had no wish to surrender lands that Lawyer had sold unfairly.

Hovering around the council grounds with his braves, Kamiakin planned to attack Stevens. He knew that Stevens was at odds with the regulars, some of whom were camped with Steptoe four miles away. Uneasy at the possibility of attack, especially since the Cayuses, Umatillas, and Teninos had just fired the grass to deny fodder to his horses, the governor moved the council nearer to Steptoe's regulars on September 14. The move was timely, for Kamiakin had planned to attack that day. The chief, leading 350 mounted and painted warriors, approached the governor, offering to shake his hand. Stevens refused to accept it because his interpreter had warned him that the Indians would stampede his horses. His mission a failure, Stevens had gone but a short distance toward The Dalles when on the nineteenth Kamiakin ordered an attack on the governor's train. A critic characterized Stevens in a general way as "the wrong man at the wrong place at the wrong time." The statement certainly fitted him in this predicament.

Qualchan and Quiltenenock led the all-day attack, forcing Stevens to form a wagon-train corral. Darkness offered him some protection from the whizzing bullets fired by the Indians, who were unskilled in night fighting. During the skirmish Qualchan called to about fifty Nez Percés who were helping shield the governor, saying that he and his braves were out to kill whites, not Indians, and that they should leave the Stevens party or suffer the consequences. Even after Steptoe moved his regulars during the night to assist the volunteers, the Indian combatants extended their firing into midmorning on September 20. When they saw Quiltenenock struck by a ball in the hip, his comrades picked him up and rode off.[3]

In yet another Walla Walla council in October, some Cayuse and Nez Percé chiefs and the Tenino headman, Stockwhitley, heard Wright assure them that troops would keep white men off their lands. "The bloody shirt shall now be washed and not a spot left on it," promised Wright. That remained to be seen. On Puget Sound authorities had dried the bloodied shirt on their own terms. Captives, such as those sent to Fox Island in July and August, were not tried in civil courts. Thus a military commission was established at Fort Steilacoom to try captured Indians and sentence those found guilty to hang or to perform hard labor.

The Puget Sound Indians had suffered the hardships of removal, and their women had traded their favors for liquor, mostly to soldiers. Other Indians were disappointed at not receiving food that had been promised them at Fort Kitsap (a blockhouse on the mainland south of Kingston, Washington, on Port Madison Reservation). They preferred to remain at their old homes on the east side of Puget Sound on the Black River (which is today nonexistent), south of Lake Washington. In December they vowed to fight for their old camps, saying, "Our fathers died here; their bones are buried here; and we also will die here." It was too late. Whites were already appropriating their lands. The Indians of the Sound naturally complained loudly that the government was giving away their lands, destroying their hunting and burial grounds. Many Indians believed the handouts that Agent Simmons distributed to them were in exchange for their lands. At this time at the Fort Kitsap Reservation, Indian Agent George Paige reduced issues to his Indians in order to make them seek their own food and abandon their "indolent habits." Special Indian Agent J. Ross Browne addressed himself to the matter after an on-the-spot inspection in 1857:

But so long as large bands of Indians, in a condition worse than pure barbarism, are permitted to roam at large, committing petty depredations wherever they can, lounging idly about the farms, consuming the substance of the settlers, affording a profitable trade to the worst possible class of whites that can infest any country, there will be very little hope for the territory of Washington.

The special agent for the Nisqually, Puyallup, and Squaxin reservations, Wesley Gosnell, refused to admit former "hostiles" onto the reservations if they were known to have killed whites. In August, Stevens met complaining

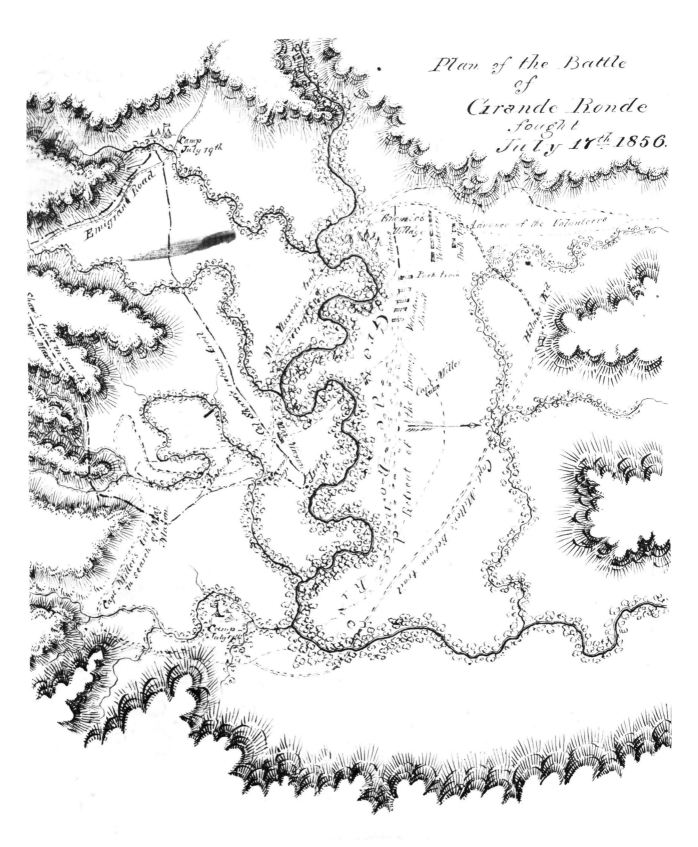

Plan of the Battle of the Grande Ronde, July 17, 1856. In the brief engagement women, children, and elderly men were massacred and their food stores destroyed by a white volunteer force. Beinecke Library, Yale University.

noncombatant Indians on Fox Island. He asked them, as he should have earlier, what they wished in the way of permanent reservations. On the basis of that Fox Island council the Puyallup and Nisqually reservations were relocated and enlarged, and a new one established for the Muckleshoots.

Leschi and his brother Quiemuth were among the last Puget Sound chiefs to hold out, having the most to lose if they were captured. After Leschi's nephew Sluggia was offered fifty blankets to coax his uncle into the woods, Leschi was captured on November 13, 1856. Then an Indian, Yelm Jim, killed Sluggia for his treachery. Turning himself in, Quiemuth was held overnight in Governor Steven's office while he awaited transfer to Steilacoom. Before he could be moved, someone forced open the door and stabbed him to death. It was strongly suspected that the killer was one James Bunton (or Joe Buntin), whose father-in-law, James McAllister, had been killed the previous year when talking with Leschi on Connell's Prairie. Bunton was freed for lack of evidence. In the meantime Leschi awaited his fate. In the spring of 1857 Yakima envoys visited Chief Seattle vainly appealing to him as an Indian to join in a renewal of the war if the Americans executed Leschi.

The aggressions of northern Indians complicated the war on Puget Sound for whites and Indians alike. They launched their attacks from canoes, which they paddled down from as far away as Alaska—and also paddled back, sometimes with human head trophies as cargo. The preoccupation of whites and Indians in their war emboldened the northerners to increase their depredations on the south. Government gunboats attempted to keep them out of the lower waters. By late 1856 the *Hancock* had driven off sixty of the marauders. When the crew of the *Massachusetts* found them that year at Port Gamble on the upper Kitsap Peninsula, her captain tried to convince them to leave, even to the point of offering to tow their canoes to Victoria. When they defiantly spurned his offer, he pressed into service the passenger steamer *Traveler*, positioning her with a launch at the upper end of their encampment. On October 20 a lieutenant carried a flag of truce to the Indians, a gesture that they took for a sign of weakness. Whereupon the men waded from the launch through breast-deep water dragging a howitzer ashore. When the Indians did not yield to the men, a fight ensued, in which the northerners fled to the cover of the woods. Two days later, after their canoes and provisions were destroyed, the chiefs surrendered. They claimed that of 117 warriors they had lost 27 killed and 21 wounded. Canoeless, they were taken to Victoria aboard the *Massachusetts*.

The killing only stimulated northern Indians to return to seek revenge and to raid and plunder. Rumors spread among Puget Sound Indians that the northerners were planning to ally with whites to exterminate the Indians of the Sound—a possibility as remote as a combination of southern Indians to exterminate whites. The Indians of Puget Sound did feel more secure from northern raiders because of the whites in their midst and, when leaving their villages, often left personal effects and valuables with them for safekeeping. In April, 1857, several massive canoes bearing about four hundred warriors, mostly male, arrived in

Puget Sound. The warriors were Stikines (a Tlingit Koluschan subdivision), Haidas, and Bellabellas (Wakashan) from far up the Northwest Coast. All armed, painted, and ready for war, they frightened whites along the northern reaches of the Sound, especially at Bellingham Bay, which was the first white settlement below the Canadian border to feel the brunt of the northern aggressors. In 1854, after a white man had killed a northern Indian in Washington Territory, his fellow Indians in revenge attacked the settlement at Bellingham Bay, killing two whites and plundering houses. Because the northern raiders laughed at the sailboats in which officials sought to pursue them, whites plead with the military for steam gunboats to prevent such attacks.

On August 11, 1857, in revenge for their Port Gamble defeat, the northern warriors selected as their victim a white "chief," Doctor J. C. Kellogg, of Whidbey Island. The choice was in keeping with their concept of blood-feud revenge, and the proposed victim also had good clothes and a good zinc boat. In Kellogg's absence they killed instead a friend of the local natives, named I. N. Ebey. They cut off his head and carried it north. Ironically, Mrs. Ebey, on observing sorties between the Skagits and the Clallams, had written in her diary that Indians knew better than to murder a white person, for fear they would be driven off or killed.[4] Reacting to the murder, officials jailed eighteen Stikines in Port Townsend as hostages. Eight were later released, and the rest dug their way to freedom. The Stikines were indignant when ordered to return Ebey's head. In Victoria, Governor James Douglas was caught up in controversy with both Washington territorial officials and United States government officials over the actions of the northern Indians. He quickly pointed out that the Stikines were Russian, not British, Indians. Agent Michael Simmons ordered Puget Sound Indians to shoot any northern Indians entering Washington Territory.[5]

The 1857 lull in the Indian war gave whites further opportunities to encroach on Indian lands, even before General W. S. Harney, commander of the Department of Oregon at Vancouver, revoked on October 31, 1858, Wool's order limiting entry into the interior. Under Wool's order some whites were licensed to trade with Indians, but many came unlicensed and uninvited. Their so-called farms in such places as the Walla Walla Valley were merely whiskey blinds. They scarcely qualified as missionaries under Wool's order; they were ruffians with bottles, not Bibles, in their saddlebags. Nor could they be called Hudson's Bay Company men, who were permitted continued residence under the order. Miners, whom Wool permitted passage through the interior, were a constant irritation to the Indians. But, bad as those violations were, the revocation of the order turned the interior into an open range for whites.

In response to the attendant increase in white encroachments, Kamiakin called a council in the spring of 1858 of Coeur d'Alenes, Palouses, Cayuses, and Nez Percés. He passionately pleaded for Indians to rise up throughout the intermontane West, warning that unless they did the military would invade their lands and enslave their women.

Shortly after the council Kamiakin and the Palouses set out to plead with the tribes to enter the conflict. Urged on by Qualchan, the Palouses killed two miners on the road to Colville and raided horses and cattle of both whites and Indians in the Walla Walla Valley. Their depredations evoked strong pleas from whites to their authorities for protection. Soon after the council the Coeur d'Alenes and Kamiakin went to Father Joseph Joset of the Sacred Heart Mission to ask if troops were coming to take their lands. Trying to allay their fears, the priest labeled such talk as rumor.

If the troops were not coming to take their lands, they were about to trespass on them. On May 6, 1858, Steptoe, now a colonel, set out for the troubled Colville country from his command post, the military Fort Walla Walla, built between September 18 and 23, 1856. He went armed with his command: 152 dragoons, five officers, and a few civilians. They were armed with three mounted howitzers, antiquated musketoons, long Mississippi Yager rifles, and insufficient ammunition. The motives for this journey northward are not clear. Possibily he wished to select a point for a fort on the forty-ninth parallel to protect the men who were engaged in the international boundary survey. Perhaps he wished to paw but not maul troublesome Indians—particularly the Palouses—who were harrying whites and even Fort Walla Walla. Perhaps he wished to drain off from winter confinement his own restless energies and those of his men, as Colonel Shaw had done with his command.

Steptoe chose an undiplomatically direct route through Spokane and Coeur d'Alène country. The troops negotiated the Snake River at Red Wolf's Crossing at the mouth of Alpowa Creek with help from the Nez Percé Timothy, who accompanied the command with his guides as they moved north. The troops were met on May 16 near present day Rosalia, Washington, by about a thousand Indians—Spokanes, Coeur d'Alènes, Palouses, Yakimas, Sinkiuses, and elements of nearly all the interior tribes except the Flatheads. The Indians were armed, painted, and defiant at the trespass; their presence revealed not only the deteriorating situation in the interior—the backwash of unratified treaties—but also the effect of Kamiakin's exhortations to keep soldiers off their lands. It had been at the suggestion of the Yakima chief that Palouse chief Tilcoax had driven stock away from Fort Walla Walla before Steptoe began his march.

The day of confrontation, May 16, was a Sunday. The sanctity of the day restrained the Indians from attack, but not from undulating alongside the command, yelling, and shaking scalps. During the confrontation the Spokanes and Coeur d'Alènes questioned Steptoe about his intentions, suspiciously eyeing his howitzers. The weapons belied his statements that his mission was peaceful, that he wished to effect good feelings between whites and Indians around Colville. His replies were obviously ad-libs in an unplanned drama in which he was forced to change his lines.

Father Joset made his entry that day on the stage where the drama was being played. His presence was of great concern to Tilcoax lest it hamper the Palouse efforts to incite the Coeur d'Alènes to war. It was a Palouse who went to the soldiers saying that the priest had brought guns and ammunition to the Coeur d'Alènes. In their continuing attempts to stir up those tribesmen, other Palouses told the Coeur d'Alènes that they had overheard Steptoe say that the Coeur d'Alènes were rich and that the Coeur d'Alène women would be captured by soldiers.

On the seventeenth, with more vocality than violence, the belligerent Indians pressured Steptoe into checking his northward progress. Joset conferred with the harried colonel, bringing some of his Coeur d'Alènes to witness the talk. In a war within the war, a Nez Percé scout, Levi, struck a blow to the Coeur d'Alène head chief, Victor. When Victor's fellow tribesman Jean Pierre Kumpasket declared the confrontation with the soldiers to be at an end, the militant Melkapsi slapped Kumpasket's face. When Victor rebuked him, the two fisticuffed until Joset broke up the fight.

At this point the Coeur d'Alène chief Stellam, who was a mutual friend of the quarreling tribesmen, fired on the troops with others of the tribe. Sporadic fighting soon became general. The Spokanes and Coeur d'Alènes positioned themselves at Steptoe's rear, the Palouses at his front. From high points the Indians worked their way along, firing at the troops in what became a running six-hour fight. At evening the Indians disengaged. Surrounded, the position of the troops seemed hopeless, and with it that of the military in the interior. At midnight the red men rushed their position. It was deserted. Managing a retreat, Steptoe and his men had slipped away in the night.

Many of the spoils of battle went to the Coeur d'Alènes: staples and about a hundred pack animals, which were taken to their Sacred Heart Mission. Around campfires they exhilarated in victory. They and their allies had killed two officers, five men, and three Indian allies, wounding several of their foe. Mixed with the sounds of victory at the mission was wailing for the nine braves killed, including the peacemakers, Victor and Zachariah, and the forty or fifty others wounded. One chief killed in the fight was Tecolekun of the Wenatchees, a signer of the 1855 Yakima treaty. He was related to Qualchan and Spokane chief Polatkin, who had been in the thick of the fight.

After that fight Joset on behalf of his Coeur d'Alènes, journeyed to Fort Vancouver to intercede with the commandant, General Newman S. Clarke. Clarke told him the Indians could have peace, but only under certain conditions: they had to confer with him or his officers, they had to permit the government to build a road through their lands on which soldiers and other Americans could travel, they had to restore property taken in the Steptoe attack, and surrender those who participated in it, and, finally, they had to drive Kamiakin out of their country. As if in defiance of Clarke's ultimatums, Kamiakin went among the Coeur d'Alènes to stir them up again to continue the fight.

On returning from Vancouver, Joset pleaded for two weeks with his red parishioners to make peace. The recalcitrant Melkapsi, wishing to rid the country of black robes and white men, generally, wrote Clarke that there could be peace if he came to the Coeur d'Alène country without troops. Such sentiments only strengthened the general's resolve to dispatch troops there. Sensing Clarke's disposition and that of the Indians, an agent wrote, "I am of the opinion we are to have a general war in the upper country."

Until such an eventuality the Indians sought vengeance against miners. The latter were moving from The Dalles to Canada in units like military troops, and in some cases they wore soldiers' uniforms to intimidate the Indians. The Indians' efforts to check the gold seekers were weakened by the Indian David's continuing thefts of Indian horses. In June, 1858, Indians at the mouth of the Wenatchee repulsed a squad of northbound miners, but, in doing so, Quiltene-nock was killed, and Qualchan was badly wounded. Later that summer Indians ambushed a similar miner expedition at McLoughlin Canyon on the Okanogan River near To-nasket, Washington, killing from one to six miners according to varying reports.[6] According to one account, Indians of the Thompson River in the British Columbia interior visited a woman of their tribe married to a French Canadian at Walla Walla, and they were the first to spread word of gold discoveries in the Fraser-Thompson river areas, setting off the rushes there.

General Clarke was so certain that the Coeur d'Alènes and their allies would reject his ultimatums that on July 4, 1858, he ordered Wright into the field to strike them from The Dalles. At the same time Clarke ordered Major Garnett north from Fort Simcoe. Garnett was the southern "fire-eater" in command of the other side of the army's two-edged sword. His orders were to punish and drive Indians toward the Spokane country.

War in the interior had diverted the army's Department of Oregon from the Mormon war with the United States. Kamiakin's talkative brother, Skloom, had told Garnett that the Mormons had twice sent emissaries among interior tribes to rouse them against the government. From the Bitterroot to the Willamette whites feared an Indian-Mormon combination against them. White mountain men had spread ugly rumors about the Mormons. The Church of Jesus Christ of Latter-day Saints had baptized and confirmed Bannocks, Shoshonis, Nez Percés, and other tribesmen as Lamanite brothers. The initial Pacific Northwestern Mormon-Indian meeting occurred as early as 1851 and had been cordial. The Saints were warmly welcomed by such Bannock chiefs as Le Grand Coquin. On June 12, 1855, the churchmen reached the Salmon River, establishing the settlement of Fort Lemhi there (near Tendoy, Idaho). It was named for Limhi, a Nephite king in the *Book of Mormon*. Their eagerness to reclaim their red brothers was evident in the permission given their men to marry Indian women.

In the summer of 1857, the Mormons, fearing that approaching United States Army troops would drive them into the desert, placed several thousand men in the field. Small detachments were dispatched to harass army troops under Colonel Albert Sidney Johnston as he entered winter quarters at Camp Scott on the Black Fork of Green River, three miles from Fort Bridger. When the Bannocks in January, 1858, began attacking Mormon livestock at the Salmon River Mission, the Mormons blamed Johnston and other

army personnel for inciting the Indians to commit the depredations. When the Nez Percés, after searching the Lemhi Valley for horses stolen by the Bannocks, began attacking the latter tribesmen, army personnel alleged that Mormons had armed the Nez Percés, and goaded them into stealing from and harassing the Bannocks, who were now joined by Northern Shoshonis in their forays. Aware of Eastern Shoshoni Chief Washakie's neutrality to whites, Johnston urged him to move his people into buffalo country during the Mormon war.

The Mormon extension of hospitality to the Nez Percés angered the Shoshonis and Bannocks; the Saints were, in the thinking of many Indians, the vanguard of a white invasion. To cap the Mormon troubles, dissident Bannocks and Shoshonis, who had failed to obtain from them guns and ammunition to fight with them as allies, struck the Mormon mission on February 25, 1858. Their attack was reminiscent of the Whitman massacre of 1847. At both places land titles had been a thorny problem. Mormon missionary efforts in the area were frustrated by the attack, two men of the mission were killed, several others were wounded, and livestock were driven off. In the spring of 1873 the Mormons attempted to balance their losses by baptizing over a hundred Shoshonis of the southern Idaho Territory. Their success was due, among other things, to the Indians' wish to escape reservations. In compliance with the wishes of their Lamanite brothers Mormons moved them to a site near Brigham City, Utah.[7]

On August 10, Garnett with nearly three-hundred troops left Fort Simcoe and its beautiful oak grove—poison oak to Indians—on his punitive mission. While tracking down Indians involved in recent brushes with miners, Garnett's troops on the upper Yakima lost a lieutenant, named Jesse K. Allen, who was believed to have been killed accidentally. Allen's party of fifteen mounted men captured twenty-one native men, about fifty of their women and children, seventy head of horses, and fifteen head of cattle, besides considerable property. Three men were shot who were recognized as participants in attacks on miners. Moving over to the Wenatchee, the command lured five Indian suspects into its camp. With no investigation or semblance of a trial the soldiers pinioned their victims for execution. Lieutenant George Crook, continuing his education as an Indian fighter on this northern war front, noted that a second lieutenant was delegated to the execution detail. As Crook put it, "This whole business was exceedingly distasteful to me," and the subordinate "rather enjoyed that kind of thing."[8]

Up the White River, a Lake Wenatchee tributary, troops during the war also pounced on ten tipis that sheltered sixty or seventy Indians gathering winter food. Before their victims could flee, the soldiers shot or hanged the men and sabre-slashed the women and children.[9] Returning to Fort Simcoe from his punitive expedition, Garnett found his wife and baby had died. He himself was to be killed in the Civil War, as was Stevens. Wright drowned in a shipwreck off the California coast. Perhaps there was retribution in the deaths. At the junction of the Snake River with the Tucannon, Fort Taylor had been built honoring a

The Battle of Spokane Plains, September 5, 1858, sketched by Gustavus Sohon. A U.S. Army force under Colonel George Wright defeated warriors of several tribes of the interior who resisted the passage of his troops. Smithsonian Institution National Anthropological Archives, Neg. No. 47,744.

captain who fell in the Steptoe fight. On August 18, 1858, Wright poised his forces to move north. A fortnight earlier he and General Clarke had met with twenty-one Nez Percé chiefs under Lawyer to sign a compact. Each party agreed not to bear arms against the other and to aid the other in case of war. Wright's forces included 190 dragoons; 400 artillery; 90 infantry, packers, and Mexican muleteers; and about 30 Nez Percé scouts. His weaponry included among other things improved long-range rifles and Minié balls and mountain howitzers.

On September 1 at Four Lakes, about twenty miles southwest of Spokane Falls, five hundred warriors readied themselves for Wright to attack—Coeur d'Alênes, Spokanes, Palouses, Yakimas, Kalispels, Colvilles, Sinkiuses, Okanagons, and scattered other tribesmen. As Wright's troops moved toward the Spokane country, some of the Indians harassed them as they had Steptoe attempting to stampede their animals. A mile and a half from the mass of waiting Indians, the troops halted, then advanced. The dragoons swung left and the Nez Percés swung right, as the main column advanced with the howitzers. With polyglot weaponry— muskets, bows and arrows, and lances—accoutered in their traditional war trappings, the braves deployed to a hill with blood-curdling yells. The right, left, and center wings were under prominent chiefs. The command under its officers deployed in a similar fashion. As the troops closed in, the warriors abandoned their vantage point, attacking as they receded, reeling and counterattacking, singling out targets in traditional native fashion.

Under the attack of the "horse-soldiers with their reins in their teeth, their knives in their right hands and their revolvers in their left, gallop[ing] madly," the Indians fled the field to a clump of woods. Broken under Wright's long-range rifle and howitzer fire, they reeled backwards for eight or ten miles carrying off their dead, abandoning piles of muskets, quivers, bows and arrows, animal robes, and horses. None of the soldiers was wounded.

On September 5 the battle shifted north to Spokane Plains, just west of Spokane Falls. To check their advancing foe, the Indians emerged from the woods again. They deployed into right, left, and center wings, firing the prairie, trying to thwart the troops and panic their animals. The horses, hooves and the troops beat out the flames as the command shot the gap. In panic the Indians fell back two miles into some woods. There Kamiakin, who was directing the fight, was knocked off his horse and injured when a howitzer shellburst sent a limb crashing down on him. The Indians' fighting spirit was shattered, and general Indian retreat followed. Foot soldiers chased them toward the Spokane River. After seven hours of fighting, which covered about fourteen miles, the field was again strewn with Indian litter, but the dead were carried away. Some Indians hurried to the Sacred Heart Mission, begging Joset to make peace overtures to Wright. The angry priest reminded them that they had twice shamed him by not keeping their word for peace, but he did give them a letter of safe conduct to carry to Wright. In response to a message carried to him, the colonel sent a letter to Joset on September 10 saying he would meet the Indians and their families at the mission if they came with their properties and accepted unconditional surrender.

After the fighting the Spokanes gathered on the right bank of their river above the Falls, as Wright advanced on the left bank trailed by the Palouses, who burned a wagon and artillery carriages. Two days after the Battle of Spokane Plains, Wright enchained Chief Polatkin as a hostage because he suspected him of participating in the murder of two Colville miners. Previously Garry, who apparently was not engaged in the recent fights, had come in to confer with Wright, only to be sent back to his people, as others were to theirs—with the colonel's warning that, if they did not give in to his demands, they would be killed.

Still in a punitive mood, Wright moved farther east, burning wheat stores and lodges and hanging an Indian suspected of killing miners. Two Indians across the Spokane River, who shouted for Polatkin's release, were fired on and wounded. A neutral Spokane group sent a tribesman named Amtoola, who had some knowledge of English, across the river swimming a horse and carrying a white flag. The soldiers shot him dead. For two days the command corralled the eight or nine hundred horses with which Tilcoax had planned to pay off those joining in war. Wright ordered all the horses except the colts knocked in the head and shot—all, that is, but a couple hundred of the better ones, which were selected for the officers and the Nez Percé scouts. About that time many horse lovers believed the reported plan of desperado Boone Helm to be far less despicable. Helm wanted to organize a Shoshoni band to help him run off "two thousand" Wallawalla horses to sell in Salt Lake City. The scheme was frustrated when a Dr. William Groves sent a word of warning to a Wallawalla chief. Thus the Indian leader had time to take precautionary measures.

The small, wirey horses that the Indians acquired from the Spanish were called cayuses after the Cayuse Indians, because those Indians were the foremost breeders of the animals. From a painting by Ralph Crawford.

Wright moved toward the mission to confer with the Coeur d'Alênes just as Donati's comet swept the heavens—an evil omen to the Indians, who feared they were about to be swept from the earth. Deep in Indian country Wright blustered the Coeur d'Alênes into signing a so-called treaty, by which they agreed to surrender all plunder, permit whites passage through their lands, and yield hostages to be taken to Walla Walla as security for the future good behavior of the tribe. With Joset's help, Wright needled the Spokanes into holding a similar treaty council. Fearing for his life if he accepted Wright's invitation to attend, Kamiakin failed to appear at the council. After failing to sign the treaty document at the mission, Melkapsi belatedly affixed his mark to it. He joined the Coeur d'Alêne hostages, who consisted of leaders in the Steptoe attack, including Coeur d'Alênes, Paschal Stellam and Hilary Peenchi, and three subchiefs and their immediate families.

On the evening of September 23, Owhi entered Wright's camp. The colonel was angered that the chief had not gathered his people on the Naches in the spring of 1856, as he had told Wright he would. He therefore clapped him in chains as a hostage and sent a message to Qualchan, who was hiding at the mouth of the Spokane River, to come in or he would hang his father, Owhi. Moses slipped away to warn Qualchan, but failed to intercept him. In the meantime Qualchan's wife, Whistalks, rode into Wright's camp on a "fine brown horse" on the twenty-fifth. She approached the colonel's tent and struck a beaded lance into the ground before riding off. Entering the camp a half-hour later, Qualchan was summarily hanged after a brief struggle in which six men pinned him down. A packmaster on the scene, Thomas Beall, later claimed that Qualchan offered him a band of horses not to put the rope around his neck, bit Beall's hand when he refused the offer, and cried like a child when about to be hanged. According to Indian tradition, the rope broke twice. Its failure to break a third time proved to the Indians that Moses had stolen Qualchan's power. Fifteen minutes elapsed between the time of the capture and the hanging . Six Palouses shared Qualchan's fate. Latah Creek, a Spokane affluent, was the scene of the hanging. No wonder that residents of the area for years to come called it Hangman Creek.

Completing his vengeance, Wright hanged four more Palouses on their river. Owhi was three miles up the Tucannon (near Starbuck, Washington). Fearing that he was about to be hanged, he dashed for freedom only to be cut down by deadly rifle fire. On October 5 in council with the Wallawallas at the wooden fort of that name, Wright selected four to be hanged. One of those who suffered that fate two days later was Wyecat (Waiecat), a participant in the Whitman killings who had escaped capture and hanging earlier. In November, De Smet was asked to return thirty-three hostages to their homes. The Spokane–Coeur d'Alêne War was over.

Kamiakin's failure to appear before white authorities was understandable, considering the fate of his Puget Sound counterpart, Leschi. Leschi was convicted, and after a stay of execution he was sentenced to hang on February 19, 1858. Shortly before his demise he said that he had failed because of lack of warriors, supplies, and ammunition in what he admitted was warfare, not murder. If it was murder, he claimed, soldiers killing Indians were also guilty. White groups as diverse as army officers, lawyers, and settlers, believed the evidence of his guilt was far from conclusive, and came to his defense, as did his own people, who raised three thousand dollars for it and an additional five hundred for acquittal. Condemned in the white men's court, he was "strangled according to law."

Wounded in the war, Kitsap came to an equally ignominious end. After incarceration in the Fort Steilacoom guardhouse, he escaped. In the company of his fellow warrior Nelson and fifteen others, he was trapped on January 6, 1859, by a military detachment in a house on the Muckleshoot Reservation. He was thrown across a stove, captured and rearrested, tried as a war criminal, and acquitted, confirming his belief that neither whites nor Indians could kill him. During his freedom he concocted a mixture of red pigment and water in emulation of a red medicine that the white men had given him. When he administered the concoction to sick Indians and they promptly died, their families shot him in retaliation, cut his throat, and severed his lower extremities.[10]

Escaping incarceration by the military in Vancouver or San Francisco, Kamiakin warily exiled himself for the rest of his life. After a brief sojourn in Canada and on the plains, he returned to the land of his birth south of the Spokane country. Thanks to the intercession of priests and other friendly whites, he was perhaps treated more charitably than he would have been in his own divided Yakima community. To the end he refused to accept the compensation due him under the 1855 treaty—even blankets to shelter him from the cold. This chief, who with horses had enticed others into the war to protect their lands, had but one horse left—that given him by Chief Garry.

"They are all savages; and they make no figure in the history of the country, over the destinies of which they have not exerted, and probably never will exert, any influence."—thus an American geographer, Robert Greenhow had written in 1844 in his *History of Oregon and California*, describing the Oregon country. At the war's end, if its Indians had done nothing else, they had given the lie to his words.

16. BROKEN BOWS

The victorious whites were unconcerned with the Indians' losses in the war of 1855 to 1858, but they were painfully aware of their own. According to nineteenth-century Oregon historian Frances Fuller Victor, such conflicts on the average cost the lives of thirty-seven whites annually over a 68-year period between 1828 and 1896. Most of them died between 1850 and 1862. The surviving victors, who profited financially from the war justified their gains as a means of preserving civilization or of padding their investments against uncertain government compensation for their goods and services. They obviously would have ignored Superintendent Joel Palmer's assessment of them at the outset of the war, which was expressed in a December 1, 1855, letter to General John E. Wool:

The future will prove that this war has been forced upon these Indians against their will; and that too, by a set of lawless vagabonds for pecuniary and political objects and sanctioned by a numerous population that regard the Treasury of the United States as a legitimate subject of plunder. The Indians...have been driven to desperation by acts of cruelty against their people. Treaties have been violated and acts of barbarity committed by those claiming to be citizens that would disgrace the most barbarous natives of the earth.[1]

On November 5, 1858, General W. S. Harney wrote: "From the different languages, interests, and jealousies existing among so many different tribes, a coalition of all of them in one common cause is impossible. It is not too much to predict that the red men of America will gradually disappear about the same time from the different sections of the country." In a similar vein another wrote, "Their inexhaustible resources have been taken from them, their bows are unstrung, and from 'lords of the soil,' they have sunk to the degredation of slaves." Another writer who traveled across the plains to Olympia in 1862, opined, "With a sure certainty their sun is declining; they are gradually passing away; a few decades more and the Indian will only be known in story." In the East such groups as the Indian Aid Association wanted no more Indian blood on American hands. Others were just as certain that God had sent Americans to destroy Indian foes like Israelites of old. Whites gradually elevated the role of the Almighty in the Indian demise to that of a force working through the relentless principles of Darwinism.

Following a traditional practice, the departments of war and the interior sought to impress Indians by inviting them to witness progress in large white communities. As early as December 29, 1856, Agent Michael Simmons had recommended to Stevens that six of the principal and "most intelligent" Puget Sound chiefs be sent to Washington, D.C.,

to show them "the great number and wealth of our people and the power of our government." De Smet believed that Indians could learn from whites, although he did not believe as some others did that they should perish from the earth. He was invited by General Harney to accompany some interior chiefs to the Vancouver-Portland area. Chiefs of the recently warring tribes were included in the group. At the same time when the priest received his invitation Flathead agent John Owen received a similar one from the superintendent of Indian affairs—another example of the rivalry rankling between those two arms of government.

On the last day of May, 1859, the chiefs were assembled at Fort Vancouver: Victor and Alexander of the Kalispels; Adolph and Francis, an Iroquois, of the Flatheads; Seltis and Bonaventure of the Coeur d'Alenes; Denis of the Kettle-Colvilles; and Garry of the Spokanes. The chiefs were duly impressed with the wonders white men had created in nearby Portland—mills, printing presses, and the magic box taking their pictures. They were impressed if not frightened by the iron-barred jails for those who broke the white man's laws. All were familiar with the guardhouse at Vancouver holding dissident Indians. On returning home, Alexander gathered his people around him, ordered the wrongdoers to step forward, and summarily whipped them before presiding at a feast. Before journeying downriver, the chiefs knew that Indians did not have to be thrown into jail to lose their freedom.

Some of the chiefs on the journey were perhaps seeing the lower settlements for the first time. Other tribesmen of the interior, as noted, had periodically visited those places. With the end of the war an ever-increasing number gravitated downriver to work in Vancouver, Portland, Salem, and other places as boatmen, porters, farmhands, and house servants. Some returned home with clothing and with wages averaging as much as thirty dollars a month. Too much of their wages went for gambling. That was nothing new to them, but it was lessened none by their association with white men. In the lower valleys some upriver Indians, such as the Spokanes, Flatheads, Palouses, and others, prostituted their women and acted as runners for white men selling liquor to Indians. Indians who hitherto had been careful not to let their women sleep with white men were forced by ruffians of the white race to abandon their traditional mores at the risk of their lives.

After the wars the Indians quite naturally returned to their old haunts. When they did, they found whites had appropriated them. Indians of the Dreamer religion at the risk of their lives defied the government to remove them from their old haunts in the rapidly filling Grande Ronde Valley east of the Cascade Mountains. Indians from the reservations returned to old haunts in the Rogue and Willamette valleys, but they did not become the farmers the government had wished them to be. One pioneer suggested ironically that "the use of the plow, and the spade should be taught them, enough of the use of the latter, at least, to dig their own graves." They fell into trouble in their old villages, which were now white settlements, but were often permitted to remain there, hiring themselves out to the ones who had appropriated their lands. The Klickitats of the Yakima Agency in Washington Territory who returned to the Willamette in the postwar period were not so fortunate, for on complaints of whites they were rounded up in 1867 and sent up the Columbia River.

Sometimes agents were ordered by their superiors to limit the number of passes issued to their charges for off-reservation travel. Those who received the permits often overstayed the time limits imposed, and many times the Indians slipped away with no passes at all. Then the military was frequently called on to help return them to confinement. In April, 1863, Superintendent J. W. Perit Huntington, using the pass system, recovered over five hundred Indians from the Willamette Valley alone.[2] He also estimated that up to three hundred escapees from the Siletz Agency and the Alsea (which was fragmented from the original Siletz) were scattered from the mouth of the Umpqua River to near Crescent City, California, playing an annual hide-and-seek game with authorities. The rationale for their migrations, as for those of so many others, was nonratification of their treaties; they were sent into confinement where they were unable to subsist by themselves. The Upper Umpquas and about half the Rogues were almost the only Indians of western Oregon with ratified treaties, and they were shipped off to Oregon reservations to live with Indians of the Oregon coast whose treaties were still unratified.

The Indians were angry at the roads built across their lands, for which they received no compensation. One of the better-known thoroughfares was the Mullan Road. Its construction was begun in 1853 and disrupted by the war, which delayed its completion for seven years. It ran 624 miles from Walla Walla to Fort Benton. At the war's end Walla Walla was a quarter-mile-long town of tawdry barrooms, billiard parlors, stores, and horse corrals. "The throng in the streets," wrote a British visitor, "consists of half-naked savages, with their squaws and children, gold-miners, settlers, American soldiers and rowdies of all sorts."

The Mullan Road little resembled a road in the modern sense. Its primary purpose was to facilitate the movement of troops, miners, settlers, and traders along its route. The Coeur d'Alênes were among the tribes most opposed to it, because it pierced their lands like a shaft. In the winter of 1858–59 after the war, a strong Coeur d'Alêne faction tried to stop the road builders from using their tribesmen as guides. Father Joset had been furnishing Indians for this purpose. The road was named for Lieutenant John Mullan, its chief engineer, who appeared among the Indians in the summer of 1859. A well-mounted party under Chief Peter Paulinas confronted the lieutenant with questions that were as piercing as the bristling weapons flourished by his men. Some Coeur d'Alênes even threatened to kill Mullan, but

they had no choice but to submit to the road building.*

With the building of the road, interior Indians had ample opportunity to see the various instruments that the engineers used, as they had those of the Stevens surveys a half dozen years before. They often opposed the driving of survey stakes into the earth, for both religious and economic reasons. In 1856, Puget Sound Indians put out the word that they wanted no such stakes driven into the earth until the government paid for it. The following year some Indians on the Sound, making good their threat, began pulling up stakes. During the summer of 1872, Indians of the Siletz Reservation opposing surveys for allotting purposes tore up corner posts, burned bearing trees, and leveled mounds, so that a new survey was required. As a result allotments were not made there until about twenty years later.[3] In August, 1867, Indians of the Puyallup Reservation seized the chain of a surveyor, Ezra Meeker, and ordered away a packer carrying his supplies. When Meeker remarked that he would be obliged to call upon the commandant of Fort Steilacoom for troops to protect him, the Indians outwardly cooled their opposition.[4] Not all reservation Indians, however, opposed the allotting process, which necessarily involved surveys. As early as 1862 those of the Grand Ronde Reservation expressed a wish to have their lands parceled out, and in 1869 a Santiam chief on that reservation, Jo Hutchins, told the Oregon superintendent of Indian affairs, "We want it divided," meaning the land. Indians there had been under an allotment system of sorts, as members of each tribe had been assigned separate houses. Indians of the Puyallup Reservation expressed a wish to have their own tracts after a potato-crop failure in 1873. They appear not to have opposed a survey of their reservation as some of them had previously.

A most important survey marked the boundary of the 1846 treaty separating the United States from British territory. It dissected several tribes in the process, such as the Semiahmoos, Okanagons, Lakes (Salishan), Kalispels, and Kutenais. Resentful that the treaty had been made without their participation, the Indians feared the border would disrupt their traditional north-south travel patterns. One Spokane chief spoke of them all when he said, "One man comes with a party from the cold side of heaven and says this is my line [while another] with his party from the warm side says the land on this side is mine; and so they settle it, and we the poor Indian have nothing to say about it."[5]

The location of the extreme western portion of the boundary remained in tenuous limbo until 1872, causing much Anglo-American tension. The controversy over its settlement, known as the San Juan Island dispute, involved the Pig War of the sixties. The antagonists considered that the Indians had a minor role in the dispute. Indians of the United States were concerned that the controversy and its settlement might in some way facilitate the southward passage of dreaded northern Indians. During the San Juan dispute natives there traded with both the Americans and the British.

---

*The Mullan Road soon reverted to "a mere pack-trail." It became overgrown with underbrush, and its bridges broke down.

Nooksack Indians near Lynden, Washington, circa 1900. Although the Nooksacks were a comparatively numerous tribe, adverse weather conditions prevented them from signing the 1855 *Point Elliott Treaty. During the 1850s gold seekers tramped through their lands en route to diggings on the Fraser River. Seattle Historical Society.*

American officials were concerned over possible opposition to their surveys at the forty-ninth parallel because of the 1857–58 Indian attacks on miners who crossed their lands en route to British gold fields. In 1858 several incidents occurred in which Indians and miners mistreated each other. Indians on the Similkameen, an Okanogan tributary, shot two miners with arrows, swinging the red beard of one as they would a scalp and helping themselves to beans and brown sugar. Near the mouth of the Nooksack River the Lummis were astonished at the great number of miners scrambling to the gold fields. The Indians who for one reason or another had visited San Francisco aboard white men's ships would not have been so surprised at the numbers. In 1857, Nooksack Indians were angered by whites who cut a road through their lands to strike the Fort Langley Trail for direct passage to the Colville mines. In 1858 miners trampled Nooksack lands over the vital Popahomy crossing, where several trails converged. The Nooksacks had traveled for years over the crossing to trade with natives on the north. Finding in the influx of miners an opportunity to gain, they sold so many fish and canoes to

them that they found themselves short of these two vital commodities. An Indian agent feared that in two months in 1858, Indians had killed no less than seven whites in the Bellingham Bay area over ferriage squabbles.[6]

The army expected troubles for their surveyors east of the Cascade Mountains because there had been so much of it already. In 1859 five companies—half a regiment of light infantry—were posted between the Similkameen River and Fort Colville. At the time of the 1846 boundary settlement and for several years thereafter Indians of the interior had crossed the border without hindrance, although they were unhappy with it. The Indians resented not only the presence of the troops for protecting the boundary surveyors but also their rooting along streams for gold. When the troops of Captain James Archer tired of digging, a chief of the Similkameen area offered to restrain his braves if the captain restrained his restless men. When the surveyors distributed gifts to the Indians, the tensions eased. Surveyors and soldiers continued on their eastward course.[7]

Expecting resistance farther east in the Colville country, the military in 1859 dispatched Major Pinkney Lugenbeel and a battalion of the Ninth Infantry there to establish a military post, Fort Colville. At the approach of the troops, several Colvilles took to the hills. They returned daily on learning that, unlike other soldiers, Lugenbeel was more friend than foe. He sought seeds and tools for them and from his own stores gave them ammunition for their hunts. He also pleaded with civil authorities to close "whiskey hells" along the upper Columbia. In the winter of 1861, early in the Civil War, with the withdrawal of regular troops from the Pacific Northwest, soldiers of Companies C and D Second Infantry, California Volunteers, replaced Lugenbeel's troops. Presumably to shield themselves from colds, but, in reality, because of cold weather and their boredom, the volunteers dosed themselves with whiskey, not a very good example for the Indians. On the day he left Colville in 1862 a member of the British boundary survey party, Lieutenant Charles Wilson, wrote that "whisky & civilization are doing their work quickly & surely amongst them, in twenty years time they will be a matter of history." A decade later a Colville agent reported that about five thousand gallons of whiskey and high wines were shipped annually into the Colville Valley, and he believed that the greater portion of it was consumed by Indians. At the time when the whiskey trade increased, that of furs slackened.* Even the trading process slowed because the Indians demanded payment for each skin separately in time-consuming transactions. The agent also believed that the Indians were peaceful only because of Lugenbeel's friendliness and aid to them.

In the later half of the nineteenth century no place in the Pacific Northwest was spared the process of white-Indian acculturation, which was quickened by the American victory in the 1855–58 Indian war. In the areas west of the Cascade Mountains and around Puget Sound, where heavy concentrations of whites mingled in close proximity with Indians, the effect of this comingling of the races was to be seen in microcosm. In 1861, when respectable whites removed some of the frontier tarnish from their civilization by establishing a Washington territorial university, it was difficult to get young Indian girls to attend the Catholic mission school on the nearby Tulalip Reservation because their parents had turned them over to prostitution. That summer, as they had and would for several years, Songish Indians from British Columbia brought ten-to-fourteen year old girls down to Washington Territory for the same purpose. Recipients of their services would not have known—nor cared—that in their kinship system a man's brothers and nephews legitimately had sexual relations with the man's wife. Also in that memorable year, 1861, to fight rampant cohabitation of employees of the Office of Indian Affairs with Indian women, that office sent down a circular to its various agencies that their personnel were not to live with nor be in a state of "concubinage" with Indian women. A main thrust of an 1873 report by General J. P. C. Shanks, chairman of the House of Indian Affairs Committee, was the tightening of laws against lax morals as evidenced in Indian polygamy and the cohabitation of white men with Indian women. At about the same time the Indian Office refused to recognize Homily as Wallawalla chief because he

had two Indian wives. It is evident that the government was no less solicitous of the morals of its Indian charges than its missionary counterparts had been.*

On Puget Sound, as elsewhere, liquor threatened the survival of the Indians. Along with firepower and fiery fever, firewater—seeking its own level—often found itself among them, forcing a surrender of their substance for little or next to nothing. It facilitated the exploitation of their labor and their women and lowered their resistence to disease. It tranquilized or exhilarated away their sense of defeat, or maddened them against whites or each other, making their lives a virtual hell on earth. At various places on Puget Sound at the time of annuity distributions agents called in troops to check the whiskey peddlers, who waited like crows or ravens on the perimeters of potlatch grounds to snatch government Indian issues in exchange for a few bottles of whiskey.

Most whites were less concerned with what drink was doing to the Indian community than what it was doing to their own. At the same time they were sensitive to criticisms that they and Indians were drinking out of the same barrel. Special Agent J. Ross Browne reported in 1858 that the Duke of York, who was maintaining his chieftaincy among the Clallams because of his skill in obtaining liquor, was no more sober than when Winthrop had seen him drunkenly lording it over his "fishy vassals." And, as if the local citizenry of Port Townsend were not bad enough, their town in Browne's opinion, was a resort for "beachcombers and outlaws of every description."

Mincing few words about the recent war, Browne reported:

Our government . . . sends up a war steamer to the Sound; this vessel drives out a few Indians, fires several rounds of ammunition into the trees back of Seattle, causes a general reverberation of large and small guns around the shores of the Sound, winds up killing some four or five Indians, informs the settler that there is no use in staying any longer and paddles back to Mare Island, where she rests from her labors for the space of one or two years.[8]

It should be noted that Browne visited the region in 1857 when the Puget Sound phase of the Indian war had ended.

The ink in Browne's pen had much less effect on Indians than the whiskey that continued to pour from white men's barrels. Besides obtaining it from whites, Indians obtained it through local Indians and "blood" intermediaries, as well as from Canadian Indians, who smuggled it across the Strait of

---

*Events in this part of the northern interior are related in Ruby and Brown, *The Spokane Indians*, p. 141ff. During the lull in the war in 1857 an agent of the Indian Office, Benjamin F. Yantis, had visited Indian fishing camps on the lower Spokane River. He recommended that four young men be sent to assist natives there in the use of hoes and spades, in the fashion of the modern Peace Corps.

*Flathead Indian agent John Owen wrote to one of his personnel that failure to heed Indian Office circulars pertaining to concubinage with Indian women would "seriously militate against the objects of the Service." Seymour Dunbar and Paul C. Phillips. eds., *The Journals and Letters of Major John Owen Pioneer of the Northwest 1850–1871 . . .*, 2: 272.

Juan de Fuca and into Puget Sound. The failure of courts to accept Indian testimony contributed to the problem. Although troops from Fort Yamhill (established near present-day Valley Junction, Oregon) and the Oregon law of 1863 helped reduce the liquor traffic in the Willamette Valley, inadequate government personnel at the same time contributed to the problem. In 1861, when a drunken white man tried to steal the wife of a Lummi chief, a general fight ensued. The Lummis pleaded with authorities to send them a subagent to protect them, as there was no government official among them to do so. Lummi chiefs knew well the pernicious effects of liquor. In 1856 one of them had canoed to Victoria for blankets because all those that his tribe had received from the government had been traded for liquor. On October 12, 1862, two men in a whiskey boat moved onto the Port Madison Reservation to ply their wares to about five hundred Indians who were gathered there at a potlatch to receive presents from the Duwamish Indians. Forced to police the situation themselves, the Indians seized and burned the boat, destroying its alcoholic cargo. A justice of the peace would not allow them to arrest the peddlers. Agent Simmons reported the incident as, "Too many of them and too few of us."

The Indians' condition would have been worse had it not been for occasional convictions of whiskey peddlers through the efforts of concerned judges, newspaper editors, clergymen-humanitarians, army officials, and Indian agents. The agents, contrary to popular notion, were not entirely oblivious to the plight of their charges. With more empathy and less biting irony than Special Agent Browne, regular Indian agents were concerned over drinking and other evils to which their Indians were exposed, which hampered them from being made over in the image of sober white men. On the Tulalip, Father Chirouse with a shepherd's care wrote the Washington Territory Superintendent of Indian Affairs on February 4, 1870, that the only way to "civilize" and protect Indians from the "emissaries of hell" was to gather them on one large reservation on Puget Sound or on reductions under the protective care of Catholic fathers.

Government efforts to remake Indians were not accepted without resistance. The Indians could not understand why the government should take their lands and force them, sometimes under pain of death, onto reservations and then compel them to work like white men. When asked about their plans, the Clallams, perhaps to antagonize whites, answered, "Cultus nannitsh, cultus mitlight" [Look about and do nothing]." Although not expressing it in their reports lest it appear that they were doing a poor job of civilizing their Indians, agents were often happy to have them return to their traditional hunting, fishing, and gathering places. Had they not done so, they would have starved because government issues were so meager or nonexistent.

The goods that they did receive were often inferior and unusable. The white and black wampum (perhaps beads) was useless when that form of money came to be replaced by silver and gold. Steel spades received were often of sheet iron. Often axes were merely of cast iron. What were passed off as good shoes often had paper soles or were three or four sizes too large. Blankets were shoddy. Scythes sent in 1861 to the Indians of the Tulalip were of little use to a people dependent upon forest and sea for food. Even the articles of good quality were unusable. Indians would not eat with the iron spoons sent them. They found the mirrors two inches square hardly large enough to see themselves and had little use for jew's harps, hair oil, and elastic garters.

Many goods were imported from the East. This raised their cost to the government and exposed them to greater damage in transit. More could have been purchased on the West Coast much nearer their Pacific Northwestern red customers. Even when they were furnished locally there were problems. In 1856 the Siletz agency obtained flour from an Oregon City mill at a government-contracted price of twenty dollars per barrel for good-quality flour. After laboriously hauling it over the mountains to the reservation, the Indians became ill on eating it. The "good-quality flour" was nothing more than "shorts and sweeps"; at the time whites used the flour for cattle feed. Another flour cargo of nearly fifty thousand pounds was of the "poorest kind of mill sweeps"; the contractor claimed to have been swindled by the mill owner. The remoteness of the Siletz had also made it difficult for ships to land there to deliver the goods.

The congressional law forbidding the purchase of goods except on the requisition of an Indian agent was systematically violated. The problem of getting goods and provisions into Indian hands during the Civil War was aggravated by the buying and selling of legal tender notes. These had depreciated and fluctuated in value, causing an apparent advance in the price of goods, which in turn reduced congressional appropriations for them from thirty to forty percent. In this chain reaction salaries of agency employees were reduced, making it difficult to hire qualified personnel.

The services received under the terms of the treaties left much to be desired. Contractors performed poor work, shortchanging not only the Indians but also the government. Buildings and equipment were in a chronic state of disrepair. Washouts, breakdowns, and fires were only some of the catastrophes plaguing agency properties. On the Grand Ronde Reservation a dam broke twenty times in fourteen years. Each time it was patched up to supply a mill. The mills were, in the words of an agent, "indispensable civilizers."

In that time before the inauguration of a federal merit system many agency personel were qualified only by their political connections. Some were dishonest or at best inefficient. They were isolated from governmental scrutiny, which would have been ineffective in any case because of the turmoil and corruption of the Civil War and of the ensuing Reconstruction era. With perhaps more insight than indignation, Siletz agent Ben Simpson in the last annual report, dated October 1, 1871, described the interior department–Indian office complex as "little better than a gigantic circumlocution office, in which everything is done by indirect and circuitous methods." The cursory examinations

Yakima Indians. This photograph, taken shortly before 1900, shows the white influence on Indian dress. Yakima Nation Media Center.

of agencies by government inspectors, which perhaps took place three times yearly, did little to improve their workers. The same isolation that permitted agency personnel great leeway in the conduct of their affairs drove many from the service. Those who remained bickered with Indians and with each other; the ramifications of their quarrels sometimes reached the national capital.

The reports required by the law were often discouraging because of the herculean task the government required of its workers. Yet for the benefit of the record reports were written so that they were not always discouraging. Agency personnel sometimes disparaged the efforts of their predecessors to make their own look better, filling their reports with such vague terms as "good progress." Had progress in farming been as great as officials reported it to have been, Indians would have become agrarians by the end of the century—which was far from the case. To have stressed, as others did,

that their charges might suffer extinction would have jeopardized the positions of the government servants.

To the Indians and the government alike the kingpin of the system was the agent. He was "just like a king, and he could do as he pleased," as an elderly Makah expressed it. The agent was the Indians' on-the-grounds representative, and he stood between them and a growing bureaucratic maze leading up to the president. By the 1860s the Indians had gotten a clearer picture of that important personage, the president, about whom they had heard so much. When Agent Browne was among the chiefs of the Siletz Reservation in October, 1857, one of three matters uppermost on their minds was the identity of the "Great White chief." Their other two concerns were the receipt of goods promised by treaty and the sickness raging among the people.

The Indians were bewildered trying to comprehend white men's laws which were so different from their own

170

traditional codes of conduct. Native juries, who were selected by agents to assist the Indians often sent to the "skookum house," or jail, Indians violating their own traditional codes or those that the agents sought for them. One graphic example of differing Indian-white codes sending a red offender to the place of incarceration occurred on the Siletz: overreacting to the sanguine admission of one Euchre Bill that he had eaten the heart of a fallen white foe, the agent physically assaulted him before confinement. From agents Indians received more orthodox punishment in the form of whipping—the practice employed by fur traders and even missionaries. Agents often delegated to chiefs the unpleasant task of administering corporal punishment. Those leaders and others designated as whippers had performed such tasks for years. On the Yakima Reservation, Chief Joe Stwire (White Swan), after severely chastising an Indian breaking an antipolygamy law, was warned by the agent, Reverend James H. Wilbur, not to mete out punishment so summarily. Indians cooperating most closely with agents in enforcing the law or in other ways were usually favored by them for the chieftaincy—another instance of how the government was able to exert its authority over the red men.

Other key government personnel were the agency physicians. Working under difficult conditions and sorely underpaid, they were often forced to turn to private practice to augment their salaries. There was no shortage of patients. Disorders scrofulic, consumptive, digestive, rheumatic, and venereal in nature, to name a few, continued to plague Indians no less severely than they had when natives first met whites. As late as 1889 bodies of the Indian victims of disease lay unburied on the upper Skagit River, just one of many places in the Pacific Northwest where smallpox continued to break out. During epidemics Indians found travel to towns restricted by quarantines designed to confine them on reservations, where at times they also came under quarantine. When smallpox broke out in the summer of 1875 among Haidas camped by Port Ludlow near the entrance to Hood Canal, authorities ordered them away and burned their shanties. On the Grand Ronde Reservation disease had been an important cause of the reduction of its natives by half.

Language difficulties prevented Indians from adquately describing the symptoms of their ailments to agency physicians. When they did communicate, they did so with gestures or in the Chinook jargon, which was far better for

Clallam Indians of the David Hunter and Henry Johnson families in fancy white-style clothing. By the twentieth century *white influences had obscured many native customs and habits.* *Penrose Library, Whitman College.*

trade than for treatment. Women suffering from venereal diseases or from the ailments peculiar to their sex found it difficult to describe their symptoms.

In an 1870 report the Skokomish Reservation physician, Dr. D. N. Egbert, described the Indian condition as a "little civilization"—which was to Indians a "rank poison." Their plight was also described as a "half civilization," in which their hybridized food, clothing, and shelter were detrimental to their health. One traveler noted that Puget Sound Indians subsisted partly on fish and partly on the government, moving around towns in cheap, ill-fitting garments, sleeping in the streets by day and sitting motionless on sidewalks for hours "like so many bundles of rags." They were, he believed, the victims of "whiskey and the law of the survival of the fittest." Joel Palmer found Indians on the Siletz in 1871 living in rude huts, eating bad fish, suffering social diseases, and generally in a worsened condition than when they first came there sixteen years before. He was describing what approached the norm for such places.

A Spokane Indian family. When they posed for this sketch in 1890, canvas tipis had replaced those of animal skins. From West Shore, *November 8, 1890.*

The "half civilization" of the Indians did not escape them even in death. Perhaps the first breakdown in native burials was interment in Hudson's Bay Company boxes. Then coffins hammered out by agency carpenters were substituted and the dead were buried in American-style cemeteries in graves decorated with yards of calicoes and other manufactured goods. The great attention that Indians paid to graves did not carry over to their graveyards. It was as if they wished those burial places to revert as quickly as possible to their natural state. When asked why he did not wish the brush cleared from an Indian cemetery, a Makah chief replied, "It would not be right, the more room the more would die."

Agency doctors pleaded with their superiors to provide funds to establish hospitals on reservations so Indians would not have to go prematurely to the graveyards. Had such medical facilities been available, Indians might not have used them. They continued to be dependent on home care provided by native doctors. Methods used by those practitioners had changed little over the years. When traditional healing failed, they sometimes resorted to the use of white men's objects, such as muskets, into which "bad spirits" were rammed and fired off.

White men's goods also found their way into "power stealings," which continued to exact the lives of rival practitioners. Instead of native concoctions to kill rivals, Indian doctors were now able to purchase poisons in small bottles at high prices at the stores of merchants who had few scruples about selling such things. Some white judges would

A Twana, or Skokomish, Indian. The acculturation process had endowed him with a white man's name, Joseph M. Spar. Penrose Library, Whitman College.

172

not prosecute the killers of native doctors if it were shown that they had killed as a matter of religious conviction. On the Yakima Reservation in 1878, Agent Wilbur opposed the findings of a grand jury that issued a true bill against an Indian for allegedly killing an Indian doctor. The bill would have brought the accused to the reservation under a law providing for the holding of such offenders on reservations for a year. Increasingly such cases came to be prosecuted by the white men's law. The cost of arresting and prosecuting suspected doctor killers prompted one white man in 1876 to advocate the settling of such matters in the old native way.

Government officials believed that the best way to civilize Indians was through schools. Initially day schools were the most common. Some of them were of the manual-labor type, such as those of the early sixties on the Siletz and Grand Ronde reservations. The philosophy behind this type of school was expressed by Superintendent Huntington when he wrote that "the hoe and the broadax will sooner civilize and Christianize them, than the Spelling Book and the Bible." On the Yakima Reservation, which was regarded as a model of Indian education, Agent Wilbur combined physical and spiritual tools in education under his slogan, "The Plow and the Bible." Boarding schools were established later to remove children even further from familial-tribal ties and influences. The words of Agent Wesley Gosnell in August, 1861, were echoed many times by whites concerned with educating young Indians: he said that the only way to succeed with them was to take them entirely away from their parents and "not to allow the influences of their savage home to counteract those of the schoolroom." When a Quinault chief said he would rather hang his children than send them to school, the teacher, William Chattin, recommended in a March 31, 1868, report that the school be removed to a prairie some distance from the Quinault Village to separate the children from parents who objected to the white men's education. When the Makahs in the mid-sixties refused to comply with their agent's order to place their children in the Neah Bay agency school, authorities moved in to force them to submit to his decree. Some Makahs who opposed sending their children to the school fled twenty miles to the remote Ozette Village. The influx raised the Ozette population and the 640-acre Ozette Reservation was established by executive order on April 12, 1893. The village was abandoned around 1900, at which time school attendance was grudgingly accepted at Neah Bay. Ozette beaches remained silent until around 1970, when excavators removed tons of mud that had inundated Ozette houses and discovered thousands of artifacts revealing the ages-old culture of a people who fashioned their lives around the pursuit of the whale. On the Tulalip, Chirouse sought to remove Indian children from pernicious whites, whom he considered a worse influence than their parents. He and other Catholic workers found that parents did not relish sending their children away to schools, even to one at Vancouver operated under government contract by the Sisters of Charity, who also operated other schools as far apart as the Tulalip and Flathead agencies.

Not the least difficult tasks of agency personnel were

Tillie Atkins, a Chehalis woman. Like other Indian women in western Washington Territory she adapted more quickly to white clothing than did her sisters of the more-remote interior. Penrose Library, Whitman College.

those performed by farmers, blacksmiths, and mechanics. Not only the Indians but also the poor soils, livestock, and equipment resisted their efforts. Resist as they might the efforts of government servants to mold them, the red men could not resist a force far more powerful—the relentless march of thousands of other purveyors of white culture. Into their path the Indians were drawn by a most vital need—that of subsistence and employment.

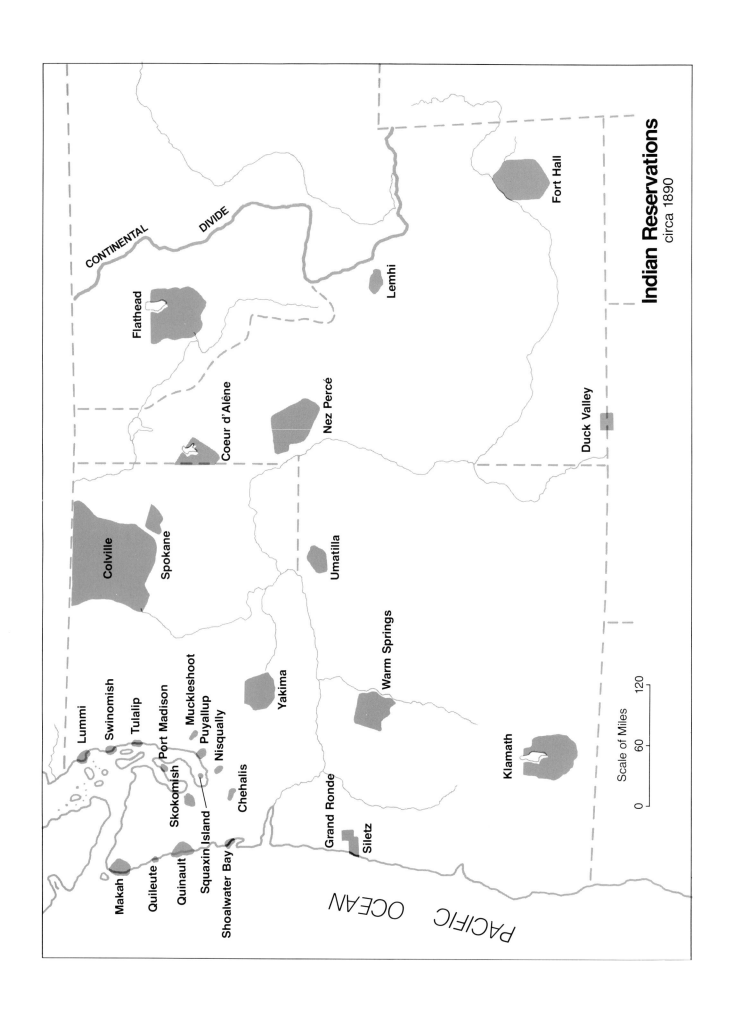

Indian Reservations
circa 1890

PACIFIC OCEAN

CONTINENTAL DIVIDE

Makah
Quileute
Quinault
Shoalwater Bay
Squaxin Island
Chehalis
Nisqually
Puyallup
Muckleshoot
Port Madison
Skokomish
Tulalip
Swinomish
Lummi

Grand Ronde
Siletz

Yakima

Warm Springs

Klamath

Colville
Spokane

Coeur d'Aléne
Nez Percé

Umatilla

Flathead

Lemhi

Fort Hall

Duck Valley

Scale of Miles

0   60   120

17. SUBSISTENCE: WITH AND WITHOUT RESERVATIONS

Of the estimated 7,000 Indians in Oregon in October, 1860, over 3,700 were not included in any treaty with the government. Similarly, of the 31,000 Indians in Washington Territory over 12,000 had not been included in treaties. When the Chehalis Reservation was established by executive order on July 8, 1864, Territorial Superintendent of Indian Affairs Thomas McKenny tried to gather on that confine all the Chehalises as well as Chinooks, Cowlitz, and scattered bands around Willapa Bay. Remnants of the Clatsops and, of the other peoples of the lower Columbia south bank, with whom the government had dealt in the unratified treaties of Tansey Point, would eventually go on Oregon reservations: the Alsea, the Siletz, and the Grand Ronde. On the lower Umpqua River there were bands outside designated reservations. In south-central and eastern Oregon three major tribes were still without treaties: the Klamaths, Modocs, and Paiutes. In eastern Washington Territory (and Idaho Territory, which was established March 4, 1863) the government had not treated with the Okanagons, Sinkiuses, Spokanes, Coeur d'Alênes, Shoshonis, and Bannocks. The recent wars—Indian and Civil—had helped delay treaty making. Also there was less pressure from whites to oust the Indians in those more-remote interior portions of the Pacific Northwest. Much of the trouble between Indians and the government stemmed from Steven's haste in effecting the treaties; he had permitted signatories to represent peoples over whom they had no hegemony. In his haste to effect the treaties Stevens did not treat with some tribes. A case in point was that of the Nooksack Indians, who because of adverse weather conditions were unable to attend the council. Without a treaty they were especially vulnerable and were caught between the reservation devil and the rising sea of white settlers. By the early seventies they had been greatly reduced in number by a smallpox epidemic, which the Lower Skagits called the Nooksack sickness. The lower and middle portions of the Nooksacks clashed with whites, who settled on the fertile tribal lands as well as those on those of individual Indians who had severed tribal relations. Early in 1874 the Indian Office, not unmindful of the influence of Father Chirouse over the Indians, ordered him as a government agent to gather on the Lummi Reservation the Nooksacks who were in the way of white settlement.* Upper Nooksacks living beyond the settlements were regarded as an inoffensive people on whom white prospectors and others depended to carry supplies.

The fertile Skagit lowlands were much coveted by land-

John Palmer, a member of the now extinct Chimakum tribe. Born near Port Townsend, Washington, about 1847, Palmer spoke English, Russian, and four native languages. He served as an interpreter on several Indian reservations until his death in 1881. Penrose Library, Whitman College.

hungry whites. Events there unfolded in much the same way as they did on the lower Nooksack River. After an altercation involving some Indians and a storekeeper on the lower Skagit River, the Indians and whites there armed themselves for battle in the summer of 1867. Early the next year the Indians assaulted a priest and drove him away. Such conflicts led to the September 9, 1873 executive order defining the northern boundary of the Swinomish Reservation, on which lived not only the Swinomishes proper but also neighboring peoples, such as the Lower Skagits, Samishes, and Kikialluses. Natives of the upper Skagit watershed were also troubled by whites encroaching on their lands. In 1870

---

*Chirouse was agent under the church-oriented Ulysses S. Grant Peace Policy discussed in Chapter 21.

A Puget Sound Indian, William Weahlup, seated near a salmon-smoking rack. Pacific Northwest Collections, University of Washington Library.

surveyors of the Northern Pacific Railroad traversed their territory. More threatening to them were other whites, who regarded not only the living Indians as obstacles but also the dead buried in native graveyards. In the mid-eighties whites burned a village of eight large cedar-bound longhouses at the confluence of the Skagit and Sauk rivers.

Between the Nooksacks of the upper Nooksack River and the Upper Skagits lived a band under an Indian known as the Mormon Prophet. Seeking to retain their isolation and to avoid working in the manner of white men, the Prophet and his followers repulsed a scientific party who were exploring their sacred mountain, Kulshan (the modern-day Mount Baker). Since the Prophet would not come from his mountain to the Tulalip Agency, several whites and Indians were dispatched to bring him in. This they did in early April, 1867. Another prophet advocating isolation from whites in his upper Skagit River homeland was Haheibalth, known to whites as Johnny Stick. Taken to the Tulalip, he failed to convince Father Chirouse that his message and teachings were from God. Chirouse had more success with one Slaybebtuk, a powerful leader of the Upper Skagits. Initially, however, Indians of that region were so suspicious of the priest that, under the urging of Indians east of the Cascade Mountains, they traveled there to visit a mission. When they returned, they built a crude church. Chirouse had some success with a former prophet, David Crockett, who around 1859 had become a Lummi chief more on the basis of piety than wealth. Across the border in Canada the Reverend Leon Fouquet, O.M.I., took a firm stand against a Fraser River prophet, Quitzkanums, who claimed to have received a strange parchment atop a moun-

tain, after which he preached against indolence and thievery. The priest spat on the parchment and cast it into the fire. The prophet, deeply insulted by the act and grieving over his favorite wife's elopement with a white man, refused to eat, wasted away, and died.

Reservations did not prove the haven for Indian subsistence that the government had hoped they would be. The continuing disappearance of native food sources became an increasing problem to reservation residents. The appropriation of fishing grounds by whites created a special legacy of troubles to plague the future of both races. Lumbermen were angered when Indian women fired the woods as they had done for years to ensure better crops of roots and berries.

The decreasing sources of subsistence and the increasing enticements and employment opportunities in the American community caused both reservation and nonreservation Indians to move toward white communities at a faster pace than ever. Over the years, as far as trade with whites was concerned, the Indians had shifted their economy away from the Hudson's Bay Company toward the Americans. The Bay Company continued operations

Old Polly, a Nooksack Indian living near Lynden, Washington, circa 1903. Whatcom Museum of History and Art, Bellingham, Washington.

below the Canadian border until the early 1870s, but now received but a fraction of the Indian trade. The bulk of the Indian market went to the Americans. From the time when American settlers first appeared on the lower Columbia and Willamette rivers, the Indians had traded them the produce of their lands. From their streams, beds, and bogs they had conducted a lively trade with the Bostons in salmon, oysters, and cranberries. In 1854 a bushel of cranberries had brought them fifty pounds of flour, which cost $2.50 in Astoria and $3.00 in Portland. Where once they had sold oysters to Americans, they shortly found themselves working at Willapa Bay for other Americans, who had appropriated their harvest of oysters. The Americans sold oysters, as others did logs and pilings, to a booming San Francisco market. In their urge to supply that market, armed oyster poachers along the Oregon coast at Yaquina Bay defied orders of the Siletz agent in 1863 and 1864 to desist from their illegal activity. At the time of his treaty making Stevens noted that Indians were sending as much as ten thousand pounds of fish daily to the Seattle market.

Boundary changes involving the Siletz Reservation had made and would continue to make it especially vulnerable to white inroads, threatening Indian subsistence on that confine. The Siletz Reservation (named later for one of many tribes inhabiting it) was established along the coast, from Cape Lookout on the north to Cape Perpetua on the south, and was first referred to simply as a "coast reservation." In 1861 a subagency, the Alsea (also named for an Indian tribe), was established at Yachats Prairie, eight miles below the Alsea River. Until then annual agency reports came from the Siletz Reservation; in 1862 they were submitted from the Siletz and Alsea agencies. A strip running twenty-five miles from north to south and twenty miles from east to west, including Yaquina Bay, was withdrawn in December, 1865, dividing the reservation. The area on the north became the Siletz, and that on the south become the Alsea. The Alsea measured twenty by thirty-one miles. On it lived 525 Indians. The withdrawal of the strip worked a hardship on Indians settling there. Despite promises of security for their persons and properties, they were ejected from their homes by force. In 1866 troops were removed from near the Siletz, and whiskey peddlers moved in. Gold hunters had been equally troublesome in the area. A March 3, 1875 congressional act stated that Indians should not be removed from the Alsea Reservation without their consent. Nevertheless, without consent the government opened the land to whites, who moved onto Indian farms at Yachats Prairie driving the Indians away without compensation, and depriving them of what little livelihood they had left.

Seeking to improve their livelihood by catching and selling sea otter, Indians from Grays Harbor north to Point Grenville were troubled by whites entering their coasts to hunt those animals. The rapid decimation of the herds, making four otter a good season's catch, by the same token greatly increased their value. Pelts brought whites about $40.00 apiece in 1860, and some Indians sold them for as little as $6.50 at about that time. Around the turn of the century a pelt brought as much as $400.00 to $600.00 to a white.

In seeking the furry wealth of the sea otter, the Quinaults and Quileutes fought whites not over wages earned in helping them hunt but because of white encroachment on native hunting grounds.[1]

After citizens of Grays Harbor in 1860 sent frantic messages to the Washington Territorial governor praying for troops to protect them from a feared combination of coastal tribes, General Harney dispatched an infantry company to the coast to cool the troubles. The arrival of the troops and the building of a blockhouse on the banks of the Quinault River in 1864 may have comforted whites, but provided the Indians little protection from those moving onto their lands. Tensions along the coast and the Strait of Juan de Fuca were increased by the killing of a white man, a Mr. Cook, by Quileutes on the Pysht River in December, 1863. A federal official talked the whites of nearby Port Angeles out of seeking their own retribution for the deed. Head Quileute chief Howyatl (Howyattle) at one time offered to surrender a person from a distant band as payment for the murder. In 1866 the Quileutes reported that Makahs and soldiers had paddled in seven large canoes down the coast, where they captured three of Cook's alleged murderers, as well as seven others who had nothing to do with the troubles. In the summer of 1857, when the son of Queets

Natives of the Pacific Northwest coast, such as the Makahs, wore cedar-bark hats with designs depicting subjects such as whale hunting, in which the Makahs were proficient. From a graphic by Keith Powell.

Makah Indians cut up a whale for distribution according to tribal rules and regulations.

Chief Hooeyastee (also known as Howayatchi or Samson) killed a Quileute, the Queets chief had offered to cover the dead. Now the Quileute chief was willing to abide by the advice of Acting Agent Joseph Hill to submit to the white man's law and have the murderer hanged.

Besides the sea otter, the salmon was another native product that Indians harvested—at such places as the entrance to the Quinault River. After salmon were first canned on the Columbia River in the 1860s, other canneries were built along that stream. In 1878 there were twenty-one in active operation. Giant wheels, nets, and other traps were installed along the river to supply the canneries, which were made ravenous for fish by technology, an expanding market, and an ample supply of Chinese rather than Indian labor. Upriver at Kettle Falls, Indians began to feel the dearth of salmon as early as 1875. They suffered thereafter from a general decrease in the numbers of that fish until the building of Grand Coulee Dam shortly before the middle of the twentieth century ended runs there forever. The Indians had devoted meticulous attention to first-run ceremonials, which they believed necessary to ensure continuing runs.

The new exploiters had no time for such superstitions. In their own fishing Indians continued to observe ancient taboos. One that they retained despite the changing times was the use of wooden spears on first-run days instead of those of metal. Sometimes to catch salmon, they used the very technology they eschewed. By 1890 the Quinaults were operating their own elaborate fish-catching contraption of ropes and pulleys built by the tribe. Each family took turns at harvesting the catch. The availability of salmon was one reason that the Quinaults historically had not engaged in whaling to the extent that the Makahs had.

Stimulated by an expanding American market, the Makahs continued whaling throughout the nineteenth century. The selling of whale products was nothing new to them, for they and the Quinaults had long sold them to non-whaling coastal peoples, such as the Chinooks, Clatsops, and Tillamooks, who depended on beached whales for their own use and trade. In 1852 alone the Makahs sold thirty thousand gallons of whale oil, most of it loaded aboard white men's ships. Because of their whale-hunting prowess, the Makahs considered themselves superior to other Indians, even the buffalo hunters of the interior. As their ancestors had, the hunters from the Makah Village of Ozette canoed bravely into the Pacific, where in the month of August, 1872, they captured nine of the huge mammals.

The new commercialism did not obviate many of the old technical and spiritual aspects of the hunt among native whale hunters. There had been but few technical changes by the late nineteenth century. Spear and lance heads made from the thick parts of mussel shells and of elk horn were still used, augmented now by pieces of metal. Still in use were harpoons, lines, and sealskin buoys of native manufacture. Hunting methods had changed but little, as had the rules and rituals pertaining to the disposition of whales, although by the twentieth century many Makah whale-killing ceremonials had lost much of their original significance. By 1870 the practice of cutting a mark across the nose of whale killers was apparently no longer observed, and shortly after the early twentieth century slivers of whale blubber were no longer put into mouths of newborn babies. Before the new century villagers, besides feasting on flesh and fat, had added potatoes to their menu, eating, as had their ancestors, until their appetites were sated. Their thirsts were now slaked by the whiskey introduced into the festivities. Some good whaling years remained for the Makahs in the later nineteenth century. In one month alone, August, 1872, they killed nine whales, and in 1885, they killed many others off Cape Flattery. A gallon of whale oil sold in the sixties and seventies on Puget Sound for as much as fifty cents. In 1885 a gallon was exchanged on the Strait for three gallons of dogfish oil.

INDIAN FISH TRAP ON QUINAULT RIVER, WASHINGTON

"Indian Fish Trap on Quinault River, Washington." Reproduced from the cover of West Shore, *October 11, 1890.*

Another enterprise in which coastal natives engaged was hunting seals for their furs. In 1882 the Neah Bay Indian agent, Captain Charles Willoughby, reported that eleven schooners owned by as many competing firms and employing Indians, had sailed out of Neah Bay to hunt seals. The Makahs at first opposed the withdrawal of those firms, but within a few years they owned and operated their own ships. In the spring of 1883 twenty vessels caught seals off Cape Flattery. The catch of each ship was around eight hundred seals and was valued at four thousand dollars. At the end of the century Indians not only owned ships but also employed whites to operate them. They also hired other Indians to tend to the pelts, paying them, as they did other Indian crewmen, a certain percentage of the catch. Such industry on their part prompted the keen observer of Indians, James Swan, to write in 1895 that their efforts "could be profitably emulated by croakers and idlers in all our towns." On the other hand a missionary among the Twanas and Clallams in 1882 opined that their profits from sealing were hampering their spiritual growth. By that reasoning they should have become more spiritual around 1890 when governmental protection of fur seals reduced the profits from that industry. The Makahs then poached seals in places as distant as Alaska. When one of their schooners was seized along with Canadian vessels in the Bering Sea, the Canadians were indemnified for their losses, but the Indians received no compensation for theirs. With the seizure of their sealing schooners, the Makahs were forced to seek other products from the sea. Then, when whites depleted the halibut from banks fifteen miles off their coast, the Makahs were forced to sail far into the Pacific to catch that fish.

In the early sixties with implementation of the 1855 treaty, Makah agents, in keeping with the government's obsession of making agrarians of Indians, urged them to raise such crops as potatoes in order to subsist. On their reservation, an unlikely place for agrarian pursuits, elderly tribesmen, who were accustomed to risking their lives on Pacific whale hunts, tried to influence younger men against farming, "jeering and ridiculing them for digging in the earth like squaws."

Indians sold whites many native goods, such as hats, mats, and baskets, which the skilled fingers of their women fabricated as their mothers had for generations. The wool was spun out on circular boards or whorls, instead of American spinning wheels, which the Indian women did not like. The native women of Puget Sound knitted socks to help supply the need for that commodity in the white community. In exchange for their products, Indians obtained white men's goods, such as bread and molasses. They had developed a taste for molasses in the early days of white trading. They also obtained coffee, but they cared less for it than for the sugar that went with it. They also traded for metal utensils and implements and for cloths, especially calicoes. Whites could never understand why goods sold to Indians adorned graves or were given away in potlatches.

Indians were involved in logging and milling just as whites were west of the Cascade Mountains. From the late forties on, Indians had logged poles for the markets in San

Makah Indian whaler holding a lance harpoon. The floats in the canoe were used to buoy up whales towed ashore.

Francisco and elsewhere. Sometimes entire Indian communities were uprooted to make room for the expanding industry. When a mill was erected in Port Ludlow in 1853, about three hundred Clallams and Chimakums were spirited away from their village there with promises that they would be supplied with all the lumber they needed to build themselves substantial houses. The Port Madison Mill owned by Messrs. Meigs and Gawley was one of many established on Puget Sound and in the lower Hood Canal region in the 1850s and 1860s. During the transition period between the trading-goods and cash-money system, Indians working there received brass sheets for their labor. Each sheet was one inch square, and had stamped on it the initials of the mill owners, M and G, and the number 50 or 25 to represent that many cents in exchange for goods at the store. A white man, finding little romanticism in Indian employment in the sawmills, wrote:

It is to be presumed the "noble red men" are too busy nowadays attending to the slabs and scantling of the saw-mills; and his chants to the moon, if he indulge in any, are drowned by the scurr of a thousand circulars converting his forests into money for the paleface. There is not much romance or sentiment, Indian or other, about a saw-mill.[2]

In 1871 the total payroll of the Indians working in the timber-bolstered coal mines of Bellingham Bay was seven hundred dollars a month in coin.

A major place of employment for Indians from all over the Pacific Northwest and as far north as Alaska was the hop fields. In September, 1890, for instance, ninety-eight canoe loads of the once-feared Alaskan natives—their fierceness lessened by missionary efforts—came down to pick hops in the Puyallup Valley. From around 1865, when the first field north of California was planted, the hop industry boomed, creating a labor shortage and forcing growers to recruit Indians to do the picking. In late summer and early fall they moved in large numbers to fields in the Willamette, Puyallup, and Yakima valleys. One observer wrote, "These Sound Indians go in the old style, in canoes, taking along whole families— men, women and children, dogs and chickens, guns, fishing lines, gambling utensils, and every

Indian basket sellers were a common sight on the streets of Seattle in the 1890s and early twentieth century. Seattle Historical Society.

other convenience, luxury and article of property incident in Indian life."[3] Natives of the interior staked their horses at various inland stations and boarded the trains of the Northern Pacific Railroad (which first crossed the Cascade Mountains in 1887) for the ride to the Puyallup hop fields.

The exodus of the natives caused ambivalent feelings among their agents. The officials were relieved that their charges could earn money to ease their subsistence problems. At the same time they worried about the adverse influences to which the Indians were exposed in the fields. Drinking and gambling there could send them home penniless. During picking times Indian schools were emptied of pupils—a situation that continued into the twentieth century, when mechanical devices obviated the need for hand labor. When school was not kept on the Yakima Reservation during the 1895 season, and reservation life was disrupted, whites sneaked sheep to graze on the southern edge of the confine. In 1889 whites burned a village of the Quileutes while the latter were away picking hops. Because of hop picking, other white employers of Indians were hard pressed to secure their services. Wages in the hop fields varied with the times. Around 1890 pickers earned a dollar per hundred pounds. In the Yakima Valley, to which much of the hop raising shifted, nonreservation Indians demanded twenty-five cents more per box than the whites had bargained for.* They were influenced by their leaders, Sohappy and Columbia Jack, who sensed that whites would rather "stand a gentle squeeze than run any risks." Around the turn of the century and up until 1912 a remnant of Nez Percés from the Colville Reservation journeyed to the Okanagan Valley in British Columbia to pick hops through arrangements with the Canadian government.

The American government had hoped that, besides subsisting on the reservations, the Indians could sell their surplus products to whites. This proved less feasible than officials had hoped. Some reservations were unsuited to agriculture, and they were often too far from markets. Although separated from Willamette Valley markets by the Coast

---

*The editor of *The Northwest* 12, no. 8 (August, 1894): 3, in an article entitled "A Siwash Strike on the Yakima," noted that the Indians had taken a "leaf from the book of the pale-face."

Indian hop pickers of the Puget Sound area. Penrose Library, Whitman College.

Range, the produce of the remote Siletz Reservation could be shipped by steamer up the coast and thence up the Columbia and Willamette rivers. Still there were other problems. In 1861 little grain was raised, and the potato crop that was scheduled for export rotted in the ground. On the Alsea Reservation, the Alsea, Siuslaw, and Umpqua bands fared little better at agriculture. The bands were parties to an as-yet-unratified treaty and were barely able to survive on "Presents, Provisions and Subsistence" from a fund for Indians in that situation.

The Tulalip Reservation farmer reported to his superiors on February 19, 1868, that in the winter of 1867 there had been about three hundred Indians on the reservation, where two years earlier there had been a thousand. In the following winter, he said, there were "hardly enough to bury the dead." The Indians had been forced to scatter to find subsistence and employment. In 1861 five-sixths of the fifteen hundred Indians scheduled to go on the Skokomish Reservation under the treaty of Point No Point found no reason for going there. They preferred to remain in various fishing villages along Hood Canal and the Strait of Juan de Fuca. Moreover, white squatters had settled on the best reservation lands, leaving the Indians nothing but sloughs and swamps.

Indians were so scattered about Puget Sound and the Strait of Juan de Fuca in the middle of the 1860s that messengers had to be dispatched to notify them of the distribution of annuity goods. Some stayed away from

An Indian woman of Puget Sound weaving a basket. Seattle Historical Society.

A battle between Clallam and Makah Indians along the Strait of Juan de Fuca. From a painting by Paul Kane. Royal Ontario Museum.

native gatherings, fearing a chance encounter with extremist shamans. In December, 1868, a Puyallup chief asked his agent, J. G. Elder, to do something about one Muckleshoot Joe, who was killing not only Indians but whites with his "bad medicine."

Intertribal conflict complicated the Indians' struggle to survive. At the least it hampered their quest for employment and their performance of various tasks. Some, remembering the old days, thought the conflicts more exciting than the monotony of employment. On Puget Sound, the strait, and the coast many found such excitement. The Indians of those places engaged in contests with neighboring tribes and with those living at great distances, such as the Haidas. Whites received some of their own medicine from the latter when the fierce northerners fired the Port Townsend post office in early December, 1865, and tried to burn down the town. Intertribal conflict erupted on March 10, 1861, when Indians along the strait at Elwha, who were in bad repute with both Indians and whites, killed the Makah chief Whalathl (or Swell). Whalathl had rescued the crew of the wrecked brig *Swiss Boy* at the entrance to the strait, saving the ship from capture by British Columbia Indians. In revenge for the killing, the Makahs threatened retribution in the old tribal way.

The Makahs paid little heed to the pleas of their newly appointed agent, Henry A. Webster, to call off the venture. They reminded him that Agent Simmons had made fools of them by warning them not to seek revenge in the old way.

They told Webster that now the Ahousahts and the Kelsemahts (both Wakashan tribes of Clayoquot Sound) and the Nitinats were calling them old women for their hesitancy in seeking revenge. All three of the threatening tribes were from Vancouver Island. With no troops or other forces at his disposal the agent was helpless to stop the Makahs. A war party of eleven canoes set out for the Elwha village on the strait. It carried about ninety warriors under the Makah chief, Cowbetsi. They were mostly blanketed and painted black, and their hair was clubbed and encircled with fir twigs like the stems and sterns of their craft. They carried about seventy guns, as well as aboriginal weapons and pitch torches with which to burn the Elwha village. To send them on their way their women and children stood atop houses beating the roofs with sticks. Three days later the warriors returned. They formed a single file with Cowbetsi at its head. A short way behind came two warriors each carrying a bloody head. They placed the heads in the sand and formed a circle around them, chanting war songs. Parading the heads to Cowbetsi's village of Tsuess, they placed them atop a pole for time, where crows completed the vengeance.

In the fall of 1865 the Makahs paddled up the Strait of Juan de Fuca in a large fifty-canoe flotilla. Their chiefs were dressed in black bearskins with rings in their noses, eagle feathers on their heads, and feather fans in their hands. On a peaceful mission this time, they were en route to attend the wedding of one of their chiefs to a Clallam girl. The Clallams came to the wedding bearing red, white, and highly prized blue blankets as gifts.

The good will between the Makahs and the Clallams was threatened by the whiskey peddlers operating along the strait between the United States and Canada. The peddlers inflamed their customers with their wares, causing no end of troubles. In early 1866, when Webster arrested an Indian who had killed a Clallam, the Indian's friends armed themselves, boarded the ship on which he was held, and released him. The troops aboard the chartered steamer, *Cyrus Walker*, arrested the killer and his rescuers, placing them aboard the steamer in irons.

Even Agent Webster became embroiled in troubles at Neah Bay. In 1869 he was in Washington, D.C., defending himself against the charge, among others, that he had bartered dogfish oil and furs to various tribesmen from his store on the edge of the reservation. Some natives of Vancouver Island had also sold him oil, for which he had exchanged blankets, thus depriving the government of legal duties on goods imported from a foreign country.

More pernicious than this trade was the slave trade that the Indians had engaged in for years. It was carried on despite restrictions on it in the Stevens treaties. In early June, 1860, Agent Simmons rescued three Haida women who had been enslaved by the "Snohome" (perhaps the Shohomish Indians), delivering them back to their people. Female slaves at that time were worth from $80 to $150 each. Not long before this, a Makah chief devised an ingenious scheme to make money. He propositioned the owners of a schooner to charter her to sail north to the Nootka or Clayoquot Sound. There he planned to invite many Indians aboard, get them drunk, and then kidnap them for sale in the south.

James Swan served as a judge at Port Townsend in the 1860s. Claiming that there was "no law between the United States and Great Britain relating to the rendition of fugitive slaves," he withheld from a Songish Indian of Vancouver Island an Indian girl of Washington Territory who had been rescued from her British Indian abductors. The Indian carried an authorization from British Governor James Douglas for the girl's release, but that did not secure it.*

Indian agents were eager to have their charges gainfully employed like white men, but at times they must have felt as if their efforts were to no avail because of continued intertribal feuding. In another of the many raids across the Strait of Juan de Fuca a canoeful of Tsimshian (or Chimmesyan) Indians of northern British Columbia landed at Dungeness a few days after some Indians from Victoria had destroyed

The buffalo was one source of nourishment for the Rocky Mountain and Columbia Plateau tribes, who fought one another for control of the hunting territory. From a painting by Chester Field.

Indian graves there. The Tsimshians had long been feuding with the Clallams and other peoples along the strait, and the Clallams fell upon them, shooting two of their number. Returning in great numbers, the Tsimshians killed two Clallams. In the later part of 1868 the Clallams attacked a Tsimshian party, killing all but one woman, who saved her life by hiding under a mat. After the fight American officials took twenty-six of the attacking Clallams to the Skokomish Reservation, where they were kept at hard labor under the agent, Charles King. The Tsimshian woman was kept by the Tsimshian wife of a white man at Dungeness. Following the Indian custom of "covering the dead," American officials sent the woman to her home on Vancouver Island, which they had amply stocked with presents for her people: $230 in United States gold coin, 226 yards of calico, ten pairs of cassimere pants, five woolen shawls, and six pairs of blankets. The gifts apparently satisfied her people.[4] Sometimes Indians of the Sound pooled their money to ransom their people kidnapped by northern tribes. Shortly after paying the "blood feud" money to the Tsimshians, the government paid Indians between Grays Harbor and the Quinault Reservation for the life of an Indian taken by a white man.

Although Indians west of the Cascade Mountains were employed working for whites, their acceptance of American ways did not come as soon or as smoothly as optimistic whites believed, or hoped, that it would. In the sparsely settled regions east of the Cascade Mountains natives exhibited even greater reluctance to yield to American ways. There the continuing contest between the "immovable object"—that is, the Indian way of life—and the "irresistible force"—the American life-style—proved to be more than theoretical.

*Such action did not lessen Swan's stature in the eyes of Indians of Washington Territory. The Makahs called him Chatic because to them he was as great an artist as a native of that name who lived at Clayoquot on the western shores of Vancouver Island.

18. BITTERROOT AND BITTER ROUTE

The Indians of the vast intermontane West that stretches from the Cascade Mountains to the Rockies continued to be caught up in a struggle born of ancient grudges aggravated by tribal mobility and shifting alliances. Tribes who were friends one year were foes the next. The increasing trespasses by whites added to the complexity of intertribal conflict. Where at one time native combatants had sought valor and victory in their wars, they now sought mostly to survive and subsist. Their many conflicts were almost too numerous to catalog. Shoshonis fought Blackfeet, Bannocks fought Kalispels, and so on. Attacks, such as that in the spring of 1857 in the buffalo country in which the Kalispels killed six Bannocks, were sure to bring retaliation. In 1861 the Crows allied with Shoshonis against the Sioux, who in turn allied with Cheyennes and Arapahos (both Algonquian) to fight back. At various times the Crows allied with the Nez Percés, Gros Ventres, and Assiniboins. Not unimportantly, the Crows became mercenaries of the United States—according to native informants—in order to save that tribe from extinction. In early 1862, Nez Percés and Crees in the predawn attacked a sleeping Kalispel camp on Milk River, a Missouri tributary, killing twenty and wounding twenty-five others. Five of the wounded died shortly. Among the fallen was the son of Chief Alexander. The attackers mutilated his body, scalping him and cutting out his heart. Elsewhere the Bannocks headed for Kalispel country to steal horses. They might have retaliated closer to their southeastern-Idaho homelands by moving against the Nez Percés, who often raided them in the Big Hole country of southwestern Montana. In 1862 on the Shields River near Bozeman, Montana, Flathead chief Moise ordered the capture of some young Piegans who had abortively raided a Salish camp for horses. For punishment some of the captives had their hair cut short, and others had pieces of their ears cut off.

Chief Washakie was caught up in the Rocky Mountain and Great Plains warfare. He was the son of a Shoshoni father and a Flathead mother and the leader of the Eastern Shoshonis, with whom the Bannocks sometimes joined in buffalo hunting and in fighting the Crows. In 1856, beyond Henry's Lake at the head of the North Fork of the Snake River, Washakie's band fought a Crow force reported at a thousand. At the end of the first hour of fighting, as the Shoshonis were pushed over a hill, the Shoshoni women entered the fight swinging butcher knives. Under such a fierce show of force the Crows began a sundown retreat with the Shoshonis in pursuit. Old Shoshoni men encircled the battlefield. They rounded up two hundred and fifty Crow horses and gathered their own dead before wolves and eagles consumed them. Two years later, in an equally fierce fight, Washakie's band defeated the Crows to help secure for themselves the Wind River Valley in western Wyoming as a hunting ground.[1] The defeats not only cost the Crows many killed and wounded but also were humiliating to those proud plainsmen. They disdained the tribes on the west, especially the Columbia River peoples, of whom they said: "On the Columbia they are poor and dirty, paddle about in canoes, and eat fish. Their teeth are worn out; they are always taking fishbones out of their mouths. Fish is poor food."[2] (Columbia River women were adept at eating salmon and spitting out the bones in one continuous process.)

Washakie sought isolation from warring tribes in the Wind River Valley, where a reservation was established for him and his people under the Fort Bridger Treaty of 1868. Fort Bridger was located in southwestern Wyoming. Washakie lived and died there a friend of Americans. His friendship was evident around the middle of the century, when westbound immigrants breaking through South Pass found him as their protector along the ensuing portion of the Immigrant Road.* In the Snake River country farther west immigrants and their animals, wearied by their trek of nearly two thousand miles from Missouri to Oregon, were less protected from attack.

Helping to make the immigrants the targets of Indian attacks in that quarter were the Shoshonis and Bannocks, who over the years had withdrawn from the diminishing buffalo ranges into mountain fastnesses under the pressure of costly wars with the Crows and Blackfeet. Scanty supplies of roots and game forced them to intensify their harassment of whites traveling the nearby Immigrant Road. In that land of short food supply the immigration of increasing numbers of Americans not only alarmed the Indians but also provided them with more targets to attack. Most of the attacks were perpetrated by small teams of young braves as private enterprises unsanctioned by responsible chieftains. Many were inspired by Indian prophets, of whom the most noteworthy was a Bannock named Pasheco (also Pashego and the like). Pasheco inspired the attack on the Mormon Salmon River mission and exerted a strong antiwhite influence over diverse Bannock-Paiute peoples from the Rockies to the Blue Mountains. He wanted Indian country to be inviolate from whites, even if it was necessary to kill them to keep it that way.

---

*Largely because of pressure from Californians, a Pacific Wagon Road office was established in the United States Department of the Interior in 1857. This in itself was unusual, since the War Department usually had charge of such roads. While a number of routes were contemplated, the main purpose of the roads was to facilitate the passage of settlers to California. One route ran from Fort Ridgely, Minnesota, to the South Pass of the Rocky Mountains; a second, central route ran west from El Paso, Texas, to Fort Yuma, California. All of the routes may be said to have composed the Pacific Wagon Road.

Lodge and encampment of Eastern Shoshoni Chief Washakie. The photograph was taken in 1870 by William H. Jackson in the Wind River Mountains, Wyoming. Washakie had a record of friendliness to Americans. Smithsonian Institution National Anthropological Archives, Neg. No. 1668.

On August 20, 1854, a band of thirty Boise Shoshoni warriors, their blood heated by their prophets, swept down on the trail-weary party of Alexander Ward twenty miles east of Fort Boise, the old fur post. They killed all but two of Ward's sons and held three children over a flaming wagon until they burned to death, throwing their charred remains to the wolves. They shot a woman in the head who tried to resist them and scalped another, bashing in her head with a club. They shot one of Ward's daughters in the head, ramming a hot iron into her body and leaving tooth marks in her cheeks. The pregnant Mrs. Ward fared no better. Her head was bashed with a tomahawk by those who had vented their lust on her and on another woman. The attack occurred the very day after Bannock-Paiutes had attacked the five-wagon Moses-Kirkland party ninety miles east of Fort Boise.

Reaction to the massacre was delayed in that time of poor communications, but came from not only the white community but also the Indians. Washakie tried to purge his people of elements hostile to traveling whites. Among those who received his scoldings were some followers of Northwestern Shoshoni chief Pocatello, whose band controlled the emigration route to Oregon and California. With scalps, clothing, and other goods stripped from immigrants, they appeared at a large Shoshoni encampment in 1854, trying to belittle Washakie, who tried to prevent conflict with whites. The long-suffering Washakie had ample reason to be provoked at whites. Immigrants had once fired on him. Once he had threatened that, if the Crow Indian agent did not control his Indians, the Shoshonis would prey upon the whites. Not the least of the provocations to him, as to other western buffalo hunters, was the chewing up of the grass by the immigrants' stock along the road, which was now rutted by their wagons. Washakie perhaps shared his problems with the United States Department of the Interior crew on the Northern Route of the Pacific Wagon Road. They wintered with him in 1858–59 and may have shared with him their own problems, not the least of which was the recent burning by the Bannocks of their supply depot, Fort Thompson, in central South Dakota.

The Oregon legislature urged that immigrants be protected on the overland route. As a result a military fort was established. Construction of Fort Boise did not begin until after July 4, 1863, when a site was selected on the Boise River forty miles up from its confluence with the Snake. In early 1859 the Bannocks and Shoshonis attacked immigrants in

Bannock Indians photographed in the 1870s by William H. Jackson on the Fort Hall Indian Reservation. On horseback at the extreme left is Buffalo Horn. Buffalo Jim is next to him. Smith- *sonian Institution, National Anthropological Archives, Bureau of American Ethnology Collection, Neg. No. 1714.*

the Goose Creek Mountains of Utah and Idaho, killing seven, wounding others, and pillaging the train. In the following year General Harney of the Department of Oregon dispatched two expeditions into the Boise area to check Indian attacks, which had resumed there. Troops under Major Enoch Steen and Captain A. J. Smith patrolled the Immigrant Road. The two forces had scarcely withdrawn for the winter when the Bannocks went on the attack. Late in the summer of 1860 a hundred of them, mostly mounted, pounced on a party of forty-four immigrants near the Salmon Falls of Snake River. Feigning hunger, they approached the train, drove off its cattle, and then attacked its members, who huddled in a hastily formed corral trying to protect themselves from the Indians pouring arrow and rifle fire at them from a cover of sage.* The fighting became known as the Salmon River, Otter, or Utter Massacre. When it ended, the train was destroyed. About nine of its members had been killed on the spot. About fifteen more were killed in flight between the Owyhee and Burnt rivers, and others survived the winter by eating their dead. Four

children were captured.

In March, 1861, Major Steen urged John Owen, the agent to the Flatheads, to search out and retrieve the captured whites. In council the Bannocks suspected of the killings told him that the Otter Massacre had been committed by Indians from the Humboldt country on the south, whose practice it was to visit the Immigrant Road about the time "the leaves commence to fall." The same Indians were also foraying on the Warm Springs Reservation.

At his Bitterroot Valley headquarters Owen had his hands full coping with agency problems.[3] Perhaps his greatest problem was keeping his Indians at home and able to subsist away from the nearby plains, where the Flatheads and other Salish Indians still risked their necks for the prized buffalo. The Flatheads had previously permitted priests to accompany them on their hunts. They now reverted to shamanistic powers to bring them within range of the buffalo and out of the range of the Blackfeet. Several forces propelled them from the Bitterroot to the plains. Most Flatheads preferred to remain in the Bitterroot Valley instead of moving to the Jocko Reservation on the north, but the crops they raised there, such as wheat and potatoes, were inadequate to sustain them. Promised annuity goods often did not

---

*This massacre of whites frequently has been referred to as the Salmon Falls Massacre and occasionally as the Myers Massacre.

arrive, or, if they did, were of little utility. Owen described them as a shipment of trash. To compound the problem, whites were aware of the agricultural possibilities of the Bitterroot and were beginning to step on Indian toes in the valley. It was also fast becoming a refuge for whiskey peddlers and other undesirable whites.

The problem of Flathead subsistence was complicated further by the Indians traversing the well-beaten valley floor en route to buffalo. They often stopped to dig roots and steal horses from both Flatheads and whites. After 1860 the Nez Percés went less to buffalo, depending more upon the Salish to do their hunting for them. The Nez Percés were excellent traders and were content to obtain buffalo products from the Salish, to whom they traded such items as watertight basketry bags. Technologists as well as traders, the Nez Percés often had money for the things they wanted, unlike other tribesmen. When other tribesmen were asked where they obtained their money, they replied, "We won it gambling with the Nez Percés."

Crowding the valley even further were Shoshonis and Bannocks. Many of them were the remnants of bands from Salmon Falls and other places. They sought subsistence from Owen in 1860 and 1861 when the Oregon and Washington superintendencies were temporarily combined. Because he gave them food and blankets, his white neighbors accused him of "trifling" with them, and he even lost some favor among his Flatheads for his action. On visiting the Shoshonis, he found the "poor miserable naked starving wretches," as he called them, living in fragile shelters of boughs and grasses. They told him that the military had frightened them and that the government had never talked with them. They said it had never given them presents, such as tobacco. Its representatives had never smoked with them as they had with the Blackfeet and others, with whom they had arranged to have roads traverse the Indians' lands for the benefit of the white men. No one, they said, had asked their permission to establish the Immigrant Road, nor had anyone compensated them for the whites' passage and pasturage along that route. Owen reported that white men committed outrages on the road "that the heart would shudder to record."

In 1862, Owen resigned in frustration after trying to protect his Indians from a host of problems. Intertribal wars had not abated. The plains were as volatile as ever. In the year when he resigned, Shoshonis and Bannocks attacked the Flatheads on their very doorstep in Hell Gate Canyon, running off horses and destroying lodges and other properties. Agency employees resorted to concubinage with Indian women. The advice of the Reverend Joseph Menetrey, S.J., who replaced Hoecken as agent on the Jocko, conflicted with the policies of the Indian office, and the difference of opinion tended to undermine Owen's position. Relations between the priests and Owen had been especially touchy since 1850. In that year the clerics had closed Saint Mary's Mission because of the Indians' inconsiderate treatment of the priests and because they were ordered to do so by their superior. Owen purchased the mission on November 5 of that year and renamed it Fort Owen. Then it was reestab-

lished as a mission in 1866. When Owen grumbled that his Flatheads "raised ten bushels of wheat to one" of the Kalispels under mission influence, the fathers suggested that his behavior had resulted from a blow to the head by a windmill blade. His behavior was made increasingly quixotic by a growing thirst for whiskey and a growing inability to cope with his problems, but he had indeed experienced too many bouts with the windmill blades of troubles. The Flatheads, however, still found him to be a friend as they struggled on with meager resources, suffering many losses. Many died by accident, or by natural causes, which struck down more of them then did their foes of the plains and Rockies.

After Owens resigned the agency was moved to the Jocko near the Saint Ignatius Mission, where for a few years it was administered by a series of weak and dishonest agents. Lumber from the reservation mill was fraudulently sold to whites. Agents falsified ledgers to hide illegal profits they had received from Kalispel and Kutenai bands on the reservation, which was thrown open to whites. The Flatheads remaining in the Bitterroot came under increasing pressure to vacate the place. Under their chiefs—Victor, Ambrose, and Adolph—they preferred scratching out a living there to removal to the Jocko. To prove his resolve to remain, Adolph in August, 1868, showed his gnarled hands to government agent William J. Cullen (who was seeking Flathead removal) and declared: "My hands—look at them. They are my tools and I scratch the ground with my nails."

The Flatheads still enjoyed a good reputation in the East. In the West, where the goodwill would have counted most, whites villified Salish speakers, especially the Kalispel buffalo hunters passing to and from the plains with the Kutenais. Fierce fights, such as that on the Teton River between Piegans and Kalispels in 1868, did not enhance the latter's reputation among whites across the Rockies. In the seventies whites in Missoula in the lower Bitterroot Valley nervously watched their town fill with Indians who were fearful of moving east because of rampaging Sioux. During the 1869–70 hunt the Salish contracted smallpox from the Gros Ventres, but managed to fight the Sioux and Crows. Sometimes truces were effected among erstwhile foes, such as that worked out in 1871 among the Flatheads, Kalispels, and Nez Percés with the Blackfeet. That arrangement worried settlers east of the Rockies, who depended on the Blackfeet to confine trans–Rocky Mountain tribes to their homelands. In 1874 the Sioux convened a council of buffalo-hunting tribes on the lower Yellowstone River to form a solid front against whites. Nearly all the tribes voted for war except the Flatheads and Nez Percés, who were traditional friends of whites. The latter claimed the fighting was too far from their lands, adding that they did not wish to ally with their Sioux foes. On a buffalo hunt in 1875 and 1876 the Flatheads allied with their Crow, Bannock, and Shoshoni foes against the Sioux, but the alliance, like others, was for temporary convenience only.

The Flatheads and other western tribes continued hunting buffalo until the early eighties, when the animals became all but extinct. Over the years the Indians' use of the animal had shifted from consuming the entire beast from horns to

Flathead Indians near Jocko, Montana, circa 1900. Dogs were a traditional part of Indian encampments. University of Oregon Library.

Coastal and Columbia Plateau tribes relied on the deer not only for food but also for its hide, from which they made moccasins, leggings, gloves, shirts, dresses, and other pieces of clothing. From a painting by Chester Fields.

hooves to taking specialized products, such as hides, many of which were sold to traders. In hopes of dissuading the Indians from hunting in exchange for a more sedentary life, the government in 1876 contracted with Montana merchants to supply buffalo meat to Indian reservations. The problem of Indian itinerancy was partially solved for the government by the diminished herds and ranges, but it was not solved for the priests on the Jocko if there is any validity to the observation of a white visitor there in the early eighties, who said that the black robes encouraged their Indians to follow the "Ishmaelitish life" because they found that the Indians took to gambling and drunkenness when confined to their little farms. "A blessing in disguise," forcing Indians to earn their living from the soil, was the way the commissioner of Indian affairs marked the passing of the buffalo in his 1879 report. Putting it another way, a white editor in 1884 wrote, "The buffalo is to be lamented, but the Indian will be redeemed."

On November 14, 1871, James Garfield, later president of the United States, was empowered to negotiate a contract between the government and the Flatheads for their removal to the Jocko—an indication that the government deemed it better to remove them than to allow them to remain in accordance with the 1855 treaty. The contract was in lieu of a treaty because the government by that time no longer recognized the sovereignty of Indian tribes. Flathead Chief Charlot (also known as Little Claw of the Grizzly Bear) was in failing health. After the recent death of his

father, Victor, in Crow country, he succeeded him. As chief he refused to sign the contract the following year. On a reconnaissance of the reservation with Garfield, he was apparently unimpressed with prospects there. Succumbing to government enticements to remove, the second chief, Arlee (or Red Night) and the third chief, Adolph both signed the contract and removed to the Jocko, as did others in succeeding years. By removing, Arlee became primary Flathead chief, greatly incensing Charlot, the hereditary tribal leader.

With removal of the Flatheads to the reservation, whites flocked into the Bitterroot Valley, where Charlot's people occupied cabins in winter and canvas tipis in summer. Impoverished from drinking and gambling, the Flatheads tried to survive on government goods and services. At the request of the government, Flathead Agent Peter Ronan in 1884 took Charlot, four other Indians, and an interpreter to Washington, D.C., where officials tried to cajole the chief into removing. They offered seed and equipment for his people and for himself, a yearly pension, and, as Victor's successor, the head chieftaincy of the Flatheads, Kalispels, and Kutenais. Charlot was warned that, if he did not remove, government subsistence would be withheld from his people. Continuing the advocacy of the Indians in his care, Ronan in 1884 sought the restoration of a western segment previously ceded from the original 1855 reservation, as well as an extension of the reservation to the Canadian border to incorporate Kutenai lands.

In the face of threats and promises Charlot remained adamantly opposed to removal, but other Flatheads continued their exodus from the Bitterroot Valley to the Jocko. Some even abandoned farms for which they had received patents. The Kutenais around Bonners Ferry in northern Idaho had not yet removed to the Jocko Reservation, but some were brought there from the area around 1900. Some Kutenais who were related to Salish peoples removed to the Colville Reservation in northeastern Washington State. Another Kutenai band under Eneas Paul was camping off the Jocko. Paul was the son of Ignace (Big Knife) and the successor to Chief Baptiste, whom the Blackfeet killed in 1876. The government pressured a number of straggling bands into removing to the Jocko. Indians of the reservation met with the Northwest Indian Commission in April, 1887, and agreed to accept Salish bands on their confine, including Spokanes. Around 1888, Chief Michael and about sixty Kalispels removed there from the Sandpoint area in northern Idaho. They feared confinement on the Coeur d'Alène Reservation if they did not do so. Other Kalispels remained in their old homelands along the lower Pend Oreille River. Pressure there from railroad builders and white settlers resulted in an executive order dated March 23, 1914, establishing a reservation for them in northeastern Washington State.

Continuing encroachments on the Jocko Reservation gave urgency to Ronan's appeals for protection of his Indians. The construction of the Northern Pacific Railroad across the confine not only facilitated the passage and arrival of more whites but also produced crimes in an area that previously had been relatively crimeless. With no more buf-

A painting by Peter Tofft of Fort Owen in the Bitterroot Valley. The fort was in the lands of the Flathead Indians and was named *for its builder, Major John Owen, who purchased the Saint Mary's Mission on the site in 1850. Museum of Fine Arts, Boston.*

falo to hunt the Indians had to hunt local game, raise beef, or starve, none of which set well with Indian traditionalists. Complaining that mission priests had put his son to work in the fields, Arlee exclaimed, "I did not send my boy there to be a squaw."

In 1891, Charlot, the best-known traditionalist of all, succumbed to removal to the Jocko, saying it was for the sake of his people. All he wanted for himself, he said, was enough ground for his grave. He later claimed that he would never have removed if General Henry B. Carrington, who came to remove him and his people, had not promised them fine horse stables, houses, and many other things. On the reservation Charlot, who was restored to the head chieftaincy, understandably did not adapt as well as others did to the white technology that was so alien to his way of life. He complained that learning English in school only helped Indians to obtain whiskey more easily.

To the end of the century the Flatheads projected the image of a moral people. They zealously kept feast days and Sundays and kept tribal control through such institutions as their "kind of general assizes or open court," in which miscreants were judged and whipped by their fellow tribesmen. When Charlot died on January 10, 1910, a priest wrote:

"Chief Charlot died this morning. He made a nice death." Through no fault of his own his life had not been so nice.

The Civil War in the early sixties did not deter the passage of immigrants westward. With the withdrawal of federal troops from the Pacific Northwest the burden of its defense and the protection of immigrants fell on state and territorial governments. In the fall of 1862, Colonel Reuben F. Maury was dispatched with three companies of the First Oregon Cavalry Volunteers to the Immigrant Road to protect travelers. The following year he was joined in that task by Colonel Justus Steinberger of the First Washington Territorial Volunteers. Both forces operated out of Fort Walla Walla, the post nearest Fort Boise on the west. The volunteers policing the Immigrant Road had to protect immigrants not only from attacking Indians but also from the devilry of outlaws, including those escaping service in the Civil War, whom a lax draft system enabled to carry out their own little wars in the largely unpoliced West. Indians were often victims of the outlaws' depredations, and usually received the blame for them.

In seeking a leader for a coalition to stem the immigrant tide engulfing their lands and lives, the Bannocks and Shoshonis passed over Washakie for Pasheco. The warriors

Flathead Chief Charlot, center, flanked by Moise, Louis, John Hill, Tom Adams, interpreter Michel Revais, and the Flathead agent, Peter Ronan. The Delegation journeyed to Washington, *D.C., in 1884. Smithsonian Institution National Anthropological Archives, Neg. No. 43,583.*

Kalispel Indians on their reservation on the east bank of the Pend Oreille River near Cusick, Washington. Pacific North-west Collections, University of Washington Library.

of the two tribes sent their families to the Salmon River Mountains in southeastern Idaho near the Montana border. They wanted them to be away from the scene of conflict as they desperately sought to save their lands from trespassing whites. In response to Indian attacks whites posted public notices warning immigrants to be on their guard.

The Indian campaign included the theft of about two hundred horses at Fort Bridger. It was so effective that immigrants, ferrymen, and even seasoned mountaineers abandoned Sublette's Cutoff, a short cut on the Immigrant Road between the Green and Bear rivers in southwestern Wyoming that bypassed Fort Bridger. After the Indians attacked and killed most of the men of an eleven-wagon California-bound train, a force of forty well-armed whites from a following train pursued the attackers in hopes of recovering stolen livestock. They were forced to retreat when they came upon three hundred warriors. Not until the harried train was reinforced to a total of seven hundred souls by joining forces with other wagons, did it proceed to the Humboldt River, and then it was under constant Indian attack.

In September, 1862, Colonel Patrick E. Connor and his California Volunteers were drawn into fighting with the Indians.[4] They had come to Salt Lake City primarily to hold rein on the Mormons in the absence of regular troops drained off by the Civil War. In December volunteers attacked a camp consisting mostly of Bannocks and Cache Valley Shoshonis in southeastern Idaho near the Bear River emptying into the Great Salt Lake. They captured four Indians and held them hostage for the return of stolen

horses. Instead of returning the horses, the Indians moved into Bear River Canyon leaving the four hostages to be shot by the volunteers. In retaliation the Indians killed a number of whites and then proceeded near to present-day Franklin, Idaho. There they demanded a handout of wheat from a Mormon bishop only to be informed by him that Connor and his cavalry and infantry were coming for them.

On January 29, 1863, Connor's cavalry swam its horses across the ice-choked Bear River and moved down a mile-long plain leading to the Indians' camp, which was in a large ravine about a mile from the ice-laden river. There they met a lone chief, who rode in front of his braves carrying a long spear from which a scalp dangled. He was perhaps Shoshoni, since Indian leaders at that place were mainly of that tribe. The warriors taunted the approaching cavalry with obscenities as they fired at them on the treeless plain that stretched for a mile between the river and the ravine where the Indians were. The mouth of the ravine led to the river. The head of the ravine led to the hills. The Indians had built fortifications of thick willows and had dug holes in the sides of the ravine from which to direct their fire. The approaching cavalry were forced to dismount and position themselves as skirmishers, joining some of Conner's infantry, who were deployed to protect the cavalry. First a frontal attack, then two detachments were deployed to prevent the Indians' escape either down the ravine and across the river, or up and over the hills.

In the ensuing fierce fight, which lasted nearly five hours, the Indians, trying to escape, were trapped in the ravine. In sharp fighting they killed a reported fifteen to

Chief Charlot (or Bear Claw), leader of those Flatheads who refused to move to the Jocko (Flathead) Indian Reservation until 1891. Smithsonian Institution National Anthropological Archives, Neg. No. 4761.

Captain Jim, a Shoshoni, in Washington, D.C., in 1880. Idaho Historical Society, Boise.

twenty-three troops and wounded forty-four to fifty-three others. About seventy-five to seventy-nine troops were incapacitated with frozen extremities. Among the many bodies that strewed the battlefield was that of Chief Bear Hunter. Two other Shoshoni chiefs, Pocatello and Sagwitch, might have suffered a similar fate if they had not left the scene the preceding day. Conner claimed 224 warriors were killed. At the same time he avoided taking credit for the women and children killed despite his reporting them as captured. If one takes into account subsequent losses, nearly 400 Shoshonis died in the battle. It was the largest number of Indians killed by the United States Army in any battle. The troops also destroyed seventy tipis hidden in some willows, captured seventy-five horses, and made off with other loot. Not the least of the Indians' casualties was the loss of their momentum to resist whites. Their situation was made no easier by the loss in March of another hundred of their people to volunteers. Scouting throughout southern Idaho, Connor met no resistance from the various bands. Too starved to resist, they were forced to treat with the government.

In April, 1863, the Bannock-Shoshonis were visited by

Utah Superintendent of Indian Affairs James D. Doty, who was invited to treat with them (he was the father of James Doty, Governor Stevens's secretary). In July, Washakie and his Eastern Shoshonis signed a peace treaty at Fort Bridger with Doty and the Fort Bridger agent, Luther Mann (who served from 1861 to 1869). In the treaty they were promised annuity goods in return for pasturage lost. During the proceedings ill-feeling mounted between the Bannocks and the Shoshonis. The Shoshonis accused the Bannocks of causing their troubles. On July 30 the Northwestern Shoshonis, one of four Northern Shoshoni groups, met under Pocatello with Doty and Connor east of the Great Salt Lake at Box Elder. They heard peace treaty terms read and interpreted, and they agreed to sign. On October 1, Western Shoshonis at Ruby Valley in northeastern Nevada also signed a treaty, which was similar in terms to the others. On October 12 the Gosiute Shoshonis of the Tuilla Valley west of Salt Lake City signed a similar pact with Doty. On October 14 at Soda Springs on Bear River, Doty and Connor treated with the Bannock chief Le Grand Coquin and two subchiefs, Taghee (or Tahgee, Tigee, and the like) and Matigund. The chiefs led a Bannock band of 150 braves and their families. The Bannock chief Tendoy (or Tindooh and the like, also known as The Climber) chose to remain hunting with his band, but sent word that he would assent to the treaty. He was the son of a Bannock father and a Sheepeater mother. Doty violated the Fort Bridger treaty by promising Le Grand Coquin five thousand dollars' worth of annuity goods from the ten thousand dollars' worth promised to Washakie on July 2 at Fort Bridger. The diminution of the annuities caused Washakie much dissatisfaction.

The Senate approved all five peace treaties with only minor changes. Except for the Bannocks, each of the groups assented to certain treaty changes. (It remained a de facto agreement for five years until another Fort Bridger treaty proclaimed February 24, 1869, replaced it.) By the 1863 Fort Bridger treaty Eastern Shoshonis under Washakie agreed not to block travel routes or molest immigrants and agreed to submit to the erection of military establishments, telegraph lines, and overland stage lines and the construction of a railroad. All the parties to the three treaties that were effected in October agreed to remove to a reservation when the government might choose for them to stop their roamings.

When he returned from fighting the Crows in the spring of 1864, Washakie discovered that the Sheepeaters, in violation of the treaties, had stolen nineteen horses from miners at Beaverhead east of the Continental Divide. They excused themselves for the thefts on the grounds of ignorance of any treaty. Pocatello was also having troubles. He was arrested by Colonel Connor on the complaint of a transportation entrepreneur, Ben Holladay. The charges were dropped, but Connor had spread word that he intended to hang the chief. In the spring of 1865, Washakie refused to join the Crows, Sioux, and Cheyennes, who sought aid in ridding the country of whites. Because of his refusal the Sioux attacked the Shoshonis that summer, capturing about four hundred horses and killing Washakie's son before his very eyes.

Regardless of treaty promises the hunger-driven Bannocks and Shoshonis reacted forcefully to white appropriation of their lands and to attacks on their persons. In 1864 a Mr. Jordan leading a twenty-man party forced some Indians into a canyon fifty miles west of Silver City in southwestern Idaho. They killed Jordan and wounded several of those with him. Such troubles prompted the Idaho Territorial Governor and Superintendent of Indian Affairs, Caleb Lyon, to treat with the Indians.[5] On October 10, 1864, a treaty was effected with the Shoshonis (who were intermarried with Paiutes) along the Boise. The tribesmen agreed to surrender all their killers and horse thieves and their lands in the Boise Valley and to remove to an as-yet-undesignated reservation. The Boise Shoshonis had been impressed by the volunteers' chastisement of the Shoshonis of southeastern Idaho Territory in 1863. Before that they had felt little inclination to sign a Fort Boise treaty. As it turned out, their 1864 treaty was not ratified. In September, 1865, Lyon invited the Bannocks and Shoshonis to meet him in council at Camas Prairie. After the council the Commissioner of Indian Affairs at Lyon's suggestion directed Lyon to appoint agents where needed and to treat with the Indians for a proposed reservation on the Snake River.

The Idaho Territorial Legislature did not check the aggressions of Bannock-Shoshonis who were angry at the government's failure to deliver goods promised in the treaties. As a result private individuals formed volunteer units to run the red men down. When the legislature declined to provide troops to fight the Indians, citizens placed bounties on them. Lyon denounced the prizes, but at the same time donated $500 to a bounty fund. One hundred dollars was offered for the scalp of a "buck," fifty dollars for that of a "squaw," and twenty-five dollars for everything "in the shape of an Indian under ten." Another of Lyon's ambivalent actions involved misappropriation of Indian funds placed at his disposal for treaty payments.

In 1866, Lyon called off a bounty-hunting party and sent it to collect Shoshonis in the Bruneau River country of southwestern Idaho Territory to effect a treaty of "perpetual peace and friendship" (by the middle of the nineteenth century the Bruneau and Boise Shoshonis had mixed with the Northern Paiute bands). The treaty was signed April 10, 1866, but was never ratified. In it the Bruneau Shoshonis agreed to cede the area of the Owyhee mines, but the treaty's terms were so nebulous that it should have been renegotiated. "During the whole negotiations," wrote Lyon, "I had to labor against a public sentiment viciously in favor of exterminating the Red men at all hazards, backed up by a press throwing ridicule upon all efforts toward tranquilizing the wronged and much abused Indians." On receipt of news that fifty Indians had been killed in Humboldt, the editor of the *Advance* of Owyhee, Idaho Territory, wrote with acid bitterness, "If some Christian gentlemen will furnish a few bales of blankets from a small-pox hospital, well innoculated, we will be distributing agent and see that no Indian is without a blanket."

On October 1, 1866, the new Idaho territorial governor, David W. Ballard, was instructed to set aside two reservations in his territory: one for the Boise and Bruneau Shoshonis and the other for the Coeur d'Alênes. On June 14, 1867, in compliance with this instruction, Ballard arranged to establish the two reserves. As a temporary measure 283 Boise Shoshonis, 300 Bruneau Shoshonis, and a 100-person Bannock band were shunted out of the way of whites to a temporary confine thirty miles up the Boise River from Boise City.

Ballard had proposed a reservation in the Fort Hall area for the Boise and Bruneau Shoshonis and the Bannocks from the Boise area.[6] By executive order on June 14, 1867, the 1.8-million-acre Fort Hall Reservation was established for those Indians under two chiefs, Bannock John and his brother, Bannock Jim. The chiefs were each married to sisters of Taghee, who had become head chief of about seven hundred Soda Spring Bannocks with the death of Le Grand Coquin. They asked their assigned agent, Charles F. Powell, for permission to hunt buffalo since without annuities they were starving. The Bruneau Shoshonis had no horses and were unable to go to hunt buffalo. With horses the starving Boise Bands were able to go to the plains, but found the game scarce there. In 1866, Washakie permitted Pocatello and a subchief, Black Bear, to accompany him on a buffalo hunt since their food supplies were low.

On August 26, 1867, the Bannocks, led by Taghee, agreed to meet with Ballard to remove by June 1, 1868, to the Fort Hall Reservation. They agreed to move on the condition that they be allowed their annual buffalo hunts, which were a necessity for them because of the government's failure to provide adequate annuities as agreed in the 1863 peace treaties. The Boise and Bruneau Shoshonis and the Bannocks came under no ratified treaties whereby they might receive annuities. The failure to implement the August 26 agreement left the Bannocks on June 1, 1868, without a reservation. Having suffered some defections among his people, Taghee roamed with his followers between Soda Springs and the Wind River country of western Wyoming, mingling at Fort Bridger with the peoples of his brother-in-law Washakie.

Agents at Boise City and Fort Bridger repeatedly requested the government to make a formal treaty with the Bannocks in order to have them removed to a reservation. The 1863 treaty provisions were now outmoded. They had served the purposes of whites, permitting their settlement, but had not provided for removing the Indians out of their way. An Indian peace commission created in 1867 was sent in 1868 to treat with the Bannocks and with Washakie's Eastern Shoshonis. When the commission arrived at Fort Bridger on June 15, the Bannocks under Taghee and the Shoshonis under Washakie were there to confer with it. The assembled Indians listened to the usual commissioner talk about how they should go to a permanent reservation to receive subsistence and live in peace with themselves and whites.

Taghee expressed a wish for a reservation in southeastern Idaho Territory in the general area of Soda Springs, Portneuf River, and Camas Prairie. One commissioner proposed to the chief that he remove permanently to Wind River to live with the Shoshonis on the reserve that Washakie had requested at that place. Taghee replied that his people were friends of the Shoshonis and hunted with them, but wanted a home of their own, something the commissioners could not understand. On July 3, 1868, the terms of a treaty were explained to the chiefs, and they signed that very day. Other treaty articles provided that, when the Bannocks wished to remove to a reservation, or when the president believed that they should be removed to one, a tract would be selected for them in their own country. They also retained the right to hunt on lands still unoccupied by whites. This Fort Bridger treaty was proclaimed February 24, 1869.

The Bannocks in the meantime were in such dire straits that four thousand dollars was immediately disbursed to them. On April 13, 1869, Agent Powell completed moving 1,150 Boise and Bruneau Shoshonis to Fort Hall, where the erection of buildings was begun. That spring Taghee and eight hundred Bannocks went off to buffalo with Washakie. Tendoy and his Shoshonis, now called the Lemhis, were in east-central Idaho Territory and western Montana Territory on no reservation at all, along with various Bannock bands

not under Taghee and a few lodges of Sheepeaters. The Lemhis were reported by Montana Territorial Governor Thomas F. Meagher to be in "misery, filth, and dire want." They signed a treaty at Virginia City, September 24, 1868. The Montana superintendent of Indian affairs had first arranged for Tendoy's people to go on the Crow Reservation, which was established by treaty on May 7, 1868. The first treaty of Fort Laramie, dated September 17, 1851, was to have established the Lemhis on that reservation, but was not ratified. Holding out for a reservation of his own, Tendoy refused to take his Shoshonis and scattered Bannocks there, as he also had refused to take them to Fort Hall. The September, 1868, treaty calling for a reservation for the Lemhis went unratified. Returning to southeastern Idaho Territory, Taghee asked that he and his people be allowed to go to the Fort Hall Reservation. On July 30, 1869, President Ulysses S. Grant signed an executive order providing them a permanent home on that confine.

Starvation, which during the sixties and seventies forced the Shoshonis, Bannocks, and Paiutes onto the lands of other peoples, produced intertribal conflict. Before making their usual buffalo kill on their annual hunt in 1867, Washakie and his people were chased by Sioux and Cheyennes back to Fort Bridger in destitute condition. The following year he and his band were again attacked, this time by three hundred Sioux, Cheyennes, and Arapahos led by the son of Sioux chief Red Cloud. Washakie had more troubles, for after the establishment of the Wind River Reservation whites plotted to oust him from a portion of it. In 1872, Indian Board Commissioner Felix Brunot asked that a northern portion of the reservation be withdrawn. Washakie yielded to the request because it was a less desirable piece of land for his Indians.

In 1869, Bannocks at Fort Hall were unhappy at having to travel to Washakie's Wind River Reservation to receive annuity goods. The Wind River Agency officials were also unhappy at their coming. It was their task to provide for the Bannocks' subsistence while they remained there through the winter on Washakie's invitation. There was friction among the Indians at Fort Hall when its agent issued treaty-authorized goods to the Boise and Bruneau Shoshonis there but not to the Bannocks, whose annuities were issued at Wind River. On the complaint of the Wind River agent the commissioner directed that, beginning in 1873, Bannock goods be sent to Fort Hall. The directive was one thing; receipt of the goods was another. For the next decade there was not enough money, food, and clothing appropriated for the Indians of either agency. Consequently the Bannocks, the Wind River Shoshonis, and other buffalo-hunting Shoshonis were forced to continue their always dangerous treks to the plains. In 1868, the Sioux, who were themselves seeking to survive on ever-narrowing buffalo ranges, drove the Bannocks and Wind River Shoshonis from the Yellowstone country. The Fort Hall agent, W. H. Danilson, had tried to carry out the wishes of the white community that Indians be confined to the reservation to subsist on its natural foods, which he believed ample for them. The new agent, J. N. High, who arrived in January, 1871, knew better. He

Jack Tendoy (Uriewici), a Shoshoni, was a member of the Bannock-Shoshoni delegation from the Lemhi and Fort Hall agencies who signed a treaty in Washington, D.C., May 14, 1880.

Smithsonian Institution National Anthropological Archives, Bureau of American Ethnology Collection, Neg. No. 1671-A.

made no complaint when his Indians left the reserve in search of food. The Lemhis crossed the Bitterroot Mountains in a single band, moving east across the Rockies to hunt in the country south of the Mussellshell River. They returned before the onset of winter. Other buffalo-hunting bands continued to leave Fort Hall in the late summer or fall during the early seventies for the same country, but they wintered on the plains not only because early Yellowstone snows blocked their homeward passage but also because they sought a few additional weeks of spring hunting. Returning to Fort Hall in May or June after a nine-month absence, they proceeded to Camas Prairie to harvest roots, after which they continued west into the Weiser country, grazing their horses until the end of summer. Returning to Fort Hall, which was well situated between hunting areas on

the north and east and root-gathering grounds on the south and west, they completed a circuit of over a thousand miles. The Boise and Bruneau Shoshonis were less inclined and equipped for buffalo hunting and were hard pressed to survive on the reservation. Their plight did not improve when other small Shoshoni bands in equally dire straits kept drifting there to live. To help solve the problem of their destitution, but perhaps more to prevent them from going to war with whites over it, the Idaho superintendent of Indian affairs wrung from the territorial government a $3,000 blanket fund for Taghee's Bannocks.

It was on a buffalo-hunting search for subsistence that Taghee died in 1871. With his death the Bannocks fragmented in their search for a successor. One group went with Bannock Jim. Most others went with Otter Beard (Pansook-

Three unidentified women beside a tipi on the Fort Hall Reservation. Photograph taken in the 1870s by William H. Jackson.

Smithsonian Institution National Anthropological Archives, Bureau of American Ethnology Collection, Neg. No. 1716-A.

motse). Many others wished to follow Taghee's son, Pat Largy (Pat Tyhee), but, as he was only sixteen years old, they went with those who joined Otter Beard. Solicitous for their welfare, Otter Beard called for a meeting with yet another agent, M. P. Berry. At that council, which was held in July, 1871, Otter Beard received only promises in response to his demands for food and clothing for his people. They were forced to winter in the buffalo country of Montana. They lost Otter Beard's intercessory services with his death in 1874. When offered the chieftaincy of the Fort Hall Bannock-Shoshonis, Tendoy refused the position. He and his people spent most of their time east of the Rockies seeking survival.

Commissioners had wished to have Tendoy become chief at Fort Hall to facilitate councils with the Bannocks and Shoshonis. The commissioner of Indian affairs arranged a meeting with them on August 25, 1873, but so few Bannocks appeared that another meeting was held from November 5 through 7. Besides wishing to reduce the Fort Hall Reservation, whose boundaries whites were already violating, the commissioner sought to abrogate Article 4 of the Fort Bridger Treaty, which guaranteed the Indians' off-reservation hunting rights. The commissioners were also eager to corral scattered Shoshonis and drive them onto the reservation. One whom they wished to confine there was Pocatello, who led about two hundred Shoshonis. In July,

1871, Agent High had sought to arrest him for depredations committed by a dozen of his so-called "outlaws" between Salt Lake City and Montana. Nevertheless, Pocatello did attend the November council. In December, High recommended that his band be confined in order to remove them from the influence of the Mormons, who encouraged Indians to commit depredations against white gentiles. Most of the Northwestern Shoshonis, whose chiefs had signed the Box Elder Treaty of July, 1863, agreed to remove to Fort Hall. Pocatello and 101 of his people removed there, as did 124 under San Pitch and 188 under Sagwitch. A 17-person band under Taviwunsher did not remove. Nearly 2,000 Western Shoshonis of Nevada and about 500 of Tendoy's followers refused to accede to the recommendation of the commissioner of Indian affairs that they be sent to Fort Hall. They held out until they were finally given a 64,000 acre reservation in the Lemhi Valley by an executive order dated February 12, 1875.

When the Bannocks of Fort Hall returned to their reservation from their winter hunt in the spring of 1874, their agent, having no food for them, sent them out on a summer hunt. In searching for food, many Indians absented themselves from the reservation for an entire year. During the winter of 1874–75 the Fort Hall beef supplies ran out, forcing many who remained there to subsist on reduced rations for the rest of the winter. In disgust the Bannocks again left to hunt buffalo. During the next winter over a third of them were east of the Rockies. By April, 1876, the absence of food issues left over a thousand Bannocks and Shoshonis to their own resources seeking food on the snow-covered countryside, begging piteously for something to feed their crying children.

With food in their own stomachs the whites accused the red men of plundering, murder, and other crimes, even blaming them for breaking away from their reservations to hunt buffalo, which was now almost a meatless undertaking. Aware of their own lack of influence on the authorities in Washington, D.C., the Indians in July, 1876, sought a conference with Idaho Territorial Governor D. P. Thompson seeking to have him intercede for them in the national capital.

Before the end of the decade increasing unrest born of deprivation of the very necessities of life would cause the Bannock-Paiute War. The cunning of the Bannocks' Paiute allies was sharpened by the struggle to survive on the harsh lands of south-central and eastern Oregon, and they were determined to remain on them no matter how difficult it was to survive. Their efforts to resist both the red and the white men who were attempting to invade and appropriate their lands make one of the most poignant annals of American Indian history.

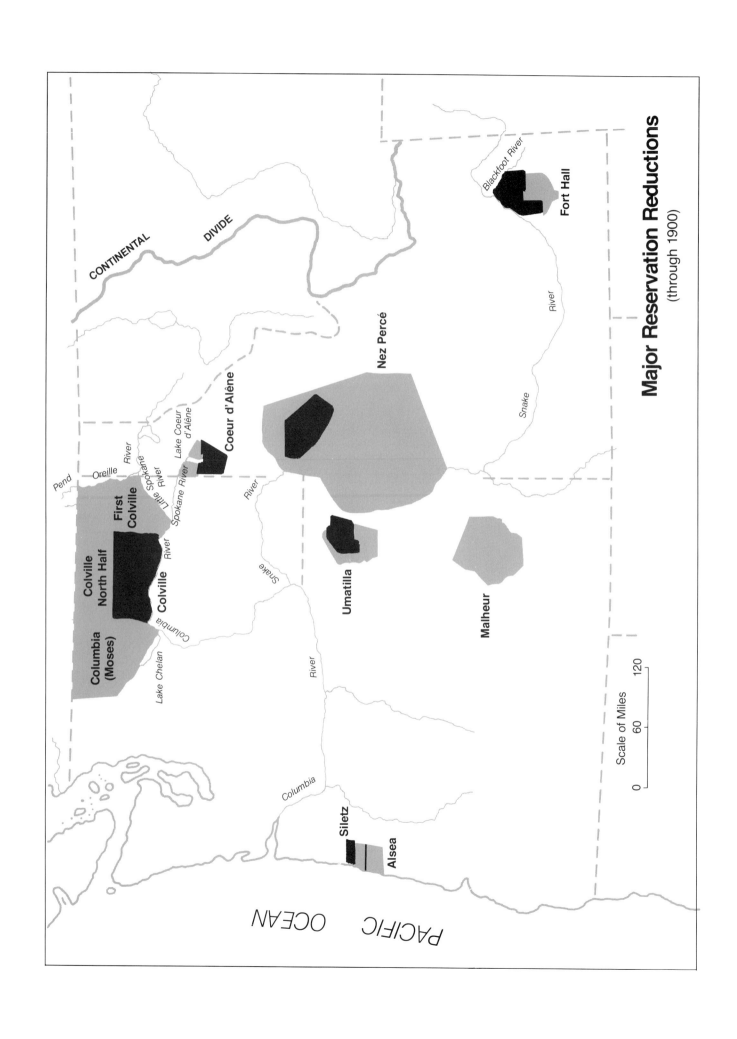

Major Reservation Reductions
(through 1900)

19. PAIUTE PREDICAMENT

At the close of the Spokane-Coeur d'Alène War in the fall of 1858 white officials had planned to open the interior to travel and settlement. The move was made possible by victories in the war and made official by General W. S. Harney's October 31, 1858, revocation of General John E. Wool's order closing the area. In anticipation of Indian opposition to the increase in American immigration, the Oregon legislature had asked for troops to patrol the Immigrant Road in Shoshoni country and for the establishment of a military post in the Fort Boise area. Shoshoni and Bannock tribesmen avoided as much as possible the military who traversed the route from Fort Vancouver to Utah, but continued to harass immigrants moving across southern Idaho Territory. At the same time the Paiutes of southeastern and south-central Oregon—which had hitherto been relatively free of white encroachment—began to see their isolation from the white men erode.[1]

The Paiutes fell into five groupings: Yahuskin (or Yahooskin and the like), Walpapi (or Woolpape, Walapi, and the like), Wahtatkin, Iukespiule, and Hoonebooey (or Woodnebooey and the like). As noted, in precontact times the Paiutes altered the lives of the natives in their way along the Columbia River. In the nineteenth century they were forced south by the Wascos and Teninos, who in 1857 began removing to the Warm Springs Reservation. A mid-century truce between the Paiutes and those peoples broke down about 1855 after the Paiutes murdered two Teninos. Paiutes began raiding the Warm Springs Reservation and its environs, which were on the periphery of Paiute territory. To avenge the depredations, which included thefts of reservation cattle and horses, the Warm Springs physician, Dr. Thomas L. Fitch, organized fifty-three Warm Springs Indians as a vigilante force. With rifles and ammunition supplied by the military at The Dalles, they set out to attack the Paiutes. It was a dangerous undertaking because the latter had increased their own supplies of arms and ammunition by raiding both whites and Indians. In April, 1859, the party attacked a Paiute camp in the John Day River country killing ten men and capturing women and children.

The situation on the Warm Springs Reservation was so explosive that on July 14, 1859, the agent, A. P. Dennison, requested the establishment of a military post there for protection from the raiding Paiutes. In early August about two hundred of these raiders swept down on the Warm Springs. They carried off agency property including many cattle and horses. They flaunted a white man's scalp in front of Dr. Fitch before driving off the stock. On August 7, Fitch wrote Agent Dennison at The Dalles: "Directed to any White man—For God's sake send some help as soon as possible. We are surrounded with Snakes—they have killed a good many Indians, and got all our stock—don't delay a single minute."

Flushed by their successes, the Paiutes continued raiding nightly from September 30 into early October. In response to frantic pleas for help, troops were dispatched to the reservation and temporarily retrieved two large herds of livestock. Other troops stationed there in the fall of 1860 quieted the situation, but their withdrawal the next year exposed the reservation and its inhabitants to renewed Paiute attacks.

The Paiutes of central Oregon had enjoyed relative isolation from whites. Their vast upland country was blocked off from seaborne moisture by the Cascade Mountains, which act, in the words of the Oregon journalist-poet Joaquin Miller, like "mighty milestones along the way of the clouds!—marble pillars pointing the road to God." The natives' relative isolation was broken in the summer of 1859 when a wagon road was constructed from The Dalles up John Day River and over to the Snake. Travelers on it avoided the steep pull through the Blue Mountains on the Immigrant Road from the Grande Ronde Valley to the Umatilla. There was heavy traffic over this central-Oregon road in 1861 and 1862: miners, freighters, packsaddle and wagon trains, and stagecoaches heading for the gold fields on the John Day, Burnt, and Powder rivers. It resembled the rush to the Boise Basin, where goldmining operations were being developed at the same time. Discoveries in the Oregon interior and southern Idaho prompted one agent to report, "Gold may be truly said to be the lever which moves the world." In this case it moved gold seekers roughshod through the Indian world, forcing native inhabitants to retaliate with an arsenal of aboriginal and American weaponry.

After gold was discovered in the Canyon City, Oregon, area in 1862, the Paiutes attacked five miners. They killed two of them west of that town on a tributary of the John Day south fork, later known as Murderers Creek, and in 1863 they attacked a packtrain fifteen miles out of Canyon City. In December of that year Oregon Governor A. C. Gibbs responded to the whites' request for troops to remove the Indian roadblocks to their progress and dispatched Oregon Cavalry Volunteers to Canyon City. From there the volunteers trailed Indians to Harney Lake in southeastern Oregon, defeating them and Paiute reinforcements from Nevada and Utah in an April, 1864, fight later known as the Battle of Harney Lake. That area was also the scene of combat in 1860 between Paiutes and army regulars under Major Enoch Steen, who was dispatched from his camp near Harney Lake to Crooked River, a Snake tributary in southeastern Oregon, to track them down. At the same time on the Owyhee a large Paiute band forced troops under Captain Smith to fall back to Harney Lake.

With Steen were Indian scouts recruited from the Warm Springs Reservation proud and itching for revenge against their ancient Paiute foes. Warm Springs braves had previously been in the government's employ. One named Billy Chinook had served with Frémont as early as 1843 because he wished to "see the whites." After Steen's scouts discovered a Paiute band on the north side of a butte called Steens Mountain, Steen's troops chased them to the summit and down the other side through a narrow gorge, where the Indians lost three men and several women and children to their pursuers.

Paiute harassment of miners and settlers continued, as did Bannock depredations in southern Idaho Territory. In 1864 whites began a concerted drive against the Indians, which was part of what were later known as the Snake Wars of 1864 to 1868. Despite the white men's fortifications dotting the Oregon interior in 1864, Indians continued their depredations as they eluded the troops. In their deadly game of hide-and-seek they had some advantages. They knew every inch of their vast, remote valley-and-mountain homeland as they did the backs of their tawny hands. The land was scorched by the summer suns and frozen under winter skies. As soldiers sweltered in summer heat, the Paiutes retreated to cool places where their people had repaired for years. The same winter that froze the soldiers' whiskers provided the Paiutes with snow on which to employ such ancient ruses as stepping in one track to make it appear that only one Indian was there. Ordinarily, when fleeing their foes, they disbanded in a dozen directions to dissolve into the silent landscape.

The winter of 1863–64 was scarcely passed before the Paiutes emerged from their fastnesses to continue their raids. In March, hunger-driven, they ate some of the hundred horses and mules that they had captured from a ranch outside Canyon City and then fled to other places to repeat their raidings and feastings. Near Rock Creek, sixty miles west of Canyon City, they captured a stagecoach, broke open an express box, and took its buckskin bindings rather than its gold—an action that in itself revealed their previous isolation from whites.

Walpapi chief Paulina (or Pahninee, Pauninna, Polini, and the like) was trailed over the Blue Mountains through Harney Valley to Steens Mountain by the forces of Lieutenant James A. Waymire and a seventy-man volunteer citizen outfit under Joaquin Miller. Paulina's band had ranged from the upper Deschutes River across Crooked River to the upper John Day River. The Indians were no strangers to white men. In 1859, Paulina had been imprisoned by Agent Dennison on the Warm Springs Reservation along with Weahwewa (Weyouwewa, Weow-wowa, Yewhaweya, and the like), the leader of a Kidutokado Paiute band whose territory was farther south and east of the Malheur and Burnt rivers and Harney Lake. In that same year they had served as guides to Captain H. D. Wallen's wagon-road expedition in central Oregon. They had escaped from the party, taking horses and rifles with them. Not much was heard of Paulina until 1864, when his people burned houses and other properties east of Warm Springs on the John Day River.

At the eastern base of Steens Mountain the combined troops of Waymire and Miller were defeated by a sizeable force under Paulina and Weahwewa. On word of the defeat General Alvord, commander of the District of Oregon, ordered Captain John M. Drake out of Fort Dalles and Captain George B. Currey out of Fort Walla Walla into the Paiute country. They were to travel by different routes to track down the Indians and then join forces near Harney Lake, where they were to attack the red men with the troops under Waymire and Miller.

On the night of May 18 the Paiutes were assembled near the crossing of Crooked River, four or five miles below the fork and about twelve miles northeast of Camp Maury (which was about 115 miles southeast of Fort Dalles and five miles above a fork of Crooked River). They sang and danced among the junipers while their horses grazed on a little flat above their camp. After midnight the singing and dancing stopped. Toward morning the camp stirred with alarm. It had been discovered by a detachment of twenty-five mounted Tenino and Wasco scouts from the Warm Springs Reservation. They were accompanying Drake's command, who had arrived at their depot, Camp Maury. As recently as early May the scouts had fought Paulina and his band near the head of McKay Creek, a Crooked River tributary, and they were eager to continue the fight.

Seeking to fortify themselves before the impending attack, the Paiutes scrambled to a rocky ledge three hundred yards from their camp. Armed with twenty rifles and bows and arrows, forty or fifty Paiutes fought desperately to defend themselves. They killed a lieutenant and two privates and wounded four other privates and a corporal. They stripped and mutilated on the spot the body of an Indian scout whom they had killed as they also did the bodies of the dead soldiers. Chief Stockwhitley, a Warm Springs scout and former inmate of the Fort Vancouver guardhouse, was cut down in a hail of bullets. He shortly died of his wounds. Three of Paulina's band were killed, and fifty-seven horses lost, as well as all the camp gear. The Warm Springs scouts still believed Paulina to be bulletproof when he and his band escaped into the hills with nothing but their guns. That night he and his followers recaptured seven of their horses from the soldiers' camp and then fled eastward into the mountains between Crooked River and the Canyon City Road. During the next month with about fifty warriors Paulina attacked and robbed whites on that road. By June 24 the band had moved farther south near Silver Lake. From there Paulina went to Sprague River Valley to try to entice the Klamaths into his war against whites.

When news of the deaths in the May 18 fight reached the Warm Springs Reservation, about seventy warriors left there to join their fellow scouts in tracking down and capturing Paiute women, children, and horses. Their treatment of captives was harsh (as was the traditional Paiute treatment of theirs). They ran sticks into them, they pinioned children to the ground and roasted them in the fire, and on one occasion, when four Tenino scouts wanted a captured Paiute girl, they cut her in enough pieces to go around. The Warm Springs braves with Currey relentlessly hunted down their Paiute foes. On June 13 the Paiutes fired on them, chasing them to within eight miles of Camp Henderson (which had

Chief Paulina, leader of Paiute bands in central Oregon. Paulina staunchly opposed the efforts of the United States government to confine him and his people on a reservation. Oregon Historical Society.

been established by Currey five miles below the mouth of Jordan River on Gibbs Creek, an Owyhee tributary). On the sixteenth, after the Paiutes had engaged the entire Camp Henderson forces in a fight, Currey abandoned the post.*

With summer the Paiutes increased their raids at various locations, including those around Canyon City. In July, at one ranch outside that place, they jerked posts from a stockade that was protecting horses from attack and made off with forty animals. To curb such attacks and to protect the Canyon City Road, the military in September established Camp Watson west of Canyon City. Perhaps lack of ammunition prevented further Paiute raids, for they had abandoned their supplies the preceding year in a defile on the Bruneau River when fleeing from a fight with troops under Colonel Maury.

---

*Camp Lyon was established the next year on Cow Creek about forty-five miles to the northeast, closer to the Owyhee mines.

Ten Cayuses joined the Washington Territorial Volunteers as scouts in the fight against their mutual Paiute foe. Like the Indians from the Warm Springs Reservation the Cayuses itched to settle old scores with the *twelka* ("enemy"), whose custom it was to steal their women, children, and horses. Near the middle of July the Cayuse scouts discovered Paulina's camp in Paulina Valley west of Canyon City. As the Cayuses and the troops moved along the south Fork of the John Day River (where the military had established Camp Lincoln on March 15), they came under Paiute rifle fire. The soldiers hoped to flush out their red foes by ascending the sides of the canyon where the Indians were positioned. An hour later the troops reached the top of the canyon, from which they chased their foes until noon the following day. By then the troops had arrived north of Burns, Oregon. The Indians fled into the Harney Lake country.

A little later in July, Paulina again turned west, where he appears to have enlisted small Paiute bands in his fight. At a small lake west of Camp Alvord on the east side of Steens Mountain in Alvord Desert, he joined twenty-three lodges of Paiutes. Later in July he moved to Goose Lake, where his band killed two men of a wagon train and captured 350 head of cattle, driving them to Warner Mountain, a Paiute stronghold. There Paulina and his people feasted on cattle and kept watch on Colonel Charles S. Drew and his troops out of Fort Klamath, who were maneuvering in the area that summer. Paulina twice planned to attack them and twice changed his mind.

As the Paiutes struggled against their pursuers, the tribes of the southern Oregon interior continued despite reversals to oppose the white pressure against them. Like other interior tribes they were affected by Paiute aggressions. Their tribalism prevented their combining with other peoples, although alliances might have checked if not prevented the Paiute attacks as well as the white aggressions. The Modocs, Klamaths, and Shastas continued to war against one another despite marital and economic ties. Slave raids on the Pit River Indians and the Shastas helped prevent the Klamaths from combining with those two peoples. Ancient hatreds also helped to prevent unification of the southern tribes with northern ones, such as those of the Warm Springs and Umatilla reservations, and with the nomadic Paiutes. The invading whites and their protectors, the military, were the beneficiaries of this factionalism, which they skillfully worked into their strategems for controlling Indians.

With the Paiute shadow always over them, the Klamaths and Modocs continued to have their troubles. The two tribes were placed under a special agent, Thomas Pyle, and permitted to remain in Jacksonville, Oregon, during the winter of 1861. They would have starved if they had returned to their homes. In the spring they were told by their agent to return home. Oregon-Washington Superintendent of Indian Affairs Edward R. Geary believed the arrangement to be humanitarian. The whites regarded it as harassment. Hitherto, when the Klamaths and Modocs had visited Jacksonville and Yreka for short stays, the white

Nettie Wright, a Klamath woman, and her daughter, Neva. Note the basket hats. *Southern Oregon Historical Society.*

citizens had been on relatively friendly terms with them, although the Indians often came, in the words of an army officer, to "barter squaws to dissolute white men." The restriction on their movements was bitter medicine to chiefs such as the Modoc Keintpoos (or Kintpush, Kintpuash, and the like). Keintpoos was nicknamed Captain Jack by Judge Elijah Steele. He was the son of a chieftain father killed fighting the Teninos near the headwaters of the Deschutes River.

The Indians did not want the citizens of white communities coming into their country, having experienced trouble with those who did. In the spring of 1859, in one of their more violent confrontations with whites, they killed five of them asleep in a camp at the head of Butte Creek in Jackson County. The Klamaths were a people two thousand strong possessing many cattle and horses. In May, 1860, they frightened a member of the British Boundary Commission, John Keast Lord, as he traversed their lands. The Klamath chief La Lakes (also Lelaks, Lalacas, and the like) appeared to Lord a "sot and sensualist...[a] flabby, red-eyed, dirt-begrimed savage...greed, cruelty, and cunning visible in every twist of the mouth and twinkle of the piglike eyes." La Lakes possessed seven wives. His emergence as head chief indicates political centralization among the

Klamaths—centralization that was soon to work to the advantage of the United States government, which encouraged it. Lord introduced himself as a King George chief of the British monarch. He warned that, if he was harmed, his king would surely burn Klamath lodges, drive off their horses, kill their braves, and perhaps hang La Lakes himself. Lord smoked the pipe with the chief and then moved north to The Dalles—with his mules and scalp intact.[2] La Lakes traveled to The Dalles shortly after, accompanied by two other Klamath headmen, George and Toontucte (or Kumtucky). For years he had traded there the women and horses he captured from Pit River Indians. He is also known to have traveled to the Willamette Valley to plead the cause of his tribesmen with white officials.

The Klamaths might have met the whites in a more hostile fashion if immigration over the South Road had not slowed during the Rogue War. In the early sixties, as travel over that road slowly resumed, the Klamaths continued to challenge white travelers. In 1861 the Modocs, who continued to resent the white immigrants, stole over nine hundred head of their stock. With ammunition purchased in Yreka and Jacksonville the Klamaths and Modocs in the summer of 1864 committed depredations against whites north and east of Klamath Lake and sold ammunition to Yahuskin Paiutes living around Summer Lake in Lake Country, Oregon. To check those activities, three military

A Columbia Plateau woman wearing the basket hat and strips of weasel fur in her braids. From a painting by William F. Reese.

expeditions were sent against the Klamaths and Modocs in the summer of 1864, and Fort Klamath was built north of Upper Klamath Lake under an order dated March 23, 1863. At that time the two tribes planned war against the whites of southern Oregon and northern California.

The two tribes may have seen some advantage in having the military in their midst. Possibly they believed the troops could protect them from the Paiutes, who were raiding both whites and Indians from one end of the Oregon interior to the other. When Lord was among the Klamaths, they had just lost seventeen of their livestock to Paiute raiders. In 1859 about half the Klamaths were reported to have considered a proposal to join the Modocs and Paiutes in a war against the whites. At the same time the Klamaths feared the Paiutes and feared their chief, Howlark (or Howlah, Howlash, Qualuck, and the like), a well-known shaman, who had led the devastating raids in early August, 1859, on the Warm Springs Reservation and who was believed capable of killing soldiers by merely waving his hand. Some Indians had considered fleeing to Jacksonville because they were so frightened of this leader, whose far-ranging band roamed from Goose Lake east to the Owyhee River and south to the Humboldt. In the summer of 1864 troops went to the Paiute country to rescue a band of prospectors, who, like the Klamaths and Modocs, were the objects of Paiute forays.

Judge Steele was now Indian agent for northern California. His intercession on behalf of the Klamaths, Modocs, and Shastas won for him their respect, but their problem of finding subsistence remained. During the winter of 1863–64 the military tried to relieve their suffering by issuing them beef and flour from stores at Fort Klamath, but hardly enough to keep them alive. In mid-February, 1864, the Klamaths under La Lakes, the Modocs under Schonchin, and the Shastas under their chiefs worked out a treaty or agreement with Judge Steele. They promised to cease intertribal squabbling and raids on the Pit River tribes, to turn over violators of the peace to the military, and to allow immigrants free passage through their country, charging them only for ferriage. They also agreed not to get drunk or steal, not to rob Chinese sluice miners, not to carry bows and arrows, not to sell their wives and children, and to come to towns only in daytime and with passes for their own protection.

Steele also intervened in a Modoc dispute over tribal leadership. Schonchin, the Modocs' old warrior chief on Sprague River, had seen the futility of fighting whites and had softened his attitude toward them. Others, such as his son John, opposed concessions to them, as did Captain Jack from the Tule Lake area. The posture of John and Captain Jack was reinforced by the teachings of a Dreamer prophet, who was like the Dreamer on the Warm Springs Reservation, the influential Tyigh prophet Queahpahmah. Through Steele's good offices an election was held pitting traditionalist antiwhites against Schonchin. When the count was tallied, Captain Jack was elected Modoc head chief. Steele also negotiated an agreement with the Modocs whereby they yielded some lands in return for assurances that they would retain their lands around Tule Lake. Since

Steele was agent for the Indians of northern California, his treaties and agreements involving Oregon tribes were unauthorized and hence went unratified.

There was much clamor from settlers, especially in the Lost River area, to have the Indians of the lake country confined through more official treaties. In August, 1864, Superintendent Huntington met Indian representatives in a preliminary session to arrange an October council at Upper Klamath Lake. At the appointed time over a thousand Indians gathered on the council grounds to effect a treaty. Huntington delivered a speech and then dangled before them various articles, such as red paint, beads, buttons, blankets, and fishhooks. He asked how much land they wished reserved for themselves. When they told him, he said it was too much. After reconsidering, they reduced their request. The chiefs signed a treaty on October 14 for about 700 Klamaths, 339 Modocs, and 22 Yahuskin Paiutes.* They yielded about 20 million acres in exchange for about 1,107,847. One reservation was designated for the three tribes. It was located in south-central Oregon along the east side of Upper Klamath Lake and extended northwest to Crater Lake. In addition, the tribes were to receive money payments for fifteen years as well as shops, mills, schools, and so on. The Klamaths, in whose country the reservation was located, were understandably more willing to be settled there than the Modocs and Yahuskins were. The Modocs were not friends of the Klamaths and might have signed less willingly had they not seen in the treaty the possibility of forming an alliance with other reservation tribes to protect themselves from Walpapi raids. After the treaty proceedings, La Lakes, acting on behalf of government officials, carried a peace message to Paulina, whose raiders were foraying against the Klamaths, Modocs, and whites passing through the Silver and Summer lake country.

The successful conclusion of the treaty for the government must have helped to convince Huntington that the government should not pursue a military hard line against the warring Paiutes.† He wrote to the secretary of the interior on December 12, 1864:

Numerous military expeditions have been sent against them, but the nature of their country, their nomadic and fierce character give the Indians such advantage that it is not exaggeration to say that

ten good soldiers *are required to wage successful war* against one Indian. *Every Indian killed or captured by the Government has cost the Government fifty thousand dollars at least. Economy then indicates that it is much cheaper to feed them than to fight them.*

About eight tons of flour were left at Fort Klamath to quiet Indians that winter and to convince them that the government was acting in good faith.

Three Paiute men, three women, and two children were overtaken in the Deschutes headwaters by the homeward-bound Huntington party. When the Paiute men tried to seize the party's guns, the latter fired on the Indians, killing one. One of those captured was Paulina's wife, who was taken to Fort Vancouver and turned over to military authorities. On November 1, 1864, Paulina sent a Paiute messenger, Skytiat-titk, to Fort Klamath to protest the killing and the capture of his people, and ten days later he came himself. The fort's commander, Captain William Kelly, had been told by Huntington to assure the chief that the Indians of the Warm Springs Reservation would not make war on him and that he should not raid that agency and should give a wide berth to what Huntington called "the Road" (Canyon City Road?) Paulina told Kelly that he was weary of war but wished to have his women, children, and horses returned from the military and that he wished to live with his people between Fort Klamath and The Dalles east of the Klamath Trail near a large mountain there (perhaps Mount Paulina).

Paulina's followers now numbered about five hundred, including the women and children. In April, 1865, Paulina sent word to Kelly that he was advising them to be friendly and that Huntington should arrange for a peace talk. With Paulina's peaceful moves Huntington brought the captured women and children to the Klamath Reservation, except for a sick woman and child, who were left at the Warm Springs Reservation. On August 12, 1865, Paulina and his people finally submitted to signing a treaty with the government. The setting for the council was Yainax ("The Mountain") in the Sprague River Valley north of the California border and east of the southern end of Upper Klamath Lake. This was an ancient gathering and trading place of interior tribes from the Columbia River to California. An Oregon historian, S. A. Clarke, wrote:

There came to Yainax, the thoroughbred tribal aristocracy; beauty had to be adorned, and no expense was spared to outfit with feathers, beads and paint candidates for matrimony of both sexes. The belles had rings on ankles, fingers and wrists, and bells on their toes, with nose quills to make up the tout ensemble———and when Octobers were gone, then the silence that ruled the region returned and possessed all nature until another autumn should come and another carnival time dawn on the sombre brown that in October clothes hills and plain at Yainax.[3]

By the terms of the treaty, which was ratified on July 5, 1866, Paulina yielded his people's vast southern-Oregon lands for confinement on the Klamath Reservation in the Sprague River Valley, where he was told to remain. He

---

*Erminie Wheeler Voegelin states that some ethnologists believe that the Yahuskins were not an aboriginal, localized, and organized group of Northern Paiutes and that they probably were just a few free-roaming Indians who were induced to treat at the council. They ceded the area of the Silver, Summer, and Abert lakes, a total of about 5,000 square miles, north of their customary range, which was around Goose Lake. The term "Yahooskin" did not appear in previous literature and was formulated at the time of the treaty to identify these people. It appears that the Indians who lived on the Klamath Reservation were "upland mixed groups of borderline Klamath-Northern Paiute" from the Sprague River Valley. The Indians who later were termed Yahuskins were a mixed group of Klamaths and Northern Paiutes who did not live in the area originally ceded by the Yahuskins. "The Northern Paiute of Central Oregon: A Chapter in Treaty-Making," *Ethnohistory* 2, no. 2, Part 1 (Spring, 1955): 95–132.

†The treaty was ratified by Congress, July 2, 1866, and proclaimed February 17, 1870.

Walark Skidat (Dave Hill), a Klamath Indian delegate to Washington, D.C., in 1875. National Archives.

agreed to release all prisoners held and "to endeavor to induce" the Hoonebooey and Wahtatkin Paiutes to cease hostilities. Agent Lindsay B. Applegate chose La Lakes and the Yahuskin chief Moshenkosket (or Mozenkaskie) to help implement the agreement and to persuade the hostile Paiute chief Howlark to come in and make peace (in which endeavor La Lakes and Moshenkosket failed).

The Klamath Agency was established in 1865 in the heart of the Klamaths' permanent winter settlement at the upper end of Upper Klamath Lake, but it was not located there until May 12, 1866. Because the agency was in the lands of the Klamaths, the Modocs remained cool toward them. Fearing Paulina's people, the Klamaths moved in the

winter of 1865–66 from their homes at the upper end of the lake down to a temporary agency. Because they received no government supplies that winter and were starving, all but four of Paulina's men and eighteen of his women and children returned to winter in their old haunts on Summer Lake and Crooked River. They promised to return to the Klamath Reservation in the spring, but warrior factions prevented them from keeping their promise. On April 22, 1866, Paulina left the reserve to join his people. His erstwhile intermediary, Moshenkosket, shortly told Major William V. Rinehart that Howlark had induced Paulina to help him fight white men by leaving the reservation and that Paulina would never return, although some Paiutes would. When the treaty that Paulina had signed was ratified, only two of his Walpapi Paiutes were on the reservation, and they were there as captives. Their numbers at that place increased after Rinehart dispatched troops to herd them in.

Eluding the military, Paulina again took to the warpath as his band and other Paiutes continued attacking stage-coaches and trains of Idaho-bound prospectors. There were extensions of Paiute bands as far south as Nevada. Regulars and volunteers were operating against Chief Paulina from as far south as the northeast corner of California, south of Warner Mountain in Oregon. They were garrisoned at Camp Bidwell in Surprise Valley just south of the California border, at Camp Alvord on the east side of Steens Mountain, and at Old Camp Warner north of Lakeview, Oregon. The same country that only sparingly provided subsistence to the natives became their ally in eluding the soldiers. The Indians were chronically short of arms and ammunition, especially lead, and they fashioned bullets from iron rods cut from captured wagons. To minimize the impact of the bullets fired into their own bodies, they fashioned small wooden plugs to insert into wounds as stoppers.

Klamath agent Lindsay Applegate set about "civilizing" the less tractable Indians in his care. Unlike their Chinook sisters, Klamath women knew on the average but a dozen English words and were unfamiliar with the Chinook jargon. This was a reflection of Klamath isolation, as was the fact that until the middle of the nineteenth century they secured few guns in trade. Applegate instituted the putting away of hereditary chiefs and the sponsoring of elections to replace them. He also tried to have the Indians cut their hair—for reasons that were more symbolic than sanitary. Cutting their hair signified for them the severance from the old ways to walk the trail of "civilization."

Paulina and various other Paiute peoples avoided that trail in their struggle to remain free. In early summer, 1866, he and his braves attacked miners and teamsters in the Owyhee River Valley and eluded the troops sent to find them. They then backtracked into Sprague River Valley and attacked Schonchin's Modoc band. Gathering his braves at Goose Lake, Paulina swept down on the Klamath Agency. The few troops there managed to drive them off. Paulina's freedom was challenged not only by government officials seeking to confine him but also by the increasing intrusions of miners, ranchers, and immigrants.

One theater in which the drama of Indians seeking survival was enacted with much violence was the Owyhee mining country of southeastern Oregon and southwestern Idaho Territory. On May 11, 1866, when he had commanded Fort Boise but two months, Major L. H. Marshall, with eighty-four men met an Indian band between the South Fork and the Middle Fork of the Owyhee. From behind rocks the Indians fired on the troops in a four-hour fight, in which seven Indians were killed and several were wounded. The Indians held their ground. Their foe lost a raft and a howitzer in crossing the river. Marshall ordered a large supply of ammunition and provisions thrown into it to render them useless to his red foes. One Indian dragged a lassoed soldier up a bluff before his fellows rescued him.

On May 19, Indians raided unarmed Chinese miners on Battle Creek, an Owyhee tributary in southwestern Idaho. They killed and scalped over fifty of their helpless quarry. The road between The Dalles and Fort Boise was filled with so many marauding Paiutes that many travelers refused to carry valuables over it. In other quarters Indians continued robbing stages and killing the passengers. On June 30 on Boulder Creek, a Jordan Creek tributary, a Paiute band fought a citizen group to a standstill and then slipped away before help arrived from Camp Lyon (which had been established June 27, 1865, in the Owyhee River country near the Idaho-Oregon border). In August about thirty Indians were killed skirmishing Marshall and his troops in the Goose Creek Mountains of south-central Idaho. Indians of southeastern Oregon met troops whom they had previously beaten on the Owyhee, but this time were themselves badly beaten. Thirty-five of their number were left hanging in trees.

On the morning of July 17 an Indian camp on Rattle-snake Creek, a Snake tributary in southwestern Idaho, was discovered by a detachment of Lieutenant R. F. Bernard's command from Camp Watson. In an ensuing clash thirteen Indians were killed, and a large number wounded, before their main camp escaped with its supplies. The troops resumed the chase, discovering the Indians in a deep canyon flanked by nearly perpendicular walls a mile from their fight with the troops two days before. In their haste to avoid entrapment the Indians abandoned everything except arms and horses and then led Bernard and thirty men on a sixty-mile chase. Those afoot fell behind rocks, losing some of their women and children to the soldiers, while the mounted ones were pursued by other troops.

Paulina and a large warrior band were under constant pressure from the military, but on August 10, 1866, they repulsed their pursuers. In the fall his and other holdout Paiute bands lessened their depredations to gather winter food supplies. By October 1 only sixteen Paiute men and forty-four of their women and children had been taken captive on the Klamath Reservation. Among them were five signers of the Walpapi treaty of the previous year. On the night of the very day when they assured officials that sixty more of their people would move onto the confine, they fled it with two horses and five guns belonging to Moshenkosket's Indians.

In the meantime whites all the way from Washington Territory to Washington, D.C., pondered how to remove the marauding roadblocks to their own occupation. To help remove them, Congress authorized the recruiting of two companies of Warm Springs scouts under the command of Dr. William McKay and John Darragh with orders to kill all "hostiles." When McKay objected to killing women, Oregon Governor George L. Woods reminded him that they were as treacherous as their men, that they roasted white children alive before the very eyes of their mothers, as they had at the Ward massacre. The scouts were promised any booty captured from their foes, a further stimulus to track them down. At the close of the war they returned to the Warm Springs Reservation with sixty-two scalps and displayed them in a great dance. Their agent, Captain John Smith, curbed such ostentatious displays, prohibiting warriors from ornamenting shot pouches with scalps.

The employment of the scouts did little to reduce Paiute forays. In September, 1866, in one of several attacks against whites in the Canyon City area, the Paiutes attacked a stage, ripped open a mail sack, and scattered its contents, including money. In that same month a Paiute war party attacked a band of Warm Springs Indians within fifteen miles of the agency. By 1866, with the end of the Civil War, government troops had phased out the volunteers. Like their predecessors the regulars found it difficult to run down the elusive Paiutes. As the citizenry began to complain loudly of the military's failure, things began to change in the end of 1866. George Crook, now a lieutenant colonel and a well-seasoned Indian fighter, arrived on the scene as the new district commander of Fort Boise and gave a new look to the war.[4] His basic plan was simple: to get to the center of operations and move out in all directions as necessity dictated. Thus he secured the advantage of operating on interior lines and conducted movements that permitted no rest to his red foe. With typical U.S. Army scorn of local troops, he wrote that he feared riding behind them because, if Indians attacked, he would be trampled to death. With forty troops and twelve Warm Springs scouts he attacked about eighty Shoshonis from the Owyhee Valley. The Indians fled leaving thirty warriors dead and their women, children, and horses captured. From this victory Crook moved down the Owyhee River, where in a daylight attack in early January, 1867, he surprised some Indians, who lost sixty of their number as well as a large number of horses. Shortly his troops discovered a small Indian camp and killed five of the occupants capturing the remainder. On January 6, 1867, in the Malheur Lake area, McKay and his Warm Springs scouts brushed with the Paiutes, killing three men and capturing horses and ammunition. Paulina believed himself safe because he was fortified on a 2,000-foot mountain covered with nearly a foot and a half of snow, but, as he paused there, another Paiute camp was discovered, and twelve of its people were killed and others captured.

By mid-March, 1867, troops had begun patrolling the Canyon City Road after the Paiutes increased their raids on whites in the area. On April 25 eight Paiutes raided farms around Canyon City, taking cattle and horses. As the Paiutes feasted on cattle in the Paulina Valley near the junction of Trout Creek (a Deschutes tributary north of Crooked River) and Little Trout Creek (north of Ashwood, Oregon, in northeastern Jefferson County), they were jumped by troops trailing them and were gunned down in an all-day battle. Paulina was one victim, killed not by soldiers but by a rancher firing a Henry rifle. Weahwewa, the Kidutokado Paiute now assumed leadership of the holdout Paiute bands with Ocheo (or Ochoho, Otsehoe, and the like), another Kidutokado Paiute.

The whites continued to hound them. In the Pueblo Mountains, south of Steens Mountain in southern Harney County, Oregon, the Paiutes were attacked in July by Crook and the Warm Springs scouts. The latter were rewarded with thirty scalps for doing much of the fighting. While campaigning with Crook, another McKay, named Donald, led Warm Springs scouts and rescued his Indian wife, Zuletta, from a three-year captivity at the hands of the Paiutes.

Crook now shifted operations to south-central Oregon, hoping to check Indian excursions between that state and California, where horses stolen by the Paiutes were traded for arms and ammunition. A short time after Crook established his fall and winter headquarters at Camp Warner, the Indians of Warner Lake stampeded and captured many of his horses. On August 16, 1867, Camp Steele had been established at the mouth of Rattlesnake Canyon, which opens into Harney Lake Valley about seventy-five miles south of Canyon City. It was renamed Camp Harney on September 14.

On September 26, on the south fork of Pit River, Crook and his troops searched out about seventy-five Paiutes, about thirty Pit River Indians, and a few Modocs holed up in a lava-rock stronghold. Two days later, after showering the soldiers with arrows, the Indians escaped through cracks and fissures, much to the surprise of the troops. Pit River chief Sieta (Sietta) was killed in this fight of the "Infernal Caverns," according to the reluctant word of a captured Indian woman. In late September, 1868, the Pit Rivers received a summons from Crook, whom they remembered from the Rogue war and who now commanded the Department of the Columbia: they were to bring their own provisions and meet him. They responded by bringing odiferous ducklings in various stages of putrefaction. They arrived at the council grounds only to be sent across the river because they smelled so bad.* Crook had summoned them because whites had been killed below Surprise Valley in their lands. When they confessed that the murderers were their people, Crook asked them to surrender the guilty ones.

Between September 2 and 22, 1867, Indians of the Silver and Abert lake areas were hunted down by troops out of Fort Klamath. Twenty-three were killed, and fourteen captured. Over in the Owyhee and Boise countries continuing Indian depredations in the winter of 1867–68 elicited more countermeasures by the military. In May, 1868, the troops surprised a ten-lodge Paiute camp on the North Fork of the Malheur River near Castle Rock. They captured a Paiute subchief named Egan (or Egante, Eghante, and the like; also known as The Blanket Wearer). Professing peace, he agreed to bring in his warriors along with Chief Weahwewa.

In July the Paiutes of the Malheur and Warner lake regions surrendered to Crook. The Winnemuccas, a Paiute band from northwestern Nevada under Chief Winnemucca, were captured in July and taken to Fort Smith in

---

*The Pit River Indians, in concert with Paiutes and Modocs, killed several whites late in the spring of 1868. The 1864 treaty with the Klamaths, Modocs, and Yahuskin Paiutes seems to have ended Klamath and Modoc spring raids on the Pit Rivers, who were more peacefully disposed than the Shastas. Before 1864 the Klamaths, after killing Pit River men, sold the women and children into slavery as far from their homelands as The Dalles and the Willamette Valley. At the latter place in 1843 the Klamaths sold their slaves for three horses apiece, and some were sold more cheaply.

southeastern Oregon. Straggling bands in southwestern Idaho Territory were not brought in until August. Weahwewa was among the chiefs attending a July council with Crook at Fort Harney. He and his Paiutes were now indeed willing to surrender. Since December, 1866, they had engaged in over forty fights with their white foes. In council they heard Crook say that he was sorry that the Indians had stopped fighting because he could replace his dead soldiers with others, but they would have to wait for their children to grow up to replace their dead warriors. Softening, he told them that they could remain free as long as they were peaceful and surrendered stolen property. Superintendent Huntington, on the other hand, wished them confined and reminded them of the 1865 treaty. The government at that time had made Paulina the spokesman for all the Paiutes, and he had promised that they would go on the Klamath Reservation. Weahwewa and the Paiutes of the Malheur country said that they wished to go on the Siletz. A small portion of the Walpapis and other Paiutes from around Warner Lake consented to live on the east side of the Klamath Reservation.

In September, 1867, a few Walpapis had been brought in by the military to the Klamath Reservation. Since only nineteen in all were gathered, it appears that their presence there was but an excuse for officials to draw on appropriations provided for them by treaty. In August, 1868, officials corralled on the reservation a few more Walpapi Paiutes from the Silver Lake area. One of those brought in by the Klamath Agency physician, Dr. William McKay, was Chocktote (or Chocktoot), the leader of the Walpapi band from Summer Lake. The two Walpapi bands on the reservation now numbered 130 souls. On December 10, 1868, a treaty with the Paiutes of southeastern Oregon and southwestern Idaho—who had not treated previously with the government—failed of ratification.

At Camp Warner in November, 1869, the new superintendent, A. B. Meacham (who had replaced Huntington the previous May 15), met with the Indians of the area to continue the task of settling them. The influential Ocheo was present at the council. He had led Paulina's band in its last fight with the soldiers, and Crook had refused to shake his hand on his surrender. At the Camp Warner council Ocheo accepted the offer of a reservation home on the condition that his captured people were released. With the promise that they would be, his band removed to the Klamath Reservation, where they were fed during the winter of 1869–70. After 1869 not only the Walpapis from Warner Mountain under Ocheo but also the Yahuskins under Moshenkosket and Schonchin's Modoc band were at Yainax, thirty-three

miles east of the Klamath Agency. In March, 1870, twelve Walpapis from the area of the Silver and Summer lakes came to live on the reservation and promised to gather others of their people on that confine.

During that winter of 1869–70 the Indians at Yainax numbered between two and three hundred. They nearly starved because the Klamaths restricted their hunting, fishing, and root gathering and because government aid was insufficient. In the fall of 1871, Ocheo's band left the reservation because of hunger and was ordered back by Major Elmer Otis, who commanded the District of the Lakes. Reduced still further in numbers, they continued struggling to survive on meager government rations, but they were propelled from the reservation by a force stronger than any government policy calling for them to remain.

After four years all the Paiute bands were either freely roaming the countryside or at various army camps. Only the small Choctote band was confined. It numbered about one hundred souls and was on the Klamath Reservation with the Yahuskins. Finally, after numerous complaints by whites about the roaming Paiutes, Major Otis in an April 15, 1872, letter to the assistant adjutant general of the Department of the Columbia recommended that a reservation be established large enough to support the different Paiute bands (except the Choctotes). The reservation was to be in their home territory—somewhere on the headwaters of the Malheur River, in the Steens Mountain country, or around Lake Warner or Lake Harney. In 1873 many bands went voluntarily to the Malheur Reservation, which was a 2,775-square-mile tract on the North Fork of the Malheur River in southeastern Oregon. It was established by executive order on September 12, 1872. The Indians there found reservation life a far cry from what they had previously known. Confinement also did not prove to be the civilizing catalyst that officials hoped it would be. In 1866 the agent on the Klamath Reservation reported that, unlike the Klamaths and Modocs, who had adjusted somewhat to white men's ways, the Paiutes were generally "as low on the scale of civilization as they were a quarter of a century ago."

Not only the Paiutes but also other Indians of the interior reaches of the Pacific Northwest would shortly be engaged in the last major Indian conflicts with the United States. Those conflicts took place scarcely a century after white men broke the aborigines' isolation on the Pacific beaches. Seeking to avoid reservation confinement, the contesting Indians sought to return to that isolation, but the citizens of the United States—expansionist, restless as a Pacific tide, and populous as the grains of sand on the Pacific beaches—tried with force to prevent such a return.

20. "BIGGEST LITTLE WAR"

In autumn 1869, Modoc Chief Captain Jack refused a summons to attend a conference with Indian Superintendent Meacham and the Klamath agent, Captain O.C. Knapp. The officials were seeking to remove him and his people to the Klamath Agency, which had been instituted on May 12, 1866. The two officials then met Jack in council on December 23, 1869, on Lost River, a Tule Lake affluent. In an all-Indian council that night a Modoc shaman, who opposed the removal of his people from the Lost River area, urged them to slay their white visitors. Despite the shaman's goadings to kill them and other whites and despite fears that the Klamaths would ridicule him and his people if they went to the Klamath Reservation, Jack, the traditionalist, and forty-three of his band finally consented to go to the Klamath with the superintendent and agent. When they arrived at the reservation, some Modocs from Schonchin's village moved in with them. The army also gathered fifteen other off-reservation Modocs and brought them there. Hoping to heal the breach between the Modocs and Klamaths, Meacham arranged for a bury-the-hatchet ceremony between Captain Jack and David, a Klamath chief appointed by whites. The Modocs' stay on the reservation was made unpleasant by the Klamath chief, Link River Jack, and others of his tribe. The Klamaths ridiculed the Modocs for surrendering their freedom, bullied them about, beat their women, and obstructed their gathering foods that the Klamaths claimed as their own. In the face of this mistreatment Captain Jack called an all-Modoc meeting in April, 1870, to propose removing to Lost River. At the same time he demanded a reservation north of Tule Lake that had been promised by Judge Elijah Steele.*

With 375 Indians, Captain Jack left the reservation. A few weeks later Schonchin, who was absent from the April Modoc meeting, drifted back to the reservation, as did about 130 other Modocs. To separate them more from the Klamaths, the agent established a subagency at Yainax in 1870. A third Modoc band, as eager as Jack and his followers to shake off reservation shackles, withdrew to the ranch of John A. Fairchild on Lower Klamath Lake. Resenting the whites occupying their lands, they took hay from the settlers' fields, turned their stock loose, entered their houses uninvited for food, and sat around on beds whooping and yelling.

When the Klamaths complained that Jack had killed their shaman for failure to cure Jack's niece, a sheriff was sent to arrest the chief. As noted above, shamans often treated the sick of more than one tribe, just as the prophets taught outside their own tribes. A Paiute prophet named Wodziwob from Walker River in Nevada was the founder of the Ghost Dance. He had a vision in 1869, and his teachings were carried to the Modocs and Klamaths from Walker Lake. The spread of the doctrine, which foretold the return of the dead, was facilitated by the performance of a certain dance, which, with its accompanying beliefs, also spread among northern California tribes and among those on the Siletz Reservation in 1871. Shortly after a prophet came to the Siletz teaching a Dreamer-like doctrine, a white man's house accidentally burned down. The Indians of the reservation proved to the Oregon Superintendent of Indian Affairs, T. B. Odeneal, that there was no need for alarm by voting to surender their arms (Odeneal had been appointed January 8, 1872, and assumed office in April). At about the same time, the Earth Lodge cult spread through northern California and southern Oregon. Unlike the Ghost Dance doctrine, which stressed world renewal, the Earth Lodge prophets foretold the end of the world. On the Siletz Reservation the movement was known as the Warm House Dance. Aware of the dangers of these movements to the Indians' progress in white men's ways,[1] Superintendent Meacham carried four hundred hats to the Klamaths to give to those who abandoned their old-time religion and cut their hair. The haircutting proposal did not set well with the Indians. Under the leadership of progressives, such as Allen David, they condescended to compromise with the superintendent by cutting their hair halfway down. (Around the turn of the century a company operating out of Shoshone, Idaho, capitalized on the luxuriance of Indian hair by selling a restorative tonic with the slogan "Did you ever hear of a baldheaded Indian?")

After midyear 1871, when Jesse Applegate refused to pay rent demanded by Jack, the chief permitted his men to raid the stock of a wagon train. Jack then agreed to attend a meeting with the new agent, John Meacham (who was Superintendent A. B. Meacham's brother). Instead of the four Modoc men whom he had promised to bring to the meeting to match the number of commissioners, Jack appeared with twenty-eight heavily armed Modocs. John Schonchin, younger brother of the old Schonchin, was at the meeting along with Hooker Jim and Curley Headed Doctor. The three favored killing the four white representatives, an action that Jack would not permit. As a result of the council Jack was told that for the time being he and his peo-

---

*For an account of the Modocs and their conflict with American military forces, see Keith A. Murray, *The Modocs and Their War*. Military reports of the conflict, although numerous, were frequently not read by the public. The public did, however, have access to popular accounts written by or about Indians and whites involved directly or indirectly with the conflict. Among the accounts were those of Edward Fox. See "Fox Among the Modocs," *Pacific Search About Nature and Man in the Pacific Northwest* 10, no. 7 (May, 1976): 12–13; Alfred B. Meacham, *Wi-Ne-Ma (The Woman-Chief.)* [Toby Riddle] *And Her People*; Jeff C. Riddle, *The Indian History of the Modoc War and the Causes that led to it*.

ple could remain in the Lost River area. During the next year, after confronting whites, he and his people were constantly pressured by the whites to remove to the Klamath Reservation. Old Schonchin later maintained that the source of white-Modoc difficulties was traceable to the whites' misunderstanding of Modoc, Paiute, and Pit River Indian operations: the Paiutes had made travel difficult for immigrants by selling their captured wagons to the Pit Rivers, who in turn sold them to the Modocs, whom immigrants believed had stolen them in the first place and on whom they took out their wrath.

When Major Otis with fifty officers and men established temporary quarters on Lost River on March 24, 1872, Jack refused to communicate with him. After Otis threatened to force Jack to a council, one of the chief's men promised to bring him in by April 3. When advised in council that he was on lands ceded to the United States by treaty in 1864, Jack promised peaceful behavior and again expressed opposition to confinement on the Klamath Reservation. He concluded his council talk by condemning the Klamaths as thieves and expressed no wish to go to Yainax, especially since Superintendent Meacham, following Judge Steele's plan, had favored a reservation for him and his people in the Lost Lake area. For espousing Steele's plan, Meacham had been replaced by Odeneal. Seeking some legal way to remain on Lost River, Jack talked with Steele and with another judge, A. M. Rosborough, in Yreka.

By September, 1872, Indian Office and military authorities had decided the time had come to force Jack and his Modocs to Yainax. On September 14 troops on a scouting expedition under Major John Green arrived at the mouth of Lost River and encamped there. Horsemen from the command rode between Jack's village and that of Hooker Jim a few hundred yards away. Jack believed that they had come to arrest him in keeping with Indian Office orders to remove him peacefully or by force if necessary. In November a rancher, Ivan Applegate, whom Jack disliked, brought him a request to meet Superintendent Odeneal at Linkville (later Klamath Falls, Oregon) between Upper and Lower Klamath lakes. Jack refused saying that he would not live under Old Schonchin at Yainax. Major Green then called for troops to force him there.

Jack's fears that soldiers would move in on his people were realized on the morning of November 29 when Scarface Charley discovered a line of troops a mile from Jack's camp. There was immediate confusion in the camp. When the soldiers arrived, the women and children were lying flat in pits to protect themselves while Jack waited in his lodge. At the same time Hooker Jim's camp, which was across Lost River from Jack's, was invaded by a band of white settlers. Hooker Jim dashed for safety, but was captured. At Jack's camp a Lieutenant F. A. Boutelle was wounded in the arm as he followed orders from Captain James A. Jackson to seize Scarface Charley's rifle. Hearing the shots, the Indians poured from their tents, firing rifles and bows and arrows. Across the river Hooker Jim's braves opened fire on the settlers. In five minutes the Battle of Lost River was over. Both whites and Indians beat hasty retreats in opposite direc-

tions. The Modocs moved into low sagebrush hills on the south. The women and children scrambled into canoes with their wounded and paddled to the south end of Tule Lake and then to their place of defense, called the Stronghold, which was in the Lava Beds near the south-central shores of the lake in northern California. A. B. Meacham described the area:

A wild jumble of rocks, where not one acre of cultivated soil could be found within its limits. . . . where only wild birds flew above, and vile reptiles in countless multitudes crept beneath, where neither wood nor grass had footing, where desolation seemed to have gathered like a great avenger to despoil it of every resource for man or beast, save only, the living swarms of fish which peopled the lake beside it.

The soldiers returned to burn Jack's village, which had been hastily abandoned by all except an elderly woman, who burned to death. In their flight Hooker Jim's people shot two settlers on the north shore of Tule Lake, wrecked settlers' houses north and east of the lake, and killed other settlers in their houses, fields, and wherever they could be found. On November 30, Hooker Jim's men joined Jack in the Lava Beds, from which they continued to venture forth to kill settlers in the area. To prevent such depredations, the Klamaths were sent from their agency to track down the Modocs. Most of Shacknasty Jim's Hot Creek Modocs (who ranged on Hot and Butte creeks and in the Lower Klamath Lake country) were unwilling to join Jack, and they moved to Yainax. A few of them fled to the Lava Beds to take their chances with Jack.

The military now geared for action. R. F. Bernard, now a captain, was stationed with troops at Land's ranch on the southeast shore of Tule Lake, about seven miles south of Bloody Point on the old South Road and about thirteen miles from Jack in the Beds. Major Green and Captain Jackson remained at Crawley's ranch on Lost River. Colonel Frank Wheaton arrived on the scene to command operations. Troops from Fort Vancouver set out for the scene of the trouble. Captain Kelly and an Oliver Applegate headed detachments of Oregon Volunteers on the scene. Under constant Indian surveillance the military brought in supplies ranging from hay for their horses to shells for the howitzers with which they hoped to blast the Modocs out of the Beds. The Modocs attacked a supply wagon train less than a mile from Bernard's camp, killing several whites and reserving a soldier's dead body for special mutilation. They would have appropriated ammunition from the train had not some cavalry appeared, from which they fled.

Wheaton arrived at Crawley's ranch on Christmas Day to establish his headquarters. In the second week of January, 1873, troops from Camp Harney also arrived for the chase. Also assembled were Klamaths and a few Modoc auxiliaries from Yainax. On January 5, Kelly's volunteers skirmished with eighteen or twenty Modocs with no casualties. There also were none in a skirmish on the thirteenth. On that day the Modocs fired on Captain David Perry and Applegate, who were leading fifty-four men on a mounted reconnaissance to the top of the bluff overlooking the Beds. The Modocs used the occasion to call to Klamath auxiliaries in the scouting party to desert the whites and join them. On the sixteenth regulars and volunteers marched to the south end of Tule Lake from their camp at the Van Bremer ranch about ten miles away. That night Jack prepared for the worst in the Stronghold. Curley Headed Doctor, claiming shamanist powers, encouraged the approximately fifty Modoc warriors holed up there to fight, assuring them his medicine would protect them from bullets. Most of the Modocs were strengthened in their fight, or possibly precipitated into it, by the belief that their dead would return to life and come to their aid, as the prophets had preached. The belief gave assurance to the thirty-seven braves who wished to continue the fight in opposition to the fourteen who sided with Jack. The latter, losing his nerve, had decided to surrender when the troops approached. The majority decision to continue the fight was also motivated by fear that the Indians would be hanged if captured because they had killed settlers. The shaman marked off an area with a red-painted tule-fiber rope and hung hawk feathers and animal skins on a limb. Then he and his followers began to dance around a fire in a step like that of the Ghost Dance. Overcome with excitement, the shaman fell convulsing to the ground.

Three howitzer shots broke the silence of a fog-shrouded January 17. Moving through the heavy mist with camouflaging sagebrush tied to their heads, the Modocs returned the soldiers' fire. In this harmless flurry the Modocs shouted to the dispirited soldiers that they should stand in order to make better targets for the Indians' muzzle-loading rifles. Each brave had two or three rifles, some of which had been taken from fleeing whites. They were ensconced behind stones piled across the rock gaps in their gigantic natural fortress, whose every fissure, cavern, and passage they knew by heart. Although the Modocs were greatly outnumbered, they proved that with their deadly rifle fire they were a difficult quarry to catch. When the fog lifted in the afternoon, they held their pursuers under their rifle muzzles. In an ensuing skirmish, emboldened by the ministrations of Curley Headed Doctor, they lost no men—a much better record than that of their foe, who had seven regulars and two volunteers killed and many wounded. Late that evening Hooker Jim ordered the braves to attack a bluff on the west. When they failed to do so, troops on the east and west sides of the stronghold withdrew under the cover of darkness. Reluctant to fight, the Klamath scouts talked back and forth with the Modocs and hid some ammunition under the rocks for them. The military sent them back to their reservation, deciding instead to hire scouts from the reservation at Warm Springs. Victorious in their first round, the Modocs fired on the troops as the soldiers moved on the twenty-second from Land's ranch to Applegate's ranch, which was on Clear Lake east of Tule Lake.

The repercussions of the Indian victory traveled telegraphically from the Lava Beds to the national capital. Wheaton was forced to yield his command to Colonel Alvan C. Gillem. In the Modoc camp the exhilaration of victory was blunted by dissensions; Curley Headed Doctor excited the war faction, and Jack refused to fight.

Also in January, 1873, the secretary of the interior appointed a peace commission, which was headed by A. B. Meacham and included Agent James H. Wilbur of the Yakima Agency and Superintendent Odeneal. The commission was to visit Jack to coax him out of the Beds. It failed, partly because of dissension within its ranks. Meacham did not like either Wilbur or Odeneal, who had replaced him as Oregon superintendent of Indian affairs. General E. R. S. Canby was commander of the Department of the Columbia, replacing Crook, who left in August, 1870, to fight the Apaches. Canby was given full authority over a reconstituted commission. Jesse Applegate and the Siletz agent, Samuel Case, replaced Wilbur and Odeneal.

Modoc dissension now increased as four rather-distinct factions emerged: one under Jack, another under Hooker Jim and Curley Headed Doctor, another under Shacknasty Jim and his Hot Creeks, and, lastly, one under John Schonchin. When Jack sent word to John Fairchild, the rancher, that he wanted to call off the war, Curley Headed Doctor correctly divined that the message was to surrender. A quarrel ensued when the shaman and Shacknasty Jim rode out to confront Jack. Unwilling to lose his leadership to Curley Headed Doctor in making the momentous decisions in the Beds for peace or war, Jack argued with the shaman all night. Curley Headed Doctor and Shacknasty Jim finally convinced Jack, Scarface Charley, Black Jim, Big Dick, and others that their only salvation lay in a last-ditch defense in the Stronghold.

After the argument, on Fairchild's word that no troops were in the vicinity, Jack rode to the rancher's place to invite settlers to return with him to the Stronghold for a conference to arrange for peace. The settlers informed him that a commission was already en route to discuss such an arrangement with him. Meanwhile at Jacksonville a grand jury met to indict Scarface Charley, Hooker Jim, Long Jim, One-eyed Mose, Curley Headed Doctor, Little Jim, Boston Charley, and Dave for killing some citizens in the November 29, 1872, Lost River fight. Some of those indicted were guilty; others were not. In preparing for the meeting with the commissioners, Jack succeeded in having Steele and Rosborough put on the commission. On February 25, 1873, communication was established between the commission and Jack. The chief sent word to Canby, who was stationed at the Fairchild ranch, that he was ready to negotiate, but only in the Lava Beds. He reasserted his wish for a reservation in the Tule Lake area. Talks continued back and forth. Canby received telegraphic orders to assume the leadership of the commission. After some resignations from that body, the general issued an ultimatum to Jack to cease negotiating and come to the military camp to surrender. Jack assented to this on March 8, but he failed to appear that day and again two days later.

On March 12, Modoc women and children tending horses at some distance from Clear Lake were driven off by troops dispatched by Canby. Thirty-three animals were lost to the soldiers from the herd, which was already diminished

FRANK LESLIE'S ILLUSTRATED NEWSPAPER

Entered according to the Act of Congress, in the year 1873, by Frank Leslie, in the office of the Librarian of Congress, at Washington.

No. 928—Vol. XXXVI.]   NEW YORK, JULY 12, 1873.   [Price, with Supplement, 10 Cents.

BOSTON CHARLEY, MURDERER OF REV. DR. THOMAS.   SHACK NASTY JIM.   HOOKER JIM, THE OPPONENT OF MR. DWYER.   SCAR-FACED CHARLEY, THE FRIEND OF STEELE.

DONALD M'KAY, THE HALF-BREED WARM SPRING
SCOUT WHO TRAILED THE MODOCS.

CAPTAIN JACK.

ONE-EYED DIXIE, THE SQUAW INTERPRETER.

SCHONCHIN, WHO TRIED TO MURDER MEACHAM.   STEAMBOAT FRANK, GEN. DAVIS'S GUIDE.   CURLY-HEADED DOCTOR, THE MODOC MEDICINE MAN.   BOGUS CHARLEY, THE MODOC BETRAYER.

THE MODOC INDIANS.—From Photographs by C. F. Watkins, San Francisco.—See Page 287.

Unlike the Pacific Northwest Indian wars of the 1850s, the Modoc War and its important Indian participants were made known to readers in the East through accounts in such publica- tions as Frank Leslie's Illustrated Newspaper. Here they are pictured on the cover page, July 12, 1873.

214

after Klamath scouts took forty of them in a skirmish before the January 17 fight. The horses were the Modocs' main means of transportation and the basis of what little wealth they had left. When the women came to the soldiers seeking to recover them, their new owners refused their request. In the meantime the troops had moved their camps closer to the Stronghold.

The commissioners now tried a new tack to get the Indians out of the Beds: they brought Old Schonchin from Yainax to try to convince his kinsmen to remove to Indian Territory in Oklahoma. The answer that he brought back was negative. After the middle of March the troops inched still closer to the Stronghold, hoping to worry the Indians out of it. After several changes the commission now consisted of Meacham, the Reverend Eleasar Thomas (a Methodist clergyman), and L. S. Dyar (a Klamath subagent). Acting in a dual role as peace commissioner and campaign general, Canby sent Donald McKay to the Warm Springs Agency to bring down its scouts. At the same time he sent a Modoc woman into the Beds to ask Jack why he had not kept his early-March appointment to come in. The Modocs returned the woman with word that they did not wish to leave their homes for a reservation. Their position was influenced perhaps by settler-circulated rumors that, when arrested, they would be burned alive.

On March 21 the Modocs were greatly agitated by a reconnaissance of Canby and Gillem to the Beds. When the troops' physician, Dr. T. T. Cabaniss, descended the bluff to talk with Scarface Charley and Jack, the latter proposed that Canby and Gillem come down and talk with them. The Indians called on Curley Headed Doctor to be their third man to match the number of the military men. The shaman and Scarface Charley carried shot pouches covered with human hair taken in the January fight—hardly peaceful trappings for a talk. Other armed Modocs appeared. In the talks Jack reiterated his request for a reservation on Lost River and asked Canby to withdraw his troops. In response to Canby's word that many presents awaited the Indians on their submission, Jack asked, if such were the case, why the three had not brought the gifts with them. The two groups then broke off the talks.

In anticipation of Modoc resistance, Bernard moved his troops from Lost River to Major E. C. Mason's camp at Scorpion Point at the southeast end of Tule Lake a short distance from the Stronghold. Several Modocs, anticipating a showdown, had escaped. In the Modoc camp the war faction decided to let the troops strike the first blow. Thus they might trap Jack into committing acts of violence from which he could not retreat. Implementing their scheme, they told Jack that they had been fired on. Ignoring the lie, he sent a request to Gillem, who was encamped at the Van Bremer ranch, that Gillem come with a ten-man delegation to meet him in the Beds on April 1. Gillem responded affirmatively to the suggestion, but, instead of coming with the ten men, brought his entire force to the bluff on March 31. On April 1 he marched them downhill into permanent quarters on the very edge of the Stronghold. Jack refused to meet with them, but sent word the next day that he would meet the

commissioners and their interpreters halfway between the Stronghold and Gillem's camp. The interpreters were Frank Riddle and his Modoc wife, Toby (sometimes called Winema). In the conference Jack asked that the soldiers be removed from the Beds, that a general amnesty be granted the members of Hooker Jim's band who had killed settlers, and that a reservation be established on Lost River. Canby's only response was that, if they surrendered as prisoners of war, the army would decide their fate.

After Jack returned to the Beds, Toby told Meacham and others that she did not trust her people—that they planned some treachery. Not until April 4 did any of the Modocs reappear. Then Boston Charley and Hooker Jim asked to confer with Meacham. Canby gave them free run of his camp, believing its gun emplacements, sentry posts, and numbers of troops would discourage them and cause them to advise their fellows to surrender. The two became violent on learning that Donald McKay was coming with a hundred Warm Spring scouts. On Saturday, April 5, Jack and his delegation arrived at the council grounds. In addressing those present, Jack said he was afraid of Canby's large force and of the Reverend Thomas, whose "medicine" might be greater than that of Curley Headed Doctor.

With a regularity that was by now monotonous to whites, Jack requested a reservation on Lost River. When told that such was out of the question, he fell back on his second proposal: a home in the Beds, where he said no one else would wish to live. Believing the request reasonable, Meacham said that, if the killers surrendered, he would try to get the Beds for the Indians. When Meacham said whites would punish the Modoc killers, Jack asked if the whites would turn over to authorities those of their own race who had killed a Modoc baby in the November 29 fight. Meacham answered in the negative, explaining that Modoc law, now moribund, was not binding on white men. Meacham was aware that no white man's court would convict a white man for killing an Indian. His explanation of this legal point virtually ended the parley. Jack refused to budge until he received some assurance of equal justice and recited wrongs committed against his people; against which, he said, they would not retaliate if permitted to remain in their Lava Bed homeland, where his father was buried.

On April 7, Toby was sent to Jack with an offer from Canby that the military would protect any who wished to surrender. The offer widened the rift between Jack and his eleven men willing to surrender and the others, who adamantly opposed such a move. Shacknasty Jim's Hot Creeks threatened anyone who went to the military. Before returning to the council tent, Toby was warned by a Modoc, William, that such a return would be risky as there was going to be bloodshed. Toby told this to her husband, who in turn carried the word to Canby and Gillem, who paid little heed to it. Mason now moved his camp to Hospital Rock, a point two miles east of Jack's Stronghold. With Gillem three and a half miles away on the west, the two forces formed a pincers with which to trap their prey. On the eighth Jack sent word through Bogus Charley and Shacknasty Jim that he would

Modoc Indians involved in the Modoc War of 1873. Left to right: Shacknasty Jim; Steamboat Frank; squawman Frank Riddle and his wife, Toby Riddle; Scarface Charley. In front:

Jeff Riddle. Smithsonian Institution National Anthropological Archives, Neg. No. 3053.

come to meet the commissioners at the council tent with but six unarmed men if the commissioners too came unarmed. When his offer was accepted, he came with the six men. At least twenty others, armed, hid in rocks on the north and south of the tent. The Modocs in council denied the charge of the Reverend Thomas that they were planning some treachery.

Now heeding Toby's warning, Canby remained in Gillem's camp. On April 9, Toby returned to the Stronghold fearing that the Modocs knew that she had passed the word to the commissioners that they planned to kill some whites. Through Riddle, Canby sent an offer of amnesty to the killers if the Modocs would accept a reservation in warmer climes. Determined to make a stand in the Stronghold, Jack tore up the message. The Modocs dried beef, piled rocks at strategic points, and waited.

On the night of April 10 the Modoc warriors decided to kill Canby and the three commissioners. In Jack's cave, men, women, and children attended a council conducted by John Schonchin and Black Jim. Jack and Scarface Charley said that they were willing to surrender and move to Yainax. At Jack's warning that no killing should take place, the warriors nearest him jumped to their feet, forced him to the ground, and dressed him in a woman's shawl and headdress—the highest insult that they could heap on him. They called him a woman, a coward, a white-faced squaw. Knuckling under this powerful peer pressure, Jack leapt to his feet and advanced a backup plan for killing Canby. A Hot Creek named Ellen's Man offered to do the killing. John Schonchin was detailed to shoot Meacham. Shacknasty Jim and a warrior named Barncho were to kill Dyar. Miller's Charley, Curley Headed Jack (not Curley Headed Doctor), and another were detailed to go east and kill Major Mason. When the plans were final, the council disbanded. Curley Headed Doctor summoned the faithful to an all-night "ghost dance."

Before daylight on Good Friday, April 11, two warriors, who had been chosen to slip up to the council tent with arms for the assassins, went into hiding near that place. Canby, Meacham, Thomas, and Dyar fearfully readied themselves for the council. Thomas paid a bill that morning in order to have no debts on his demise. Meacham penned a note to his wife, saying that she might become a widow that day. Jack asserted that it was his prerogative, not that of Ellen's Man, to fire the first shot at Canby. Boston Charley and Bogus Charley, having spent the morning in the commissioners' quarters, hurried to the tent ahead of them. Bogus asserted that killing the commissioners would frighten the soldiers away and end the war. The commissioners, Toby, and Frank Riddle then arrived at the tent. There in silence to meet them were Jack, the two Charleys, John Schonchin, Ellen's Man, and the three Jims—Hooker, Shacknasty, and

Black. The council began. Jack again asked the soldiers to leave. Meacham said that they could not. After shuffling about, the Indians settled down. There was talk from both sides. On the pretense of answering a call of nature, Jack left the council. He returned and signaled. The two with the arms came running. When Meacham asked the meaning of those moves, Jack said nothing, but pulled out a hidden revolver and aimed it at Canby. The trigger failed to release. He recocked his gun. This time it discharged, striking the general below the left eye. Canby rose, staggered a distance of over a hundred feet, and was felled by fire from Ellen's Man's gun, which had been brought to him by the two in hiding. Boston Charley shot Thomas in the chest with a rifle that had been smuggled into the council despite the ban on arms there. As Thomas ran, a fatal shot struck him in the back of the head. A shot tore off part of Meacham's beard, and he fell unconscious from a ricocheting bullet to his forehead. The Indians believed him dead. Dyar was targeted for extinction from Hooker Jim's rifle fire, but escaped. When Toby falsely warned the Indians, who were stripping

Indian scouts, including Teninos and members of other tribes from the Warm Springs Reservation, in the lava beds along the *Oregon-California border in 1873. Smithsonian Institution.*

217

Oister, formerly of the Warm Springs Reservation, resided on the Yakima Reservation. He was one of the Warm Springs scouts serving under Donald McKay in the Modoc War of 1873. Holland Library, Washington State University.

the bodies preparatory to scalping them, that soldiers were coming, they fled to the Stronghold with their prizes, over which they later quarreled. At Mason's camp Miller's Charley and Curley Headed Jack drew two officers from the camp under some pretence and fire on them. Three days later one of them died from his wounds.

The rapid-fire events sent troops marching westward toward the Stronghold. They stopped a short way from the council tent, where they believed the Modocs would not return fire. In the meantime Meacham revived. The troops chose to attack on the next day, April 12, when Donald McKay and his Warm Springs scouts were expected to arrive. On that day the Indians fired the first shot—at a sentry. East of the Stronghold they followed a scouting party into the Lava Beds south of Hospital Rock, firing on them somewhere between Juniper Butte and Three Sisters Butte. When the soldiers returned the fire, the attackers scurried to the

Beds. Sporadic firing continued throughout April 12 and into Easter Sunday. Canby's scalp was attached to a medicine pole in the Modoc camp—a part of the Indians' own religious celebration. A few hours after the bodies of Canby and Thomas were taken to Yreka for embalming, McKay and seventy-two scouts reached Hospital Rock. Among the scouts were thirty-two Wascos, twenty-four Tyighs, eleven Teninos, an Umatilla, a Nez Percé, a Yakima, and a Paiute. The Paiute was the young son of Paulina.

On Monday morning, the fourteenth, plans were formulated for the attack on the Stronghold. The Warm Springs scouts were now soldier-uniformed to distinguish them from the Modocs, who were aware of their presence. The scouts were to move south and on the next day swing across the southern edge of the lava flow known as Black Ledge (Schonchin Flow). They were to attack as the two pincer columns attacked on the east and west. Curley Headed Doctor assured his people that no foe would cross the magic red-tule rope marking the boundaries of their lands. On Tuesday morning they spied the advancing troops, who were commanded by Colonel Jefferson C. Davis, who was sent out by General of the Army William Tecumseh Sherman as Canby's replacement. The women and children huddled in caves. The warriors bound themselves with rawhide bandages to protect their bodies from jagged rocks as they maneuvered about in the Beds. After midnight two troop companies moved up undetected to Hovey Point a mile west of the Stronghold.

As the two pincer columns inched toward the Stronghold, Jack ordered eight men to fire long-range volleys to delay their advance. A soldier fell. His rifle accidentally fired the first shot. At a signal the Modocs began mass firing. The troops, now about four hundred strong, stopped and took cover. By noon they were about a half mile from the "medicine" flat outside Jack's cave. Their advance was slowed by fire from less than a hundred braves. At day's end three soldiers lay dead, and six were wounded. As Jack anticipated, they did not withdraw for the night. Throughout the next day, April 16, both troop columns futilely fired at Jack's positions from behind rock fortifications, hurling insults at their red foes, who returned the verbal missiles in good English.

Mason's plan of ending the war was completely frustrated on the sixteenth. During that night a Modoc was killed, giving the lie to Curley Headed Doctor's claim that his "medicine" would protect them from death. As the troops reached the magic red-tule rope, the Modocs, dispirited, turned to Jack as undisputed leader. At 9:00 P.M. he ordered the men to break through to Tule Lake for much-needed drinking water. When they failed to do so, Jack ordered his people to evacuate the Stronghold. About midnight braves, women, and children crept southward through a 400-to-500-yard gap in the encircling troops where the Warm Springs scouts would have been stationed if Mason had followed Gillem's orders. For some reason the scouts also failed to report to their officers the sounds of children crying on the Modocs' four-mile evacuation trek to Black Ledge. Not until 11:00 A.M. on April 17 were the troops aware that their quarry had slipped away. They had left behind an elderly man and woman, whom the soldiers killed. Hooker Jim and a few picked braves swung back to Gillem's camp on the west, causing little stir until they killed a packer.

After the Modoc escape fresh troops were dispatched from California posts under Captains H. C. Hasbrouck and John Mendenhall to join in the chase. Except for occasional forays the Modocs remained hidden until April 19, when they attacked a supply train, killing a soldier. Spotted at Black Ledge by Warm Springs scouts, Jack and his people kept retreating toward a lava plateau. They halted in crevices just short of some pumice buttes less than a dozen miles south of Tule Lake. After the scouts rediscovered them, Gillem ordered a howitzer to blast them out of the area. On April 26, sixty-four officers and men, besides McKay and twelve of his scouts, assembled under Captain Evan Thomas to pursue the foe. The captain led the column between the formidable Black Ledge and an even-rougher lava flow, which was aptly named The Devil's Homestead. Twenty-four Modocs, assigned by Jack to keep the moving troops under surveillance, crawled through lava cracks keeping pace with them. At noon the troop columns, unaware of the Modoc presence, were less than a half mile from them. Unknown to the troops, the Indian warriors had abandoned the flow to join Jack and the others, who were atop and around Harden Butte, the obvious objective

of the soldiers. On the east and west sides of the base of the butte other Modocs were poised to fire on the troops when they halted for lunch. As the soldiers ate, waiting for McKay and his scouts to catch up with them, Lieutenant George M. Harris and two men climbed the hill toward Scarface Charley's hiding place, signaling Gillem's camp that they could find no Indians. As two men, under orders from Captain Thomas Wright (son of the late General George Wright), climbed a little ridge on the east to scout for Modocs, Jack and another brave fired on them. On the detail to signal Gillem, Thomas and his men, hearing the shots, ran down the ridge flashing the message that the Indians had been found.

Firing now became general, but desultory. To shorten their range, the Modocs ran downhill toward the troops. In leading an infantry charge to the west, Wright was shot down. Running from a thicket, a squad of six men under Lieutenant Arthur Cranston was cut down to the man by yelling and screaming Modocs. On reaching the ridge that Wright had been ordered to take, Thomas and Lieutenant Albion Howe could not find the slain Cranston. The Modocs fired a flurry of shots killing Thomas and most of his men. Scarface Charley called down to his foe: "All you fellows that ain't dead had better go home. We don't want to kill you all in one day." Evidently not, for he called off the fighting.

The only military uniforms that the Warm Springs

Donald McKay, center, flanked by scouts from the Warm Springs Reservation. McKay and the Warm Springs scouts were *instrumental in the capture of Captain Jack and other Modoc Indians in the Modoc War. University of Oregon Library.*

scouts now wore were their hats, making it difficult for the soldiers to distinguish them from their red foe. The soldiers disdained the military efforts of their red auxiliaries. Help finally reached the wounded, who had been lying out all night, from Mason's camp and from Gillem's. The latter was about four miles from the battle scene. The Modocs withheld their fire as the soldiers retrieved the bodies of their dead. Wright's body was one of those recovered. The bodies of Cranston and his five men were not found for ten days.

In this fight, which is known as the Battle of Hardin Butte, four officers (Wright, Cranston, Thomas, and Howe), eighteen men, and a civilian packer were killed, and nineteen were wounded. The Modoc fighters suffered none killed. On April 27, McKay and his scouts led the crippled army forces out of the battle area. When the Modocs found a brush-covered pile of soldiers' bodies abandoned by the retreating survivors, they burned the corpses. Blamed for the recent disaster, Gillem turned his command over to Colonel Davis.

In their hour of victory the 166 Modocs faced many problems. A most pressing one was subsistence. To meet it, Jack shifted his camp to the place between a lava flow and Juniper Butte known as Captain Jack's Cave. When its ice was exhausted three days later, he shifted his people four miles south to the Caldwell Ice Cave. Five days later they had consumed its ice also. Around May 8 they moved east to a point almost due south of the army camp on Scorpion Point. The Warm Springs scouts in the meantime had lost the Modocs' trail. Two Indian women sent from the army camp to find them returned in three days with no trace of them, but reported finding the bodies of Cranston and his five men.

To keep from starving, about twenty Modocs seized three supply wagons en route to Scorpion Point. Three men, two infantry and one cavalry, were wounded in this encounter, known as the Second Battle of Scorpion Point. Under orders to move out with the Warm Springs scouts against the Modocs, Captain Hasbrouck advanced to Dry Lake (formerly known as Sorass Lake). He had divided his cavalry and artillery. On the night of May 9, Jack prepared a surprise attack on those troops by moving his men silently around the lake after nightfall to assume positions on a ridge about four hundred yards north of the cavalry camp on the north side of the lake. The troops were so positioned that, if they tried to escape, they would be forced into lakeshore mud on the south or directly into Modoc gunfire on the north. Shortly before dawn the next day at a signal from Jack, who was wearing Canby's uniform out of necessity rather than vanity, the Modocs crawled closer to the soldiers' camp. With a yell they fired on their sleeping foe. Demoralized, the soldiers rushed for the lake. In their fight they lost three of Captain Jackson's men killed and three wounded. Their horses broke loose and stampeded. After this confusion the troops regrouped. Advancing two hundred yards, they caught the Modocs by surprise, killing Ellen's Man. Two scouts were killed, and one was wounded, as McKay and his red auxiliaries outflanked the Modocs in the savage fighting of the Dry Lake Fight. When soldiers

dragged a dead Modoc to camp by a rope around the neck, the scouts hacked him to pieces at the joints, as they did another whom they had trailed in revenge. Before the victim died, they scalped him and cut off his legs. Their treachery had also included dropping rocks on Modocs who were hiding in lava caves to plug their escape, leaving them to suffocate.

Hasbrouck ordered McKay and his scouts to chase the now-retreating Modocs, a maneuver in which they were aided by the regrouped cavalry. The Modocs lost no one in retreat, but did lose two dozen horses and supplies, including precious ammunition and blankets, which the scouts took home as war spoils along with captured guns. Lack of supplies and horses hampered the Modocs' escape from then on. The dissension that had smouldered within their ranks from the beginning was laid aside long enough to dispose of the body of Ellen's Man, on whose wrist was Canby's watch. Dissension then resumed as Bogus Charley, Hooker Jim, Shacknasty Jim, and Steamboat Frank denounced Jack for causing Ellen's Man's death. Hooker Jim and thirteen followers deserted Jack and rode about forty miles out of the war zone to the west of Butte Valley, twelve miles south of Dorris, California. Jack's band rode west a few miles to camp on May 10 at Big Sand Butte at the edge of the lava flow.

About 3:30 P.M. on May 12, Mason with about 150 troops reached Big Sand Butte, whose top Jack and his band held. That night Jack moved them a few hundred yards north and west to lava flows at the base of the butte. His band was now reduced to a mere thirty-three broken and destitute souls. Their food and water were nearly gone, their weapons were worn out, and their clothing was in tatters. Jack knew his fighting now had to be purely defensive. On May 14, Hasbrouck and Mason readied their troops for the kill as they awaited the return of the Warm Springs scouts from a reconnaissance. When the scouts returned, they reported that they had not found the Modocs and believed that they might have escaped the lava flow altogether.

Jack had indeed escaped, moving west and south with his band. On May 16, Colonel Davis ordered Mason to break camp at the Butte and move his men to Gillem's camp. Three days later on the west side of the valley opposite Bone Mountain, Hasbrouck's men trailed fresh tracks of Hooker Jim's band returning from their camp on Sheep Mountain. The Modocs opened fire on their pursuers, and the shouting brought the Warm Springs scouts on the gallop. An ensuing chase took the Indians nearly eight miles along the ridge to a point opposite the Van Bremer ranch, where they scattered among the junipers. Captain Jackson and his men captured five women and five children. Avoiding capture, Hooker Jim and his men doubled back north of where the skirmish began, firing on a teamster carrying mail to Gillem's camp. The women assured the soldiers that the band was coming to surrender and were released to tell their people to do so immediately and unconditionally. Hasbrouck promised that, if they did so, the men would not be killed. The women went out and returned with word that the band refused to surrender; they did not believe Hasbrouck's promise.

On May 22, the Modocs sent word that, if their friend Fairchild would assure their safety, they would come in. The rancher went out and returned with but a dozen men wearing parts of army uniforms. The women wore clothing taken from settlers' homes the previous November. Their faces were daubed with pitch in mourning for their defeat. On inquiring about Jack, Davis was told that he had left the group. When Davis inquired about Hooker Jim, Bogus Charley replied that he was dead, as was Boston Charley. Steamboat Frank, Shacknasty Jim, and Curley Headed Doctor nodded in agreement. The chiefs were taken to the Davis tent for further interrogation. At this point Hooker Jim rushed breathless to the tent confessing that he had advised the Indians to say he was dead until he could see what kind of treatment they received. That night the Warm Springs scouts frightened the captives by honing their knives on their moccasins whenever they caught the prisoners watching.

By the fourth week of May three companies of Oregon Volunteers had joined in the search for Jack's band. With the possibility it might have headed south, the governor of California dispatched volunteers to join the search there. Unbeknownst to the troops, Jack and his thirty-two warriors had separated into several groups east of Clear Lake. Under questioning by Davis, the captured Modocs said that they believed Jack was east of Clear Lake at Willow Creek or south of that lake at Coyote Springs or possibly at Boiling Springs or on Pit River. Jackson and his cavalry were dispatched to Scorpion Point in hopes of finding him there. On Sunday, May 25, Davis with two armed civilians, five soldiers, and four Hot Creek Modocs set out from Fairchild's for the camp of Lieutenant W. H. Boyle near Scorpion Point. Two days later, after being armed and provisioned with four days' rations, the four Modocs were sent out to find Jack. They scouted south of Tule Lake and past Horse Mountain in the direction of Clear Lake.

Hooker Jim suspected that Jack was not running away, but planning to raid the ranches of Ivan and Oliver Applegate on Clear Lake in retaliation for their opposition to him in the early stages of the war. Working on that assumption, a squad was dispatched about thirty miles to the Applegates to prevent such retaliation. Hooker Jim's suspicion proved to be correct: the Hot Creeks discovered four of Jack's sentries, who accompanied them to Jack. The chief told them that the Hot Creeks could stay in his camp despite their desertion in May after the Dry Lake fight, provided they surrendered their arms and became his prisoners. At their refusal to do so Jack was angry; it was they who had put the woman's shawl and hat on him in April. At their suggestion that he surrender, Jack said that, if he were to die, it would be by a gun in his own hands and not a rope around his neck, that they could go and live like white men if they wished, but, if they ever returned, he would shoot them down like dogs. Ironically, it was Curley Headed Doctor and Hooker Jim who had refused Jack's pleas to surrender in February. Finally, Bogus Charley asked Jack to leave so the Hot Creek could talk to his men without interference. At this suggestion Jack ordered Bogus Charley and the others

to leave. Scarface Charley, who was with Jack, said he would talk with the four Hot Creeks despite Jack's order to the contrary. Scarface told Bogus Charley that most of Jack's twenty-four men, who were living like animals, were tired of fighting, running, and starving. Bogus said soldiers and Warm Springs scouts were en route to Jack's camp. One of Jack's men asked Bogus if he had led them there. He refused to answer, saying merely that they were coming. When they returned to Tule Lake, where they met Captains Jackson and Hasbrouck, the four Hot Creeks were told to wait at the Applegate ranch. The soldiers reached there on May 29 and then moved to where Jack's band had been. Accompanying the troops were the Hot Creeks, who were acting as if they had been on the side of the soldiers throughout the war. Heeding the Hot Creeks' warning of possible ambush, the troops divided into three detachments, each with a squad of Warm Springs scouts. Hooker Jim guided the detachment on the north, Steamboat Frank was on the south, and two Modocs were with the troops who moved up a creek valley between them.

The troops did not spot Jack's sentries until they were within a mile of his camp. On the advice of Steamboat Frank they halted and then approached Jack's camp unobserved. When the Warm Springs scouts were within three hundred yards of the camp, three of Jack's men ordered them and the troops to halt, asking why so many had come. Fairchild, Bogus Charley, and Shacknasty Jim tried to induce a Modoc to come closer and surrender. The Modoc was none other than the supposedly deceased Boston Charley, who, very much alive, laid down his gun at the rancher's feet. The Warm Springs scouts also laid down their guns to relieve Boston Charley's fears that he would be killed on the spot. In gratitude he shook their hands, but the gesture was no assurance of surrender. Others of Jack's band moved in closer. It was reported that, as Steamboat Frank moved to his horse, his gun hammer caught in a shrub and discharged sending some Modocs fleeing in the belief that Boston Charley had been shot. Boston was told to round them up, but in doing so ran into Hasbrouck's men, who had been on the north side of the mountain. Unaware of what Boston Charley was up to, they seized him and held him prisoner. Fairchild sent Donald McKay to find out what had happened to him. When he found out, and Boston Charley was released, it was late. Except for a few women and children the Modocs had fled. When Boston returned that evening, he told Fairchild that some women and children would surrender. On the next day the fleeing Modocs were rounded up by twos and threes.

The scouts discovered Jack and twelve men hiding in a canyon. They and Dr. Cabaniss held a long talk with some of the Modocs. Coming off the hillside from Jack's hideout, Scarface Charley told the doctor that his people were tired and hungry. The doctor then went to talk with Jack in his hiding place. The chief asked what would happen to him on surrender. Unauthorized to reply to that query, Cabaniss said he would return with food and clothing, since the Modocs had promised to surrender the next morning. True to his word, the doctor returned with food and clothing, and he spent the night with Jack's band. The soldiers pulled back five miles. Before Cabaniss awoke, Jack had slipped away, telling his fellows that, unprepared to surrender, he could not bear to watch them do so. Throwing down his gun, Scarface Charley surrendered to the soldiers. John Schonchin and nine or ten others followed suit, as did others later that day, turning over their arms.

The prisoners were taken to Colonel Davis at the Applegate ranch. The biggest quarry of all, Captain Jack, was still at large. Searchers found that he had doubled back to Lost River and from there had moved east to Langell's Valley northeast of Tule Lake and then on east to the Willow Creek hiding place where Frank and Bogus Charley had first found him. Five miles up Willow Creek, Humpty Joe, Jack's half brother, stepped out of the brush only to be warned that the place was surrounded and that Jack had best surrender. A guide led Major Joel Trimble and Humpty Joe up the creek to call out to Jack. The Modoc chief stepped out on a ledge, rifle in hand. Jack obeyed Trimble's order to turn over his weapon. He repeated several times, "Jack's legs gave out." A Warm Springs scout is said to have sung a song prompting his decision to surrender. Jack's two wives and child were among those coming out of hiding with him.

The Modoc War was over. The few free-scattered Modocs posed no threat to the Lost River Valley ranchers. The victory song that the Warm Springs scouts sang grew louder as the party bringing in the captives approached the headquarters of Colonel Davis. Late on that afternoon, June 1, the leg shackles confining Jack were also clamped onto John Schonchin. As Fairchild was taking four surrendering Modocs and their families to the peninsula at the southeast edge of Tule Lake, which was now abandoned by the troops, two unidentified whites held the rancher at gunpoint beyond Lost River Ford and fired into the Indians, killing four and wounding another.

The captives were taken to Fort Klamath. The fort and agency buildings stood close to the shadow of a mountain, separated by a lovely prairie from the mountains that enclosed the valley on three sides. The Indians called the area Beautiful Land of Flowing Waters. The barren Lava Beds bore no comparison to it, yet Jack and his fellow captives preferred the free barrenness of the Beds to the beauties surrounding their Klamath prison. Shacknasty Jim, and Steamboat Frank were allowed to remain outside the fort stockade. Captain Jack, Boston Charley, Black Jim, John Schonchin, Slolux, Barncho, and seven others were confined to the guardhouse. Only the six Modocs who participated in the murder of Canby and Thomas stood trial before a military commission from July 1 to July 9. It was the decision of the United States attorney general to try only the murderers of Canby and Thomas and not the others. The military panel found all six guilty—Captain Jack, John Schonchin, Black Jim, Boston Charley, Barncho, and Slolux—and sentenced them to die. Most fortunate of all, Hooker Jim, Bogus Charley, Shacknasty Jim, and Steamboat Frank escaped trial and punishment.

Maintaining that he had committed no crime, Jack burned with anger that the others had gone free. When asked whom he wished to replace him as chief, he said he could trust no one. Boston Charley was also angry that Steamboat Frank and Bogus Charley were free since they had helped kill Thomas, an act that Charley blamed on young Modocs.

Execution was set for October 3. On an open meadow a scaffold was erected with six ropes hanging from beams. Graves were dug outside the guardhouse in full view of the prisoners. On the day before the execution General Wheaton accompanied a Roman Catholic priest to inform the doomed of their fate. On the execution day all the Modoc prisoners were forced to watch the grisly proceedings. Four coffins were placed on wagons to be drawn to the scaffold. Still shackled, Jack sat atop one coffin; Schonchin on a second; Black Jim on a third; and Boston Charley, Barncho, and Slolux on a fourth. Barncho and Slolux were left sitting on the coffin as the other four, with their shackles removed, were marched up the steps to the dangling ropes. At 10:00 A.M. the execution order was read. The death sentences of Slolux and Barncho were commuted to life imprisonment on Alcatraz Island. After a chaplain's prayer the axeman severed the rope. Four bodies were placed in their coffins.

In that same month 153 Modoc prisoners were settled on the Quapaw Agency in the Indian Territory. By congressional action on March 3, 1909, they were permitted to sell their lands on the Quapaw Reservation or to lease those that the government had allotted them in a period not to exceed five years, and they were permitted to return to Yainax if they wished to do so. Those who chose to return recieved allotments on the Klamath Reservation in 1909.

A late nineteenth-century historian called the Modoc War "The Biggest Little War in American History."[2] Not only was the Modoc force shattered, but also Joaquin Miller's dream of an Indian confederacy of Modocs, Pit River Indians, and Shastas in an Indian Republic, which was to be "a wheel within a wheel, with the grand old cone, Mount Shasta in the midst."[3] White men shattered Miller's plan by believing that on the American continent only they were divinely appointed to dream dreams. In their plans, unlike that of Miller, there was no room for Indians.

As a supreme indignity to the Modocs and to Captain Jack, who was trapped by his own warriors as much as the military, his body was exhumed, embalmed, and exhibited as a carnival attraction before going to the Army Medical Museum in Washington, D.C. As if this were not indignity enough, the treacherous Warm Springs scouts who helped bring about his demise were lionized in Europe in 1874 and again two years later as glorified sideshow attractions at the Philadelphia Centennial Exposition. A March 8, 1890, directive from Commissioner of Indian Affairs T. J. Morgan warned agents that certain shows of the Wild West variety were "evil" for Indians. They could never have been more evil than the real live Wild West show performed by Captain Jack and his Modocs in their center ring in the lava beds.

Modoc war leaders in chains: Captain Jack, left, and Schonchin John. Both were hanged at Fort Klamath, October 3, 1873. Smithsonian Institution National Anthropological Archives, Neg. No. 3052.

A group picture taken at the Colville Agency. Front row, second from left, the Colville agent, Captain John McA. Webster, *front row, right, Chief Eneas in an ermine-spotted cape.*

21. PROPHETS AND POLITICIANS

Reverberations of the Modoc War reached all the corners of the Pacific Northwest, especially the interior, which was now dotted with ranches and small settlements. The residents there, having read exaggerated newspaper accounts, feared Captain Jack's resistance would spread to other red men as far north as Canada and trap them in an all-out Indian war. Indians on reservations were disgruntled with the government for its failure to keep its promises. Nonreservation Indians were apprehensive at the prospect of going onto a reservation. In 1870, Colville agent W. P. ("Park") Winans warned his superiors that several upper–Columbia River bands below the Canadian border had talked in stormy councils of going to war with whites to stop settlement along a proposed route of the Northern Pacific Railroad. The Northern Pacific's promoters combined surveys and stratagems to put lines through Indians lands. Unhappy with the stakes driven into their lands, the Indians were unimpressed when told that the railroads would bring them more quickly in touch with the Great White Father.[1]

To help ease Indian acceptance of the proposed Northern Pacific Railroad line, Duncan McDonald was engaged to pacify and prepare them for the anticipated line. McDonald was the son of trader Angus McDonald and like his father had traveled with the Indians to hunt buffalo. The railroad company finally withdrew its right-of-way along the northern route, freeing lands in present-day northeastern Washington for the establishment of the Colville Indian Reservation, which was established by executive order on April 9, 1872. Before the year was out, land-hungry settlers in the Colville Valley had pressured the government into restoring the area to white settlement. Then the president by executive order on July 2, 1872, established another Colville Reservation, which was west and north of the Columbia River and east of the Okanogan and which extended north to the Canadian border.

Winans soon discovered that his nontreaty Indians were wary of going on a reservation. In response to his efforts to take a census in his district in 1870, a Sanpoil-Nespelem chief, Qualitikun (or Ouytulakin and the like) expressed the feeling of most Indians, telling Winans: "I recognize no chief but God and he has already numbered them. . . . No man shall number them." Two years later another Sanpoil chief, Kimatalekyah, told the agent: "We don't want anything to do with your President or any of his Agents. God is our agent and is all the one we want, and all the one we will listen to. . . ." In 1880, farther down the Columbia, off-reservation bands drove a census taker from their camps, threatening his life. Seeking subsistence on seasonal rounds in the old way, the nontreaty Indians were not only hard to enumerate but also wary of the government, whose presents they feared were given in exchange for their lands.

Chief Moses emerged as the leader of the nontreaty Indians of the mid-Columbia. He would have liked to extend his chieftaincy, but found such peoples as the Sanpoils and Nespelems as wary of him as they were of the government. After the Spokane-Coeur d'Alène War he and his people marked time in their isolation, awaiting the inevitable white settlement of their country. Until that time they kept a grudging eye on the hundreds of Chinese who were patiently working the bars of the Columbia and its tributaries looking for gold. The *Spokane Times* of July 24, 1879, reported between five and seven hundred "Celestials" working Columbia River bars at various points between the Wenatchee and Spokane rivers.

The Indians also kept a wary eye on cattlemen driving herds from the lower ranges, such as the Yakima Valley, northward to Canadian mines. Already the Yakima cattlemen were casting covetous eyes on the Columbia and Okanogan grasslands in order to supply a growing coastal market. The cattlemen's heyday was from the 1860s to the 1880s, after which their industry was forced to change its methods. They often hired Indians in canoes to wrangle herds across the Columbia on drives to Canadian mines, or to hack out westward roads across Snoqualmie Pass for drives to the coastal markets. Expanding their herds, the cattlemen feared the establishment of an Indian reservation in the interior. Some of them called it an Indian Botany Bay depriving whites of rangelands for their cattle. The one-armed General O. O. Howard, (a veteran of the Civil War, in which he had suffered the casualty), now commanded the Department of the Columbia. The cattlemen were incensed in September, 1878, when, in council with Chief Moses at Priest Rapids, Howard restricted the cattlemen from occupying lands on which Moses and his people roamed between the mouths of the Spokane and Yakima rivers. The establishment of reservations did not prevent cattlemen from illegally driving herds onto lands set aside for Indians. Klamath agent Joseph Emery complained in 1888 to the commissioner of Indian affairs that nowhere on the continent was the military more needed to guard against the encroachments of cattlemen than on his reservation. He was echoing the sentiments of other agents.

On the lower mid-Columbia several nontreaty Indian leaders resisted government pressures to round them up like cattle and send them to the Yakima, Umatilla, and Nez Percé reservations. Influential in stimulating them to resist such moves were the teachings of a *yanchta* (leader and spiritual advisor) named Smohalla (Big Talk on Four Mountains), a hunchbacked Wanapum prophet. He was a distinctive kind of nontreaty Indian, neither a realist nor a politician. He avoided dealings with the government and relied on dreams, visions, and promises of restoration of his people's lands from the whites to hold his followers. As those

Wanapum Indians are led in the washat *ceremony by Puck Hyatoot, a direct descendant of Smohalla. Smohalla's drummer and dreamer religion spread rapidly during the second half of* *the nineteenth century, espoused by traditionalists who saw their land engulfed by whites.*

lands disappeared, Smohalla's teachings gathered momentum and spread to other tribes.[2] The powerful Queahpahmah was influenced by them. He had been arrested by government officials and cruelly treated in confinement, and on November 8, 1861, after trial and sentencing in the circuit court for Wasco Country, Oregon, four of his men were hanged for killing some white men.

In 1862 a tiny knot of traditionalists in the Grande Ronde Valley clashed with the settlers, who were quickly filtering into the valley to appropriate the fertile lands that formerly belonged to the Indians. Four Indians were killed trying to elude troops of the First Oregon Cavalry under Captain George B. Currey, dispatched there at the settlers' request to arrest them. Tenounis, "The Dreamer," was one of those killed. In the brazen attack on their camp Tenounis, another man near him, and two others were shot as Currey and his men carried out their vengeance. Apparently it was Currey's policy to shoot first and ask questions later. Complaints circulated among whites two years later in Boise that his command had killed seven friendly Indians. Another officer subscribing to the "shoot first–talk later" policy was

Army Lieutenant Marcus A. Reno. His command captured two Columbia River "renegades" in the winter of 1860–61 and hung them in front of their own people, who were horrified at this cowardly way to die.

Natives flocked to Smohalla's P'na village ("a fish weir") at Priest Rapids to dance the *washat*, the ritualistic dance of Smohalla's Dreamer religion, and listen to his predictions that Indians would someday reinherit the earth. Smohalla told a Methodist preacher that the Indians were first on the earth and that all people came from one Indian mother. To another white man he said: "My young men shall never work.... Men who work cannot dream, and wisdom comes to us in dreams." To a military officer he elaborated his beliefs still further, declaiming: "You ask me to plough the ground! Shall I take a knife and tear my mother's bosom.... You ask me to dig for stone! Shall I dig under her skin for her body to be born again. You ask me to cut grass and make hay and sell it, and be rich like white men, but how dare I cut off my mother's hair?"

Hereditary chieftains, whether they were traditionalist or progressive, were characteristically bitter toward prophets. Moses was the successor of the great Sulktalthscosum, and, when he went down to P'na village, he reportedly beat Smohalla to within an inch of his life. One story has it that an Indian had whipped and hunched Smohalla's back for supposed indiscretions with the attacker's wife. After the beatings the prophet was said to have wandered throughout the West, including the Mormon country, from which he returned a greater *yanchta* than ever, extending his influence by predicting such events as eclipses. Such prophesies were based on information supplied him by a white man with an almanac. When he passed on the information to his followers, his stature was greatly enhanced in their eyes.

Smohalla reportedly predicted a major earthquake that rocked the Pacific Northwest on the night of December 14, 1872. One group of present-day scientists believes the epicenter was in the Lake Chelan country and northward. In any case, the quake dislodged a cliff, temporarily blocking the Columbia River north of Entiat, Washington, and sending the Indians of the area scrambling in terror to higher ground. Another crippled prophet, the Sanpoil Dreamer Skolaskin, was also reported to have predicted the quake. Skolaskin controlled his followers with stratagems, such as piling logs in front of his lodge, with which, he told them, he would build an ark to save them from a second flood. Catholic priests were among the greatest threats to his authority. They were the only Christian missionaries to whom the Sanpoils and most other upper-Columbia-River Indians were exposed since the 1848 departure of Walker and Eells. Because of his control over the Indians and his defiance of governmental authority, Skolaskin was hustled off in late 1889 by the military and finally incarcerated at Alcatraz. He predicted a severe winter as he left. The winter was one of the coldest on record.

A mysterious Wenatchee River prophet, Patoi, also used the earthquake and its aftershocks (which continued well into 1873) to advance his teachings. When he told the Reverend Urban Grassi, S.J., that during a prayer after the tremors he had seen three persons clad in white, the priest, seeking some way to gather Patoi and his followers into the Catholic fold, told him that he, Grassi, was the third person.* Besides running to the hills in fright, Indians responded to the earth shaking by seeking out priests for baptism and vowing to abandon polygamy forever. The prophets' effective use of the earthquake was evident when many followers of Chief Moses succumbed to the teachings of Patoi and when the chief himself hurried down to the P'na village to dance the *washat*. Moses feared God's punishment for his sins, which he believed included permitting whites to enter his lands. Priests in the Chelan country in the early eighties found that the quake had not shaken into reformation at least one important personage, Chelan chief Nmosize (Innomoseecha Bill), a traditionalist, burned

down the mission house that the Reverend Alexander Diomedi, S.J., had built in his absence.

Protestant missionary efforts among Pacific Northwest Indians were renewed shortly before the quake. A general malaise among the Indians at the decline of their culture, punctuated by the prophets' forebodings of dire things to come, helped prepare the way for the missionary effort. Reverend Henry H. Spalding returned to the Nez Percé Agency in 1861 and again in 1871 as superintendent of education and sought to harvest the seed that he had sown among the Nez Percés a quarter century earlier. The spiritual grounds had been replowed in June, 1870, by four Christian Yakimas under one George Waters. Eighteen months after they arrived on the Nez Percé Reservation to preach the gospel, over six hundred Nez Percés had been received into the Presbyterian Church on confession of faith. Revival also appears to have helped the Catholics in their quest of Nez Percé souls. In May, 1872, the Nez Percé agent, J. B. Monteith, reported to the commissioner of Indian affairs the existence of about thirty to forty Catholic Nez Percés, a number he wished no larger. He attempted to curb the ministrations of the Reverend Joseph Cataldo, S.J., who had come in 1867 and in the following year built the first Catholic church for the Nez Percés near their reservation. In May, 1872, Cataldo baptized thirty-two Nez Percés in a church at Lewiston and others in their camps. In 1874 the first Catholic church was dedicated on the reservation, Saint Joseph's. From the Yakima, or Simcoe, Reservation, Waters shortly carried the revival flames to the Puyallup and the Chehalis reserves. One Thomas Pearne carried the word from the Yakima reservation to the Klamath, and Yakima delegations preached on the Warm Springs Reservation. At the time there was also a spiritual awakening on the Siletz.

When Spalding returned the revival to the Simcoe Agency on the Yakima Reservation in 1872, Chief Moses avoided that place. He was afraid not so much of facing his old mission teacher as of facing "Father" James H. Wilbur, who was appointed Simcoe agent in 1864 (he was called Father because the Yakimas had been Christianized by Catholic fathers). Wilbur wished to gather the chief and other nonreservation Indians under his plow-and-Bible standard. He believed it the humanitarian and Christian thing to do in the light of the Indians' associations with undesirable whites and the rapid erosion of their off-reservation resources. Especially disturbing to him was the presence of Smohalla's followers at Union Gap at the very edge of the reservation, to which he feared the prophet's teachings would spread, putting dust on the Bible and rust on the plow. In 1860, when employed as teacher on the Simcoe, Wilbur had faced Dreamers holding services only four miles from the agency.

Captain Jack's initial success in his war had strengthened Smohalla's opposition to Wilbur. Jack's defeats did not minimize the whites' fear of Smohalla, whose followers, now widespread, frightened them by feathering themselves and beating drums. Smohalla's Wanapums, however, were so reduced in number that for them to have attacked white men would have been suicidal. The barrenness and unat-

---

*The *Pacific Christian Advocate*, May 8, 1873, reported an Indian living north of Priest Rapids as saying: "You see us. We crying. This world makes us cry, because it is always an earthquake and never to stop. One time I dream and I saw the angel flying about me. He had a long sword in his hand, and the angel said: 'If ye all do not pray to God, he will destroy the world.'"

tractiveness of Smohalla's Priest Rapids homeland helped him to avoid confinement. He was also helped by the military men, who cared no more for work than he did and opposed the confinement that the Indian Office sought for him. Wilbur was a strong believer in the work ethic and feared that nonworking and misbehaving soldiers were exerting an adverse effect on nonreservation Indians. He once remarked that he wished troops no nearer the Indians than the Rocky Mountains. From the military, Indians learned of their rights under the Indian Homestead Acts of March 3, 1875 (18 Stat 402) and July 4, 1884 (23 Stat 76). The first act required them to sever tribal relations in order to homestead, and the second permitted them to homestead without severing those ties. It is doubtful that Wilbur told them of such laws in his zeal to confine them, which was not only a matter of personal pride but also to protect them from unprincipled whites trying to sell them lands inferior to those of the reservation. Dispatched by General Nelson A. Miles, commander of the Department of the Columbia, Major J. W. MacMurray explained to Indians their options under the laws. When a military interpreter, Arthur Chapman, encouraged them to homestead, Yakima Agent R. H.

Louie Wapato, a Chelan Indian, circa 1907. At that time he was reported to be the only Indian lawyer in the state of Washington. North Central Washington Museum Association.

Milroy called him "an unprincipled squawman." Milroy continued Wilbur's policies.

The only treaty that Smohalla's rapidly diminishing people ever signed was an agreement with the Grant County (Washington) Public Utility District, dated January 15, 1957. According to the agreement the agency paid them $20,000 for the rights to the site of Priest Rapids Dam on the Columbia River and provided them with other considerations.

Once an Indian named Colwash began dreaming and drumming across from The Dalles, and the zealous Wilbur went down to put a stop to it. With little resemblance to his laying on of hands in his religious services, the reverend's arms began revolving "like the fans of a great windmill" as he seized the Dreamer by the nape of the neck, handcuffed him, and returned him to the agency in a hack. A teller of the story wrote: "the act was characteristic of the man. He feared God only." In the late seventies Skimiah (Skamiah and the like), the Dreamer leader of a small band near Celilo, was thrown into the Fort Vancouver guardhouse, and his people were removed to the Yakima Reservation.

In the Spokane country Chief Garry's natives were still frightened by the quake, and on March 27, 1873, Garry sent word to Spalding inviting him "to baptize his people and marry them according to the laws." In response to the invitation Spalding went to Pine Creek, where he met Chief Moses. The two embraced warmly. Spalding hoped that Moses would spiritually exhort his hearers in the Christian faith and lead them in it because of his position as chief, but in fact Moses could not, having abandoned the missionary's teachings. Instead he launched into a tirade against white slanderers associating him with Captain Jack. He feared such rumors would force him and his followers onto a reservation.

In April, 1873, Wilbur informed the Dreamer Hush-hushcote (also Husicuit, Hosiskue, and the like, or "The Baldhead"), that the law required that Hush-hushcote and his people go onto a reservation. Hush-hushcote was a Palouse chief of little bands that farmed for sixty miles up and down the Snake River. They refused to go on the reservation, claiming that the government had not fulfilled its treaty obligations by failing to evaluate their properties. Like Wilbur, the Warm Springs agent, John Smith, was eager to gather dissidents under his watchful eye. He was especially wary of the Indian leader Hackney (or Hehaney; perhaps Highnea), who spent considerable time in the seventies not only in the Warm Springs skookum-house but also in the jail at Fort Vancouver. Once, when confined in May, 1871, he filed off his chains and escaped. On April 15, 1879, Smith arrested an Indian named Hehaney, who perhaps was Hackney, releasing him eight days later on the intercession of various Indians, including Queahpahmah. The latter, abandoning his several wives and the Smohalla religion, had returned to the Warm Springs Reservation. He had been away for seven years on the Umatilla and Yakima reservations, where his presence caused great concern among officials, who feared the spread of his teachings.

Near Thorn Hollow on the Umatilla Reservation there

was in effect a school of Dreamer religion, where such Dreamers as the Wallawalla Homily and the Umatilla Talles held sway. Nez Percés often came there from their Wallowa homeland in northeastern Oregon to hear teachings enhancing their own nonreservation status. A prominent Nez Percé Dreamer, who was gaining a following among dissidents, was Toohoolsote (or Toohulhulsote and the like). His antagonist, General Howard, called him a "cross-grained growler" and a "savage of the worst type." His followers included Old Joseph and Young Joseph (Hinmahtooyahlatkekht, Thunder Traveling to Loftier Mountain Heights). To them he represented the old Indian way at its best, while to Howard he represented its worst.

Like other Pacific Northwestern Indians, the Dreamers found the government's new approach in the management of Indian affairs no more palatable than its previous policies. The controversial Ulysses S. Grant Peace Policy operated from 1870 until 1882 at various agencies throughout the country. It was predicated on the principle that in the complex American society rapidly developing after the Civil War red men could be saved from extinction only through an enlightened church-oriented policy in the management of their affairs. Pacific Northwestern Indians were, indeed, faced with the threat of extinction. When treating with bands of the lower Columbia in the summer of 1851, Superintendent Anson Dart reported that the people were wasting away and could not be persuaded to fix a time beyond ten years to receive moneys due them in exchange for their lands. Nearly two thousand Indians had been on the Grand Ronde Reservation in 1856. They were the remnants of eight tribes located there. Only five of the tribes had treaties and received annuities; the remainder depended on the funds that the agent might spare them from appropriations for their removal and subsistence. Within a decade of their removal to the reservation a third of the Grand Ronde Indians had died. It was not until 1865 that a special committee of Congress officially recognized that Indians were decreasing by disease, intemperance, war, starvation, and oppression by unscrupulous whites. Between 1849 and 1861 there had been twenty-two campaigns against American Indians in addition to many lesser conflicts.

General Alfred Sully was a painter, a West Point graduate, and a soldier in the Mexican and Civil wars as well as the conflicts with Indians on the Great Plains. In 1864 he wrote that the best way to exterminate an Indian was to "civilize" him. The Indians were incapable of adjusting to American culture as rapidly as whites expected that they would, and they were aware of it long before the whites realized the difficulties of fusing the two cultures. On the Siletz Reservation, Indians expressed a willingness to resume hostilities because, in their words, they had so much to gain by free roaming off the reservations and by warring against whites and so little to lose. Also on the Siletz Reservation the Indians had a saying, "It is your peace that is killing us."

There were stirrings, mostly outside Congress, to save Indians from extinction. To overcome the Indian agency problems, President Grant, from a Civil War surplus, appointed military officers as Indian agents. As a consequence

nearly all the Pacific Northwestern Indian agents in 1869 were military men. Unhappy with this encroachment on its patronage powers, Congress on July 15, 1870, enacted legislation prohibiting the appointment of army officers to top agency posts. The Society of Friends, or Quakers, had been successful in operating some agencies before military men were assigned to them, and they had enough clout to cause the posts to be filled once again by nonmilitary men; however, at the end of the nineteenth century, during the administration of Secretary of Interior Hoke Smith, military men replaced civilian personnel for a time.

Shifts in the administration of Indian policy revealed the pitfalls inherent in trying to assimilate Indians into the mainstream of American life. There were, however, many who optimistically clung to hopes of such assimilation, especially churchmen, who believed it could be achieved through the application of Christian principles. In 1864, Washington Superintendent of Indian Affairs W. H. Waterman expounded this viewpoint by declaring that only Christian influence could save the Indians from extinction. Among the reformers who now clambered aboard the Indian "civilizing" bandwagon were some who had jettisoned the black cause for the red. After the midsixties Episcopal churchmen joined Quakers in a concern for Indian welfare. The Indian Office was itself composed of churchmen, and they hired church-sponsored teachers for the agencies. Like their employer these personnel believed that they could dictate morals and assimilate Indians by such means as dispensing domestic articles amongst them. The Board of Indian Commissioners, established in 1869 to exercise joint control in the disbursement of Indian funds and to advise the commissioner of Indian affairs, consisted of church-appointed members.

Grant's Peace Policy was the culmination of those shifts in administration. It was launched by a two-million-dollar appropriation on April 10, 1869, and was designed to gather Indians on reservations and promote Indian efforts toward self-sufficiency. In 1872 the policy of driving Pacific Northwestern Indians to reservations was carried out by the Military Division of the Pacific and its Department of the Columbia. Whether they liked it or not, the peace politicians were thus backed up by the military and knew that the Rifle had joined the Bible as adjuncts to the Plow.

In 1866 two Supreme Court decisions (72 U.S. [Wall. 5], 737, 1866, and 72 U.S. [Wall. 5], 761, 1866) guaranteed rights under the Constitution to Indians. On the recommendations of the Board of Indian Commissioners in its 1869 report and on the recommendation of President Grant, Congress passed an act on March 3, 1871 (16 Stat 566), declaring that the United States no longer recognized Indian tribes as sovereign. From then on the government dealt with the tribes through executive orders. The last treaty ratified by the Senate for Pacific Northwestern Indians was with the Nez Percés on August 13, 1868.

The assigning of Indian agencies to various religious denominations was not only the policy's most unique characteristic but also its most controversial. It angered churchmen even more than it bewildered the Indians that the agencies were shuffled among the churches like so many decks of cards. Especially unhappy were Catholic churchmen, who, seeking only to propagate their faith, had taken no part in the reform movement from which the policy evolved. The Catholics came out scarcely better in the Pacific Northwest than in the nation at large in the church-shuffling contest with the Protestants. They were assigned the Flathead Agency in Montana Territory, the Colville and Tulalip agencies in Washington Territory, and the Umatilla and Grand Ronde agencies in Oregon. Under the supervision of the Methodist Episcopal Church were the Fort Hall and Lemhi agencies in Idaho Territory, the Yakima and Quinault agencies in Washington Territory, and the Klamath and Siletz agencies in Oregon. The Skokomish Agency in Washington Territory was under the Congregationalist Church (initially it was under the Methodists). The agencies under the United Presbyterian Church were the Nez Percé in Idaho Territory, the Warm Springs in Oregon, and the Puyallup in Washington Territory. Agencies under the Christian Union were the Malheur in Oregon and the Makah in Washington Territory.

More Indian agencies fell to the Methodists than to any other church although that denomination at that time had come to believe its greatest mission prospects were in Africa and Asia rather than America. According to the Methodist *Pacific Christian Advocate* of November 16, 1872, the Indians' "inaptitude and distaste for improvement" had smitten them with such a deep-seated "depravation of character" that their redemption was impossible.

The change in agency appointees from strictly politicians to churchmen made little difference in the management of Indian affairs. As before, some agency officials were good, some were bad, and many were indifferent. Before Ben Simpson turned over his office as agent to Joel Palmer after eight years of service on the Siletz, he warned in his last annual report of October 1, 1871, that, "in the search for piety in those who aspire to office, certain other very respectable and necessary qualities may be lost sight of" and a "talent for affairs" did not always follow godliness. The Reverend Lawrence Palladino, S.J., wrote that for an agent he preferred "an honest, liberal-minded Protestant to a poor Catholic." Palladino was appointed first to the Saint Ignatius Mission in 1867, and he later served elsewhere in Montana. His church mistrusted the Peace Policy to the point of advancing one of its own. As early as 1865, Superintendent J. W. Perit Huntington had believed the type of school to be more important than the denomination of the church administering it. Only boarding schools, he opined, could effectively educate the children of his superintendency, where, because of competition among "Catholics, Protestants and Professors...*not one Christianized or an educated Indian is to be found.*"

Under the Peace Policy "talent for affairs" (to use Simpson's words) usually meant the degree of efficiency and effectiveness with which an agent and his aides could remake the Indian in the white man's image. At no place was the effort more evident than at the Simcoe agency. Methodists justified their presence there on the grounds that Jason Lee had ministered to the natives before the first Catholic missionaries, Blanchet and Demers, appeared in the country in 1838. Methodists claimed that their missionaries had been the first to preach to the Indians who eventually went to the Grand Ronde Reservation; thus, the Methodists believed, they should have been given that place to administer also. In their anger that the Catholics were awarded the Umatilla Agency after the Whitmans laid down their lives ministering to many of its natives, Protestants overlooked the fact that Catholic missionaries had remained to Christianize the Indians after the Protestant mission had failed.

There had been much squabbling among Simcoe Agency personnel.* Trouble again flared after the Catholics reopened their war-shattered Saint Joseph's Mission.† Simcoe agent, "Father" Wilbur, kept the priests away from the confine and the Indians away from Saint Joseph's. Those clinging to the Catholic faith found themselves denied agricultural implements—the only tangible offense with which Wilbur can be charged. His intolerance of Catholics matched his intolerance of the natives' culture, which, he believed, had to be destroyed to assure their survival. Like those of other agents he used his reports as a good vehicle to catalog the accomplishments of his charges. Like a general parading his troops he displayed a phalanx of statistics favorably padded for the world to see and for the forces of darkness to tremble at: so many acres under cultivation, so many cattle raised and sold to purchase farm machinery and additional livestock, so many board feet of timber sawn and so many bushels of flour ground at the mill, so much money earned from leased rangelands, so much agency work performed, so many children in school and adults in church, and so on. Cooperating with Wilbur was the Klickitat Joe Stwire, who became chief of the Yakimas on January 1, 1868. Unlike his predecessor, the Klickitat Spencer, Stwire was elected by important men casting colored ribbons to show their preference. Pointing out his people's houses and farms, he told some visiting Sioux that they too could be happy and avoid destruction if they emulated the Yakimas. He would later get into trouble with his fellow tribesmen for favoring sales of Yakima lands.

When permission was granted to the Bureau of Catholic Indian Missions in 1873 to establish churches on the Yakima and Nez Percé reservations, their respective agents

---

*How the Peace Policy worked on the Yakima Reservation, where it proved to be a bone of contention, is explained in Grant L. Whitner, "Grant's Indian Peace Policy on the Yakima Reservation," *Pacific Northwest Quarterly* 50, no. 4 (October, 1959): 135–42.

†After the failure of the Methodist mission at The Dalles, which was established in 1838 and terminated in 1847, Indians at the Catholic Saint Peter's Mission received the ministrations of the Reverend Toussaint Mesplié, who kept many of them out of the Yakima War. They also received the ministrations of Father Adrian Croquet, who accompanied Mesplié on an apostolic expedition among several Indian tribes along the banks of the Columbia River in the area of Mount Hood, where they "were everywhere most affectionately received, the chiefs honoring [them] by offering the calumet." Edwin V. O'Hara, *Pioneer Catholic History of Oregon*, p. 179.

Joe Stwire, or White Swan, who assumed the Yakima chieftaincy, January 1, 1868.

strongly opposed it. Agent Monteith was a Peace Policy appointee to the Nez Percés, and he carried out with sectarian vengeance opposition to Catholics or any other denomination not professing aid to the Presbyterian cause. With equal zeal he tried to prevent Indians from severing tribal ties and homesteading off the reservation. The reaction of Protestant partisans to Catholics was so strong that Secretary of the Interior Columbus Delano withdrew permission for the latter to build churches on the two reservations. After subsequent requests by Catholics to build the churches were also denied, they asked the commissioner of Indian affairs for funds to support a boarding school in Yakima City, a mile from the reservation boundary. When that request was likewise denied, the Catholics removed students of Catholic parentage to the Umatilla, Colville, and Coeur d'Alène reservations, a move that Agent Milroy in 1884 termed "unexampled imprudence." Not until 1880 did the Indian Office permit all denominations access to all reservations.

If they had not known it before, the Indians soon learned that the Peace Policy contained as much rancor as it did religion. When asked if his people wanted churches in the Wallowa country of northeast Oregon Young Chief Joseph replied that they did not. Churches, he said, would only teach them to quarrel about God like Catholics and Protestants. The basic bone of contention between the two branches of the Christian faith in their dealings with Indians pertained to their spiritual welfare. Basic theological differences smoldering from early mission days resurfaced to center around such concepts as conversion. On the Warm Springs Reservation, Agent Smith believed that Catholics admitted unregenerate Indians to their churches, permitting them to hear mass in the mornings and run horses and play cards the rest of the day—all under the eye of the priests. "I have my doubts," wrote Smith, "if a single Indian can be found on this coast that has been made any better by the Catholics."

Caught up in the revivalism of the later nineteenth century some Protestant groups tended to equate progress with religious zeal. The conscientious agent Joel Palmer was made aware of this when he arrived on the Siletz Reservation on April 30, 1871, to assume his duties as agent after an unsuccessful attempt to win the Oregon governorship. Believing that secular progress did not come to Indian camps through camp meetings, Palmer came under the attack of a young preacher named John Howard, who was employed as agency farmer. Howard reported Palmer to his superior as unfit to be agent. To Howard, Palmer's unfitness was his inability to prove the superiority of Methodism over Catholicism. Methodist officials tolerantly retained both men in their positions and permitted the "Methodist mutiny" to brew on the Siletz, from which they hoped it would not boil over.

Rival Protestant and Catholic groups agreed that both the spiritual and physical welfare of the Indians had to be advanced. Even the Protestant stalwart, General Howard, a preacher in his own right, was impressed with Catholic efforts. Howard noted the effectiveness of the Reverend Adrian Croquet (whose ministrations were muzzled on the Methodist Siletz). As Howard put it, priests were effective because they did not try to draw "the broad line that we [Protestants] do between the converted and the unconverted." The general was impressed by the teaching efforts of the sisters on the Grand Ronde, where Croquet had founded Saint Michael's Mission in the early sixties. An Indian spoke for Howard's benefit on the Grand Ronde Reservation, saying, "You can see we dress like you, we have a school and a church, we have houses and lands, teams and plows; we are no longer 'wild Indians.'" Even the *Pacific Christian Advocate* echoed this sentiment on April 4, 1872, by noting the statement of a Methodist missionary that not one blanket-wearing Indian lived on the Grand Ronde.

General Howard was encouraged by the progress that Indian children on the Grand Ronde were making in speaking English, although during his visit they passed his words on to their parents in the Chinook jargon. The Peace Policy had worked no magic in eliminating the babel of tongues on the reservations. On the Skokomish Reservation, the Sunday School, in the words of its Peace Policy missionary, the Reverend Myron Eells, began with: "Four songs in the Chinook jargon; then three in English, accompanied by an organ and violin. The prayer was in Nisqually, and the lesson was read by all in English...." Sometimes the Indians of the region united popular hymn tunes with erotic and bacchanalian ditties taught them by white men whose ideas of propriety were hardly those of the missionaries.

Also impressed with the Catholic efforts was Indian inspector E. C. Kemble. After visiting the mission school on the Tulalip Agency, he hailed it as "the best Indian school probably this side of the Rocky Mountains." Even the editor of the *Pacific Christian Advocate*, on April 4, 1872, admitted great progress on the Tulalip. Not so impressed with progress there were some Protestant critics. They and their Catholic counter critics engaged in a tiresome recital of accomplishments at that and other agencies and of the lack of progress on the agencies of their rivals. The storm of controversy centered over personalities, particularly Wilbur and Chirouse, as their supporters cheered them on from opposing sides. By defending Wilbur's policies, the *Advocate* became embroiled in the controversy involving the sorest of all points to the Catholics, the Simcoe Agency. The editor rated progress among the Simcoe Indians as substantial. He rated progress among the Indians on the Warm Springs and Siletz also as substantial, but saw only moderate progress on the Klamath Reservation, where there was "a little advance toward civilization," and poor progress at Neah Bay. One minister in a March 31, 1874, letter to him had reported the Neah Bay Indians as "filthy in their persons, diseased in their bodies, squalid in their houses, and destitute of all ambition to rise above the low hut in which they were born." Lending its editorial voice in the advocacy and defense of Catholic agencies was the *Catholic Sentinel* of Portland, Oregon. Only Catholics, it maintained, conducted the true Peace Policy. "It is a remarkable fact," wrote its editor on April 25, 1873, "that the Indians under Catholic Agents, or who have Catholic misionaries among them, are the most peaceable and tractable in the country."

Spokane Indian Agency police at Fort Spokane with a captive secured by a ball and chain around the ankles. Cull White Collection.

When Howard visited the Grand Ronde, older Indians told him that nothing offended them so much as white men attempting to take their women. To the Indians who clung to polygamy despite missionary preachments against the practice it appeared that the agents were trying to destroy their family life by stripping them of their wives. On the Warm Springs Reservation, Smith set about rescuing the Indians from such pagan practices, which had not been reduced at all, he believed, by the military personnel managing the agency in 1869 and 1870. In one meeting he dramatically plead with the Indians to become monogamous. Bewildered, Chief Mark said:

I love all my women. My old wife is a mother to the others. . . . I can't send her away to die. This woman [pointing to another] cost me ten horses. . . . I can't do without her. That woman [pointing to still another] cost me eight horses. . . . She will take care of me when I am old. I don't know how to do. I want to do right. I am not a bad man. I know your new law is good; The old one is bad. We must be like the white men. I am a man; I will put away the old law.

On hearing those assurances, Smith, in the words of a Protestant missionary, behaved like an old-fashioned Methodist, shouting, "Thank God, thank God, the ice is broke." The ice jam of bewilderment among the others melted somewhat at Mark's concession, as they began jumping on the "one-wife" bandwagon. Billy Chinook, who had been a scholar at the Methodist mission at The Dalles and in faraway Philadelphia, said: "I have two wives. . . . If anyone

wants one of my wives, he can have her; if he don't, she can stay." The surrender seemed complete the next day when Pianoose, who had previously watched the proceedings in sullen silence, rose and threw aside his blanket, declaiming, "I am going to be a white man." Unable to restrain his joy at this disclosure, Smith slapped his hand on the desk as his eyes filled with tears. To cap the ceremonies, he called his employees to a meeting attended by some of the Indians to exhort them to right living. Very shortly he had to merge his joy with the sobering responsibility of enforcing the changes. A head chief and six men were selected and charged with enforcing Smith's decrees, such as the requirement that couples marry before living together and the prohibitions on drinking ardent spirits, playing cards, and gambling. Violators were fined twenty-five dollars and forced to work ten days on agency roads. Small wonder that Smith exultantly reported that by 1873 the Warm Springs guardhouse had fallen into ruins.[3]

Progress in attaining such goals did not come as quickly for Smith or any other agent as they hoped or believed it would, causing them at times to resort to force as well as faith to bring it about. Remembering the recent Indian wars, Pacific Northwestern settlers favored force more than they did faith in the conduct of Indian affairs—more so than the Indian agents did. The settlers' pleas and petitions for troops and military installations were legion. Typical was an 1873 complaint of citizens of Idaho Territory that fifty soldiers at Fort Boise were inadequate to protect them from Shoshoni-Bannock bands who were "endangering their lives" and by now, in most cases, "their economic well being." Many citizens viewed the Peace Policy with pragmatic rather than humanitarian eyes as an economic godsend for their trade and commerce until more distant markets and sources of supplies could be tapped with improved transportation.

Although relying on the military for aid, such agents as Smith had encouraged trusted Indians to become policemen and jurists. Authorized by federal legislation on May 27, 1878 (20 Stat 63, at 86), the Indian police system was instituted at the various agencies to achieve the goals of the Peace Policy. The duties of Indian policemen ranged from protecting annuities and other properties to running down thieves, whiskey peddlers, errant spouses, and truant school children. Another innovation was the Court of Indian Offenses created by the secretary of the interior on March 30, 1883. New administrative vehicles, such as the native courts and police, were established for social control. They were similar to traditional native institutions only now they were used to effect cultural change.

Under the Peace Policy, agents sought to mold their Indians into loyal subjects of god and country. Where they had once assembled at different places for their socioeconomic activities, the government, seeking to make agrarians of them, discouraged or prohibited the roamings and gatherings that were traditionally so much a part of their lives. Aware of the Indians' need to assemble, the Catholic fathers, who were more concerned with making them subjects of god than of country, continued to encourage them to come to the missions to observe the holy days of the Church, especially Christmas, Good Friday, Easter, Whitsunday, and the Feast of Corpus Christi. They were encouraged to celebrate those occasions with Christian dignity. At the Kettle Falls–Colville area, which was a longtime gathering place of Indians, natives from as far away as three hundred miles were saluted by gunfire on their arrival and welcomed by the native residents with much protocol. The Reverend P. G. Guidi, S.J., on August 17, 1875, wrote that Indians gathering there a week before the Feast of Corpus Christi had been forbidden by their leaders to engage in "unnecessary or distracting occupations in the camp." In practice such orders were seldom strictly observed. In recounting the celebrations the *Stevens County* (Washington) *Standard*, June 3, 1893, reported the words of an observer: "I have seen Indians go there with fifteen head of horses, saddle, blankets, robes. . . .and walk away penniless losing everything. . . ." Arriving in the region in 1889, the Reverend Augustine Laure, S.J., like most clerics, was not as concerned with the Indians' nonreligious activities at the Kettle Falls celebration as he was with their devotional responses. On the Flathead Reservation, besides observing other traditional holy days, Indians observed the day of the patron saint of the mission, Ignatius. On this and other special days over a thousand communicants traveled to the mission from as far away as three hundred miles to participate in the services. After the services were over, piety deferred to pleasure as at Kettle Falls as the Indians raced horses and gambled.

One type of socioeconomic gathering that peace politicians sought to disparage was the potlatch ceremony of

Puget Sound and the Strait of Juan de Fuca. They believed it the antithesis of the government's wish to encourage the Indians to work in order to save because the Indians gave away their resources in the ceremony. Formerly the ceremony had been part of a welfare system practiced by and for the wealthy in a high social milieu. In the second half of the nineteenth century it became increasingly difficult for important personages to amass great wealth for potlatching purposes—not a discouraging thing to the government in its wish to effect a leveling of Indian classes. By the 1880s the traditional potlatch was seldom practiced on Puget Sound or the strait, although natives continued some of their traditions. Annuity goods now found their way onto potlatch piles. The natives arrived on the grounds banging the sides of their canoes with paddles and singing special songs to announce their arrival at the ceremonies. In July, 1891, Old Patsy, a Squaxin at Port Hadlock (six miles below Port Townsend), tried to revive the potlatch by distributing articles during a week-long Fourth of July celebration that attracted bands of Quileutes, Snohomishes, Skokomishes, Lummis, Suquamishes, and Clallams.

On the Puyallup Reservation, like others, the Fourth of July celebration was being substituted for the traditional potlatches. In 1874 a chief of the Muckleshoot Reservation, Nelson, said that he had learned more on the Fourth than he had during his previous life. The Declaration of Independence is Thomas Jefferson's castigation of King George III for seeking to unleash on American frontiersmen "the merciless Indian savages, whose known rule of warfare is an undistinguished destruction of all ages, sexes, and conditions." Perhaps this section of the document, like its other tedious indictments of King George, was left unread.

Indians found in the raucous celebrations of the Fourth a reasonable substitute for government-banned traditional festivities. It gave them a chance to mix fireworks and fire water. On July 4, 1869, the Duke of York with his followers paraded an American flag upside down and then boarded a cutter to break his resolve never to drink again. Instead of creating unity, as the government hoped they would, the celebrations often intensified and exposed divisions on the reservations. The centennial independence celebration among the Nez Percés scandalized their teacher, Kate McBeth, prompting her to institute a counter celebration more like the decorous ones sponsored by the Presbyterian Church. Although McBeth believed traditional Nez Percé culture had to be overturned to preserve the people, she did see the fairness of permitting them to parade in their pagan clothing and trappings—as long as they returned them when the celebrations were over. Three years later Nez Percé chiefs and elders would not permit "blanket" tribesmen to join the celebration at Kamiah. The conflict between the Christian and the largely traditionalist non-Christian Nez Percés surfaced in the Fourth of July celebrations. When word of it reached the commissioner of Indian affairs, he issued a directive in 1891 expelling "heathen elements" from the celebrations.[4]

The Indian wars of the seventies made whites fearful lest Indian celebrants become violent. As late as 1889, in the Big

Young Indian girls from the Colville and Spokane reservations are taught the clothes care of a culture new to them at the Fort *Spokane boarding school.*

Bend town of Wilbur near the Columbia River in Washington Territory, when Chief Moses raised his gun to signal the start of a Fourth of July horse race, a frightened citizenry believed he was signaling his men to begin hostilities. On the Quinault Reservation in 1885 the possibility of war was more remote. Agent Charles Willoughby and visiting dignitaries were carried in a parade on blankets held at the four corners by athletic Indians. On the Warm Springs Reservation that same year the agent, Alonzo Gesner, was pleased with what he believed to be a spirit of harmony prevailing there, noting that the various tribes celebrated the Fourth together for the first time. Around the turn of the century the Warm Springs melting pot had amalgamated the Wascos, Teninos, and Paiutes to such an extent that it was impossible to obtain their statistics by tribe. A similar amalgamation was taking place on all the other reservations with varying degrees of rapidity. By the mid-eighties Father

Anthony Ravalli noted that every Flathead was of mixed lineage.

Officials used holidays for purposes that were practical as well as patriotic and religious. At the Fourth of July celebrations they often tried to enumerate the Indians under their supervision. During the 1857 Christmas holiday period Agent Richard H. Lansdale asked Wishram chiefs Sinawah and Colwash to provide him the numbers of their people. In return for providing the census, Lansdale issued Sinawah presents and provisions for his people. To Colwash he issued some sugar, coffee, flour, and molasses for his people's New Year's dinner celebration. The French-Canadian and Scottish fur men had regarded New Year's Day as an occasion for bigger celebrations than Christmas, thus influencing many Indians to observe the beginning of the new year. After a celebration in 1880 the Chelan chief Nmosize childed Father Diomedi: "Go away from my land;

Cayuse women and children, circa 1900. One of the women, Wenix, was the sister of the half blood Donald McKay. Smithsonian Institution National Anthropological Archives, Bureau of American Ethnology Collection, Neg. No. 3073-B-79.

Boys and girls from the Colville and Spokane reservations lose their individuality at the Fort Spokane boarding school.

you always come here to reprove us for your customs. You Americans spent New-Year's day worse than we did. I saw them drunk and still drinking, quarrelling and fighting. You are worse than we are, and yet you come here and urge us to become Christians."* George Washington's birthday was also celebrated by "Bostons" and Indians alike.

Officials used the schools to foster and perpetuate special-day celebrations. Carrying out educational programs in their broadest sense proved far more difficult. Unlike the informal instruction of earlier times Indian children, isolated from their elders, were subjected to unfamiliar formalized education in coeducational classrooms. In schools academic subjects, such as the three R's, were to be balanced with practical subjects, such as manual training for boys and domestic sciences for girls. Besides the many reservation schools others were established to educate children from a wider area of the Pacific Northwest and even from Alaska. One of those was at Chemawa near Salem, Oregon. After establishment at Forest Grove, Oregon, in 1880 as the Indian Training School, it was removed to the more healthful environs of Chemawa, from which it was hoped its pupils would return to diffuse American culture among their peoples. Its founder, Lieutenant Melville Wilkinson, Third Infantry, United States Army, scoured the Pacific Northwest for students from what one white observer called Wilkinson's "Christian nursery" for "wigwam babies." At the school the children received English names, and the "native tongue [was] never heard." Heaviest attendance was from the children nearest the school. The mortality rate of the students from the interior was high. It was believed that this was because they were exposed to diseases endemic to the lower altitude at Chemawa. In December, 1883, Agent Joseph Emery reported that of the nineteen children transported from his Klamath agency to Chemawa during the previous three years eleven had died. Spokane chief Lot stated in the early nineties that of twenty-one children of his tribe sent there all but five had died, confirming among his people the truth of their saying that "to go to Chemawa is to die."† Despite these human sacrifices on the altar of American acculturation, the proponents of such schools believed that they would return their graduates to their people as "so

many lanterns of civilization and Christianity." Some Pacific Northwestern Indians also studied—and endured homesickness far from their native lands—at the Carlisle Indian School established in 1884 at Carlisle, Pennsylvania, and at the Haskell Institute established in 1884 at Lawrence, Kansas. Not all whites and Indians believed that their lanterns burned brightly on their return to the reservations, where many were demoralized rather than motivated by their experience in two cultural worlds. A number of students returned to their homes orphaned by the deaths of their parents during their absence.

Especially opposed to sending children to government schools were officials of the Roman Catholic Church. The situation on the Umatilla was similar to that on other reservations. The Catholic agent, R. H. Fay, and the resident priest, Reverend Louis Conrardy (or Conrardi), had tried unsuccessfully in 1881 to resist Wilkinson's attempts to garner the reservation's children for the school at Forest Grove. Catholic agents looked unfavorably on the growing secularization of education, which threatened their long-standing religious educational policies. In 1886 an act of Catholic agent Bartholomew Coffey on the Umatilla symbolized the advent of secular education: under order from superiors in Washington, D. C., he had "the cross removed from the school." He was excommunicated for rendering unto Caesar what his church believed should have been rendered to God.[5]

Secularization was but one of many reasons that the Peace Policy, so nobly conceived and so ignobly ended, failed for both Protestants and Catholics. Other forces playing a part in the policy's demise were sectarianism, Americanism, and agrarianism. The settlers and the military also contributed to its failure. Superintendent Alfred B. Meacham cited the failure of the Indian Office to provide "well-defined regulations" for its operations. Lastly, contributing to the failure of this program dedicated to peace was its very antithesis, war. Even before it had a chance to succeed or fail, dissident Indians seeking to retain their traditional ways of life continued in the seventies their fight against the government, which sought to regain its primacy in controlling Indians even if it meant killing them.

---

*Military camps, around which liquor flowed freely, were a source of great trouble to Indians and of much concern to their chiefs. Chelan chief Nmosize is most likely referring here to the behavior of troops at the newly established Camp Chelan at the lower end of the lake of that name.

---

†Another Pacific Northwestern government-supported Indian School was Cushman Indian School, originally named Puyallup Indian School. Its first buildings were constructed in 1878. In 1910 the name was changed to Cushman.

22. NEZ PERCÉ HOUSE: A HIATUS

Because of its poignancy and drama, the war involving the Nez Percés and the United States is the best known of all later Pacific Northwestern Indian wars. Although the conflict involved but a portion of the tribe, the setting in which it erupted involved all the Nez Percé peoples. In contrast to the natives of central Oregon, the Nez Percés were traditionally friendly to Americans and met gold seekers with less conflict than other tribes did. This did not, however, imply a lack of firmness on their part in confronting outsiders. When Henri Chase, who is credited with discovering gold on a creek flowing into the Grande Ronde River, planned to settle on the Touchet River, the Indians told him that they wanted no farmers or gold seekers in that country. In July, 1856, Major John Owen had received a letter from Chase saying that the Nez Percés had refused to allow whites in their country and wanted no more of their gifts. Instead of settling on Nez Percé lands, some whites moved north to the friendlier climate of the Bitterroot Valley.

In 1860 "Captain" E. D. Pierce and a small party of prospectors discovered gold on the Nez Percé Reservation on Orofino (or Oro Fino) Creek, a branch of the Clearwater. News of the discovery spread on October 21, 1860, to the nearest town, Walla Walla, and the rush was on. To reach the diggings, miners had to cross the Nez Percé Reservation. Led by Lawyer, who still bore the wound he had received in battle with the Blackfeet at Pierre's Hole on July 18, 1832, chiefs from the northern portions of the reservation answered a call from Oregon-Washington Superintendent of Indian Affairs Edward Geary to attend a meeting at Lapwai in early April, 1861, to sign a treaty. Never ratified, it provided for opening the reservation to whites for mining purposes and retaining for "the exclusive use and benefit to the Indians" that portion of the reservation lying north of the Snake, the Clearwater, the South Fork of the Clearwater, and the trail from the South Fork via the Weippe root grounds across the Bitterroot Mountains. By the treaty the Indians agreed to permit access to the mines and agreed to the establishment of a fort on the reservation for their protection.[1]

The Nez Percés began to have mixed feelings about the miners. Unwanted, the latter nevertheless provided the tribe a lucrative market for their horses and for surplus produce from the small garden patches that they had cultivated since mission days along stream beds. The moneys thus earned enabled the Nez Percés to buy much-wanted white men's goods. Even the Nez Percé aristocracy contributed to the advancement of mining. Jane, the daughter of the white-oriented Chief Timothy, guided the miners to gold fields. A Nez Percé headman, Reuben (or Tipyahlanah Oikelazikin and White Bird of the Mountain), built a warehouse at the mouth of the Clearwater and established a ferry for the pas-

sage of miners over that stream. A tent town laid out there in October, 1861, bore the name Lewiston for the American explorer Meriwether Lewis, who had visited there. It was better known to the Nez Percés as Tsceminicum (The Meeting Place).

Nez Percé enterprise impressed a visiting newspaper man. "They are not mendicants," he wrote. "They do not steal, and there again they are superior to the whites." Yet Robert Newell, who knew them well, opined, "The Nez Percés are more dissipated than formerly." After associating with rough white men, they had lost some of the decorum and formality with which they had formerly demeaned themselves.

Prowhite Chief Lawyer was receptive to permitting miners entry to his northern portion of the reservation. On its southern portion Chief Eagle from the Light who had not been invited to the Geary council, opposed the entry of intruders who violated the treaty by slipping south across the Clearwater to mine. To counter the violations, he went so far as to call on the Shoshonis, who were his enemies and longtime raiders of Nez Percé lands. He endeavored to solicit their participation in an alliance to rid the country of miners and others whom the miners brought with them. As miners filled their pouches with dust from the diggings and dampened the dust in their throats with whiskey, they set a poor example to the Indians. To meet the problem of liquor and license, Eagle from the Light called a war council at Lapwai in August, 1861. The miners and their whiskey kept coming. In 1862, miners were pouring in from points as distant as the Fraser River goldfields and those of the California Sierras. In 1861 a "fire boat," the steamer *Colonel Wright*, churned up the Columbia, Snake, and Clearwater rivers carrying miners and supplies. She was followed in 1862 by others in her wake. The *Oregonian*, a newspaper of Portland (which was an important outfitting town for the miners), reported on January 1, 1862, that at that time three million dollars' worth of gold had been shipped there from the Idaho country.

In 1862, Indians were chased from the mouth of the Clearwater by the miners, who were blind in their lust for gold to the rights of the native inhabitants standing in their way. Pack-carrying miners—Boston Jackasses, the Nez Percés called them—traveled the road daily from Lewiston to Florence in the upper Salmon River country. A road was

laid out from Lewiston to Culdesac east of Lapwai and to Orofino on Orofino Creek. Besides Florence, other mining camps were established on the reservation at Pierce City, Salmon, Elk City, and Warren.* In 1863 miners established several more camps on the Salmon River.

Greatly incensed at the increasing flood of miners and at the October, 1863, establishment of Fort Lapwai in keeping with the Geary treaty, Eagle from the Light strengthened his ties with elements of the Shoshonis, Cayuses, Yakimas, Klickitats, Flatheads, and Palouses in an effort to check the intruders. On Camas Prairie he personally stopped miners en route to the Salmon River diggings, warning them not to trespass on Nez Percé lands.

The government not only permitted miners such trespasses, but also planned to appropriate a portion of the Nez Percé Reservation lands. Seeking to ward off this move, Nez Percé chiefs late in 1861 requested a council with government officials but Lawyer opposed it. In 1862 the tribesmen were called by government officials to a council at Lapwai. Arriving there, the Indians found the officials unprepared to deal with them, causing a postponement of the council until the following May, 1863. When that time came, more than two thousand Indians, some from as far away as the Okanogan River, and about twenty thousand horses were on the council grounds. To forestall a possible Indian outbreak, six troop companies were poised in the valley. Representing the government on the grounds were Washington Superintendent of Indian Affairs Calvin H. Hale and his fellow commissioners Charles Hutchins and S. D. Howe. Also present were Robert Newell and William Craig, a son-in-law of the Nez Percé Big Thunder (or James), as intermediaries seeking to prevent possible violence.

Opening the council, the commissioners proposed reducing the reservation by what amounted to a staggering ninety percent. Their friendly disposition to whites notwithstanding, Lawyer and Utsinmalikin, representing the tribes of the north portion, were jarred by the proposal. Sharply questioning Hale, the commission spokesman, they asked why the government had not honored its obligations under the 1855 treaty. The only response that Hale and the other commissioners could give was to assure that the treaty would not be abrogated. On the Indians' request that several whites be ejected from the Lewiston area, Colonel Justus Steinberger, commanding six volunteer companies, removed the trespassers. In ensuing council sessions Lawyer and the subchiefs continued sparring verbally with Hale. Why, asked Lawyer, did tribes who had fought the United States receive more benefits from it than its Nez Percé allies had? "Dig the gold and look at the country," he said, "but we cannot give you the country you ask for." Alluding to the failure of the government to abide by its 1855 treaty obliga-

tions, he told the commissioners that all he had seen on the reservation were the mills. A sawmill to which he referred would shortly supply lumber—mainly to whites.

On Lawyer's refusal to accept Hale's offer, the council recessed. Six days later on June 3 it reopened, this time with a thousand more Indians on the grounds, including antiwhite traditionalists under Eagle from the Light, Red Owl, Old Joseph, White Bird, and Big Thunder. In their own councils the chiefs argued bitterly whether or not to sell their lands and, if they did, which ones and how much of them. From those minicouncils a strong current of militancy emerged among the traditionalists. Helping foster their militancy was the Delaware Tom Hill, who had come among the Nez Percés in the forties. He had opposed Whitman's ministrations and he also had opposed the 1855 treaty. He had even persuaded about a hundred Nez Percé lodges to recognize him as their chief. Ellis and other Christian-oriented Nez Percés believed him to be demented.

Faced with resistance to their proposals and a consequent stalemate, the commissioners were forced to change their strategy by meeting with individual chiefs in small councils. The first chief with whom they conferred was Lawyer, who was followed by several others. Anticipating trouble, the commissioners called on Colonel Steinberger to dispatch troops to the council grounds. Responding, the colonel sent in a detachment of the Oregon Cavalry under Captain Currey. When the Indians failed to reach agreement among themselves, Big Thunder walked out of their council—a move symbolizing the rupture of Nez Percé unity. The bands agreed that they should no longer be considered a unified people, reverting instead to their status before their 1842 pact with Dr. Elijah White, when they had agreed to have but one head chief. Each leader now spoke for his own band. Claiming no part of the proposed treaty, Big Thunder shook hands with Lawyer, saying that they would continue as friends despite their differences. As he left one of the sessions with the commissioners, he said, "I am very sick, and spitting blood, excuse me." More anti-Lawyer than anti-treaty, Big Thunder had left not wishing to lose face to his rival. All the traditionalists departed without signing the treaty. Among those who signed the June 9 document were Lawyer and fifty-one of his followers. Except for Timothy and Jason none of the signatories lived outside the confines of the reduced reservation. In signing, Lawyer and the others surrendered all of their reservation lands except for 756,968 acres (1,182.76 square miles).

The treaty remained unratified until 1867, four years after its signing. The 1855 treaty ratification had been similarly delayed. In August, 1868, Lawyer, Timothy, and Jason signed a supplemental treaty (ratified in February, 1869) permitting off-reservation Indians to be moved to the confine, where they were to be given parcels of land. The treaty also provided for congressional restoration of squandered school funds.

Lawyer signed the 1863 treaty believing he had done so only for his own faction, which represented only a third of the Nez Percés. To the present day many of the tribe believe he tricked their ancestors into accepting the diminished res-

---

*Because of its high altitude, the Florence area was unfrequented by Indians. Pierce City was off their beaten paths. Elk City was on the Nez Percé trail to hunt buffalo and was a contact point for whites. Pierce City nonetheless was on Indian land, and Elk City perhaps was also because the Nez Percés claimed an area that extended east of Lewiston to a vague boundary that was called in their 1855 treaty "the spurs of the Bitter Root Mountains."

ervation. Lawyer was also accused by reds and whites alike of obtaining large numbers of signatures to the treaty to make it appear that the Indians overwhelmingly favored it. Not to be overlooked, however, were the efforts of the commissioners. Like Stevens and Palmer before them, they had used bandwagon and bantering techniques to secure the signatures.

After the council the troops moved south to select a site for Fort Boise. Miners were already flocking into the area. Antitreaty Nez Percés returned to their villages to ponder what had transpired. Those of Chief White Bird went to villages on Salmon River; those of Looking Glass to villages on Clear Lake, a branch of the Middle Fork of the Clearwater; and those of Old Joseph to villages in the Wallowa country.

During the ensuing decade the Nez Percé camps steamed like pent-up volcanoes as whites moved onto their surrendered lands to mine, farm, and complain to the government about the Indian "nuisance." Heading the whites' complaints, officials pressured the Indians into leaving their homes for the shrunken confine. Increasing pressures for removal brought a corresponding reaction from the Indians as they pondered a quarter century of mistreatment. Had not Stevens and Palmer told them that the reservation was theirs? If so, why had it been reduced? Why had stage roads, stations, and now the whispering wires of the telegraph marked up their lands? Why had white men cut down their trees? Why had moneys appropriated for them been squandered? In short, why had the government treated them so poorly? Their complaints were more than justified. As noted, the sawmill provided them by the 1855 treaty furnished lumber primarily to whites. The schoolhouse had been traded to Robert Newell, and until 1864 the teacher did not teach. The agency doctor doubled as the Fort Lapwai surgeon and worked no more than three hours a week for the Indians. Five agency farmers had not even produced enough for their own subsistence despite good soils. The blacksmith knew little of his trade. The agency had no gunsmith or wagon makers' shop.

Thanks to tutoring by Spalding and other whites, the Nez Percés had developed a sophistication in assessing the worth of annuity goods,many of which they quickly detected as substandard. When they unburdened their complaints on Governor Lyon in 1864, he told them to till the soil and avoid three things: the predatory life, drinking whiskey, and other pitfalls dug by whites. After the Senate ratified the 1863 treaty of Governor David W. Ballard's council with Nez Percé tribesmen at Lewiston on June 19, 1867, to implement provisions of the treaty was dubbed by his critics "a magnificent fizzle." Hampering Ballard's efforts had been Lyon's theft of Indian funds for implementing the treaty and the failure of the United States to fulfill its treaty obligations. No wonder the Indians talked saucy to Ballard. His political foes did so too, even blaming him for continuing the Snake War.

In the Wallowa country, where Young Joseph had assumed the chieftaincy on the death of his father, Old Joseph, in August, 1871, there was much talk of war. The father had admonished the son never to surrender the land covering his bones. War talk was fanned by the failure of the government to remove settlers on Nez Percé lands between the Snake, the Grande Ronde, and the West Fork of the Wallowa River—the area that President Grant on June 16, 1873, had ordered set aside as a reservation for Joseph and his people. In an August 2 meeting at Lapwai with John P. C. Shanks, who headed a three-man commission, Joseph, refusing schools on his Wallowa Reservation, delivered his classic indictment that his people were taught to quarrel by Christians of Protestant and Catholic churches. His hopes for isolation from white influences seemed doomed. Increased white pressures to have his reservation withdrawn were officially expressed in a letter from Oregon Governor Lafayette F. Grover to Secretary of the Interior Delano. An order of June 10, 1875, withdrew the reservation.

The task of breaking to Joseph the news of the government order fell to Agent Monteith. In effect, the order meant that he and his people had to remove themselves to the Nez Percé Reservation. Joseph was sullen. Back in the

Chief Joseph, well known for his leadership of the Nez Percés in their flight from the U.S. Army in 1877. This photograph was taken when Joseph lived on the Colville Indian Reservation, where he and some of his people went in 1885 after confinement in Indian Territory in Oklahoma. Museum of Native American Cultures.

Wallowa Valley a council was held of important nontreaty chiefs: Joseph, Eagle from the Light, White Bird, and Looking Glass. Also present was the Dreamer Toohoolsote counseling for war. On learning from Agent Monteith the incendiary nature of the situation, General O. O. Howard dispatched two cavalry companies to the Wallowa. On the Umatilla Reservation in the spring of that year, 1875, Joseph talked with the general, who had opposed stripping him of his Wallowa lands.

In June, 1876, rapidly moving events translated the Nez Percé resentment into action after two whites killed an Indian in the Wallowa country. In revenge for the killing and other depredations and encroachments of whites, young Nez Percé braves called for their extermination. Trying to prevent such retaliation, Monteith asked Joseph to come to Lapwai. After a conference there between the chief and the agent, Monteith believed a crisis was at hand and again asked Howard to dispatch troops to the Wallowa. Howard ordered Captain David Perry, the commander of the troops at Fort Lapwai, to visit Joseph to see what was needed to preserve the peace.

In November, 1876, Joseph consented to a meeting at Lapwai with a commission, of which General Howard was a member, to discuss a move onto the reduced Nez Percé Reservation. During the deliberations the chief was on the point of acceding to the move when he was dissuaded from it by Toohoolsote. In early 1877, Joseph sent word to the Umatilla agent, Narcisse Cornoyer, that transactions at the council had been poorly interpreted. Advised of this by Cornoyer, Howard requested that Joseph come down to the Umatilla to talk with one of his aides, since he himself was in Portland. Countering this move, Joseph sent his brother Ollicut (or Ollikut, Olokut, and the like) to meet with the aide, Lieutenant William H. Boyle. As Joseph sent word that he had been promised an interview with Howard in the spring, the general planned to meet him at Walla Walla in April. At the same time Monteith had given Joseph until the first of that month to gather his people and stock and remove to the reservation. Joseph believed this ultimatum to be the final wrong done to his people not only by white men but also by treaty Nez Percés, amongst whom the government now wanted them to live.

Those anxieties and the jockeying with the military regarding times and places of confrontations only increased the tensions in Joseph and his people, causing Howard to plan a military post in the Wallowas—which, in turn, only created more tension among the Indians. Without waiting for a hoped-for reservation and favorable treatment by the government, Joseph's Nez Percés bought guns from farmers in exchange for cayuses, and Looking Glass set about recruiting an army of warriors. At the April 19 Walla Walla meeting with Howard, Ollicut again substituted for Joseph, this time because the latter was ill. He asked for more time to remove from the Wallowa. On Howard's refusal to grant the extension of time, Ollicut suggested that the Umatilla Reservation be dissolved and its Indians removed to the Wallowas. The Nez Percés were intermarried with the Indians on the Umatilla. For a time it looked like such a transfer

would be effected, especially since from the beginning of the seventies whites had been discovering the rich soils beneath the lush Umatilla grasses—which soon would make it one of the greatest wheat-producing regions on earth. Since the Indians of that reservation were more interested in grazing horses than in growing wheat, it was small wonder that the editor of a newspaper in Pendleton, which would be withdrawn from the Umatilla Reservation, wrote on August 5, 1882, "We favor their removal as it is a burning shame to keep this fine body of land for a few worthless Indians."

In the April 19 meeting with Howard, Ollicut requested that the general meet with the entire nontreaty Nez Percé band. After several futile attempts to gain the ear of the general, who was now avoiding Smohalla for fear of treachery, the Dreamer went to Howard with word from Toohoolsote that the nontreaty Nez Percés wanted freedom to roam at large. Although Joseph lived farthest from Lapwai, where Howard had promised to meet him on May 3, he was the first to arrive. He was accompanied by Ollicut, the Dreamer-influenced Cayuse Young Chief, and about fifty members of his band. On the following day White Bird joined the parley.

From the opening of the council, when he insisted that Perrin Whitman (nephew of the missionary) interpret correctly, Toohoolsote dominated the proceedings with often-repeated declamations that the earth, the Indians' mother, should not be plowed or otherwise disturbed. On the third day of the proceedings, May 7, the Dreamer declaimed: "What the treaty Indians talk about was born of to-day! it isn't true law at all. You white people get together, measure the earth, and then divide it; so I want you to talk directly what you mean!" To this Monteith replied: "The law is, you must come to the reservation; the law is made in Washington. We don't make it." To this Toohoolsote answered: "We never have made any trade. Part of the Indians gave up their land. I never did. The earth is part of my body, and I never gave up the earth."

The dialogue in council reveals that Nez Percé traditionalists believed that the government's aggressive and acquisitive policies did not square with the teachings of Christianity that white men purported to follow. Old Joseph had been one of Spalding's first two converts (besides Timothy). He had expressed symbolically his anger and disillusionment at the divergence between what white men practiced and what they preached when he tore up a treaty and his New Testament and "turned back to Egypt." Old Joseph's rejection of Christianity had produced a spiritual void that was a fertile soil for the cultivation of the Dreamer faith, causing trouble for the government in its dealings with traditionalist Indians.

Failing to see that the Indians' nativist religion was inexorably associated with their lands, Howard claimed that the government did not wish to interfere with their religion, reminding Toohoolsote that he knew very well the government "had set apart a reservation, and that the Indians must go upon it." Howard continued: "If an Indian, becomes a citizen, like old Timothy of Alpowa he can have land like any other citizen outside, but he has to leave his tribe, and take lands precisely as a white man does. The government has set apart this large reservation for you and your children, that you may live in peace, and prosper." At this Toohoolsote became furious, demanding to know, "What person pretends to divide the land, and put me on it?" Howard replied: "I am the man. I stand here for the President, and there is no spirit good or bad that will hinder me. My orders are plain and will be executed. I hoped that the Indians had good sense enough to make me their friend, and not their enemy."

When Looking Glass and White Bird concurred with Toohoolsote, stating that they would not go on the Nez Percé Reservation, Howard gave them an ultimatum to remove to that confine, and, after threatening the Dreamer with confinement in the Indian Territory, he arrested him. During his incarceration the nontreaty chiefs went with Howard to look over the reservation, as though resigning themselves to going there. At the same time, White Bird and Looking Glass pled for Toohoolsote's release. Howard was apparently unwilling to risk the wrath of Toohoolsote's followers, and, on receipt of the Dreamer's promise to conform and to give his people "good advice," Howard released him from a five-day confinement. The nontreaty Nez Percés were causing great concern not only to Howard but also to the treaty Nez Percés as well. Should trouble erupt between the two factions, the treaty Indians had only shotguns, where the others had breech-loading rifles and pistols. Outweighing this disparity in arms, the treaty bands outnumbered the nontreaty bands by three or four to one.

The government at this time sought to confine not just the nontreaty Nez Percés but all nontreaty and nonreservation Indians. The independence of those along the Columbia River—whom the whites called "renegades"—was affecting surrounding tribes. To curb their disaffecton, Howard assigned an inspector of Indian affairs, E. C. Watkins, the task of rounding them up for removal. In early June, 1877, various Columbia River peoples, including the rivals, Smohalla and Moses, met Howard at Fort Simcoe to hear his statement that they had to go to a reservation.

The Fort Simcoe council was held in the twenty-day interval that had been given Joseph to remove his people to the reservation. Joseph and his band reluctantly left the Wallowa country with Toohoolsote's tempting war talk in their ears. In their haste to meet the unrealistic June 14 deadline for removal, they abandoned livestock and much household and ranch equipment for the trek to confinement. Crossing the flood-swollen Snake River in makeshift rafts, they lost no lives, but some of their horses stampeded back to their old ranges, from which they were never recovered. Across the Snake the band trailed to Salmon River, ferrying that stream and moving to a Tolo Lake meadow about six miles west of Grangeville, Idaho, where other nontreaty Nez Percés met them. Until the final day set for removal they tried to prepare for winter.

A brooding, drinking young brave named Wahlitits (Wal-lai-its and the like) rode about camp. The whites had killed his father, Eagle Robe, the previous year on the Salmon River. His horse trampled some bulbs that an Indian woman was curing. Incensed at a rebuke from her husband, the young brave rode down on June 13 to Salmon River to avenge his father's death. He was accompanied by his cousins, Red Moccasin Tops (Sarpsis Ilppilp) and Swan Necklace (Wetyetmas, Wyakaikt, and the like). Unable to find the killer, a white man named Larry Ott (who had fled), they shot a settler, killed three other white men, and wounded another. On the next day the three revenge-seekers were joined by several more Indians, mostly of White Bird's band, and the group committed a dozen atrocities—all of which were unauthorized by Joseph, who at the time was off with Ollicut butchering beef for their people. On learning of the killings, Joseph knew that they meant war.

Joseph moved with his band to a camp at the bottom of White Bird Canyon[2] north of the Salmon River, a place that was well chosen for defense. They were now refugees. Only seventy of the braves had arms with which to fire the precious ammunition that they had been secretly hoarding. Early on the morning of June 17 they deployed atop eminences and prepared to meet Captain Perry's troops, which numbered nearly a hundred. A coyote call signaled them to charge the troops. The latter met their advance with rifle fire. The Nez Percés counterfired, killing the trumpeter, John Jones. The eternal peace envisioned by their forefathers and Lewis and Clark was now broken. In heavy firing a dozen troops fell from their mounts. In the confusion following the killing of a second trumpeter, Lieutenant Edward R. Theller and eighteen of his men were shot down on the spot. Regrouping, the shattered command hastily withdrew. The Indians lost none killed. Two were wounded.

On June 27, Howard, assuming field command, reached the Salmon River several miles upstream from White Bird Creek and established a camp opposite that of the Indians. On July 1, as the troops were crossing the Salmon with some difficulty, their red foes fled into camp at Craig's Ferry twenty-five miles downstream. On the next day the Indians crossed the Salmon to camp at Aipadass, having put some distance between themselves and Howard, who did not reach Craig's Ferry until July 5. Joseph wished the one-armed general to follow his band across the Salmon, whereupon he planned to cut off the troops' supplies. Rather than cross the river, the general moved from Craig's Ferry back upstream, recrossing it at the mouth of White Bird Creek. He reached Grangeville on July 8. Captain Stephen G. Whipple was dispatched to find Looking Glass, who was absent on his home ground near the Middle Fork of the Clearwater during the fight. As troops commanded Looking Glass to come forth, general firing erupted. One of the chief's men was shot in the thigh, a young man and a woman and her baby were killed, and two others wounded. The Indians abandoned their camp to the troops, who moved in to pillage it, trample gardens, and capture many horses.

On July 3 advance guards of Joseph's and White Bird's bands emerged from the Salmon River. Their rifle fire downed one of two civilians whom Captain Whipple had dispatched to scout Mahoney Creek for roaming Indians. Nez Percé scouts had been kept on Camas Prairie to guard the trails used by the main Joseph–White Bird bands to cross the Clearwater. At noon on July 5 they attacked a seventeen-man volunteer party returning to Cottonwood. By the time Howard had emerged from Salmon River, the Nez Percés had reached eighty volunteers from Mount Idaho near Grangeville. Ollicut's men withstood the volunteers' attack, in what the whites called the Misery Hill Fight. Joining forces, Joseph and White Bird camped with their people just above the confluence of the South and Middle forks of the Clearwater. Their combined warrior strength was a mere two hundred and fifty braves, an insufficient force to cope with their attackers in the three-day fight led by Toohoolsote that began on July 11. In meeting the cavalry charge on the twelfth they deployed too far left, exposing themselves. Several troop sorties sent them tumbling through woods and over rocks, ravines, and ridges into the river. With no time for the women to pack their camp, the band moved fighting downstream, crossing the Clearwater on July 13, from which they escaped to Wieppe Prairie.

With their defeat on the Clearwater, the various chiefs began to argue about what they should do next. Four options lay open to them: they could counterattack the troops, surrender, return to the Wallowa, or move east to Crow country. It would be a difficult problem in logistics to move the nearly seven hundred refugees, whatever course they chose.

At Weippe Prairie on July 14 they met Red Heart and his Nez Percé band returning from hunting buffalo. Red Heart did not join them in flight. Instead he returned with some of the refugees to Kamiah, where they were captured by General Howard. After much controversy the chiefs decided on July 15 to move east to the land of the Crows. Believing that tribe would receive them as brothers, Looking Glass, Toohoolsote, Five Crows, Rainbow, and Five Wounds argued for going there. Reluctant to concur in the decision, Joseph, who was now approaching his fortieth year, deferred to Looking Glass to command the band.

The refugees moved along the Lolo Trail. On July 17 five warriors serving as a rearguard attacked a scouting unit of the troop command, who retreated to Kamiah. The Indians paused to rest when they reached Lolo Creek, a point within an easy day's travel of its confluence with the Bitterroot. There they were surprised by troops of Captain Charles C. Rawn. Joseph, White Bird, and Looking Glass conferred with Rawn on July 27 and 28 at Fort Missoula, which had just been established on June 7, 1877. It was later dubbed Fort Fizzle. The captain had been dispatched to the fort to strengthen it. The Nez Percés agreed with Rawn to move through the Bitterroot without disturbing settlers during their passage. Chief Charlot ordered them to leave the valley immediately, even refusing to shake the proffered hand of Looking Glass, on which he said was "the blood of the white man." The presence of Eagle from the Light among the Flatheads during the war greatly disturbed Bitterroot settlers.

Reaching the Big Hole Basin, where they expected a respite of several days, the Nez Percés established a village camp of about ninety lodges along the east bank of the Big Hole River. There the women gathered firewood and cut lodge and travois poles while their men fished. Their strength was somewhat renewed, and they danced in exhilaration at their respite, unaware that troops were hot on their trail. On August 4, the day after arriving at Fort Missoula, Colonel John Gibbon led his command up the Bitterroot Valley in the direction of the Nez Percés. Howard and his command reached the Bitterroot four days later.

The Nez Percés failed to heed Five Wounds' warning that they post sentinels around their camp. On August 9 soldiers shot a Nez Percé out looking for horses. Gibbon's troops, finding their quarry, rushed the camp, attacking swiftly and scattering the Indians in all directions. Many went to the cover of the willow-lined river, into which they jumped behind its banks and bushes. Others, confused, were cut down before they could escape from their lodges, whose dampness kept the troops from firing them. In close-quarter combat the Indians fired into their attackers, clubbing them down. About noon they rushed for a howitzer on a hill. Escaping two blasts from the lumbering weapon, they dismantled it and rolled it into a ravine. Attacking, they crept behind their enemy's line and also captured a pack mule carrying over two thousand rounds of Springfield rifle ammunition. The ammunition was a valuable prize since they collected a number of the rifles from the battlefield to augment that their fighting women picked up from their fallen husbands. In the howitzer skirmish they killed a corporal, wounded two sergeants, and sent six others fleeing to their badly mauled command. Gibbon himself suffered a flesh wound in the side. Among the approximately eighty-seven Indians killed were thirty-three warriors. Ironically, one of them, Five Wounds, had urged the posting of sentinels to prevent a surprise attack. Others who fell were Red Moccasin Tops, Rainbow, and Wahlitits and his wife. Wives of Joseph and Ollicut were also cut down. Nearly all the lodges were destroyed.

After the Big Hole fight the battered Nez Percés limped up Pioneer Creek, crossed Skinner Meadows and over a pass, and descended South Bloody Dick Creek to the mouth of Stevenson's Canyon. From there they crossed a ridge on the west to Horse Prairie in Montana, where they camped on August 12. South of the Big Hole at Bannock City, Montana, which Howard reached on August 14, the citizenry readied their defenses. Their fears were not unlike those of others where the Nez Percés might have passed or sent emissaries seeking reinforcements. On June 19, two days after hostilities began, two Nez Percés had visited Coeur d'Alène chief Seltis and Spokane Garry, seeking to entice them into hostilities, as whites huddled for safety on Havermale Island in the Spokane River and others scurried to the safety of the settlements. When Seltis refused to let them camp at the mission, a Nez Percé band moved northward across the Spokane River. On the south war hysteria and rumors that troops were coming to fight Indians had spread to Fort Hall, whose Bannocks the Indian Office had tried to confine during the troubles, as it had Indians on other reservations. Some Bannocks under Buffalo Horn scouted for Howard during the conflict. Farther south Indians of the Malheur Reservation did not openly engage in the war. Their greatest fear was that the Nez Percés might steal their horses.

Under Nez Percé pressure to join his old friend Joseph, Chief Moses displayed a bent for diplomacy rather than war characteristic of his younger days and withheld his people from hostilities. The Catholic missionaries Joset and Cataldo and the Protestant ministers, the Reverends Henry T. Cowley and S. G. Havermale, were among the whites quieting the Indians of the northern Interior, where Garry and Seltis were using their influence for peace. After a council with Colonel Frank Wheaton at Spokane Falls, which began on August 15 and was attended by several interior tribesmen, the Indians turned over eight prisoners whom they described as "Nez Percés and bad Indians."

The fleeing Nez Percé combatants could have used the services even of neutrals in their flight, which took them through Bannock Pass back over the Continental Divide and down Cruikshank Canyon into Idaho. As they detoured in the areas of the upper Lemhi River and Birch Creek, Idaho, Bannock Chief Tendoy nudged them through that country. Bands under Looking Glass and White Bird reached Junction, Idaho, south of Salmon City, on August 13, establishing a camp near present-day Leadore. The women, children, and elderly under Joseph's care trailed several hours behind.

As at other camps, the Nez Percés set their defenses against attack. Moving rapidly now, they evaded their ever-nearer pursuers. On August 15, in Birch Creek Canyon they stumbled onto a frieighter outfit, whose supplies, guns and kegs of whiskey an advance guard had appropriated. On Joseph's orders the kegs were broken open denying the braves their inflammatory contents. Even without them the braves killed five freighters, freeing two Chinamen. From Birch Creek, on the evening of the seventeeth after skirting foothills on the southeast, they reached the stage road a mile north of Hole-in-Rock station. On the nineteenth Howard's pursuing command camped on Camas Creek just south of the Continental Divide (west of Yellowstone National Park, Wyoming). As they did when confronting the Blackfeet, Nez Percé raiders crept to the soldier camp and unloosened picketed horses. They made off with two hundred mules as a hundred horsemen chased them northward at dawn.

After an easterly crossing of the Continental Divide through Targhee Pass, they camped on August 22 at present-day West Yellowstone, Montana, along the upper Madison River, which the chiefs elected to follow. Shortly they came upon a white prospector, a Mr. Shively, who would remain with them until Aug. 31. All the time they were trailed by fifty Bannocks scouting for Howard. On the morning of August 24 they came upon a white family named Cowans, and on the following day they captured a white man named Irwin. On September 8, surrounded by the Bannock scouts, they made a "precipitous exit" from the Absaroka Mountains on the eastern borders of present-day Yellowstone National Park. On reaching Clark Fork, a Yellowstone tributary, Looking Glass, who boasted of friendship with the Crows, went ahead to seek that tribe's help only to have their chiefs spurn his pleas to them to fight their allies the Long Knife Americans. Their refusal diminished Looking Glass's already reduced position among

Dave Williams, a Nez Percé who went through the Nez Percé War as a young man in 1877.

his people.

Moving toward the mouth of Canyon Creek north of the Yellowstone River (west of Billings, Montana), the Nez Percé warriors began firing on the troops of Colonel Samuel D. Sturgis and 360 other troops of General George Custer's old Seventh Cavalry command. As they raced toward them, other warriors directed by Looking Glass formed a steady-firing rearguard. Various commands by now had been dispatched over Montana and Wyoming to run them down. The skirmishing at the mouth of Canyon Creek was brief as the pursued ones kept moving until after dark. Accompanied by the Crows, Sturgis disengaged to camp at the mouth of the creek, then resumed the chase for several days until the troops reached the Musselshell River. North of Canyon Creek on September 14 about one hundred Crows and Bannocks with Sturgis attacked the Nez Percé rearguard in a fast-moving two-day skirmish.

245

Besides Howard and Sturgis, the Nez Percés were about to face Colonel Nelson A. Miles, who was moving from Fort Keogh at the mouth of Tongue River near Miles City, Montana, to intercept them. After failing to cast their fortunes with the Crows, the Nez Percés, instead of moving east, swung north in hopes of joining the Sioux chief Sitting Bull in sanctuary exile across the Canadian border. Believing that they had reached the border, they rested at Bear Paw Mountain eight miles south of Milk River near present-day Chinook, Montana. They were actually about forty miles short of their destination. Spurning Poker Joe's urgent pleas to push north, Looking Glass, feeling secure, allowed his tired and starving camp a slow retreat. Spotted by Miles's Cheyenne scouts, the Nez Percés faced Miles's command charging down on them, dissecting their camp, and capturing most of their horses. Dazed and confused, many warriors were unable to round up their ponies to escape. Joseph's twelve-year-old daughter was able to find a horse to join those fleeing into Canada.

Fighting now moved to close quarters. The combatants were sometimes only twenty paces apart. Repulsing the soldiers, the Nez Percés captured much of their arms and ammunition. During the first day and night of combat the Nez Percés lost twenty-two killed. Six of them died at the feet of Joseph, who, with his wife and children, dashed unarmed through the soldier line. Several others were killed as the soldiers rushed their lodges. Others with camas hooks and butcher knives tried to save themselves in trenches, from which they shoveled the dirt with pans. During the first day of the attack Miles lost fifty-three killed and forty wounded—lethal proof of the Nez Percés' fighting spirit and accurate rifle fire. Among the twenty-two Nez Percés killed were Ollicut, Toohoolsote, and Poker Joe. Three of the twenty-two were shot by the Palouse Dreamer, Hushhushcote, who mistook them for Cheyenne scouts.

On October 1, across a landscape whitened by recent snow, the Nez Percés saw a truce flag flying from the soldier camp. Later they heard a voice calling out in the Chinook jargon that Miles wished to talk with Joseph. After conferring with White Bird and Looking Glass, Joseph prepared to parley with the colonel. The other two chiefs opposed such a talk lest Joseph surrender the band, whereupon they might all be shot or hanged. Before Joseph went over to parley, the Nez Percés sent Tom HIll, their interpreter, to talk with Miles. On receipt through Hill of Miles's assurances of Joseph's safety, the chief and the interpreter crossed over to Miles, who waited halfway from the Indian camp. At the meeting Joseph refused to surrender his people's arms, but, on the condition that the band be returned to the Wallowas, he acceded to Miles's demand that they cease fighting. Miles said that he would take Joseph and his people to Fort Keogh for the winter, releasing them in the spring. On Joseph's continued refusal to surrender, Miles ordered his men to bind his hands and feet.

When Joseph was in Miles' camp, a Lieutenant Lovell H. Jerome reconnoitered the Indian camp. On learning that Miles had detained Joseph, the Nez Percés detained Jerome as hostage. That same day the soldiers captured some Nez

Percé fleeing northward, and some Assiniboins killed a couple of fleeing Nez Percés and drove others away. On that day the troops fired cannon into the Nez Percé ranks. That night more snow fell on the Indians' fireless camp—a chilly contrast to that of the soldiers, where the men warmed themselves around fires, found cover in their tents, and ate warm food. The Nez Percés expectantly awaited aid from Sitting Bull, to whom they had sent a call for help. They clung to the hope that the Sioux Chief would sweep down from Canada with an Indian force to rescue them. On October 2, Joseph and Jerome were exchanged. On his release Joseph conferred with White Bird and Looking Glass, who were fearful that Joseph had committed himself to surrender. During the day gunfire between the soldier and Indian camps was accompanied by the cries of Indian children suffering from cold and hunger.

On October 4, Howard joined Miles at Bear Paw. The general was accompanied by two treaty Nez Percés, Captain John and Old George. On the next day, wearing feathered caps and white men's clothes, the two treaty Indians rode carrying a flag to the Nez Percé lines. The Nez Percés restrained one of their groups from shooting the approaching envoys. The warriors called a council to discuss the request of Captain John and Old George that they surrender. Looking Glass and White Bird remained averse to such a move, unlike Joseph, who wished to surrender to alleviate the suffering in their camp. From the soldier camp Howard asked why they did not surrender. For a second time Captain John and Old George rode into the Nez Percé camp with a truce flag to tell Joseph that Howard wished a talk—that he wished to stop fighting. At this the Indians reasoned that there would be a stalemate permitting them to break off hostilities and return to their homeland. Looking Glass and White Bird opposed any truce lest they be shot or hanged as Wright had done to his captives after the Spokane–Coeur d'Alène War. Looking Glass warned Joseph that their two-tongued foe would destroy them and, seeing his flight ending, decided with White Bird to flee into Canada. Of the three, only White Bird made good his escape. Looking Glass hoped that some approaching Indians were Sitting Bull's braves. They proved to be Miles's scouts. They shot and killed him to end his journeyings forever.

Sickened by those developments and having so few warriors, Joseph announced to his people that he was calling a halt to the fighting. With five warriors he rode out to meet Howard and Miles on a hill. Behind the officers stood a courier ready to carry the surrender news to Fort Keogh. Joseph rode up and handed his rifle to Howard, who in turn handed it to Miles, his superior. Accompanying that symbol of surrender was Joseph's speech, a classic of American literature, in which he declared the plight of his people and his avowal to "fight no more forever."

Instead of returning west, 79 men, 78 women, and 174 children were taken to Fort Keogh. From there they traveled down the Yellowstone River to the Missouri and down that river to Fort Lincoln (Bismark, North Dakota). Among the captives was the son of the explorer Clark, who nearly three-

*Yellow Bull, a Nez Percé subchief during the Nez Percé War.
Like Chief Joseph he returned from Indian Territory to live on the
Colville Indian Reservation. Photograph by Frank Avery, circa
1900.*

quarters of a century earlier had ascended that stream. At Fort Lincoln the captives were lionized by whites. Very fine—but it did not prevent their being taken to Fort Leavenworth, Kansas, whence they were shipped in July, 1878, to the Quapaw and later the Ponca agency in Indian Territory. The humidity of that land, contrasting sharply with the rarefied atmosphere of their beloved Wallowa Mountains, caused them to succumb to melancholia and other diseases.

Seeking relief for their people, Joseph, Yellow Bull, and an interpreter journeyed to the national capital in January, 1879. They received from its officials more promise than per-

formance and more acclaim than accommodation. In that same year three Christian Nez Percés, including James Reuben, a student of the Presbyterian missionary Sue McBeth, arrived from Lapwai under government auspices to teach and preach among the captives. Reuben also pled with government officials in the capital to return the Nez Percés to their homeland. The government was more influenced by the settlers who wanted them out of the Wallowas than by Reuben and others who wanted them in that country, and it failed to act on their removal, although twenty-nine Nez Percés (two of them old men and the others mostly widows) were permitted to return to the Nez Percé Reservation. In

Nez Percé warriors en route to Indian Territory in Oklahoma after being captured at the end of the Nez Percé war with the *United States in 1877. Museum of Native American Cultures.*

the meantime, as members of the national Presbyterian Church increased efforts on behalf of Joseph and his people, the chief sent emissaries westward to arrange for their return. Until such a time they clung to hopes that a deliverer would rescue them from their exile with all its troubles, not the least of which were the white man's labor and the laws that were imposed on them during confinement.

Eight long years after the retreat that took them half a continent from their homes, the Nez Percés returned to the west. After reaching Wallula Junction on the Columbia River by rail on May 27, 1885, 92 adults, 12 children, and 14 infants were returned to Lapwai. Joseph, his second-in-command (Yellow Bull), 118 other adults, 16 children, and 14 infants were sent to the Colville Reservation. The move was pleasing not only to many whites of Idaho Territory but also to some Indians of the Nez Percé Agency who did not want them there. Considerable opposition to their coming

on the Colville was shown by its original inhabitants, the San Poils and Nespelems, who castigated Chief Moses for welcoming and harboring them on that confine.

In 1904, Joseph died—of a broken heart, according to the Colville Agency physician—and he was buried on that confine at Nespelem, where his bones lie far from those of his father in the Wallowas. White men were one day to name a Columbia River dam for him. The token, albeit sincere, ill fits this one who remained a traditionalist until he died.

The defeat and confinement of Joseph and his people proved that the government had a strong arm to control dissident Indians. By contrast its hand to sustain them was weak. As Joseph and his followers bore their confinement with sullen resignation, other Indians, under no such vows as his at Bear Paw to "fight no more forever," would try to bite the hand that was not feeding them. One consequence was the Bannock-Paiute War.

23. BANNOCK-PAIUTES: EMBATTLED TRIBESMEN

During the Nez Percé War the Indian Office sought to induce the Paiutes of the Pacific Northwest to go on reservations. In July, 1877, Idaho Territorial Governor Mason Brayman persuaded Chief Egan of the Malheur Agency to come to the southwestern part of his territory to try to induce over a hundred Paiutes or Weiser River Shoshonis under Chiefs Eagle Eye and Bear Skin to go on the Malheur. Evidence of the Indian Office's wish to confine the Paiutes was seen in the visit of a special agent to the Priest Rapids lodge of Smohalla. The agent was trying to lure onto a reservation one of the hunchbacked prophet's disciples, the Paiute Waltsac, who was a terror to whites in the John Day Valley. Waltsac told the agent that like white men he wanted to go and do as he pleased.

Winnemucca and some of his people roamed along the Owyhee River in southeastern Idaho. Other Paiutes under subchief Leggins had spent a cold winter in 1876–77 on the Malheur Reservation with no government distribution of blankets. Winnemucca abandoned his original plan of taking his people to make permanent homes at the Duck Valley Agency in Nevada, since it was to be set aside by executive order on April 16, 1877, for Western Shoshonis. When given an ultimatum to move either to Pyramid Lake Reservation in Northwestern Nevada or to the Malheur, he chose the latter. The Malheur Reservation was to him the lesser of the two evils, although a Smohalla-influenced Paiute, Oytes, lived there, and Winnemucca disclaimed his Dreamer practices.

The Paiutes often moved to military camps at the insistence of whites who were seeking protection from the Indians. Chief Ocheo, for instance, went to Camp Bidwell, which was in California south of the former Paiute stronghold in the Warner Mountains. Indians also went to Camp McDermit in northern Nevada, where they did not have to work as Indians did at the reservations. Winnemucca and half his people wintered at Camp McDermit in 1874–75. In the winter of 1877–78 Eagle Eye and Bear Skin's Weisers were on the Malheur Reservation, as were some of Winnemucca's Paiutes. Among those who wintered with Ocheo north of Camp Bidwell in Warner Valley were Waltsac, some of Winnemucca's people, and nearly two hundred Paiutes who were not tied down on any reservation. The white settlers angrily objected to Indian horses grazing the ranges, but failed to see the injustice when they, in turn, drove their livestock onto Indian reservations to graze. In 1878 stockmen ran 1,400 horses and 10,839 cattle on the Malheur Reservation alone. To satisfy the complaints of the settlers clamoring for the opening of the western portion of that reservation, where their stock grazed, the Malheur agent, Major W. V. Rinehart, suggested that the whites lease the land to settle the immediate problem. On June 28,

1876, Rinehart had replaced Sam B. Parrish, who had served as agent since August, 1874.

The military Fort Hall had been established on May 27, 1870, about twenty-five miles from the old fur-trading Fort Hall and fifteen miles from the Fort Hall Agency. In May, 1878, troops from the fort were sent to garrison Camp Douglas in Utah. The Fort Hall agent, W. H. Danilson, feared that the absence of troops from the area would subject the country to Bannock aggressions. He had reason to be apprehensive, for during the height of the Nez Percé war frenzy, a Bannock, in retaliation for the rape of his sister, shot two white men. When the attacker was arrested on November 23, 1877, at the Fort Hall Reservation, one of his Indian friends, Tambiago, shot a white man delivering cattle to the reservation. On the next morning Indians at the agency found in their midst Captain A. H. Bainbridge and fifteen soldiers from Fort Hall. By December 5 three infantry companies had arrived at the reservation. They gave the Indians just ten days to deliver the murderer. Eventually they turned him over to be tried in Malad City, Idaho Territory. The tension created by those events caused nearby whites to build stockades for protection. Some Shoshonis even left the reservation in fear of the Bannocks. On January 16, 1878, Colonel John E. Smith directed three cavalry companies to surprise two 32-lodge Bannock villages, from which they captured fifty-three men, thirty-two guns, and nearly three hundred horses. After some consideration the military released all of the Indians except Tambiago's family and returned the confiscated horses, but they kept the guns. Tambiago was hanged on June 28.

During the Nez Percé War over five hundred Bannocks and a thousand Shoshonis had been kept under surveillance on the Fort Hall Reservation to prevent them from joining the Nez Percés. The Paiutes and Western Shoshonis ranged over southern Idaho Territory, eastern Oregon, and northern Nevada, although reservations had been established for them—Pyramid Lake, Duck Valley, Walker River, and the Malheur. On the Lemhi Reservation nearly nine hundred Bannocks and Shoshonis had also been watched by nervous whites during the war.

General George Crook had divined the deeper cause of Indian aggressions: their starving condition. Subsisting was virtually impossible on the reservations for these migratory peoples. They had two agonizing alternatives, in the words of Crook: "the war path or starvation." Their ill feeling was intensified by the government's failure to provide them adequately with annuity goods and by its policy of confinement, which hindered them from fending for themselves. Subsidies designated by treaties were not only meager but also disproportionate. The Shoshonis, for example, were given more goods per person than the Bannocks were. A rising young traditionalist Bannock warrior, Buffalo Horn, and his people, whose braves had scouted the Nez Percés for General Howard, received stale tobacco in lieu of their promised pay. In the spring of 1878, Buffalo Horn, leading a band of angry Bannocks, joined other Bannocks and some of Tendoy's people from the Lemhi Reservation in a desperate search for food. They met at Camas Prairie about ninety miles east of Boise, Idaho. Buffalo Horn ordered whites to clear 2,500 cattle and 80 horses off the prairie root grounds. Before the stockmen could leave the prairie, two drunken Indians entered their camp on May 30 and seriously wounded two of them.

In council the Bannocks decided that the time had come to take the warpath.[1] After some Bannocks returned to the Fort Hall Reservation, and some of Tendoy's Lemhis returned to theirs, Buffalo Horn and a war party of over 150 followers headed south to Snake River. Before departing they killed a white man, who was carrying the news of the shooting of the two cattlemen. They were joined by Paiutes from the Malheur Reservation. When the Fort Hall troubles had broken out during the previous fall, the Fort Hall Indians had visited Paiutes on the Malheur, with whom they had close ties, carrying word of their troubles. Responding to Bannock calls for help in March and April, 1878, several Cayuses, Umatillas, and Wallawallas of the Umatilla Reservation, as well as Smohalla-influenced "renegades" from along the lower-middle Columbia River, joined the Bannock war party.

In March, after two Indians from Fort Hall brought word of the Bannock's intent to go to war, the Paiutes gathered on the Malheur Reservation. Thus more of them were there in April than had wintered there. By June 1 forty-six Bannocks were on the Malheur demanding food. The traditionalist Paiute chief Egan was the leader of like-minded traditionalist warriors and was sympathetic to the Bannock cause. He demanded rations of Agent Rinehart only to be refused them. On June 5 the Indians left their reservation tasks to join nonworking Indians on the next day twenty miles away on the Malheur River. When no one appeared at the agency for the June beef slaughter, Rinehart, sensing trouble brewing, prepared to abandon the place. By June 11 it was deserted by whites and Indians alike. The military at Fort Harney, which was fifty miles away north of Malheur Lake, later moved in to make a supply and prisoner depot of the agency.

Buffalo Horn and his war-bent followers, with six hundred horses, were en route to the Bruneau Valley. On crossing Snake River at Glenns Ferry, they pillaged a house and store, sank the ferry, killed a number of whites, and then ran off livestock in the Bruneau Valley. About six miles from the small mining town of South Mountain, Idaho Territory (near the Oregon border about fifty miles north of the southwest corner of Idaho), they ran into twenty-six volunteers under Captain J. B. Harper from Silver City, Idaho Territory. In an ensuing fight on June 8 several of the approximately sixty warriors were killed, including Buffalo Horn, who was a much greater loss to his followers than anything they might have gained by the killing of two volunteers in

that engagement. Escaping down the Owyhee River, the main Bannock force joined the Paiutes from the Malheur Reservation. The Paiutes had been en route to the north end of Steens Mountain (which they reached on June 17) to rendezvous with Buffalo Horn's people. On the way they had killed an old man, fired his house in Happy Valley, and increased their firepower by stealing two boxes of Winchester rifles and ammunition from a stagecoach. At Juniper Lake on the northeast side of Steens Mountain, 450 Bannock-Paiute warriors assembled in a band of about 700 Indians. They heard the pleas of "peace chief" Winnemucca to refrain from hostilities and Oytes's haranguing rebuttal that they should rise up in war to destroy whites and restore lost Indian lands. Some Bannocks went so far as to confiscate the weapons of wavering Paiutes, holding their arms until their owners consented to enter the war. Egan remained somewhat neutral until it appeared that the majority were inclined to fight. Then he assumed leadership of the combined Bannock-Paiute war faction.

Winnemucca's daughter, Sarah, wished to frustrate such war designs. She offered her services to Captain Bernard, the commander of Fort Boise. Troops from the fort

The antelope provided sustenance and material for tipis and clothing for Pacific Northwest Indians. From a painting by Chester Fields.

250

Paiute woman grinding seeds in the entry of a thatched hut, circa 1872. National Archives.

were then dispatched to the field to chase the Bannocks.* Sarah carried messages from the military to the Paiutes and read signal fires for the officers. At Howard's bidding she had also been paid to dissuade the Indians from entering the war. Her father became a prisoner among war-frenzied Paiutes. With a Bannock price on her head, she escaped with him, her brother, and several hundred noncombatant Paiutes. Some of the force were overtaken by the fighting elements and forced to return short of their destination (Camp Lyon) between the Owyhee and Jordan rivers near the Oregon–Idaho Territory border. After June 15, when she rode into General Howard's Sheep Ranch camp a hundred miles south of Boise, Sarah accompanied the general throughout most of the Bannock-Paiute campaign. At Steens Mountain, Ocheo's people had also decided to refrain from hostilities.

Beginning at Fort Hall, which was within General

Crook's Department of the Platte, the conflict had shifted to areas under Howard's Department of the Columbia. As its commander, Howard was charged with the responsibility of preventing actions harmful to whites, and he set out to neutralize the tribes who were being contacted by the combatants to join their cause. He ordered artillery and infantry troops from Forts Vancouver, Canby, and Townsend in Washington Territory and Fort Stevens in Oregon to assist Captain Bernard in the field.

Pulling out ahead of the troops, the combatants left Juniper Lake to join the Umatillas and other militant traditionalists on the north. They were first sighted on Saturday, June 22, by Bernard's cavalry near the site of Camp Curry (which was operative during the mid-sixties at Silver Creek thirty miles west of Burns, Oregon). On Sunday morning a combined force of about two hundred men, including Indian scouts under Colonel Orlando Robbins, readied themselves to meet their foe, who were led by Egan and Oytes. During an all-day fight known as the Battle of Camp Curry, the Indians were repulsed in three successive cavalry charges, rallying after each one. During the charges Egan was wounded. During the night the warrior force slipped northward up Silver Creek, across to the South Fork of the John Day, and traveled about thirty miles downstream to the main river. From there they turned upriver to a point near Canyon City, from which they moved north across the Long Creek country, the John Day Middle Fork, and then on its North Fork, which they crossed at a point then called Dale, nearly fifty miles south of Pendleton. In their northward flight they scattered widely, touching down here and there like twisters with tornadic fury, killing freighters, plundering wagons, running off horses, stealing cattle, frightening settlers, and burning their buildings. On June 29 they engaged John Day Valley whites in a running fight, sending them scurrying into mine shafts and stockades to await rescue by regular troops.

On June 26, Howard, having linked his forces with Bernard's, sent a message to General Frank Wheaton at Fort Walla Walla to move his troops to intercept the Bannock-Paiutes in Camas Meadows south of Pendleton. He also ordered gunboats to patrol the Columbia to prevent the combatants from crossing that stream to join the renegades. In keeping with its policy of utilizing ancient tribal animosities, the military tried to recruit Warm Springs Indians to pursue their old enemies. Possibly one reason that the Warm Springs warriors failed to respond to the request was the loss in the Modoc War of two of their scouts, whose families and heirs the government had not provided for as it had promised. Fifteen Nez Percés and several Umatillas with some reluctance signed on as scouts.

Apprized of the advance of the combatants, Pendleton volunteers geared for action. An Indian, decked out in war bonnet and astride a painted horse, spotted the advancing volunteers on Willow Springs, a headwater branch of Birch Creek, near Albee, Oregon, twenty-five miles south of Pendleton. In attempting to flee, he was shot down, sending about a hundred of his fellows bursting from the woods firing into his attackers. Outnumbered, the volunteers fled to

Pendleton. Their retreat was embarrassing for those western American minutemen. It was the Fourth of July.

Two days later in the same area about 150 Indians attacked a 45-man volunteer camp. The volunteers were under the command of "Captain" John Sperry, who was Umatilla County sheriff, and they were under the authorization of the Oregon governor. A third of them were mounted. During the six-hour fight known as the Battle of Willow Springs about a dozen men breached the Indian line, as others kept up the fight from the cover of a sheep shed. After the Indians withdrew, all remained quiet until near midnight, when the volunteers broke ranks and fled. Sporadic fighting continued throughout the night. Under Indian fire the volunteers retreated. Most of them were afoot. They suffered several casualties, including at least two men killed. Help was on its way as Captain Charles B. Throckmorton and some troops dispatched by Colonel Wheaton from Walla Walla arrived in Pendleton on July 6 and as Howard, under constant Bannock-Paiute surveillance, advanced with troops from the south. The Battle of Willow Springs prevented the warring Indians from joining their allies on the Umatilla Reservation. There the Indians seemed unaware of the delays in the Bannock-Paiute advance and paraded about in war paint and feathers in the area of Cayuse Station, about a dozen miles east of Pendleton.

On July 7, Howard joined forces with the troops under Throckmorton to meet the warriors circulating in the Pilot Rock area south of Pendleton. The latter were seeking to join the Umatillas and other allies on the north. They prepared for combat by posting themselves on a hill, from which they returned the fire of the advancing troops, emptying some saddles of riders and killing many horses. Despite the Indians' strong defensive positions, the troops managed to reach the top of the hill, forcing their red foe to flee to lava-rock defenses on a still-higher hill. Within twenty minutes they were routed from this position also, abandoning in their flight many spare horses, ammunition, provisions, and camp gear. They now scurried to a third defensive position, a thick stand of pines. Under cavalry pressure on their front and flank, the Indians were dislodged and pushed five miles west into the mountains. Thus they were defeated in this Battle of Birch Creek. The harsh terrain of their escape route forced their fatigued pursuers to abandon further attack.

On the day of the Birch Creek fight and in the ensuing days groups of Bannock-Paiutes tried to cross the Columbia at the mouth of Willow Creek in their flight northward. Some were hoping to reach Canada to escape capture. Patrolling gunboats, the *Spokane* and the *Northwest*, quickly detected them and poured fire into their canoes, killing several and destroying the craft. At one place the Indians were charged by crews debarking from one of the gunboats. At another place Indians fired on the pilot house of the *Spokane*. To clear fugitives from the river, the gunboats without warning fired into a peaceful camp, scattering corpses in all directions, and killing several old men and women. Others received gunboat fire at fishing sites near the mouth of the

Umatilla River on the Oregon shore. The Indians' plan to swim about two hundred horses across the Columbia at Long Island (near Coyote Station, Oregon) was frustrated when volunteers captured the animals as well as packs, canvas, and other properties, which they destroyed. Thus they caused some Indians and many horses to drown in their retreat across the broad stream. Joining in the Indian chase, apparently without military authorization, were vigilante cattlemen from the areas. They sought to remove the Indians and their stock from nearby ranges so that they could move onto them. Some Indians of northeastern Oregon who were trying to avoid association with the warring bands became the targets of indiscriminate white attackers. From these and other victims whites took many finely worked buckskin dresses and shirts to saloons in Portland and Vancouver—trophies of their indiscriminate vengeance along the Columbia River.

Once across the Columbia, seven Umatillas on July 10 wreaked their own vengeance by killing a white named Alonzo Perkins and his wife—"the pregnant one", the Indians still call her—as the couple fled from the mid-Columbia to Yakima amidst rumors that warriors were sweeping through the country. One consequence of the murders was the capture and jailing of Chief Moses in Yakima for alleged complicity in the crime, a move that satisfied settlers and stockmen seeking to appropriate his lands. At the time of the chief's council with Howard in September, 1878, Agent Wilbur had been in Washington, D.C., expressing to Commissioner of Indian Affairs E. H. Hayt his wish to have the chief removed to the Yakima Reservation. In 1879 the chief returned from the capital with the Great Father's promise of a reservation to be called the Moses or Columbia, which was to be located between Lake Chelan and the Canadian border and from the summit of the Cascade Mountains east to the Okanogan River.

The Bannock-Paiutes, their forces somewhat depleted, finally linked up with the Umatillas. Eleven Umatillas under their chief, Umapine, and about fifty Columbia River renegades burned Cayuse Station and killed a white settler. They had learned that troops were well out of the area trying to prevent combatants from escaping eastward. The foot-soldier command of Captain Evan Miles moved toward the Umatilla Reservation and arrived at the agency at 2:00 A.M. on July 13. The captain conferred with Agent Cornoyer. As daylight approached, the Umatillas found that the troops were deployed within easy musket range and sent them a flag of truce requesting a parley. At the parley and throughout the day they demonstrated good intentions. Then, decked in war paint and feathers, they moved to a vantage point on the hill overlooking the agency as the troops innocently moved onto the agency grounds and leisurely drank coffee. They had scarcely lit their fires when Bannock-Paiute warriors rushed toward them from the east. Approaching within rifle range of each other, the two forces commenced firing. They continued until 2:00 P.M., when the warriors fled toward the mountains. The troops pursued them the next day, but returned to the agency on learning that they planned to swing around to burn its buildings and drive off its stock. Between July 13 and 15, wishing to disengage themselves from the dissident tribesmen, the Umatillas came to Miles professing friendship and offering help, which he accepted.

It appears that, with the region occupied by the military and escape routes blocked, the Umatilla militants saw their demise approaching and knew that they would be severely punished if captured. Thus they sent a representative to bargain with Cornoyer for their pardon in return for decoying the combatants into captivity. Their wish to dissociate themselves from the Bannock-Paiutes seems to have led to an agreement whereby they betrayed Egan. Other reservation Indians, particularly the Cayuses, offered to help capture him and his followers. The question arises why they should want to capture the Paiute chief. Perhaps they were aware of the $2,000 reward for Egan's scalp offered by Albert H. Robie, a private citizen and son-in-law of former mountain man William Craig. The monetary motive perhaps weighed more heavily than previous Paiute aggressions or Egan's Cayuse parentage. His Cayuse associations were weakened by his long absence as a captive among the Paiutes, whose chief he had become.

Nearly forty Umatilla Reservation Indians and others left on July 14 to follow the warring Bannock-Paiutes. On the next morning they met Egan and his people in the Blue Mountains about two miles southeast of present-day Meacham Station. The Umatillas lured the chief aside to parley on the pretext that they would join him. Out of range of fire from most of Egan's warriors, the Umatillas seized him, telling him they were taking him to white authorities. Resisting, he was shot down. His killers returned that day to Cornoyer and Miles with his scalp and those of several of his comrades—more scalps than the Bannock-Paiutes had sliced from the heads of seven teamsters along the road to Meacham (strewing the contents of the wagons for six miles along their retreat route). The Cayuse Yatiniawitz (or Yettinewitz), who was married to the daughter of Cayuse chief Howlish Wampo, paraded Egan's scalp before the authorities. Besides many captured horses, there were other human trophies, including six or seven women, mostly with children. The Cayuse among the Umatillas lashed the mothers with serviceberry withes until they drew blood and then divided their human prizes as slave wives.

The Umatilla Reservation Indian Umapine handed Egan's scalp to Miles. From it trailed a thirty-inch, single-braided cluster of hair strands tied with a strip of red blanket. Wallawalla chief Homily is often credited with firing the fatal shot at Egan. Since a number of guns were leveled at the chiefs it is small wonder that besides Umapine the Cayuse, Five Crows also claimed the honor, as did a Yakima-Cayuse named Wahsack. Egan's body was punctured by many wounds, and his wrist was bound in willow splints.

After crossing the North Fork of the John Day River, the defeated Bannock-Paiute warriors descended a hill on the south side of the fork and discovered that they were pursued by an advance guard of Col. James W. Forsyth's command, who shortly fired upon them. The Indians fortified themselves on the brow of a hill, from which they returned the fire for an hour and a half before escaping. Crossing the John Day River east of Canyon City, they moved east of the Malheur Reservation. At that point their coalition splintered. The Paiutes remained in southeastern Oregon, and the Bannocks moved into Idaho Territory north of Boise. Agent Rinehart found the Malheur Agency in shambles on his return there in August. Soldiers had stolen and sold off its properties, a crime for which at least one of them would be prosecuted. That was a matter of little moment perhaps to Winnemucca's followers and to other Paiute survivors of the war who returned there to live under military guard.

Fleeing Bannocks were discovered on an island in Bennett Creek in southwestern Idaho, fourteen miles up from Snake River near Bennett Mountain. After leaving a trail of bloodshed and destruction in their flight, they were found there on August 9 by troops under Captain William Edgar Dove, reinforced by those under Captain Harry E. Egbert. In a four-hour skirmish they managed to keep their numbers intact by shielding themselves behind trees, and they eluded their pursuers in nearby mountains. They had hoped to find refuge among the Lemhi Shoshonis on their Salmon River reservation, but the Lemhis were friendly to the whites during the war and offered little comfort to dissidents. Some remained with them, however, while others fled to Fort Hall.

The Lemhis' neutrality during the war earned them no favors from the government—in fact, the very opposite. Under white pressure to appropriate their reservation an executive order was issued on January 7, 1879, to force them to remove to Fort Hall. When Tendoy returned in May from hunting buffalo, he protested the change, threatening the warpath in lieu of removal. The Indian Office next tried to remove Tendoy's Lemhis to the Crow Reservation in Montana Territory, but the Crows would not accept them. Next the government, hoping to impress Lemhi leaders with its power, brought them to Washington, D.C. There they were intimidated into signing an agreement dated May 14, 1880, which was not ratified until February 23, 1889, whereby they were to remove from the Lemhi Reservation to Fort Hall and be allotted lands. The first group would not go there until April, 1907. Tendoy said he would never leave his home in the Salmon River country. He died there in May, 1907. His removal was spared by a decree from a power greater than the government of the United States.

More concerned at the moment with the troops on their trail than with white encroachment on their hands, twenty lodges of stubborn Bannock resisters moved to the northeast. They had decided on flight into Canada, possibly to join Sitting Bull, who was still in exile there. Near Heart Mountain on the Clarks Fork of the Yellowstone River in Northwestern Wyoming the holdouts were tracked down by seventy-five booty-seeking Crow scouts engaged by Colonel Nelson A. Miles, the commander of the Yellowstone District. In a bloody fight on September 5 twenty-eight Bannocks were killed. About forty were captured on the landscape scarred by cannon fire, and others were captured in flight by troops of Lieutenant Hole S. Bishop. Those who managed to escape those encounters and the Heart Mountain fight were surrounded on September 12 at Dry Fork, a

The delegation from the Lemhi and Fort Hall agencies who signed the treaty of May 14, 1880, in Washington, D.C. Standing, left to right: Ti Hee (Tyhee), Bannock delegation leader; John A. Wright, U.S. Indian agent; Charles Rainey, acting interpreter. Sitting: Jack Tendoy (Uriewici); Captain Jim; Tendoy, chief of the Lemhi band of Bannocks, Shoshonis, and Sheepeaters; Grouse Pete; Jack Gibson; Tesedemit (Tisidimit). Smithsonian Institution National Anthropological Archives, Bureau of American Ethnology Collection, Neg. No. 1704-B.

Snake tributary in Wyoming. There the weary Bannock remnant decided to surrender. As they did so, several were mowed down by gunfire, which ended their lives and their three-and-a-half-month war with the United States. Their survivors and other surviving Bannocks were imprisoned at various military posts: Fort Washakie and Camp Brown, Wyoming Territory; Fort Keogh, Montana Territory; Omaha Barracks, Nebraska; and Fort Hall, Idaho Territory. Still others disappeared, and their relatives never learned of their whereabouts.

The Bannock drive for food, which precipitated the war in the first place, did not end with peace. Seeking subsistence, those of Fort Hall regularly trekked east to hunt for game. Angry over the dwindling of the elk herds on which the Bannocks survived, whites fined and jailed the red hunters from

the west in the summer of 1895 after a fight in which one Bannock was killed and six others were wounded.

Like the Bannocks, whose tribal solidarity was disrupted, the Paiutes found themselves in far-flung places at the war's end. On September 27, 1879, after detention at Fort Vancouver, thirty-eight Paiute war prisoners arrived on the Warm Springs Reservation. Their acceptance there was surprisingly friendly, considering its inhabitants long-standing hatred of the Paiutes. On arrival Oytes went to visit relatives on the Yakima Reservation, where Agent Wilbur detained him. The Paiutes in southern Oregon were also detained—at Fort Harney under the watchful eye of soldiers. The troops became obnoxious to them, as the soldiers on the Malheur Reservation did to its Indians. The Malheur held bad memories for the Paiutes. Major Rinehart, unlike

Parrish, had been of little comfort to them. His numerous relatives did little to improve his image as they outfitted themselves from the agency warehouse. In poker games Rinehart and his cronies had appropriated what little the Indians owned, and he had gotten them to farm for him, paying them off in government goods.

Sarah Winnemucca came to the aid of the Paiutes in their postwar plight. Among her people were noncombatants under Leggins, a bitter foe of Oytes. Sarah had been influential in gathering about half the Paiute refugees on the Malheur Reservation. The other half took their chances in northwestern Nevada. Suspicious at Paiute detention at Fort Harney, Sarah discovered with anguished horror that, contrary to government promises and despite her services during the war, the Paiutes were to be forcibly marched 350 miles to the Yakima Reservation, which Paiutes as well as renegade Columbia River Indians had found an anathema. The Paiutes never forgot that the Yakimas and other Shahaptian and Salish peoples had been their ancient foes.

Increasing Sarah's anguish was the Paiute belief that she had deceived them. Despite their suspicions she accompanied them through deep snows to the Simcoe Agency. It proved to be a death march for a number of the people. They were poorly clad. Children froze to death, and mothers died during childbirth along the way. The Indians were not even allowed to bury their dead. On February 2, 1879, 543 Paiutes stumbled into the Simcoe Agency, where they were herded into cold sheds "like so many horses and cattle," as Sarah bitterly recorded. Far from their homelands, they were among an alien people speaking a different tongue, and from the eldest to the youngest the Yakimas were contemptuous of the Paiutes. The latter's inadequate weekly rations forced them to steal to survive, while refusing Wilbur's offer of lands in severalty. Sarah regained her people's goodwill by demanding food, clothing, and shelter for them. Defying a Wilbur directive, she paraded them nude, bringing a "nude revue" into the reverend's revival meetings in front of dignitaries he was trying to impress as leader of a model reservation of "civilized" Indians. One somewhat acculturated Indian by now was Oytes, who was apparently trying to adjust to reservation life. By contrast, his adversary, the once-progressive Leggins, who was the leader of 100 of the 543 Paiutes arriving on the Simcoe, was disgruntled with prisoner status and constantly sought to escape confinement.

The removal of Indians from the Malheur stirred rumors that it would be opened to settlers. When off the reservation in July, 1878, Rinehart had suggested its closure. With the Indians absent, the angry, landhungry settlers had flocked onto the confine. At Camp McDermit, where Winnemucca and his people went (and where some worked for a dollar a day and board), whites kept telling them not to return to the Malheur. In 1880, Ocheo and Winnemucca were with their people at Camps Bidwell and McDermit. Futile attempts had been made the previous year to get them to return to the Malheur. Had they gone there, they would have suffered the same fate as Leggins—exile to the Yakima country. The Weiser River Indians had left the Malheur for their homelands led by Chief Eagle Eye.

By 1880 about seventy Paiutes had fled the hostile Yakima environment. Also leaving that year was Sarah, who went with her father to Washington, D.C., to seek the release of their people. In the capital her embarrassing speeches about her dirty, ragged people pressed Interior Department Secretary Carl Schurz to bribe her to refrain from speechmaking. He promised her release of the Simcoe Paiutes and allotments to their adult males of 160 acres and enough canvas for each family to make a lodge. The Paiutes still at liberty later camped around the railroad station at Lovelock, Nevada, waiting for the canvas, which never came.

Sarah returned to Simcoe with an executive order signed by President Rutherford B. Hayes—with whom she was not impressed—authorizing the promises of Schurz. Wilbur refused to honor the paper, and Schurz reneged on his promise: the Indians were not released. Not all government officials, however, turned a deaf ear to their plight. One who espoused their cause was General Howard. Another was Nelson A. Miles, now a general, who early in 1882 requested that the Simcoe Paiutes be sent to Camp McDermit or the Warm Springs Agency. Three hundred Paiutes were released from the Simcoe Reservation. Most of them settled on the outskirts of Bend, Oregon, since they could not return to the Malheur. That reservation was restored to the public domain by executive order on May 21, 1883, except for a 320-acre portion of the reserve of the former Camp Harney military post. Even that post reserve was restored by a similar order on March 2, 1889. To compound the Paiute anguish, the tribe received no proceeds from the sales of those lands. In 1896 and 1897, 115 homeless Paiutes received individual 160-acre allotments between fifteen and twenty-five miles east of Burns. The allotments were primarily to provide them a tribal land base and a legal framework within which to participate in federal Indian programs. Over the years some of the allotments were alienated so that in 1924 only seventy-one scattered ones remained, totaling 11,014 acres. By 1935 an additional 761 acres northeast of Burns had been purchased by the Paiutes to form what later became the Burns Paiute Reservation.

In late June, 1884, Paddy Cap with a band of fifty Paiutes left Simcoe for the Duck Valley Reservation, where they became the major element of the Miller Creek Paiutes. With seventy followers, minus some who remained for the hop harvest, Oytes left on August 15 for the Warm Springs Reservation. On that reservation, the ancient hunting grounds of his people, the former Dreamer prophet and war advocate became an agency policeman. Of all the Warm Springs peoples at the turn of the century the Paiutes, occupying the southern portion of the reservation, were the only ones to wear long hair and blankets. They clung most tenaciously to the old ways. Warm Springs leaders were selected from among the more-progressive and supposedly more-cooperative Wascos, not from among the Paiutes.

The Bannock-Paiute War did not teach its red belligerents the lessons that the victor, the United States, hoped it would. In their rush to develop the country, the American community continued to be more concerned with its own

255

progress than with that of red men. The Indians resisted Americanization in many ways. For example, those of the Fort Hall Reservation used government issues for purposes other than those for which they were intended. Flannels issued to women were often used by their men for horse trimmings, leggings, and breechclouts. They often sold farm equipment to white farmers on the borders of the reservations at a fraction of its value when their agents' eyes were closed or their backs were turned. Often everything from hoes to harvesters gathered rust and dust at the agencies when not disposed of in this manner. In 1886 Fort Hall agent Peter Gallagher termed the Indian response to farming a "burlesque on civilization."

Sarah Winnemucca helped Indians, especially their young, to make some adjustment to the inevitable white culture. Among those who received her ministrations at Fort Vancouver were refugees of the Bannock-Paiute War who were captured in their own 1879 conflict, the Sheepeater War—which was fought in the lands of the fiercely independent Sheepeaters.

By the mid-1860s gold seekers roamed the Sheepeater country. With little investigation whites blamed the native inhabitants for many depredations, including the February 12, 1879, murder of five Chinese miners on Loon Creek eighty miles northeast of Boise, although it was never proven that they had committed the act. It was not unusual for whites to do away with competing Chinese miners, blaming the murders on Indians. The murder of the Chinese as well as that of two whites on the South Fork of the Salmon River (southeast of Warren in central Idaho) precipitated military action, although deep snows in the mountains delayed attempts to search out the refugees in the Sheepeater country. These were less mobile Sheepeaters from the mountains of Idaho who had not joined the Lemhi Shoshonis. With improving weather, military units began converging on the Sheepeater lands. A company of fifty-seven cavalry under Captain Bernard left Boise Barracks for the mountains (Fort Boise was renamed Boise Barracks on April 5, 1879). With twenty Cayuses and Umatillas whom Bernard had enlisted on June 9, Lieutenant E. S. Farrow prowled the mountains in an independent maneuver, Lieutenant Henry Catley with fifty mounted infantry left Camp Howard near Grangeville, Idaho, on a similar expedition.

On July 29 the refugees at the mouth of Big Creek, a tributary of the Middle Fork of the Salmon River, discovered troops of Catley's command moving up the north side of Big Creek Canyon. The troops had spotted them the previous day. The refugee band had a mere fifty-one souls, only fifteen of whom were warriors. They chose to make their stand at a rock fortress that they had built on a cliff across Big Creek. As the troops advanced single file down the narrow Sheepeater trail, the Indians opened fire from a distance of a hundred yards. In returning the fire, two soldiers were wounded. The troops hastily retreated up and out of the canyon. On the next morning the Indians reached a rocky eminence as the troops struggled to a point that is now called Vinegar Hill (because the troops sipped vinegar there for lack of water). As their gunfire was ineffective, the refugees

set fire to the base of the hill. To save themselves from the flames moving swiftly uphill, the troops set rings of backfire so then, after being pinned down for fourteen hours, they abandoned their baggage and twenty-three pack mules and continued their retreat early in the morning on July 31.[2]

Following their brush with the troops, the refugees in mid-August killed some whites in the South Fork of the Salmon River, burned buildings, and stole livestock before repairing to their canyon stronghold. Bernard, Catley, and Farrow joined forces in mid-August and converged on that area. Discovered before daylight on August 19, in Big Creek Canyon by Indian scouts, the beleaguered red men fired on the Indian mercenaries. As the scouts forced the refugees uphill, the troops joined the chase and reached a well-watered plateau of several acres, now called Soldier Bar, where the scouts looted several food caches. After destroying ten lodges, the troops remained there for the night. At daybreak on August 20, the refugees were discovered by the scouts, who were out rounding up the soldiers' horses. They fled, abandoning twenty-nine horses and mules to the scouts, who poured a few shots into the Sheepeaters. In their flight the hunted ones abandoned caches of saddles and a hundred pounds of flour, which the scouts discovered. On the same day they circled back, creeping over rocks, to fire on the troops, as the latter were breaking camp. They wounded a soldier, who later died. No match for their soldier foes, they fled down the Middle Fork of the Salmon River.

Terrain and weather took a toll of both the hunters and the hunted. The Indians lost supplies: salmon from traps on Big Creek, flour, and bacon, and many horses slain, strayed, or captured. The soldiers lost forty-five pack mules and eighteen horses on this second expedition into the area. Yet the refugees had no respite from them, for the military decided to wage one more campaign against them before the onset of winter. On September 21, west of the Salmon Middle Fork and south of the main Salmon River, two Indian women, two boys, and an infant were discovered by Farrow's command. All were captured save one boy, who escaped. The others, some mounted, some afoot, hastily abandoned their camps. At one camp a dog barked at midnight. Fearing detection, its masters extinguished their fire, abandoned four horses (stabbing one with a butcher knife, which they left in the animal), and fled. They abandoned six hundred pounds of partly cured elk and venison, on which the troops feasted when they entered the camp. For revealing their location, the Indians killed the dog and hung its carcass in a tree over the trail.

One of the captured women was released by the troops to seek out her people. Her infant was retained as a hostage to ensure her return. She did return, saying she could not find her people, and then moved from one camp to another. The troops finally discovered the fugitives in the general area of Papoose Gulch (a Middle Salmon tributary) under their leader, Tamanmo, a Bannock-Nez Percé. He had been on the Malheur Reservation at the outbreak of the Bannock-Paiute War. Unable to return to Fort Hall on abandoning that conflict, he had fled to join the refugees

Sheepeater Indians. These people lost their fight with the military in the wilds of mountainous central Idaho. Idaho Historical Society.

whose leadership he assumed. On the evening of September 24, with winter already setting in, he walked out of the timber toward the troops. A half mile from them he uttered a loud yell. Lieutenant William C. Brown and an Umatilla scout, Wahtiskowkow, walked out unarmed toward him. When he was within a hundred yards of the two, Tamanmo dropped his Henry rifle at their command. Concealed at his back was a revolver. He inquired of the scout the identity of Brown. When told, he advanced and shook hands with the lieutenant. He told Farrow, over whose tent a white flag flew, that the pursued ones had planned to raid the soldiers' horses that very night. He was pursuaded to ride a fresh horse to an Indian camp at the mouth of Big Creek to gather its people. On the next day, August 26, carrying a white flag, Tamanmo came in with one Indian, Buoyer, who was the husband of one of the captured women. Not all that familiar with the country, Tamanmo had been unable to find nine men with their families. Another group of twenty was still scattered. Leaving his gun, Buoyer went out to find those who were holding out.

On October 1, Tamanmo entered the soldier camp with four lodges of Indians. Their bodies were covered with paint and feathers. A total of thirty-nine captives were now in the camp with eleven others and thus ended the Sheepeater War. A severe environment had contributed to the Indians' defeat. It was no great victory for their captors, achieved at much expense to the government. Agreeing to go to the Fort Hall Agency, the captives were taken to Fort Vancouver for the winter. During the campaign of 1879, while the military chased renegades from various Shoshonean tribes in central Idaho, Eagle Eye and his people hid out above the forks of the Payette River in Dry Buck Valley.

Reverberations of the Bannock-Paiute War and of other white-Indian conflicts of the seventies reached both races in the Pacific Northwest and the rest of the country. As late as 1879 whites in Pacific Northwestern coastal regions still believed that the Cascade Mountains were too low to shield them from Indian wars and rumors of them. In December, 1879, a worried Tulalip agent wrote the commissioner of Indian affairs that an upper-Skagit chief, John Campbell, who was the son of Chief Sahkumiku, with a mere dozen followers was in touch with dissidents east of the Cascade Mountains and that he was urging Indians to avoid reservations and take up their muskets and fight. East of the mountains roaming treaty and nontreaty Indians, prizing their freedom and the last vestiges of their own way of life, continued to avoid the very antithesis of their quest—Indian reservations. On the other hand, as far as whites were concerned, the economic and social realities of life in the Pacific Northwest could not afford such freedom to the vast majority of the region's native inhabitants. Thus on over a score of reservations they were confined to a way of life from which they found little escape. Their responses to the reality of such unmerited confinement marks one of the most agonizing periods of their long history.

257

Indian lodges near the Celilo fisheries at The Dalles on the Columbia River, circa 1900. University of Oregon Library.

24. RESERVED FOR INDIANS

On the reservations the United States government sought to replace the Indian blanket with the vestments of civilization. Instead the reservations became patchwork quilts of federal Indian policy. Some tribes residing on them were under treaty; some were not. Some treaties had been ratified; others had not. A most important consequence of those variations was confusion in the patterns of subsistence provided by the government. The subsistence varied with tribal status and was complicated by the failure of reservations to provide adequate means of survival to their residents. The Indians were often reluctant to adopt agriculture because the lands were unsuited to that type of economy. Out of necessity or by tradition Indians were forced off reservations to survive.

One consequence of the Indians' efforts to seek off-reservation subsistence was the continuing Fish War, a struggle between Indians and whites and between the states and the federal government. Under the original treaties Indians were guaranteed the right to fish at "usual and accustomed places" in common with citizens of the territory. They shortly encountered trouble with those citizens and later with local governments on behalf of those citizens. The first Washington state law pertaining to Indian fishing was an 1891 session statute (1891 Washington State Session Laws, 171). It guaranteed to the white citizens of Washington and of any state having concurrent jurisdiction over or upon any rivers or waters the right to fish if they produced evidence of citizenship or if they declared their intention of becoming citizens after living in the state six months. The law specifically excluded Indians. Despite this, Indians were treated as noncitizens and arrested off reservations for fishing and hunting without licenses.*

As a consequence of the Washington state legislation, Lummi Indians, for example, were arrested even as late as the early twentieth century for fishing off their reservation, as were Indians off the Tulalip Reservation for fishing and for shooting ducks. In most cases the Indians were exonerated, but only after the expense and humiliation of going to court. Conflict was present in all Pacific Northwestern salmon waters, but was especialy bitter in Puget Sound and on the Columbia River. Complicating the situation for Indians, especially those fishing in the Columbia River, was the advantage that whites had over them by their use of salmon-trapping devices, such as fish wheels. The latter had been operated on the East Coast since 1829, but were not introduced along the Columbia until fifty years later. Within two decades of their introduction there were seventy-six in operation, mainly at The Cascades and between The Dalles and Celilo. The year 1894 was an exceptionally good one for the wheels. Between May 17 and July 31 one wheel swept up nearly a quarter of a million pounds of salmon. They were positioned along rocky shorelines where natives for generations had dipnetted and speared salmon, and they easily surpassed their human competitors in the harvests. The state of Washington in 1893 had laws authorizing the construction and maintenance of such devices, but they were later outlawed in Oregon.

In the eighties the Yakimas complained that a fence maintained by a certain Frank Taylor obstructed the land approaches to their Tum Water fishery and its adjacent village site in The Dalles area, preventing them from exercising their rights under the June 9, 1855, treaty. A January 25, 1887, appeals-court decision (*United States* v. *Taylor*, 3 Wash. T. 88) reversed a district-court decision and forced Taylor to remove the obstruction. The operations of Audubon and Linneus Winans were a threat to Indians in The Dalles area. The Winanses had established fish wheels there around 1890, besides blasting out a large rock from which Indians had customarily fished in the Wishram area on the Columbia north bank. Around 1895 the Winanses restricted Indians from the area, telling them to fish at other places along the river. To reach the other places, Indians had to cross lands held by whites. The Yakimas' catches had some days run to as many as fifteen hundred salmon, which they used for their own consumption and for sale to canneries, and, when they were deprived of them, the Yakimas began to complain. Receiving little satisfaction from their agent, they brought suit against the Winanses in the United States Circuit Court, District of Washington, Southern Division. The case was argued on April 3 and 4, 1905, and decided on May 15. The court ruled that Indians could not be excluded from their usual and customary fishing places. (*United States* v. *Winans*, 198 U.S. 371, 25 Sup. Ct. 662, 49 L.Ed. 1089). The license issued by the state to maintain fish wheels thus did not empower owners of fishing operations to exclude Indian fishing.

On Puget Sound opportunities for off-reservation fishing were restricted. When some Indians of the Swinomish Reservation obtained a license in 1898 to reef net at fishing grounds off Lopez Island in the San Juan Islands, they discovered whites there driving pilings preparatory to installing fish traps. Similar devices were being installed at other

---

*During the nineteenth century few whites advocated Indian rights. By the turn of the century the number of Indian advocates had increased, and they had become more vocal. Among those concerned with Indian rights at this time, especially in the Puget Sound area, was Charles M. Buchanan, whose address, "Rights of the Puget Sound Indians to Game and Fish," was sent to the Washington state legislature in 1915. *Washington Historical Quarterly* 6, no. 2 (April, 1915): 109–115. In a similar vein are Lewis H. St. John, "The Present Status and Probable Future of the Indians of Puget Sound," *Washington Historical Quarterly* 5, no. 1 (January, 1914): 12–21, and William J. Trimble, "American and British Treatment of the Indians in the Pacific Northwest," *Washington Historical Quarterly* 5, no. 1 (January, 1914): 32–54.

places on Puget Sound. Some were on the perimeters of the reservations, where fish entrepreneurs claimed the right to operate above the extreme low-water mark. Countering Indian claims that such lands were theirs under the treaties, whites claimed that they had become state lands because the Washington State enabling act had provided for cession to the state of all tidelands. Under this interpretation the White Crest Canning Company of Anacortes operated in waters off the Tulalip Reservation. In 1900, Lummi Indians complained of whites setting nets at their customary fishing grounds at the mouth of the Nooksack River.

North of the Nooksack River the Alaska Packers' Association leased the lands of a certain Kate Waller on Point Roberts, the extremity of a peninsula extending into the Gulf of Georgia. There they constructed fish traps—rows of pilings supporting nets to funnel and trap the sockeye salmon bound for the Fraser River. An ensuing circuit-court case—*United States* v. *Alaska Packers' Association* [(C.C.) 79 Fed. Rep. 152]—was heard on March 12, 1897. It pitted Lummi Indians claiming federal treaty rights against a corporation claiming rights granted by the state. In rendering his opinion, Judge Cornelius H. Hanford conceded that, although fish traps impeded Indian fishing, they were authorized and licensed by the state pursuant to laws enacted to regulate fisheries within the state's jurisdiction. He concluded that the Indian rights guaranteed under the fifth article of their treaty provided for Indian fishing rights coequal with those of state citizens and that, since Lummi rights had not been invaded by whites, the court could not by injunction interfere with the Alaska Packers' trapping operations.*

It was to avoid such confrontations that the government wished to make agrarians of the Indians. It was a difficult task, especially on such reservations as the Makah, where the people lived on nonagricultural lands and secured most of their subsistence from the sea. On other reservations, such as the Spokane, government officials would have been wiser to have encouraged the Indians to graze cattle rather than farm. The Spokanes had been sent to that reservation, which had been selected by the government for them because of its undesirability for whites. In the twentieth century tribesmen found revenues there not only from timber but also from uranium. The ore mined and processed there to meet the needs of the atomic age provides fortunes for a few Spokanes and tribal revenues and employment for others.

Indian residency on reservations was complicated by troubles arising over boundaries, especially those that were not clearly defined by geographic features. A case in point was the Warm Springs Reservation, whose boundaries had been written into the Warm Springs Treaty after its 1855 signing—the delay was in itself a source of trouble. The

northern boundary proved extremely troublesome. In 1871 a boundary survey was made by a man named T. B. Handley. The Indians were dissatisfied with this survey, which was made south of where they believed the boundary to be, and south of the Wapinitia ridge, where an agent had shown them it lay. One of their agents, Jason Wheeler, carried word of their displeasure to the commissioner of Indian affairs, and Congress on October 16, 1886, authorized a resurvey and remarking of reservation metes and bounds. In the following year twenty Indians joined a John A. McQuinn on a survey extending the boundary north of the Handley line. On February 6, 1888, before the McQuinn survey was approved, the General Land Office transmitted a report recommending a compromise boundary between those laid out by Handley and McQuinn. Commissioners rejected the recommendation, believing that the boundary should be established as McQuinn had surveyed it. Whites were angry since the McQuinn survey enlarged the reservation. Endeavoring to bring some order to the conflict, a three-man commission was appointed in 1890 to review and resurvey the line. After lengthy consultations with the commissioners the Indians insisted that the line be set from an oak tree blazed by an early agent and that the line on the north side of the Wapinitia veer back along that ridge. One Indian named Schooly testified that he had even helped stack rocks along that line shortly after the 1855 treaty had been signed. On June 6, 1894, Congress finally declared the correct boundary line to be that of Handley. In that same year McQuinn signed a contract to survey the reservation western boundary, which was also contested.

In 1919 the General Land Office accepted the Handley line as the reservation boundary. Eleven years later Congress authorized the dissatisfied tribe to present its case to the Court of Claims, which in 1941 accepted the McQuinn line except for a small triangular tract on the northeast corner. Nearly 80,000 acres were left between the McQuinn and Handley lines, and 17,251 of the acres were in private hands. In 1948, Congress enacted legislation enabling the Indians to receive the net income from 61,360 acres of government land within the disputed area, but it was not until 1972 that a Senate bill established the modified McQuinn line as the northern and western reservation boundaries.[1]

The case of the Muckleshoots was a typical example of Indians fearing unfavorable reservation boundaries. In 1897 their agent returned their boundary complaints with a decree that they make no more trouble. An example of a reservation boundary settled after long delay was that of the Yakimas. It was not until the 1930s that an original map, presumably made at the time of the treaty, was found in the Bureau of Indian Affairs files. It showed the western boundary of the Yakima Reservation to have differed from that surveyed. Included in the Gifford Pinchot National Forest (established in 1897) were about 121,500 acres of reservation lands. Of this acreage approximately 98,000 acres fell into private hands. 2,500 acres of scattered tracts remained in tribal ownership, and about 21,000 acres were still in the public domain under the control of the United States Forest Service. In 1968 the Indian Claims Commission ruled that the

---

*Judge Hanford's court was in Seattle, Washington. The judge held that the treaty guaranteed to the Indians common rights when fishing in the state, subject to the same restrictions as were imposed upon citizens. Determinations in subsequent cases taken to the Supreme Court directly reversed this holding; for example, *U.S.* v. *Winans*, 198 U.S., 371.

Fish was a staple of Indian diets. Here Indians gather salmon at Celilo Falls on the Columbia River, where their ancestors had fished from ancient times. The falls are now under water. North Central Washington Museum Association.

entire 121,500 acres should have been included in the reservation as the area shown on the recovered map. The Yakima Nation settled for fifty cents an acre for the 98,000 acres that had passed into private hands, but refused to sell the 21,008.66 Forest Service acres, which included Mount Adams. President Richard Nixon returned that acreage to the Yakima Nation by executive order on May 20, 1972.

Indians continued to fear not only that boundary lines would be readjusted for white occupancy under white pressure, but also that entire reservations would be taken from them, as the Malheur had been. Some reservation diminutions involved townsites. Pendleton was withdrawn from the Umatilla, and Pocatello from the Fort Hall. Under the demands of whites, larger portions were withdrawn for their occupation or for transportation corridors. In many cases whites already occupied the portions of reservations that they wished withdrawn.

The Moses, or Columbia, Reservation was reduced because of prior occupation by miners. The Okanogan and Similkameen Mining District was organized two decades before the reservation was established on April 18, 1879, and before it was enlarged on March 6, 1880, and before a federal mining law of May 10, 1872, permitted free and open exploration, occupation, and possession by locators. On learning

of the establishment of the reservation, miners called meetings and sent protests to the government demanding that the reservation be abolished. Cattlemen were a lesser threat to Chief Moses: the enterprising chief extracted fees from those who intruded on the lands of local Indians; his own people did not take up residence there. Anticipating troubles, the military in 1880 established short lived Camp Chelan at the lower end of Lake Chelan. Miners continued to pressure Congress to restore at least a portion of the reserve and to give Moses lands on the Colville in exchange. Those were less audacious proposals than that of Washington Territorial governor William A. Newell, who suggested in an address on October 5, 1881, that all reservations be abolished and opened for settlement. Under such pressures President Chester A. Arthur on February 23, 1883, issued an executive order restoring a fifteen-mile strip to the public domain. Unaware of the presidential action, the native owners, who were now trespassers on the strip, suffered insults, indignities, and property damages from intruders.

Because of the turmoil Moses and other Indian leaders of the area were called to Washington, D.C., to sign a July 9, 1883, agreement permitting the government to purchase the entire Columbia Reservation and assigning the chief and his people to the Colville. An act of Congress, dated July 4, 1884, officially restored Moses's former reservation to the public domain; the official opening was May 1, 1886. Moses allegorized the events that lost him the reservation, which Secretary Carl Schurz had said would last as long as the Cascade Mountains. Two white men, the chief said, came one day to look at the reservation's rocky surface. As he was telling them that it was a present from the whites, a rock fell into the hands of one of the visitors and broke open exposing gold and silver inside. The two men began fighting for the precious metal, telling Moses that he could have what was on the outside.

The Colville Reservation, to which Moses and his people were removed, itself suffered reduction. A mere two decades after its establishment its North Half was withdrawn by an act of Congress on July 1, 1892 (without presidential signature). The Indians there were permitted allotments on their individual holdings—which were essentially little Indian islands in a sea of whites. The act also provided that money from sales of surplus lands could be granted to the state of Washington for Indian education in lieu of taxes on the allotments in the area thrown open. In 1926 and 1928 congressional deficiency appropriations implemented the 1892 act by providing moneys to certain counties of the state. That was presumably the only instance of federal grants to local governments in lieu of Indian taxes.

On February 23, 1896, the North Half of the Colville Reservation was thrown open to mineral entry. White men used many devious methods to establish mineral claims there—in many cases before the official opening date. One method was to claim marriage to Indian women. The North Half was thrown open for homesteading in 1900. On July 1, 1898, the Colville South Half was thrown open to mineral entry, sending miners swarming over it like termites seeking a place to burrow. Their blasting interfered with Indian fishing in the Sanpoil River, and they took Indian women and cattle. As the Colville was surrounded on three sides by the Columbia and Okanogan rivers, stockmen could not excuse their illegal entry as they had on the Nez Percé Reservation on the grounds that Indians had not fenced its boundaries. With the opening of the area for mining, there was a burgeoning of ferryboats on the Columbia. Many of them were run by Indians operating as dummy owners for whites, who operated their craft to the reservation in violation of federal law.

In the mineral-rich northern Idaho Territory, the Coeur d'Alênes suffered diminution of their lands—to which Governor David Ballard had advocated that they be restricted in order to end their roaming ways. On June 14, 1867, about the time squatters began appearing on the Coeur d'Alêne lands, President Andrew Johnson ordered the creation of a quarter-million-acre reserve for the Coeur d'Alênes within a twenty-square-mile area. Unlike its western boundary, which was the well-marked line of Washington Territory, the reservation's boundary was an imaginary line from the mouth of the Saint Joe River south to the headwaters of Latah Creek. The southern boundary was a short line from the headwaters of the Latah to the Washington

line. The northern boundary ran to the Washington line from the mouth of the Saint Joe. No attempt was made at that time to remove the Coeur d'Alênes there. When they became aware of the reservation in 1871, the tribe refused to accept it, claiming it was much too small. In 1873 a three-man commission was appointed to deal with the tribe. In council, at the old mission site at the mouth of the Saint Joe, an agreement was reached whereby a tract of land was given to the Coeur d'Alênes. It included not only the area set aside in 1867 but also an extension of the eastern line northeast to a second mission site on the Coeur d'Alêne River. On the northwest it was extended to the northern reaches of Lake Coeur d'Alêne and along the Spokane River to the eastern boundary of Washington Territory. For ceding their lands, the tribe was promised the usual mills, schools, and so on with corresponding personnel. When Congress failed to ratify the creation of the reservation, the president established the confine by executive order on November 8, 1873—without remuneration to the Indians for the lands ceded.

A rush of miners to the reservation between 1882 and 1885 resulted in the establishment of several settlements on the confine. The army established Camp Coeur d'Alêne (later Fort Sherman) in 1879 to cool possible troubles involving tribesmen and whites. It established Fort Spokane for the same reason the following year on a bluff overlooking the Spokane Reservation at the confluence of the Columbia and Spokane rivers. Whites also acquired much of the northern half of the Coeur d'Alêne Reservation, staking claims and cutting timber. Chief Seltis requested that someone be sent to negotiate with his people to clear the land of unwanted settlers. It was not a little ironical that John Mullan, whose road had opened the Coeur d'Alêne lands in the first place, acted on behalf of the Coeur d'Alênes in the national capital. In the face of their protests whites suggested that the tribesmen receive allotments in severalty and that the lands remaining be made available to settlers.

After meeting with another commission, the Coeur d'Alênes signed an order on March 26, 1887, to retain the area included in the 1873 executive order, agreeing at the same time to permit a portion of the Spokane tribe, who were not going to the Spokane or Flathead reservations, to come there. Under the agreement no part of the reservation was to be sold, occupied, or opened to white settlement without the Indians' consent. Again the treaty failed to receive congressional approval. Under persistent pressure from Chief Seltis to have the agreement approved, still another commission came to meet with the Coeur d'Alênes. At the first session on August 14, 1889, at De Smet, Idaho, the tribe learned that the commissioners had come to purchase a portion of the reserve. Reminded by Seltis of the government's failure to ratify treaties, the commissioners promised to stipulate that the 1887 agreement with the Coeur d'Alênes be approved before any agreement was made for the sale of their lands. Seltis requested a conference with the president. The commissioners acceded to that request, but the meeting was to take place only after an agreement was made. After three more sessions with Seltis the commissioners requested the purchase at $1.25 per acre of 184,960 acres on the northern portion of the reservation, including much of Lake Coeur d'Alêne. Seltis held out for $5.00 per acre, pointing out that the government should treat separately with about a half dozen of his tribesmen who held claims there. The commissioners dismissed his contention, saying that those people could be paid for their lands from tribal funds. More haggling followed. Seltis refused a $150,000 offer for the area, but finally agreed to accept it, to pay the Indian families in the northern portion, and to accept $500,000 for the portion of the reservation thrown back into the public domain. The agreement, which called for acceptance of the 1887 agreement, was ratified by the Senate on March 3, 1891. The Coeur d'Alênes yielded 2,389,924 acres of their lands, or nearly forty percent of the northern portion of their reservation, where whites had established themselves.

A significant diminution of a reservation for purposes of transportation was on the Klamath. In June, 1864, under federal law the Oregon legislature had been granted permission to build a wagon road.[2] The land grant and the permission to build the road were awarded to the Oregon Central Military Wagon Road Company. Completed in 1872, the road traversed the Klamath Reservation from north to south, then turned to the east and left the confine. Soon after construction of the road Oregon Central sold its land grant of alternate reservation sections, and ownership rested with the California and Oregon Land Company, which was controlled by a timber firm. Because of a 1900 timber-land boom that company then attempted to trade to the Klamaths its scattered 110,000 acres, which consisted mostly of grazing land, for a consolidated 87,000 acres of thick ponderosa pine in the Yamsey Mountain area. In 1900, Congress authorized the secretary of the interior to deal with the Klamaths for the trade. Two years later Congress authorized a $108,750 payment to the Klamaths for the transaction. The Klamaths later claimed that their signatures on the transfer were obtained under duress when their superintendent, H. G. Wilson, intimated it was a choice of signing and obtaining the $108,750 or not signing and getting nothing. In 1925 the Klamaths filed suit against the government. On April 8, 1935, a Court of Claims dismissed their claims for compensation for the alienated lands at a 1906 timber value for the ponderosa pine of $1.50 per thousand board feet, or an estimated $2,980,000. The Supreme Court on April 25, 1938, awarded the tribe $5,313,347.32. Ironically the road that precipitated all the trouble never served any real purpose.

A late nineteenth-century railroad promoter wrote "When the locomotive came the red man knew his fight against civilization was at an end." The statement was an oversimplification, yet railroads had important repercussions on reservation Indians, as they did on the population at large. The railroads' conquest of the Indians was completed by the end of the nineteenth century with the passage of an act on March 2, 1899 (30 Stat. 990), by which railroad companies could receive blanket approval from the secretary of the interior for rights-of-way through Indian lands.

The first transcontinental railroad to the Pacific Northwest, the Northern Pacific, reached the West Coast in 1883, three decades after the Stevens surveys for such a road, which had given urgency to his treaty making with Indians of the interior. The road was completed to Puget Sound in 1887. It crossed not only the Cascade Mountains but also the Yakima Indian Reservation. On May 2, 1894, nearly a decade after it crossed the reservation, Yakima agent L. T. Erwin complained to the commissioner of Indian affairs that not one dollar had been paid for Indian stock killed on the reservation. Of the six or seven Indians with whom the railroad company had made the agreement for the reservation crossing all but one of those with whom Erwin had talked had said that, whereas the company had agreed to pay them for stock destroyed, nothing at the time had been said about fences or cattle guards. "You can readily understand," wrote Erwin, "how a lot of ignorant Indians could have been deceived in a skillfully drawn instrument." Erwin added that promised warehouse facilities had never been built with the result that harvested crops were left uncovered awaiting shipment. A promise of free passage for the Indians and their produce was not realized. As for free passage for themselves, the Yakimas were less fortunate than the Coeur d'Alênes, who with passes traveled the fifty-seven miles from Cataldo, Idaho, to Tekoa, Washington, thanks to provisions of an 1889 contract with the Harriman interests securing the railroad a right-of-way across the Coeur d'Alêne Reservation. The Northern Pacific took temporary lumps from the Department of the Interior in the summer of 1887 when it was stopped from surveying the Nez Percé Reservation for a road. After receiving congressional approval for a right-of-way, the company resumed its surveys.

Among the many reservation Indians involved with railroad problems were the Shoshonis and Bannocks on the Fort Hall. In 1878 they discovered that the Utah and Northern Railroad Company (authorized by acts of Congress on March 3, 1873, and June 20, 1878) was building a road from Salt Lake City across their reservation to tap the Montana goldfields. Seeking to pacify the Indians for the construction across the reservation, railroad officials met with them to obtain their consent for the project in exchange for a promised five hundred head of good cattle. The Indians later received no compensation for the right-of-way across their reserve.[3]

On July 2, 1881, the Indians were called into council to learn that Utah and Northern wanted to cross the reservation with an east-west line. The Indians agreed to its survey, and in council on July 18 they agreed to grant the right-of-way. On reconvening, the Bannocks refused to sign, complaining that the Shoshonis had done all the negotiating. When they did sign, it was only on assurances that settlers along the north-south line would be removed. By signing the red men ceded 670 acres for the line and an additional 102 acres for stations and sidings. For the east-west line land the company paid the Indians $6,000, which was deposited with the United States treasurer after the agreement was approved on July 3, 1882.

Through its Oregon Short Line Railroad subsidiary, the

Union Pacific Railroad received by transfer from Utah and Northern that company's reservation right-of-way. The Indians had never been compensated for the north-south right-of-way. A thousand people had already settled at Pocatello Station, where the two lines crossed. Thus the Oregon Short Line and Utah and Northern wanted additional land for a townsite there, and a commission was sent to meet the Indians. In council the Bannocks resisted surrendering more of their lands, wanting to know, as did the Shoshonis, why whites kept crowding in on them. Led by Taghee, who favored selling more lands, the leaders on May 27, 1887, signed an agreement surrendering 840 acres for the Pocatello townsite. Utah and Northern agreed at this time to compensate the Indians for the north-south right-of-way. Under the agreement, which was approved by Congress on September 1, 1888, that company paid $7,621.04 for the right-of-way and three years later paid another $13,182.72 for an additional 150 acres for the Pocatello townsite.

With the rapid passing of the American frontier in the late nineteenth century the government assumed an interest in the irrigation of western lands, including Indian reservations. In 1889, a year of severe summer drought, Flathead agent Peter Ronan wrote "Proper irrigation of this reservation is the most essential thing to be undertaken by the Department [of the Interior] to give the Indians productive farms." Ronan's efforts understandably surpassed those of his priestly predecessors, such as De Smet, who had ditches dug at Saint Mary's, and Spalding and Whitman, who had them dug at their missions. In 1892, Ronan was given permission to enlarge one canal, and with Indian labor he dug another at a cost of $5,870 to divert waters from Finlay Creek and the Jocko River. Four years later two more ditches were laid out.

The time between the building of the earliest ditches and the later more substantial ones had been upwards of half a century. Even at a later date on some reservations a great deal of time passed between their advocacy and their construction. After Klamath agent Linus M. Nickerson advocated the building of a ditch in 1884, a small one was finally dug sixteen years later. Despite riparian strife among allottees, other canals were built on the Klamath in the twentieth century. On the Fort Hall Reservation about $3,000 was spent for irrigation in 1887 and 1888. In 1889, Agent Peter Gallagher called for the construction and development of canals, ditches, and reservoirs for both Indians and whites. He even put a notice in the newspapers requesting readers' suggestions in anticipation of a visit by a Senate committee on irrigation and reclamation of arid lands. That same year Gallagher proposed building a canal to carry Snake River waters to lands on and off the reservation. The Department of the Interior in 1892 purchased five hundred miner's inches of water for $1,500 for a hundred new reservation acres to be put in wheat, oats, and grasses.

The first official record of irrigation on the Warm Springs Reservation was a May 22, 1893, authorization for the expenditure of $200.00 on an irrigation ditch. In May and June, 1885, about 850 acres on the Lemhi Reservation were under irrigation at a cost of $913.27, over two-thirds of

which went to pay Indians for their work on the ditches. That year Indians had to pay for seed out of their own pockets. In 1890 a thousand Lemhi Reservation acres were under irrigation, some of them cultivated by forty-five Indians. More acreage might have been tilled if the government had prepared the land and built ditches.

In the Yakima country, where priests a quarter-century earlier had taught irrigation to the Indians farming on the Ahtanum Creek, whites had left Indians only a quarter of its flow. They had diverted its waters as they had those of numerous other streams throughout the interior. In one of many irrigation projects in the Yakima Valley the Northern Pacific, Kittitas & Yakima Irrigation Company in 1891 built a dam three miles southeast of Union Gap across the Yakima river to the Yakima Reservation, constructing what was known as the Sunnyside Canal, through which waters flowed to irrigate off-reservation lands. The project, authorized by the Department of the Interior, drew the ire of Indians and their supporters because it hampered not only their own smaller irrigation projects but also their fishing. The fight between the Yakimas and whites over the waters of the Yakima River evoked a second Battle of Union Gap—this one involved less physical force than that of the Yakima War.

Seeking to establish the Yakimas more firmly in irrigation agriculture, Agent Erwin constructed the Erwin Ditch in 1896. Years later his ashes would be scattered over it. He believed it to be the greatest accomplishment of his life. What had been a monument to him became a monument to tribal dissension. The twenty-thousand dollars needed to build the ditch were diverted from tribal funds derived from the sale of the Wenatchee fisheries. Traditionalist Yakimas were angry at the sale. Angriest of all were the Wenatchee Indians seeking compensation for the sale of their fisheries, which had been reserved under the 1855 Yakima Treaty. Indians of the upper Yakima River had used the fisheries for ages along with their Wenatchee neighbors.

As Indians wrestled with problems of reservation life, government officials continued to wrestle with problems of administration. Seeking to simplify their tasks, officials combined several reservations under a single agency. For example, the Coeur d'Alêne, Spokane, and Colville reservations were combined under the Colville Agency. One of the largest agencies, the Puyallup, comprised the former Puyallup, Chehalis, Nisqually, Squaxin, and Skokomish reservations. Officials continued seeking assistance from Indians in the management of agency affairs. On the reservations the tribal courts operated with varying degrees of success. On the Yakima Reservation cases could be appealed from district courts to three justices and beyond that to Agent R. H. Milroy, who declared himself a "supreme court". On the Fort Hall Reservation, where Indians in 1884 had been unwilling to serve as tribal judges without pay, Agent Gallagher in 1888 declared the court a failure because it consumed too much time dealing with petty offenses. On the other hand, the Siletz agent in the same year was happy that his court spent so much time dealing with petty offenses because it freed him from having to deal with them. In 1889,

Gallagher in a turnabout expressed the belief that the Fort Hall court performed "moderately well." Agent Ronan did not concur in that assessment in evaluating his court's performance on the Flathead. In 1888, of the three Colville Agency reservations, there was a tribal court only on the Spokane. Chief Lot was influential in its establishment. He set an example of what the government wanted in native jurists, for when his son violated a new American law that was not the same as the old native one, the chief refused to uphold him. On the Quinault Reservation judges would not serve in cases involving medicine men because they were afraid of receiving bad "medicine" from them.

Assessments of the effectiveness of the Indian police also varied from reservation to reservation. In 1883 the Lemhi agent discharged his force for "incompetency," claiming that the Indians got along better without it. In most cases "incompetency" meant failure of policemen to enforce patterns of cultural change dictated by the Indian Office. In 1893 the Warm Springs agent reported that the effectiveness of reservation police was reduced by medicine men frightening them as they had tribal judges, such as those on the Quinault. Yet Fort Hall agent S. G. Fisher reported in 1890 that his fifteen policemen were rendering valuable service in maintaining order.

The conduct of educational programs on all reservations before the turn of the century was made difficult by traditionalists who opposed their operations. On the Fort Hall Reservation, Shoshoni traditionalists, led by their medicine men, were even more averse than the Bannocks were to sending their children to school. Time, however, continued to erode Bannock-Shoshonis separatism, and by 1885 there had been so much Bannock-Shoshoni intermarriage that it was difficult to find a full-blooded Bannock. On the Lemhi Reservation, where buildings were run-down, the boarding school was discontinued on June 30, 1889. The proximity of the school to Indian lodges had tempted children to escape to their homes. Their flight was encouraged by their elders, who disrupted the educational process whenever they could. In 1890 Agent Fisher reported the Indians as "strongly prejudiced" against educating their children—small wonder because the death rate for those attending school was greater than that for those living in tipis with their parents. The Indian Office responded to these failures by increasing its efforts and appropriations for Indian schooling. On the Jocko the Flatheads requested a government school, and the government attempted to eliminate the mission school at Saint Ignatius. Nevertheless, between 1886 and 1899 with annual federal contracts the mission was able to educate as many as three hundred boys and girls a year at an annual cost of $150 each. This was at a time when the Bureau of Catholic Indian Missions was beginning to retrench the funding of its schools.

While the government sought to make Indian education fit the vocational mold into which it tried to force the Indians, there appeared, as there had periodically, certain Indians who believed the greatest learning comes not through practical education, be it native or American, but through inspiration. One such Indian was John Slocum

(Squasachtun), a Squaxin. In 1882 he "returned from heaven" with a strong injunction to his people to live circumspect lives by avoiding certain evils, such as alcohol. His religion, Shakerism, was a substitute for the now forbidden native religions. Its practices incorporated certain native, as well as Roman Catholic, forms, and in some instances they became spiritual substitutes for the native religions. Finding the spirit more powerful than spirits, one Shaker exulted, "Come into it, come into it, it is as good as getting drunk." The reaction of Indian agents to the new religion, which they called the "Shakes," was at first negative. Their opposition was moderated somewhat as the Shaker Indians evinced a morality that lessened the tasks of the government officials. Complaints against Shakerism continued, however. In 1898 the Tulalip agent reported that healers were taking credit for cures effected by agency doctors. The Shaker movement eventually spread into Oregon and eastward to The Dalles. It spread more widely in the twentieth century despite differences among its followers, who were divided over whether the Bible was more efficacious than the Indians' traditional nonwritten word.

Unlike Shakerism, the religion of the Paiute preacher Wovoka, "The Cutter" (Jack Wilson), proclaimed the coming return of the dead to reclaim lost Indian lands and was rooted in nativism. When working in Oregon hopfields, Wovoka must have gained some knowledge of Smohalla's teachings, some of which he incorporated into his religion. Oregon Indians may also have visited Wovoka near Walker Lake. In the 1880s Wovoka's religion spread to the Fort Hall Reservation, where many Bannocks became his converts. The Bannocks were able to speak the Shoshoni tongue and they had so intermarried with the Southern Shoshonis that it was difficult to find a pure-blooded Bannock. Thus they became intermediaries between Wovoka and Plains tribes on the east. At the height of the Ghost Dance fervor, Bannocks returned from the plains with the message of the resurrection of the dead, and, when Plains tribes visited Wovoka, they took Fort Hall Bannocks with them as interpreters to facilitate the spread of the Ghost Dance religion.

Most Pacific Northwestern Indians had grievances aplenty to attract them to the Ghost Dance faith with its promise for their future. In the early nineties rumors were rife that the Ghost Dance was spreading throughout the Pacific Northwest. It had spread to the Sioux Indians, whose "Ghost Shirts" proved vulnerable to soldier bullets in the infamous Wounded Knee Massacre of December 29, 1890. Before the massacre they had carried the doctrine as far west as the Columbia River, having been present at an Indian powwow at the mouth of the Wenatchee River in August of 1890. Those as far west as the Okanogan reportedly sent emissaries to the plains to learn of the doctrine. When a white freighter was killed in mid-October, 1890, in a remote corner of the Colville Reservation, his supposed killer was lynched by vigilantes. The Indians of the area began dancing what the rumor-riddled white community believed to be the Ghost, or Messiah, Dance, despite the assurances of Chiefs Moses and Joseph that they were merely performing traditional winter dances. The white community took no chances, and in 1891 units of the Washington National Guard were dispatched to the Okanogan country. Tensions were eased thanks to the efforts of Indian chiefs and the Reverend Stephen De Rouge, S.J.

Of all things effecting reservation life perhaps none was more important than the allotting of lands. Allotments involved surveys, which were initially regarded by Indians as attempts by whites to steal their land. In 1866 the Yakima agent reported that a few years previously Indians had been so hostile to allotting that they had pulled up surveyors' stakes "almost as fast as they were driven"—a practice of Indians on other reservations as well. Slowly Indians began to tolerate the allotment system, finding in it a measure of territorial security.

Provisions had been made in the treaties for Indians to take up farming on lands that had been withheld from those held in common by tribes. Before the Dawes Indian Severalty Act of February 8, 1887 (24 Stat 388), 109 Indians and "mixed bloods" on the Grand Ronde were allotted twenty-acre plots. Without official titles they made no improvements on them.* In his 1886 report Grand Ronde agent Amos Harvey had expressed the wish that Indian families have their own parcels of reservation lands, since those who had them did not roam as much as those without them. In 1867, Superintendent Huntington had urged allotments for his Oregon Indians, but in 1885, in three councils, Umatilla Reservation tribes rejected allotments six years after their chiefs had gone to Washington, D.C. seeking them.

The Dawes Act was calculated to hasten the process of making Indians more individualistic in the American style by breaking down tribal entities. Allotments were held in fee simple for twenty-five-year periods, which some agents wished reduced for "advanced" Indians. The Puyallups, however, were allotted by the authority of their treaty in 1886. As a result, pressure on Congress from Tacoma, Washington, businessmen produced federal legislation on March 3, 1893 (27 Stat 633), whereby individual allotments on the Puyallup Reservation could be sold after a ten-year trust period. Buyers made quick and large profits purchasing the former Indian lands. In the decade after 1895 Commissioners sold about seven thousand Puyallup acres amounting to about forty percent of the tribe's alloted lands—and for less than a half million dollars ($420,503). Some of the land was valuable waterfront property along Commencement Bay in Tacoma and along the Puyallup River. Land purchased was gradually concentrated in the possession of various railroad, lumber, and land companies and other enterprises.

On some reservations the Indian response to implementation of the Dawes Act was scarcely enthusiastic. According to an account in the *Yakima Herald*, February 8, 1894, the Yakimas gave a government representative a cool reception. A tribal spokesman said to him: "The lands were given us by the Great Father of the Sun. They are ours. We will not give up another inch of them. We are weary of the pale faces' treaties. Go! we never want to see you again. There is the way. Go!" Despite the rhetoric the Yakimas submitted to allotting. Their records show that 4,556 allotments were made between 1892 and 1915.

The Klamaths were assembled in 1888 to hear a commissioner who used every possible argument in favor of their accepting the provisions of the Dawes Act. In the next year Agent Emery reported that over eight hundred of the tribe had signed an agreement to take lands in severalty in face of opposition from elderly traditionalists. In 1889, Flathead chiefs and headmen opposed taking lands in severalty, shrewdly divining that, after allotments were made, the remaining reservations lands would be sold to whites and thus the territorial integrity of their reservation would be destroyed. Because of pressure from whites, the Flathead Reservation was allotted in 1904. It was officially opened to white settlement six years later. Unique among reservation Indians were those of Fort Hall, who wisely had included in their allotment agreement the provision that they retain ownership of the tribal lands beyond those marked for allotment.

The rate at which the allotting proceeded varied from reservation to reservation. On the Siletz in 1887, the year that the Dawes Act was passed, Special Agent M. C. Connelly was allotting from September until December, but the promptness with which the process got underway did not ensure swiftness: in January, 1890, the Siletz agent reported only seventy-two allotments made. After being allotted, the Indians of the Siletz petitioned the government to grant them full title to their lands. Under this urging, Congress on March 3, 1901, passed legislation permitting termination of trust control of the allotted Siletz lands. By 1953 only seventy-six trust allotments, or 5,390 acres of the former Siletz Reservation, had by remaining in trust, escaped land-grabbing whites.

A most colorful allotting agent was Alice Fletcher, The "Measuring Woman." An anthropologist from Harvard's Peabody Museum, she was sent to the Nez Percés in May, 1889, five months after allotting the Winnebagos (Siouan). Because of considerable opposition at Lapwai to allotting, she worked out of Kamiah from her headquarters, Camp McBeth. She still met considerable opposition although the Nez Percés had inquired the previous year why allotments had not been made. At that time it had been explained that until 1887 the eastern line of the reservation had not been resurveyed from its original surveys of many years before. In Fletcher's final council for the year in November, 1889, some Indians appeared with knives concealed beneath blankets, and a medicine man put an evil eye on her. His failure to harm her enhanced her mystique among the Nez Percés, who ambivalently awaited her return another year. On a fourth and last visit after three and a half round trips across the continent and nearly twenty-two months of exhaustive

---

*The Dawes Severalty Act of 1887 permitted the allotting of all reservation lands to tribal Indians. Few tribes, however, had previously been permitted to allot adequate acreages on reservations under the provisions of their treaties with the government. The Puyallups, for instance, received allotments in January, 1886, when the president issued restricted fee patents to members of the tribe pursuant to authority granted in article 6 of their Medicine Creek Treaty.

Delegation to Washington, D.C., in December, 1889. Front row, left to right: Peo (Umatilla), Homily (Wallawalla), and Young Chief (Umatilla). Back row, left to right: John McBain (inter- *preter), Showaway (Cayuse), Wolf (Palouse), and Lee Moorhouse (Umatilla agent). University of Oregon Library.*

labors, she finished her task in 1892. On leaving, she received a council pipe that had been smoked in over three decades of tribal deliberations. Among the Colville Nez Percés who were allotted on the Nez Percé Reservation was Joseph's lieutenant, Yellow Bull. Joseph came down to see Fletcher, saying he would allot only in his beloved Wallowas.

The allotment system created many problems for not only those receiving tracts but also those administering them. The Indian Office was swamped with numerous inquiries from agents, many of which pertained to people's eligibility for allotments. Some agents, such as Fisher in 1890 at Fort Hall, questioned the advisability of the Indians taking in severalty lands that would be untillable until they received irrigation. In 1886 the Puyallup agent credited the Indian Office with protecting Indian land patents in the face of

strong railroad and land-company opposition, but in 1895 the Tulalip agent wrote that many patent-holding Indians, especially those who had been absent from the reservation for years, had never improved their lands and that in some cases they did not even know where their allotments were. As a result, he believed, citizenship was thrust on the Indians prematurely, as it removed them from the restraints of tribal courts and agents, allowing them to get "gloriously drunk." In 1894 the Umatilla agent lamented the languishing state of agriculture on his reservation, particularly among full bloods. Mixed bloods on the Umatilla farmed their allotments with livestock, machinery, and provisions furnished by bankers and merchants, who took mortgages on the crops and then the crops themselves.

The Siletz agent in 1901 reported that some Indians had the mistaken idea that they could transfer their allotments

267

Coeur d'Alêne Chief Peter Moctelme. Eastern Washington State Historical Society.

to other Indians and lease them to whites entirely on their own initiative. A number of Indians did not live beyond the trust periods to receive their patents. The Siletz agent reported that of the 880 allotments completed on his reservation by 1893, 196 allottees had died leaving about 17,000 acres of inherited lands. On the deaths of the allottees the heirs in big families received negligible income from leases when the lands were divided. By the middle of the twentieth century heirship had become a problem that only radical legislation could correct. With holdings so small and unmanageable, owners saw no purpose in farming, and this no-purpose farming perhaps contributed to the fragmentation of lands. Securing agreements to sell lands under multiple ownership was another problem. Amendments to the Dawes Act in 1891, 1897, and 1900 permitted the leasing of allotted lands, frustrating the government's wish to make the Indians into farmers. Other factors, such as poor farm prices during most of the later nineteenth century and the absence of draft animals and equipment, contributed to the Indians' longstanding unwillingness to farm. Many owners sold their allotments after obtaining unrestricted titles to them when the trust periods expired.

There were some Indians with large farm holdings who quite naturally opposed allotments of 160 acres. One of these, Coeur d'Alêne Chief Peter Moctelme followed the admonition of Catholic fathers to his people to farm. Al-

though he and his people opposed allotments even to the point of pulling up survey stakes, they were allotted in 1905 and 1906. Moctelme was even opposed to the allotting on the Coeur d'Alêne Reservation of the Spokanes who had been sent there by the 1889 agreement partly because of their Catholic faith.

Indian landholdings in the United States were reduced by nearly two-thirds between 1887 and 1934. The process was reversed by passage of the Wheeler-Howard Indian Reorganization Act of 1934 (48 Stat 984). Thirty years after passage of the Dawes Act approximately three million reservation acres had been alienated in Washington, Oregon, and Idaho alone.

In response to a petition by some Yakima Valley businessmen to the secretary of the interior that Indians be given patents in fee simple and treated as American citizens, the Yakima Indian advocate L. V. McWhorter warned in effect, "The white man with much booze and very little money will speedily 'eliminate' the 'Indian factor' from the Yakima Valley forever." McWhorter's protectionism for Indians was understandable in the light of the numerous wrongs done them. His statement raised a key question: How long and to what extent would Indians succumb to the policies of a patronizing government while they sought the independence it denied them? With this legacy of the nineteenth century the twentieth would have to deal.

A *Coeur d'Alêne hunter with his quarry and two very-much-alive passengers. Museum of Native American Cultures.*

Two legacies of the Indians' past remained: fishing was involved in Judge George Boldt's February 12, 1974, decision in *United States* v. *Washington* (384 Supp. 312), and gambling in the Indian Gaming Regulatory Act of 1989. *United States* v. *Winans* (see p. 259) had assured Indians the right to fish off-reservation in common with non-Indians and guaranteed them access to their fishing places. During the first half of the 20th century, off-reservation Indian fishing was subject to state regulations for non-Indians that required license fees, adherence to fishing seasons, and use of certain fishing gear. In 1942 the United States Supreme Court ruled in *Tulee* v. *Washington* (315 U.S. 681, 1942) that states could not impose license fees on Indians, but could limit types of fishing gear in order to conserve fish.

In the 1950s and 1960s litigation continued regarding states' restrictions on off-reservation Indian fishing, and incomes of non-Indian commercial fishermen were failing. At that time western Washington Puyallup and Nisqually Indians, supported by others including entertainment figures, clashed with Washington state officials enforcing regulations on Indians and clogged rivers with boats and nets in protest demonstrations. On October 13, 1965, at Frank's Landing on the Nisqually River, six Indians were arrested and jailed. In what was in essence a riot, some law enforcers were injured so badly that they required hospitalization and one badly beaten Indian woman died.

Neither the Washington Department of Game nor its Department of Fisheries protested the Indians' right to fish on their reservations—the problem was off-reservation fishing. The Department of Game brought suit against the Puyallups, declaring them a "non-tribe" since their reservation had been sold off, but in 1957 the state's Supreme Court ruled that the Puyallups were still a tribe. Following other suits and appeals involving both Nisquallys and Puyallups, their combined cases were taken to the U.S. Supreme Court on May 27, 1968, for a ruling in *Department of Game* v. *Puyallup Tribe* (391 U.S. 392). The Court opined that the state had jurisdiction over off-reservation fishing but could close their rivers to fishing when necessary for conservation. But while the Department of Fisheries changed its regulations to permit Indians to set nets for salmon on the Puyallup River, the Department of Game, classifying steelhead as a game fish, assumed authority to refuse Indians the use of fishing nets.

The U.S. Supreme Court refused to review a 1963 decision of the Ninth Circuit Court in an Oregon case, *Maison* v. *Confederated Tribes of the Umatilla Indian Reservation* (314 F.2d 169), which sustained state jurisdictional regulations over Indian fishing only after limitation or prohibition of non-Indian fishing. Meanwhile other legal battles were being waged in Oregon. In 1969 the Sohappy family, salmon gillnetters on the lower Columbia, sued Anthony Smith, Oregon Fish Commissioner (*Sohappy* v. *Smith*, USDC D Oregon 68-409), and the Justice Department joined in the suit as *United States* v. *Oregon* (USDC D Oregon 68-513). In U.S. District Court in Oregon it was ruled that treaty tribes, who had rights to fish in usual and accustomed places, were entitled to an (undefinable) fair and equitable share of all fish from given runs—at that time Indians were catching only 5 percent.

As the 1970s approached, violence between Indians and enforcement officials continued on the Puyallup and other rivers. In these "wars" people were shot and nets and boats damaged. Officials retaliated with tear gas, and there were many arrests. On behalf of seven western tribes, the Justice Department sued the State of Washington in the U.S. District Court in Tacoma. Before the case was adjudicated seven more tribes had joined the suit. Presided over by Judge Boldt, the three-year trial began in 1970. Intense preparations had produced 250 documents entered as exhibits with testimony of over 500 factual and legal conclusions.

Department of Game officials now contended that treaty rights did not entitle Indians to rights and privileges greater than those of non-Indians and that Indians could not net steelheads since they were game fish. The Department of Fisheries did not dispute Indian treaty rights to fish, but following *Sohappy* v. *Smith* and *United States* v. *Oregon* it wanted clarification of what constituted fair and equitable shares of fish harvests. In *United States* v. *Washington* Judge Boldt handed down a landmark ruling that assured Indians salmon and steelhead fishing rights. Judge Boldt interpreted words such as "fair and equitable" to mean "equally." As equals Indians were entitled to 50 percent of harvestable migrating fish. The Boldt decision limited non-Indians from fishing beyond the terminal point of fish migration not only in the ocean, where fishing was mostly commercial, but also on the lower Columbia and in Puget Sound. Indians were permitted to regulate their own fisheries, issue their own permits, set their seasons, and designate their gear.

Although the "wars" ceased, the post-Boldt era saw intense debate as Departments of Fisheries and Game sought to overturn the decision with appeals on behalf of mostly non-Indian commercial and sports fishermen. A year

later Judge Boldt asked the tribes to talk out their differences and reach a common consensus. Two years later a task force was established to study the situation and recommend tribal fishing zones. Specifically, on Puget Sound and its affluents, some tribes could fish to the exclusion of others.

The Justice Department supported a review of the Boldt decision. After agreeing in October 1978 to review it, on July 2, 1979, the U.S. Supreme Court ruled six to three to uphold the decision with minor modifications. The Indians' 50 percent share of fish had not included salmon caught for ceremonial purposes or on reservations, but the Court altered the decision to include those catches.

As Pacific Northwest fishing had involved creeks and courts, gambling involved casinos and courts. A 1979 court case brought by Florida Seminoles caused expansion of high-stakes bingo operations that reached the Pacific Northwest. The Tulalips were the first in the region to offer this form of gambling, and by 1990 seven reservations offered it. Then the Cabazon Band of Indians of California sought to establish casino gambling on their reservation. When county and state officials denied their request the Cabazons sued, holding that as a sovereign tribal entity they could legally operate bingo as well as casino gambling on their reservation. In 1987 their case reached the U.S. Supreme Court. The Court sided with the Cabazons, who had not surrendered the jurisdictional rights of their reservation to the state of California under Public Law 280, and ruled that gambling on their reservation was a civil regulatory function rather than a criminal activity since the state did not prohibit all forms of gambling.

Nevada gambling interests pressured Congress into legislating some controls over reservation gambling, resulting in the 1989 Indian Gaming Regulatory Act, which covered games other than bingo, stick games, and non-banking gambling. However, tribes or bands had to negotiate contracts with the states and give them control over amounts wagered and operating hours, as well as general control to prevent criminal takeovers.

When Siletz Indians, whose reservation was near the Oregon coast, wanted to conduct casino gambling on lands they proposed to buy in the busy I-5 corridor at Salem, Governor Barbara Roberts refused their request. When the Spokane tribe was at variance with Washington State over slot machine use, the issue came down to one of money versus morality. The same dilemma faced their Idaho neighbors, the Coeur d'Alênes, who proposed a national lottery. The moral issue was not lost on everyone; Yakima Nation tribal members were reluctant to establish gambling because of its destructive nature. Nevertheless, a separate group of pro-gambling Yakimas pushed for negotiations with the state gambling commission. When the commission allowed increased wager amounts and extended casino gambling hours, the Washington legislature demanded participation in Indian gambling negotiations. Despite promises that gambling would be free of criminal elements, there was increasing sentiment that these forces would move in, and in January 1995 a bill was introduced in Congress that sought to deny Indians their El Dorado.

25. EPILOGUE: A CHANGE OF WORLDS

In the fall of 1853, Chief Seattle and his people met Governor Isaac Stevens, who introduced himself as the new superintendent of Indian affairs for Washington Territory. The chief concluded his responses to Stevens by saying that there was a change of worlds for man. He was referring to both the present world and to that which follows death. For Indians even more than Stevens and his successors there was change in the present world. By the twentieth century the Indian world had been all but replaced by that of the white men, whose civilization, also changing, raced on at a quickening pace sweeping Indian traditionalists aside. In huts or on street corners the Indians often sat in sullen silence dreaming of the past as the white men rushing by them planned for the future. The once-proud horsemen of the interior, dreaming of their free-riding past, saw their equestrian prizes rounded up and shipped off to canneries. Indians saw road and town builders destroy their ossuaries or found them destroyed by relic hunters.

Caught up in the progressivism of the period, the officials charged with the management of Indian affairs carried out their tasks with an efficiency hitherto unknown, serving more effectively to change traditional Indian ways. Many officials sincerely sought to make the Indians coheirs of the rapidly advancing technology of the period. On some reservations in the vast arid portions of the Pacific Northwest the Indians learned to practice irrigation agriculture on a scale never dreamed of by their fathers, to whom missionaries had introduced it a half century before. Indians inherited twentieth-century technology only slowly, however. Utilities on reservation lands were initially built to serve white men, not Indians.

Seeking redress for their grievances, Indians continued their pilgrimages to the Great Father in Washington. They were spurred by some previous successes, but often resigned because of previous failures. Until the twentieth century officials welcomed chiefs at the national capital, intimidating them with the power of the government and the spectacle of an endless stream of whites. In an 1909 council a Cayuse chief, with perhaps more futility than fidelity, ceremoniously declaimed, "I have great love for you, President Taft, although I never saw your face." The presidents began wooing the Indians with Great Father paternalism as the nation with patriotic fervor approached the First World War. Thanks to an invention of Thomas Edison (who condemned the wrongs done to Indians), President Woodrow Wilson talked to them by phonograph, calling them his brothers and not his children. Some Pacific Northwestern red men responded to his call to join their other brothers in the crusade to make the world safe for democracy, as others had scouted for the government to make the Pacific Northwest safe for white men. In 1892 fifteen Nez Percés enlisted in the cavalry, putting their equestrian skills to good use. In the

following year some Spokanes and Colvilles were discharged from the service for being absent without leave from Fort Spokane. Five years later, without the restriction of ill-fitting uniforms, several Spokanes appeared at that fort in paint and feathers to volunteer their services in the Spanish-American War. About two decades later their successors wore khaki on the battlefields of France, where some traditionalists believed they were being sacrificed by the same government that had fought their fathers.

In 1924 the government responded to the Indians' war service by an act (43 Stat 253) extending citizenship to the Indian community. In 1931 a commissioner of Indian affairs spoke for the first time of helping Indians to adapt successfully to modern life with as little cultural change as possible. In a period when antidemocratic forces were soon to catapult the world into the second great war of the century, the government sought to live up to its own democratic principles and instituted the Indian Reorganization Act of 1934. Regarded suspiciously by the Indian traditionalists, the act returned to the tribes some autonomy and some lands that were alienated under the Dawes Act. A provision of the act and subsequent federal legislation permitting Indian socio-economic programs only meant further assimilation of white culture. The commissioner's words, "as little cultural change as possible," had become an impossibility.

By World War II the opposition of the Indian community to their young serving in the American armed forces had all but disappeared. Examples of Indian valor in that conflict are many. Two will suffice. A Spokane Indian, Louie Adrian, died a few feet from the top of Mount Surabachi so that the American Flag could be raised there. Walter Lawyer, a descendent of the Chief Lawyer who was severely wounded by Blackfeet, died in 1945 from wounds sustained in Germany. The war drew many Indians to Pacific Northwestern cities to face for the first time the complexities of urban life. Some sought escape from the alienation suffered there by returning to their reservations in hopes of finding security among their people on the land. The inadequate economic base of most reservations, however, continues to propel tribesmen to the cities to swell the ranks of those classified as urban Indians.

In the postwar era the government was entangled more deeply than ever by conflicting ideologies in its Indian policies. Some spokesmen continued the suppression of traditional Indian culture; others tried to rectify previous wrongs done to red men. Through the Indian Claims Commission some tribes received compensation for some of their original lands at a percentage of their true value. A program in the 1950s to terminate reservations, albeit honestly conceived, failed to take into account the basic Indian need for land. The tragic failure of the Klamath Indians in the 1960s to retain their lands was a lesson to others not only to retain theirs but also to continue pressing their claims. Pressing claims was one of the many new legal types of warfare that Indians began to wage. In early 1974 the tiny Kutenai tribe declared war against the United State with publicity as its major weapon, and it received some concessions from the enemy.

Other wars involving Pacific Northwestern Indians are largely jurisdictional in nature and still rage between the tribes and local, state, and federal governments. The federal Bureau of Indian Affairs, despite declining powers and concessions, is to many Indians more an adversary than an advocate. Conflict continues to swirl around tribal water rights. The ink had scarcely dried on the Stevens treaties, which promised Indians the right to fish in their "usual and accustomed places, in common with citizens of the Territory," when controversy arose. Controversy has continued into the present over the percentages of the allotment of salmon to Indian and non-Indian fishermen. Technology has helped to precipitate the conflict by diminishing the fish runs. Less than a century after they were promised their grounds in perpetuity, Indians in June, 1940, observed their Ceremony of Tears for Kettle Falls, whose fishery Grand Coulee Dam had destroyed. Fifty years earlier a white publicist had compared the supposedly more civilized method of taking fish by wheels to the methods used by Indians, which he described as barbarous. Today there is hope that fishery enhancement programs, applied by Indians and non-Indians alike, will restore the runs.

The greatest of all the Indian wars is their struggle to adapt to a world not of their choosing. On some reservations the adaptation has only recently been effected—and it has been so effective in some cases that Indians who formerly were encouraged to adopt the ways of the white man now fear that such acceptance will destroy the last vestiges of their culture. The physical survival of the Indians was assured around the turn of the century when improved health programs turned the tide of decreasing populations. The turnabout disappointed some whites, surprised others, and vindicated some Indians whose prophets had predicted that red men would one day reinherit the earth. Indian blood, which ran strongly in early times, continues, however, to lose it quantum. Although some tribal languages have been preserved, those who speak them become fewer with each passing year. Some Indians, like white men, from whom they learned their responses, seek alcohol to numb themselves to their losses. Some turn to suicide to end the struggle born of familial-societal disorganization.

The struggle for Indian identity continues. The Nez Percés gathered at White Bird on June 17, 1977, a century to the day after they fought the United States at that place. With a confidence born of a newly found sense of identity, they commemorated their confrontation with white men in a sacred rite conducted on the battlefield, from which they returned to their homes with a resolve to conduct their own affairs and fashion their own destiny in an aura of revived spiritism and tribalism. Several hitherto-landless tribes have today achieved federal acknowledgment that—as Indian tribes they are "unique political entities". Others seek such an acknowledgment and a land base to give them fishing rights and other benefits.

After their 200-year association with the Indians of the Pacific Northwest, white men of the region like men elsewhere, suffer misgivings about the liberties taken with science and technology. When the telegraph appeared in the region, Indians believed the "whispering wires" had evil eyes to harm them. In the mid twenties Indians were afraid when water first roared over a dam on a Skagit River tributary, the Baker, which had flowed untrammeled past their villages for ages. When the locomotive first crossed the plateau, Indians heard white men say the iron monster would leave its tracks and run them down. How white men laughed when Indians hid behind trees and bushes in terror! Today no one laughs. An untracked technology is man's greatest danger. Both Indians and whites pray it will not blast them out of this world into the next before their time.

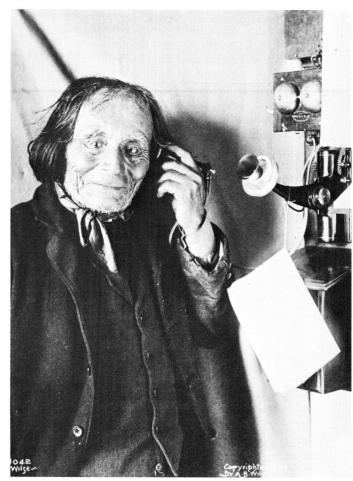

An Indian using a telephone in Seattle, circa 1900. Seattle Historical Society.

272

Notes

CHAPTER 1

1. For an account of the complex ritual and protocol of the China trade, see Robert H. Ruby and John A. Brown, *The Chinook Indians*, pp. 75–76.

2. "Dr. John Scouler's Journal of a Voyage to N.W. America," *Oregon Historical Quarterly* 6, no. 2 (June, 1907): 196.

3. The tradition is related in Martin J. Sampson, *Indians of Skagit County*, p. 28.

CHAPTER 2

1. Helpful to the reader following the exploits of the Lewis and Clark Expedition are: Elliott Coues, ed., *History of the Expedition under the command of Lewis and Clark*, vol. 2, and Bernard DeVoto, ed., *The Journals of Lewis and Clark*.

2. For sources dealing with the spread of the horse among Indian tribes of the interior, see Robert H. Ruby and John A. Brown, *The Cayuse Indians*, pp. 7 and 11n.

3. Relations between Plains peoples, such as the Blackfeet, and the Shoshonis are narrated by the British trader-explorer David Thompson, who in the early nineteenth century talked with members of the Plains tribes, who told him about those relationships at the time and in the eighteenth century. David Thompson, *The Publications of the Champlain Society David Thompson's Narrative 1784–1812*, ed., Richard Glover, p. 221ff.

4. W. A. Ferris, *Life in the Rocky Mountains A Diary of Wanderings on the sources of the Rivers Missouri, Columbia, and Colorado from February, to November, 1835*, pp. 324–25.

5. Charles Wilkes, U.S.N., *Narrative of the United States Exploring Expedition During the Years 1838, 1839, 1840, 1841, 1842*, 4: 456.

6. Madge Wolfenden, ed., "John Tod: 'Career of a Scotch Boy,'" *British Columbia Historical Quarterly* 18, nos. 3–4 (July-October, 1954): 217–18.

7. Elliott Coues, ed., *New Light on the Early History of the Greater Northwest: The Manuscript Journals of Alexander Henry, Fur Trader of the Northwest Company, and of David Thompson, Official Geographer and Explorer of the Same Country, 1799–1814*, 2: 836

CHAPTER 3

1. Early nineteenth-century developments among the Spokanes and their Salish-speaking neighbors are described in Robert H. Ruby and John A. Brown, *The Spokane Indians*, p. 34ff.

2. Thomas Farnham, *Travels in the Great Western Prairies* 1: 264, in *Early Western Travels 1784–1846*, ed. Reuben Gold Thwaites, vol. 28.

3. The events attending the founding of Astoria and subsequent events in the area of that post as they pertain to its natives are chronicled in Ruby and Brown, *The Chinook Indians*, p. 128ff.

CHAPTER 4

1. There are several accounts of the expedition, among which there is considerable variation. Among them are Gabriel Franchère, *Adventure at Astoria, 1810–1814*, ed. Hoyt C. Franchère, pp. 96–99; Jesse E. Douglas, ed., "Matthews' Adventures on the Columbia," *Oregon Historical Quarterly* 40, no. 2 (June, 1939): 137; and Alexander Henry, *Journal*, ed. Elliot Coues, vol. 2, 790–808.

2. The event and others involving fur trader–Indian relationships in the general area of the Columbia-Snake river confluence are found in Alexander Ross, *Adventures of the First Settlers on the Oregon or Columbia River*, p. 214.

3. Ross Cox, *Adventures on the Columbia River . . .* 1: p. 346–47.

4. Alexander Ross, *The Fur Hunters of the Far West*, p. 151. McKenzie's exploits are discussed in Jean C. Nielson, "Donald McKenzie in the Snake Country Fur Trade, 1816–1821," *Pacific Northwest Quarterly* 31, no. 2 (April, 1940): 161–79.

CHAPTER 5

1. An evaluation of the Pacific Northwestern fur trade by Simpson and the narration of his experiences in the region are presented in Frederick Merk, ed. *Fur Trade and Empire George Simpson's Journal*, p. 41.

2. The expedition is narrated in Ross, *Fur Hunters*, pp. 208–93.

3. Cox, *Adventures* 1: 321.

4. Sally Snyder, "Quest for the Sacred in Northern Puget Sound: An Interpretation of Potlatch," *Ethnology* 14, no. 2 (April, 1975): 149–61.

5. An account of this episode appears in S. A. Clarke, *Pioneer Days of Oregon History*, pp. 231–35.

6. A good account of intertribal conflict is found in Merrill D. Beal and Merle W. Wells, *History of Idaho* 1: 109ff.

7. Bonneville's experiences among Pacific Northwestern natives are related in Washington Irving, *The Adventures of Captain Bonneville, U.S.A. in the Rocky Mountains and the Far*

West, ed. Edgeley W. Todd.

8. Townsend's opinions regarding the treatment of red men are expressed in his *Narrative of a Journey across the Rocky Mountains to the Columbia River*, in *Early Western Travels 1784–1846*, ed. Reuben Gold Thwaites, 21: 214–15.

CHAPTER 6

1. Frank Ermatinger, "Earliest Expeditions Against Puget Sound Indians," *Washington Historical Quarterly* 1, no. 2 (January, 1907): 16–19. For a discussion of McLoughlin's relations with the Indians, including the dispatching of punitive expeditions against them, see Dorothy O. Johansen, "McLoughlin and the Indians," *Beaver*, Outfit 277, no. 1 (June, 1946), pp. 18–21.

2. Peter Corney, *Early Voyages in the North Pacific 1813–1818 by Peter Corney*, pp. 162–64.

3. William Fraser Tolmie, *The Journals of William Fraser Tolmie, Physician and Fur Trader*, ed. R. G. Large, p. 176.

4. Events at Fort Nisqually are narrated by its chief trader, William Fraser Tolmie, in *The Journals of William Fraser Tolmie*, p. 171ff.

CHAPTER 7

1. Virginia Cole Trenholm, and Maurine Carley, *The Shoshonis*, p. 85.

2. Verne F. Ray, "The Bluejay Character in the Plateau Spirit Dance, *American Anthropologist* 39, no. 4 (October-December, 1937): 593–601; Leslie Spier, *The Prophet Dance of the Northwest and Its Derivatives, the Source of the Ghost Dance*, American Anthropological Association, General Series in Anthropology, no. 1, pp. 20, 35.

3. "Journal of Occurrences at Nisqually House," *Washington Historical Quarterly* 7, no. 2 (April, 1916): 157–58.

4. John Fahey, *The Flathead Indians*, p. 66.

5. Mission activities of Lee and his aides are recorded in numerous writings. Among these, besides letters and journals, are: Gustavus Hines, *Life on the Plains of the Pacific*; D. Lee and J. H. Frost, *Ten Years in Oregon*. Mission life is also presented in Zechariah Atwell Mudge, *Sketches of Mission Life among the Indians of Oregon*.

6. Quoted in Harvey E. Tobie, "From the Missouri to the Columbia," *Oregon Historical Quarterly* 38, no. 2 (June, 1937): 156–57.

7. Jonathan S. Green, *Journal of a Tour on the North West Coast of America in the Year 1829*, pp. 90, 100–101n. See also George Verne Blue, "Green's Missionary Report on Oregon, 1829," *Oregon Historical Quarterly* 30, no. 3 (September, 1929): 259–71.

8. Parker's account of his missionary travels is found in Samuel Parker, *Journal of an Exploring Tour beyond the Rocky Mountains, Under the Direction of the A.B.C.F.M.*

9. Much has been written about the Whitman Mission because of the martyrdom of its founders. A compact account of its founding, activity, and demise is in Ruby and Brown, *The Cayuse Indians*, p. 63ff.

10. For an account of American Board activity among the Spokanes and surrounding Salish peoples, see Ruby and Brown, *The Spokane Indians*, pp. 59–82, and Clifford M. Drury, *Nine Years with the Spokane Indians The Diary 1838–1848, of Elkanah Walker*.

CHAPTER 8

1. Exploits of these missionaries are found in F. N. Blanchet et al., *Notices and Voyages of the Famed Quebec Mission to the Pacific Northwest . . .*

2. Among writings of De Smet in which his missionary activity is recorded is his *Letters and Sketches: With a Narrative of a Year's Residence among the Indian Tribes of the Rocky Mountains.*

3. For a discussion of mission reductions among Indians of the Pacific Northwestern interior, see Robert Ignatius Burns, S.J., *The Jesuits and the Indian Wars of the Northwest*, pp. 48–55.

4. W. P. CLark, *The Indian Sign Language . . .*, p. 310.

5. Quoted in Fahey, *The Flathead Indians*, p. 75.

6. *Wilderness Kingdom Indian Life in the Rocky Mountains: 1840–1847 The Journals and Paintings of Nicolas Point, S.J.*, ed. Joseph P. Donnelly, S.J., p. 109.

7. A(lexander) Diomedi, S.J., *Sketches of Modern Indian Life*, p. 52ff.

8. Denton R. Bedford, "The Fight at 'Mountains on Both Sides,'" *The Indian Historian* 8, no. 2 (Fall, 1975): 13ff.

9. Robert H. Ruby and John A. Brown, *Half-Sun on the Columbia*, pp. 23–24.

CHAPTER 9

1. A manuscript (P-B 206:10 in the Bancroft Library, University of California, Berkeley) tells of this early settler in a letter from John Broyles to a Mr. Taylor, President, Bellingham Bay & British Columbia Railroad, July 25, 1908.

2. James L. Ratcliff, "What Happened to the Kalapuya? A Study of the Depletion of Their Economic Base," *The Indian Historian* 6, no. 3 (Summer, 1973): 27–33. A good account of early Indian life in the Willamette Valley is Stepen Dow Beckham, *The Indians of Western Oregon This Land Was Theirs*, pp. 1–93.

3. Wilkes's observations may be found in Edmond S. Meany, ed., "Diary of Wilkes in the Northwest," *Washington Historical Quarterly* 16, no. 1 (January, 1925): 49–61, no. 2 (April, 1925): 137–45, no. 3 (July, 1925): 206–23, and no. 4 (October, 1925): 290–301.

4. For an account of the law giver, see Elijah White, *Ten Years in Oregon*, pp. 172–200.

5. Lansford W. Hastings, *Narratives of the Trans-Mississippi Frontier*, p. 59.

6. Ibid., pp. 58–59.

7. P. J. De Smet, S.J., *Oregon Missions and Travels over the Rocky Mountains*, in *Early Western Travels 1748–1846*, ed. Reuben Gold Thwaites, 29: 236–38.

CHAPTER 10

1. Edwin Bryant, *What I saw in California . . .* (New York, 1849), pp. 273–74; Joseph Warren Revere, *Naval Duty in California*, pp. 125–31. See also Robert Fleming Heizer, "Walla Walla Indian Expeditions to the Sacramento Valley," *California Historical Quarterly* 21, no. 1 (March, 1942): 1–7, and John Adam Hussey and George Walcott Ames, Jr., "California Preparations to Meet the Walla Walla Invasion, 1846," ibid., pp. 9–17.

2. The governance of the distant Oregon country was marked by delay on the part of the United States. At the time of the Cayuse War the United States was involved in the Mexican War, and the Oregon Territory did not come under direct American governance until March 3, 1849, when the territorial government became effective.

CHAPTER 11

1. Mildred Baker Burcham, "Scott's and Applegate's Old South Road," *Oregon Historical Quarterly* 41, no. 4 (December, 1940): 405–23. See also, Buena Cobbstone, "Southern Route Into Oregon: Notes and a New Map," *Oregon Historical Quarterly* 47, no. 2 (June, 1946): 135–54.

2. "The California Recollections of Casper T. Hopkins," *California Historical Quarterly* 25, no. 2 (June, 1946): 113–20.

3. Treaty making and its consequences in Oregon are discussed in C. F. Coan, "The Adoption of the Reservation Policy in Pacific Northwest, 1853–1855," *Oregon Historical Quarterly* 23, no. 1 (March, 1922): 1–38, and in Coan, "The First Stage of the Federal Indian Policy in the Pacific Northwest, 1849–1852," *Oregon Historical Quarterly* 22, no. 1 (March, 1921): 46–86, and in Jerry A. O'Callaghan, "Extinguishing Indian Land Title on the Oregon Coast," *Oregon Historical Quarterly* 52, no. 3 (September, 1951): 139–44, and in William G. Robbins, "Extinguishing Indian Land Title in Western Oregon," *The Indian Historian* 7, no. 2 (Spring, 1974): 10–14.

4. George Crook, *General George Crook His Autobiography*, ed. Martin F. Schmitt, pp. 39–42.

5. Quoted in Preston E. Onstad, "The Fort on the

Luckiamute: A Resurvey of Fort Hoskins," *Oregon Historical Quarterly* 65, no. 2 (June, 1964): 178.

CHAPTER 12

1. Ezra Meeker, *The Busy Life of Eighty-Five Years of Ezra Meeker*, p. 114.

2. William S. Lewis and Paul C. Phillips, eds., *The Journal of John Work A chief-trader of the Hudson's Bay Co. during his expedition from Vancouver to the Flatheads and the Blackfeet of the Pacific Northwest*, p. 47.

3. These and other Roman Catholic missions of the Pacific Northwest are presented in Wilfred P. Schoenberg, S.J., *A Chronicle of Catholic History of the Pacific Northwest 1743–1960*.

4. Kamiakin's biography is *Ka-Mi-akin, The Last Hero of the Yakimas*, by A. J. Splawn.

5. Hancock's observations are recorded in *The Narrative of Samuel Hancock 1845–1860*, pp. 181–84.

6. B[enjamin] Alvord, "The Doctor Killing Oregons," *Harpers*, February, 1884, pp. 364–66.

7. For locations of routes to buffalo, see *Reports of Explorations and Surveys, to Ascertain the Most Practicable and Economical Route for a Railroad from the Mississippi River to the Pacific Ocean, 1853–55*, vol. 12, pt. 1, pp. 118–27, and vol. 1, p. 97. See also George A. Buffey, *Eighty-One Years in the West*, pp. 77–78.

8. Hines, *Life on the Plains of the Pacific*, pp. 173–74.

9. *Reports of Explorations and Surveys* 1: 424.

CHAPTER 13

1. Steven's treaty making is recorded not only in his official reports but also in his biography, Hazard Stevens, *The Life of Isaac Ingalls Stevens*, 1: 448–80 and 2: 1–119.

2. Edward Curtis, *The North American Indian*, 9: 25–28. Edmond S. Meany, "Legends, Traditions and Present Condition of Lummi Indians," *Seattle Post Intelligencer*, October 1, 1905. Among more recent publications dealing with the Lummis are Bernhard J. Stern, *The Lummi Indians of Northwest Washington*, and Wayne Suttles, "Post-Contact Culture Change among the Lummi Indians," *British Columbia Historical Quarterly* 18, nos. 1 and 2 (January-April, 1954).

3. James G. Swan, *The Northwest Coast: or, Three Years' Residence in Washington Territory*, p. 166.

4. Proceedings at the May-June Walla Walla Council and treaties evolving from it are presented in several works. Among them are Alvin M. Josephy, Jr., *The Nez Perce Indians and the Opening of the Northwest*, pp. 283–332, and Ruby and Brown, *The Cayuse Indians*, pp. 189–204.

5. Quoted in Charles H. Carey, *General History of Oregon Through Early Statehood*, p. 576.

6. Using primary and secondary sources, Fahey dis-

cusses the Flathead Council in *The Flathead Indians*, pp. 89–112. The council is also discussed in Burns, *The Jesuits and the Indian Wars of the Northwest*, pp. 82–116.

CHAPTER 14

1. For an account of the council, see Ruby and Brown, *The Spokane Indians*, pp. 98–101.

2. Curtis, *The North American Indian* 7: 65.

3. Events at the mission during this period are narrated in Denys Nelson, "Yakima Days," *Washington Historical Quarterly* 19, no. 2 (April, 1928): 125–86.

4. War developments in the Walla Walla Valley and the surrounding area are narrated in Ruby and Brown, *The Cayuse Indians*, pp. 224–41.

5. For the reader who does not have access to official documents of the war, a factual account may be found in Edmond S. Meany, *History of the State of Washington*, pp. 176–219. It was written about forty years ago and from the point of view of whites.

CHAPTER 15

1. The attack on The Cascades is chronicled in numerous secondary sources, including Meany, *History of the State of Washington*, pp. 193–96.

2. P. H. Sheridan, *Personal memoirs of P. H. Sheridan, General, U.S. Army* 1: 112.

3. The attack is narrated in Ruby and Brown, *The Cayuse Indians*, pp. 248–52.

4. Victor J. Farrar, ed., "Diary Kept by Colonel and Mrs. I. N. Ebey," *Washington Historical Quarterly* 8, no. 2 (April, 1917): 140.

5. Documents pertaining to the incursions of northern Indians are found in "Defending Puget Sound against the Northern Indians," *Pacific Northwest Quarterly* 36, no. 1 (January, 1945): 69–78.

6. Events along the mid-Columbia during the Yakima War are recorded in Ruby and Brown, *Half-Sun on the Columbia*, p. 36ff.

7. The Mormon mission at Lemhi, the conflict there, and its consequences are discussed in Brigham D. Madsen, *The Bannock of Idaho*, p. 48ff.; Lawrence G. Coates, "Mormons and Social Change Among the Shoshoni, 1853–1900," *Idaho Yesterdays* 15, no. 4 (Winter, 1972); 1–11; John D. Nash, "Salmon River Mission of 1855: A Reappraisal," *Idaho Yesterdays* 2, no. 1 (Spring, 1967): 22–31; and W. W. Henderson, ed., "The Salmon River Mission: Organization and Founding," *Utah Historical Quarterly* 5, no. 1 (January, 1932): 22ff.

8. Crook, *General George Crook: His Autobiography*, pp. 59–68.

9. The White River Massacre was narrated by a forester,

A. H. Sylvester. Typescript copy in possession of Bernice Greene, Wenatchee, Washington. The massacre is also described in a letter to her from Moses George, January 30, 1975. The George account differs from that of Sylvester because George states that the Indian victims were noncombatants.

10. "The Indian Chief Kitsap," *Washington Historical Quarterly* 25, no. 4 (October, 1934): 297–301.

CHAPTER 16

1. Oregon Superintendency of Indian Affairs, Letter Book, D:10, National Archives, Washington, D.C.

2. Huntington, *Report*, September 12, 1863; Oregon Superintendency of Indian Affairs, Letter Book, H:10, National Archives, Washington, D.C.

3. T. W. Davenport, "Recollections of an Indian Agent," *Oregon Historical Quarterly* 8, no. 3 (September, 1907): 242.

4. *Washington Standard* (Olympia, W. T.), August 17, 1867, p. 2.

5. Burns, *The Jesuits and the Indian Wars of the Northwest*, p. 161; Ruby and Brown, *The Spokane Indians*, p. 103.

6. Michael Simmons, agent, to James Nesmith, superintendent, August 29, 1858. Records of the Washington Superintendency of Indian Affairs, 1853–1874; Letters from Agents Assigned to the Puget Sound District as a Whole, December 4, 1853–August 16, 1862. National Archives, Washington, D.C.

7. Events attending the boundary survey are found in Federal Archives, Letters Sent by U.S. Commissioner Archibald Campbell, February 27, 1857–November 8, 1869; Records Relating to the First Northwest Boundary Survey Commission, 1853–69. Microcopy No. T-606.

8. Browne's investigation of Pacific Northwestern Indian affairs is found in David Michael Goodman, *A Western Panorama 1849–1875 the travels, writing and influence of J. Ross Browne . . .*, pp. 121–37.

CHAPTER 17

1. Among sources dealing with sea-otter hunting is "Hunting the Sea Otter . . .," *The Northwest* 8, no.7 (July, 1890): 11. Among those dealing with seal hunting is one appearing on page 7 of the same periodical entitled "Indian Seal Hunters."

2. George W. France, *The Struggles For Life and Home In the North-West*, pp. 206–207.

3. *Weekly Pacific Tribune* (Tacoma, W.T.), August 31, 1877, p. 3.

4. The eipsode is discussed in Robert H. Ruby and John A. Brown, *Myron Eells and the Puget Sound Indians*, in a chapter entitled "War and the Chase" based on an Eells manuscript.

CHAPTER 18

1. The Shoshoni-Crow fights are narrated in Trenholm and Carley, *The Shoshonis: Sentinels of the Rockies*, p. 173ff.

2. Quoted in Washington Irving, *The Adventures of Captain Bonneville*, p. 165.

3. Owen's activities among the Flatheads are found in Dunbar and Phillips, *The Journals and Letters of Major John Owen*. A good secondary source for the Flatheads at this and other periods is Fahey, *The Flathead Indians*.

4. Basing his account on primary and secondary sources, Madsen gives an account of the fight in *The Bannock of Idaho*, p. 133ff.

5. Lyon's activities involving Indians of Idaho Territory are discussed in Merle W. Wells, "Caleb Lyon's Indian Policy," *Pacific Northwest Quarterly* 61, no. 4 (October, 1970): 193–200.

6. For developments among the Bannocks and Shoshonis at this time see Madsen, *The Bannock of Idaho*, p. 150ff.

CHAPTER 19

1. Omer C. Stewart has a good presentation of the Paiutes in "The Northern Paiute Bands," *Anthropological Records* 2, no. 3: 127–49. See also Erminie Wheeler Voegelin, "The Northern Paiute of Central Oregon: A Chapter in Treaty-Making," in three parts in *Ethnohistory* 2, no. 2 (Spring, 1955): 95–132 and no. 3 (Summer, 1955): 241–72; and vol. 3, no. 1 (Winter, 1956): 1–10.

2. John Keast Lord, *The Naturalist in Vancouver Island and British Columbia*, 1: 271–79.

3. S. A. Clarke, *Pioneer Days of Oregon History*, p. 120.

4. Crook narrated his experiences in the war, as he did his previous military experiences in the Pacific Northwest, in *General George Crook: His Autobiography*, p. 142ff.

CHAPTER 20

1. The movements are discussed in Lee Sackett, "The Siletz Indian Shaker Church," *Pacific Northwest Quarterly* 60, no. 3 (July, 1973): 120.

2. J. Henry Brown, "The Biggest Little War in American History," *Oregon Historical Quarterly* 43, no. 1 (March, 1942): 37–39.

3. Joaquin Miller, *My Own Story*, p. 206–207.

CHAPTER 21

1. Events on the upper middle Columbia River at this time are discussed in Ruby and Brown, *Half-Sun on the Columbia*, pp. 43–63.

2. An account of Smohalla and his Dreamer movement may be found in Click Relander, *Drummers and Dreamers.*

3. Developments at the Warm Springs and other Protestant missions at this time are discussed in Myron Eells, *History of Indian Missions on the Pacific Coast: Oregon, Washington and Idaho.*

4. For an explanation of conflict arising over Nez Percé Fourth of July celebrations, see Allen and Eleanor Morrill, "Talmaks," *Idaho Yesterday* 8, no. 3 (Fall, 1964): 4ff.

5. Ruby and Brown, *The Cayuse Indians*, p. 292.

CHAPTER 22

1. Standard works on Nez Percé history are Francis Haines, *The Nez Percés: Tribesmen of the Columbia Plateau*, and Alvin M. Josephy Jr., *The Nez Perce Indians and the Opening of the Northwest*. The two works that are anthropological in nature are instructive: Herbert Joseph Spinden, *The Nez Percé Indians, Memoirs of the American Anthropological Association* 2, Part 3 (November, 1908): 165–274, and Deward Walker, *Conflict and Schism in Nez Percé Acculturation; A Study of Religion and Politics.*

2. Nearly a dozen full-length works have chronicled the Nez Percé, or Joseph War because of its poignancy and drama, although the Indian combatants composed but a small portion of the tribe. A brief summary of relationships between the Nez Percés and the government may be found in Francis Haines, "The Nez Percé Tribe versus the United States," *Idaho Yesterdays* 8, no. 1 (Spring, 1964): 18–25.

CHAPTER 23

1. A standard account of the war is George F. Brimlow, *The Bannock Indian War of 1878*. See also Madsen, *The Bannock of Idaho*, p. 204ff.

2. An account of the campaign may be found in W. C. Brown, "The Sheepeater Campaign," *Tenth Biennial Report of the Board of Trustees of the State Historical Society of Idaho, for 1925–26*. See also Carl Yeckel, "The Sheepeater Campaign," *Idaho Yesterdays* 15, no. 2 (Summer, 1971): 1–9.

CHAPTER 24

1. On the Warm Springs Reservation on November 22, 1972, on the occasion of the Thanksgiving Celebration commemorating the return of the McQuinn Strip lands to tribal ownership, a booklet written by Gordon McNab was published entitled *A History of the McQuinn Strip.*

2. The road as it affected the Klamaths is presented in Jerry A. O'Callaghan, "Klamath Indians and the Oregon Wagon Road Grant, 1864–1938," *Oregon Historical Quarterly* 53, no. 1 (March, 1952): 23–28.

3. Madsen, *The Bannock of Idaho*, p. 234.

Bibliography

ALVORD, B(enjamin). "The Doctor Killing Oregons," *Harpers Magazine*, February, 1884.

BAKER, PAUL E. *The Forgotten Kutenai.* Boise, Idaho, 1955.

BAKKEN, LAVOLA J. *Land of the Umpquas Peaceful Indians of the West.* Grants Pass, Ore., 1973.

BANCROFT, HUBERT HOWE. *The Works of Hubert Howe Bancroft, 3 volumes. History of Oregon 1834-1848.* San Francisco, 1886. *History of Oregon 1848-1888.* San Francisco, 1888. *History of Washington, Idaho, and Montana 1845-1889.* San Francisco, 1890.

BARRY, J. NEILSON. "Ko-come-ne Pe-ca, the Letter Carrier, *Washington Historical Quarterly* 20, no. 3 (July, 1929).

BEAL, MERRILL D. *"I Will Fight No More Forever": Chief Joseph and the Nez Perce War.* Seattle, 1963.

– –.and WELLS, MERLE W. *History of Idaho.* 3 vols. New York, 1959.

BECKHAM, STEPHEN DOW. *Requiem For a People: The Rogue Indians and the Frontiersmen.* Norman, Okla., 1971.

– –. *The Indians of Western Oregon This Land Was Theirs.* Coos Bay, Ore., 1977.

BEDFORD, DENTON R. "The Fight at 'Mountains on Both Sides,'" *The Indian Historian* 8, no. 2 (Fall, 1975).

BEESON, JOHN. *A Plea for the Indians; with Facts and Features of the Late War in Oregon.* New York, 1858 [1857].

BERREMAN, JOEL V. *Tribal Distribution in Oregon.* Memoirs of the American Anthropological Association, no. 47. Menasha, Wisc., 1937.

BIGART, ROBERT. "The Salish Flathead Indians During The Period of Adjustment, 1850-1891," *Idaho Yesterdays* 17, no. 3 (Fall, 1973).

BLACK, W. W., ed., *The Indian Miscellany; Containing Papers on the History, Antiquities, Arts, Languages, Religions, Traditions and Superstitions of the American Aborigines.* Albany, N.Y., 1877.

BLAINE, DAVID E., and BLAINE, KATE P. *Letters From the Pacific Northwest Written by David E. Blaine and Kate P. Blaine 1854-1858.* Mimeographed. Seattle. University of Washington Library.

BLANCHET, F. N., et al. *Notices and Voyages of the Famed Quebec Mission to the Pacific Northwest, Being the Correspondence, Notices, etc., of Fathers Blanchet and Demers, Together with Those of Fathers Bolduc and Langlois . . . 1838 to 1847 . . .* Portland, Ore., 1956.

BLINMAH, ERIC; COLSON, ELIZABETH; and HEIZER, ROBERT, "A Makah Epic Journey," *Pacific Northwest Quarterly* 68, no. 4 (October, 1977).

BLUE, GEORGE VERNE. "Green's Missionary Report on Oregon, 1829," *Oregon Historical Quarterly* 30 (1929).

BRIMLOW, George F. *The Bannock Indian War of 1878.* Caldwell, Idaho, 1938.

BROWN, J. HENRY. "The Biggest Little War in American History," *Oregon Historical Quarterly* 43, no. 1 (March, 1942).

BROWN, W. C. "The Sheepeater Campaign," *Tenth Biennial Report of the Board of Trustees of the State Historical Society of Idaho, for 1925-26.* Boise, Idaho, 1926.

BUCHANAN, CHARLES M. "Rights of the Puget Sound Indians to Game and Fish," *Washington Historical Quarterly* 6, no. 2 (April, 1915).

BUFFEY, GEORGE A. *Eighty-One Years in the West.* Butte, Mont., 1925.

BURCHAM, MILDRED BAKER. "Scott's And Applegate's Old South Road," *Oregon Historical Quarterly* 41, no. 4 (December, 1940).

BURNS, ROBERT IGNATIUS, S.J. *The Jesuits and the Indian Wars of the Northwest.* New Haven, 1966.

CAREY, CHARLES H. *General History of Oregon Through Early Statehood.* Portland, Ore., 1971.

CHEVIGNY, HECTOR. *Russian America: The Great Alaskan Venture, 1741-1867.* New York, 1965.

CLARK, W. P. *The Indian Sign Language . . . .* Philadelphia, 1885.

CLARKE, S. A. *Pioneer Days of Oregon History.* Portland, Ore., 1905.

COAN, C. F. "The Adoption of the Reservation Policy in Pacific Northwest, 1853-1855," *Oregon Historical Quarterly*, 23, no. 1 (March, 1922).

– –. "The First Stage of the Federal Indian Policy in the Pacific Northwest, 1849-1852," *Oregon Historical Quarterly* 22, no. 1 (March, 1921).

"Coast Whaling," *The Overland Monthly* 6, no. 2 (February, 1871).

COATES, LAWRENCE G. "Mormons and Social Change Among the Shoshoni, 1853-1900," *Idaho Yesterdays* 15, no. 4 (Winter, 1972).

COBRONEO, ROSS R., and DOZIER, JACK. "A Time of Disintegration: The Coeur d'Alene and the Dawes Act," *Western Historical Quarterly* 5, no. 4 (October, 1974).

CONN, RICHARD T. "The Iroquois in the West," *Pacific Northwesterner* 4, no. 4 (Fall, 1960).

CORNEY, PETER. *Early Voyages in the North Pacific 1813-1818.* Fairfield, Wash., 1965.

COUES, ELLIOTT, ed. *History of the Expedition under the command of Lewis and Clark.* 3 vols. Magnolia, Mass., 1965.

– –. *New Light on the Early History of the Greater Northwest: The Manuscript Journals of Alexander Henry, Fur Trader of the Northwest Company, and of David Thompson, Official Geographer and Explorer of the Same Company, 1799-1814.* 3 vols. Minneapolis, 1965.

COX, ROSS. *Adventures on the Columbia River, Including the Narrative of a Residence of Six Years on the Western Side of the Rocky Mountains, among Various Tribes of Indians Hitherto Unknown; Together with a Journey across the American Continent.* 2 vols. London, 1831.

CROOK, GENERAL GEORGE. *General George Crook: His Autobiography.* Ed. by Martin F. Schmitt. Norman, Okla., 1946.

CURTIS, EDWARD. *The North American Indian, Being a Series of Volumes Picturing and Describing the Indians of the United States and Alaska.* 20 vols. Norwood, Mass., 1907-1930.

DAVENPORT, T. W. "Recollections of an Indian Agent," *Oregon Historical Quarterly* 8, no. 3 (September, 1907).

DAVIES, K. G. *Peter Skene Ogden's Snake Country Journal 1826-27.* London, 1961.

"Defending Puget Sound against the Northern Indians," *Pacific Northwest Quarterly* 26, no. 1 (January, 1945).

DE SMET, PIERRE JEAN, S.J. *Letters and Sketches: With a Narrative of a Year's Residence among the Indian Tribes of the Rocky Mountains.* Philadelphia: 1843.

– –. *Life, Letters and Travels of Father Pierre-Jean de Smet, S.J., 1810-1873.* Edited by

Hiram Martin Chittenden and Alfred Talbot Richardson. 2 vols. New York, 1905.

– –. *Oregon Missions and Travels Over the Rocky Mountains, In 1845–46 By Father P. J. De Smet, Of the Society of Jesus. Early Western Travels 1784–1846*, edited by Reuben Gold Thwaites, vol. 29. New York, 1907. Fairfield, Wash., 1978.

– –. *Origin, Progress, and Prospects of the Catholic Mission to the Rocky Mountains*. Philadelphia, 1843.

– –. *Western Missions and Missionaries: A Series of Letters, By Rev. P. J. De Smet*. Totowa, N.J., 1972.

DEUTSCH, HERMAN J. "Indian and White in the Inland Empire The Contest for the Land," *Pacific Northwest Quarterly* 47, no. 2 (April, 1956).

DEVOTO, BERNARD, ed. *The Journals of Lewis and Clark*. Cambridge, Mass., 1953.

DIOMEDI A(LEXANDER), S.J. *Sketches of Modern Indian Life*. Woodstock, Md., 1884.

DOIG, IVAN. "Fox Among the Modocs," *Pacific Search About Nature and Man in the Pacific Northwest* 10, no. 7 (May, 1976).

DOUGLAS, DAVID. *Journal Kept by David Douglas during His Travels in North America in 1823–1827*. New York, 1959.

DOUGLAS, JESSE E., ed. "Matthews' Adventures on the Columbia," *Oregon Historical Quarterly* 40, no. 2 (June, 1939).

DRUCKER, PHILIP. *Indians of the Northwest Coast*. New York, 1955.

DRURY, CLIFFORD M. *Diaries and Letters of Spalding and Smith Relating to the Nez Perce Mission, 1838–1842*. Glendale, Calif., 1958.

– –. *Henry Harmon Spalding, Pioneer of Old Oregon*. Caldwell, Idaho, 1936.

– –. *Marcus and Narcissa Whitman and the Opening of Old Oregon. Glendale, Calif., 1973.*

– –. *Nine Years with the Spokane Indians The Diary, 1838–1848, of Elkanah Walker*. Glendale, Calif., 1976.

DUNBAR, SEYMOUR and PHILLIPS, PAUL C., eds. *The Journals and Letters of Major John Owen Pioneer of the Northwest 1850–1871.* . . . 2 vols. New York, 1927.

DUNN, JOHN. *History of the Oregon Territory and British North-American Fur Trade, with an Account of the Habits and Customs of the Principal Native Tribes on the Northern Continent*. London, 1846.

EDSON, LELAH JACKSON. *Fourth Corner; Highlights From Early Northwest*. Bellingham, Wash., 1951.

EELLS, MYRON. *History of the Indian Missions on the Pacific Coast: Oregon, Washington and Idaho*. Philadelphia, 1882.

ELLIOTT, E. C., ed. "Journal of John Work, November and December, 1824," *Washington Historical Quarterly* 3, no. 3 (July, 1912).

ELYEA, WINIFRED. "The History of Tatoosh Island," *Washington Historical Quarterly* 20, no. 3 (July, 1929).

ERMATINGER, FRANK. "Earliest Expeditions Against Puget Sound Indians," *Washington Historical Quarterly* 1, no. 2 (January, 1907).

EVANS, ELWOOD. *History of the Pacific Northwest: Oregon and Washington*. 2 vols. Portland, Ore., 1889.

FAHEY, JOHN. *The Flathead Indians*. Norman, Okla., 1974.

FERRIS, W. A. *Life in the Rocky Mountains A Diary of Wanderings on the sources of the Rivers Missouri, Columbia, and Colorado from February, 1830, to November, 1835*. Denver, 1940.

FRANCE, GEORGE W. *The Struggles For Life and Home In the North-west*. New York: 1890.

FRANCHÈRE, GABRIEL. *Adventure at Astoria, 1810–1814*. Edited by Hoyt C. Franchère. Norman, Okla., 1967.

– –. *Narrative of a Voyage to the Northwest Coast of America in the Years 1811, 1812, 1813, and 1814; or, the First American Settlement on the Pacific*. Edited by J. V. Huntington. New York, 1854.

FRÉMONT, J. C. *Oregon and California: The Exploring Expedition to the Rocky Mountains, Oregon and California*. Buffalo, 1850.

GATSCHET, SAMUEL ALBERT. *The Klamath Indians of Southwestern Oregon. Department of the Interior U.S. Geographical and Geological Survey of the Rocky Mountain Region* . . . Washington, D.C., 1890.

GOODMAN, DAVID MICHAEL. *A Western Panorama 1849–1875 the travels, writing and influence of J. Ross Brown*. Glendale, Calif.: 1956.

GREEN, JONATHAN S. *Journal of a Tour on the North West Coast of America in the Year 1829*. New York, 1915.

GREENHOW, ROBERT. *The History of Oregon and California, and the Other Territories on the North-West Coast of North America*. London, 1844.

HAINES, FRANCIS. *The Nez Percés: Tribesmen of the Columbia Plateau*, Norman, Okla., 1955.

– –. "The Nez Perce Tribe versus the United States," *Idaho Yesterdays* 8, no. 1 (Spring, 1964).

HANCOCK, SAMUEL. *The Narrative of Samuel Hancock 1845–1860*. New York, 1927.

HASTINGS, LANSFORD W. *Narratives of the Trans-Mississippi Frontier: The Emigrants' Guide to Oregon and California*. Cincinnati, 1845.

HAYDEN, WILLARD C. "The Battle of Pierre's Hole," *Idaho Yesterdays* 16, no. 2 (Summer, 1972).

HEIZER, ROBERT FLEMING. "Walla Walla Indian Expeditions to the Sacramento Valley," *California Historical Quarterly* 21, no. 1 (March, 1942).

HENDERSON, W. W., ed. "The Salmon River Mission: Organization and Founding," *Utah Historical Quarterly* 5, no. 1 (January, 1932).

HINES, GUSTAVUS. *Life on the Plains of the Pacific: Oregon, Its History, Condition and Prospects*. Buffalo, 1851.

– –. *Wild Life in Oregon*. New York, 1887.

HOBUCKET, HARRY. "Quillayute Indian Tradition," *Washington Historical Quarterly* 25, no. 1 (January, 1934).

HODGE, FREDERICK WEBB, ed. *Handbook of American Indians North of Mexico*. 2 vols. Washington, D.C., 1971.

HOONAN, CHARLES. *Neah Bay Washington, A Brief Historical Sketch*. N.p., 1964.

HOPKINS, SARAH WINNEMUCCA. *Life Among the Piutes: Their Wrongs and Claims*. New York, 1883.

HOWAY, F. W. "The Dog's Hair Blankets of the Coast Salish," *Washington Historical Quarterly* 9, no. 2 (April, 1918).

HOWISON, NEIL M. *Report of Lieut. Neil M. Howison, United States Navy, to the Commander of the Pacific Squadron* . . . Washington, D.C., 1848.

"Hunting the Sea Otter . . . ," *The Northwest* 8, no. 7 (July, 1890).

HUSSEY, JOHN ADAM. *Champoeg: Place of Transition*. Portland, Ore., 1967.

– –, and AMES, GEORGE WALCOTT, JR. "California Preparations to Meet the Walla Walla Invasion, 1846," *California Historical Quarterly* 21, no. 1 (March, 1942).

"The Indian Chief Kitsap." *Washington Historical Quarterly* 25, no. 4 (October, 1934).

"Indian Seal Hunters," *The Northwest* 12, no. 7 (July, 1894).

IRVING, WASHINGTON. *The Adventures of Captain Bonneville, U.S.A. in the Rocky Mountains and the Far West*. Edited by

Bibliography

Edgeley W. Todd. Norman, Okla., 1961.

JACKSON, HELEN HUNT. *A Century of Dishonor: A Sketch of the United States Government's Dealings with Some of the Indian Tribes.* Boston, 1890.

JEFFCOTT, P. R. *Nooksack Tales and Trails.* Sedro-Woolley, Wash., 1945.

JESSET, THOMAS E. *Chief Spokan Garry, 1811-1892, Christian, Statesman, Friend of the White Man.* Minneapolis, 1960.

JOHANSEN, DOROTHY O. "J. Ross Browne," *Pacific Northwest Quarterly* 32, no. 4 (October, 1941).

— —."McLoughlin and the Indians," *Beaver,* Outfit 277, No. 1 (June, 1946).

— —.and GATES, CHARLES M. *Empire of the Columbia: A History of the Pacific Northwest.* New York, 1957.

JOSEPHY, ALVIN M., JR. *The Nez Perce Indians and the Opening of the Northwest.* New Haven, 1965.

KANE, PAUL. *Wanderings of an Artist Among the Indians of North America From Canada to Vancouver's Island and Oregon Through the Hudson's Bay Company's Territory and Back Again by Paul Kane.* Toronto, 1925.

KAPPLER, CHARLES J., ed. *Indian Affairs, Laws and Treaties.* 2 vols. Washington, D.C., 1904.

KIP, LAWRENCE. *The Indian Council at Walla Walla, May and June, 1855. Sources of History of Oregon,* vol. 1, pt. 2. Contributions of the Department of Economics and History of the University of Oregon. Eugene, Ore., 1897.

KIRK, RUTH, and DAUGHERTY, RICHARD. *Hunters of the Whale.* New York, 1974.

KNUTH, PRISCILLA, and GATES, CHARLES M. "Oregon Territory in 1849-1850," *Pacific Northwest Quarterly* 40, no. 1 (January, 1949).

LANG, H. O., ed. *History of the Willamette Valley, Being a Description of the Valley and its Resources, with an account of its Discovery and Settlement by White Men, and its Subsequent History. . .*Portland, Ore., 1885.

LEE, D., and FROST, J. H. *Ten Years in Oregon.* New York, 1844.

LEWIS, ALBERT BUELL. *Tribes of the Columbia Valley and the Coast of Washington and Oregon.* Memoirs of the American Anthropological Association, vol. 1, pt. 2. Lancaster, Pa., 1906.

LEWIS, WILLIAM S., and PHILLIPS, PAUL C., eds. *The Journal of John Work A chief-trader of the Hudson's Bay Co. during his expedition from Vancouver to the Flatheads and the Blackfeet of the Pacific Northwest.* Cleveland, 1923.

LORD, JOHN KEAST. *The Naturalist in Vancouver Island and British Columbia.* 2 vols. London, 1866.

LOWIE, ROBERT H. "The Northern Shoshone," *Anthropological Papers of the American Museum of Natural History* 2, pt. 2 (1909).

McBETH, KATE C. *The Nez Perces Since Lewis and Clark.* New York, 1908.

McNAB, GORDON. *A History of the McQuinn Strip.* Portland, Ore.[?], 1972.

McWHORTER, LUCULLUS VIRGIL. *Tragedy of the Wahk-Shum The Death of Andrew J. Bolon, Indian Agent to the Yakima Nation, in mid-September, 1855.* Yakima, Wash., 1937.

MACKEY, HAROLD. *The Kalapuyans: A Sourcebook on the Indians of the Willamette Valley.* Salem, Ore., 1974.

MADSEN, BRIGHAM D. *The Bannock of Idaho.* Caldwell, Idaho, 1958.

MALONEY, ALICE BAY, ed. *Fur Brigade to the Bonaventura: John Work's California Expedition, 1832-1833, for the Hudson's Bay Company.* San Francisco, 1945.

MALOUF, CARLING. "Early Kutenai History," *Montana Magazine of History* 2, no. 2 (Spring, 1953).

MANRING, B. F. *The Conquest of the Coeur D'Alenes, Spokanes and Palouses: The Expeditions of Colonels E. J. Steptoe and George Wright Against the "Northern Indians" in 1858.* Spokane, 1912.

MEACHAM, ALFRED B. *Wigwam and War-Path; Or the Royal Chief in Chains.* Boston, 1875.

— —.*Wi-Ne-Ma (The Woman Chief.)* [Toby Riddle] *And Her People.* Hartford, Conn., 1876.

MEANY, EDMOND S., ed. *A New Vancouver Journal on the Discovery of Puget Sound By A Member of the Chatham's Crew.* Seattle, 1915.

— —."Chief Patkanim," *Washington Historical Quarterly* 15, no. 3 (July, 1924).

— —.ed. "Diary of Wilkes in the Northwest," *Washington Historical Quarterly* 16, no. 1 (January, 1925), no. 2 (April, 1925), no. 3 (July, 1925), no. 4 (October, 1925).

— —.*History of the State of Washington.* New York, 1941.

— —.*Vancouver's Discovery of Puget Sound.* Portland, Ore., 1957.

MEEKER, EZRA. *The Busy Life of Eighty-Five Years of Ezra Meeker.* Indianapolis, 1916.

MERK, FREDERICK, ed. *Fur Trade and Empire: George Simpson's Journal.* Cambridge, Mass., 1968.

— —.ed. *Narrative of a Journey Round The World, During The Years 1841 and 1842.* 2 vols. London, 1847.

MILLER, JOAQUIN. *My Own Story.* London, 1891.

MOONEY, JAMES. *The Ghost Dance Religion: The Shakers of Puget Sound.* Seattle, n.d.

MORRILL, ALLEN and ELEANOR. "Talmaks," *Idaho Yesterdays* 8, no. 3 (Fall, 1964).

MUDGE, ZECHARIAH ATWELL. *Sketches of Mission Life among the Indians of Oregon.* New York, 1854.

MURRAY, KEITH A. *The Modocs and Their War.* Norman, Okla., 1959.

NALTY, BERNARD C., and STRO-BRIDGE, TRUMAN R.,"The Defense of Seattle, 1856 'And Down Came the Indians,'" *Pacific Northwest Quarterly* 55, no. 3 (July, 1964).

NASH, JOHN D. "Salmon River Mission of 1855: A Reappraisal," *Idaho Yesterdays* 2, no. 1 (Spring, 1967).

NELSON, DENYS. "Yakima Days," *Washington Historical Quarterly* 19, no. 2 (April, 1928).

NIELSON, JEAN C. "Donald McKenzie in the Snake Country Fur Trade, 1816-1821," *Pacific Northwest Quarterly* 31, no. 2 (April, 1940).

"The Nisqually Journal," *Washington Historical Quarterly* 10, no. 3 (July, 1919).

O'CALLAGHAN, JERRY A. "Extinguishing Indian Title on the Oregon Coast," *Oregon Historical Quarterly* 52, no. 3 (September, 1951).

— —."Klamath Indians and the Oregon Wagon Road Grant, 1864-1938," *Oregon Historical Quarterly* 53, no. 1 (March, 1952).

OGDEN, PETER SKENE. *Traits of American Indian Life & Character, By a Fur Trader.* San Francisco, 1933.

O'HARA, EDWIN V. *Pioneer Catholic History of Oregon.* Portland, Ore., 1911.

"Old Fort Nisqually," *The Northwest* 8, no. 2 (February, 1980).

OLSON, RONALD L. *The Quinault Indians.* University of Washington Publications in Anthropology 6, no. 1. Seattle, 1936.

OTIS, D. S. *The Dawes Act and the Allotment of Indian Lands.* Norman, Okla., 1973.

OVERHOLT, THOMAS W. "The Ghost Dance of 1890 and the Nature of the Prophetic Process," *Ethnohistory* 21, no. 1 (Winter, 1974).

PALLADINO, L. B., S.J. *Indian and White In*

The Northwest: A History of Catholicity In Montana 1831 to 1891. Lancaster, Pa., 1922.

PARKER, SAMUEL. Journal of an Exploring Tour beyond the Rocky Mountains, Under the Direction of the A.B.C.F.M. Ithaca, N.Y., 1838.

PHILLIPS, PAUL C., ed. Forty Years on the Frontier as seen in the Journals and Reminiscences of Granville Stuart Gold-Miner, Trader, Merchant, Rancher and Politician. 2 vols. Cleveland, 1925.

POINT, NICOLAS, S.J. Wilderness Kingdom Indian Life in the Rocky Mountains: The Journals and Paintings of Nicolas Point, S.J. 1840-1847, Edited by Joseph P. Donnelly, S.J. Chicago, 1967.

POWELL, FRED WILBUR. Hall J. Kelley on Oregon. Princeton, N.J., 1932.

RATCLIFF, JAMES L. "What Happened to the Kalapuya? A Study of the Depletion of Their Economic Base," The Indian Historian 6, no. 3 (Summer, 1973).

RAY, VERNE F. "The Bluejay Character in the Plateau Spirit Dance," American Anthropologist 39, no. 4 (October-December, 1937).

– –. The Sanpoil and Nespelem: Salishan Peoples of Northeastern Washington. University of Washington Publications in Anthropology no. 5. Seattle, 1933.

REAGAN, ALBERT B. "Tradition of the Hoh and Quillayute Indians," Washington Historical Quarterly 20, no. 3 (July, 1929).

RELANDER, CLICK. Drummers and Dreamers. Caldwell, Idaho, 1956.

Reports of Explorations and Surveys, to Ascertain the Most Practicable and Economical Route for a Railroad from the Mississippi River to the Pacific Ocean 1853-55. 12 vols. Washington, D.C. 1855-60.

REVERE, JOSEPH WARREN. Naval Duty in California. Oakland, 1947.

RICH, E. E., ed. Eden Colvile's Letters 1849-52. Publications of the Hudson's Bay Record Society. London, 1956.

– –. McLoughlin's Fort Vancouver Letters: First Series, 1825-38. Publications of the Champlain Society. Toronto, 1941.

– –. ed. Peter Skene Ogden's Snake Country Journals, 1824-25 and 1825-26. London, 1950.

– –. ed. Simpson's 1828 Journey to the Columbia. Publications of the Champlain Society, Toronto, 1947.

RICHEY, ELINOR. "Sagebrush Princess with a Cause: Sarah Winnemucca," The American West 12, no. 6 (November, 1975).

RICKARD, T. A. "Indian Participation in the Gold Discoveries," British Columbia His-

torical Quarterly 2, no. 1 (January, 1938).

RIDDLE, GEORGE W. History of Early Days in Oregon by George W. Riddle. Riddle, Ore., 1920.

RIDDLE, JEFF C. The Indian History of the Modoc War and the Causes that led to it. N.p., 1914.

ROBBINS, WILLIAM G. "Extinguishing Indian Land Title in Western Oregon," The Indian Historian 7, no. 2 (Spring, 1974).

ROLLINS, PHILIP ASHTON, ed. The Discovery of the Oregon Trail: Robert Stuart's Narratives of his Overland Trip Eastward from Astoria in 1812-13. New York, 1935.

RONAN, PETER. Historical Sketch of the Flathead Nation. Minneapolis, 1890.

ROSS, ALEXANDER. Adventures of the First Settlers on the Oregon or Columbia River. . . . London, 1849.

RUBY, ROBERT H., and BROWN, JOHN A. Half-Sun on the Columbia: A Biography of Chief Moses. Norman, Okla., 1965.

– –. The Spokane Indians: Children of the Sun. Norman, Okla., 1970.

– –. The Cayuse Indians: Imperial Tribesmen of Old Oregon. Norman, Okla., 1972.

– –. The Chinook Indians: Traders of the Lower Columbia River. Norman, Okla., 1976.

– –. Myron Eells and the Puget Sound Indians. Seattle, 1976.

SACKETT, LEE. "The Siletz Indian Shaker Church," Pacific Northwest Quarterly 60, no. 3 (July, 1973).

ST. JOHN, LEWIS H. "The Present Status and Probable Future of the Indians of Puget Sound," Washington Historical Quarterly 5, no. 1 (January, 1914).

SAMPSON, MARTIN J. Indians of Skagit County. Mt. Vernon, Wash., 1972.

SAUM, LEWIS O. The Fur Trader and the Indian. Seattle, 1965.

SCHAEFFER, CLAUDE. "The First Jesuit Mission to the Flathead, 1840-1850: A Study in Culture Conflicts," Pacific Northwest Quarterly 28, no. 3 (July, 1937).

SCHOENBERG, WILFRED P., S.J. A Chronicle of Catholic History of the Pacific Northwest 1743-1960. Portland, Ore., 1962.

SCOULER, JOHN. "Dr. John Scouler's Journal of a Voyage to N.W. America," Oregon Historical Quarterly 6, no. 2 (June, 1907).

"Seattle's First Taste of Battle, 1856," Pacific Northwest Quarterly 47, no. 1 (January, 1856).

SETTLE, RAYMOND W., ed. The March of the Mounted Riflemen, First United States Military Expedition to travel the full length

of the Oregon Trail, From Fort Leavenworth to Fort Vancouver, May to October, 1849, as recorded in the journals of Major Osborne Cross and George Gibbs and the official report of Colonel Loring. Glendale, Calif., 1940.

SHANE, RALPH M., and LENO, RUBY D. A History of the Warm Springs Indian Reservation, Oregon. Mimeographed. Portland, Ore., Oregon Historical Society, 1949.

SHERIDAN, P. H. Personal memoirs of P. H. Sheridan, General, U.S. Army. 2 vols. New York, 1888.

SIERRA, BENITO DE LA, FRAY. "Fray Benito De La Sierra's Account of the Hezeta Expedition to the Northwest Coast in 1775," California Historical Quarterly 9, no. 3 (September, 1930).

"A Siwash Strike on the Yakima," The Northwest 12, no. 8 (August, 1894).

SLACUM, WILLIAM A. Memorial of William A. Slacum, Praying Compensation for His Services in Obtaining Information in Relation to the Settlements on the Oregon River. Washington, D.C., 1837.

SLATER, G. HOLLIS. "New Light on Herbert Beaver," British Columbia Historical Quarterly 6, no. 1 (January, 1942).

SMITH, MARIAN W. "The Coast Salish of Puget Sound." American Anthropologist 47 (1941).

– –. "The Nooksack, the Chilliwack, and the Middle Fraser," Pacific Northwest Quarterly 41, no. 4 (October, 1950).

– –. The Puyallup-Nisqually. Columbia University, Contributions to Anthropology, vol. 32.

SNYDER, SALLY, "Quest for the Sacred in Northern Puget Sound: An Interpretation of Potlatch," Ethnology 14, no. 2 (April, 1975).

SPAULDING, KENNETH, ed. On the Oregon Trail: Robert Stuart's Journey of Discovery, 1812-1813. Norman, Okla., 1953.

SPECK, GORDON. Northwest Explorations. Portland, Ore., 1954.

SPIER, LESLIE. The Prophet Dance of the Northwest and Its Derivatives; the Source of the Ghost Dance. American Anthropological Association, General Series in Anthropology no. 1. Menasha, Wisc., 1935.

– –. Tribal Distribution in Washington. American Anthropological Association, General Series in Anthropology no. 3. Menasha, Wisc., 1936.

SPINDEN, HERBERT JOSEPH. The Nez Percé Indians. Memoirs of the American Anthropological Association 2, pt. 3. Lancaster, Pa., November, 1908.

SPLAWN, A. J. Ka-Mi-akin, The Last Hero of the Yakimas. Portland, Ore., 1917.

Bibliography

STEEVES, SARAH HUNT. *Book of Remembrance of Marion County, Oregon. 1840–1860*. Portland, Ore., 1927.

STERN, BERNHARD J. *The Lummi Indians of Northwest Washington*. New York, 1969.

STERN, THEODORE. *The Klamath Tribe: A People and Their Reservation*. Seattle, 1965.

STEVENS, HAZARD. *The Life of Isaac Ingalls Stevens*. 2 vols. Boston, 1901.

STEWARD, JULIAN H. *Basin-Plateau Aboriginal Sociopolitical Groups*. Smithsonian Institution Bureau of American Ethnology Bulletin no. 120. Washington, D.C., 1938.

STEWART, OMER C. "The Northern Paiute Bands," *Anthropological Records* 2, no. 3 (1939).

SUTTLES, WAYNE. "Post-Contact Culture Change among the Lummi Indians," *British Columbia Historical Quarterly* 18, nos. 1 and 2 (January-April, 1954).

SUTTON, DOROTHY, and SUTTON, JACK, eds. *Indian Wars of the Rogue River*. Grants Pass, Ore., 1969.

SWAN, JAMES G. "The Indians of Cape Flattery, at the Entrance of the Strait of Fuca, Washington Territory," *Smithsonian Contributions to Knowledge* 16, no. 8 (1870).

− −.*The Northwest Coast; or, Three Year's Residence in Washington Territory*. New York, 1857.

SWANTON, JOHN R. *The Indian Tribes of North America*. Smithsonian Institution, Bureau of American Ethnology Bulletin, no. 145. Washington, D.C., 1953.

TAYLOR, HERBERT C., JR. "Aboriginal Populations of the Lower Northwest Coast," *Pacific Northwest Quarterly* 54, no. 4 (October, 1963).

TEIT, JAMES H. *The Middle Columbia Salish*. University of Washington Publications in Anthropology 2, no. 4. Seattle, 1928.

− −.*The Salishan Tribes of the Western Plateaus*. Forty-fifth Annual Report of the Bureau of American Ethnology, 1927-28. Washing-

ton, D.C., 1930.

THOMPSON, A. W. "New Light on Donald Mackenzie's Post on the Clearwater, 1812-1813," *Idaho Yesterdays* 18, no. 3 (Fall, 1974).

THWAITES, REUBEN GOLD, ed. *Early Western Travels 1784-1846*. Vol. 21, New York, 1966.

TOBIE, HARVEY E. "From the Missouri to the Columbia," *Oregon Historical Quarterly* 38, no. 2 (June, 1937).

TOLMIE, WILLIAM FRASER. "Journal of William Fraser Tolmie—1853," *Washington Historical Quarterly* 3, no. 3 (July, 1912).

− −."Journal of Occurrences at Nisqually House," *Washington Historical Quarterly* 7, no. 2 (April, 1916).

− −.*The Journals of William Fraser Tolmie, Physician and Fur Trader*. Edited by R. G. Large. Vancouver, B.C., 1963.

TOWNSEND, JOHN K. *Narrative of a Journey across the Rocky Mountains to the Columbia River. Early Western Travels 1784-1846*, edited by Reuben Gold Thwaites. Cleveland, 1905.

TRENHOLM, VIRGINIA COLE, and CARLEY, MAURINE. *The Shoshonis: Sentinels of the Rockies*. Norman, Okla., 1964.

TURNEY-HIGH, HARRY HOLBERT. *The Flathead Indians of Montana*. Memoirs of the American Anthropological Association, Contributions From Montana State University. Supplement to *American Anthropologist* 39, no. 4; pt. 2, no. 48.

VOEGELIN, ERMINIE WHEELER. "The Northern Paiute of Central Oregon: A Chapter in Treaty-Making," *Ethnohistory*, vol. 2, no. 2 (Spring, 1955), no. 3 (Summer, 1955); vol. 3, no. 1 (Winter, 1956).

WAGNER, HENRY R. *Spanish Explorations in the Strait of Juan de Fuca*. Santa Ana, Calif., 1933.

− −."The Last Spanish Explorations of the Northwest Coast and the Attempt to

Colonize Bodega Bay," *California Historical Quarterly* 10, no. 4 (December, 1931).

WALKER, DEWARD. *Conflict and Schism in Nez Percé Acculturation; A Study of Religion and Politics*. Pullman, Wash., 1968.

Washington D.C. Federal Archives. Records Relating to the First Northwest Boundary Survey Commission, 1853-69. Microcopy in Federal Archives, Seattle.

Washington, D.C. National Archives. *Records of the Washington Superintendence of Indian Affairs, 1853-1874*, no. 5, Roll 9. Letters from Agents Assigned to the Puget Sound District as a Whole December 4, 1853–August 16, 1862.

WATERMAN, T. T. "The Whaling Equipment of the Makah Indians." *University of Washington Publications in Anthropology* 1, no. 1 (1920): 1-67.

WEATHERFORD, MARK V. *Bannock-Piute War: The Campaign and Battles*. Corvallis, Ore., 1957.

WELLS, MERLE W. "Caleb Lyon's Indian Policy," *Pacific Northwest Quarterly* 61, no. 4 (October, 1970).

WHITE, ELIJAH. *Ten years in Oregon: Travels and Adventures of Doctor E. White and Lady West of the Rocky Mountains*. Ithaca, N.Y., 1848.

WHITNER, GRANT L. "Grant's Indian Peace Policy on the Yakima Reservation," *Pacific Northwest Quarterly* 50, no. 4 (October, 1959).

WILKES, CHARLES, U.S.N. *Narrative of the United States Exploring Expedition During the years 1838, 1839, 1840, 1841, 1842*. 5 vols. Philadelphia, 1845.

WINTHROP, THEODORE. *The Canoe and the Saddle*. Tacoma, Wash., 1913.

WOLFENDEN, MADGE, ed. "John Tod: 'Career of a Scotch Boy,'" *British Columbia Historical Quarterly* 18, nos. 3-4 (July-October, 1954).

YECKEL, CARL. "The Sheepeater Campaign," *Idaho Yesterdays* 15, no. 2 (Summer, 1971).

Index

Index